Extremisms in Africa

Extremisms in Africa

Edited by
Alain Tschudin, Stephen Buchanan-Clarke,
Lloyd Coutts, Susan Russell, Mandla Tyala

First published by Fanele, an imprint of Jacana Media (Pty) Ltd, in 2018

10 Orange Street
Sunnyside
Auckland Park 2092
South Africa
+27 11 628 3200

www.jacana.co.za

© Good Governance Africa, 2018

All rights reserved.

ISBN 978-1-928232-61-2

Cover design by Shawn Paikin
Editing by Glenda Younge
Proofreading by Tessa Botha
Index by Tessa Botha
Set in Bembo 10.9/14pt
Printed by Print on Demand (Pty) Ltd
Job no. 003295

See a complete list of Jacana titles at www.jacana.co.za

Contents

List of figures and tables vii
List of contributors ix
List of acronyms and abbreviations xii
Acknowledgements xvii
Introduction 1
About Good Governance Africa 7

Chapter 1 Between rhetoric and reality: Strategic approaches to counterterrorism (Peter Knoope) 9

Chapter 2 Public opinion on security and terrorism in Africa (Rorisang Lekalake) 36

Chapter 3 Terrorism in North Africa and the Sahel (Richard Chelin) 81

Chapter 4 The Sahel's ungoverned spaces and the ascent of AQIM, Al-Mourabitoun and MUJAO in Mali and Niger (Celeste Hicks) 107

Chapter 5 Why the Tuareg have been demonised (Jeremy Keenan) 140

Chapter 6 Visions of an alternative world: Understanding the background to Boko Haram (Graham Furniss) 162

Chapter 7 Boko Haram and counter-insurgency in Nigeria (Stephen Johnson) 176

Chapter 8 The rise of ISIS and its implications for East Africa (Stephen Buchanan-Clarke) 205

Chapter 9 The evolving threat of violent extremism and terrorism in the SADC region (Richard Chelin & Stephen Buchanan-Clarke) .. 227

Chapter 10 Identity politics and the re-emergence of South Africa's far-right (Stephen Buchanan-Clarke) 258

Chapter 11 The rehabilitation and reintegration of children associated with armed groups in Borno State, Nigeria (Emmanuel Bosah & Mustapha al-Hassan) 284

Chapter 12 Accounting for the rise and trajectory of Islamist extremism in Africa (Hussein Solomon)..............................302

Chapter 13 Transnational evangelical Christianity and political culture in sub-Saharan Africa (Robert A. Dowd)............................327

Chapter 14 The United States' approach to countering terrorism and violent extremism (Lindsay Cohn)..............................351

Index 363

Figures and tables

FIGURES

Figure 2.1 Summary of key indicators of security context, 36 countries, 2014/15
Figure 2.2 Citizen prioritisation of security concerns, Kenya, Mali and Nigeria, 2002–2017
Figure 2.3 Public distrust in public security agencies, Kenya, Mali and Nigeria, 2000–2017
Figure 2.4 Perceived impact of the Arab Spring, five North African countries, 2015
Figure 2.5 Citizen preferences on ensuring security vs strengthening democracy and protecting human rights, Tunisia, 2015
Figure 2.6 Evaluations of Kenya's counterterrorism strategies, 2011–2016
Figure 2.7 Support for Kenyan Defence Forces' involvement in Somalia, Kenya, 2014 vs 2016
Figure 2.8 Perceived usefulness of various security forces in restoring territorial integrity, Mali, 2013 vs 2017
Figure 2.9 Reported victimisation during security crisis, Mali, 2017
Figure 2.10 Perceived motivations for joining extremist groups, Nigeria, 2014 vs 2017
Figure 2.11 Perceived effectiveness of government counter-extremist efforts in Nigeria, 2014 vs 2017
Figure 9.1 Conflict events and fatalities, Tanzania, 2010–2016
Figure 11.1 School operational status and children's enrolment in Borno State

TABLES

Table 2.1 Summary of citizen evaluations of security context, five North African countries, 2013 vs 2015
Table 2.2 Public opinion on violent extremism in North Africa, 2015
Table 2.3 Citizen preferences on addressing terrorist suspects, four North African countries, 2015
Table 2.4 Evaluations of security context in Kenya by key demographic

	indicators, 2016
Table 2.5	Support for KDFs' involvement in Somalia, by key demographic variables, Kenya, 2016
Table 2.6	Evaluations of security context in Mali, by key demographic indicators, 2017
Table 2.7	Predicted consequences of the security crisis, Mali, 2017
Table 2.8	Evaluations of the security context in Nigeria, by key demographic indicators, 2017
Table 2.9	Perceived political and social support for extremist organisations, Nigeria, 2014 vs 2017
Table 2.10	Suggested improvements to government counter-extremist efforts, Nigeria, 2014 vs 2017
Table 2A.1	Afrobarometer Round 6 fieldwork dates and leading security indicators
Table 2A.2	Key public opinion indicators on security | 36 countries | 2014/15
Table 2A.3	Public confidence in security forces | 36 countries | 2014/15
Table 2A.4	Frequency and impact of terrorism in featured countries in 2014
Table 2A.5	Citizen perceptions of the armed forces | 3 countries | 2016/17
Table 2A.6	Frequency and impact of terrorism on North Africa in 2015
Table 2A.7	Perceived threat of extremist groups | by key demographic indicators | 5 countries | 2015
Table 2A.8	Overall direction of country | 3 countries | 2012–2017
Table 2A.9	Fear of violence | 3 countries | 2016/17
Table 2A.10	Reported victimisation during security crisis in Mali | by region | 2017
Table 2A.11	Key indicators of insecurity in Nigeria | by residence | 2017
Table 9.1	List of terror-related attacks in Tanzania and Zanzibar

Contributors

MUSTAPHA AL-HASSAN AND EMMANUEL BOSAH are Senior Programme Officers responsible for the coordination and implementation of the Neem Foundation's community-based socio-economic rehabilitation and reintegration programme aimed at children associated with the armed forces and armed groups (CAAFAG) in northeast Nigeria. This programme is part of the Neem Foundation's commitment to preventing violent extremism by providing and raising the standard of psychosocial care and education, research and policy, advocacy and communications, and community peace-building and reintegration in northern Nigeria.

STEPHEN BUCHANAN-CLARKE is Lead Researcher for the National Security Project at Good Governance Africa. Additionally, since 2016, he has managed a comparative research project on perceptions and responses to violent extremism in the Central African Republic, Kenya and Nigeria. He has published widely on the topic of peace and security in Africa with a particular focus on terrorism and non-conventional security threats.

RICHARD CHELIN is an independent researcher. He is a post-graduate scholar from the University of KwaZulu-Natal. His research interests are in the field of transitional justice, civil wars, social justice and post-conflict reconstruction. He is also a conflict analyst for various news channels, focusing on political and security issues in Africa.

LINDSAY COHN is an Associate Professor at the United States Naval War College. Her research and publications focus on military organisations, civil–military relations, international law of war and foreign policy/public opinion, and she has taught courses on terrorism, insurgency and politics of the Middle East. She spent a year working for the Deputy Assistant Secretary of Defense for Special Operations and Combating Terrorism, as a Council on Foreign Relations Fellow, where she was responsible for security cooperation programmes in the Middle East, Europe and Africa.

ROBERT A. DOWD is an Associate Professor of Political Science at the University of Notre Dame, founding Director of the Ford Family Program in Human Development Studies and Solidarity, and a faculty fellow at both the Kellog Institute for International Studies and the Kroc Institute for International Studies. Author of the book *Christianity, Islam, and Liberal Democracy: Lessons from sub-Saharan Africa*, his research interests include African politics, ethnic politics, and the impact of religion on development outcomes and political institutions.

GRAHAM FURNISS is Emeritus Professor of African Language Literature at SOAS, University of London. He was SOAS' first Dean of the Faculty of Languages and Cultures and the first Head of the Language Centre. His research and teaching has focused on popular culture and oral and written literature in Hausa. He was the founding President of the International Society for Oral Literature in Africa (ISOLA), and founding editor of the *Journal of African Cultural Studies*.

CELESTE HICKS is a freelance journalist whose primary focus is the Sahel and North Africa. She is a former BBC correspondent in Chad and Mali and Editor on BBC News in Africa service. She is the author of *Africa's New Oil; Power, pipelines and future fortunes* published by Zed Books in 2015.

STEPHEN JOHNSON is the Programme Officer for The Programme for African Leadership at the Firoz Lalji Centre for Africa at the London School of Economics and Political Science. He previously worked as a research coordinator for Good Governance Africa, where his research focused on defence, security and political instability. Additionally, he has also worked for higher education institutions in South Africa and the United Kingdom, including the University of Cape Town, King's College and Birkbeck College.

JEREMY KEENAN is a social anthropologist and currently a professorial research associate in the Department of Social Anthropology and Sociology at SOAS, University of London and visiting professor, School of Law, Queen Mary University London (QMUL). A recognised authority on the Sahara and its peoples, especially the Tuareg, he has over 300 academic publications, including a number of full-length documentary films and professional reports, to his name.

Peter Knoope is a career diplomat who was, inter alia, Head of Mission to Afghanistan and headed the Humanitarian Aid section at the Dutch Ministry of Foreign Affairs. He was the Director of the International Centre for Counter-terrorism (ICCT), The Hague, from its inception until August 2014. Prior to the ICCT, he was Deputy Director of the Policy and Strategy Department of the Dutch National Coordinator for Counter-terrorism (NCTb).

Rorisang Lekalake is a doctoral student at the Massachusetts Institute of Technology (MIT). She conducts research in comparative politics, with primary interests in democratisation and governance in sub-Saharan Africa. Prior to attending MIT, Rorisang worked as Afrobarometer's assistant project manager for the southern African region based in Cape Town, South Africa. She is the author of several publications, analysing Afrobarometer data in a number of research areas, including citizen support for democratic governance, the evolving landscape of political participation on the continent and security-related issues.

Hussein Solomon lectures in the Department of Political Studies and Governance at the University of the Free State, South Africa. He is also Visiting Professor at Osaka University in Japan, Senior Research Associate of Research on Islam and Muslims in Africa (RIMA) in Israel and Research Fellow of the Security Institute for Governance and Leadership in Africa (SIGLA) at Stellenbosch University.

Acronyms and abbreviations

ACSRT	African Centre for the Study and Research on Terrorism (CAERT in French)
ACLED	Armed Conflict Location and Event Database
ACR	Association for Church Renewal
ADF-NALU	Alliance of Democratic Forces-National Army for the Liberation of Uganda
AEC	African Economic Community
AFRICOM	United States Africa Command
AIAI	Al-Itihaad al-Islamiya (Somalia)
AIC	African-initiated churches (AICs)
AIS	Islamic Salvation Army (Algeria)
AMISOM	African Union Mission in Somalia
ANT	National Army of Chad
AQAP	Al-Qaeda in the Arabian Peninsula
AQI	Al-Qaeda in Iraq
AQIM	Al-Qaeda in the Islamic Maghreb
ATAWT	Association des Agences de Tourisme Wilaya de Tamanrasset
ATNMC	Alliance Tuareg du Nord-Mali pour le Changement
AU	African Union
CAAFAG	children associated with armed forces and armed groups
CAN	Christian Association of Nigeria
CAR	Central African Republic
CBN	Christian Broadcasting Network
CCZ	Christian Council of Zambia
CERD	Committee on Eliminating Racial Discrimination (UN)
CFA	Colonies Française d'Afrique
CJA	Congrès pour la Justice dans l'Azawad (Tuareg)
CJTF	Civilian Joint Task Force
CMA	Coordination of Movements of Azawad (Mali)
CMFPR	Coordination des Mouvements et Forces Patriotiques de Résistance (Tuareg)
CNCDH	National Human Rights Commission (France)

CPA	Coalition du Peuple pour l'Azawad (Tuareg)
CTITF	Counter-Terrorism Implementation Task Force (UN)
DRC	Democratic Republic of Congo
DRS	Département du Renseignement et de la Sécurité (Algeria)
EC	European Commission
ECDB	Extremist Crime Database (USA)
EFZ	Evangelical Fellowship of Zambia
EPLO	European Peacebuilding Liaison Office
EU	European Union
EUAFR	European Union Agency for Fundamental Rights
EUCOM	United States European Command
FAMA	Forces Armées et de Sécurité du Mali
FAN	Niger's Armed Forces
FARC	Revolutionary Armed Forces of Colombia
FATF	Financial Action Task Force (framework)
FBI	Federal Bureau of Investigation (USA)
FBO	faith-based organisation
FFS	Socialist Forces Front (Algeria)
FIS	Islamic Salvation Front/Front Islamique du Salut (Algeria)
FLAA	Front de Libération de l'Aïr et de l'Azawak (Niger)
FLM	Macina Liberation Front (Mali)
FLN	National Liberation Front (Algeria)
FLN	Forces de Libération du Nord du Mali
GATIA	Groupe Autodéfense Touareg Imghad et Alliés (Tuareg)
GCTF	Global Counterterrorism Forum (USA)
GDP	gross domestic product
GIA	Armed Islamic Group/Groupe Islamique Armee (Algeria)
GITOC	Global Initiative against Transnational Organized Crime
GOA	Governmental Accountability Office (USA)
GSPC	Salafist Group for Preaching and Combat/Groupe Salafiste pour la Prédication et le Combat (Algeria)
GTD	Global Terrorism Database
GTI	Global Terrorism Index
GWOT	Global War on Terrorism
HCUA	Haut Conseil pour l'Unité de l'Azawad (Tuareg)
HDI	Human Development Index (UN Development Programme)
I-ACT	Integrated Assistance on Countering Terrorism (UN)
ICG	International Crisis Group
ICU	Islamic Courts Union
IDP	internally displaced person

IED	improvised explosive device
IIAG	Ibrahim Index of African Governance
IIRO	International Islamic Relief Organization
IJR	Institute for Justice and Reconciliation
ILO	International Labour Organization
IRCU	Inter-Religious Council of Uganda
IRD	Institute on Religion and Democracy
ISAF	International Security Assistance Force (UN)
ISDSC	Inter-State Defence and Security Committee (SADC)
ISIS	Islamic State of Iraq and Syria
ISWAP	Islamic State of West Africa Province
JTF	Joint Military Task Force (Nigeria)
KIA	Kenyan Intelligence Agency
KKK	Ku Klux Klan
LRA	Lord's Resistance Army (Uganda)
MAA	Mouvement Arabe de l'Azawad
MAK	Maktab al-Khidamat
MENA	Middle East and North Africa
MIA	Armed Islamic Movement/Movement Islamique du Azawad
MMD	Movement for Multiparty Democracy (Zambia)
MINUSMA	United Nations Multidisciplinary Integrated Stabilization Mission in Mali
MNJ	Nigerien Movement for Justice/Mouvement des Nigériens pour la Justice
MNJTF	Multinational Joint Task Force
MNLA	National Movement for the Liberation of Azawad/Mouvement Nationale pour la Liberation d'Azawad
MUJAO	Movement for Unity and Jihad in West Africa/Movement for Oneness and Jihad in West Africa
MWL	Saudi Muslim World League (Saudi Arabia)
NATO	North Atlantic Treaty Organization
NCNC	National Council for Nigeria and the Cameroons
NCTC	National Counterterrorism Centre (Tanzania)
NEPA	Nigerian Electric Power Authority
NPC	Northern People's Congress (Nigeria)
OAU	Organisation of African Unity
OPSD	Organ on Politics, Security, and Defence (SADC)
OIC	Organization of the Islamic Conference
OSCE	Organization for Security and Cooperation in Europe
PAGAD	People Against Gangsterism and Drugs (South Africa)

P/CVE	preventing and countering violent extremism
PEPFAR	President's Emergency Plan for AIDS Relief (USA)
PFN	Pentecostal Fellowship of Nigeria
PKK	Kurdistan Workers' Party
PLO	Palestinian Liberation Organization
PSC	Peace and Security Council (AU)
PSI	Pan-Sahel Initiative
PSPSDN	Special Programme for Peace, Security and Development in Northern Mali
RAN	Radicalisation Awareness Network (Europe)
REC	Regional Economic Community
RFI	Radio France Internationale
RUF	Revolutionary United Front (Sierra Leone)
SADC	Southern African Development Community
SADCC	Southern African Development Coordinating Conference
SAVE	Sisters Against Violent Extremism Mother Schools
SCM	Sovereign Citizen Movement (USA)
SPLC	Southern Poverty Law Centre (USA)
START	National Consortium for the Study of Terrorism and Responses to Terrorism (University of Maryland)
SUBEB	State Universal Basic Education Board (Nigeria)
TBN	Trinity Broadcasting Network
TCC	troop contributing country
TFG	Transitional Federal Government (of Somalia)
TOCU	transnational organised crime unit
TSCTI	Trans-Saharan Counterterrorism Initiative
TSCTP	Trans-Sahara Counterterrorism Partnership
UAE	United Arab Emirates
UAMSHO	The Association for Islamic Mobilisation and Propagation/Jumikior Jumuiya ya Uamsho na mihadhara ya kiislam
UJCC	Uganda Joint Christian Council
UN	United Nations
UNATA	Union Nationale des Associations des Agences de Tourisme Alternatif
UNCCT	United Nations Counterterrorism Centre
UN DESA	United Nations Department of Economic and Social Affairs
UNDP	United Nations Development Programme
UNDP-HDI	United Nations Development Programme – Human Development Index
UNESCO	United Nations Educational, Scientific and Cultural

	Organisation
UNGA	United Nations General Assembly
UNHCR	United Nations High Commissioner for Refugees
UNICEF	United Nations Children's Fund
UN OCHA	United Nations Office for the Coordination of Humanitarian Affairs (UN)
UNODC	United Nations Office on Drugs and Crime
USIP	United Institute for Peace
VEO	violent extremism organisation
WAMY	World Assembly of Muslim Youth
WPEV	Women Preventing Extremist Violence
ZEC	Zambian Episcopal Conference

Acknowledgements

On behalf of the GGA team, I would like to thank all of our contributors to this volume for your innovative approaches, continued exchanges and demonstrable grit to endure – this has been a marathon and not a sprint. Accordingly, we salute you!

To our Board of Directors, thank you for your support and likewise to our acting General Manager, Michelle Venter, and to the heads of Programmes and Publications, Mandla Tyala and Lloyd Coutts, to our sub-editor, Susan Russell, and to our lead researcher, Stephen Buchanan-Clarke, for taking the initiative and for contributing thoroughly throughout this process.

We are sincerely grateful to our partners at Jacana Media, and specifically to Bridget Impey and colleagues, for the continued collaboration and to the editor of this book, Glenda Younge.

We are thankful for broader dialogue with a range of committed and credible conversation partners, advisers and associates, and we look forward to advancing fact-based knowledge and action on this and related themes with you.

Topics under consideration include cyberterrorism and cybersecurity; geopolitics and state-sponsored extremism; online recruitment and radicalisation; and the impact of anti-terrorism legislation on immigrant communities.

Alain Tschudin, PhD
Executive Director
GGA SADC March 2018

Introduction

This anthology, *Extremisms in Africa*, is the first in a series of publications Good Governance Africa (GGA) will be offering as part of our National Security programme. Globally, it is recognised that a straight line exists between poor governance, transnational crime and extremist threats to stability and security. This applies equally on the African continent and, if anything, is magnified by the additional threats posed by internal conflicts and wars and diverse natural and human disasters on a landmass that covers 20 per cent of the Earth's surface.

We argue that the prevailing militarised narrative of the Global War on Terrorism or GWOT, which informs and dominates the response to extremist and radical threats in Africa and elsewhere, serves only to put a Band-Aid on an arterial bleed. Unless a serious and sustained attempt is made to explore and identify the push and pull factors that make radicalisation and recruitment attractive to those who are marginalised (youth and ethnic minorities, for example), all the spend in the world (currently US$50 million a day) will not stem the bloodletting.

To this end, our volume is timely. It is book-ended with an introduction by a counterterrorism specialist and a conclusion by a military strategist. Ambassador Peter Knoope sets the scene with a clarion call for alternatives other than a purely militarily loaded response. Professor Lindsay Cohn skilfully reflects on the various chapters and correlates this with the situation on the ground. She suggests how gains from the current approach could provide a refreshing shift of engagement for those who see the state as greater than its defence department. In between, we offer a wide array of analysis on both a regional and a thematic basis. This is an introductory anthology and the first of its kind on this topic to be authored and published on the African continent.

In his polemical book, *The Spirit of Terrorism*, penned in the aftermath of 9/11, French thinker Jean Baudrillard poses a question and offers a definition of contemporary terrorism that is worth entertaining:

> When global power monopolises the situation to this extent, when there is such a formidable condensation of all functions in the technocratic machinery, and when no alternative form of thinking is allowed, what

other way is there but a *terroristic situational transfer*? It was the system itself which created the objective conditions for this brutal retaliation. By seizing all the cards for itself, it forced the Other to change the rules. And the new rules are fierce ones, because the stakes are fierce. To a system whose very excess of power poses an insoluble challenge, the terrorists respond with a definitive act which is also not susceptible of exchange. Terrorism is the act that restores an irreducible singularity to the heart of a system of generalised exchange … This is terror against terror – there is no longer any ideology behind it. We are far beyond ideology and politics now. No ideology, no cause – not even the Islamic cause – can account for the energy which fuels terror. The aim is no longer even to transform the world, but (as the heresies did in their day) to radicalise the world by sacrifice. Whereas the system aims to realise it by force.[1]

Rather than dismiss Baudrillard's assertion as left-leaning and anti-Western, we should take the call to consider the multifaceted complexity of the situation at hand seriously. Any attempt to engage the difficult and perplexing topic of extremisms has to consider the broad and deep factors involved. These range from the varied historical, cultural and social contexts, to the political and economic legacies involved and incorporate intricate interplays of direct and indirect violence (the latter including structural and cultural violence) between perpetrators and victims, colonisers and colonised, 'supermen' and the powerless. As we in South Africa learnt painfully in the days of apartheid, one person's 'terrorist' is another's 'freedom fighter'.

Given that this is an introductory volume, we would like it to serve as a catalyst for further collegial dialogue and balanced scholarship. For this reason we have drawn on a wide range of writers. Besides the aforementioned security-sector specialists, we have included, among others, conflict analysts, journalists, international relations and governance specialists, political scientists, social anthropologists, psychologists and theologians.

Akin to the popular mantra that 'Africa is not a country', there is not only one extremism that can boast exclusivity on this continent – there are a plethora of extremisms. We consider so-called offshoots of both Christianity and Islam in the forms of radicalised movements such as the LRA and AQIM, ISIS, Al-Shabaab and Boko Haram. Although we consider both Christian and Muslim responses to radicalised religion, we are cognisant of the fact that extremisms also extend to ethnicity and race. As a result, we examine the potential for a resurgence of white

---

1   Baudrillard, 2012, pp. 7–8.

extremism on the south of the continent, given the recent aspirations of the Alt-Right in the United States. We also offer regional analyses of the situations in the west, east and north of the African continent. Going beyond this, we look at interventions such as psychosocial support for survivors of extremism, at returning combatants, at popular culture and at self-determination aspirations gone wrong.

To expand a little. In our introductory chapter, Ambassador Knoope argues that although 9/11 and 2001 is benchmarked as the defining moment, the so-called fourth 'religious' wave of international terrorism began several years earlier, with the bombings of US embassies and the related military response against perpetrators from inception. Arguing for a 'softer' approach, Ambassador Knoope traces the recent history of this fourth wave, focusing on Al-Qaeda, the Taliban and ISIS. He distinguishes between counterterrorism and spoof-counterterrorism practices, along with military versus alternative tactics. Noting the conspicuous absence of 'soft' approaches, he proposes the value of these.

In Chapter 2, Rorisang Lekalake presents data relating to public opinion on security and terrorism in Africa. Hers is an analysis that speaks to geographic epicentres or 'hotspots' for terror, and speaks to public dissatisfaction with governance around crime reduction. Whereas people seem more or less satisfied with their militaries, they do not have a high regard for the police. While citizen security concerns are on the decline in Kenya and Nigeria, they are on the rise again in Mali. Interestingly, poverty appears to be the prime driver of recruitment for ISIS in North Africa. This chapter provides a wealth of statistical insights and trends.

Chapter 3 presents an analysis of terror in North Africa and the Sahel by former GGA national security researcher Richard Chelin. Tracing roots back to returning jihadis from Afghanistan in the 1990s, this chapter looks at how Al-Qaeda and ISIS-affiliated groups have exploited the fractured colonial legacy, grievances against authoritarian regimes, Gaddafi's fall in Libya, complex clan rivalries and criminal networks to entrench themselves. Since 2015, ISIS's quest for domination in Libya has been boosted by surging jihadis entering from Iraq and Syria. Coordinated responsive security measures and political will are necessary to tackle the root causes of recruitment.

In Chapter 4, Celeste Hicks documents the rise of AQIM, Al-Mourabitoun and MUJAO in Mali and Niger. With a journalistic eye, she shows how arbitrary boundaries are meaningless here, and observes the region has hosted a continuum of trade over centuries. The root cause of lawlessness is the failure of Sahelian states to control their borders and territorial integrity. It is not that this is an ungoverned space insofar as it is an alternatively governed space. The arrival of jihadis, subsequent events in Libya, and mixed and shifting Tuareg ambitions marked a sea change in the region. As always, poor governance is implicated in the ensuing chaos.

Professor Jeremy Keenan focuses on the Tuareg in Chapter 5 and specifically on how ambitions for self-determination have been spectacularly undermined by ongoing events. He argues that the Tuareg have been made the scapegoat for the terror surge in the Sahel. In 1992, their ecotourism aspirations were radically disrupted when the Algerian military annulled the first democratic elections in that country. Just as there was a glimmer of hope for a return of tourism in the late 1990s, an Al-Qaeda-affiliated kidnapping of 32 tourists in 2003 wrought havoc. Although the leading jihadi in the region is a Tuareg, Keenan argues that the GWOT has led to rent-seeking governments in the Sahel provoking minority and opposition groups to receive ongoing funding, at the expense of the Tuareg.

In Chapter 6 there is a regional shift of focus to West Africa and, more specifically, an examination of the background to Boko Haram. Professor Graham Furniss uses a career's worth of experience to place the organisation within the complex context of the history of the region, particularly as it relates to the Muslim population's sense of being under siege and to previous jihads. After a probing analysis of local history and popular culture in Nigeria, he poses a pivotal question: can a modern nation state accommodate an ideology and a group of committed individuals who wish to have nothing to do with the daily manifestations of that state?

The thematic focus on Boko Haram and Nigeria continues in Chapter 7, where Stephen Johnson provides an analysis of the counter-insurgency. He argues that the Nigerian government's claims to have defeated Boko Haram are exaggerated and that the organisation still poses a significant threat to peace and stability in the country, particularly in the north where it has been able to devastate the local population. To defeat Boko Haram, the government has to commit to better governance, security-sector reform and economic development. It has to alleviate the poverty divide between the impoverished north and more affluent south – which is also evident along rural/urban lines – and it has to give people the space to air their grievances.

Moving from west to east, in Chapter 8, our analyst Stephen Buchanan-Clarke considers how the spread and proliferation of militant Islamic groups (Al-Qaeda, Al-Shabaab and ISIS) have had a profound effect on East Africa as a region. Salafism and Wahhabism, imported ideologies from the Gulf states, have relied on weak governance, corruption, ethnic tensions, poverty and youth unemployment, all of which combine to form a potent, nasty cocktail that encourages recruitment. The jockeying for power between Al-Qaeda and ISIS poses a significant threat to regional security, with the former appealing to

Introduction

sheiks and clerics, and the latter to the youth.

Chapter 9 provides an overview of the Southern African Development Community (SADC). Chelin and Buchanan-Clarke examine the potential threat to the region posed by organisations such as Al-Qaeda and ISIS. The recent attacks in northern Mozambique by a group claiming to be Al-Shabaab are telling, especially as oil and gas reserves are of increasing interest to international investors. The chapter considers case studies from Tanzania and South Africa, which have respectively seen increasing militancy in recent years and served as a logistical hub for organisation like Al-Qaeda and ISIS. On the whole, the SADC's response to transnational extremism appears to be largely theoretical.

Maintaining a southern African focus in Chapter 10, we consider the resurgence of white extremism in South Africa. More specifically, Stephen Buchanan-Clarke considers how identity politics and the white far right are being bolstered by recent developments, particularly in the United States and Europe. Although this receives less publicity than violent Islamist groups, far-right parties and organisations have also been growing of late, and pose a threat to the advancement of democracy. In the South African context, while society might become more fractious, there is little to suggest that a powerful resurgence of the white far-right is likely, especially given that this group is such a minority.

Chapter 11 looks at the psychosocial support for survivors and the attempts to heal children affected by armed conflict in Nigeria's north-east region. Emmanuel Bosah and Mustapha Al-Hassan, who work for the NEEM foundation, examine the motivations and mechanics of a community-based, socio-economic rehabilitation and reintegration programme aimed at children associated with armed forces and groups such as Boko Haram. They present various elements of the programme, trauma counselling and psychosocial support, religious counselling and creative education and play therapy. It is hoped that this programme could be adapted for use in other conflict contexts.

In Chapter 12, Professor Hussein Solomon, a pre-eminent scholar, writes on the rise of Islamist extremism in Africa and considers its origins and trajectory before making recommendations on how it can be engaged. He provides an overview of Islamist ideologies before diving deeper into internal and external factors responsible for the recent escalation in related extremist movements. He identifies Arabism and Islamism, along with the ideological indoctrination of so-called charities from the Gulf, as among the reasons for the rise in Islamist extremism, while its trajectory revolves around poverty and an economic slowdown, accompanied by a lack of democracy. Existing counterterrorism strategies also do little to help. The appeal of Sufism as a traditionally more moderate form of Islam helps to counterbalance a potentially explosive militarised balloon.

In Chapter 13, Professor Robert A. Dowd writes on evangelical Christianity and political culture in sub-Saharan Africa. After exploring this phenomenon and its growth on the African continent, where from American roots it has been largely indigenised, he argues that while the evangelicals advocated for political rights, they discouraged the advancement of some basic civil liberties. He considers in greater detail the country contexts; for instance, in Nigeria, politically aggressive Christianity counters politically aggressive Islam, whereas in Uganda and Zambia, there is an endeavour to steer away from Western secular liberalism, as witnessed in the attempts to suppress homosexuality. In the face of a political agenda that promotes an 'illiberal democracy', Dowd calls for an approach that would foster greater social tolerance.

In our ultimate chapter, Professor Lindsay Cohn provides a response to the overall themes raised in our anthology from the perspective of military strategy. She notes the broad consensus that poor governance plays a significant role in the emergence and spread of violent extremism in Africa, with dysfunctional post-colonial governments, neo-patrimonialism, patronage systems and a 'Big Man' culture all playing a role. While the United States does provide significant aid to African states, when it comes to countering violent extremism, precedence is given to a 'militarised' approach rather than 'softer' approaches such as the EU's four-pillar Countering Violent Extremism (CVE) strategy. This is due to historical structural factors in US political culture, which is problematic insofar as the Defence Department appears to be given precedence over the State Department.

It is clear from this outline, and the diverse and difficult ground covered, that much greater balance is required than the predominant GWOT paradigm employed to date. Accordingly, our programme will seek to explore and advance non-military alternatives in preventing, countering and eventually overcoming extremisms in Africa.

Alain Tschudin, PhD
Executive Director
GGA SADC
March 2018

About Good Governance Africa

Good Governance Africa is a leading research and advocacy non-profit organisation, which seeks to build a bridge between government and the private sector in all African countries, while strengthening civil society and promoting democracy.

See www.gga.org
SADC Office, The Mall Offices, 11 Cradock Avenue, Rosebank, 2196
SADC Tel +27 11 268 0479 Nigeria Tel +234 1 4627411-3 West Africa Tel +233 302 672925
Fax +27 11 268 0478 Email info@gga.org

Chapter 1

Between rhetoric and reality: Strategic approaches to counterterrorism

Peter Knoope

Introduction

As David Rapoport wrote in his seminal 2004 essay on the four waves of modern terrorism, 'September 11, 2001 is the most destructive day in the long, bloody history of terrorism. The casualties, economic damage, and outrage were unprecedented.'[1] The attack led President GW Bush to declare a 'war [that] would not end until every terrorist group of global reach has been found, stopped and defeated'.[2] The Global War on Terrorism (GWOT) was on. And Rapoport was right. September 11, 2001 has come to be a defining moment in modern history.

The 11 September attacks have been regarded by several scholars of political violence and terrorism as the start of a fourth 'religious wave' of international terrorism. Rapoport (2004) identifies three preceding waves, which include an 'anarchist' wave beginning in the 1880s, an 'anti-colonial' wave beginning around the 1920s, and a 'new-left' wave of international terrorism beginning around the 1960s and declining towards the end of the 20th century.[3] However, there is a strong argument to be made that the fourth wave of 'religious terrorism' started considerably earlier than 2001. For example, on 8 August 1998, Al-Qaeda, led by Osama bin Laden, carried out simultaneous bombings on United States embassies in Nairobi, Kenya and Dar es Salaam, Tanzania.[4] This attack, which left 224 people dead and roughly 5 000 injured, was indicative of the threat to come. Just 13 days later, on 20 August 1998, the United States launched cruise missiles at suspected terrorist targets in Afghanistan and Sudan in retaliation.[5]

This kinetic military response to the first large-scale Al-Qaeda attack would come to define the way in which states react to this new wave of international terrorism in the 21st century. As Rapoport predicted, the September 9/11 attacks were a defining moment in modern history. However, this has been due more to the responses of states to acts of terrorism, than the organisations responsible for the acts themselves.

This chapter provides a brief overview of the emergence and evolution of the 'fourth religious wave of terrorism', with a focus on Al-Qaeda and its affiliates. Drawing on my experience as national coordinator for counterterrorism in the Netherlands and many years spent working on security issues in the heart of government, I provide a taxonomy of counterterrorism policy options from which governments commonly choose when faced with the threat of terrorism, and some of the environmental pressures that shape these decisions. Finally, this chapter provides an overview of recent developments in 'soft approaches' to counterterrorism, and some of the opportunities and challenges involved in introducing them in African contexts.

Al-Qaeda and the increasingly deadly fourth wave of terrorism

Al-Qaeda emerged out of the Soviet occupation of Afghanistan during the Cold War, which was maintained by Moscow's 'atheist/Marxist' regime – a natural enemy for Al-Qaeda. The Soviet withdrawal from Afghanistan in early 1989 was viewed by Bin Laden as a major victory. Bolstered by this perceived victory over a major power, and confident the organisation could fight and win anywhere in the world, Bin Laden chose not to dissolve Al-Qaeda. Instead, he found refuge in Sudan, where he began linking up with groups from all over the Middle East and North Africa, laying the groundwork for his international jihad against the West.[6] For example, in 1996, Al-Qaeda merged with the Egyptian Islamist Jihad organisation, headed by Ayman al-Zawahiri, who would later lead Al-Qaeda after the death of Bin Laden. Over the last decade of the 20th century, Al-Qaeda became increasingly active in staging attacks against Western targets, the majority of which were American. In 1993, Al-Qaeda trainers were suspected of aiding in downing two American Black Hawk helicopters in Somalia.[7] That same year, the organisation took credit for the bombing of the World Trade Centre in New York, which left six dead. In 1998, Al-Qaeda associates were responsible for the aforementioned attacks in East Africa, and just two years later, they launched an attack on the *USS Cole* stationed in Yemen, killing 17 US sailors. In 1996, Bin Laden returned to Afghanistan where he forged a close relationship with the Taliban, led by Mullah Mohammed Omar. Under the protection of the Taliban, he began to rebuild his network and prepare for the 9/11 attacks.[8]

The response to 9/11 was the United Nations Security Council Resolution 1386, which established the International Security Assistance Force (ISAF), laying the groundwork for the subsequent invasion of Afghanistan, which chased Al-Qaeda from the country but not the region.[9] Rather, the organisation went into hiding in neighbouring Pakistan and started to work in decentralised units or 'chapters'. These units, with more or less independent operational commanders and cell leaders, made the organisation less vulnerable to detection. The strategy worked, and the number of attacks attributed to Al-Qaeda and its affiliates rose dramatically over the next decade.[10] The detection of Bin Laden's hideout in

Pakistan in 2011 and the substantial degrading of Al-Qaeda Central's operational capabilities was only due to the presence of thousands of US troops in the region for over a decade.

However, several of Al-Qaeda's decentralised units are still highly active. Al-Qaeda in the Islamic Maghreb (AQIM), for example, continues to stage attacks across a growing number of states in North Africa and the Sahel. Al-Qaeda in the Arabian Peninsula (AQAP) is also considered a major threat to US interests in the region and, according to a recent International Crisis Group (ICG) report, is 'stronger than ever'.[11] Jemaah Islamiyah, the Islamic Movement of Uzbekistan and the Islamic Army for Iraq are also among the many groups and affiliate organisations that are (or were) ideologically and strategically connected to Al-Qaeda Central.[12]

The international environment changed dramatically for Al-Qaeda in 2011. Not only was the organisation's founder tracked and killed in Pakistan by US Navy Seals, but the so-called 'Arab Spring' rocked the political landscape in the Middle East and North Africa (MENA) region. The leaders of the Arab world, as the 'near enemy', which had long been targeted by violent Islamist organisations like Al-Qaeda for being 'corrupted by the West', were now confronted by widespread resistance from ordinary civilians and other non-religious actors.[13] The days of Al-Qaeda's relevance seemed over, and commentators were ready to announce that the organisation would fall in the spring.[14] Instead, however, something completely unpredicted and unexpected occurred.

As detailed in Jessica Stern and JM Berger's book, *ISIS: The state of terror*, a debate had been raging between the leader of Al-Qaeda in Iraq (AQI) and Al-Qaeda Central.[15] Led by Abu Musab al-Zarqawi, AQI had established itself as Al-Qaeda's chapter in Iraq and was effective in attracting a large number of foreign fighters to its cause. However, despite the group's successes, both Bin Laden and his then second-in-command, Ayman al-Zawahiri, were troubled by Al-Zarqawi's brutality, especially in targeting Muslims he personally deemed '*takfir*'.[16] While Al-Zarqawi was killed in 2006 by a US-targeted bombing, and his successor in 2010 by a joint American-Iraqi operation in Tikrit, the relationship between AQI (which became the Islamic State of Iraq and Syria [ISIS] under Abu Bakr al-Baghdadi) and Al-Qaeda Central was beyond repair, and in 2013, Al-Zawahiri publically disowned ISIS.

According to General Douglas Stone, the major general responsible for in-country interrogation and detention in Iraq, the way in which detention facilities were established and operated during this period only contributed to radicalisation and the organisation of jihadi movements. Abu Bakr al-Baghdadi, for example, was arrested in 2004 and detained in Abu Ghraib and Camp Bukka detention facilities for two years.[17] During this period, Al-Baghdadi was able to recruit from the prison population, many of whom were disenfranchised former Ba'athists and bitter opponents of the newly elected regime. The network of recruits Al-Baghdadi was able to build, his standing as a former US prisoner, and his claim to be a direct descendant of the Prophet Muhammad made him the perfect leader of ISIS and the caliphate.[18]

Both the rapid territorial expansion of ISIS and the hard line it took on those organisations deemed to be the 'the enemy' was startling. All opponents, Muslim or otherwise, of the proposed new caliphate were deemed infidels and met with extreme violence. ISIS actively sought to destroy state borders in the region and challenge the existing world order. The organisation's early successes and slick propaganda campaigns helped to attract an estimated 30 000 to 40 000 foreign fighters to its cause from across the world.[19]

The instability in Iraq and Syria, as well as in Arab Spring countries in general, helped to expand the geographic reach of the organisation, and by 2017, ISIS had managed to carry out attacks in 29 countries, from Afghanistan to Libya.[20] Since the recent military defeat of ISIS in Mosul, the caliphate project has ended. However, the ideology and traction of the organisation are still very relevant. ISIS fighters returning to their home countries pose a significant threat to countries across the world, but to the MENA region in particular. In addition to active ISIS cells, those inspired by their ideology can operate largely on their own, whenever and wherever they have the opportunity, with little operational oversight from ISIS leadership other than encouragement to attack their enemies.

While the global number of terrorist incidents reached its peak in 2014 at 16 800 and dropped to 13 000 in 2016, this is still a 300 per cent increase from just a decade ago.[21] The spread of terrorist organisations to countries, which until now had been relatively insulated, shows that the 'fourth wave' of terrorism is still raging and has been able to adapt to the ever-expanding global war on terror. What then were the strategies that got us to this point? What can be learned from the past 16 years and what changes need to be made going forward?

The 'so-called' counterterrorism strategies
The US government started to push for United Nations sanctions against the Taliban from the late 1990s. This was largely in response to the US Embassy bombings in East Africa and the close ties between the Taliban and Osama bin Laden. The US government introduced Executive Order 13129, which froze Taliban assets in the United States, prohibited US trade with Taliban-controlled Afghanistan, and put an international flight ban on Ariana Afghan Airlines, Afghanistan's national carrier.[22] The UN adopted the sanctions regime in 1999. Its measures are laid out in UN Security Council Resolution 1267.[23] These measures, in addition to the human rights violations perpetrated in Taliban-

controlled regions of Afghanistan, led to the country becoming what Paul Holtom calls a 'pariah state'.[24]

Today, these financial sanctions, freezing of assets and 'listings' make up a large part of global counterterrorism approaches. There is a UN consolidated sanctions list that includes all individuals and entities subject to sanctions measures imposed by the Security Council. Similar lists exist in individual countries and in the European Union (EU). The sanctions regime is maintained by the so-called 1267 Committee, a sub-committee of the Security Council. This committee possesses discretionary powers to list and delist targeted individuals and entities.

However, it is relevant to ask whether these sanctions listings are a well thought-out strategy and if creating a pariah state in Afghanistan has been effective in curbing terrorism. Governments and some (rare) individuals listed have critically analysed the measures and (more specifically) the procedures, arguing that certain procedures are incompatible with internationally recognised due-process guarantees. Some individuals, like Saudi businessman Yassin Abdullah Kadi,[25] have successfully fought the procedure, leading to the appointment of an ombudsperson to monitor the UN sanctions regime. However, much more research is needed to evaluate the strategic value of sanctions listings.

A major strategic shift, over and above sanctions and isolation, designed to target terrorists and those who 'sponsor' terrorism more aggressively was introduced after the 9/11 attacks. In the wake of the attacks, the GWOT strategy was announced as a necessary response to combat Al-Qaeda and states or entities that 'sponsor terrorism'. By drawing on the North Atlantic Treaty Organization (NATO) charter which stipulates that 'an attack on one is an attack on all', the 9/11 attacks were framed as an act of aggression against all NATO member states, which were then encouraged to support this new strategy.[26]

The UN established the International Security Assistance Force (ISAF) through UNSCR Resolution 1386 and mandated ISAF to 'support international efforts to root out terrorism, in keeping with the charter of the United Nations'.[27] The establishment of ISAF follows UNSCR 1373 (28-11-2001), which 'reaffirms the inherent right of individual or collective self-defence as recognised by the charter of the United Nations'.[28] This helped to frame military responses to the 9/11 attacks as an act of self-defence in response to an imminent threat, apparently emanating from Afghanistan.

Sanctions in the 1990s failed to hamper or diminish the threat of Al-Qaeda, and the organisation continued to spread and find a home in Sudan, Yemen and Afghanistan. This, along with the friendly relations between the Taliban and Osama bin Laden and the subsequent 9/11 attacks, all contributed to the enormous sense of humiliation that shocked the Unites States and the world.

Following the attacks, the United States claimed that they deserved NATO solidarity and framed the invasion of Afghanistan as an act of self-defence. However, the question of whether a military response would be more effective than further sanctions or other possible strategic options was not asked. In part, this was due to it being considered politically incorrect at the time to talk about the 'root causes' of terrorism. As Paul Ehrlich wrote in 2002:

> Little attention has been paid (at least in the US government) to what must be a critically important part of a long war – changing the basic conditions that generate terrorist acts. While thoughtful people realise that those atrocities were connected to a variety of underlying factors, social scientists are far from understanding exactly what circumstances trigger such violent acts.[29]

Another reason why the discussion of the root causes of terrorism was difficult to have at the time was due to the term 'terrorist' remaining largely undefined. Even today, there is no international agreement on a definition of the term. For example, the question of whether a sovereign state could (under certain conditions) ever be considered a terrorist actor and whether violence against a foreign occupation should be defined as an act of terrorism is still disputed. However, despite these various disagreements in defining the term, it has managed to gain a common understanding at the policy level.[30]

In September 2006, the UN adopted (in consensus) a global counterterrorism strategy.[31] The document is worth reading. It comprises four pillars, which call for: (1) 'Addressing the conditions conducive to the spread of terrorism'; (2) 'Preventing and combating terrorism'; (3) 'Building states' capacity and strengthening the role of the United Nations'; and (4) 'Ensuring human rights and the rule of law'.[32] Nowhere in the document is there reference to enforce, create or advocate military response mechanisms to terrorism. On the contrary, the kinetic responses central to the GWOT strategy are absent, while preventative and law enforcement approaches are emphasised.

The UN global counterterrorism strategy was not the first document of its kind to downplay military approaches to counterterrorism and place emphasis on prevention and law enforcement. On 30 November 2005, the EU published its counterterrorism strategy. It, too, is composed of four pillars: prevent, protect, pursue and respond. Long lists of activities, coordinated or promoted from the European Commission (EC) or EU council secretariat in Brussels, fall under each pillar.[33] While the UN created a coordinating mechanism to implement its strategic approach in the Counter-Terrorism Implementation Task Force (CTITF), the EU relied on existing coordinating bodies and appointed a counterterrorism coordinator that works within the structure of the Secretariat of the Council. Many national counterterrorism strategies have been developed since 2005. Most are tailored around the pillars of the above-mentioned EU and UN strategies, and share similarities in several respects.

Despite the development of these counterterrorism 'strategies', in reality, they are unworthy of the term. After all, a 'strategy' is the optimal combination of an objective with the effective use of the means needed to attain the said objective. Neither the EU nor the UN 'counterterrorism strategies' give clear answers to the question of how the objectives are defined or how to most effectively use the means needed to achieve them. On the contrary, the 'strategies' are simply lists of potential activities divided into different pillars. These pillars are categories of (potential) activities. Nowhere in these documents is there any indication of what to prioritise or how the pillars are connected, let alone the required costs, financial or other.

As expected, this has led analysts such as Oldrich Bures to conclude that the EU counterterrorism strategy is 'more of a paper tiger than an effective counterterrorism device',[34] while the inability of the CTITF to 'make a difference' is clearly described by Hendrik Hegemann in his book on counterterrorism bureaucracies.[35] It is therefore disheartening to see that many national counterterrorism strategies today often read as hasty reproductions of the aforementioned UN and EU examples. However, while often not reflected in UN and EU documents, governments *are* able to make strategic choices when it comes to addressing terrorism and violent extremism. But from what menu of realistic strategic options can governments choose? Let us have a look at the reality behind the paper tigers.

Strategic options in counterterrorism

A taxonomy of counterterrorism strategies has been well described by the National Consortium for the Study of Terrorism and Responses to Terrorism (START), based at the University of Maryland. In a 2015 report, Amy Pate provides an empirical evaluation of counterterrorism, counter-insurgency, and countering violent extremism policies designed to undermine the ability or motivation of non-state actors to engage in acts of terrorism.[36]

While her conclusions are interesting, they are unsurprising. However, the author's synthesis and summary of counterterrorism measures is refreshing and informative. Pate draws on various frameworks for categorising policies, including the 'escalation ladder of coerciveness of influence' typology developed by Paul Davis and Brian Jenkins, the DIMEFIL schema, and a multi-level schema developed by Jeffrey Knopf.[37] As a result, her review identifies six categories of policies that range from 'hard' military measures on one side, to 'soft' power approaches on the other.

These categories represent the potential counterterrorism policies from which governments (and communities) commonly choose. Writing about the efficacy of these policies, Pate says 'most literature addressing counterterrorism, counterinsurgency and/or countering violent extremism does not include empirical evaluations of specific policies'.[38] This means that more than 14 years into the GWOT strategy, one of the most important fields of international and national policy development since 9/11, there is no clear picture as to whether policies developed have been successful. Pate's review finds only that the 'majority of studies *with* (emphasis added) evaluation find that the use of coercive methods, such as repression, tend to produce backlash effects'.[39]

This lack of data on the efficacy of counterterrorism policies should trouble policy-makers and raises a host of questions surrounding the rationale behind choices that have been made in the 'war on terror'. More on this will be discussed. First, however, it is important to briefly identify the seven categories of counterterrorism policy interventions identified in Pate's work.

1. Military deterrence/coercion
1.1 Direct punishment
1.1.1 Retaliation against the violent extremism organisation (VEO)
Examples of retaliatory strikes against VEOs in response to acts of terrorism are well known. This choice has been at the centre of the GWOT strategy and early examples of it can be seen in Operation Infinite Reach, the codename given to US cruise missile strikes on Khost, Afghanistan, and the Al-Shifa pharmaceutical factory in Khartoum, Sudan, in response to the US embassy bombings in East Africa.[40] With the advent of drone technology, retaliatory strikes have become commonplace in Pakistan, Yemen, Somalia and elsewhere.[41] While the US-led invasion of Iraq itself was in part framed as retaliation against an 'axis of evil' state that supported terrorism, governments in Cameroon, China, Kenya, Nigeria, Russia and elsewhere have responded similarly to local terrorist incidents. Indeed, to date, retaliatory strikes against VEOs in response to acts of terrorism are perhaps the most commonly used policy response in counterterrorism following the 'denial' option discussed below.

1.1.2 Retaliation against the community/society which the VEO claims to represent
A more severe policy option than retaliation against the VEO is to target the broader community perceived to be supporting it. According to Amnesty International, the Nigerian army, in their operations against Boko Haram intended to target the Kanuri to deter alleged support for the organisation by Kanuri communities in northern Nigeria.[42] Similarly, Kenya's Operation

Usalama Watch, while billed as a 'crackdown on terrorism' in the country, led to the arbitrary arrest, harassment, extortion, and ill-treatment of thousands of Somalis in what many considered to be a retaliation for Somali communities' *alleged* support of Al-Shabaab.[43]

1.2 Indirect punishment
1.2.1 Against state sponsors/enablers
The 2001 US-led invasion of Afghanistan, aimed at dismantling Al-Qaeda and denying it a base from which to operate by removing the Taliban from power, is a clear example of this policy. The term 'axis of evil' (first used by President GW Bush in his State of the Union address in 2002) was itself developed to rally public support for the GWOT against states that 'sponsored' terrorism. Initially, these 'axis states' included Iran, Iraq and North Korea. However, increasingly, Libya and Syria were also identified as sponsors of terrorism and therefore a legitimate target in the GWOT. The indirect result of this was regime change in the former, and a bloody civil war in the latter. In both cases, these countries are unstable today and more prone to the emergence and spread of terrorist organisations.

1.2.2 Against private supporters/enablers
Sometimes, targeted military action is taken against individuals alleged to be enablers or supporters of VEOs. One example was the US targeted drone strike, which killed Anwar al-Awlaki on 30 September 2002. Al-Awlaki was an American and Yemeni Islamic lecturer, known for his fiery diatribes against the West, and described by one Saudi newspaper, *al-Aribiya*, as the 'Bin Laden of the internet'.[44]

2. Non-military deterrence/coercion
2.1 Denial
Apart from military action in the form of retaliation against VEOs, the 'denial' strategy is probably the most developed and commonly used. To be effective, it requires in-depth knowledge of the strategies, tactics and plans of the terrorist organisation(s) that is being targeted. This is usually obtained through intelligence gathering, using both open and undercover 'human intelligence' sources. Over the past two decades, many governments have developed fusion centres where information from different sources can be collected and synthesised to improve their information. Collected information on recruitment strategies, types of attack, timing, and VEOs' other modi operandi creates the opportunity to intervene on three levels: (1) the strategic (such as the protection of potential targets, prevention of recruitment, denial or disruption of preparatory spaces,

prevention of mobility/immigration, etc); (2) the operational (such as direct intervention to disrupt the preparation and planning of an attack); and (3) the tactical (such as the denial of access to source funding, equipment, operationals and information necessary for a VEO to carry out an attack).

2.2 Alternative (non-military) punishment threats

Unlike the US, the EU has always advocated non-military approaches to counterterrorism. These have primarily taken the form of both *legal measures* and *financial sanctions*, in addition to rules to reinforce checks at external borders, enhance firearm controls, the creation of a dedicated body to curb terrorist propaganda online, and measures to improve information sharing and collaboration between EU member states. For example, the EU is currently working on its fourth iteration of their anti-money-laundering directive, designed to prevent money laundering and terrorist financing. Similarly, after 2001, the EU developed a list of people, groups and entities involved in terrorist acts and subject to restrictive measures. The individuals, groups and entities on this list are liable to have funds and other financial assets frozen, as well as face enhanced measures related to police and judicial cooperation in criminal matters. EU legal measures are constantly updated and amended due to the evolving nature of terrorist threats.[45]

3. Bargaining/negotiations/dialogue
3.1 Negotiations
3.1.1 With the VEO as a whole

Several conflicts, where non-state actors have routinely engaged in acts of terrorism, have been resolved through political negotiations, and there are some impressive examples of this. The Revolutionary Armed Forces of Colombia (FARC) is perhaps the most recent example of a political negotiation between a state and a non-state actor to end a decades-old insurgency. Similarly, the Turkish government stood ready to negotiate a peace deal with the Kurdistan Workers' Party (PKK) after many years. While the Turkish government has abandoned this approach, it could very well be adopted again in the future.

There are notably fewer examples of negotiations brokered in conflicts where religion is an important factor, even though the case of Northern Ireland and the Irish Republican Army could serve as an example. However, negotiations with ISIS, Al-Qaeda and their affiliates are made difficult, if not impossible, because their demands are unclear. Negotiations with the Iranian government helped to reduce US-Iranian tensions, while there are ongoing talks between the United States and both the Taliban and the Syrian government. Israel, who for many decades has publically opposed negotiations with 'terrorist organisations', talked in secret with members of its longest-standing rival, the Palestinian Liberation Organization (PLO), in 1993 and signed accords in Oslo, Norway. In Nigeria, the government has tried to initiate negotiations with Boko Haram, which gained increased traction after the Chibok schoolgirls were kidnapped. However, they have largely failed to achieve any significant outcomes.

The Material Support Act in the United States has hampered contact between terrorist groups and officials. This act stipulates that assistance or contacts (for whatever reason) with terrorist organisations is illegal and is a violation of US law. Under this Act, anybody who engages with an organisation on the US terrorism watch list can be charged and extradited to appear before a US court.[46]

3.1.2 Third parties who can influence the VEO
Sometimes, intermediates can help to identify the leaders that are open for a conversation. This is a well-established strategy that can prove useful, especially in initial phases of negotiations. Egypt, for example, has a track record of negotiations with violent jihadist groups, some of which have been successful. Mohamed Morsi, during his brief spell as president in 2012, was successful in using former jihadist militants as intermediaries in dealing with radical Islamists operating in the Sinai Peninsula: in exchange for an end to violence, the Egyptian military agreed to suspend its anti-terror operation in the Sinai.[47]

3.1.3 Attempts to identify and separate out moderates
Former combatants and moderates have been used as important intermediaries between the state and VEOs. Separating hardliners from moderates on the basis of their ideology and stated goals can be the first step towards identifying potential partners for fruitful dialogue. As Panait (2014) argues, 'In terms of constituency, moderates play a vital role in tempering the fires and lofty goals of groups once they intermingle with extremists. When moderates represent the bulk and extremists are included, they feel more inclined to choose a more moderate course for fear of becoming too isolated or unrepresentative. However, the reverse of this thinking is the polarising "war on terror" mentality, which often alienates moderates from the process.'[48] In Northern Ireland, for example, peace talks began between the government and more moderate Ulster Unionist Party and Catholic SDLP, while it concluded with an agreement between the more hard-line Democratic Unionist Party and Sinn Fein.[49]

3.2 Dialogue
3.2.1 Promote dialogue among groups
VEOs often deliberately increase tensions between different (religious) societal factions or groups. Increased polarisation creates an environment where there

are clear sides and a specific enemy: this can be advantageous for recruitment and propaganda purposes. Under the leadership of Abu Musab al-Zarqawi, for example, Al-Qaeda in Iraq (which would later become ISIS) specifically targeted Shi'a Muslims and Shi'a holy sites as a means of instigating a sectarian war in Iraq and thereby gaining recruits, material and ideological support.[50] This has been seen in the case of Christians and Muslims in Nigeria, between Coptic Christians and Muslims in Egypt, between immigrant communities in Europe, to name a few. Facilitating public dialogue between communities can help to reduce intercommunal tensions, ensure moderate voices prevail, and help increase the resilience of communities to ideological and political manipulation. There are several initiatives that can be drawn on as examples of dialogue promotion.[51]

4. Persuasion and counter-narrative
4.1 Persuasion
4.1.1 Deradicalisation

The term 'radicalisation' is still somewhat disputed. Radicalism and extremism are, of course, relative terms and therefore mean different things to different people, depending on the environment. However, while disputed, radicalisation is generally understood as 'a process whereby individuals (and even groups) develop, over time, a mindset that can – under the right circumstances and opportunities – increase the risk that he or she will engage in violent extremism or terrorism'.[52] It then follows that 'deradicalisation' can be used to refer to the 'methods and techniques used to undermine and reverse the completed radicalisation process, thereby reducing the potential risk to society from terrorism'.[53] There are a number of examples of deradicalisation programmes worldwide. However, in response to the roughly 2 500 Saudis that have travelled to Syria to fight for ISIS, the government established and developed what has been called 'the best funded and longest continuously running counter-radicalisation programme in existence'.[54] The programme's central objective is to persuade extremists housed within the country's prison system that their jihadist interpretation of the Qur'an is incorrect. While the programme is not without its detractors, it has claimed some success, and is able to report very low recidivism rates among participants.[55]

5. Deterrence by counter-narrative/delegitimisation
5.1 WMD focus

There are a wide variety of counter-narratives that can and have been used to undermine or delegitimise the political demands or extremist ideologies that animate VEOs. These can, for example, include the analysis and refutation of specific readings of religious texts. In the case of the aforementioned Saudi Arabian deradicalisation programme, religious scholars and clerics are used to refute ISIS's interpretation of *takfirism* – a concept used by the organisation to distinguish someone, Muslim or otherwise, as an unbeliever and thus deserving of death.[56] Other counter-narratives can be used to expose the use of certain weapons or the pursuit of specific political objectives as counterproductive, such as the consequences of using weapons of mass destruction.

6. Positive incentives/opening up alternative options

Based on a thorough conflict analysis, which exposes the root causes, drivers and dynamics of a given conflict, action can be undertaken to address any underlying grievances and causes that might persuade individuals to join a VEO. According to research by, among others, the Global Centre on Cooperative Security, many counterterrorism efforts are based on assumptions and lack a basis in strong prior-conflict analysis.[57] This can render counterterrorism initiatives ineffective, or worse, counterproductive. However, there are examples where measures to address the root causes of conflict have produced favourable results. Often, providing economic *development and incentives* to communities that feel marginalised may serve to at least address the economic root causes of recruitment into VEOs. However, where grievances are political, and not purely economic, these measures need to be accompanied by *peaceful political change*. The Kenyan government, for example, introduced a new Constitution in 2013, which divided the country's formally eight provinces into 46 districts. One of the motivations for doing this was to increase the responsiveness of government to address the economic grievances of communities at the local level, and create further space for political dialogue.[58]

7. Democracy promotion

A government can take a number of measures to promote democracy, ranging from promoting civil society and ensuring freedom of the press, to institutional reform and guaranteeing free and fair elections. While the causal link between low levels of democracy and the emergence of VEOs is contested, there is a strong argument to be made that democratic institutions and procedures, by promoting inclusivity, enabling the peaceful airing of grievances, and providing channels for participation in policy-making, can help to address the underlying grievances that fuel the rise of terrorism.[59] For example, in Iraq, the failure to include Sunni Arabs in the post-2003 political settlement is frequently identified as a cause of the 2006–2007 civil war and the later rise of the Islamic State of Iraq and Syria (ISIS).[60]

As can be seen above, the policy options a government can choose to address the threat posed by VEOs stretch from kinetic, 'hard' military measures to introducing policy change that address the perceived 'root causes' of terrorism. However, while there is a range of options in theory, in reality, the options available are often limited by a number of environmental considerations. How then do policy choices come about?

Strategic choices: The considerations

The real considerations governments face when drawing from the above list to develop national counterterrorism policy are often difficult to identify. They can also be obscured by the official statements that governments are obliged to make, and the reality of the policies they ultimately choose to adopt. For example, there are formal UN and EU counterterrorism strategies, but measures taken on the ground often do not reflect the intentions or the objectives outlined in the documents.

Furthermore, as has been identified in academic reviews of counterterrorism policy development, there is still a paucity of understanding about what actually works. For example, in a systematic review on evaluation research on counterterrorism strategies, Lum (2006) found that not only was there an almost complete absence of evaluative research on counterterrorism interventions, but from those few found, it also appeared that many interventions either did not achieve the outcomes sought, or sometimes increased the likelihood of terrorism occurring.[61] Her findings dramatically emphasise the need for government leaders, policy-makers, researchers and funding agencies to support outcome evaluations of these programmes and efforts to develop an infrastructure to foster counterterrorism evaluative research.[62]

Overall, what can be drawn from this and other studies, is that counterterrorism strategies are generally haphazard and often unrelated to the desired objectives they seek. However, from my own experience, during my time at the office of the National Coordinator for Counterterrorism in the Netherlands, and based on my contacts with foreign governments over the past decade, I have seen how choices in counterterrorism measures are often based on and limited by a number of important environmental considerations.

1. The actions of terrorists

The operational tactics of terrorist organisations have to be taken into consideration when choosing between various counterterrorism policy choices. However, these tactics are not static, and evolve over time. While intelligence services, analysts and police officers follow terrorist suspects closely to try and garner information on operational planning and modi operandi, security services often do not have access to perfect information and will inevitably be taken by surprise. As captured in the phrase that security agencies are 'trying to win the last war, not the following one', the constant evolution in terrorist organisations' operational tactics often precedes and motivates advances in policing tactics. Aviation security serves as a good example of this 'technical race' between security officials and the terrorists. As subsequent terrorist plots to detonate or take control of an aircraft are uncovered, new policies are formulated to regulate what one can and cannot carry onto an aircraft.

2. Availability of instruments and financial resources

As with any other field of policy development, the range of available measures is limited by the availability of resources and capacity. Where resources are scarce, policy priorities must be set. Usually, the most direct, operationally relevant and affordable measures push themselves to the front of policy debates. However, the most obvious, direct or affordable policy choice is not always the most effective in the long term. Often, the pressure to immediately prevent casualties by, for example, increasing airport security, may in fact drain resources that could be better spent on longer-term policies. Furthermore, terrorist organisations will use the knowledge that resources and capacity are finite to their operational advantage.

3. External pressure

There are a number of external pressures that act on national policy development, and several examples where governments were pressured into adopting certain counterterrorism policies by other governments or intergovernmental organisations. These policies can often lead to 'blowback' on the adoptees. The Kenyan government's decision to engage militarily in Somalia and subsequent Al-Shabaab reprisal attacks in Kenya is one example of this.[63] Another example of the effects of external pressure on national counterterrorism policy development is the Financial Action Task Force (FATF) framework. Originally established in 1989, the objective of this intergovernmental body was to promote effective implementation of legal, regulatory and operational measures for combating money laundering. However, after 9/11, the FATF has increasingly expanded its mission to target terrorism financing. The FATF uses the policy of 'debanking', where an individual or organisation suspected of ties with a terrorist organisation is immediately excluded from regular banking services and susceptible to further financial sanctions. Several reports have been published, outlining the negative and counterproductive effects of this approach.[64]

4. Public and political support and/or pressure

Democratically elected governments are beholden to their citizens to provide security. However, the democratic election cycle provides politicians with recurrent opportunities to draw on citizens' fears and prejudices to garner support by elevating one counterterrorism policy over another. However, citizens' understanding of the complexity of counterterrorism or, in fact, the real threat terrorist organisations pose to their personal security, is often flawed. Governments also have to balance effective counterterrorism against the potentially negative blowback caused by privacy infringements, additional policing of public spaces and increased surveillance. Public support will, therefore, always exert substantial pressure on a government's choices in strategic counterterrorism policy development.

5. Chance

Policy development does not always follow a logical pattern, nor is the best policy, after rigorous analysis, always the one that is adopted. During my years working in the heart of government on security issues, I have noticed that the development and adoption of policies is often based largely on 'chance'. Somebody within the ministry or department will come up with an innovative or attractive idea and turn it into a policy note that then arrives on the desk of their superior. If the superior likes the idea, a taskforce might be established, and later a development plan for the new policy. It can be as simple as that. However, as mentioned earlier, this often does not result in the best or most researched ideas reaching the front of the policy queue.

6. Political culture

The last factor that can profoundly shape the decision on counterterrorism policy choices is political culture. In a culture of political polarisation, anxiety and fear, policy choices are often reflexive rather than a result of careful consideration. In a study by Orehek et al (2012), it was found that 'reminders of terrorist attacks elevate the need for closure and the need for closure may enhance in-group identification; interdependence with others; out-group derogation; and support for tough and decisive counterterrorism policies and for leaders likely to carry out such policies'.[65] This trend is evident in many nations where terrorism is pronounced. However, the response mechanism in the face of acts of terrorism differs between countries, depending on their political culture.

As Hofstede has identified, every culture has dominant values that can be expressed along six dimensions: power distance, individualism, uncertainty avoidance, long-term orientation, masculinity, and indulgence vs restraint.[66]

These dominant value systems will be reflected in the political culture and compete with reflexive or regressive policy discourse in times of crisis, such as acts of terrorism. The difference in European and US response mechanisms after major terrorist attacks are both indicative of, and serve to shed light on, the different political cultures in these regions. Similar differences can be seen in the way in which France and Scandinavia, and Russia and the Arab world have developed response mechanisms to terrorism. Terrorist organisations will exploit social polarisation and reflexive political culture to their own ends. Al-Qaeda's 9/11 attack was specifically designed with the presumption that the United States would be drawn into a long-term war that they could not win.[67]

If response mechanisms are largely determined by a combination of political culture and tendency towards reflexive and regressive decision-making, it will require wisdom, courage and analytical rigour to create and advocate for more efficient approaches. After all, military approaches to counterterrorism since 9/11 have been extremely costly, often counterproductive, and largely under-evaluated. However, in recent years, due to a growing awareness of the limits of military approaches to addressing violent extremism, preventing and countering violent extremism (P/CVE) has emerged as a new field of policy development that seeks more effective, efficient and evaluative approaches to addressing the root causes of violent extremism.

Preventing and countering violent extremism: How it came about, and where we are today

It is my own experience that in the years immediately following the 9/11 attacks, discussion or debate around the possible root causes of terrorism was largely taboo. Just asking the question was considered politically incorrect, as by implication, this could be interpreted as justifying political violence. I remember vividly the panic when MP Lousewies van der Laan asked the Dutch government, via a motion presented before parliament in 2005, to give an analysis of what could be considered the breeding ground for international terrorism. While the text of her motion was one sentence, it took a full year for the government to present an answer. During that year we, as civil servants, struggled to come up with an academically rooted and plausible analysis. A full five years had gone by since 9/11, and there was little if any understanding within policy circles of the common motivational factors, ideological narratives, and 'push and pull' factors, which drive recruitment and enable VEOs to operate. This was due almost entirely to one reason: in the wake of 9/11, it was politically incorrect to have this discussion. The United States was attacked on its own soil. There was no justification. The war was on and any attempts to seek a deeper understanding of motivational factors relevant to terrorist recruitment and operations was seen as giving legitimacy to their cause. However, MP Van der Laan was courageous enough to ignore the taboo, which forced the Dutch government to look into the question and begin doing some desperately needed analysis on the topic.

In 2007, the office of the National Coordinator for Counterterrorism in The Hague, under the leadership of Tjibbe Joustra, organised one of the first international gatherings on what later became known as 'radicalisation'. The meeting brought over 200 representatives together from a number of Muslim majority states, including Kuwait and Saudi Arabia, the EU and European member states, the United States, UN bodies, the Organization for Security and Cooperation in Europe (OSCE) and many others. This, and other early meetings, in addition to the publications that arose out of them, helped to generate discussion among policy-makers of the motivations behind terrorist organisations, or, as the politically correct language of the UN puts it, 'factors conducive to the spread of terrorism'.

Today, there is a much-improved understanding of the various pathways into extremism. There is a consensus among policy-makers that the trajectories differ and are specific to certain environments, and an analysis of the specifics of the given environment is required to tailor effective initiatives to prevent and counter recruitment and radicalisation. No two environments are the same and it is counterproductive to assume that they are.[68]

In 2011, the year of the Arab Spring, the death of Osama bin Laden, and a decade after 9/11, both the United States and the EU independently presented an alternative to the military-centred GWOT strategy. The European initiative is called the Radicalisation Awareness Network (RAN) and the US initiative is known as the Global Counterterrorism Forum (GCTF). The RAN is a large network of governmental and non-governmental groups and individuals that have developed projects and approaches related to counter radicalisation.[69] These include deradicalisation initiatives; training and early warning mechanisms; and developing the role that health-care workers, prison staff, former combatants and victims can play in addressing recruitment into violent extremism. The network effectively seeks to increase know-how and promotes the exchange of expertise among European actors. Today, the RAN also has an external pillar, linking some MENA countries to the network.

The GCTF comprises 30 member states.[70] Central to the forum's overarching mission is the promotion of strategic, long-term approaches to counterterrorism and the ideologies that animate VEOs.[71] Understanding motivational factors and drivers for extremism is part and parcel of the GCTF's approach. The forum has developed inspirational material for policy-makers, and several institutes have been created to advance its work.[72] Since 2011, the US government has pushed the CVE agenda as an alternative to purely military approaches to counterterrorism. In more recent years, this has led to more funding for programming in this field. The United Nations Development Programme (UNDP), for instance, has a US$100 million fund available for CVE work in Africa.

While the policy frameworks are in place and funding is available, monitoring and evaluation for P/CVE programming is still underdeveloped and deserves attention. As iterated earlier, analysis and evaluation of policy efficacy is vital to refine initiatives and ensure they evolve with changing environments.

To this end, in 2017, the Institute for Justice and Reconciliation (IJR) undertook a comparative research project in the Central African Republic (CAR), Kenya, and Nigeria, which sought to evaluate the efficacy of local P/CVE programmes and determine to what extent P/CVE frameworks on paper have been operational on the ground.[73] The conclusions were not optimistic. In both Kenya and Nigeria, there are ample official government policies, which include common P/CVE policy approaches, such as counter-narrative, deradicalisation and early warning initiatives, to name a few. However, in reality, these policies had not been working on the ground. In the CAR the situation is even worse. A proper conflict analysis exercise has, so far, been largely absent from government's policy development planning. Although there is agreement that peace-building efforts need to get off the ground as soon as possible, there is no common understanding – or debate – of the root causes of conflict in the CAR. In the absence of such analysis and debate, fixing the problem through non-military means is a difficult task.

Conclusion

The unpleasant conclusion is that despite all the talk there is still no walk. Soft approaches to counterterrorism, especially outside of Europe, and more significantly in sub-Saharan Africa, exist on paper and are discussed in policy circles, but are simply not part of the reality.

One reason why soft approaches to counterterrorism have had difficulty in gaining traction in Africa might be the characteristic of the relationship between the state and its citizens in many African countries. As Leonard et al write: 'The historical and foundational social contract for most Africans is not between the state and individuals but is instead with communities.'[74] In the absence of a social contract between the state and its citizens, the state may be reluctant to invest in the economic and political reform required to bring down the level of political violence and address grievances that fuel violent extremism.

Rather, governments in the region often choose 'hard' security approaches to counterterrorism, given precedent by the GWOT, and which have roots in the state-building project of colonial rule. However, the more the state asserts itself in the lives of its citizens, the more it emphasises its illegitimacy, and the cycle of violence continues. Breaking this cycle will take both analytical and innovative thinking to develop policies that speak to the unique environments in which violent extremism emerges.

Endnotes

1. Rapoport DC (2004) The four waves of rebel terror and September 11, *Anthropoetics*, **8** (1), p. 46. Available at: www.anthropoetics.ucla.edu/ap0801/terror.htm
2. Bush, GW (2001) Address to a Joint Session of Congress and the American People, 20 September 2001. Available at: https://georgewbush-whitehouse.archives.gov/news/releases/2001/09/20010920-8.html
3. Rapoport (2004) p. 47.
4. CNN (2017) 1998 USD Embassy bombings in Africa: Fast fact. Published 8 August 2017. Available at: http://edition.cnn.com/2013/10/06/world/africa/africa-embassy-bombings-fast-facts/index.html
5. Ibid.
6. Reidel, B (2008) *In Search of Al-Qaeda: Its leadership ideology and future*. Washington, DC: Brookings Institution Press.
7. Hansen, SJ (2013) *The History and Ideology of a Militant Islamist Group*. Oxford: Oxford University Press.
8. PBS (2017) Brief history of Al-Qaeda. Available at: www.pbs.org/moyers/journal/07272007/alqaeda.html
9. UN Security Council (2001) *Security Council Resolution 1386 (2001) [on the situation in Afghanistan]*, 20 December 2001, S/RES/1386 (2001). Available at: http://www.refworld.org/docid/3c4e94571c.html
10. National Consortium for the Study of Terrorism and Responses to Terrorism (START) (2016) *Global Terrorism Database*. Published on 19 September 2017. Available at: https://www.start.umd.edu/gtd
11. International Crisis Group (ICG) (2017) Yemen's al-Qaeda: Expanding the base. Published 2 February 2017. Middle East Report No. 174. Available at: http://refworld.org/docid/58933e434.html
12. Ibid.
13. For an explanation of the concepts of 'Near' and 'Far' enemy, see, Gerges, FA (2005) *The Far Enemy: Why the jihad went global*. Cambridge: Cambridge University Press.
14. CNN (2014) Why Arab Spring could be Al-Qaeda's fall. Published 21 February 2014. Available at: http://edition.cnn.com/2011/WORLD/meast/02/21/arab.unrest.alqaeda.analysis/index.html
15. Stern, J and Berger, JM (2016) *ISIS: The state of terrorism*. New York: Harper Collins.
16. Ibid.
17. Ibid.
18. *The Guardian* (2014) ISIS: The inside story. Published 11 December 2014. Available at: https://www.theguardian.com/world/2014/dec/11/-sp-isis-the-inside-story
19. Byman, DL (2017) Frustrated foreign fighters. Brookings Institute. Published 13 July 2017. Available at: https://www.brookings.edu/blog/order-from-chaos/2017/07/13/frustrated-foreign-fighters/
20. CNN (2017) ISIS goes global: 143 attacks in 29 countries have killed 2,043. Published 13 February 2017. Available at: http://edition.cnn.com/2015/12/17/world/mapping-isis-

attacks-around-the-world/index.html
21 Institute for Economics and Peace (2016) *Global Terrorism Index, 2016.* Available at: http://economicsandpeace.org/reports/
22 Presidential Order 13129, Blocking Property and Prohibiting Transactions with the Taliban, 4 July 1999. Available at: https://fas.org/irp/offdocs/eo/eo-13129.htm
23 United Nations Security Council (1999) *Security Council Resolution 1267 (1999) [Afghanistan].* Published 15 October 1999. Available at: http://www.refworld.org/docid/3b00f2298.html
24 The Taliban movement was formed in Sunni Islamic madrassas in Pakistan in 1993 by predominantly Afghan Pashtun mujahideen, with the aim of restoring peace to Afghanistan, disarming the population, enforcing sharia law, and defending the integrity and Islamic character of Afghanistan. See: Fruchart, D, Holtom, P and Wezeman, ST (2006) *United Nations Arms Embargoes: Their impact on arms flows and target behaviour.* Stockholm International Peace Research Institute and Uppsala University, Sweden.
25 The *Kadi and Al Barakaat International Foundation v Council and Commission* (2008) EU law case, concerning the hierarchy between international law and general principles of EU law has received much attention in this regard, to which there are several publications dedicated. See, for example: Kokott, J and Sobotta, C (2012) The *Kadi* Case: Constitutional core values and international law – Finding the balance? *European Journal of International Law,* **23** (4), pp. 1015–1024.
26 North Atlantic Treaty Organization (1949) The North Atlantic Treaty: Article 5. 4 April 1949. Available at: http://www.nato.int/cps/en/natohq/official_texts_17120.htm
27 United Nations Security Council (1999) *Security Council Resolution 1267 (1999) [Afghanistan].* Published 15 October 1999. Available at: http://www.refworld.org/docid/3b00f2298.html
28 Ibid.
29 Ehrlich, P and Liu, J (2002) Some roots of terrorism, *Population and Environment,* **24** (2), pp. 183–192.
30 Schmid, A (2004) Terrorism – The definitional problem, 36 Case W. Res, *Journal of International Law,* **375**. Available at: http://scholarlycommons.law.case.edu/jil/vol36/iss2/8
31 United Nations (2006) *Global Counter-Terrorism Strategy.* Available at: https://www.un.org/counterterrorism/ctitf/en/un-global-counter-terrorism-strategy
32 Ibid.
33 European Union: Council of the European Union (2005) *The European Union Counter-Terrorism Strategy.* Published 30 November 2005. Available at: https://refworld.org
34 Bures, O (2011) *EU Counterterrorism Policy: A paper tiger?* Farnham: Ashgate Publishing, p. 2.
35 Hegemann, H (2014) *International Counterterrorism Bureaucracies in the United Nations and the European Union.* Hamburg: Institute for Security and Peace Research, University of Hamburg.
36 Pate, A (2015) Surveying the Literature on Counter-Terrorism, Counter-Insurgency, and Countering Violent Extremism: A summary report with a focus on Africa. Report to the Strategic Multilayer Assessment Office, Department of Defense, and the Office of University Programs, Department of Homeland Security. Available at: www.start.umd.edu/pubs/START_SMA-AFRICOM_LiteratureReview_Jan2015.pdf
37 See: Davis, P and Jenkins, B (2002) *Deterrence and Influence in Counterterrorism: A component in the war on Al-Qaeda.* RAND Monograph Reports 9 &10. Available at: http://www.rand.org/content/dam/rand/pubs/monograph_reports/2005/MR1619.pdf; Ackerman, GA and Pinson, LE (2011) *I-VEO Empirical Assessment: Literature review and knowledge matrix.* START, University of Maryland. Available at: http://www.start.umd.edu/data-tools/iveo-knowledge-matrix

38 Pate (2015).
39 Ibid.
40 Perl, R (1998) Terrorism: US response to bombings in Kenya and Tanzania: A new policy direction? Document 6, National Security Archive. Washington, DC: Congressional Research Service. Available at: https://digital.library.unt.edu/ark:/67531/metacrs603/
41 The Bureau of Investigative Journalism (2017) *Drone Warfare*. Available at: https://digital.library.unt.edu/ark:/67531/metacrs603/
42 RFI (2011) Civilians killed in Nigerian military's fight with Boko Haram, claim human rights groups. Published 23 November 2011. Available at: en.rfi.fr/africa/20111122-military-might-brings-misery-maiduguri; Amnesty International (2015) Stars on their shoulders. Blood on their hands. War crimes committed by the Nigerian military. Available at: https://www.amnesty.org/en/documents/afr44/1657/2015/en/
43 Amnesty International (2014) Kenya: Somalis scapegoated in counter-terror crackdown. 27 May 2014. Available at: https://www.amnesty.org/en/articles/news/2014/05/kenya-somalis-scapegoated-counter-terror-crackdown/
44 *The Washington Post* (2011) Anwar al-Aulaqi, U.S.-born cleric linked to al-Qaeda, killed in Yemen. Published 1 October 2011. Available at: https://www.washingtonpost.com/world/middle-east/anwar-al-aulaqi-us-born-cleric-linked-to-al-qaeda-killed-yemen-says/2011/09/30/gIQAsoWO9K_story.html?utm_term=.1415658ef60c
45 European Union: Council of the European Union (2005) *The European Union Counter-Terrorism Strategy*. Published 30 November 2005. Available at: https://refworld.org
46 Legal Information Institute (2017) 18 US Code No. 2339A – Providing material support to terrorists. Available at: https://www.law.cornell.edu/uscode/text/18/2339A
47 Haaretz (2012) Egypt's Morsi using former Islamists as intermediaries in negotiations with Sinai militants. Published 29 August 2012. Available at: http://www.haaretz.com/middle-east-news/egypt-s-morsi-using-former-islamists-as-intermediaries-in-negotiations-with-sinai-militants-1.461453
48 Panait, A (2014) Negotiating with terrorists considered: A review of scholarly literature, *Perspectives* 2014. Available at: https://cola.unh.edu/sites/cola.unh.edu/files/student-journals/Perspectives2014_Panait.pdf
49 *The Atlantic* (2015) Negotiate with ISIS. Published 7 December 2015. Available at: https://www.theatlantic.com/international/archive/2015/12/negotiate-with-isis/419157/
50 Weaver, MA (2006) The short, violent life of Abu Musab al-Zarqawi, *The Atlantic*. Published July/August 2006. Available at: https://www.theatlantic.com/magazine/archive/2006/07/the-short-violent-life-of-abu-musab-al-zarqawi/304983/
51 See, for example, the Women Preventing Extremist Violence (WPEV) and the Sisters Against Violent Extremism Mother Schools (SAVE) programmes funded by the United Institute for Peace (USIP). Available at: https://www.usip.org/publications/2015/03/dialogue-women-countering-violent-extremism. More information can be found at: http://opportunitydesk.org/2017/02/01/cve-centre-for-youth-dialogues-in-kenya
52 RAND (2013) *Scientific Approach to Finding Indicators for and Responses to Radicalisation: Project information*. Available at: https://www.rand.org/randeurope/research/projects/safire-radicalisation.html
53 Ibid.
54 Boucek, C (2008) *Saudi Arabia's 'Soft' Counterterrorism Strategy: Prevention, rehabilitation, and aftercare*. Carnegie Papers, Middle East Program, Carnegie Endowment for International Peace. Published 2 September 2008. Available at: http://carnegieendowment.org/2008/09/22/saudi-arabia-s-soft-counterterrorism-strategy-prevention-rehabilitation-and-aftercare-pub-22155
55 Ibid.

56 Ibid.
57 Global Centre on Cooperative Security (2015) *Does CVE work? Lessons learned from the global effort to counter violent extremism.* Published September 2015. Available at: http://www.globalcenter.org/wp-content/uploads/2015/09/Does-CVE-Work_2015.pdf
58 Ghai, YP and Cottrell Gahi, J (2011) *Kenya's Constitution: An instrument for change.* Nairobi: Katiba Institute.
59 Collier, P, Elliott, E, Hegre, H, Reynal-Querol, M and Sambanis, N (2003) *Breaking the Conflict Trap: Civil war and development policy.* Washington, DC: World Bank.
60 Stern, J and Berger, JM (2016) *ISIS: The state of terrorism.* New York: Harper Collins.
61 Lum, C (2006) Are counter-terrorism strategies effective? The results of the Campbell systematic review on counter-terrorism evaluation research, *Journal of Experimental Criminology*, **2** (4), pp. 489–516.
62 Ibid.
63 National Consortium for the Study of Terrorism and Responses to Terrorism (START) (2015) Al-Shabaab Attack on Garissa University in Kenya. Background report, START, University of Maryland. Published April 2015. Available at: https://www.start.umd.edu/pubs/STARTBackgroundReport_alShabaabGarissaU_April2015.pdf
64 Centre for Global Development (2015) *Unintended Consequences of Anti-Money Laundering Policies for Poor Countries.* A CGD Working Group Report. Available at: https://www.cgdev.org/sites/default/files/CGD-WG-Report-Unintended-Consequences-AML-Policies-2015.pdf
65 Orehek, E, Fishman, S, Dechesne, M, Doosje, B, Kruglanski, AW and Cole, AP (2012) Need for closure and social responses to terrorism, *Basic and Applied Social Psychology*, **23** (4), pp. 279–290.
66 Hofstede, G (2001) *Culture's Consequences: Comparing values, behaviors, institutions and organizations across nations*, 2nd edn. Thousand Oaks, CA: Sage Publications.
67 Wrights, L (2006) *The Looming Tower: Al-Qaeda and the road to 9/11.* New York: Knopf Doubleday.
68 Global Centre for Cooperative Security (2015) *Does CVE Work? Lessons learned from the global effort to counter violent extremism.* Published September 2015. Available at: http://www.globalcenter.org/wp-content/uploads/2015/09/Does-CVE-Work_2015.pdf
69 See: Radicalization Awareness Network. About us. Available at: https://ec.europa.eu/home-affairs/what-we-do/networks/radicalisation_awareness_network_en
70 The 30 founding members of the GCTF are: Algeria, France, The Netherlands, Spain, Australia, Germany, New Zealand, Switzerland, Canada, India, Nigeria, Turkey, China, Indonesia, Pakistan, United Arab Emirates (UAE), Colombia, Italy, Qatar, United Kingdom (UK), Denmark, Japan, Russia, United States (US), Egypt, Jordan, Saudi Arabia, European Union (EU), Morocco and South Africa.
71 See: Global Counter Terrorism Forum (GCTF) About us. Available at: https://www.thegctf.org/
72 Among others, these include Hedayah CoE in Abu Dhabi and the International Institute for Justice in Malta.
73 See: Knoope, P and Buchanan-Clarke, S (2017) *Central African Republic: A conflict misunderstood.* Institute for Justice and Reconciliation, Occasional Paper No. 22. Available at: http://www.ijr.org.za/portfolio-items/central-african-republic-a-conflict-misunderstood/; Buchanan-Clarke, S and Knoope, P (2017) *The Boko Haram Insurgency: From short-term gains to long-term solutions.* Institute for Justice and Reconciliation, Occasional Paper No. 23. Available at: http://www.ijr.org.za/portfolio-items/the-boko-haram-insurgency-from-short-term-gains-to-long-term-solutions/
74 Leonard, DK, Mushi, MF and Vincent, J (2011) *Social Contracts and Security in Sub-Saharan*

African Conflict States: The Democratic Republic of Congo, Sierra Leone and Somalia. Paper for presentation to the African Studies Association, Washington DC, November 2011

References

Ackerman, GA and Pinson, LE (2011) *I-VEO Empirical Assessment: Literature review and knowledge matrix*. START, University of Maryland. Available at: http://www.start.umd.edu/data-tools/iveo-knowledge-matrix

Amnesty International (2014) Kenya: Somalis scapegoated in counter-terror crackdown. Published 27 May 2014. Available at: https://www.amnesty.org/en/articles/news/2014/05/kenya-somalis-scapegoated-counter-terror-crackdown/

Amnesty International (2015) Stars on their shoulders. Blood on their hands. War crimes committed by the Nigerian military. Available at: https://www.amnesty.org/en/documents/afr44/1657/2015/en/

Boucek, C (2008) *Saudi Arabia's 'Soft' Counterterrorism Strategy: Prevention, rehabilitation, and aftercare*. Middle East Program, Carnegie Endowment for International Peace. Published 2 September 2008. Available at: http://carnegieendowment.org/2008/09/22/saudi-arabia-s-soft-counterterrorism-strategy-prevention-rehabilitation-and-aftercare-pub-22155

Buchanan-Clarke, S and Knoope, P (2017) *The Boko Haram Insurgency: From short-term gains to long-term solutions*. Institute for Justice and Reconciliation, Occasional Paper No. 23. Available at: http://www.ijr.org.za/portfolio-items/the-boko-haram-insurgency-from-short-term-gains-to-long-term-solutions/

Bures, O (2011) *EU Counterterrorism Policy: A paper tiger?* Farnham: Ashgate Publishing.

Bush, GW (2001) Address to a Joint Session of Congress and the American People. 20 September 2001. Available at: https://georgewbush-whitehouse.archives.gov/news/releases/2001/09/20010920-8.html

Byman, DL (2017) Frustrated foreign fighters. Brookings Institute. Published 13 July 2017. Available at: https://www.brookings.edu/blog/order-from-chaos/2017/07/13/frustrated-foreign-fighters/

Centre for Global Development (2015) *Unintended Consequences of Anti-Money Laundering Policies for Poor Countries*. A CGD Working Group Report. Available at: https://www.cgdev.org/sites/default/files/CGD-WG-Report-Unintended-Consequences-AML-Policies-2015.pdf

CNN (2014) Why Arab Spring could be Al-Qaeda's Fall. Published 21 February 2014. Available at: http://edition.cnn.com/2011/WORLD/meast/02/21/arab.unrest.alqaeda.analysis/index.html

CNN (2017) 1998 USD Embassy bombings in Africa: Fast fact. Published 8 August 2017. Available at: http://edition.cnn.com/2013/10/06/world/africa/africa-embassy-bombings-fast-facts/index.html

CNN (2017) ISIS goes global: 143 attacks in 29 countries have killed 2 043. Published 13 February 2017. Available at: http://edition.cnn.com/2015/12/17/world/mapping-isis-attacks-around-the-world/index.html

Collier, P, Elliott, E, Hegre, H, Reynal-Querol, M and Sambanis, N (2003) *Breaking the Conflict Trap: Civil war and development policy*. Washington, DC: World Bank.

Davis, P and Jenkins, B (2002) *Deterrence and Influence in Counterterrorism: A component in the war on Al-Qaeda*. RAND Monograph Reports 9 &10. Available http://www.rand.org/content/dam/rand/pubs/monograph_reports/2005/MR1619.pdf

Ehrlich, P and Liu, J (2002) Some roots of terrorism, *Population and Environment*, **24** (2), pp. 183–192.

European Union: Council of the European Union (2005) *The European Union Counter-Terrorism Strategy*. Published 30 November 2005. Available at: https://refworld.org

Fruchart, D, Holtom, P and Wezeman, ST (2006) *United Nations Arms Embargoes: Their impact on arms flows and target behaviour*. Stockholm International Peace Research Institute and

Uppsala University, Sweden.

Gerges, FA (2005) *The Far Enemy: Why the jihad went global.* Cambridge: Cambridge University Press.

Ghai, YP and Cottrell Gahi, J (2011) *Kenya's Constitution: An instrument for change.* Nairobi: Katiba Institute.

Global Centre for Cooperative Security (2015) *Does CVE work? Lessons learned from the global effort to counter violent extremism.* Published September 2015. Available at: http://www.globalcenter.org/wp-content/uploads/2015/09/Does-CVE-Work_2015.pdf

Haaretz (2012) Egypt's Morsi using former Islamists as intermediaries in negotiations with Sinai militants. Published 29 August 2012. Available at: http://www.haaretz.com/middle-east-news/egypt-s-morsi-using-former-islamists-as-intermediaries-in-negotiations-with-sinai-militants-1.461453

Hansen, SJ (2013) *The History and Ideology of a Militant Islamist Group.* Oxford: Oxford University Press.

Hegemann, H (2014) *International Counterterrorism Bureaucracies in the United Nations and the European Union.* Hamburg: Institute for Security and Peace Research, University of Hamburg.

Hofstede, G (2001) *Culture's Consequences: Comparing values, behaviors, institutions, and organizations across nations,* 2nd edn. Thousand Oaks, CA: Sage Publications.

Institute for Economics and Peace (2016) *Global Terrorism Index 2016.* Available at: http://economicsandpeace.org/reports/

International Crisis Group (ICG) (2017) Yemen's al-Qaeda: Expanding the base. Published 2 February 2017. Middle East Report No. 174. Available at: http://refworld.org/docid/58933e434.html.

Knoope, P and Buchanan-Clarke, S (2017) *Central African Republic: A conflict misunderstood.* Institute for Justice and Reconciliation. Occasional Paper No. 22. Available at: http://www.ijr.org.za/portfolio-items/central-african-republic-a-conflict-misunderstood/

Kokott, J and Sobotta, C (2012) The *Kadi* Case: Constitutional core values and international law – Finding the balance? *European Journal of International Law,* **23** (4), pp. 1015–1024.

Legal Information Institute (2017) 18 US Code No.2339A – Providing material support to terrorists. Available at: https://www.law.cornell.edu/uscode/text/18/2339A

Leonard, DK, Mushi, MF and Vincent, J (2011) *Social Contracts and Security in Sub-Saharan African Conflict States: The Democratic Republic of Congo, Sierra Leone and Somalia.* Paper for presentation to the African Studies Association, Washington DC, November 2011

Lum, C (2006) Are counter-terrorism strategies effective? The results of the Campbell systematic review on counter-terrorism evaluation research, *Journal of Experimental Criminology,* **2** (4), pp. 489–516.

Michaelsen, C (2010) The Security Council's Al-Qaeda and Taliban sanctions regime: 'Essential tool' or increasing liability for the UN's counterterrorism efforts? *Studies in Conflict & Terrorism,* **33** (5), pp. 448–463.

National Consortium for the Study of Terrorism and Responses to Terrorism (START) (2015) Al-Shabaab Attack on Garissa University in Kenya. Background report START, University of Maryland. Published April 2015. Available at: https://www.start.umd.edu/pubs/STARTBackgroundReport_alShabaabGarissaU_April2015.pdf

National Consortium for the Study of Terrorism and Responses to Terrorism (START) (2016) *Global Terrorism Database.* Published 19 September 2017. Available at: https://www.start.umd.edu/gtd

North Atlantic Treaty Organization (1949) The North Atlantic Treaty: Article 5, 4 April 1949. Available at: http://www.nato.int/cps/en/natohq/official_texts_17120.htm

Orehek, E, Fishman, S, Dechesne, M, Doosje, B, Kruglanski, AW and Cole, AP (2012) Need for closure and social responses to terrorism *Basic and Applied Social Psychology*, **23** (4), pp. 279–290.

Panait, A (2014) Negotiating with terrorists considered: A review of scholarly literature, *Perspectives* 2014. Available at: https://cola.unh.edu/sites/cola.unh.edu/files/student-journals/Perspectives2014_Panait.pdf

Pate, A (2015) Surveying the Literature on Counter-Terrorism, Counter-Insurgency, and Countering Violent Extremism: A summary report with a focus on Africa. Report to the Strategic Multilayer Assessment Office, Department of Defense and the Office of University Programs, Department of Homeland Security. Available at: www.start.umd.edu/pubs/START_SMA-AFRICOM_LiteratureReview_Jan2015.pdf

PBS (2017) Brief history of Al-Qaeda. Available at: www.pbs.org/moyers/journal/07272007/alqaeda.html

Perl, R (1998) Terrorism: US response to bombings in Kenya and Tanzania: A new policy direction? Document 6, National Security Archive. Washington, DC: Congressional Research Service. Available at: https://digital.library.unt.edu/ark:/67531/metacrs603/

Presidential Order 13129, Blocking Property and Prohibiting Transactions With the Taliban, 4 July 1999. Available at: https://fas.org/irp/offdocs/eo/eo-13129.htm

Rapoport DC (2004) The four waves of rebel terror and September 11, *Anthropoetics*, **8** (1), p. 46. Available at: www.anthropoetics.ucla.edu/ap0801/terror.htm

RAND (2013) *Scientific Approach to Finding Indicators for and Responses to Radicalisation: Project information*. Available at: https://www.rand.org/randeurope/research/projects/safire-radicalisation.html

Reidel, B (2008) *In Search of Al-Qaeda: Its leadership ideology and future*. Washington, DC: Brooking Institution Press.

RFI (2011) Civilians killed in Nigerian military's fight with Boko Haram, claim human rights groups. Published 23 November 2011. Available at: en.rfi.fr/africa/20111122-military-might-brings-misery-maiduguri

Schmid, A (2004) Terrorism: The definitional problem, 36 Case W. Res., *Journal of International Law*, **375**. Available at: http://scholarlycommons.law.case.edu/jil/vol36/iss2/8

Stern, J and Berger, JM (2016) *ISIS: The state of terrorism*. New York: Harper Collins.

The Atlantic (2015) Negotiate with ISIS. Published 7 December 2017. Available at: https://www.theatlantic.com/international/archive/2015/12/negotiate-with-isis/419157/

The Bureau of Investigative Journalism (2017) *Drone Warfare*. Available at: https://digital.library.unt.edu/ark:/67531/metacrs603/

The Guardian (2014) ISIS: The inside story. Published 11 December 2014. Available at: https://www.theguardian.com/world/2014/dec/11/-sp-isis-the-inside-story

The Washington Post (2011) Anwar al-Aulaqi, U.S.-born cleric linked to al-Qaeda, killed in Yemen. Published 1 October 2011. Available at: https://www.washingtonpost.com/world/middle-east/anwar-al-aulaqi-us-born-cleric-linked-to-al-qaeda-killed-yemen-says/2011/09/30/gIQAsoWO9K_story.html?utm_term=.1415658ef60c

United Nations (2006) *Global Counter-Terrorism Strategy*. Available at: https://www.un.org/counterterrorism/ctitf/en/un-global-counter-terrorism-strategy

United Nations Security Council (1999) *Security Council Resolution 1267 (1999) [Afghanistan]*. Published 15 October 1999. Available at: http://www.refworld.org/docid/3b00f2298.html

UN Security Council (2001) *Security Council Resolution 1386 (2001) [on the situation in Afghanistan]*, 20 December 2001, S/RES/1386 (2001). Available at: http://www.refworld.org/docid/3c4e94571c.html [Accessed 19 September 2017].

Weaver, MA (2006) The short, violent life of Abu Musab al-Zarqawi, *The Atlantic*. Published July/August 2006. Available at: https://www.theatlantic.com/magazine/archive/2006/

07/the-short-violent-life-of-abu-musab-al-zarqawi/304983/
Wrights, L (2006) *The Looming Tower: Al-Qaeda and the road to 9/11*. New York: Knopf Doubleday.

Chapter 2

Public opinion on security and terrorism in Africa

Rorisang Lekalake

Introduction

In recent years, Africa has experienced a substantial escalation in the threat posed by violent extremist groups to local populations. Incident data from the Global Terrorism Database (GTD) show a dramatic growth in the number of attacks targeting civilians on the continent since 2011, with particularly high levels of violence in 2014 and 2015.[1] Despite this increase in the overall frequency of incidents, terrorism is a largely geographically concentrated phenomenon, with the majority of attacks occurring in relatively small areas or 'hot spots' of extremist activity, leading to wide variations in its impact on citizens both across and within African countries. This chapter employs public opinion data from more than 30 African countries to address public perceptions of the current security context in the region and to gauge the impact of terrorist activity on ordinary citizens in a selection of the countries most affected by terrorist activity, before presenting the findings of the most recent research in three key contexts: Kenya, Mali and Nigeria.

Afrobarometer is a pan-African, non-partisan research network founded in 1999, which measures public attitudes towards democracy, governance, economic conditions and related issues. The majority of Afrobarometer survey items are asked in all countries and core questions are repeated, which allows for comparisons across country and time. Afrobarometer conducted about 54 000 interviews between March 2014 and December 2015 (see Appendix, Table 2A.1 for fieldwork dates), which correspond with the surge in the number of terrorist attacks on the continent.[2] The dataset therefore provides important insights into citizen attitudes, perceptions and evaluations in a crucial time period of escalated terrorist threat. The Nigeria survey was the most affected by levels of insecurity at the time of data collection and the team was unable to conduct data collection in the three most affected states, while fieldwork also corresponded with elevated threat levels in Kenya and Tunisia. However, since then, fieldwork has taken place in Kenya (December 2016), Mali (February 2017) and Nigeria (April/May 2017).[3]

Despite the recent growth in the number of extremist attacks and casualties on the continent, an analysis of the leading English-language literature on terrorism worldwide indicates that African countries represent seven of the 10 countries in which further research is most critically needed.[4] Afrobarometer conducts surveys in five of these seven countries, which offer crucial insights into terrorism's impact on ordinary citizens. This analysis will begin by summarising the findings from the 2014/15 round of surveys in Africa as a whole and in the North African region in particular, before presenting the latest data from 2016 and 2017 in three featured countries. It will focus on providing a purely descriptive analysis of the findings while highlighting opportunities for further causal analysis and research in this area.

Public opinion and the security context in Africa, 2014/15

Prior to analysing public opinion on terrorism in specific regions and countries, it is important to establish a baseline understanding of popular perceptions of the security context in Africa. Evidence from Afrobarometer indicates that security is not a primary concern for the majority of Africans. In 2014/15, unemployment was the most widely cited problem facing African countries, followed by health, education, infrastructure/transport, water, poverty, farming/agriculture, food shortages, and then crime and security.[5] Concern about security varied widely across the 36 countries. On average, one in five survey respondents identified a security related issue among the top three problems facing their country, while a similar proportion (17 per cent) supported further investment into security infrastructure (Figure 2.1). Prioritisation of further investment into security services also ranged widely, from only 3 per cent in Sierra Leone to 45 per cent in Tunisia (see Appendix, Table 2A.2).

These differences reflect the divergence in national contexts across the continent. The Ibrahim Index of African Governance (IIAG) provides composite scores for measures of personal security and national security for all African countries based on a combination of objective and perception data (including Afrobarometer surveys), and found that this area of governance deteriorated the most between 2005 and 2015.[6] Many of the countries that score poorly on the IIAG's national-security measure have faced a growing threat from extremist activity (eg, Sudan, Kenya, Nigeria and Cameroon), but comparing overall scores on this measure to those on personal security, indicates that the latter is the greater challenge for most African states (Appendix, Table 2A.1).

Half of Afrobarometer respondents in 2014/15 said their government was handling crime reduction 'very' or 'fairly' badly, and a fairly substantial minority reported feeling unsafe in their communities (37 per cent) or homes (30 per cent) at least once in the previous year. While about 25 per cent had been a victim of theft, only 9 per cent reported being physically assaulted.

Category	Indicator	%
Citizen priorities	Cite security among most important problems	19%
	Support investment into security services	17%
Personal safety	Govt handling reducing crime "very" or "fairly" badly	51%
	Felt unsafe walking in neighbourhood at least once	37%
	Feared crime in home at least once	30%
	Had something stolen from house	26%
	Physically assaulted	9%
Lack of confidence in security institutions	Trust the police "just a little" or "not at all"	47%
	"All" or "most" police are corrupt	45%
	Trust the army "just a little" or "not at all"	33%

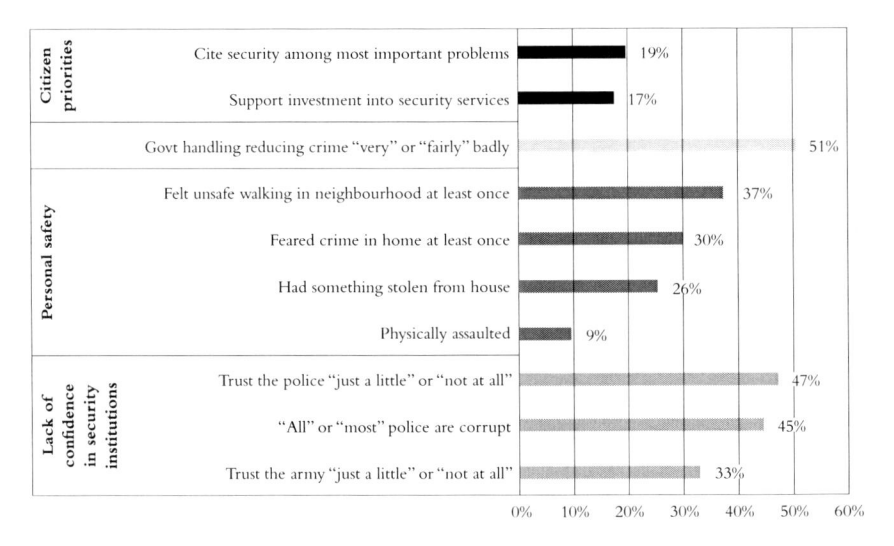

Figure 2.1: Summary of key indicators of security context, 36 countries, 2014/15

Respondents were asked:

1. In your opinion, what are the most important problems facing this country that government should address?[7]
2. If the government of this country could increase its spending, which of the following areas do you think should be the top priority for additional investment? And which would be your second priority?

(percentage who cited security as one of their two priorities)

3. Over the past year, how often, if ever, have you or anyone in your family:
    a. Felt unsafe walking in your neighbourhood?
    b. Feared crime in your own home?

(percentage 'just once or twice')

4. During the past year, have you or anyone in your family:
    a. Had something stolen from your house?
    b. Been physically attacked?

(percentage 'yes')

5. How much do you trust each of the following, or haven't you heard enough about them to say:
    a. The police?
    b. The army?

('just a little' or 'not at all')

Figure 2.1 also indicates relatively low confidence in state security forces. While only a third of respondents reported distrusting the military in their respective countries, almost half (47 per cent) said they trusted the police 'just a little' or 'not at all'. Furthermore, the police are seen as the most corrupt institution or societal group in Africa: 45 per cent of respondents said they believe 'all' or 'most of them' to be corrupt, and 27 per cent of those who came into contact with the police in the preceding year said they had to 'pay a bribe, give a gift or provide a favour' to get the help that they needed.[8] This is of particular importance in countries threatened by terrorist activity due to the greater role the police forces play in preventing and countering violent extremism (P/CVE) programming than in traditional counterterrorism strategies.[9]

P/CVE strategies emphasise the role of local communities as vital partners in the fight against terrorism, which requires a productive working relationship with both the military and police. These findings suggest that many countries would face significant challenges in convincing local communities to cooperate with the police in particular.

Public opinion and the security context: Key trends in Kenya, Mali and Nigeria

Figure 2.1 provides a useful 'snapshot' of public opinion across the region in 2014/15. However, a number of countries have been surveyed repeatedly since the first round and, therefore, there are data on the trends in public perceptions and evaluations since 2000. This is particularly useful in evaluating citizen responses to the evolving context in three of the countries most affected by terrorism in Africa: Kenya, Mali and Nigeria. Of the three, Nigeria has experienced the highest number of terrorism-related casualties, injuries and infrastructural damage in recent years (see Appendix, Table 2A.4).

Results across survey rounds in Nigeria show that citizen concern about security declined between 2002 and 2008 before surging to its highest level (39 per cent) in 2014 (Figure 2.2). Since then, however, there has been a similarly dramatic decline to only 13 per cent in 2017. As in Nigeria, fewer Kenyans ranked security among their primary concerns in their most recent survey (2016) compared to 2014, while Mali experienced an increase on this measure. These results will be contextualised and contrasted in the latter sections of this analysis.

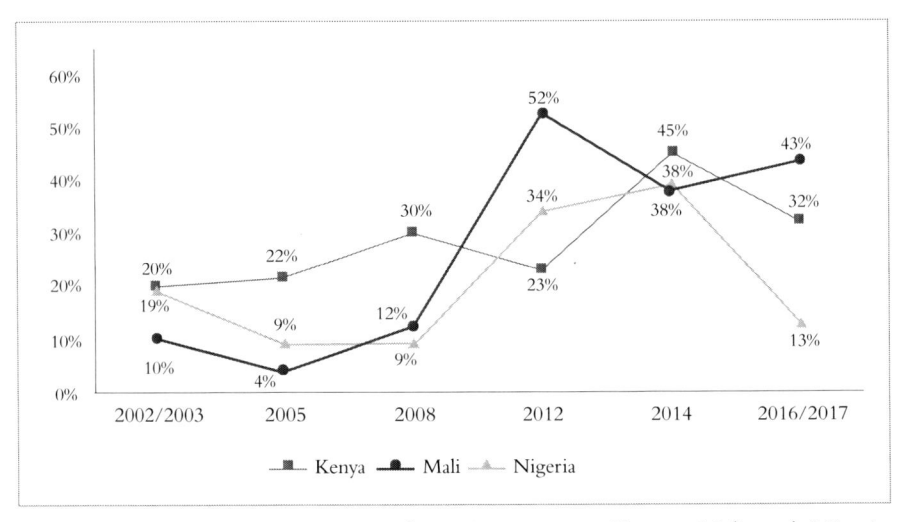

Figure 2.2: Citizen prioritisation of security concerns, Kenya, Mali and Nigeria, 2002–2017
(percentage of respondents who cite security related concerns among top three problems facing the country)

As shown above, improving citizens' perceptions of the police is particularly important in the countries facing the most significant threat from terrorism in order to implement successful P/CVE initiatives. Among the five countries surveyed by Afrobarometer that are at greatest risk of terrorist violence (based on their global GTI ranking), public distrust in the police and military was highest in Nigeria (68 per cent on average, across the two institutions), followed by Kenya (45 per cent), Cameroon (38 per cent), Egypt (27 per cent) and Niger (10 per cent) (see Appendix, Table 2A.3). Comparison of public opinion data from the three featured countries in the second half of this chapter indicates substantial differences in average levels by country and across time. Nigerians were generally more likely to distrust both the police and military, although confidence in the armed forces has improved significantly since 2012 (Figure 2.3). Mali also experienced a decline in distrust of the military between 2012 and 2017, but lack of public confidence in the armed forces started at a much lower baseline than in Nigeria.

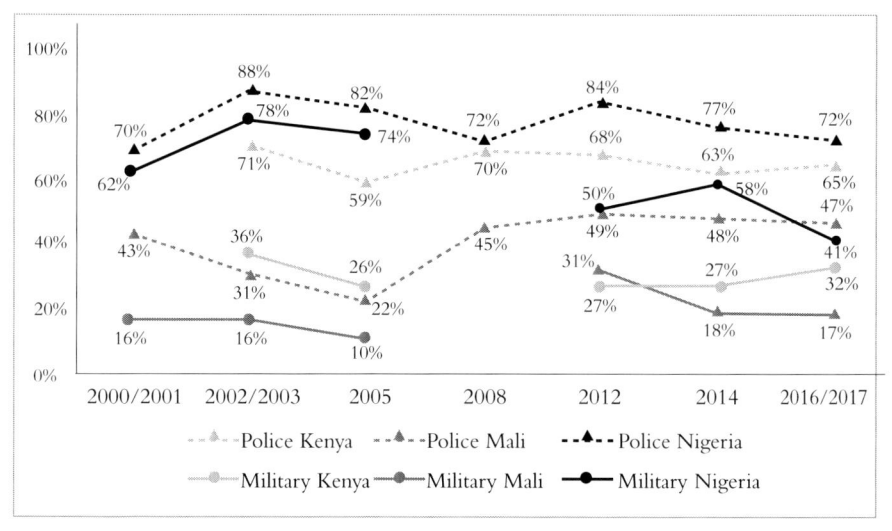

Figure 2.3: Public distrust in public security agencies, Kenya,[10] *Mali and Nigeria, 2000–2017*
(percentage reporting 'a little' or 'not at all')

While these results are promising, there is still room for improvement in how local communities relate to the armed forces. The most recent Afrobarometer questionnaire (2016/18) introduced new questions about the armed forces' efficacy, access to resources and conduct. While seven in 10 respondents said the Malian armed forces are 'often' or 'always' professional and respectful to the public, just under half said so in both Nigeria (49 per cent) and Kenya (47 per cent) (see Appendix, Table 2A.5).

This section provides useful insights into public opinion regarding the general security context across Africa in 2014/15. In addition to these standardised items, the survey instrument also includes a limited number of 'country specific questions' that address topical issues in that country at the time of research. Questions related to terrorism and armed extremism were asked in 11 countries in 2014/15 and addressed in two 2016 Afrobarometer publications.[11] The following section presents findings from five North African countries: Algeria, Egypt, Morocco, Sudan and Tunisia.

Public opinion and terrorism: Key trends in North Africa[12]

The Middle East and North Africa (MENA) has been heavily affected by violent extremism and North African countries, in particular, have become a focus of extremist activity in recent years. In part, this has been a result of the political upheaval following the overthrow of Libya's long-time ruler, Muammar Gaddafi, during the Arab Spring protests of 2011.[13] In recent years, Libya has experienced an exponential growth in terrorist-related violence. Moreover, violent extremist organisations have taken advantage of the country's power vacuum, and the wider region's porous borders, to increase their geographic scope and the intensity of their activities throughout North Africa and in adjacent regions such as the Sahel and the Lake Chad Basin.

On average, the five North African countries surveyed by Afrobarometer in 2015 scored 60.2 points on the IIAG national security measure, compared to a continental average of 75.2 points. This partly reflects the elevated threat of terrorism that these countries face overall compared to most other African nations: the Global Terrorism Database (GTD) recorded 990 attacks perpetrated by terrorist organisations in the region in 2015, which led to over 1 500 recorded casualties (Appendix, Table 2A.6).

In 2015, four in 10 (41 per cent) respondents felt that the Arab Spring had had a 'negative' or 'very negative' impact on the region, while three in 10 (29 per cent) said the same about its impact on their country (Figure 2.4). These levels varied substantially by country, with Tunisians reporting the greatest perceived negative impact on both measures, despite being the only MENA country to have successfully democratised following the Arab Spring protests.[14] Furthermore, one-third of respondents in Tunisia said that law, order and stability had declined in the country since the period prior to the initial protests in 2011, which is significantly higher than the average levels in the other four countries (17 per cent).

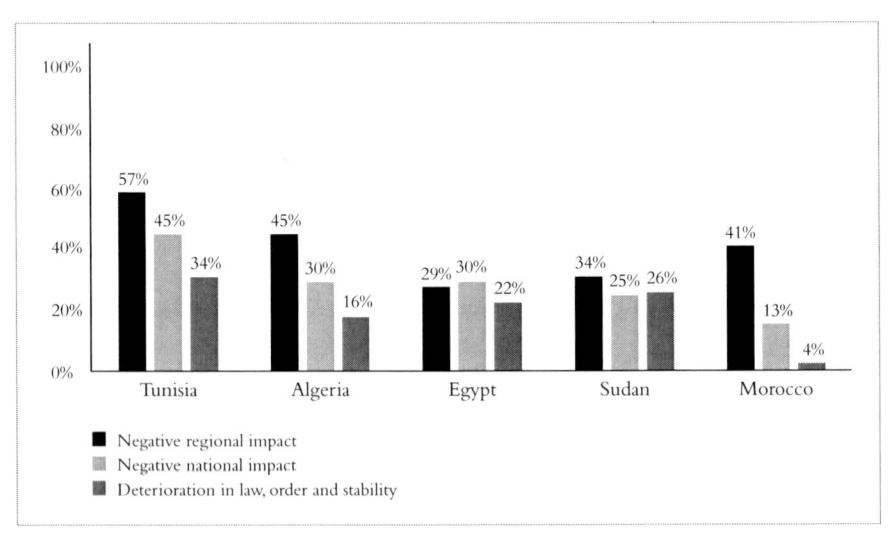

Figure 2.4: Perceived impact of the Arab Spring, five North African countries, 2015

Respondents were asked:
1. During 2011, several Arab countries in North Africa witnessed a wave of popular protests demanding democracy and improvements in human rights, popularly known as the 'Arab Spring'. Do you think the Arab Spring has had a positive impact, a negative impact or no impact on:
   a. The North African region?
   b. [Your country]?
(percentage reporting 'somewhat negative' or 'very negative')
2. Comparing the situation in your country today to how things were four years ago before the Arab Spring, do you think the following things have increased, decreased or stayed the same: the preservation of law, order and stability?
(percentage reporting 'decreased somewhat' or 'decreased a lot')

Egypt and Libya were ranked ninth and tenth among the countries most affected by extremism globally in 2015, while Tunisia was ranked 35th overall.[15] While this might suggest that concern about security would be lower in Tunisia, that year the country experienced its highest number of terrorism-related deaths since 2000, and extremist groups carried out three major attacks on civilian and military targets in March (at the Bardo National Museum in Tunis, 22 fatalities); June (a hotel in the resort town of Sousse, 38 fatalities), and November (the bombing of a bus transporting presidential guards in Tunis, 12 fatalities).[16] This appears to have had a significant impact on public opinion regarding the country's general security context.

Tunisia was the only country in the region in which a majority of citizens said their country was going in the wrong direction in 2015 and had the highest proportion of citizens who cited security related issues among their top national priorities (Table 2.1). However, criticism of the government's efforts to reduce crime and inequality declined between 2013 and 2015, and public distrust in the army was extremely low (5 per cent vs a regional average of 27 per cent). Despite being the country that was most affected by terrorism in the region surveyed by Afrobarometer, Egypt experienced a dramatic improvement in public evaluations of the country's overall trajectory: 73 per cent of respondents gave a negative evaluation in 2013 compared to only 18 per cent in 2015.

Table 2.1: Summary of citizen evaluations of security context, five North African countries, 2013 vs 2015

	Country 'going in the wrong direction'		Security concerns among most important problems		Govt handling reducing crime 'fairly badly' or 'very badly'[17]		Trust the army 'just a little' or 'not at all'	
	2013	2015	2013	2015	2013	2015	2013	2015
Algeria	10%	42%	4%	12%	40%	47%	11%	38%
Egypt	73%	18%	17%	20%	88%	44%	14%	17%
Morocco	29%	26%	4%	9%	69%	49%	48%	40%
Sudan	55%	47%	13%	33%	59%	–	31%	36%
Tunisia	67%	61%	20%	47%	73%	58%	14%	5%
Average	47%	39%	12%	24%	66%	50%	24%	27%

Respondents were asked:
1. Let's start with your general view about the current direction of our country. Some people might think the country is going in the wrong direction. Others may feel it is going in the right direction. So let me ask YOU about the overall direction of the country: would you say that the country is going in the wrong direction or going in the right direction?
2. How well or badly would you say the current government is handling the following matters, or haven't you heard enough to say? Reducing crime.

These contrasting findings highlight the importance of timing in interpreting the results of public opinion data, particularly when comparing results to prior or future surveys and to those in other countries. The Afrobarometer survey in Tunisia was conducted in April–May 2015, following the Bardo Museum attack. In Egypt, data collection was held in June–July 2015. Despite experiencing a higher number of terrorist attacks during 2015 than many other North African countries, the country had seen a monthly decline in terrorist incidents since its highest point in July 2014.[18] Further research in both countries is, therefore, required to provide a systematic explanation for these differences.

Public perceptions of the threat posed by terrorism are important due to the fact that civilians are generally the primary target for this type of violence. Survey data can, therefore, highlight which social groups feel the most vulnerable to which terrorist organisations, what type of terrorist activity, and why. For example, about four in 10 citizens in the five countries surveyed by Afrobarometer thought that the Islamic State (42 per cent) and AQIM (37 per cent) were at least 'somewhat active' in 2015, and a similar proportion perceived these groups to pose a national security threat (Table 2.2). All three measures were significantly higher in Tunisia. Further analysis of these results by key demographic indicators shows that, on average, there are no differences in responses by urban–rural location or gender, but that this perceived threat increases with both age and levels of socio-economic insecurity, as measured by Afrobarometer's measure of 'lived poverty' (Appendix, Table 2A.7).[19]

Table 2.2: Public opinion on violent extremism in North Africa, 2015

	Level of extremist activity ISIS	Level of extremist activity AQIM	Threat posed by ISIL (ISIS) and AQIM	Top 4 perceived motivations for joining ISIL (ISIS) Poverty	Religious beliefs	Unemployment	Lack of education
Algeria	32%	36%	39%	18%	19%	16%	15%
Egypt	59%	49%	51%	20%	21%	15%	13%
Morocco	25%	13%	32%	32%	18%	10%	11%
Sudan	28%	24%	24%	23%	16%	18%	7%
Tunisia	66%	62%	77%	32%	17%	18%	6%
Average	42%	37%	45%	25%	18%	15%	10%

Respondents were asked:
1. How active do you think each of the following Islamic movements are in [your country]:
   a. The Islamic State of Iraq and the Levant, known as ISIL?
   b. Al-Qaeda in the Islamic Maghreb, known as AQIM?
   (percentage reporting 'somewhat active' or 'very active')
2. In your opinion, to what extent does ISIL or AQIM pose a threat to [your country's] security? (per cent 'somewhat' or 'a lot')
3. There is much talk about the Islamic State of Iraq and the Levant, or ISIL, which is attracting members and fighters from a number of countries. In your opinion, what is the main reason that some [people from your country] join this group?

Respondents were also asked what they believed were the primary reasons for their fellow citizens joining terrorist organisations. Poverty was the most frequently cited motivation for joining ISIL (ISIS) (25 per cent), followed by religious beliefs (18 per cent), unemployment (15 per cent) and a lack of education (10 per cent). Citizens living under high levels of material deprivation were significantly more likely to say that poverty was the primary driver of recruitment into these organisations, while there were no differences by education attainment.[20]

In addition to its human and economic costs, terrorism poses a significant threat to general political stability, and Freedom House's most recent assessment of the global state of political rights and civil liberties cites this violence as among the leading factors in undermining democratic standards and human rights in the region.[21] In 2015, Afrobarometer explored the tension between respecting individual rights and assuring collective peace and security. Overall, public opinion was split between those who said that governments should be free to treat individuals suspected of extremist activity 'in any way necessary to ensure peace and security' (47 per cent) and those who agreed that human rights should be inviolable, even in the case of national security (43 per cent) (Table 2.3).

Egyptians were the most likely to prioritise ensuring peace and security over suspected extremists' rights (59 per cent), followed by citizens in Morocco (55 per cent), Sudan (41 per cent) and Algeria (34 per cent).

Table 2.3: Citizen preferences on addressing terrorist suspects, four North African countries, 2015

	Algeria	Egypt	Morocco	Sudan	Average
Government can violate human rights to ensure peace and security	34%	59%	55%	41%	47%
Government should never violate individuals' human rights	51%	31%	34%	55%	43%
Agree with neither	7%	2%	4%	1%	4%
Don't know	8%	8%	7%	3%	7%

Respondents were asked:
Which of the following statements is closest to your view? Choose Statement 1 or Statement 2.

Statement 1: Government should be free to deal with suspected persons connected with terrorism in any way necessary to ensure peace and security, even if it means violating their rights.

Statement 2: Government should never violate individuals' human rights, even when it comes to ensuring peace and security for the country.

In Tunisia, citizens were asked a slightly different question, contrasting government prioritisation on ensuring security and fighting terrorism with prioritising protecting human rights and further strengthening the country's fledgling democracy. As with the question above, the findings suggest that public opinion is divided on the appropriate balance between security and civil liberties: a slight majority of survey respondents (53 per cent) agreed that the government should prioritise security and counterterrorist efforts (Figure 2.5). However, Tunisian human-rights organisations have frequently warned that the country's extended state of emergency has led to severe human-rights violations[22] and that recent anti-terrorism legislation gives excessive powers to security forces.[23] These survey findings suggest that a substantial proportion of the Tunisian public was supportive of these types of measures and indicate the need for further research in this area in the country.

Response	Percentage
Ensuring security and fighting terrorism	53%
Protecting democracy and human rights	44%
Agree with neither	1%
Don't know	2%

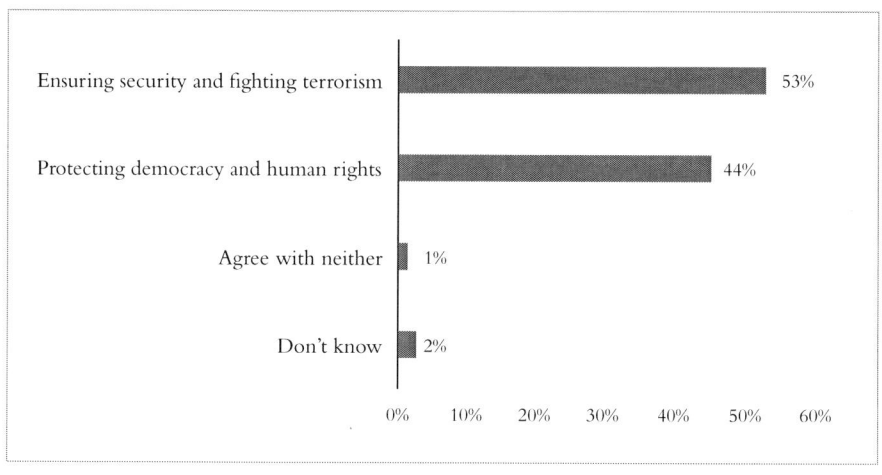

Figure 2.5: Citizen preferences on ensuring security vs strengthening democracy and protecting human rights, Tunisia, 2015

Respondents were asked:
Which of the following statements is closest to your view? Choose Statement 1 or Statement 2.

Statement 1: Government should prioritise ensuring security and fighting terrorism, even if it undermines democracy and human rights.

Statement 2: Government should prioritise strengthening democracy and protecting human rights, even if this undermines security and the fight against terrorism.

Overall, these findings show that follow-up research is crucial in both Egypt and Tunisia to evaluate the medium- to long-term effects of terrorist violence on societal norms and values, as the 2015 data suggest diverging trends between the two countries. Tunisia, in particular, faces a large influx of returning ex-combatants from foreign conflicts (most notably Libya and Syria), which poses a significant potential threat to social and political stability if their deradicalisation and reintegration is not appropriately addressed.[24] While Egyptians faced a significantly higher threat from terrorist organisations than their fellow citizens in the other North-African countries surveyed by Afrobarometer, both the economic and political context were more stable in 2015 than in 2013 which, given objective data on terrorist attacks, appears to have led to better than expected evaluations.[25]

Kenya: Lowered citizen concern with security amid improved evaluations of government counterterrorism efforts

In 1998, Egyptian Al-Qaeda affiliates bombed US embassies in Nairobi, Kenya and Dar es Salaam, Tanzania, in an apparent response to American involvement in the arrest and extradition of several of their members. Contemporary concern about terrorism in Kenya, however, relates to a different foreign group from neighbouring Somalia, Al-Shabaab. Al-Shabaab's transformation from a nationally based insurgency into a transnational organisation, with links to international jihadist networks, is linked to the Kenyan government's decision to launch a military offensive against the group, Operation Linda Nchi ('Protect the Country') in 2011,[26] and to join the African Union Mission to Somalia (AMISOM), whose mandate is to support the Somali government in its fight against the organisation.

In 2014, Kenya experienced its highest level of terrorist activity since Al-Shabaab reprisals began in 2012. During this period, and often in collaboration with a local Islamist organisation, Al-Hijra, the group was responsible for about 228 successful attacks, 73 of which took place in 2014 – including an attack at Garissa University College that killed 147 people.[27] The group also gained significant international attention the previous year when it attacked Westgate Shopping Mall in Nairobi. In addition to the human cost, the terrorist threat posed by Al-Shabaab has also had economic consequences due to its impact on tourism, which is a major sector of the national economy.[28]

Afrobarometer conducted its most recent survey (at the time of publication) in September/October 2016. The research found that Kenyans were divided on the country's overall trajectory: 47 per cent of respondents said the country was headed in the right direction, while 48 per cent said the opposite. However, this still represents a significant increase in approval since 2011 (24 per cent) (see Appendix, Table 2A.8). The results further indicate that respondents were generally positive about the country's security climate in 2016: only minorities reported a decline in their personal safety (22 per cent), and believed that the armed forces were 'never,' 'rarely' or only 'sometimes' able to protect the public from security threats, or said that they feared an armed attack by political or religious extremist groups like Al-Shabaab (33 per cent) (Table 2.4). Furthermore, fewer respondents in Kenya (4 per cent) said that they had experienced terrorism-related violence than in Mali (8 per cent) or Nigeria (11 per cent) (Appendix, Table 2A.9).

Table 2.4: Evaluations of security context in Kenya by key demographic indicators, 2016

	Personal safety is 'worse' or 'much worse'	Feared violence by extremists	Armed forces 'never', 'rarely' or 'sometimes' protect the public	Govt handling countering extremist violence 'fairly' or 'very' badly
Average	22%	33%	28%	35%
Urban	25%	37%	34%	36%
Rural	21%	30%	25%	35%
Male	23%	34%	28%	36%
Female	21%	31%	28%	34%
18–35 years	20%	34%	30%	36%
36–55 years	23%	33%	27%	34%
56 and older	31%	27%	26%	35%
No formal education	18%	26%	21%	25%
Primary education	24%	28%	24%	40%
Secondary education	23%	39%	34%	35%
Post-secondary education	19%	33%	30%	30%
No lived poverty	20%	22%	34%	32%
Low lived poverty	20%	36%	27%	34%
Moderate lived poverty	25%	32%	28%	38%
High lived poverty	24%	31%	28%	38%

Respondents were asked:
1. Please tell me if the following things are worse or better now than they were a few years ago, or are they about the same? Your personal safety from crime and violence.
2. In any society, people will sometimes disagree with one another. These disagreements occasionally escalate into physical violence. Please tell me whether, in the past two years, you have ever personally feared any of the following types of violence? An armed attack by political or religious extremists.
3. In your opinion, to what extent do the armed forces of our country keep our country safe from external and internal security threats?
4. How well or badly would you say the current government is handling the following matters, or haven't you heard enough to say? Countering political violence from armed extremist groups.

Further analysis of these results by key social and demographic variables indicates that urban residents were more likely to report worsened personal safety, to say that they had feared an armed attack, and to say that the armed forces 'never,' 'rarely' or 'sometimes' protected the public. Older Kenyans (aged at least 56 years) and those living under moderate or high levels of lived poverty were also more likely to report feelings of increased insecurity. However, citizens aged 18 to 55 years were more likely to say they had feared an armed attack and there was no clear pattern on this particular measure by poverty level.

In 2011, 82 per cent of survey respondents approved of the handling of the threat posed by Al-Shabaab (Figure 2.6). However, the survey took place in November of that year, shortly after the government launched Operation Linda Nchi and subsequent Al-Shabaab activity began to take place in Kenya. In 2016, only 35 per cent of Kenyans said that the government was countering violence from armed extremist groups 'fairly' or 'very' badly, while a majority of respondents (52 per cent) had expressed dissatisfaction with counterterrorism efforts in 2014. This suggests that citizen confidence in the government's capabilities is being restored. Respondents living under moderate or high levels of lived poverty were more likely to be critical of government efforts (38 per cent vs 33 per cent), but there were no other distinct patterns in citizen evaluations by demographic indicators (Table 2.4).

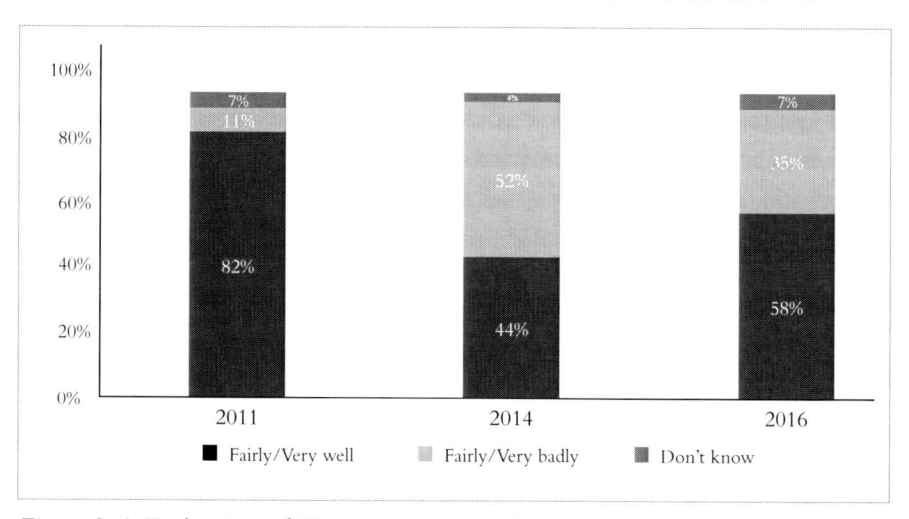

Figure 2.6: Evaluations of Kenya's counterterrorism strategies, 2011–2016

Respondents were asked:
How well or badly would you say the current government is handling the following matters, or haven't you heard enough to say?
- Addressing terrorist threats by Al-Shabaab terror group (2011).
- Fighting terrorism in Kenya (2014).
- Countering political violence from armed extremist groups (2016).

Given the origins of Al-Shabaab's activity in Kenya, Afrobarometer asked citizens in the 2014 and 2016 surveys about their opinion on the country's intervention in Somalia. While a majority of Kenyans said that the Kenya Defence Forces' (KDFs') involvement in Somali affairs had been 'necessary in spite of the terrorist problems resulting from it' in both surveys, support levels have declined since 2014 (57 per cent vs 66 per cent) (Figure 2.7). Only four in 10 respondents disagreed with a potential withdrawal from Somalia in both years.

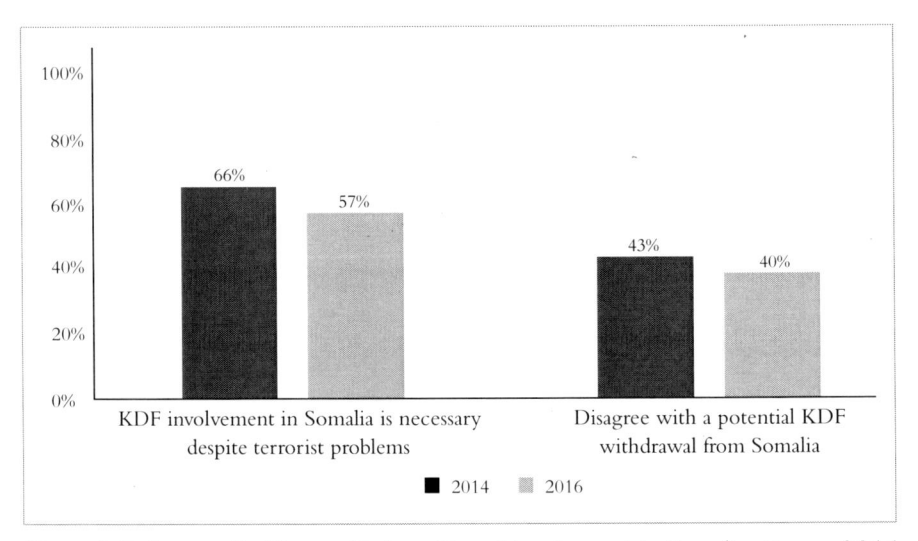

Figure 2.7: Support for Kenyan Defence Forces' involvement in Somalia, Kenya, 2014 vs 2016

Respondents were asked:
For each of the following statements, please tell me whether you disagree or agree, or haven't you heard enough to say?
- The involvement of the Kenya Defence Forces or KDF in Somalia is necessary in spite of the terrorist problems resulting from it (percentage citing 'agree' or 'strongly agree').
- The Kenya Defence Forces should pull out of Somalia (percentage citing 'disagree' or 'strongly disagree').

Endorsement of the KDFs' involvement was higher among men than women (61 per cent vs 53 per cent) and somewhat higher among survey respondents aged 55 years or younger (Table 2.5). In addition, support increased with educational attainment and levels of socio-economic security. Interestingly, while similar patterns by education and lived poverty levels can be seen for the direct rejection of a KDF withdrawal from Somalia, there is no clear pattern by age, and women were more likely to express this view. These somewhat contradictory results indicate either a lack of coherence in citizen attitudes or differing interpretations of what each question poses. Further analysis of these patterns or qualitative research could help to explain these differences.

Table 2.5: Support for KDFs' involvement in Somalia, by key demographic variables, Kenya, 2016

	KDF involvement is necessary	KDF should not withdraw from Somalia
Average	57%	40%
Urban	58%	40%
Rural	56%	39%
Male	61%	43%
Female	53%	49%
18–35 years	58%	42%
36–55 years	57%	37%
56 and older	53%	39%
No formal education	45%	31%
Primary education	53%	35%
Secondary education	61%	43%
Post-secondary education	62%	47%
No lived poverty	62%	46%
Low lived poverty	61%	44%
Moderate lived poverty	54%	35%
High lived poverty	47%	32%

Overall, 2016 survey results show that Kenyans expressed less concern about their personal security and national security than in 2014 and that evaluations of the government's counterterrorism efforts were relatively high. However, public opinion continued to be mixed on the consequences of the KDFs' involvement in Somalia. Despite these promising results, public opinion may have changed since the time of data collection due to the increase in Al-Shabaab attacks in 2017, particularly in the coastal region. Al-Shabaab improvised explosive devices (IED) killed 40 people between February and March 2017, while, for the first time, the group employed beheading in the country during a July attack.[29] Furthermore, like Tunisia, the Kenyan government faces the potential threat of ex-combatants returning from ISIS activity in Libya and Middle Eastern conflicts if they are not appropriately reintegrated into Kenyan society.[30]

Mali: Waning optimism amid renewed sense of insecurity

Over the past decade, the Sahel region has become a 'hot spot' of violent extremism due to a combination of economic, geographic and political factors. Countries in the region, including Mali, are among the world's poorest nations.

Moreover, with few natural resources, high population growth and changing regional weather patterns, these nations have become increasingly vulnerable to sporadic food shortages.[31] In addition, the human and physical geography of Sahelian states is extremely challenging for political stability as no state has been able to exert full control over their large areas of sparsely populated territory or their long desert borders.[32]

Northern Mali has a long history of secessionist movements due to the southern-based central government's persistent failure to address the grievances of local semi-nomadic pastoralist groups. The country experienced major Tuareg rebellions in 1963, 1990–1995 and 2006, primarily precipitated by demands for greater autonomy from Bamako.[33] Since 2007, transnational jihadist groups have exploited these local grievances, taking advantage of the country's weak governance and security structures to establish their presence in northern Mali.[34] This mix of terrorist and secessionist activity in the region came to a head in 2012 when the government was suddenly unable to address the rapid influx of returning Tuareg militants following the collapse of the Gaddafi regime in Libya.

The combination of the two threats led to a rapid succession of military defeats for the state, but conflict between the Tuareg separatist and jihadist groups, combined with the deployment of French troops, helped the Malian armed forces (Forces Armées et de Sécurité du Mali, FAMA) stop the capture of the capital and helped the government regain control over much of the region by January 2013.[35] In June, the government signed a ceasefire with the Tuareg separatists.

In December 2012, Afrobarometer conducted its first of four post-crisis surveys in Mali, although data collection could not take place in some areas due to ongoing violence. At the time, three-quarters of respondents said that the country was going in the wrong direction overall, which declined to only 31 per cent in the 2013 survey.[36] This surge in optimism is unsurprising given that data collection took place in late 2013 and early 2014, after the recapture of key strategic cities by French and Chadian forces and the deployment of the United Nations Multidisciplinary Integrated Stabilization Mission in Mali (MINUSMA) (Appendix, Table 2A.8). However, amid growing public concern about security, the number of respondents who stated that the country was going in the right direction has declined from 69 per cent in 2013 to only 28 per cent in 2017 (see Figure 2.2).

AQIM and other Islamist groups (Al-Mourabitoun, Ansar al-Din) have continued to carry out attacks on both military and civilian targets in Mali, despite the presence of French, regional and international troops – including an attack at an upmarket hotel in the capital in November 2015.[37] Furthermore, the groups officially declared their intention to unite their forces and renew their allegiance to

Al-Qaeda and continue their insurgency throughout the Sahel in March 2017.[38] It is likely that this continued threat has led to the substantially higher proportion of respondents in Mali who said that their personal safety had deteriorated (41 per cent) and that they feared violent extremist groups (45 per cent) in 2017 (Table 2.6) than those in Kenya.

Table 2.6: Evaluations of security context in Mali, by key demographic indicators, 2017

	Personal safety is 'worse' or 'much worse'	Feared violence by extremists	Armed forces 'never', 'rarely' or 'sometimes' protect the public	Govt handling countering extremist violence 'fairly' or 'very' badly
Average	41%	45%	19%	58%
Urban	40%	41%	24%	58%
Rural	42%	46%	18%	59%
Male	45%	47%	20%	59%
Female	38%	44%	18%	58%
18–35 years	40%	46%	20%	59%
36–55 years	40%	43%	17%	56%
56 and older	47%	47%	20%	61%
No formal education	38%	46%	17%	56%
Primary education	52%	48%	18%	61%
Secondary education	34%	42%	23%	66%
Post-secondary education	46%	39%	31%	68%
No lived poverty	35%	33%	12%	49%
Low lived poverty	39%	41%	16%	58%
Moderate lived poverty	44%	41%	21%	58%
High lived poverty	47%	68%	27%	64%

Men were more likely to report deteriorated personal safety than women, as were respondents aged 56 years and older, and those living under higher levels of material deprivation. In contrast to Kenya, a larger proportion of urban residents said that they had feared an armed attack in 2017, and there was a clear pattern in responses by poverty level: over twice as many Malian respondents living with frequent shortages of basic goods and services (ie, 'high lived poverty') said so, compared to those who did not experience these shortages ('no lived poverty'). Furthermore, perceptions of lack of protection from the armed forces and negative evaluations of the government's counter-extremist efforts rose with poverty levels. This suggests that poorer Malians are the most vulnerable social group in the face of violence. While more educated citizens were also likely to be critical of FAMA and the government's strategy, perceptions of vulnerability do not seem to vary directly with education attainment.

A majority of citizens surveyed in 2017 (58 per cent) said that the Malian government was handling the threat of violent extremism poorly, despite continuing to indicate that the national armed forces deserve the greatest credit for the progress made toward restoring national territorial integrity and unity (Figure 2.8). Interestingly, there were substantial increases in the proportion of survey respondents who saw MINUSMA and self-defence groups as playing a useful role, while significantly fewer credit the French armed forces for any success (55 per cent, down from 92 per cent in 2013).[39] This is in spite of the critical role that these troops have played in supporting the national forces against this threat since its onset.

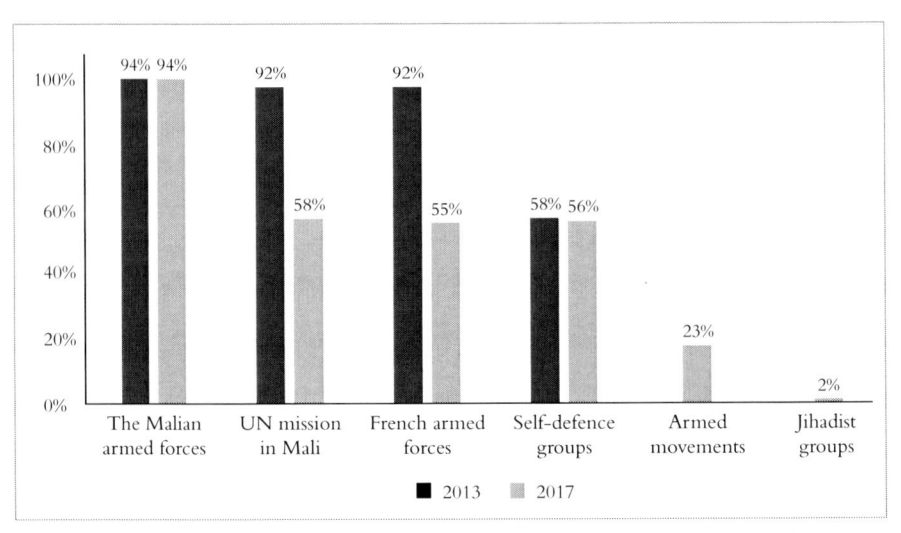

Figure 2.8: Perceived usefulness of various security forces in restoring territorial integrity, Mali, 2013 vs 2017

Respondents were asked:
In your opinion, how useful have the following forces been in helping Mali to recover its territorial integrity and national unity, or haven't you heard enough to say?[40]

Of those surveyed in 2017, one in five respondents was the victim of intimidation or threats as a result of the crisis, while 15 per cent reported witnessing beatings or killings, and at least one in 10 respondents were either directly affected by displacement (12 per cent left their homes for another location in Mali and 6 per cent left the country) or supported internally displaced persons (IDPs) (Figure 2.9). These findings further show the economic impact of the security crisis, including the proportion of respondents who experienced the loss of employment (14 per cent) or their business (13 per cent), or experienced an occupational change (12 per cent). These relatively small proportions likely reflect the highly geographically concentrated nature of the conflict, as residents of Tombouctou and Gao in particular make up a disproportionate number of affirmative responses (Appendix, Table 2A.10).

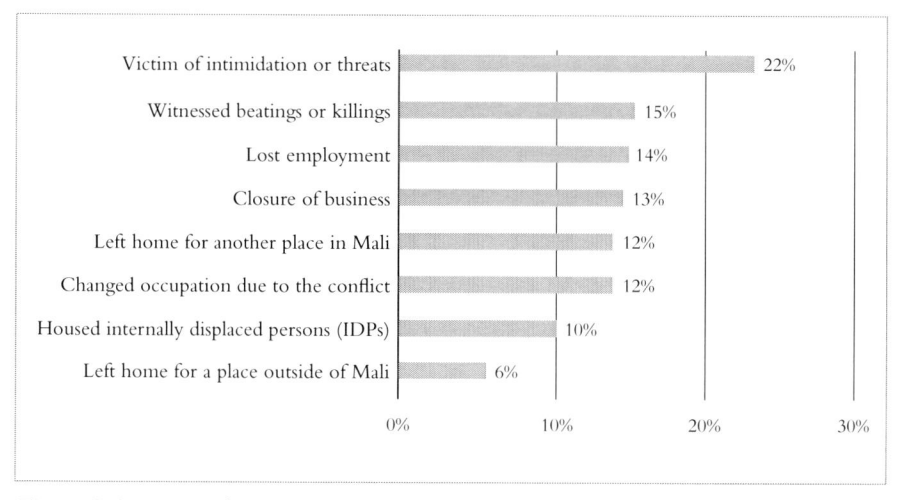

Category	Percentage
Victim of intimidation or threats	22%
Witnessed beatings or killings	15%
Lost employment	14%
Closure of business	13%
Left home for another place in Mali	12%
Changed occupation due to the conflict	12%
Housed internally displaced persons (IDPs)	10%
Left home for a place outside of Mali	6%

Figure 2.9: Reported victimisation during security crisis, Mali, 2017

Respondents were asked:
Please tell me if you personally or if members of your family have been affected by the crisis in the north of Mali in one of the following ways?[41]

When asked about their predictions for the future, a third of the total responses were related to threats to state integrity via territorial loss (19 per cent), the loss of independence or sovereignty (12 per cent), or dissolution into several independent states (3 per cent) (Table 2.7). Citizens also expressed concern that the country would lose its national unity (10 per cent) or highlighted the threat of interfaith or interethnic conflict. This further highlights the level of public concern regarding the security context at the time, despite significant improvements since 2012.

Table 2.7: Predicted consequences of the security crisis, Mali, 2017

	First response	**Second response**	**% of total responses**
Mali will lose an area of its territory	38%	–	19%
Mali will lose significant independence	10%	12%	12%
Mali will lose its national unity	5%	2%	10%
Mali will experience more interfaith conflict	3%	5%	7%
Mali will be a federal state	2%	1%	4%
Mali to lose weight in the United Nations	1%	2%	3%
Economic consequences	6%	2%	3%
Mali will break into several independent states	3%	4%	3%
Social consequences	5%	3%	2%
Mali to face more interethnic conflict	13%	15%	2%
Other	2%	2%	1%
None/no further reply	6%	55%	31%
Refused	0%	–	0%
Don't know	5%	–	3%

Respondents were asked:
What do you think the effects of the conflict in the north might be for Mali?[42]

Overall, the most recent public-opinion data from Mali indicate a reversal in the initial optimism levels measured in 2013. As noted above, this is likely a reflection of persisting extremist activity in the country and across the Sahelian region in general, which the recent merger of Al-Qaeda-affiliated networks may exacerbate. Despite the high levels of citizen confidence in the national security forces, regional and international troops have been essential to achieving relative stability since the onset of the crisis and will continue to be crucial in leading the response to AQIM and Al-Mourabitoun's expanded operational footprint in countries like Côte d'Ivoire and Burkina Faso. The French reorganised their military presence in West Africa in July 2014 and MINUSMA is authorised to remain in the country until June 2018.[43] Moreover, the Sahel G5 states (Burkina Faso, Chad, Mali, Mauritania and Niger) announced their intention to establish a joint counterterrorism force in northern Mali and neighbouring states in February 2017.

One of the most important areas for further research, however, is an exploration of the reasons for the substantial decline in citizen perceptions of the utility of the French forces' contributions to restoring national territorial integrity between Operation Serval (2013–2014) and Operation Barkhane (2014 to present) given their continued leadership in this area.[44] A similar drop in confidence in MINUSMA may indicate that continued stated belief in FAMA's utility may be reflexive support for the armed forces, particularly given the fact that a majority of citizens disapprove of the government's performance in countering extremist violence.

Nigeria: Improved evaluations of government performance and growing confidence in armed forces

Boko Haram has waged an insurgency against the Nigerian state since 2010 that has claimed the lives of over 20 000 civilians and displaced roughly two million more across northern Nigeria, while increasing its geographic presence throughout the Lake Chad Basin in recent years.[45] The peak of the insurgency was in 2014, a year in which Boko Haram was estimated to control an area roughly 17 700 km^2 across Borno, Adamwa and Yobe states and was responsible for more civilian deaths than any violent extremist organisation internationally.[46] In 2014 and early 2015, Boko Haram also gained global notoriety for a number of incidents, which gained international media attention, including the kidnapping of the Chibok girls (April 2014), and a series of large-scale attacks in the region which led to the postponement of the 2015 presidential elections.

On 28 March 2015, the former military general Muhammadu Buhari defeated the incumbent Nigerian president, Goodluck Jonathan, after successfully campaigning on a platform of defeating Boko Haram and curbing corruption. After his election, President Buhari acted to deliver on his campaign promises by relocating the military command from Abuja to Maiduguri, overhauling the military's entire counter-insurgency strategy, and pushing through a Bill to support supplementary military spending.[47] Since then, the Nigerian military has been able to push Boko Haram from their strongholds across northern Nigeria and has severely diminished the group's ability to hold territory, which has led to a substantial reduction in the number of deaths attributed to their attacks.[48] However, despite these significant military gains, Boko Haram continues to carry out regular attacks and remains a significant asymmetrical threat in the country and the wider region.

Afrobarometer conducted its 2014 survey in Nigeria during a period of intense insecurity in the country's north-eastern region; therefore (as in Mali's 2012 survey) data collection could not take place in the three states most heavily affected (ie, Borno, Adamwa and Yobe). That year, almost three-quarters of survey respondents said that the country was heading in the wrong direction. Citizens were less critical in 2017 than in the previous two rounds, but negative evaluations remain the majority, at 63 per cent (Appendix, Table 2A.8). Despite Boko Haram's prolific nature, fewer Nigerians than Kenyans expressed concern about security related issues in 2014, and this dropped to only 13 per cent in 2017 (Figure 2.2).

About 25 per cent of survey respondents said that their personal safety from crime and violence was worse in 2017 than in preceding years and 37 per cent said they feared an armed attack (Table 2.8). Those with at least secondary education were more likely to report deteriorated personal security conditions, along with poorer Nigerians. As in Mali (and in contrast to Kenya), fear of extremist violence was higher among rural residents (39 per cent vs 34 per cent) and men (39 per cent vs 35 per cent).

Table 2.8: Evaluations of the security context in Nigeria, by key demographic indicators, 2017

	Personal safety is 'worse' or 'much worse'	Feared violence by extremists	Armed forces 'never,' 'rarely' or 'sometimes' protect the public	Govt handling countering extremist violence 'fairly' or 'very' badly
Average	24%	37%	39%	44%
Urban	25%	34%	37%	44%
Rural	23%	39%	42%	44%
Male	23%	39%	37%	42%
Female	25%	35%	42%	46%
18–35 years	26%	36%	34%	45%
36–55 years	20%	41%	39%	42%
56 and older	22%	30%	43%	43%
No formal education	17%	36%	34%	30%
Primary education	22%	40%	39%	38%
Secondary education	27%	37%	43%	51%
Post-secondary education	24%	36%	37%	45%

	Personal safety is 'worse' or 'much worse'	Feared violence by extremists	Armed forces 'never,' 'rarely' or 'sometimes' protect the public	Govt handling countering extremist violence 'fairly' or 'very' badly
No lived poverty	21%	38%	43%	50%
Low lived poverty	19%	33%	33%	38%
Moderate lived poverty	31%	40%	43%	49%
High lived poverty	36%	43%	52%	53%

Nigerians were significantly more likely than their counterparts in Kenya or Mali to say the armed forces 'never', 'rarely' or 'sometimes' protect the public, with rural residents, women and older respondents reporting higher levels on this indicator. However, citizens were less critical of the government's overall handling of extremist violence than in Mali (44 per cent vs 58 per cent).

As Table 2.9 shows, perceptions that terrorist groups like Boko Haram enjoy support among local political and social leaders declined on all measures in Nigeria between 2014 and 2017.[49] In contrast, more citizens in 2017 said that 'most' or 'all' members of international extremist groups support their local counterparts (52 per cent vs 43 per cent) (Table 2.9). This may be a reflection of Boko Haram's increasingly visible ties to international jihadist networks, particularly since it declared its official affiliation with ISIS.

Table 2.9: Perceived political and social support for extremist organisations, Nigeria, 2014 vs 2017

	2014			2017		
	Most/All	Some	None	Most/All	Some	None
International extremist groups	43%	33%	10%	52%	35%	11%
Senior officials in federal government	38%	40%	11%	33%	46%	17%
National Assembly members	35%	41%	12%	33%	46%	17%
Nigerian Muslims	37%	35%	16%	31%	38%	26%
Members of Nigerian military	32%	44%	13%	25%	48%	23%

	2014			2017		
	Most/All	Some	None	Most/All	Some	None
Local government officials	24%	37%	23%	21%	48%	27%
Traditional leaders	20%	39%	26%	18%	47%	32%

Respondents were asked:
How many of the following people do you think are involved in supporting and assisting the extremist groups that have launched attacks and kidnappings in Nigeria, or haven't you heard enough about them to say?

When asked about the motivations for joining terrorist organisations, poverty was the most frequently cited cause in 2017 (31 per cent), followed by unemployment (26 per cent), religious beliefs (17 per cent), a lack of education (8 per cent), a sense of injustice or mistreatment (7 per cent), and various other possible explanations (Figure 2.10). This is very similar to the pattern in North Africa, as reported earlier. Citizens' perceptions were generally similar to those in 2014, but a higher proportion cited religious beliefs in the most recent survey (17 per cent vs 11 per cent).

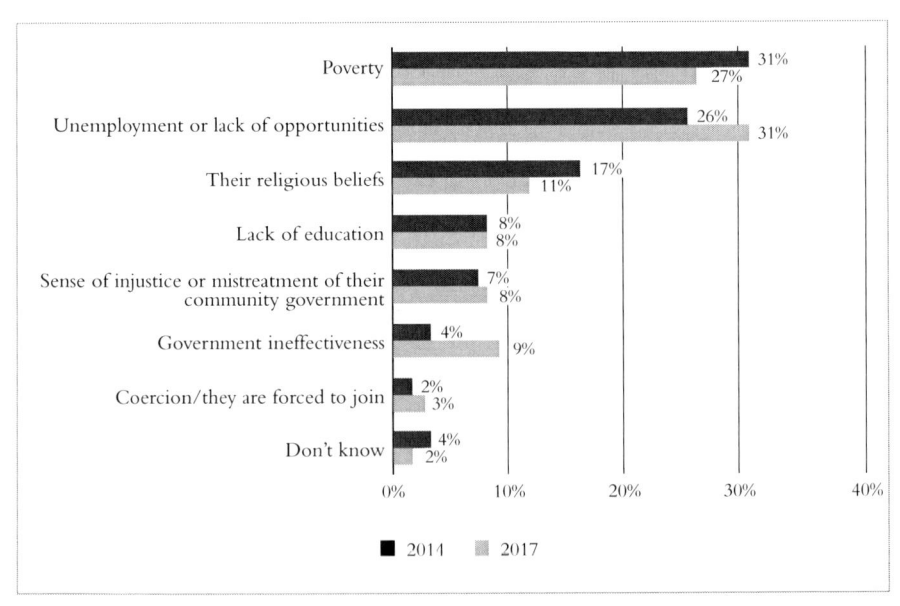

Motivation	2014	2017
Poverty	31%	27%
Unemployment or lack of opportunities	26%	31%
Their religious beliefs	17%	11%
Lack of education	8%	8%
Sense of injustice or mistreatment of their community government	7%	8%
Government ineffectiveness	4%	9%
Coercion/they are forced to join	2%	3%
Don't know	4%	2%

Figure 2.10: Perceived motivations for joining extremist groups, Nigeria, 2014 vs 2017

Respondents were asked:
In your opinion, what is the main reason why some Nigerians join extremist groups?

The Nigerian questionnaire also included an alternative measure of citizen evaluations of the government's counterterrorism strategy, which asks how *effective* respondents thought these efforts had been. Three-quarters (74 per cent) said that they had been 'somewhat' or 'very' effective in 2017, which is a substantial improvement from 2014 when only 42 per cent of respondents said the same (Figure 2.11). Furthermore, 72 per cent of respondents in 2017 said the government's performance in handling the insurgency in the north-eastern region had improved since the previous year.

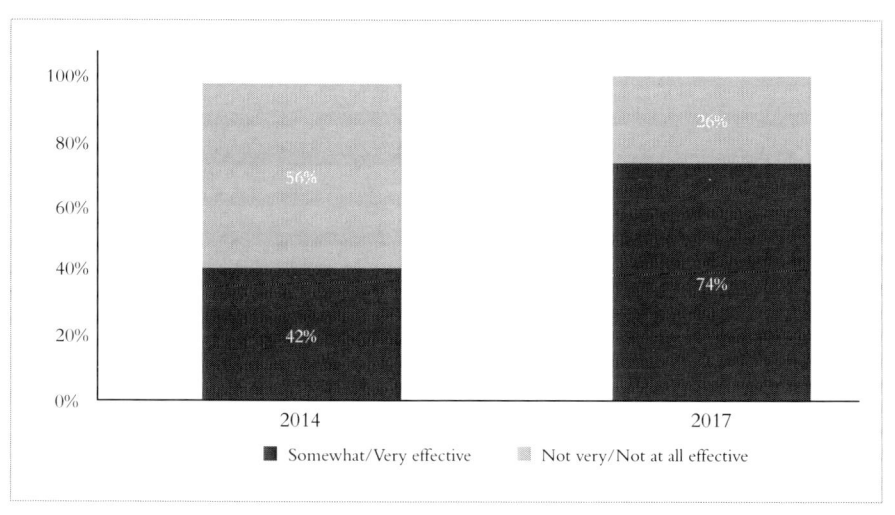

Figure 2.11: Perceived effectiveness of government counter-extremist efforts in Nigeria, 2014 vs 2017

Respondents were asked:
How effective do you think the Nigerian government has been in its efforts to address the problem of armed extremists in this country?

Citizens continued to recommend strengthening military-led counterterrorism strategies and military capacity as the leading suggested improvements to government efforts (31 per cent), followed by overall economic development and job creation (24 per cent), and collaboration with religious or traditional leaders (15 per cent) (Table 2.10). The results were similar to those in 2014. A majority of respondents said the country's armed forces 'always' or 'often' protect the public (60 per cent) and that they receive the necessary resources (55 per cent). However, only 49 per cent reported that military personnel are regularly professional and respectful to citizens, which leaves significant room for improvement to promote more effective collaboration with local communities (Appendix, Table 2A.5).

Table 2.10: Suggested improvements to government counter-extremist efforts, Nigeria, 2014 vs 2017

	2014	2017
Nothing/government is already effective in combating them	5%	8%
Strengthen the military response or military capabilities	29%	31%
Improve the economy and create more jobs	19%	24%
Work together with traditional/religious leaders to address the issue	17%	15%
Govern more effectively/provide better government services	7%	7%
Improve education standards	7%	4%
Treat the communities the extremists come from more fairly	3%	2%
Cooperate more with other countries in our region to address the issue	3%	2%
Cooperate more with the international community to address the issue	4%	2%
Split the country	1%	2%
Give more power to local governments to make their own decisions	2%	1%
Increase resources distributed to states and local communities	1%	1%
Other	1%	1%
Don't know/refused to answer	2%	1%

Respondents were asked:
In your opinion, what do you think would be the best way for the government to be more effective in addressing the problem of armed extremists in our country? And what would be the second most important reason?

Analysis of indicators of insecurity in Nigeria by geographic location shows that residents of the three most affected states in 2014, and the north-eastern zone in general, were actually marginally less likely to report worsened personal safety than the national average in 2017 (Appendix, Table 2A.11). This further reflects improvements made in the past few years in these areas. Citizens in the three states were still, however, more likely to have feared an armed attack by terrorist organisations in 2017. Although perceptions that armed forces 'never', 'rarely' or only 'sometimes' protect the public were higher among those living closest to Boko Haram, they were less critical of the government's efforts.

Summing up, the 2017 survey results indicate relatively low levels of perceived insecurity in Nigeria as a whole, although rural residents and those in the north-eastern zones were more likely to fear an armed attack. Men were also more likely to indicate feeling vulnerable to this threat. Further statistical analysis and qualitative research could help to further explain these findings. The section also shows that Nigerians are somewhat less likely to believe that terrorist organisations are supported by local elites than in 2014 and that they are less critical of the government's counterterrorism efforts under the Buhari administration. While there is considerable support for a more holistic approach to the problem, strengthening military capabilities remains the most supported suggested improvement. It is crucial, however, that the government works toward improving citizen confidence in both the armed forces and police if it is to fully address the challenge posed by Boko Haram, particularly in remote areas.

Conclusion

Findings from the Afrobarometer surveys show that public opinion regarding security varies widely in Africa, depending on the national context, and that citizens' attitudes toward terrorism in particular are likely even more sensitive to the timing of data collection. While nationally representative surveys provide crucial insights into citizen perceptions, evaluations and preferences by offering a 'snapshot' of these views at a particular time, they are best used in conjunction with other forms of research. Given the highly concentrated nature of many forms of violence, including terrorism, local-level quantitative or qualitative research is crucial.

The results from North Africa show the importance of relative levels of terrorist threat in shaping citizen perceptions and evaluations. While Egypt experienced a greater objective threat from terrorism in 2015 than Tunisia, public-opinion data indicate far greater concern in the latter. This is due to their diverging contexts relative to recent events. Egypt's economic and political context improved substantially between 2013 and 2015, while Tunisia experienced its highest number of attacks and related casualties in 2015. Furthermore, a major attack in the capital near parliament close to the date when the survey was undertaken is likely to have exacerbated citizen concern.

The Kenyan results indicate major progress towards assuring citizens of their safety from terrorism since the 2014 survey, which took place during a period of heightened security threats. In contrast, citizens reported relatively low levels of concern about security related issues in 2017, and confidence in the government's capabilities increased significantly – although the public remains ambivalent about Kenya's involvement in Somalia's fight against Al-Shabaab. Nigeria, similarly, showed improvement across most measures reflected in the survey and appears to show the clearest indication of the impact successful military intervention has had on public perceptions regarding the threat posed by terrorism and on evaluations of government performance. As terrorism is highly concentrated, it would be useful to have larger-scale research that concentrates on the specific areas in each country where the threat of terrorism is most prevalent.

Mali's survey results, in contrast to those in Kenya and Nigeria, show the negative impact of a continued threat from terrorism. Respondents in Mali reported the highest levels of deteriorated personal security and fear of an armed attack of the three countries, and was the only context in which a majority of citizens were critical of government counter-extremist efforts in 2016/17. This is concerning for the prospects of restoring political rights and civil liberties in the country after Mali's improbable successful democratisation prior to the 2012 crisis. Interestingly, despite the current conditions, government forces have managed to gain overwhelming citizen support, which may help the state to implement successful P/CVE programming. In contrast, Malians were significantly more critical of French and UN forces in 2017 than in 2013.

While these findings present important insights into public opinion on security and terrorism in Africa in recent years, they represent a starting point for future research in this area. Nationally representative surveys are useful for presenting an overall picture of citizen attitudes, preferences and evaluations at a given moment, but they often have only a relatively small sub-sample in geographic areas of interest for this type of work. Terrorism in Africa tends to be concentrated in sparsely populated areas far from government control. It is, therefore, crucial that follow-up research in these areas be conducted. Furthermore, it is difficult to establish causal connections between different results without using experimental methods or other forms of observational data in conjunction with survey results. Given the dearth of studies on terrorism in key African countries, it is essential that further vigorous quantitative or qualitative research take place, particularly comparative studies that can shed light on the divergences within and between contexts.

Appendix

Table 2A.1: Afrobarometer Round 6 fieldwork dates and leading security indicators

Country	Months when Round 6 fieldwork was conducted	Ibrahim Index of African Governance (IIAG) score (/100)				Global Terrorism Index (GTI) ranking	
		Personal safety		National security			
		2014	2015	2014	2015	2014	2015
Algeria	May–Jun 2015	51.7	51.9	77.9	78.3	34	42

Country	Months when Round 6 fieldwork was conducted	Ibrahim Index of African Governance (IIAG) score (/100) Personal safety 2014	2015	National security 2014	2015	Global Terrorism Index (GTI) ranking 2014	2015
Benin	May–Jun 2014	57.7	60.5	89.8	87.9	124	130
Botswana	Jun–Jul 2014	62.6	62.6	100.0	99.9	124	130
Burkina Faso	Apr–May 2015	49.7	42.4	85.4	83.4	107	63
Burundi	Sep–Oct 2014	45.6	34.5	69.1	44.8	55	31
Cameroon	Jan–Feb 2015	41.6	47.3	74.9	62.8	20	13
Cape Verde	Nov–Dec 2014	59.2	59.2	100.0	100.0	N/A	N/A
Côte d'Ivoire	Aug–Sep 2014	58.4	54.9	76.1	79.4	58	72
Egypt	Jun–Jul 2015	30.8	41.5	62.7	62.4	13	9
Gabon	Sep 2015	58.1	46.1	91.6	91.6	124	130
Ghana	May–Jun 2014	61.0	56.6	87.1	85.2	93	106
Guinea	Mar–Apr 2015	39.0	37.5	88.6	86.7	98	85
Kenya	Nov–Dec 2014	42.9	49.7	61.1	59.2	18	19
Lesotho	May 2014	52.7	53.0	91.4	87.4	124	95
Liberia	May 2015	52.2	50.4	86.9	85.9	96	110
Madagascar	Dec 2014–Jan 2015	36.0	37.8	89.3	86.4	69	81
Malawi	Mar–Apr 2014	54.6	49.6	95.2	95.1	124	130
Mali	Dec 2014–Jan 2015	50.9	50.9	70.1	65.7	26	25
Mauritius	Jun–Jul 2014	66.7	62.5	100.0	100.0	124	130
Morocco	Nov 2015	43.9	53.2	83.1	81.2	92	95
Mozambique	Jun–Aug 2015	51.9	48.9	85.2	87.3	37	51
Namibia	Aug–Sep 2014	57.7	60.5	95.6	99.7	124	130
Niger	Mar–Apr 2015	60.2	61.2	71.1	61.0	51	16
Nigeria	Dec 2014–Jan 2015	29.9	33.5	57.7	50.8	3	3
São Tomé and Príncipe	Jul–Aug 2015	73.3	68.4	94.9	94.9	N/A	N/A
Senegal	Nov–Dec 2014	61.0	57.1	79.9	78.5	52	64
Sierra Leone	May–Jun 2015	63.5	60.2	87.0	85.4	124	130
South Africa	Aug–Sep 2015	36.9	37.2	72.5	75.0	38	52
Sudan	Jun 2015	22.2	27.5	30.8	29.5	16	18

Country	Months when Round 6 fieldwork was conducted	Ibrahim Index of African Governance (IIAG) score (/100)				Global Terrorism Index (GTI) ranking	
		Personal safety		National security			
		2014	2015	2014	2015	2014	2015
Swaziland	Apr 2015	50.5	54.8	91.6	91.6	124	130
Tanzania	Aug–Nov 2014	51.5	54.3	90.5	90.9	45	49
Togo	Oct 2014	58.0	58.0	88.9	87.4	124	130
Tunisia	April–May 2015	42.8	46.5	83.0	78.5	47	35
Uganda	May 2015	56.9	57.8	77.4	82.0	30	40
Zambia	Oct 2014	55.8	56.5	94.3	93.8	124	130
Zimbabwe	Nov 2014	40.1	36.1	79.0	76.7	87	104

Sources: Afrobarometer (2016), Institute for Economics and Peace (2016), Mo Ibrahim Foundation (2016)

Table 2A.2: Key public opinion indicators on security | 36 countries | 2014/15

Country	Citizen priorities		Personal safety				
	Cite security among top 3 problems	Support investment in security	Govt handling reducing crime 'very badly' or 'fairly badly'	Felt unsafe walking in neighbourhood	Feared crime in home	Had something stolen from house	Physically assaulted
Algeria	12%	22%	46%	28%	18%	21%	12%
Benin	10%	10%	52%	41%	29%	26%	7%
Botswana	13%	15%	32%	44%	44%	26%	12%
Burkina Faso	11%	12%	43%	37%	27%	22%	4%
Burundi	34%	20%	45%	17%	14%	18%	4%
Cameroon	22%	22%	38%	46%	37%	44%	15%
Cape Verde	39%	34%	63%	36%	27%	17%	9%
Côte d'Ivoire	22%	18%	42%	36%	21%	18%	9%
Egypt	20%	22%	44%	39%	23%	12%	5%
Gabon	13%	7%	81%	52%	37%	40%	12%
Ghana	5%	6%	57%	25%	24%	28%	7%
Guinea	8%	11%	62%	27%	20%	14%	3%
Kenya	45%	34%	55%	49%	41%	26%	9%

Country	Citizen priorities — Cite security among top 3 problems	Support investment in security	Govt handling reducing crime 'very badly' or 'fairly badly'	Personal safety — Felt unsafe walking in neighbourhood	Feared crime in home	Had something stolen from house	Physically assaulted
Lesotho	14%	10%	45%	35%	38%	22%	7%
Liberia	4%	12%	55%	50%	42%	63%	37%
Madagascar	43%	34%	75%	72%	60%	18%	4%
Malawi	14%	15%	64%	44%	48%	37%	14%
Mali	38%	21%	50%	35%	29%	20%	3%
Mauritius	48%	35%	77%	17%	6%	9%	2%
Morocco	9%	17%	49%	47%	29%	26%	19%
Mozambique	12%	11%	43%	49%	37%	33%	13%
Namibia	15%	14%	44%	43%	30%	33%	16%
Niger	14%	19%	14%	15%	6%	17%	3%
Nigeria	39%	43%	71%	39%	33%	31%	19%
São Tomé and Príncipe	7%	7%	41%	17%	10%	21%	5%
Senegal	10%	10%	53%	43%	24%	29%	4%
Sierra Leone	3%	3%	54%	26%	24%	28%	7%
South Africa	29%	20%	77%	60%	53%	28%	13%
Sudan	33%	17%	N/A	37%	32%	41%	15%
Swaziland	8%	8%	32%	38%	36%	22%	8%
Tanzania	9%	14%	39%	21%	16%	22%	6%
Togo	7%	6%	50%	33%	25%	30%	5%
Tunisia	47%	45%	58%	43%	24%	9%	5%
Uganda	10%	12%	25%	31%	36%	38%	10%
Zambia	6%	6%	48%	44%	34%	31%	11%
Zimbabwe	7%	5%	50%	27%	33%	28%	6%
Average	19%	17%	51%	37%	30%	26%	9%

Table 2A.3: Public confidence in security forces | 36 countries | 2014/15

Country	Trust the police 'not at all' or 'just a little'	Trust the army 'not at all' or 'just a little'	Say 'all' or 'most' police are corrupt
Algeria	40%	38%	25%
Benin	47%	41%	54%
Botswana	40%	28%	34%
Burkina Faso	27%	26%	28%
Burundi	26%	9%	41%
Cameroon	49%	28%	55%
Cape Verde	40%	29%	19%
Côte d'Ivoire	58%	59%	49%
Egypt	36%	17%	26%
Gabon	59%	56%	63%
Ghana	62%	41%	64%
Guinea	50%	45%	38%
Kenya	63%	27%	75%
Lesotho	40%	29%	39%
Liberia	76%	55%	77%
Madagascar	63%	56%	49%
Malawi	38%	18%	39%
Mali	48%	18%	53%
Mauritius	40%	32%	22%
Morocco	50%	41%	34%
Mozambique	48%	44%	43%
Namibia	30%	25%	40%
Niger	12%	7%	27%
Nigeria	78%	59%	72%
São Tomé and Príncipe	68%	54%	28%
Senegal	26%	10%	31%
Sierra Leone	65%	38%	59%
South Africa	54%	26%	48%
Sudan	49%	36%	42%
Swaziland	37%	38%	42%
Tanzania	38%	17%	50%
Togo	56%	55%	44%
Tunisia	31%	6%	26%

Country	Trust the police 'not at all' or 'just a little'	Trust the army 'not at all' or 'just a little'	Say 'all' or 'most' police are corrupt
Uganda	42%	17%	64%
Zambia	52%	35%	51%
Zimbabwe	49%	34%	58%
Average	47%	33%	45%

Table 2A.4: Frequency and impact of terrorism in featured countries in 2014

	Number of terror attacks*	Number of fatalities due to terror attacks*	Global Terrorism Index (GTI) score**	GTI global ranking	IIAG national security score (/100)
Kenya	95	287	6.660	18	61.1
Mali	55	117	5.871	26	70.1
Nigeria	621	7 461	9.213	3	57.7

Sources: START (2015), Institute for Peace and Economics (2015) and Mo Ibrahim Foundation (2016)

* Numbers were derived using all three criteria used to define a terrorism incident in the Global Terrorism Database: An act must (1) 'be aimed at attaining a political, economic, religious, or social goal', (2) 'be evidence of an intention to coerce, intimidate, or convey some other message to a larger audience (or audiences) than the immediate victims', and (3) 'be outside the context of legitimate warfare activities, i.e. the act must be outside the parameters permitted by international humanitarian law' (National Consortium for the Study of Terrorism and Responses to Terrorism, 2016). Ambiguous cases were excluded from the search criteria.

** A country's Global Terrorism Index (GTI) (2015) score is based on the number of attacks, fatalities, and injuries, as well as the amount of property damage attributed to terrorists in a given year (Institute for Economics and Peace, 2016).

Table 2A.5: Citizen perceptions of the armed forces | 3 countries | 2016/17

	Kenya	Mali	Nigeria
Armed forces protect from security threats			
Often/Always	67%	81%	60%
Rarely/Sometimes	25%	17%	34%
Never	3%	2%	5%
Don't know	5%	1%	0%
Armed forces get necessary resources			
Often/Always	56%	32%	55%
Rarely/Sometimes	24%	38%	39%

	Kenya	Mali	Nigeria
Never	3%	21%	4%
Don't know	16%	9%	1%
Armed forces are professional and respectful to citizens			
Often/Always	47%	70%	49%
Rarely/Sometimes	38%	19%	44%
Never	5%	6%	6%
Don't know	10%	6%	1%

Table 2A.6: Frequency and impact of terrorism on North Africa in 2015[1]

	Number of terror attacks	Number of fatalities due to terror attacks	Global Terrorism Index (GTI) score	GTI global ranking	IIAG national security score (/100)
Algeria	16	21	4.282	42	78.3
Egypt	346	790	7.328	9	62.4
Libya	451	460	7.283	10	31.0
Morocco	1	0	0.892	95	81.2
Sudan	159	210	6.600	18	29.5
Tunisia	17	103	4.963	35	78.5

Source: START (2016) and Institute for Economics and Peace (2016)

Table 2A.7: Perceived threat of extremist groups | by key demographic indicators | 5 countries | 2015

	Algeria	Egypt	Morocco	Sudan	Tunisia	Average
Urban	38%	54%	31%	17%	74%	45%
Rural	37%	46%	32%	30%	82%	43%
Male	39%	50%	32%	28%	72%	44%
Female	36%	49%	31%	23%	82%	44%
18–35 years	36%	51%	33%	25%	77%	41%
36–55 years	38%	49%	31%	27%	79%	47%
56 and older	42%	42%	25%	29%	74%	49%

---

1 For more information on how these figures were calculated and what they report, see Buchanan-Clarke and Lekalake (2016).

	Algeria	Egypt	Morocco	Sudan	Tunisia	Average
No formal education	45%	41%	28%	24%	79%	44%
Primary education	39%	56%	29%	24%	78%	48%
Secondary education	37%	52%	32%	25%	74%	43%
Post-secondary education	36%	56%	36%	26%	76%	42%
No lived poverty	35%	51%	26%	20%	76%	41%
Low lived poverty	45%	50%	30%	19%	76%	44%
Moderate lived poverty	41%	52%	42%	28%	79%	48%
High lived poverty	56%	43%	40%	35%	84%	52%

Table 2A.8: Overall direction of country | 3 countries | 2012–2017

		2011/2012	2014	2016/2017
Kenya	Wrong direction	68%	55%	47%
	Right direction	24%	43%	48%
Mali	Wrong direction	75%	52%	72%
	Right direction	24%	48%	28%
Nigeria	Wrong direction	70%	74%	63%
	Right direction	26%	23%	37%

Respondents were asked:
Let's start with your general view about the current direction of our country. Some people might think the country is going in the wrong direction. Others may feel it is going in the right direction. So let me ask YOU about the overall direction of the country: Would you say that the country is going in the wrong direction or going in the right direction?

Table 2A.9: Fear of violence | 3 countries | 2016/17

	Kenya	Mali	Nigeria
Feared violence in neighbourhood			
No, never	53%	70%	60%
Feared but didn't experience	32%	26%	21%
Feared and experienced	15%	5%	19%
Feared violence at political event			
No, never	53%	72%	52%

	Kenya	Mali	Nigeria
Feared but didn't experience	33%	24%	30%
Feared and experienced	12%	3%	18%
Feared violence during public protest			
No, never	58%	75%	60%
Feared but didn't experience	32%	22%	26%
Feared and experienced	8%	2%	14%
Feared violence by extremists			
No, never	66%	51%	62%
Feared but didn't experience	29%	37%	26%
Feared and experienced	4%	8%	11%

Table 2A.10: Reported victimisation during security crisis in Mali | by region | 2017

	Bamako	Kayes	Koulikoro	Sikasso	Ségou	Mopti	Tombouctou	Gao	Kidal
Left home for another place in Mali	14%	20%	6%	4%	13%	15%	15%	13%	0%
Left home for a place outside of Mali	18%	15%	8%	1%	7%	10%	23%	16%	3%
Supported internally displaced persons (IDPs)	21%	7%	3%	3%	16%	25%	10%	15%	0%
Closure of business	12%	16%	3%	2%	14%	11%	19%	22%	2%
Lost employment	14%	19%	3%	4%	15%	11%	19%	14%	2%
Changed occupation due to the conflict	15%	14%	3%	1%	15%	14%	17%	19%	2%
Victim of intimidation or threats	12%	24%	1%	15%	13%	13%	14%	7%	1%
Witnessed beatings or killings	11%	16%	0%	6%	15%	15%	17%	18%	2%
Proportion of sample	13%	14%	17%	18%	16%	14%	5%	4%	0%

Table 2A.11: Key indicators of insecurity in Nigeria | by residence | 2017

	Most affected states	North East	Nigeria
Personal safety is 'worse' or 'much worse' than 5 years ago	22%	20%	24%
Feared violence by extremists	43%	48%	37%
Armed forces 'never,' 'rarely' or 'sometimes' protect the public	55%	52%	39%
Government handling countering extremist violence 'fairly' or 'very badly'	37%	38%	44%
Government handling of insurgency in northeastern region 'worse' or 'much worse' compared to 12 months ago	14%	11%	12%
Government 'not very' or 'not at all' effective at addressing armed extremists	11%	13%	26%

Endnotes

1. National Consortium for the Study of Terrorism and Responses to Terrorism (2016) *Global Terrorism Database*. Available at: http://www.start.umd.edu/gtd
2. Six rounds of surveys have been conducted in a growing number of countries, increasing from 12 in 1999/2000 to 36 in 2014/15. Round 7 surveys were ongoing at the time of this book's publication. Afrobarometer surveys are conducted by national partners in each country via face-to-face interviews in the language of the respondent's choice. Samples are representative of adult citizens (ie, aged 18 years and above), yielding country-level results with margins of error of +/-2 per cent (for samples of 2 400) or +/-3 per cent (for samples of 1 200) at a 95 per cent confidence level (for full details of the survey and network, including sampling principles, see www.afrobarometer.org).
3. Okenyodo, K, Gondyi, N and Lewis, P (2015) Security and armed extremism in Nigeria: Setting a new agenda. Afrobarometer Dispatch No. 29. Available at: http://afrobarometer.org/sites/default/files/publications/Dispatches/ab_r6_dispatchno29_security_and_extremism_nigeria.pdf
4. These are: Somalia, Libya, Algeria, Tunisia, Nigeria, Kenya and Mali. The report combines automated and manual text-mining analysis on over 3 000 peer-reviewed journal articles published 1998–2016. Afrobarometer does not conduct surveys in Somalia or Libya. See: Douglass, RW and Rondeaux, C (2017) *Mining the Gaps: A text mining-based meta-analysis of the current state of research on violent extremism*. Resolve Network. Available at: http://resolvenet.org/wp-content/uploads/2017/02/RSVEMiningGapsCVEAnalysis_DouglassRondeaux_20170208.pdf
5. Bentley, T, Olapade, M, Wambua, P and Charron, N (2015) Where to start? Aligning Sustainable Development Goals with citizen priorities. Afrobarometer Dispatch No. 67. Available at: http://afrobarometer.org/sites/default/files/publications/Dispatches/ab_r6_dispatchno67_african_priorities_en.pdf
6. Mo Ibrahim Foundation (2016) *A Decade of African Governance 2006–2015*. 2016 Ibrahim Index of African Governance Index Report. Available at: http://mo.ibrahim.foundation/iiag/

7   Respondents could give up to three responses. Figure 2.1 shows the percentage of respondents who cited each issue among their top three problems. 'Security-related issues' combines the categories of crime and security, political violence, political instability, ethnic tensions, interstate war, civil war and terrorism.
8   The question was also asked about the president and officials in his office, members of parliament, government officials, local government councillors, tax officials, judges and magistrates, traditional and religious leaders, and business executives.
9   Transparency International (2015) *People and Corruption: Africa survey 2015*. Available at: http://www.transparency.org/whatwedo/publication/people_and_corruption_africa_survey_2015
10 Kenya was first surveyed by Afrobarometer in 2003.
11 See: Buchanan-Clarke, S and Lekalake, R (2016) *Violent Extremism in Africa: Public opinion from the Sahel, Lake Chad and the Horn*. Afrobarometer Policy Paper No. 32; Bentley, T, Lekalake, R and Buchanan-Clarke, S (2016) Threat of violent extremism from a 'grassroots' perspective: Evidence from North Africa. Afrobarometer Dispatch No. 100. Available at: http://afrobarometer.org/sites/default/files/publications/Dispatches/ab-r6-dispatchno100-violent-extremism-nth-africa-en.pdf
12 An earlier version of this analysis was published as Lekalake, R (2018) Preventing and Countering Violent Extremism in North Africa: 'Grassroots' insights from the 2015 Afrobarometer Survey. In L Sayed and J Barnes (eds) *Contemporary P/CVE Research and Practice*. Hedayah Center. Available at: http://www.hedayahcenter.org/Admin/Content/File-222018131552.pdf
13 Gartenstein-Ross, D, Barr, N, Willcoxon, G and Basuni, N (2015) *The Crisis in North Africa: Implications for Europe and options for EU policy-makers*. Den Haag: Clingendael Netherlands Institute of International Relations.
14 Diamond, L (2015) Facing up to the democratic recession, *Journal of Democracy*, **26** (1), pp. 141–155.
15 Institute for Economics and Peace (2016) *Global Terrorism Index 2016: Measuring and understanding the impact of terrorism*. Available at: http://economicsandpeace.org/wp-content/uploads/2016/11/Global-Terrorism-Index-2016.2.pdf
16 Al Jazeera (2015) Deadly explosion hits presidential guard bus in Tunis. 25 November 2015. Available at: http://www.aljazeera.com/news/2015/11/explosion-tunisia-151124164711388.htm
17 This question was not asked in Sudan.
18 Institute for Economics and Peace (2016). *Global Terrorism Index 2016: Measuring and understanding the impact of terrorism*. Available at: http://economicsandpeace.org/wp-content/uploads/2016/11/Global-Terrorism-Index-2016.2.pdf
19 The Lived Poverty Index (LPI) measures respondents' levels of material deprivation by asking them how often they or their family members went without enough food, enough clean water, medicines or medical treatment, enough cooking fuel, and a cash income during the previous year. 'No lived poverty' refers to full access to all five basic necessities, while 'high lived poverty' refers to regular shortages of these goods and services. (For more information on the LPI, see Afrobarometer Policy Paper No. 29. Available at: www.afrobarometer.org)
20 Bentley et al (2016) p. 8.
21 Freedom House (2017) *Freedom in the World 2017. Populists and autocrats: The dual threat to global democracy*. Available at: https://freedomhouse.org/sites/default/files/FH_FIW_2017_Report_Final.pdf
22 Amnesty International (2017) 'We want an end to the fear': Abuses under Tunisia's state of emergency. Available at: https://www.amnesty.org/en/documents/mde30/4911/2017/en/
23 Human Rights Watch (2015) *Tunisia: Counterterror law endangers rights. Legislate safeguards*

against abuse. Available at: https://www.hrw.org/news/2015/07/31/tunisia-counterterror-law-endangers-rights

24 See: The Soufan Group (2015) *Foreign Fighters: An updated assessment of the flow of foreign fighters into Syria and Iraq*. Available at: http://soufangroup.com/wp-content/uploads/2015/12/TSG_ForeignFightersUpdate3.pdf; Dodwell, B, Milton, D and Rassler, D (2016) *The Caliphate's Global Workforce: An inside look at the Islamic State's foreign fighter paper trail*. New York: Combating Terrorism Center at West Point.

25 Middle East Eye (2016) Analysis: Egypt's economy five years after the revolution. Published 23 January 2016. Available at: http://www.middleeasteye.net/news/analysis-egypts-economy-5-years-after-revolution-1084797209

26 Al Jazeera (2011) Kenya says making gains against al-Shabab. Published 19 October 2011. Available at: http://www.aljazeera.com/news/africa/2011/10/2011101942627768243.html

27 National Consortium for the Study of Terrorism and Responses to Terrorism (2016) *Global Terrorism Database*. Available at: http://www.start.umd.edu/gtd

28 *The Telegraph* (2015) Kenya visitor numbers fall 25 per cent as terrorism hits tourism. Published 12 June 2015. Available at: http://www.telegraph.co.uk/travel/destinations/africa/kenya/articles/Kenya-visitor-numbers-fall-25-per-cent-as-terrorism-hits-tourism/

29 *Daily Maverick* (2017) Kenya: Nine villagers beheaded in brutal al-Shabaab attack. Published 10 July 2017. Available at: https://www.dailymaverick.co.za/article/2017-07-10-kenya-nine-villagers-beheaded-in-a-brutal-al-shabaab-attack/

30 News24 (2016) ISIS make inroads in Kenya. Published 30 July 2016. Available at: http://www.news24.com/Africa/News/isis-makes-inroads-into-kenya-20160630

31 UNODC (2017) The Sahel Programme. Available at: https://www.unodc.org/westandcentralafrica/en/newrosenwebsite/sahel-programme/sahel-programme.html

32 Herbst, J (2014) *States and Power in Africa: Comparative lessons in authority and control*. Princeton, NJ: Princeton University Press.

33 De Albuquerque, AL (2014) Explaining the 2012 Tuareg rebellion in Mali and lack thereof in Niger. FOI Memo No. 5099. Available at: https://www.foi.se/download/18.7920f8c915921957088a2ca/1484060671072/foi%20_5099.pdf

34 Cilliers, J (2015). *Violent Islamist Extremism and Terror in Africa*. Institute for Security Studies Paper No. 286. Available at: https://www.issafrica.org/uploads/Paper%20286%20_v3.pdf

35 BBC (2017) Mali profile: Timeline. Last updated 28 June 2017. Available at: http://www.bbc.com/news/world-africa-13881978

36 The 2013 survey was a special round specifically designed to measure democracy, governance and reconciliation in Mali. Data collection took place between 17 December 2013 and 5 January 2014. About one in five (18 per cent) of the respondents came from previously occupied areas that could not be surveyed in 2012.

37 Melly, P (2017) Terrorism in the Sahel is not fading away. Chatham House. Published 20 January 2016. Available at: https://www.chathamhouse.org/expert/comment/jihadism-sahel-not-fading-away

38 Weiss, C (2017) Analysis: Merger of Al-Qaeda groups threatens security in West Africa, *Long Wars Journal*. Published 18 March 2017. Available at: https://www.longwarjournal.org/archives/2017/03/analysis-merger-of-al-qaeda-groups-threatens-security-in-west-africa.php

39 In response to increasing violence and instability in Mali since 2013, increasing numbers of communities have taken up arms to form 'self-defence' groups to protect themselves against the threat posed by jihadist groups and the growing prevalence of inter-community violence. In several cases, these have been supported by Malian security forces and local elites. See: International Crisis Group (2016) *Central Mali: An uprising in the making?* Africa

Report No. 238. Available at: https://d2071andvip0wj.cloudfront.net/central-mali-an-uprising-in-the-making.pdf
40 Original text: *A votre avis, combien les forces suivantes sont-elles utiles pour aider le Mali à recouvrer son intégrité territoriale et son unité nationale, ou n'en avez-vous pas suffisamment entendu parler pour vous prononcer?*
41 Original text: *S'il vous plaît, dites-moi si vous PERSONNELLEMENT ou des MEMBRES de votre FAMILLE ont été affectés par la crise et le conflit du Nord, d'une des manières suivantes?*
42 Original text: *Quelles pourraient être, selon vous, les séquelles de la crise et du conflit du Nord sur le Mali?*
43 http://www.un.org/en/peacekeeping/missions/minusma/facts.shtml
44 The operation names were specified in each questionnaire.
45 Council on Foreign Relations (2017) *Nigeria Security Tracker*. Available at: http://www.cfr.org/nigeria/nigeria-security-tracker/p29483
46 Institute for Economics & Peace (2016) *Global Terrorism Index 2015*. Available at: http://economicsandpeace.org/reports/
47 Federal Ministry of Budget and National Planning (2016) Full Text of President Muhammadu Buhari's 2016 Budget Address at the National Assembly. Available at: http://www.nationalplanning.gov.ng/index.php/news-media/news/current-news/494-full-text-of-president-muhammadu-buhari-s-2016-budget-address-at-the-national-assembly
48 Institute for Economics & Peace (2016) *Global Terrorism Index 2016: Measuring and understanding the impact of terrorism*. Available at: http://economicsandpeace.org/reports/
49 For comparison of 2014 results on this question and others related to terrorism in Nigeria, Niger and Cameroon, see Buchanan-Clarke and Lekalake (2016).

References

Al Jazeera (2011) Kenya says making gains against al-Shabab. Published 19 October 2011. Available at: http://www.aljazeera.com/news/africa/2011/10/2011101942627768243.html

Al Jazeera (2015) Deadly explosion hits presidential guard bus in Tunis. 25 November 2015. Available at: http://www.aljazeera.com/news/2015/11/explosion-tunisia-151124164711388.htm

Amnesty International (2017) 'We want an end to the fear': Abuses under Tunisia's state of emergency. Available at: https://www.amnesty.org/en/documents/mde30/4911/2017/en/

BBC (2017) Mali profile: Timeline. Last updated 28 June 2017. Available at: http://www.bbc.com/news/world-africa-13881978

Bentley, T, Lekalake, R and Buchanan-Clarke, S (2016) Threat of violent extremism from a 'grassroots' perspective: Evidence from North Africa. Afrobarometer Dispatch No. 100. Available at: http://afrobarometer.org/sites/default/files/publications/Dispatches/ab-r6-dispatchno100-violent-extremism-nth-africa-en.pdf

Bentley, T, Olapade, M, Wambua, P and Charron, N (2015) Where to start? Aligning Sustainable Development Goals with citizen priorities. Afrobarometer Dispatch No. 67. Available at: http://afrobarometer.org/sites/default/files/publications/Dispatches/ab_r6_dispatchno67_african_priorities_en.pdf

Buchanan-Clarke, S and Lekalake, R (2016) *Violent Extremism in Africa: Public opinion from the Sahel, Lake Chad, and the Horn*. Afrobarometer Policy Paper No. 32.

Cilliers, J (2015) *Violent Islamist Extremism and Terror in Africa*. Institute for Security Studies Paper No. 286. Available at: https://www.issafrica.org/uploads/Paper%20286%20_v3.pdf

Council on Foreign Relations (2017) *Nigeria Security Tracker*. Available at: http://www.cfr.org/nigeria/nigeria-security-tracker/p29483

Daily Maverick (2017) Kenya: Nine villagers beheaded in brutal al-Shabaab attack. Published

10 July 2017. Available at: https://www.dailymaverick.co.za/article/2017-07-10-kenya-nine-villagers-beheaded-in-a-brutal-al-shabaab-attack/
De Albuquerque, AL (2014) Explaining the 2012 Tuareg rebellion in Mali and lack thereof in Niger. FOI Memo No. 5099. Available at: https://www.foi.se/download/18.7920f8c915921957088a2ca/1484060671072/foi%20_5099.pdf
Diamond, L (2015) Facing up to the democratic recession, *Journal of Democracy*, **26** (1), pp. 141–155.
Dodwell, B, Milton, D and Rassler, D (2016) *The Caliphate's Global Workforce: An inside look at the Islamic State's foreign fighter paper trail.* New York: Combating Terrorism Center at West Point.
Douglass, RW and Rondeaux, C (2017) *Mining the Gaps: A text mining-based meta-analysis of the current state of research on violent extremism.* Resolve Network. Available at: http://resolvenet.org/wp-content/uploads/2017/02/RSVEMiningGapsCVEAnalysis_DouglassRondeaux_20170208.pdf
Federal Ministry of Budget and National Planning (2016) Full Text of President Muhammadu Buhari's 2016 Budget Address at the National Assembly. Available at: http://www.nationalplanning.gov.ng/index.php/news-media/news/current-news/494-full-text-of-president-muhammadu-buhari-s-2016-budget-address-at-the-national-assembly
Freedom House (2017) *Freedom in the World 2017: Populists and autocrats: The dual threat to global democracy.* Available at: https://freedomhouse.org/sites/default/files/FH_FIW_2017_Report_Final.pdf
Gartenstein-Ross, D, Barr, N, Willcoxon, G and Basuni, N (2015) *The Crisis in North Africa: Implications for Europe and options for EU policymakers.* Den Haag: Clingendael Netherlands Institute of International Relations.
Herbst, J (2014) *States and Power in Africa: Comparative lessons in authority and control.* Princeton, NJ: Princeton University Press.
Human Rights Watch (2015) *Tunisia: Counterterror law endangers rights. Legislate safeguards against abuse.* Available at: https://www.hrw.org/news/2015/07/31/tunisia-counterterror-law-endangers-rights
Institute for Economics and Peace (2015) *Global Terrorism Index 2015.* Available at: http://economicsandpeace.org/reports/
Institute for Economics and Peace (2016) *Global Terrorism Index 2016: Measuring and understanding the impact of terrorism.* Available at: http://economicsandpeace.org/wp-content/uploads/2016/11/Global-Terrorism-Index-2016.2.pdf
International Crisis Group (2016) *Central Mali: An uprising in the making?* Africa Report No. 238. Available at: https://d2071andvip0wj.cloudfront.net/central-mali-an-uprising-in-the-making.pdf
Lekalake, R (2018) Preventing and countering violent extremism in North Africa: 'Grassroots' insights from the 2015 Afrobarometer Survey. In L Sayed and J Barnes *Contemporary P/CVE Research and Practice.* Hedayah Center. Available at: http://www.hedayahcenter.org/Admin/Content/File-222018131552.pdf
Melly, P (2017) Terrorism in the Sahel is not fading away. Chatham House. Published 20 January 2016. Available at: https://www.chathamhouse.org/expert/comment/jihadism-sahel-not-fading-away
Middle East Eye (2016) Analysis: Egypt's economy five years after the revolution. Published 23 January 2016. Available at: http://www.middleeasteye.net/news/analysis-egypts-economy-5-years-after-revolution-1084797209
Mo Ibrahim Foundation (2016) *A Decade of African Governance 2006–2015.* 2016 Ibrahim Index of African Governance Index Report. Available at: http://mo.ibrahim.foundation/iiag/
National Consortium for the Study of Terrorism and Responses to Terrorism (2016) *Global Terrorism Database.* Available at: http://www.start.umd.edu/gtd

News24 (2016) ISIS make inroads in Kenya. Published 30 July 2016. Available at: http://www.news24.com/Africa/News/isis-makes-inroads-into-kenya-20160630

Okenyodo, K, Gondyi, N and Lewis, P (2015). Security and armed extremism in Nigeria: Setting a new agenda. Afrobarometer Dispatch No. 29. Available at: http://afrobarometer.org/sites/default/files/publications/Dispatches/ab_r6_dispatchno29_security_and_extremism_nigeria.pdf

The Soufan Group (2015) *Foreign Fighters: An updated assessment of the flow of foreign fighters into Syria and Iraq*. Available at: http://soufangroup.com/wp-content/uploads/2015/12/TSG_ForeignFightersUpdate3.pdf

The Telegraph (2015) Kenya visitor numbers fall 25 per cent as terrorism hits tourism. Published: 12 June 2015. Available at: http://www.telegraph.co.uk/travel/destinations/africa/kenya/articles/Kenya-visitor-numbers-fall-25-per-cent-as-terrorism-hits-tourism/

Transparency International (2015) *People and Corruption: Africa survey 2015*. Available at: http://www.transparency.org/whatwedo/publication/people_and_corruption_africa_survey_2015

UNODC (2017) The Sahel Programme. Available at: https://www.unodc.org/westandcentralafrica/en/newrosenwebsite/sahel-programme/sahel-programme.html

Weiss, C (2017) Analysis: Merger of Al-Qaeda groups threatens security in West Africa, *Long Wars Journal*. Published 18 March 2017. Available at: https://www.longwarjournal.org/archives/2017/03/analysis-merger-of-al-qaeda-groups-threatens-security-in-west-africa.php

Chapter 3
Terrorism in North Africa and the Sahel

Richard Chelin

Introduction

Over the past decade, North Africa has become a hot bed of terrorist activity, creating an arc of instability stretching across the Sahel. Terrorism is not new to the region. In the early 1990s, Algerian mujahideen, returning from fighting alongside Al-Qaeda against the Soviet Union in Afghanistan, helped to form the Armed Islamic Group (GIA), which quickly began a campaign of terrorism in a bid to transform Algeria into an Islamic state ruled by sharia law. However, in recent years, North Africa and the Sahel region have experienced a rapid increase in the frequency of terrorist attacks and prevalence of violent jihadist organisations. Al-Qaeda in the Islamic Maghreb (AQIM) and, more recently, the Islamic State of Iraq and Syria (ISIS) in Libya, are two of the most prominent organisations operating in the region today.

There are a number of common structural, social and economic drivers which, to varying degrees, make countries in this region vulnerable to instability, criminal trafficking and violent extremism. However, to gain a better understanding of why violent jihadist organisations have been so successful in North Africa and the Sahel, it is important to examine both the colonial and post-colonial history of its countries, as well as the often complex trajectories and relationships between the various criminal and militant organisations, which have entrenched themselves in the region. In Mali, for example, AQIM has proven adept at fielding loyalty and developing relationships with local jihadist organisations, embedding itself with groups in the north who have grievances against the state, exploiting local clan conflicts, and creating connections with the criminal networks that maintain the region's trafficking routes. In contrast, ISIS in Libya has used the chaos caused by the fall of Muammar Gaddafi, and relied on the magnetism of its extremist narrative, attention to communications, and the drawing power of its grand idea to create a 'caliphate', to establish itself in the country.[1]

Noting the complexity of the security landscape in North Africa and the Sahel, and the importance of understanding the diverse goals and modi operandi of the militant groups that operate within it, this chapter seeks to provide a history and overview of both AQIM and ISIS in the region, including their distinctive strategies, historical origins, ideological differences, and recent successes and failures. In addition, several other, less prominent, violent jihadist groups are discussed, as well as what strategies might best serve both governments and civil society to improve security in the region.

Setting the scene

North Africa is a broad region that extends from the Atlantic Ocean on the western coast of Morocco to the Suez Canal and the Red Sea on the northeast of the African continent. The region includes the modern-day countries of Morocco, Algeria, Tunisia, Libya, Egypt and Sudan, as well as the territory of western Sahara. The French referred to the region as *Afrique du Nord* during the colonial period, while the Arabs named it the Maghreb, which translates from Arabic as the 'place of setting (of the sun), and hence West'.[2] A salient feature of the Maghreb region are the mountain ranges that dominate its landscapes, including the Rif in Morocco, the Tellian Atlas in northern Tunisia and the Aures in Algeria.

Despite the fact that the Berbers were the first to dwell there, the majority of the inhabitants in the region today identify themselves as Arabs. Berbers are an ethnic group that can be traced back to the Roman occupation of North Africa, their name being derived from *barbari,* denoting the non-Latin speaking people of the region.[3] After conquering the Maghreb in 705, the Arabs named the local ethnic group the Barbar (Berber), borrowing the term from the previous occupiers.

Culturally and religiously, the Arab Muslim conquerors had a greater influence over the local population than their predecessors. As McKenna (2011) notes, within less than four centuries after the Arab conquest, 'Berbers had become Islamised and in part also Arabised. The region's indigenous Christian communities, which prior to the Arab conquest had constituted an important part of the Christian world, ceased to exist.'[4] It is important to note that the Berbers were not forcibly converted to Islam, nor were they systematically indoctrinated, as previous conquerors had attempted.[5] The Maghreb remained under Muslim rule until the advent of European colonisation in 1830, which is encapsulated by the French capture of Algiers.

Despite the French occupying, often brutally, the wider region for more than a century, Islamic religious and cultural practices remained strong. After studying the cultural history of the Maghreb region, Zartman (1973) presciently noted, 'the basic ingredient of North African attitudes is the area's Islamic background'.[6] When assessing the present-day situation through the lens of colonial history, it is clear that during the period, the oppressed found a sense of identity and belonging through their religion and its values.

Further south of the Maghreb is the Sahel-Sahara zone that connects the Mediterranean world and sub-Saharan Africa. Geographically, the Sahel belt comprises parts of North and West Africa and passes through Algeria, Mali, Niger, Mauritania, as well as parts of Libya, Burkina Faso and Chad. The Tuaregs – descendants of ancient Berber speakers – are one of the most prominent ethnic tribes that call the Sahel home and the main inhabitants of the region, with their traditional range extending 'through five countries, Algeria, Mali, Libya, Niger, and Burkina Faso'.[7]

The other major ethnic groups in the Sahel include the Hassaniyya-speaking Arabs, the Fulbe/Fulani and the Songhai. Home to such a variety of ethnic groups, the Sahel has always been a trading hub. As Gregoire (1997) notes, 'sustained trade has linked the Sahel with North Africa for many centuries' with a multitude of products being exchanged, including gold, ivory, cotton and ostrich feathers.[8] With these vast trade routes connecting various market cities in different countries, both products and ideas were exchanged.

While trade and commerce in the Sahel may have preceded Islam, North African Muslims, who played a crucial role in the trans-Saharan trade, helped to spread the religion in West Africa. The population of the Sahel subsisted on agriculture and hunting. However, this would change drastically with the advent of colonisation as it spelt an end to the trans-Saharan trade. In the mid-19th century, the French would occupy most of the Sahel. In 1879, they began the conquest of *Soudan Française* (which would later become Mali).

In 1895, the French established an administrative grouping under its rule known as the Federation of French West Africa, which comprised the modern-day states of Benin, Burkina Faso, Guinea, Ivory Coast, Mali, Mauritania, Niger and Senegal. By the 1920s, the French forces had effectively gained control over the remotest corners of the Sahara Desert.[9] In the aftermath of the Second World War, there was an increase in nationalist movements who opposed colonial rule in French West Africa. These movements were demanding self-determination in the form of independence from their colonisers, and by the 1960s, all of France's former colonies had become independent republics.

After the independence of its colonies, France still wanted to maintain its presence in Africa so it designed a project to establish a partnership with its former subjects. The *Loi Cadre* (a law passed by the French government that provided each colony with semi-responsible government in 1956) set the foundation for such a project. This has been critical in the formulation of a framework for French foreign policy in Africa in the post-colonial period.

As Chafer (2002) highlights, the aim of the framework was to 'protect French strategic interests by maintaining France's presence in the region, but without incurring the costs of direct colonial rule'.[10] This was achieved through the signing of defence, military, technical and cultural assistance accords and the maintenance of the Franc zone.[11] Additionally, the French government also established an African currency in the form of the franc CFA (*Colonies Française d'Afrique* – French Colonies of Africa) with a view to protect Africa from some of the effects of the devaluation of the franc.[12] This ensured that France would maintain a solid form of economic control over its former colonies. The remnants of this influence remain prevalent within the context of counterterrorism operations conducted by France in some of its former colonies today (Mauritania, Mali, Niger and Chad).

The euphoria, which African states felt after obtaining independence, soon turned to anguish as leaders began to realise the fragile nature of the states they had inherited. To assert control, many African leaders became more focused on retaining power than developing their countries. As a result, the emergence of dictatorships and coups d'état became a regular phenomenon in many francophone states, such as Burkina Faso, Central African Republic and Benin, among others.[13] Mali, a weak state that has undergone both terrorist attacks and a recent attempted coup, is a prime example of both the impact of France's colonial legacy and the poor governance that has characterised the country in its post-independence years. Incidentally, the French were the first to come to the aid of the Malian government during the 2013 attempted coup by violent jihadists who, having taken control of the northern part of the country, were advancing on the capital.

As will be illustrated in the following sections, colonialism and post-colonialism played a major role in fostering extremist groups. However, it is also noteworthy to emphasise that colonialism or post-colonialism are but one of many factors that have contributed to the rise of terrorist organisations in the region.

Al-Qaeda in the Islamic Maghreb

Exactly seven months after 9/11, on 11 April 2002, Al-Qaeda launched its first attack on North African soil. The target was the El Ghriba synagogue on the Tunisian island of Djerba, which left 21 people dead.[14] The Tunisian attack not only signalled the emergence of Al-Qaeda in North Africa but also marked the beginning of the group's reign of terror that would leave an indelible imprint in the Maghreb region. It is within this context that this section will examine the ideology and historical origins of Al-Qaeda in the Islamic Maghreb (AQIM).

AQIM's ideology is rooted in militant Islamic fundamentalism that amalgamates Salafi-jihadist dogma with a North African overtone that includes references to the early Islamic conquest of the Maghreb.[15] Abdelmalek Droukdal, the group's current leader, reiterated these objectives when he renewed AQIM's loyalty to the leader of Al-Qaeda, Al-Zawahiri on 4 July 2014, pledging 'an allegiance to jihad to liberate Muslim lands and affirm Islamic sharia law in it and bring back the caliphate that is based on prophetic principles'.[16] Since both Salafism and Wahhabism have a great influence on the ideology and objectives of AQIM, it is important to analyse the underlying tenets of these teachings.

Salafism, an ideology that advocates a return to the original teachings and practices of Islam as it was in the days of the prophet Muhammad, emerged from the writings of the 19th century Muslim scholar Jamal al-Din al-Afghani.[17] During his epoch, Al-Afghani witnessed the decline of Islamic civilisation vis-à-vis the emergence of Western technological and cultural advances. This weakening of Islamic power, according to Al-Afghani, was a result of Muslims turning away from the true path of Islam. Spiritual revival, he asserted, was the remedy and therefore 'by looking back to the past it is possible to put Islam on the path to renewal and return Islamic society to its rightful dominant position'.[18] The writings of Al-Afghani have influenced subsequent generations of Salafist thinkers. Of these scholars, two notable figures, Sayyid Qutb and Maulana Mawdudi, appear to be the most influential in defining the Salafi-jihadi doctrine that would become the foundation of the ideology of Al-Qaeda and other similar groups.

Sayyid Qutb declared that 'the oneness and sovereignty of God preclude human rule, which should be violently overturned if necessary and that the only legitimate form of government over Muslims is an Islamic state'.[19] Mawdudi, supplementing Qutb's perspective, advocated that a state's governance be based purely on the principles of Allah and sharia law. He further believed that the five pillars of Islam – profession of faith, prayer, fasting for Ramadan, pilgrimage and almsgiving – were phases of training and preparation for jihad. 'Jihad' is an Arabic word which literally translates to 'struggle' or 'effort'. More specifically, it is a struggle in the path of Allah.[20] However, despite the complexity of the word jihad, Salafi militant groups singularly interpret the term to mean 'holy war' (which is only one of its meanings) and adopt it as the only method to achieve spiritual revival.

In a document titled *Join the Caravan,* the late Osama bin Laden exemplifies this mode of thought when he writes: 'When the enemy enters that land of the Muslims, *jihad* becomes individually obligatory ... When *jihad* becomes obligatory, no permission of parents is required ... *Jihad* is a collective act of worship'.[21]

Muhammad ibn Abd al-Wahhab, the founder of Wahhabism, advocated a puritanical form of Islam based on the literal interpretation of the Qur'an.[22] Similar to the Salafists, Wahhabist scholars ascribe the decline of Islamic civilisation to a deviation from the 'right path' and claim Islam can regain its glory only when Muslims return to the way of Allah. Moreover, Wahhabists reject reinterpretations or readjustments of Islamic laws or doctrines that attempt to account for changes in the contemporary world.[23] To justify political extension and legitimise the use of jihad against infidels, Wahhabists differentiate between true believers and unbelievers by classifying the world into *dar al-Islam* (abode of Islam) and *dar al-harb* (abode of war) and often resort to the concept of *takfir* or excommunication.[24]

Takfir, the act of declaring a Muslim an infidel, has been interpreted by some as a way to justify violence and the use of jihad against Muslims who do not live according to the Qur'an and the Sunna, and fall within the *dar al-harb* category.[25] Subsequently, the ideology behind Salafi-jihadi groups like AQIM incorporates tenets of both Salafism (spiritual reform through the use of *jihad*) and Wahhabism (the concept of *takfir*) to create an Islamic state founded on the principles of the Qur'an and the Sharia. However, equally important to understanding the ideology of AQIM, is to understand the recent history of its country of origin, Algeria, and the predecessor organisations which helped give rise to it.

AQIM's Algerian roots

After 132 years of colonial rule, on 5 July 1962, Algeria gained political independence from France after a war that lasted eight years, during which at least a million people were killed or wounded.[26] The National Liberation Front (FLN), given the notable role it played in Algeria's independence, arrogated control of the country to itself. Algeria became a one-party state, with the FLN as the ruling party and Ben Bella as president of the country.[27] However, three years later, Colonel Houari Boumediene seized power through a coup d'état. After Boumediene's death, Chadli Bendjedid assumed office in 1979, but was deposed by the military for his perceived role in a crisis that would trigger a decades-long civil war.[28]

For almost 30 years after independence, to the outside world, Algeria seemed to be 'enjoying a degree of political stability and economic and social development', while its citizens faced 'economic hardship, social malaise and a changing international environment'.[29] This situation precipitated a decline in support for the FLN. People began searching for change and reform that would resurrect Algeria from its socio-economic woes brought on by decades of mismanagement and corruption by the FLN. This change would come in the form of the Islamic Salvation Front (FIS).

The Islamic Salvation Front

In June 1990, Algeria held elections. The results awoke the FLN from their slumber, as the FIS won 54 per cent of the votes to the FLN's 28 per cent.[30] Late in the evening of 26 December 1991, the results were made official: out of the 231 contested seats in the national assembly (430 in total), the FIS won 188; the FFS (Socialist Forces Front), the main opposition party, captured 25; and the FLN came third with 15 seats.[31] Not only did the FIS win by a huge margin but they also won by a majority, which meant they would have the power to change the constitution. The people had made their choice and the results were proof that they believed the FIS would bring about the change that Algeria needed. Consequently, a change in the political horizon was imminent.

In 1992, the FIS, positioned to win the second round of the general elections and become the first democratically elected government, was denied victory. The military seized control and forced President Chadli to tender his resignation.[32] Furthermore, the leaders of FIS were imprisoned and the party was banned, forcing the group's members into hiding. Consequently, when the military banned Islamist political parties from the political platform, the only option to achieve change was through violent clashes with the state.

The FIS struggled to regain its original unity after the coup as its leaders were imprisoned. It eventually splintered and the majority of its members joined militant Islamist groups to lead an armed resistance against the state. Among these militant groups was the Islamic Salvation Army (AIS), which was considered the military wing of the FIS, and the Armed Islamic Group (GIA). The latter not only consisted of Salafist members who were disenchanted with the ideals of the FIS, but also Algerian veterans who had returned from the Afghan jihad, fighting alongside Al-Qaeda against the Soviet Union.[33]

The Armed Islamic Group (GIA)

The GIA, formed in 1993, and led by Abdelhak Layada, became one of the most dangerous and feared Islamic militant groups during the Algerian civil war. Its attacks, based on the concept of *takfir*, included both local (government and civilians) and transnational (French) targets. The tactics of the GIA were diametrically opposed to those of the MIA (Armed Islamic Movement) or the AIS – who were both prepared to negotiate with the government in their bid to ascend to power. Another tenet that separated the GIA from other armed groups such as the MIA or the AIS was the group's adoption of violence. According to Rudolph (2008), the 'sweeping use of *takfir*' meant that any person who did not participate in the fight against the government was perceived as an enemy of the GIA and hence Islam.[34] Although the GIA and the MIA shared the same goal of Islamising Algeria, their means to achieving this end differed radically.

The GIA for its part rejected any means of dialogue or compromise with the Algerian government in its bid to transform Algeria into an Islamic state ruled by sharia. To attain these objectives, the GIA preferred 'short-term, spectacular terrorist attacks' that extended to suicide bombing and transnational terrorism.[35] In the beginning, the group killed 'diplomats, clergy, industrialists, intellectuals, journalists, priests, and foreigners. However, from 1996 they murdered tens of thousands of innocent Algerians.'[36] A campaign that began as a quest for an Islamic state in Algeria spiralled into an uncontrollable and brutal massacre that shocked the Islamic world.

The GIA became the first group to export jihadi terrorism to France. The first GIA attack on the soil of its European nemesis led to four dead and more than 80 injured when the group detonated a bomb at the Saint-Michel–Notre Dame metro station in Paris on 25 July 1995.[37] Two weeks later, a nail bomb at the Arc de Triomphe injured 17 people, among whom were 11 tourists. The GIA went on to detonate a further eight bombs in France between July and December 1995, three of which went off in Paris metro stations, killing 10 and injuring over 200 people.[38] The GIA was as relentless on the local scene as it was abroad. In March 1995, a bomb exploded outside the police station in Algiers resulting in 40 fatalities.[39] Between 1992 and 1997, the GIA's inexorable campaign claimed the lives of over 200 000 people, and as a result, popular support for the group dwindled, precipitating an eventual collapse. Support for, and the legitimacy of, the GIA reached its nadir after the group perpetuated an act that shocked even the most extreme fundamentalists. In March 1996, GIA militants raided a Trappist monastery in the village of Tibhirine and kidnapped seven monks. When the French government did not succumb to GIA's demands, its leader ordered that the monks be killed.[40] This was a crippling blow to the image of the GIA from which it never recovered. Soon afterwards, Al-Qaeda, which hitherto had supported the GIA, issued a communiqué denouncing the group's brutality and violence before severing all ties with them.

The Salafist Group for Preaching and Combat (GSPC)
In 1998, Hassan Hattab, the former head of the GIA network in Europe, broke away from the group and established the Salafist Group for Preaching and Combat (GSPC) as a reaction to the undiscerning and excessive violence of the GIA.[41] Similar to the GIA, the GSPC adhered to Salafist ideology and aimed to convert Algeria into an Islamic state governed purely by sharia law. To enhance their support among local people, the GSPC changed their tactics by attacking government and military targets only and in the process tried to mend the Salafi-jihadi image that the GIA had tarnished. The fact that the GSPC had become Algeria's most prominent terrorist group can be attributed

to two factors. The group had the support of Al-Qaeda and was able to operate outside of Algeria by drawing on its European networks.[42] Both sides realised that a partnership would not only be important but also mutually beneficial. The GSPC saw this partnership as producing global exposure and legitimacy in the eyes of the worldwide Salafi-jihadist movement. For Al-Qaeda, it had a practical basis as the group sought to access the widespread network of GSPC cells in Europe.[43]

In 2003, Nabil Sahraoui replaced Hattab as leader of the GSPC, and a few months later, orchestrated the kidnapping of 32 foreign tourists in the Sahara Desert.[44] In 2004, Sahraoui was killed by Algerian forces, resulting in Abdelmalek Droukdal assuming leadership of the organisation. Unlike his predecessors, Droukdal pursued closer relations with Al-Qaeda. The 2003 US invasion of Iraq, according to Harmon (2010), 'became a major recruiting tool for the global *jihad* … [and] brought the GSPC and other national resistance *jihads* in line with al-Qaeda'.[45] Furthermore, the kidnapping and execution of two Algerian diplomats in Baghdad in July 2005 signalled a rapprochement between Droukdal and Al-Zarqawi (the former leader of the Al-Qaeda branch in Iraq [AQI]). As such, an accord between the GSPC and AQI was sealed.[46]

Al-Qaeda in the Islamic Maghreb: Merger and operations

On 11 September 2006, Al-Qaeda's second-in-command, Al-Zawahiri, formalised the merger between Al-Qaeda and the GSPC. In response, the GSPC released a communiqué announcing 'the merging of the Salafist Group for Prayer and Combat in Algeria with Al-Qaeda, and swearing *bayat* [an oath of allegiance] to the Shaykh Usama Bin Laden'.[47] Hereafter, the group changed its name from GSPC to Al-Qaeda in the Islamic Maghreb (AQIM).[48]

AQIM opened its campaign of terror on 13 February 2007 with seven synchronised bomb attacks targeting police stations across Algeria, killing six people.[49] On 11 April 2007, AQIM led three simultaneous suicide bombings in Algiers, targeting the government palace, a police station, and a *gendarmerie* post.[50] At the government building, a dozen people were killed and approximately 118 injured, while the attack at the police station claimed the lives of 11 people and injured more than 40.[51] These attacks demonstrated the professionalism of AQIM in their use of explosives, car bombs, remote-control devices and suicide bombers. Prior to the emergence of AQIM, groups such as the GIA and GSPC hardly resorted to suicide bombings as a weapon of attack. Nonetheless, in an interview on Al Jazeera, Droukdal defended the group's use of suicide bombings, despite some members of AQIM disagreeing with him.[52]

After two coordinated suicide attacks on a United Nations office and the Constitutional Court in Algiers in December 2007, which killed over

60 people and injured approximately 180, AQIM claimed responsibility and released a statement labelling the foreigners who were killed as 'crusaders who are plundering our land and resources'.[53] The period between 2008 and 2009 witnessed a significant increase in suicide attacks on indiscriminate targets. To justify their methods of attack, AQIM appealed to the notion of sacrifice, extolling suicide bombers as 'the knights of the faith with their blood in defence of the wounded nation of Islam'.[54] As with the GIA, AQIM appealed to the concept of *takfir* to justify their attacks. However, the indiscriminate nature of these operations had a negative impact on the image of AQIM. Support for the group began to weaken among locals and its recruiting capacity was dealt a major setback. As a result, the group began to refrain from using suicide bombing as a method of attack.[55]

AQIM resorted to a range of activities to raise funds for their operations. These primarily included kidnapping and drug smuggling.[56] For instance, to name a few cases, the group has been responsible for kidnapping two Austrian tourists in Tunisia, two UN diplomats in northern Niger, and three Spanish aid workers in Mauritania.[57] In recent years, the number of attacks claimed or attributed to AQIM has declined – with the exception of the northern Mali insurgency in 2013. Some scholars attribute this to the fact that AQIM is moving away from terrorism towards organised crime. However, others argue that terrorist attacks are outsourced to smaller groups linked to AQIM.[58] An example is Al-Mourabitoun, led by Mokhtar Belmokhtar, the former commander of AQIM. The group claimed responsibility for the assault on a natural gas facility at Ain Amenas in January 2013 that claimed the lives of 67 people. They also claimed responsibility for restaurant attacks in Mali on 8 March 2015, where five people were killed.[59] In November 2015, Al-Qaeda and Al-Mourabitoun launched a joint operation, besieging the Radisson Blu hotel in the Malian capital, Bamako. A month later, Al-Mourabitoun merged with AQIM. The newly merged group conducted their first attack on two hotels in Ouagadougou on 15 January 2016. On 13 March 2016, AQIM launched their first attack in Ivory Coast when gunmen opened fire on tourists at the resort of Grand Bassam, killing 18 people and injuring 33.[60] These operations by AQIM not only signalled a resurgence of the group with the aim of consolidating Al-Qaeda's hold in West Africa, but also sent a message of defiance to ISIS, which has been rapidly expanding in power and influence in recent years.

On 2 March 2017, the AQIM Sahara branch merged with Ansar al-Din, Al-Mourabitoun and the Macina Liberation Front to form the *Jama'at Nusrat al-Islam wal-Muslimin* (Group for the Support of Islam and Muslims). The leader of the group is the former Ansar al-Din leader, Iyad ag Ghali, who was instrumental in the Burkina Faso attacks. To commemorate the inception of the group, he pledged his allegiance as follows: 'On this blessed occasion, we renew our pledge of allegiance (*bayat*) to our honourable emirs and sheikhs: Abu Musab Abdel Wadoud (*emir of AQIM*), our beloved and wise sheikh Ayman al-Zawahiri (*emir of Al Qaeda*) and … the emir of the Islamic Emirate in Afghanistan, Mullah Haibatullah, may Allah protect them and support them.'[61]

The merger comes in the wake of growing insurgency in northern Mali, which since 2015, has seen 257 Al-Qaeda-linked attacks. In 2016, there were 150 per cent more jihadist activities in the greater region than there were the previous year, with the majority occurring in northern Mali, Burkina Faso, Ivory Coast and Niger.[62] All of the constituent groups have engaged in guerrilla warfare, using typical insurgent tactics such as ambushes and bombings with improvised explosive devices (IEDs). However, Al-Mourabitoun, with Mokhtar Belmokhtar as its leader, is usually the subgroup that is behind the larger, more spectacular assaults. This includes, for example, the massive suicide attack on a Malian military base in Gao, which left at least 50 people dead in January 2017.

According to data compiled by FDD's *Long War Journal* (2017), in the first few months of 2017, over 50 Al-Qaeda-linked attacks in Mali and neighbouring countries were recorded. Most of the operations were carried out inside Mali, mainly in the southern half of the country. However, at least 12 were perpetrated in Burkina Faso and Niger. Depending on whether these groups will be willing to assert their presence, the most likely scenario is a continuation of localised attacks in northern and central Mali, as well as in the country's extended border regions.[63]

AQIM continues to transform and adapt to the changing conditions of the Maghreb and is currently venturing into West Africa, with the attacks in Burkina Faso being the first major operation in the country by any Al-Qaeda affiliate. It is this ability to survive that makes the group an inherent danger to North African countries and the wider Sahel region. However, in recent years, Al-Qaeda's former associate, the Islamic State of Iraq and Syria (ISIS), has challenged its dominance in the Middle East by controlling large swathes of land in Syria and Iraq. ISIS has also received pledges of allegiance from groups that were formerly allied to Al-Qaeda, such as Boko Haram and Ansar al-Sharia in Tunisia. However, while ISIS as an entity has not replicated their territorial accomplishments in the Middle East on the African continent, they, nonetheless, have managed to secure a point of entry in Libya.

The Islamic State of Iraq and Syria (ISIS)

ISIS is an extremist group formed from an Al-Qaeda offshoot in Iraq and Syria. While ISIS's immediate aim is to create an Islamic state in the Levant, a region consisting of Syria, Lebanon, Israel, Jordan, Cyprus and southern Turkey, its long-term goal is to bring all Muslims under its rule. Aside from being a terrorist group, it is also a political and military organisation that holds a radical interpretation of Islam as a political philosophy and seeks to impose that worldview by force on Muslims and non-Muslims alike. Expelled from Al-Qaeda for being too extreme, ISIS claims to be the legitimate ruler of all Sunni Muslims worldwide. From its emergence in 2014, ISIS has established what they regard as a state, which includes large swathes of territory in Syria and Iraq, governed from Raqqa in Syria.[64]

Originally led by Musab al-Zarqawi, the one-time head of Al-Qaeda in Iraq, ISIS gained support within Iraq as a Sunni insurgency group fighting a partisan Shiite-led Iraqi government, which was often perceived by Sunni locals to be a US-puppet government. In 2013, the group joined the Syrian civil war, but rather than focus on defeating the regime of Bashar al-Assad, they quickly began their Islamic state. ISIS rapidly became a dominant regional force, and was able to recruit more than 20 000 fighters from around the world.[65] On 29 June 2014, ISIS officially declared the territory under its control in Iraq and Syria as a caliphate and the group's new leader, Abu Bakr al-Baghdadi, as caliph. In his acceptance speech for the caliphate, Al-Baghdadi made it clear that ISIS's activities were not limited to any one region, as the group sought global governance of all Muslims. Controlling territories stretching from north of Aleppo to south of Baghdad, including the cities of Raqqa in Syria and Mosul in Iraq, in 2014, there were roughly six million people on either side of the Syrian and Iraqi border living under ISIS's rule.

Similar to its predecessor in Iraq (Al-Qaeda), ISIS's governance structure is hierarchical, multi-faceted and comprehensive. It consists of a core leadership group, a *Shura* council, 24 governors and various subordinate councils, which include military, security, intelligence, religious affairs, finance and media. This structure is further mirrored at each of the lower-level provincial, district and town levels.[66] ISIS divides governance into two main categories, namely administration (religious education and enforcement, courts and punishment) and services (humanitarian aid, essential food supplies and key infrastructure, such as power and water).[67] In the early stages of governing an area, ISIS focuses on religious administrative matters and eliminating opposition, a process first used to rebuild its influence in Iraq's Sunni areas and counter the impact of the 'tribal awakening'.

ISIS's overarching belief centres on re-establishing an Islamic caliphate. Unlike Al-Qaeda, which views a global caliphate as a long-term goal, ISIS considers the present conditions ripe for its immediate establishment. Since its official founding in June 2014, this doctrinal commitment has been translated into a successful quest for territory across Iraq and Syria.[68] Similar to other Salafi-jihadist groups, ISIS adheres to a literalist interpretation of Sunni Islam, specifically embracing an extremist Salafi vision. ISIS also seeks a return to the days of the *salaf*, but is explicitly willing to use violence to achieve it, based on the conviction that violence is divinely ordained. ISIS supplements its Salafist worldview with a belief in the revival of *takfiri* practices. As a Salafi-Takfiri group, the 'enemies of Islam' may be Muslims too. Thus, according to ISIS doctrine, almost 200 million Shiite Muslims, as well as Sufis, Yazidis and Ba'hai, are all apostates and deserve death.[69]

Due to its extreme use of violence against innocents, 'notorious intractability', and Al-Baghdadi's refusal to operate under Al-Qaeda's umbrella and take orders from Al-Zawahiri, Al-Qaeda disavowed the group in February 2014.[70] Undeterred by this abjuration, ISIS continued to expand and take control of new territories as it gradually set its sights on extending its caliphate beyond Iraq and Syria. The next target was North Africa, more specifically, Libya.

ISIS in Libya

Libya is ISIS's third largest stronghold after Syria and Iraq. In Libya, a context of rampant instability and a complete absence of statehood has facilitated the group's expansion and provided an ideal haven in which to function. ISIS began its operations in Derna on the Mediterranean coast, a stronghold for jihadist and *takfiri* thought. However, the group is now expanding towards Sirte and has its sights set on other strategic points, such as major oil fields along Libya's coast.[71] During 2015, ISIS gained control of about 200 to 300 km of coastline between Sirte and Ben Jawwad. Their numbers also began to surge in Libya after June 2015, as battle-hardened ISIS fighters returned from Syria and Iraq.[72]

While some commentators tend to portray the rise of ISIS in Libya as the result of a ruthless and brilliant strategy, its advance appears to be largely opportunistic, occasioned by the fissures, distraction and incapacity of rival factions. Furthermore, the growing number of ISIS fighters in Libya has been helped by the support of Libyan nationals who have returned from fighting in Iraq and Syria, foreign fighters from the Maghreb and defectors from local Libyan militant groups.

Unlike its counterpart in Syria and Iraq, ISIS in Libya does not appear to have a coherent strategy except for weakening other Islamist groups to present itself as the only viable alternative for Islamists in the country. However, Qsiyer (2015) asserts that 'the purpose of the group's activity in Libya is not only to expand internally, as their basic strategy remains to build a base for IS expansion in the African north, and reach out to other extremist groups they can bring into their fold in the Sahara and north Africa coastal regions'.[73] The delegate leader of ISIS in Libya has publically stated that the reason Libya remains an important part of ISIS's overall strategy is due both to its location and abundant resources.[74]

According to the United Nations Security Council (2015), ISIS in Syria and Iraq has a close relationship with its members in Libya. A significant number of Libyan nationals, about 800, who fought for ISIS in Syria and Iraq, now fight for ISIS in Libya. Furthermore, 'ISIS in Iraq and the Syrian Arab Republic continues to send emissaries with instructions, albeit infrequently, to ISIS in Libya'.[75] This pattern of ISIS in Iraq and Syria sending emissaries has not been observed in other areas in which other ISIS affiliates operate.

One of the major milestones of the Islamic State's 'official' presence in Libya came immediately after the Islamic Youth Shura Council, a militant group that had been in control of Derna, declared allegiance to Abu Bakr al-Baghdadi, the leader of ISIS in Iraq and Syria, and Ansar al-Sharia in Derna, in October 2014.[76] The Islamic Youth Shura Council or *Majlis Shura Shabab al-Islam* (MSSI) announced its existence on 4 April 2014, when masked members of the group took to the streets of Derna.[77] In the spring of 2014, an ISIS delegation visited the Islamic Youth Shura Council in Derna and talked them into pledging allegiance to Abu Bakr al-Baghdadi. Soon afterwards, the council declared eastern Libya an ISIS '*wilayat*', naming it the *Barqa* (Cyrenaica) province. In addition to the declaration of this new province in eastern Libya, ISIS prioritised its expansion in the west. On 19 February 2015, a convoy of Islamic State vehicles arrived at Sirte in central Libya and declared it *Wilayat Tarablus* (Tripoli Province).[78]

In Derna, ISIS attempted to consolidate control through a campaign of intimidation and violent clashes with militia and tribal rivals. Soon, they began displaying their traditional style of draconian governance in the city. The group confiscated cigarettes and other banned items, and set up its own police force and court system. They segregated schools, banned certain subjects from the curriculum, and implemented a strict dress code for women. They also carried out public lashings and executions.[79] Due to its style of governance, the group soon faced strong resistance from local tribes. In return, ISIS retaliated by attacking its opponents, using tactics that included beheadings and crucifixion. As indicated in a special report by the Crisis Group: '[ISIS] Militants began to publicly execute security officials and residents accused of spying or engaging in unIslamic practices; demand young girls be handed over for forced marriage and de-facto rape; and, at checkpoints along Libya's main coastal road, arrest individuals identified as state employees or oil sector workers.'[80]

While it is a challenge to uncover ISIS's funding sources in Libya, some commentators believe that the group imposes local taxes (including on smuggling), loots banks, has wealthy sponsors and uses extortion and kidnapping to fund themselves. According to the Crisis Group, although ISIS ransacked oil fields and attacked ports and refineries, there is little evidence to confirm the group smuggles oil.[81] ISIS in Libya also sources funds by taxing and facilitating migrant smuggling. A 2016 report by the Global Initiative against Transnational Organized Crime (GITOC) noted that, 'this creates incentives whereby the Islamic State can increase profit by exacerbating the migration flow by targeted attacks on civilians in their stronghold areas'.[82] The report further indicates that in 2015, 'illegal migrants coming to Europe by crossing the Mediterranean from Libya (the so-called 'Central Mediterranean Route'), make up roughly 60% of all illegal migrants to Europe'.[83]

Drug smuggling and arms trafficking are other forms of funding for ISIS in Libya. ISIS and Ansar al-Sharia coordinate with criminal groups and benefit from local criminality in the areas under their control. Azoulay (2015) writes that ISIS has 'nurtured alliances with Al-Qaeda-linked groups, profiting from criminal activities to expand its reach in the country'.[84] ISIS in Libya managed to overcome the dissension between Al-Qaeda and ISIS by co-opting local jihadi groups and nurturing alliances with Al-Qaeda-linked groups.[85] Ansar al-Sharia, which remains loyal to the Al-Qaeda leadership, provides assistance to ISIS in Sirte, Dernia and Benghazi, while thus far managing to preserve its identity separate from ISIS.[86]

The long-term goals of ISIS in Libya

It is important to note that ISIS's choice to expand along the Libyan coastline, starting from Derna all the way to Sirte, was part of a greater plan. This decision forms part of the group's overall strategy to take areas where human traffickers are highly active to ensure themselves an ever-fresh and steady supply of foreign recruits. Furthermore, given the group's propensity to attack and seek control of oil-production facilities, it can be safely anticipated that they will continue sweeping along the coast to gain control of as much of Libya's oil as they can. Since oil has been their preferred source of funding in Syria and in Iraq, it is highly likely to be the same in Libya, where Sirte is one of the major points of interest in the 'oil crescent' region.[87]

ISIS habitually divides countries in which they have a military presence into '*wilayat*', or 'provinces'. In Libya, ISIS divided its territory into three: Barqa (encompassing the east), Tripoli (the central and western parts) and Fezzan (the south). Given the political and military context, these are not provinces in the true sense of the word as much as they are part of the group's propaganda attempt to use geography and history to create a political and military status quo. The primary strategic objectives of ISIS in Libya are to eradicate the borders between Libya, Egypt and Tunisia, thereby turning the region into a strategic gateway to the Islamic State of Iraq and Syria.[88] In the words of Abu Irhayyim al-Libi, a former high-ranking leader within Al-Qaeda and supporter of ISIS in Libya: 'There are some who don't realise the (strategic) importance of Libya, which encompasses sea, desert and mountains, and provides access to Egypt, Sudan, Chad, Niger, Algeria and Tunisia.'[89]

Despite the gains made by ISIS in Libya, there are two main obstacles that hinder the organisation's primary objective. First, ISIS is unable to leverage the sort of broad-based sectarian grievances that have fuelled Sunni support for the group in Syria and Iraq. Unlike Syria and Iraq, Libya has a homogenously Sunni population, and does not suffer from sectarian conflict between Sunni and Shiite Muslims. Second, ISIS in Libya currently lacks the capacity to provide administrative and social services to local populations. In war-torn Iraq and Syria, ISIS was able to raise money through ransoms and the control of oil. In Libya, however, oil continues to be controlled by the state-run National Oil Company. The government controls foreign oil sales and then distributes revenues to both the rival Tobruk- and Tripoli-based governments.[90]

With this in mind, it is more probable for ISIS in Libya to raise the appeal of its brand through high-profile attacks to attract supporters from Libya's defecting jihadist movements. Meanwhile, it will continue to attack oil fields and destabilise the country, hoping to create an environment conducive to attaining its objectives.

Countering ISIS in Libya

As demonstrated in Iraq and Syria, degrading and ultimately destroying ISIS has proved to be a difficult task for the United States and its allies. Yet, through several counterterrorism measures the United States has been able to make strategic gains in limiting ISIS's access to funding, its recruitment pool and its strategic territory.[91] The expansion of aerial bombing campaigns and targeted drone strikes in Iraq and Syria has greatly contributed to restricting the momentum of the rapid ISIS advance.

As Hashim (2014) pointedly remarks, 'It [the campaign of airstrikes] has even allowed the dispirited Iraqi army and the vastly overrated Kurdish Peshmerga to push IS back from some of the territories it had conquered.'[92] Although ISIS was driven from its main areas of control in Libya in December 2016, and oil production has rebounded to a three-year high, Libya still remains polarised and more fragmented than ever.

It is important to note that over-reliance on airpower is not the solution to destroying ISIS. Airpower can degrade but it cannot uproot an entire system of control by ISIS over territory, people and infrastructure. ISIS militants have learnt to disperse, to tunnel, to use camouflage and to go to ground in the cities. ISIS is capable of reverting to pure terrorism, a tactic in which it is thoroughly adept.[93] According to US officials and the Pentagon's Africa command, the fact that ISIS was driven from its stronghold in Sirte has resulted in several hundred fighters dispersing across Libya, who now pose a threat to the country, its neighbours and potentially Europe.[94]

ISIS is a prime example of how, over the past few years, violent jihadist movements have become more powerful than ever. Standard counterterrorism measures such as designations, financial sanctions, travel bans, targeted killings and special-forces operations, among others, are insufficient against movements that control cities, towns and supply lines, provide public goods, generate revenue locally and have tens of thousands of fighters. Furthermore, some jihadist leaders' ideology and aspirations prevent a situation where they can be engaged politically to formulate a peace agreement.

Reversing jihadist gains in Libya will depend on resolving rivalries between local forces and persuading them to collaborate against ISIS. This may also involve giving areas associated with the Gaddafi regime, which are most vulnerable to ISIS recruitment, a stronger position in the national fabric, and probably also self-defence capabilities. As demonstrated in Syria and Iraq, a bombing campaign could hamper ISIS operations, especially near oil facilities, and thereby degrade its revenues. In the context of Libya, such targeted strikes may make sense. However, as long as rivalries between its enemies persist, it will continue to hold the area around Sirte and may extend further east.

As Crisis Group (2016) have noted, 'If the USA or others decide to press ahead with heavier bombing, better they do so without demanding that the fledging, contested unity government invite or endorse foreign military action'.[95] Doing so may contribute to reducing the credibility of the unity government among the local population. Rather, more can be done to engage with diverse Libyan security actors – and promote contact between them – to build support for the political process and find potential partners against ISIS.

As noted earlier, airstrikes and targeted killing by drone strikes may be effective if used in a limited manner. Another military measure commonly used to combat jihadist groups is the elimination of the group's leaders, often referred to as 'decapitation'.[96] Targeted killings can disrupt extremist networks and their ability to undertake sophisticated attacks and, in the case of drones, do so without immediate risk to military personnel – as has been demonstrated in the targeted killings of several prominent Al-Shabaab leaders in recent years. Certainly, they have disrupted Al-Qaeda in the Pakistani tribal areas and appear to have impacted ISIS's ability to operate in Afghanistan by hindering leaders' movements. However, their greatest strength is also a weakness. The deaths of non-combatants in drone strikes have, in several cases, destabilised local political conditions and fuelled anger among local civilians. Hence, unless they are integrated into a broader strategy to calm a conflict, their tactical gains come at a cost.

Despite the fact that assassinations can help disrupt a leader's and the groups' ability to operate, they tend to be high risk and have little impact.[97] The impact is particularly uncertain against large insurgent movements in war zones, particularly those like ISIS whose inner workings and command structures are opaque. Although in some instances it may fragment a group, in the case of a well-organised organisation such as ISIS, a more radical and violent replacement is likely to quickly emerge.[98] In short, there is little evidence that targeted killings are helpful in ending conflicts with jihadists or that they decisively weaken their movements.

Another method to combat ISIS in Libya is to do so on the ideological level. The failure of purely military approaches to combat terrorism has seen the emergence of preventing and countering violent extremism (P/CVE) initiatives in recent years. P/CVE agendas tend to include: (1) civic engagement with communities; (2) a push-back or a 'counter-narrative' against intolerant strands of religion; (3) a focus on stemming the flow of foreign fighters; and (4) efforts to address the perceived 'root causes' of radicalisation.[99]

Different states and international bodies, including the United Nations (UN), emphasise different aspects in their P/CVE agendas. These range from socio-economic root causes, to countering specific ideological and religious recruitment narratives. For instance, the UN Secretary-General's recent Plan of Action on Preventing Violent Extremism calls on states to develop their own plans of action, which include measures that address diverse sources of fragility.[100]

While it is important to recognise the diverse factors that can drive extremism, and shift resources toward efforts to tackle them, there are some important caveats to remember. First, while creating jobs for youth is sensible, it prevents them from joining extremist groups in only some and not all environments. Second, helping marginalised communities is a vital component of reconstruction, but if the motivation behind the project is to win support against extremists, it can work against the provision of aid and those delivering it. Third, in many instances, governments and the UN may not be best positioned to develop locally relevant counter-narratives. Furthermore, co-opting 'friendly' imams may result in them losing legitimacy among their followers and thereby empower more radical religious voices.

Governments should allow, and protect space, for diverse Muslim voices, Salafi and otherwise. Perhaps more importantly, ideology's role in driving the rise of extremists is not straightforward. Although Salafi proselytising and often state-sponsored Islamisation of parts of society have helped set the stage, the consolidation of groups such as ISIS owes more to the jihadists' exploitation of war and state collapse, or armed groups adopting more extreme tactics as crises deepen. During crises, the support extremists may enjoy from communities is, in most cases, based less on shared values and more on what else they provide when things fall apart. These include protection against a hated regime, quick dispute resolution, social advancement or opportunity for profit.

Despite some of its setbacks, the P/CVE agenda has value. It can be an effective tool in tackling ISIS recruitment, which in many places pivots less on imams and religion than on social media and appeals to fraternity, belonging and purpose. It might, for example, advance deradicalisation in prisons where many are radicalised and recruited, and contribute to assisting particularly vulnerable youth groups, which are often a primary target of ISIS recruiters.

In developing approaches to counter the influence of extremist movements, governments and civil society actors should narrow P/CVE to a handful of context-specific activities and contribute to funding research on radicalisation and its patterns – a subject which is under-researched. Additionally, there should be a greater focus on efforts to address the root causes of instability and conflict. In this regard, donors can usefully shift resources from military and security spending to addressing those underlying factors. A wide range of stakeholders should be engaged whenever possible, and efforts made to draw from civil society, the religious community, women and youth groups, and other relevant parties.

Conclusion

The rise of ISIS in Libya and the growing strength of Al-Qaeda-linked groups over the last few years pose a significant threat to both state and human security across North Africa and the Sahel. In recent years, countries like Burkina Faso and Ivory Coast, which until now have been relatively isolated from terrorism, have been a target of AQIM's expanding operational footprint, while ISIS networks now run through Egypt, Libya and into Algeria.

These organisations continue to destabilise nations desperately trying to consolidate democracy, while discouraging tourism and economic growth. The extreme ideologies they espouse make mediation difficult and traditional peace agreements improbable. Furthermore, their links to transnational criminal networks serves to perpetuate illicit drug and human-trafficking networks that generate immense suffering across the region.

Defeating organisations such as AQIM and ISIS is difficult, and there seem to be few precedents from which lessons can be learnt. What is clear is that military responses are not enough. Both organisations have proven their ability to adapt and survive in the face of massive military pressure. AQIM, for example, has a long track record of finding new local conflicts into which they can insert themselves to leverage power and gain support, while ISIS has been able to attract support and recruits from around the world through deft communication, propaganda and recruitment strategies.

Defeating these organisations will ultimately require both coordinated and responsive security measures *and* a concerted effort by governments in the region to identify and address the root causes which make people susceptible to recruitment. Countries in North Africa and the Sahel share similar colonial and post-colonial histories and many suffer the same structural and economic difficulties. However, instead of generating oversimplified theories and models of 'key factors' that give rise to terrorism, care must be taken to study both the unique organisational history and constant adaptations of these groups, as well as the history of the regions in which they operate.

Endnotes

1. Canadian Security Intelligence Services (2016) *Terrorism in North African and the Sahel: The expansion of a regional threat?* World Watch: Expert Notes series, publication No. 2016-12-05. Available at: https://www.csis-scrs.gc.ca/pblctns/wrldwtch/2016/2016-12-19/TERRORISM-IN-NORTH-AND-WEST-AFRICA_REPORT_ENG.pdf
2. Hourani, A (2013) *A History of the Arab Peoples*. Cambridge, MA: Harvard University Press.
3. McKenna, A (2011) *The History of Northern Africa*. New York: Britannica Educational Publishing, p. 3.
4. Ibid, p. 38.
5. Ibid, p. 41.
6. Zartman, W (1973) (ed) *Man, State and Society in the Contemporary Maghrib*. New York: Praeger Publishers, pp. 16–18.
7. Harmon, S (2010) From GSPC to AQIM: The evolution of an Algerian Islamist terrorist group into an Al-Qai'da affiliate, *Concerned African Scholars*, **85**: p. 5.
8. Gregoire, E (1997) Major Sahelian trade networks: Past and present. In C Raynaut (ed) *Societies and Nature in the Sahel*. London: Routledge.
9. Hall, BS (2011) *A History of Race in Muslim West Africa*. Cambridge: Cambridge University Press, p. 105.
10. Chafer, T (2002) *The End of Empire in French West Africa: France's successful decolonization?* Oxford: Berg Publishers, p. 232.
11. Ibid, p. 233.
12. Mortimar, RA (1972) From federalism to Francophonia: Senghor's African policy, *African Studies Review*, **15** (2), pp. 283–306.
13. Meridith, M (2014) *The Fortunes of Africa: A 5000-year history of wealth, greed, and endeavour*. London: Simon and Schuster, p. 601.
14. *The Guardian* (2002) Deadly attack keeps world on alert. Published 4 September 2002. Available at: http://www.theguardian.com/world/2002/sep/04/september11.usa
15. Porter, G (2011) AQIM Objectives in North Africa, *CTC Sentinel*, **4** (2), pp. 5–9.
16. Terrorism Research & Analysis Consortium (TRAC) (2014) *Reorganization of Jihadist Groups in Maghreb and Sahel*, p. 1. Available at: http://www.trackingterrorism.org/

17 Turner, J (2010) From cottage industry to international organisation: The evolution of Salafi Jihadism and the emergence of the Al-Qaeda ideology, *Terrorism and Political Violence*, **22**, p. 543.
18 Ibid, p. 544.
19 Botha, A (2008) *Terrorism in the Maghreb: The transnationalisation of domestic terrorism*. ISS Monograph Series, No. 144. Pretoria: Institute of Security Studies, p. 15.
20 Turner (2010) p. 544.
21 Cited in Gunaratna, R (2002) *Inside Al Qaeda: Global network of terror*. New York: Columbia University Press, p. 87.
22 Alvi, H (2014) The diffusion of intra-Islamic violence and terrorism: The impact of the proliferation of Salafi/Wahhabi ideologies, *Middle East Review of International Affairs*, **18** (2), p. 40.
23 Ibid.
24 Ibid.
25 Botha (2008) p. 17.
26 Le Sueur, J (2010) *Algeria Since 1989: Between terror and democracy*. London: Zed Books, p. 11.
27 Werenfels, I (2007) *Managing Instability in Algeria: Elites and political change since 1995*. New York: Routledge, p. 32.
28 Ibid, p. 35.
29 Aghrout, A and Bougherira, R (2004) (eds) *Algeria in Transition: Reforms and development prospects*. London: Routledge Curzon, pp. 1–5.
30 See, Le Sueur (2010) p. 42; Volpi, F (2003) *Islam and Democracy: The failure of dialogue in Algeria*. London: Pluto Press, p. 52.
31 Le Sueur (2010) p. 51.
32 Zoubir, Y (2004) The dialectics of Algeria's foreign relations, 1992 to the present. In A Aghrout and R Bougherira (2004) (eds) *Algeria in Transition: Reforms and development prospects*. London: Routledge Curzon, pp. 154–184.
33 Le Sueur (2010) p. 124.
34 Rudolph, RM (2008) The Islamic Salvation Front: Transition FIS-Style. In A van Engeland and RM Rudolph (eds) *From Terrorism to Politics*. New York: Routledge, p. 126.
35 Stone, M (1997) *The Agony of Algeria*. London: Hurst & Company, p. 184.
36 Gunaratna (2002) p. 137.
37 Le Sueur (2010) p. 131.
38 Gunaratna (2002) p. 122.
39 Stone (1997) p. 193.
40 Le Sueur (2010) pp. 132–133.
41 Botha (2008) p. 39.
42 Gunaratna (2002) p. 115.
43 Le Sueur (2010) p. 155.
44 Ibid, p. 152.
45 Harmon, S (2010) p. 15.
46 Filiu, JP (2009) *Al-Qaeda in the Islamic Maghreb: Algerian challenge or global threat?* Carnegie Endowment Papers No. 104. Washington, DC: Carnegie Endowment for International Peace, p. 156.
47 Kohlmann, E (2007) *Two Decades of Jihad in Algeria: The GIA, the GSPC and Al Qaeda*. New York: The NEFA Foundation. Available at: www.nefafoundation.orginfo, p. 21.
48 Le Sueur (2010) p. 156.
49 Ibid, p. 164.
50 Filiu (2009) p. 6.

51 Le Sueur (2010) p. 164.
52 Ibid, p. 165.
53 Filiu (2009) p. 23.
54 Botha (2008) p. 58.
55 Europol (2010) *European Union Terrorism Situation and Trend Report (TE-SAT) 2010*. Available at: https://www.consilium.europa.eu/uedocs/cmsUpload/TE-SAT%202010.pdf
56 See: Harmon (2010) p. 19; Chivvis, C and Liepman, A (2013) *North Africa's Menace: AQIM evolution and US Policy Response*. Rand Corporation Research Report, p. 5.
57 *The Guardian* (2014) France's last hostage freed by Al-Qaida in Mali. Published 9 December 2014. Available at: http://www.theguardian.com/world/2014/dec/09/serge-lazarevic-last-french-hostage-released-al-qaida-mali
58 Echeverría, C (2012) Al-Qaeda terrorism in the Islamic Maghreb(AQIM): An example of survival and adaptability, *Journal of the Higher School of National Defense Studies*, **0**, p. 163.
59 Al Jazeera (2015) A-Qaeda linked group claims Mali restaurant attack. Published 9 March 2015. Available at: http://www.aljazeera.com/news/2015/03/al-qaeda-linked-group-claims-mali-restaurant-attack-150309072613760.html
60 Reuters (2016) Death toll in Ivory Coast militant attack rises to 18: Government. Published 14 March 2016.
61 Joscelyn, T (2017) Analysis: Al-Qaeda groups reorganize in West Africa, *FDD's Long War Journal*. Available at: http://www.longwarjournal.org/archives/2017/03/analysis-al-qaeda-groups-reorganize-in-west-africa.php
62 Weiss, C (2017) Merger of Al-Qaeda groups threatens security in West Africa. Available at: http://www.longwarjournal.org/archives/2017/03/analysis-merger-of-al-qaeda-groups-threatens-security-in-west-africa.php
63 Assanvo, W (2015) *Mali's Jihadist Merger: Desperate or dangerous?* ISS Situation Analysis, 10 April 2015. Available at: https://issafrica.org/pscreport/situation-analysis
64 Barret, R (2014) *The Islamic State*. New York: The Soufan Group, p. 29.
65 Counter Extremism Project (2014) ISIS. Available at: https://www.counterextremism.com/threat/isis, p. 2.
66 Barret (2014) p. 34.
67 Caris, C and Reynolds, S (2014) *ISIS Governance in Syria*. Washington, DC: Institute for the Study of War, p. 4.
68 March, A and Revkin, M (2015) A caliphate of law, *Foreign Affairs*. Available at: https://www.foreignaffairs.com/articles/syria/2015-04-15/caliphate-law
69 Barret (2014) p. 34.
70 *The Washington Post* (2014) Al-Qaeda disavows any ties with radical Islamist, ISIS group in Syria. Published 3 February 2014. Available at: https://www.washingtonpost.com/world/middle_east/al-qaeda-disavows-any-ties-with-radical-islamist-isis-group-in-syria-iraq/2014/02/03/2c9afc3a-8cef-11e3-98ab-fe5228217bd1_story.html
71 Qsiyer, K (2015) *The Islamic State (IS) in Libya: Expansion by political crisis*. Al Jazeera Centre for Studies. Published 23 June 17. Available at: http://studies.aljazeera.net/en/reports/2015/06/201562310837854715.html
72 Crisis Group (2016) *Exploiting Disorder: Al-Qaeda and the Islamic State*. Special Report, 14 March. Available at: www.crisisgroup.com
73 Qsiyer (2015) p. 3.
74 United Nations Security Council (2015) Report of the Analytical Support and Sanctions Monitoring Team submitted pursuant to paragraph 13 of Security Council Resolution 2 214 (2015) concerning the terrorism threat in Libya posed by the Islamic State of Iraq

and the Levant, Ansar al Charia, and all other Al-Qaeda associates, p. 6.
75 Ibid, p. 7.
76 Wehrey, F and Alrababa'h, A (2015) *Splitting the Islamists: The Islamic State's creeping advance in Libya*. Carnegie Middle East Centre. Published 19 June 2015. Available at: http://carnegie-mec.org/diwan/60447
77 Ibid, p. 1.
78 Ibid, p. 2.
79 Ibid, p. 3.
80 Crisis Group (2016) p. 19.
81 Ibid, p. 20.
82 Global Initiative against Transnational Organized Crime (GITOC) (2015) *Libya: A growing hub for criminal economies and terrorist financing in the Trans-Sahara*, Policy Brief, 11 May 2015.
83 Ibid, p. 3.
84 Azoulay, R (2015) Islamic State franchising. Available at: http://www.clingendael.nl/sites/default/files/Rivka-Azoulay_Islamic_State_expansion_CRU_April2015.pdf
85 United Nations Security Council (2015) p. 16.
86 Azoulay (2015) p. 35.
87 Qsiyer (2015) p. 7.
88 Ibid.
89 Ibid, p. 8.
90 Wehrey and Alrababa'h (2015) p. 3.
91 Bouzis, K (2015) Countering the Islamic State: US counterterrorism measures, *Studies in Conflict and Terrorism*, **38**, p. 894.
92 Hashim, A (2014) The Islamic State: From A-Qaeda affiliate to caliphate, *Middle East Policy*, **21** (4), p. 76.
93 Ibid, p. 78.
94 Schmitt, E (2016) ISIS remains threat in Libya despite defeat in Sirte, *The New York Times*. Available at: https://www.nytimes.com/2016/12/08/us/politics/libya-isis-sirte.html p. 1.
95 Crisis Group (2016) p. 34.
96 Ibid, p. 36.
97 Ibid, p. 35.
98 Boot, M (2013) *Invisible Armies: An epic history of guerrilla warfare from ancient times to present*. New York: Liveright.
99 Holmes, G (2013) *Countering Violent Extremism: A peacebuilding perspective*. Special Report No. 336. Washington, DC: US Institute of Peace.
100 Crisis Group (2016) p. 35.

References

Agbiboa, D (2014) Peace at daggers drawn? Boko Haram and the State of Emergency in Nigeria, *Studies in Conflict & Terrorism*, **37**, pp. 41–67.

Aghrout, A and Bougherira, R (eds) (2004) *Algeria in Transition: Reforms and development prospects*. London: Routledge Curzon.

Al Jazeera (2015) Al-Qaeda-linked group claims Mali restaurant attack. Published 9 March 2015. Available at: http://www.aljazeera.com/news/2015/03/al-qaeda-linked-group-claims-mali-restaurant-attack-150309072613760.html

Al Jazeera (2016) Tunisia: Deadly clashes erupt in Ben Gardane near Libya. Published 3 March 2016. Available at: http://www.aljazeera.com/news/2016/03/tunisia-ben-gardane-clashes-160307070914234.html

Alvi, H (2014) The diffusion of intra-Islamic violence and terrorism: The impact of the proliferation of Salafi/Wahhabi ideologies, *Middle East Review of International Affairs*,

18 (2), pp. 38–50.

Assanvo, W (2015) *Mali's Jihadist Merger: Desperate or dangerous?* Institute for Security Studies, Situation Analysis. Pretoria: Institute for Security Studies. Published 10 April 2015. Available at: https://issafrica.org/pscreport/situation-analysis

Azoulay, R (2015) Islamic State franchising. Available at: http://www.clingendael.nl/sites/default/files/Rivka-Azoulay_Islamic_State_expansion_CRU_April2015.pdf

Barret, R (2014) *The Islamic State*. New York: The Soufan Group.

Benjamin, D (2012) *LRA, Boko Haram, Al-Shabaab, Aqim, and Other Sources of Instability in Africa*. US Department of State. Published 25 April 2012. Available at: http://www.state.gov/j/ct/rls/rm/2012/188816.htm

Boot, M (2013) *Invisible Armies: An epic history of guerrilla warfare from ancient times to present*. New York: Liveright Publishing.

Botha, A (2008) *Terrorism in the Maghreb: The transnationalisation of domestic terrorism*. ISS Monograph Series, No. 144. Pretoria: Institute for Security Studies.

Bouzis, K (2015) Countering the Islamic State: US counterterrorism measures, *Studies in Conflict and Terrorism*, **38**, pp. 885–897.

Canadian Security Intelligence Services (2016) *Terrorism in North African and the Sahel: The expansion of a regional threat?* World Watch: Expert Notes Series Publication No. 2016-12-05. Available at: https://www.csis-scrs.gc.ca/pblctns/wrldwtch/2016/2016-12-19/TERRORISM-IN-NORTH-AND-WEST-AFRICA_REPORT_ENG.pdf

Caris, C and Reynolds, S (2014) *ISIS Governance in Syria*. Washington, DC: Institute for the Study of War.

Chafer, T (2002) *The End of Empire in French West Africa: France's successful decolonization?* Oxford: Berg Publications.

Chivvis, C and Liepman, A (2013) *North Africa's Menace: AQIM evolution and US policy response*. Rand Corporation Research Report. Santa Monica, CA: Rand Corporation.

Counter Extremism Project (2014) ISIS. Available at: https://www.counterextremism.com/threat/isis, p. 2.

Crisis Group (2016) *Exploiting Disorder: Al-Qaeda and the Islamic State*. Special Report. Published 14 March 2016. Available at: www.crisisgroup.com

Echeverría, C (2012) Al-Qaeda terrorism in the Islamic Maghreb (AQIM): An example of survival and adaptability, *Journal of the Higher School of National Defense Studies*, **0**, pp. 167–177.

Economic Community of West African States (ECOWAS) (2013) *The Political Economy of Conflicts in Northern Mali*. Institute for Security Studies. ECOWAS Peace and Security Report No. 2. Published April 2013.

Europol (2010) *European Union Terrorism Situation and Trend Report (TE-SAT) 2010*. Available at: https://www.consilium.europa.eu/uedocs/cmsUpload/TE-SAT%202010.pdf

Filiu, JP (2009) *Al-Qaeda in the Islamic Maghreb: Algerian challenge or global threat?* Carnegie Endowment for International Peace. Carnegie Endowment Papers, No. 104. Washington, DC: Carnegie Foundation.

Global Initiative against Transnational Organized Crime (GITOC) (2015) *Libya: A growing hub for criminal economies and terrorist financing in the Trans-Sahara*, Policy Brief, 11 May.

Global Terrorism Index (2014) *Measuring and Understanding the Impact of Terrorism*. Sydney: Institute for Economics and Peace.

Gregoire, E (1997) Major Sahelian trade networks: Past and present. In: C Raynaut (ed) *Societies and Nature in the Sahel*. London: Routledge.

Gunaratna, R (2002) *Inside Al Qaeda: Global network of terror*. New York: Columbia University Press.

Hall, BS (2011) *A History of Race in Muslim West Africa*. Cambridge: Cambridge University Press.

Harmon, S (2010) From GSPC to AQIM: The evolution of an Algerian Islamist terrorist group

into an Al Qai'da affiliate, *Concerned African Scholars*, **85**, pp. 12–29.
Hashim, A (2014) The Islamic State: From A-Qaeda affiliate to Caliphte, *Middle East Policy*, **21** (4), pp. 69–83.
Holmes, G (2013) *Countering Violent Extremism: A peacebuilding perspective*. United States Institute of Peace, Special Report No. 336. Washington, DC: United States Institute of Peace.
Hourani, A (2013) *A History of the Arab Peoples*. Cambridge, MA: Harvard University Press.
Investigative Project on Terrorism (IPT) (2011) Clinton: Al-Shabaab 'tries to work with' AQ's North African Branch. Published 12 August 2011. Available at: http://www.investigativeproject.org/3102/
Jeune Afrique (2015) Tunisie – Attentat du Bardot: AQMI derriere l'atentat? Published 26 March 2015. Available at: http://www.jeuneafrique.com/Article/ARTJAWEB20150326103759/
Joscelyn, T (2017) Analysis: A-Qaeda groups reorganize in West Africa, *FDD's Long War Journal*. Available at: http://www.longwarjournal.org/archives/2017/03/analysis-al-qaeda-groups-reorganize-in-west-africa.php
Kohlmann, E (2007) *Two Decades of Jihad in Algeria: The GIA, the GSPC and Al Qaeda*. New York: The NEFA Foundation. Available at: www.nefafoundation.orginfo
Le Sueur, J (2010) *Algeria Since 1989: Between terror and democracy*. London: Zed Books.
March, A and Revkin, M (2015) A Caliphate of Law. *Foreign Affairs*. Published 15 April 2015. Available at: https://www.foreignaffairs.com/articles/syria/2015-04-15/caliphate-law
McKenna, A (2011) *The History of Northern Africa*. New York: Britannica Educational Publishing.
Meridith, M (2014) *The Fortunes of Africa: A 5000-year history of wealth, greed, and endeavour*. London: Simon and Schuster.
Morsy, M (1984) *North Africa 1800–1900: A survey from the Nile Valley to the Atlantic*. New York: Longman.
Mortimar, RA (1972) From federalism to Francophonia: Senghor's African policy, *African Studies Review*, **15** (2), pp. 283–306.
Pham, P (2011) The dangerous 'pragmatism' of Al-Qaeda in the Islamic Maghreb, *Journal of Middle East and Africa*, **2**, pp. 15–29.
Porter, G (2011) AQIM objectives in North Africa, *CTC Sentinel*, **4** (2), pp. 5–9.
Qsiyer, K (2015) *The Islamic State (IS) in Libya: Expansion by Political Crisis*. Al Jazeera Centre for Studies. Published 23 June 17. Available at: http://studies.aljazeera.net/en/reports/2015/06/201562310837854715.html
Reuters (2016) Death toll in Ivory Coast militant attack rises to 18: Government. Published 14 March 2016. Available at: https://www.google.co.za/
Rudolph, RM (2008) The Islamic Salvation Front: Transition FIS-Style. In A van Engeland and RM Rudolph (eds) *From Terrorism to Politics*. Routledge: New York.
Stone, M (1997) *The Agony of Algeria*. London: Hurst & Company, p. 184.
Terrorism Research & Analysis Consortium (TRAC) (2014) *Reorganization of Jihadist Groups in Maghreb and Sahel*, p. 1. Available at: http://www.trackingterrorism.org/
The Guardian (2002) Deadly attack keeps world on alert. Published 4 September. Available at: http://www.theguardian.com/world/2002/sep/04/september11.usa
The Guardian (2014) France's last hostage freed by Al-Qaida in Mali. Published 9 December. Available at: http://www.theguardian.com/world/2014/dec/09/serge-lazarevic-last-french-hostage-released-al-qaida-mali
Turner, J (2010) From cottage industry to international organisation: The evolution of Salafi Jihadism and the emergence of the Al-Qaeda ideology, *Terrorism and Political Violence*, **22**, p. 543.
United Nations Security Council (2015) Report of the Analytical Support and Sanctions Monitoring Team submitted pursuant to paragraph 13 of Security Council Resolution 2 214 (2015) concerning the terrorism threat in Libya posed by the Islamic State of Iraq and

the Levant, Ansar al Charia, and all other Al-Qaida associates, p. 6.

Volpi, F (2003) *Islam and Democracy: The failure of dialogue in Algeria*. London: Pluto Press, p. 52.

Weiss, C (2017) Merger of Al-Qaeda groups threatens security in West Africa. Available at: http://www.longwarjournal.org/archives/2017/03/analysis-merger-of-al-qaeda-groups-threatens-security-in-west-africa.php

Werenfels, I (2007) *Managing Instability in Algeria: Elites and political change since 1995*. New York: Routledge, p. 32.

Zartman, W (1973) (ed) *Man, State and Society in the Contemporary Maghrib*. New York: Praeger Publishers, pp. 3–18.

Zoubir, Y (2004) The dialectics of Algeria's foreign relations, 1992 to the present. In A Aghrout and R Bougherira (eds) *Algeria in Transition: Reforms and development prospects*. London: Routledge Curzon, pp. 154–184.

Chapter 4

The Sahel's ungoverned spaces and the ascent of AQIM, Al-Mourabitoun and MUJAO in Mali and Niger

Celeste Hicks

Introduction

On 14 March 2016 gunmen stormed the Grand Bassam beach resort in Ivory Coast, 40 km south of the capital, Abidjan. Firing outside the Hotel L'Etoile du Sud, which was full of expats and beachgoers, the armed men killed 16 people, including four foreigners, before the attack was brought under control. The attack followed hot on the heels of two similar incidents. In November 2015, armed men broke past security at the upmarket Radisson Blu hotel in Mali's capital, Bamako, stormed the lobby and took a number of hostages, killing a total of 21 people. In January 2016, gunmen attacked the Splendid Hotel and Cappuccino Café in downtown Ouagadougou in Burkina Faso, spots popular with foreigners, set off explosives and shot at customers. Over 30 people, including six members of one Canadian family, were killed.

All three attacks were claimed by Al-Qaeda in the Islamic Maghreb (AQIM) and its affiliate Al-Mourabitoun, which in the aftermath of the Mali attack announced it was remerging with AQIM. These were the kinds of attacks that diplomats, governments and any observer of West Africa's Sahel region had been anticipating for several years. In March 2017, the threat level in the Sahel region increased further when leaders of AQIM, Al-Mourabitoun and Ansar al-Din officially announced that they would be merging.

This chapter seeks to understand how it is that groups such as AQIM and Al-Mourabitoun have been able to rise to such prominence in the Sahel, move freely almost anywhere in the West African region and to drive into the heart of capital cities. Fundamental to an understanding of this is an appreciation of the implications of long-standing poor governance in Sahelian countries, most notably in Mali and Niger, but also in Burkina Faso, northern Nigeria and Chad. This has left many marginalised groups in the region without job opportunities or hope for economic advancement, and created an environment where long-standing criminal trafficking networks and militant jihadist groups can flourish. Poor governance has also resulted in the failure of governments to respond adequately to secessionist claims from groups such as the Tuareg, as well as leaving national armies and border security forces unable to adequately defend national territories.

This chapter covers the period from 2007 onwards, when Islamist groups such as AQIM moved into the Sahel region from their bases in Algeria. While this chapter considers the circumstances in other Sahelian countries that have contributed to the rise of jihadist groups, namely Niger, Mauritania and the southern fringes of Libya and Chad, it focuses primarily on the vast deserts of northern Mali. It documents how a prolonged period of neglect and lack of effective governance in this area created a crucible of chaos in which the numerous rebel and violent jihadist groups, which now dominate the Sahel, have been able to foment.

Borders

The Sahel ('shore' in Arabic) is a vast semi-desert zone to the south of the Sahara, which stretches from Mauritania in the west to Sudan in the east. Trade routes across the Sahara Desert have existed for centuries, carrying people, goods and ideas between the Arab and Berber populations of North Africa and the black sub-Saharan populations to the south. From the 9th century onwards, Islamic pilgrims began to tread these routes, often travelling from centres of learning such as Fes in Morocco or Egypt to modern-day Mali and Niger. Before West Africa's coastal links to Europe developed, merchants exchanged gold, salt and slaves between North and West Africa, while students and scholars travelled to the prestigious university at Timbuktu in modern-day Mali. Today, traders living in the semi-desert fringes of the Sahara still use these routes, some to smuggle consumer goods, fuel, cigarettes, and a growing number of people, to and from the North African market, often with Europe as the final destination.

In the 1990s, the use of these routes by drug traffickers multiplied.[1] Reliable estimates of the quantities of drugs being trafficked across the Sahel are difficult to find. However, it has been widely documented that large quantities of hashish are grown in northern Morocco's Rif Mountains and transported across the Sahel.[2] Drug traffickers started taking circuitous routes to smuggle cocaine into Europe, picking up shipments from South America in the port of Bissau in the barely functioning nation of Guinea-Bissau, and carrying them across the Malian deserts and on to Europe. Others chose routes whereby drug shipments arrived in the Mauritanian port of Nouadhibou, before being picked up by Chadian traders who would then pass them on to their networks in Sudan and Egypt. The United Nations Office on Drugs and Crime (UNODC) estimates that in 2008, 14 per cent of the cocaine that arrived in Europe had transited through West Africa.³

As drugs and contraband smuggling grew, the region also saw an explosion in the number of weapons circulating from conflicts across Africa, such as in western Sahara, Chad, Nigeria and Sudan. A devastating period of drought, which ebbed and flowed in the 1970s and 1980s, led to the displacement of Sahel populations, whose traditional livelihoods in semi-nomadic pastoralism and small-scale farming came under threat. During these years, thousands of young Tuaregs left northern Mali and Niger and travelled to Libya, where they joined other African groups in being trained and armed in Colonel Muammar Gaddafi's 'Islamic Legion', his vision for a united Africa under the patronage of Libya.⁴

Added to the mix was an increase in human trafficking as people-smuggling gangs started to multiply in the 1990s and 2000s, facilitating the passage of thousands of sub-Saharan migrants keen to reach Europe. Many of these migrants, from Ghana, Nigeria, southern Mali and elsewhere, came to congregate in remote desert towns, such as Agades in Niger, before attempting a several-day crossing of the Sahara. In the early 2000s, many of these migrants were aiming for the Spanish enclaves of Melilla and Ceuta on the Moroccan coast. However, in later years, as Morocco and Spain began to clamp down, migrants began to target Libya. Some would take perilous sea journeys in small boats across the Mediterranean into Italian ports such as Lampedusa, while others sought low-paid domestic work in Algeria and Libya.

The root cause of this enduring lawlessness lies in Sahelian countries' inability to control their own borders and territorial integrity. In much of the Sahel, borders are nothing more than a line in the sand. The distances involved are vast, with most border crossings lying in inhospitable, featureless desert. Mali, for example, shares a total of 7 243 km of land boundaries with seven bordering states, including Algeria (1 376 km to the north and northeast), Niger (821 km to the east), and Burkina Faso (1 000 km to the southeast). Niger has a 951 km border with Algeria, and a 1 196 km border with Chad – most of it cutting through remote, mountainous desert. As some of the poorest countries on Earth (Niger, for example, came bottom of the United Nations Development Programme Human Development Index [UNDP-HDI] in 2015), Sahelian countries have very little means with which to train and deploy effective border forces. For example, Niger's army numbers only around 5 000 soldiers, with no dedicated border force.⁵ Similarly, in Mali, while some border crossings are patrolled by (the) *gendarmerie*, the national army comprises only around 6 000 soldiers.

While it is important to underline that the drug traffickers, people smugglers, cigarette smugglers, violent jihadists and tribal rebels, who have been able to operate in the Sahelian deserts for many years are by no means one and the same, there are clear links between the groups. In the absence of effective state control, intricate webs of relations have been able to develop to a remarkable degree using traditional systems of trading networks, family links and reciprocity. These networks are so well-developed that they prompted the United Kingdom Foreign Office to state that it would be wrong to characterise the furthest reaches of the Sahel as an 'ungoverned space', but more accurately that '[i]t is governed, just not in the conventional sense'.[6] Jihadists, traffickers and rebels often work closely to achieve their separate goals. For example, Mokhtar Belmokhtar, the one-eyed leader of an AQIM off-shoot, Al-Mua'qi'oon Biddam (The Signed in Blood Battalion), which in 2013 merged with elements of the Movement for Unity and Jihad in West Africa (MUJAO) to form Al-Mourabitoun (The Sentinels), has been dubbed 'Mr Marlborough' for his long history of involvement in cigarette smuggling. During the late 2000s, AQIM is known to have demanded protection money for guaranteeing the safe passage of drug consignments through territory that it controls, while a range of Arab drug traders supported MUJAO's occupation of Gao in 2012.[7]

It would be wrong to assume this cauldron of problems had escaped the attention of the international community. World powers have seemed aware of the dangers inherent in such a vast, poorly controlled space since at least the early 2000s. From 2007 onwards, foreign diplomats based in Mali's capital, Bamako, were sounding the alarm about the potential for Islamist extremism in northern Mali. The United States began its focus on the region even earlier, following the September 11 terrorist attacks. In 2002, the Pan-Sahel Initiative was launched, which aimed to promote peace and security in the region.[8] This was later replaced by the Trans-Saharan Counterterrorism Initiative (TSCTI) and after that the Trans-Saharan Counterterrorism Partnership (TSCTP). While these initiatives have paid noteworthy attention to democracy and governance projects, such as supporting local media and institution-building, their primary focus has been on the military, delivering counter-insurgency training to thousands of troops from Sahelian nations since 2006. Operation Flintlock, which is managed through the Stuttgart-based United States Africa Command (AFRICOM), is an annual three-week-long training course for roughly 1 000 troops from Sahelian states, the focus of which is small-unit combat training, counterterrorism surveillance methods and medical assistance. Former West African colonial power France has also continued to have a strong military presence in the region. Despite formally decolonising the region in the 1960s, France retained a number of military advisers and intelligence personnel in countries such as Mali, Burkina Faso, Chad and Niger. A 1 000-strong contingent known as Operation Epervier, with intelligence-gathering drones and surveillance equipment, was based in Chad's capital, N'Djamena, from the late 1980s until 2013. Both France and the United States have been running intelligence-gathering drone flights across the Sahel for several years.[9]

Into the cauldron

Mali's history has been marked by a failure to adequately address the grievances and demands for greater autonomy from the northern semi-nomadic pastoralist and small-scale farming communities such as the Tuareg, Songhai and Peul, among several others. Since the creation of Mali in 1960, following a brief union with Senegal, some in these northern communities have continued to feel marginalised and excluded by Mali's southern-based central government. Social and cultural connections are sometimes weaker with people in the south who are mostly sedentary farmers in the fertile Niger River basin. The term 'Tuareg' is often used loosely and fails to sum up the complex network of ties between hundreds of generally Berber-speaking tribes across the Sahara and Sahel, which stretch up into southern Algeria and into southern Morocco. Within these communities, every shade of opinion can be found (including strong loyalty to Bamako). However, one world view which has emerged is that the historical Tuareg homeland in the cross-border regions of six countries (Mali, Niger, Algeria, Burkina Faso, Mauritania and Libya) was effectively carved up by the creation of the new Malian state in 1960.

As evidence of this, the first of several Tuareg rebellions took place in 1963 as the nascent Malian state was taking steps to assert itself. The Malian army dealt with it brutally, moving en masse into Kidal and sending thousands of people fleeing as refugees, further fomenting grievances against the state, which would only build through the years.[10] Government's inadequate response to severe drought, which wracked the country through the 1970s and 1980s, led to a crisis for the traditional semi-nomadic pastoralist way of life, and further exacerbated northern communities' anger and feelings of abandonment towards the government. In the 1990s, skirmishes and attacks by armed groups in the north culminated in a full-blown rebellion in 2006/07 by the Alliance Tuareg du Nord-Mali pour le Changement (ATNMC), led by veteran rebels Ibrahim Ag Bahanga and Hassan Faggaga. At its height, the ATNMC rebellion succeeded in briefly capturing Kidal and Menaka and taking 40 Malian army soldiers hostage.

The central government's attempts to deal with this series of rebellions often involved a military approach, where rebels clashed with the national army until some kind of defeat or impasse was reached. Once both sides seemed ready to talk, there would be peace conferences, which periodically switched venue from Algeria to Libya (where they would often be hosted by

Colonel Gaddafi). Sometimes dragging on for months, these conferences would lead to a negotiated agreement (such as the 2006 and 2008 Algiers Accords) signed by both sides, which included a number of measures such as pledges to incorporate former rebels into the national army, proposals to increase regional autonomy for the north, and pledges of extra spending to develop the region. Some important steps were taken as a result of these Accords, such as increasing the number of northern officers in the national army and providing more representation for Tuaregs in national politics. In fact, in 2002, the first Tuareg prime minister was elected and northern communities began to receive more financial support from government. However, this quickly led to some in Mali's south to feel that the north was receiving too much financial support, relative to its population.

Nevertheless, as one of the poorest countries on Earth, Mali was unable to provide the level of security and development needed to bring all northern rebels into the fold. Peace deals were thus often characterised by attempts to placate some of the prominent local families, rewarding those who shouted loudest, as opposed to serious well-funded attempts to engage with entire communities and address developmental concerns. It has been argued that under the government of Amadou Toumani Touré (ATT) 'relations between the centre of power in Bamako and the periphery rested on a loose network of personal, clientelistic, even mafia-style alliances with regional elites with reversible loyalties'.[11] With each subsequent rebellion, the contentious issues of how these groups were becoming more and more implicated in criminality, in smuggling and, in later years, transformed into violent jihadist groups, were largely skirted. As the renewed outbreak of rebellion in 2011 led by the MNLA (National Movement for the Liberation of Azawad/Mouvement Nationale pour la Liberation d'Azawad) quite clearly showed, no peace-building or reconciliation efforts over the 50 years since Mali's independence have succeeded in producing a lasting and comprehensive solution.

The Islamists

From 2006 onwards, this already deeply problematic situation was further complicated by the emergence of a number of violent jihadist groups, who must surely have realised the potential for basing themselves in a region where the central government was unable to fully assert its presence. The most prominent of these groups was Al-Qaeda in the Islamic Maghreb, known by its acronym AQIM.

Long enjoying a reputation as a fearsome and brutal operation, AQIM started life in 1992 after the French-backed Algerian military cancelled a second round of parliamentary elections when it looked as if the Islamist political party, Front Islamique du Salut (FIS), was about to win. The Groupe Islamique Armee (GIA or Armed Islamic Group), a conglomerate of militant jihadist groups, formed under the command of Abdelhak Layada. The leader of one of these groups, Hassan Hattab, broke away from the GIA to form the Groupe Salafiste pour la Predication et le Combat (Salafist Group for Preaching and Combat or GSPC). Hattab was pushed aside in favour of Nabil Sahraoui, and then Abdelmalek Droukdel (also known as Abu Musab Abdel Wadoud) who became the new leader after Sahrawi was killed by Algerian security forces in 2004. For several years the GSPC held Algeria and Algiers as their primary target, but following a number of severe crackdowns by the Algerian security forces, they began to move south and eventually crossed the border into Mali's northern desert. As successive governments in Bamako – more than 1 500 km away from the Algerian border – continued to neglect the north and failed to bring trafficking, criminality and secessionist rebellions under control, the GSPC was able to consolidate its position and grow.

From 2008 onwards, the group set up bases in the Wagadou Forest area on the border between Mauritania and Mali, which allowed its lightly armed, highly mobile fighters to operate quite freely over an enormous area stretching from Mauritania in the west, into Libya to the northeast, and as far as eastern Niger. Although the group was still capable of conducting attacks in Algeria – such as a twin suicide car bomb attack in Algiers in 2007 – its focus began to shift towards the Sahel. With connections between GSPC fighters and those who had fought against the Soviet Union in Afghanistan in the 1980s, the GSPC formally allied itself with Al-Qaeda in 2006, and rebranded itself as Al-Qaeda in the Islamic Maghreb.[12] While AQIM's internal workings are largely shrouded in secrecy, there appears to have been a long power struggle at its core between Droukdel and Mokhtar Belmokhtar, an almost legendary figure in the minds of some in West Africa for his ability to evade capture or attempts to kill him.

As AQIM consolidated its presence in northern Mali from 2008 onwards, it began a lucrative line in hostage-taking. This began with the kidnapping of a United Nations diplomat in Niger in 2008, seven employees of the French nuclear firm Areva at the Arlit uranium mine in northern Niger in September 2010, and several businessmen in the town of Hombori in northern Mali in late 2012. New criminal groups, recognising the profits to be made from kidnapping foreigners, sprang up and took hostages which they could sell to AQIM. It has been claimed that AQIM is one of the richest groups in the world thanks to this business, in addition to its control of regional drugs and weapons smuggling networks.[13] Western governments, particularly France, have been criticised for their willingness to pay large sums to secure the release of hostages. For example, in 2013, the former US ambassador to Mali criticised France for paying more than US$11 million to secure the release of four hostages, saying it was directly contributing to the group's ability to operate.[14]

A stage set for collapse

In 2011, the Arab Spring protests broke out across North Africa. The world watched wide-eyed as Zine el-Abidine Ben Ali of Tunisia and Hosni Mubarak of Egypt fell under popular pressure. But it was the collapse of Colonel Muammar Gaddafi's regime in Libya that was to have the most severe impact on the Sahel region. Gaddafi's rule had been marked by his vision for a united Africa. During his time in power, Libyan diplomats travelled to many corners of Africa, offering finance for a number of important infrastructure and development projects, while thousands of Africans travelled to the country to work in low-paid jobs. Gaddafi intervened personally in a number of internal political conflicts in sub-Saharan Africa, often prolonging and complicating them. In the 1980s and 1990s, Libyan troops were sent to conflicts as diverse as the Democratic Republic of Congo (DRC), Central African Republic (CAR) and northern Chad. Rebels from Burkina Faso, Mali, Chad and others moved freely in Tripoli. Gaddafi's long association with northern Mali paid off when Tripoli and Sirte fell to the Libyan rebels during the revolution in 2011. A number of Tuareg, including a future leader of the MNLA, Mohamed ag Najem (a cousin of the last Tuareg leader Ibrahim Ag Bahanga), stayed loyal to the colonel to the end and reportedly fought alongside his presidential guard.[15]

However, when it finally became obvious that Gaddafi's days were numbered, hundreds of these Tuareg fighters fled back to the deserts and mountains of northern Mali, taking with them weapons and ammunition seized from Libyan stockpiles.[16] The birth of the most powerful Tuareg rebel group to date, the MNLA, primarily made up of rebels from previous conflicts such as Ag Najem, was announced a few days before Gaddafi's death in October 2011. Within months they had attacked and conquered the northern Malian towns of Anderamboukane, Menaka, Tessalit and Niafunke, routing the Malian army and forcing thousands of people to seek refuge in neighbouring Mauritania, Niger and Burkina Faso.

A decisive moment in MNLA's advance came on 17 January 2012, when over 100 Malian soldiers were executed in the remote northern town of Aguelhoc. Controversy still surrounds exactly what happened that day, but the Malian government blamed an alliance between AQIM and MNLA.[17] As the army reeled and troops began to flee, the rebels continued to advance, claiming more towns in the north. The army was in disarray and rapidly losing ground. One day in March, seemingly disillusioned at the government's failure to protect them, a group of mutinous soldiers staged a protest, firing in the air when Mali's defence minister tried to visit them at the Kati barracks outside Bamako. On 22 March, in what has been dubbed an 'accidental coup', an angry group of relatively low-ranking soldiers made their way up Didé Koulouba hill, a cool oasis on the outskirts of Bamako.[18] When they arrived at the gates of the presidential palace, it seemed they encountered little resistance from the 'red beret' presidential guard. A few hours later, after the state broadcaster, Office de Radiodiffusion-Télévision du Mali (ORTM), had shown several hours of unscheduled wildlife documentaries, a slightly stunned-looking Captain Amadou Sanogo appeared on camera with a group of soldiers to announce that President Amadou Toumani Touré had been overthrown, just weeks before he was due to step down in a national election. As infighting within army ranks continued and most of the political class seemed at a loss, the MNLA chose their moment and struck hard. By April, the rebels declared they were in control of northern Mali, effectively half the country's territory north of a line running through Mopti and Sévaré.[19] In May, the interim president, Dioncounda Traoré, was beaten up by disgruntled soldiers in his own office. Attempts by African leaders to negotiate a settlement to the crisis stalled, and the international community looked on aghast.

Just as these alliances between the jihadists, smugglers and rebels in northern Mali had shifted to allow a brief period of cooperation between the MNLA and AQIM, the rules changed again. Into the mix appeared a new rebel group, Ansar al-Din (Defenders of the Faith), formed by the veteran Tuareg rebel leader Iyad ag Ghali in early 2012. Ag Ghali is a member of the prominent Tuareg Ifoghas clan and his father was killed in the first Tuareg uprising of 1963. Throughout the 1990s, he was secular and was seen as a key leader of the Tuareg rebellions and part-time hostage release negotiator.[20] However, in the late 1990s he began to learn about the Salafi doctrines of a Pakistani missionary organisation called Tablighi Jamaat and was slowly re-incarnated as a committed Islamist. In the early days of the MNLA's takeover of northern Mali, it seems that Ag Ghali tried to position himself as the new group's leader, but his attempts were rebuffed by an organisation that has largely remained secular. In revenge, Ag Ghali created Ansar al-Din, pledged allegiance to AQIM and declared that the group's aim was to impose sharia across the whole of northern Mali. Ag Ghali's group carried much weight and influence in the region. While AQIM has often been associated with 'foreigners' because of its primarily Algerian leadership, Ansar al-Din comprised mostly Malians, with a number of Mauritanians and other foreign fighters among its ranks.

Finally, a third group known as MUJAO emerged in 2011. Also originally an AQIM offshoot, the group's first prominent act was the abduction of three humanitarian workers from the Tindouf refugee camp for Sahrawi refugees in Algeria in 2011.[21] Led by Ahmed al-Tilemsi, the group appeared to have a number of Mauritanians and Malian Arabs among its ranks, possibly as a result of its early focus on Mauritania.[22] MUJAO's presence in Gao was first reported in early 2012, where it also tried to impose sharia law on the local population. The group was behind the abduction of seven Algerian diplomats from Gao, one of whom was later killed, but also claimed responsibility for a number of attacks inside Algerian territory.

An alliance between the broadly secular MNLA and the more ideologically driven jihadist groups was unlikely to last, and in May and June 2012, AQIM and Ansar al-Din began to turn on their erstwhile allies. Seemingly no match for the Islamists, the MNLA were forced to hastily retreat towards the traditional Tuareg homelands around Kidal. By July 2012, the map of northern Mali had been completely redrawn again, to show Ansar al-Din and AQIM largely in charge in Timbuktu, MUJAO in Gao, and the MNLA in and around Kidal. It was not long before the horror stories about life under sharia in northern Mali began to emerge. Media headlines screamed of thieves having their hands cut off, and Ansar al-Din began a systematic attack on sites of significant cultural and emotional value in Timbuktu, including a number of Sufi shrines and mosques which were considered to be un-Islamic.[23]

However, the world was forced to sit up and take notice in early January 2013, when the Islamists reached central Mali.[24] Ansar al-Din announced on 10 January that it had taken Konna, and was moving on Douentza, which had been in the hands of MUJAO since late December when they had defeated a Songhai self-defence militia, the Ganda Iso. These two towns lie on the main route south to Bamako, in a region which is seen psychologically as the dividing line between north and south in Mali. Panic struck at the heart of politics in Bamako. With the army still in disarray and little progress in establishing a UN peacekeeping force for Mali, the interim president, Dioncounda Traoré, called on France for help. Within a few days, France announced the launching of Operation Serval with the objective of preventing an Islamist take-over of Mali.

Operational Serval

French troops were quickly deployed, using surveillance and transport planes which had been based in N'Djamena, Chad, since the late 1980s as part of France's 1 000-strong Operation Epervier (Sparrowhawk). The initial goal was to halt the advance of the Islamists, but it quickly shifted to an attempt to oust AQIM, MUJAO and Ansar al-Din from the north of Mali, thereby creating an opportunity for the Malian government to re-establish control.[25] Within days, France was joined by about 2 000 troops from the National Army of Chad

(ANT) who moved into northern Mali from Niger. The operation had a number of notable early successes – by 14 January 2013 they had retaken Konna and by the end of the month, French and Chadian soldiers had taken strategic locations in Gao, Timbuktu and Kidal. By 8 February they had reached Tessalit, near the border with Algeria. The speed of Serval's advance was credited to the French forces, which had long experience in the desert environment, supported by the ANT, which had been battling rebel groups in its own eastern desert for several years. Faced with such superior firepower, it seems the Islamists decided on a tactical withdrawal, and simply melted into the most inaccessible corners of the Sahara Desert.

Despite these early successes, the mission's further objectives seemed to remain frustratingly out of reach. Repeated attempts by French and Chadian soldiers to flush out the remaining fighters from Adrar des Ifoghas failed. Within weeks of the fall of the main towns, suicide bombers attacked French and Chadian army targets in Timbuktu and Kidal, using tactics that many observers had predicted from the start. After successfully securing Kidal airport and forcing the Islamists to leave the town, the French and Chadian army reached an impasse with remnants of the MNLA and new Tuareg groupings such as MIA (Movement Islamique du Azawad), who refused to relinquish control of the town. The French were under no illusion as to the advantage that groups such as AQIM had in the extreme desert environment – after all, they had been moving freely around these areas for more than 10 years. As the Islamists disappeared into the sand dunes, early claims that Serval would be wound up and withdrawn within a few months proved premature.

It was not until July 2014 that France announced the end of Operation Serval, but by this time French military commanders appeared to have appreciated that a complete withdrawal would be disastrous for the region, as the Malian army had not been able to fully redeploy to the north. Serval was replaced by Operation Barkhane, a significant reorganisation of France's entire military presence in West Africa, which included 3 000 troops stationed over five Sahelian countries – Chad, Niger, Mali, Burkina Faso and Mauritania. This followed the Security Council Resolution 2 100 in April 2013, which had authorised the deployment of just over 11 000 international troops under the United Nations Multidisciplinary Integrated Stabilization Mission in Mali (MINUSMA).[26]

Although they no longer held territory, the Islamists appeared to go from strength to strength. Within days after the start of Operation Serval, Mokhtar Belmokhtar 'the uncatchable' delivered stunning proof of the group's ability to operate across almost unimaginably large areas of hostile desert, even as his 'colleagues' in AQIM were apparently battling for survival in Mali. On 16 January 2013, Belmokhtar's group, the 'Signed in Blood Battalion', attacked the Tigantourine gas plant near In Amenas in the remote Algerian Desert. By the end of the four-day crisis, 39 foreign workers were dead, and several dozen more captured. Four months later, neighbouring Niger was hit by twin attacks. A suicide bombing at a military barracks in Agades northern Niger, which killed 18 Nigerien soldiers, was quickly followed by an attack on the Somair uranium mine near Arlit, which is operated by the French state-owned nuclear firm Areva. The attack was claimed by Belmohktar and MUJAO in retaliation for Niger's support of France's operations in Mali. A few days later, 22 people escaped from a prison in Niamey after suspected members of MUJAO staged a prison break. Among them was Cheibane Ould Hama who had been convicted of killing four Saudis and a US citizen.[27]

The ability of MUJAO and the Signed in Blood Battalion to survive, evade capture, and to move weapons, supplies and loyal followers in extreme conditions over immense distances did not appear to have been significantly impacted. In August 2013, MUJAO and the Signed in Blood Battalion finally announced that they were merging to create a new group, Al-Mourabitoun (the Sentinels) which also included some smaller armed groups loyal to Belmokhtar.[28] Reports said that Belmokhtar and Al-Tilemsi jointly agreed to leave leadership to an Egyptian, Abu Bakr al-Masri, in a bid to prevent future power struggles.[29] Al-Mourabitoun appears to have offered Belmokhtar some of the independence from AQIM that he craved, following a series of power struggles with top leadership during the occupation of Mali and tensions over the ethnic composition of the group. Belmokhtar's repeated affirmations of loyalty to Al-Qaeda Central under Ayman al-Zawahiri showed the strength of his ambitions.[30] From late 2013, the group began to post a series of audio messages and communiqués via Mauritanian media outlets signalling their determination to defend Islam across Africa, singling out France and other foreign targets as the number one enemy. Al-Mourabitoun's intentions could not have been plainer.

Why were the Islamists able to thrive?
Over the years, there have been many attempts to dismiss groups such as AQIM as 'narco-traffiquants' and 'bandits'.[31] As with all radical Islamist groups, the extent to which AQIM members wholeheartedly believe in a religious ideology has been hotly debated, with some arguing that their motivations lie in the promise of making money through kidnapping and drug smuggling, and not in defending the faith.[32] Relatively little was known about the precise nature of the group's ideology, the personal piety of its fighters, or the interpretation of sharia law they intended to impose.

Within weeks of the Islamist take-over of northern Mali in 2012, a narrative began to emerge. One of their first widely condemned acts was stoning to death a young unmarried couple in Aguelhok for having sexual relations, even though the couple had children and had been living together. Reports began to emerge of thieves having limbs sliced off using machetes, smokers and prostitutes being publicly whipped, women being beaten for walking unveiled, and the banning of Western music.[33] Across the north, from Timbuktu to Kidal, armed men went into people's houses, took their musical instruments and smashed or burnt them. This was a bitter pill to swallow in Mali, which has long prided itself on its rich musical tradition. The Islamists threatened to destroy tens of thousands of ancient Arabic manuscripts, which have been guarded by the people of Timbuktu for centuries. Fortunately, through a remarkable secret campaign, only a small number were destroyed while thousands of the most precious texts were smuggled out of the city by residents to safe houses in other parts of Mali.[34] At the same time, Ansar al-Din launched a campaign of destroying 'idolatrous' Sufi shrines and tombs in Timbuktu, the city of 333 saints, posting videos of their fighters reducing the tombs to rubble with pick axes. Media outlets wasted no time in comparing the destruction to the blowing up of the Buddhas of Bamiyan by the Taliban in 2001. The jihadist threat was given a pan-African dynamic – editorials and experts attempted to show that AQIM was working with Boko Haram in Nigeria and even Al-Shabaab in Somalia, reviving the hackneyed narrative of the Sahelian 'Arc of Instability'.[35]

However, it is important to note that there is a fierce debate about the extent to which the outcry against the imposition of sharia law was hyperbole, particularly when the scale of the actions of AQIM, Ansar al-Din and MUJAO are compared to the senseless violence of another Islamist-inspired group, Boko Haram, who have killed thousands in northeastern Nigeria over the last six years.[36] Part of the Malian narrative was undeniably seen through the prism of threats to Western citizens from kidnapping, and the possible damage to French business interests. Many were convinced by the rhetoric of politicians such as France's defence minister, Jean Yves Le Drian, who claimed on several occasions that the Islamists posed a credible threat on European soil.[37]

This is an important point to appreciate when attempting to evaluate how Malians experienced the brief imposition of sharia law. Mali's relationship with Islam dates back hundreds of years. Islam first arrived in the 9th century, brought to the territory we now call Mali by Berber and Tuareg traders moving across the Sahara from northwest Africa. The religion was able to adapt to the local conditions in West Africa and won a number of early converts. By the 13th century, the area covered by present-day Mali was unquestionably Muslim. The fabulously rich Mansa Moussa, the Islamic king of the Malian empire (modern-day Ghana and southern Mali), caused a storm when he arrived laden with gold in Mecca in 1244. On his way home, accompanied by a retinue of Muslim scholars and academics, he conquered a small trading post at Timbuktu which, within a few hundred years, rose to be a centre of Islamic learning with one of the region's oldest universities. Timbuktu was to go on to become an important crossroads in the Sahara for Muslim pilgrims travelling from the north to the south.

Malian Islam is often characterised as a traditionally tolerant form of Malikite Islam. It is also heavily influenced by Sufi teachings, often described as the more 'mystical' aspect of Islam. Sufi Brotherhoods, such as the Qadriyia and the Tidjania, are also very popular in Senegal and Mali, and there is deep respect for accomplished sheikhs who have followed a Sufi education. Malian Islam is also influenced by traditional animist practices which pre-date the arrival of Islam, and a famous saying goes that Mali is 98 per cent Muslim, 2 per cent Christian and 100 per cent animist.[38] Hunters, griots (praise-singers) and blacksmiths have traditionally important roles in Malian society (as in other parts of West Africa), and these 'African' roles have created a very distinct form of Islam, which often includes syncretic practices.

The region also has a long history of more conservative religious movements. Present-day Mali bordered the Sokoto caliphate created by the jihad of Usman dan Fodio in the early 19th century. In the mid-19th century, a jihad led by El Hadj Umar Tall conquered the Bamana Empire of southern Mali, making Segou the capital of the Toucouleur Empire. A number of villages around the northern town of Gao, particularly Fulbe villages, have seen a revival in interest in a rigorous reading of Islam dating back to the 1960s. Mali has also not escaped the Salafist influence, in particular from Wahhabist groups which advocate the use of the Qur'an and the Hadiths as the sole source of Muslim belief and practise.[39] From the 1950s onwards, preachers from Saudi Arabia began to arrive in Bamako, where they built a number of new mosques in the city – including the city's impressive Grand Mosque. These mosques and their accompanying madrassas have a reputation for following a strict form of Islam.

The take-over of groups such as AQIM in northern Mali and their application of sharia law caused something of a spiritual crisis in Mali in 2012/13, exposing the underlying fault lines in the well-manicured image of Mali's tolerant, laid-back Islam.[40] The country's spiritual authority, the High Islamic Council (HIC), is led by the Wahhabi-influenced Imam Mahmoud Dicko.[41] In 2009/10, Dicko led popular demonstrations against the attempts by former president Amadou Toumani Touré to introduce a modern Family Code which would have, among other things, increased women's rights in inheritance: the first time in modern Mali's history that thousands took to the streets in support of a religious leader. In the early days of the jihadist take-over in 2013, Dicko gave somewhat mixed messages about the imposition of sharia law. A subtle war of words broke out between Dicko and the vice-president of the HIC, Mali's best known Sufi Sheikh Cherif Ousmane Haidara, whose movement Ansar al-Din (not to be confused with Ag Ghali's group) has thousands of followers across mostly southern Mali and beyond. Haidara has built an enormous mosque in the Djelibougou quartier of Bamako, where every day crowds of pilgrims come to seek benediction and sit patiently outside. As the Islamists swept to power, Haidara made subtle references to Dicko's lukewarm denunciations of violence. Dicko was openly criticised by more progressive groups, and the growing flow of people fleeing their homes in the north and arriving in Bamako and other southern centres, such as Mopti, further raised tensions.

Nevertheless, alternative viewpoints did begin to emerge, particularly in the months after AQIM, Ansar al-Din and MUJAO had been dislodged from the main urban centres. Serious consideration began to be given to the idea that the rise of the Islamists had to have been, to a certain extent, facilitated by the local population. Instead of the Islamists being primarily viewed as 'foreign occupiers', they had been able to easily recruit from local populations. Malians from all ethnic groups – and indeed from north and south – were indisputably an important force in Ansar al-Din, and to a lesser extent in AQIM and MUJAO. Many lower-ranking young recruits appear to have been attracted to the groups by the promise of getting powerful positions.[42]

AQIM and MUJAO had spent many years operating in the region and establishing a network of relationships with existing local elites. According to researcher Andrew Lebovich, through its almost 10-year period of relatively easy movement in the Sahel, AQIM had 'worked to establish itself within local social and economic structures in the region'.[43] Crucially, several of their leaders have married into local tribes, such as Mokhtar Belmokhtar who married into the Arab Berabiche tribe.[44] Iyad ag Ghali and his Ansar al-Din network were seen as a credible authority in the north. These relationships were used to gain the cooperation of local elites, consolidate power and set up alternative governance systems.

It is undeniable that the relatively small number of violent acts in response to public order offences and the imposition of sharia law did, in fact, scare and anger many. However, it is important to appreciate that this narrative was often emerging from the south of Mali, where the syncretic, tolerant, 'Sufi' form of Islam is more prevalent, and, indeed, from international actors invoking echoes of the war on terror. Even in 2015, political figures in Bamako were still keen to maintain the image of a secular government and continued to argue that 'Mali's Muslims will never again accept this kind of foreign jihadism'.[45] However, it is merely too simplistic to see the brief Islamist take-over as something that was universally rejected and despised by the local northern populations. To understand why some in these communities, and in particular local leaders, may have felt that religious rule under a group of rebels, with many foreigners among their ranks, was preferable to life under a government in Bamako, we need to return to the question of the role of governance.

The role of governance

To answer the question of the extent to which governance – or the lack of it – has facilitated the rise of Islamist groups in the Sahel, it is necessary to recognise two distinct areas. First, there is the question of how poor governance has created a veritable vortex of political authority in large swathes of the Sahel, a space in which non-state armed groups have been able to thrive. The second consideration is the extent to which weak state institutions have been unable to give ordinary people a strong sense of citizenship, let alone an effective education, health services or the promise of a job. Across the Sahel many communities feel locked out of power and political dialogue, elections are often a sham, and there is deep cynicism that those in power look after their own tribes and families at the expense of everyone else. Mali, Chad and Niger all featured in the 'worsening category' of the 2015 Fragile State Index, with Mali ranking 30th, Niger 19th and Chad 6th in the 'Alert' category.[46]

We have already noted how, over the course of many years, Sahelian states have consistently failed to control their own territories. No Sahelian country is able to exercise full control over those crossing their long desert border. To avoid an official border post, all that is required is to drive a few kilometres further into an otherwise featureless desert and find another route through. The rampant trafficking of goods, people and drugs through these areas has carried on unhindered, largely undetected by weak police and border agencies. This point is crucial in understanding how the Signed in Blood battalion reached In Amenas in Algeria just days after the French intervention began in Mali; how MUJAO fighters managed to kidnap aid workers in the western Sahara refugee camp in western Algeria; how hundreds of heavily armed Tuareg fighters were able to cross back into northern Mali from Libya following the 2011 revolution; and more recently, how Al-Mouribatoun were free to drive into Grand Bassam on the Gulf of Guinea coast, central Bamako and Ouagadougou, heavily armed.

Once these poorly controlled spaces were colonised by criminal trafficking networks, there was little that the weak and cash-strapped Sahelian governments could do to reassert control. The weaknesses inherent in all of the Sahel's national armies are clear: as Mali's soldiers squabbled in their barracks in Bamako in the wake of the 'accidental' coup, directing their anger at Mali's 'old guard' political class, the MNLA captured huge swathes of territory with barely a fight. Several sources describe Malian soldiers simply running away when faced with the determination of the Islamists, something which caused a deep sense of humiliation among many in Mali.[47] In the latter years of Touré's rule, serious problems of corruption had begun to plague the higher echelons of the Malian army and many accused the president of mismanagement and nepotism.[48]

In Niger, at least two serious coup plots have been uncovered in the higher ranks of the army since President Issoufou came to power in 2011. Some efforts have been made by initiatives such as the TSCTP's Operation Flintlock to give the national armies of the Sahel specialist counterterrorism training, but the forces remain weak and divided. Only the Chadian army has the capability to fight effectively in a desert environment.

Intelligence-gathering capability has also been extremely poor. Sahelian states have often relied on the French military to provide them with intelligence. For example, Chad's President Idriss Déby Itno narrowly escaped being toppled in a coup in 2008 after using satellite images provided by French surveillance jets based in N'Djamena, which showed the position of rebel columns approaching from the east. French military advisers have been present in all Sahelian countries for many years, and more recently began to step up the information provided to governments through surveillance drone flights across the Sahel. The United States has also increased its intelligence-gathering networks. Surveillance drone flights have been carried out in northern Niger near Agades since at least 2011, and in 2013 and 2014 the United States announced the opening of two drones bases in Niger to carry out intelligence gathering.[49]

Poor governance in Mali

Mali emerged as a democracy in 1991 after the regime of Moussa Traoré was overthrown in a coup led by Lieutenant Colonel Amadou Toumani Touré (ATT). Touré duly stepped aside to allow elections to take place, which veteran diplomat Alpha Oumar Konare won, but he returned to the political scene a decade later to contest the 2002 elections when Konaré voluntarily left office. Mali continued to hold elections every few years, busily hoisting the billboards and sending politicians into villages to hold high-profile, noisy rallies. However, these elections were not always what they seemed. Whoever lost would usually cry foul, citing irregularities, and local news reports would claim that voters had been paid to choose a particular candidate.[50] Although Mali's elections were generally given the all clear by international observers, turnout was generally low at about 40 per cent. Furthermore, tribal loyalties also hold considerable sway with citizens. In remote rural areas, many people lack the basic civic knowledge to make an informed choice based on policy success and are more inclined to vote for someone they had at least heard of.[51]

Mali's experience again proves the maxim that democracy is not just about holding elections. As argued by International Crisis Group (ICG) in a report following the 2012 coup, 'The consolidation of democracy ... did not lead to the consolidation of the state.'[52] As we have seen, the army, police and intelligence services were neglected, but the effect on schools and health care for the average Malian was acute. Mali's human development indicators are very poor: life expectancy is just 58 years, the under-five mortality rate is 122 per 1 000 live births, the adult literacy rate is just 33 per cent, and secondary school enrolment is under half of the youth population.[53] The wider Sahel region, particularly Niger, has experienced three serious food crises linked to erratic rainfall and desertification over the last 10 years, at its worst leaving over 5 million people in need of food assistance. Across the region, economic development and job creation stalled, along with ordinary people's expectations about what democracy could deliver in terms of improving their everyday lives.

The effect of all this was marked in Mali's north – in the furthest reaches from Gao to Kidal and outside of Timbuktu, where there are no paved roads. Clinics and schools are sparsely dotted across the barren Sahelian scrub, few fields are irrigated, and most homes are poorly constructed out of concrete and breezeblock or mud. It has often been argued that the best chance the north had for inclusive development was the 'The National Pact', which promised the integration of the rebels into the national army and economic development measures for the marginalised north after a Tuareg rebellion in the early 1990s. However, the plan was never given proper financing and its implementation was continuously postponed, a factor that is often cited as the reason for the resurgence of the Tuareg rebellion under Ibrahim Ag Bahanga in the 2000s. However, it is important to note here that there are many people in the south who feel that the north has received a disproportionate amount of funding and political attention, feelings which were exacerbated by the perception that it was the activities of the MNLA that had brought Mali to its knees in 2012.

During the rule of Touré, the choice was often a policy of 'hands-off' governance in the north – partly because the challenges were so huge and because resources were limited. This policy relied on the cooperation of regional elites who often had questionable loyalty to the central government. As security deteriorated, it even meant the creation of Arab self-defence militias.[54]

Efforts were made to increase the state presence in the north, but they were roundly criticised for militarising relations between north and south and not sufficiently consulting local populations. In 2011, the government launched the €50 million Special Programme for Peace, Security and Development in Northern Mali (PSPSDN), which aimed to promote inclusive development for the northern communities. It envisaged the creation of 11 secure government and development centres across the north, where security forces were to be stationed as infrastructure projects were undertaken. While the project laudably identified that state presence should be reinforced in the north, it came under fire from many communities (some of which included future members of the MNLA) who rejected the notion of a 'top-down' centralised programme.[55] The project was eventually abandoned in early 2012 as the MNLA swept across the north.

Poor governance in Niger
It is interesting here to compare Mali's efforts with neighbouring Niger, which has also been beset by Tuareg rebellions and jihadist activity in its northern Sahelian zone. Many of the conditions described in the sections on Mali – lack of adequate border control, uneven development in periphery regions, and the lack of services and jobs – are just as important in creating the potential for instability in Niger.

The last major Tuareg revolt in Niger started in 2007 and was led by Aghlay ag Alambo's MNJ (Nigerien Movement for Justice), which was fighting for a greater share of the wealth created by Niger's important uranium mines – located deep in the Sahara Desert near the town of Arlit, close to the Algerian border. Northern Niger is as remote and underdeveloped as northern Mali, with towns such as Agades serving as the main embarkation points for a crossing of the Sahara Desert. The MNJ appeared to be inspired by the success of Ag Bahanga's brief rebellion in Mali, which had broken out the previous year, and there were many rumours of links between the groups. Northern Niger's Sahel region around Agades and the Air Mountains is very similar to northern Mali, with largely pastoralist communities living in the less developed fringes of semi-desert and mountains. Furthermore, Niger's Tuareg communities – as well as Tubu and Fulani – have felt similar isolation from the centre of power in Niamey, especially as southern Niger is dominated by the Hausa group, which originates in northern Nigeria. Over two years, the MNJ, which also included Tubu and Fulani, led a series of attacks against army positions in the north, killing around 45 people and taking numerous Nigerien soldiers hostage. They also targeted uranium facilities in the north, including those owned by China, and the French nuclear giant Areva.

The Nigerien government, then led by President Mamadou Tandja, initially chose to respond to the rebellion with force. A state of emergency was declared in 2007 and the military pursued a crackdown on the rebels, restricting access to the zone for journalists and humanitarian actors. The desert tourist industry in the region dried up overnight and civilians fled from their homes. In 2008, a repressive new anti-terror law was passed, which gave extended powers to the army and police. Once again, Colonel Gaddafi attempted to mediate in the crisis and a series of half-hearted peace conferences began. Eventually, however, it was splits in the rebel movement itself that served to undermine its strength, with a new faction being formed by Rhissa ag Boula. By May 2009, President Tandja was able to make a visit to Agades and the rebellion appeared to run out of steam.

In early 2012, as the MNLA rebellion was in full force in neighbouring Mali, Niger was on high alert for a rekindling of the MNJ rebellion through association with the MNLA.[56] In a story with powerful echoes of the return of the MNLA to Mali, press reports accused Ag Boula's men of helping one of Colonel Gaddafi's sons, Al-Saadi, to escape southern Libya in a heavily armed convoy, bringing him to Agades and then Niamey, where he was to live under house arrest for several years before being extradited. Thousands of Tuareg refugees and other groups began to flee over the border from Mali to the safety of camps in northern Niger. Many observers feared the worst and expected northern Niger to fall as well. Nevertheless, the expected uprising did not take place. What had Niger done that Mali had not?

Just six months after the MNJ rebellion ended, President Tandja provoked a national crisis in October 2009 by attempting to change the Constitution to allow him to stand again for president. In February 2016, he was overthrown by a group of disgruntled generals, who significantly stepped aside the following year to allow elections to take place, which were won by Niger's current president, Mahamadou Issoufou. Although Tandja had crushed the rebellion by force, Issoufou's initial moves indicated a more conciliatory approach, which can be credited in part for helping to prevent the outbreak of a similar Tuareg rebellion in Niger. Both Rhissa ag Boula and Aghlay ag Alambo were brought into the political fold through the creation of special positions as presidential advisers. Brigi Rafini from Iferouane, deep in Niger's Tuareg region, was made prime minister, a position he still holds in 2016. Rhissa Feltou became mayor of Agades and Mohamed Anacko, another former rebel, was made president of the Regional Council of Agades. Ag Alambo was charged with the process of bringing Tuareg fighters back from Libya and reintegrating them into the national army. In addition, credible claims have been made that the Nigerien government – well aware of the evolution of the crisis in Mali – proactively stepped up border patrols in the north to disarm any fighters coming back from Libya.[57]

Despite these important steps, which helped the country prevent a spill-over of the crisis in Mali, Niger remains in danger of a similar state collapse if another toxic mix of circumstances, such as those seen in Mali, are allowed to develop. Niger's record on promoting democracy and state-building is poor. The country has seen four coups and a significant part of its post-independence history has been spent under military rule. Although the country was returned to civilian rule in 2011, in a widely praised election in which challenger Seyni Oumarou gracefully accepted his defeat, in recent years old political habits in the country have begun to return. Authorities claim to have uncovered at least two serious coup plots in 2011 and late 2015, and cracked down hard on members of the military believed to have been behind them. In 2013, the governing coalition broke down, and a former staunch ally of the president and leader of the opposition Moden Lumana party, Hama Amadou, fled into exile in Paris after being charged with involvement in a baby-trafficking scandal in the lead up to Niger's presidential election in 2016. When Amadou returned to Niger in late 2015 to contest the election, he was promptly arrested and found himself fighting his campaign from prison. Unable to organise his supporters, Amadou pulled out of a second round run-off, leaving Issoufou free to win the vote in February 2015. The cast of characters who stood for president – Issoufou, Amadou, Seyni Oumarou, Mahamane Ousmane – are all members of a tiny political class who have spent the best part of 20 years moving in and out of government.[58] As in Mali and also in Chad, Niger's political opposition is accused of being ineffective and unrepresentative.

Despite clear commitments in a new Constitution, passed by popular vote in 2010, to increase transparency in the country's lucrative extractive sector, the government has failed to publish new contracts it drew up with the French nuclear giant Areva. Hundreds of people were tear-gassed and arrested in demonstrations calling for greater transparency. Supporters of Hama Amadou have been arrested while calling for his release. Similar protests calling for greater democracy and denouncing Issoufou's rule broke out in 2014 and 2015, some of which were broken up by the security forces. Despite worthy commitments to free speech, journalists have also been targeted, with at least five arrested in 2015.

Niger, like Mali, has consistently failed to deliver equitable development for its people, scoring the lowest human development indicators in the world on the UN's 2015 Human Development Index. The country's infant mortality rate is 102 per 1 000 live births, while the average number of years of schooling for a Nigerien is just five. With regards to the literacy rate, 85 per cent of the adult population cannot read or write.[59] The population grew by 3.9 per cent in 2014 and is set to double within 18 years, as the country has the world's highest fertility rate. This will undoubtedly put immense strain on services such as schools and education, lead to further degradation of grazing lands and agricultural areas, and create a rural exodus to the main urban centres. Many of these people will choose to make the perilous journey to Europe in search of a better life.

Niger has suffered from three major food crises in less than 10 years, and almost six million people were at risk of hunger in 2012 after the annual rains failed. The country is more than 50 per cent dependent on international donors for its budget, yet repeated commitments by the government to invest in health, education and development have failed to materialise, including the ambitious 'Renaissance' plan announced by President Issoufou on his election in 2011.[60] Almost half the money Niger received from donors was unspent in 2014,[61] and money that was originally earmarked for development has been diverted to increase the military budget as the twin threats of AQIM and Boko Haram have increased. The country's 2012 budget was increased by 52.7 per cent with doubled defence spending and US$60 million cuts in resources for food security, health and education.[62]

President Issoufou has worked hard in recent years to promote Niger as a reliable partner in the fight against regional terrorist groups such as AQIM, appealing directly to the international community for assistance and allowing France and the United States to increase their military presence on Nigerien soil. Niger has joined a number of regional coalitions combating terrorism, and contributed troops to fight the northern Mali rebels and the insurgency led by the Islamist group Boko Haram in northeastern Nigeria. However, while the country had a lucky escape by avoiding the potential for spill-over from Mali's MNLA rebellion, it has not escaped from AQIM, which has operated in Niger since the early days of the GSPC's move from Algeria. The twin suicide attacks in 2013 and continuing hostage-taking in the north have shown how the group is still able to strike in Niger unhindered. Furthermore, Niger is now affected by the activities of the Nigerian Islamist group Boko Haram, which since 2014 has moved outside its traditional area of operation in Nigeria's three northeastern states. At least 50 attacks took place on Nigerien territory in 2015, mostly in the remote eastern province of Diffa. This has displaced thousands of Nigeriens along the border. The government and relief agencies have struggled to provide for them, with the increased number of people putting pressure on already poor local health and education services and food stocks.

In trying to contain these threats, Niger suffers from many of the same challenges as Mali. Governance is lacking and has failed to deliver equitable development, and large sections of the population feel marginalised and isolated. There is a small but growing movement of religious protest groups, which appear to be developing to fill the space left by an almost invisible political opposition. 'With no alternative means of expressing discontent, citizens increasingly turn to Islamist groups to channel dissent,' argues the International Crisis Group.[63] A group known as the Yan Izala – a Salafi-oriented reform movement – were believed to have been behind some of the unrest in Niger that followed the attack on the Charlie Hebdo office in Paris. In the days after the attack, a number of churches across Niger were attacked and burned and Christians targeted in public. In addition, as Boko Haram evolves in eastern Niger, there are fears that local young people, without jobs and who feel alienated from the centre of power, are choosing to join the group. Furthermore, as the formal national education system is increasingly under strain, a network of highly conservative Quranic schools have been able to gain traction. These schools may further change the religious and cultural landscape of the region in years to come and provide pools of potential recruits to AQIM and its affiliates.

To what extent can failures of governance be blamed for the rise in Islamist violence in the Sahel? Since independence, Sahelian governments have consistently failed to build effective state institutions such as armies and border forces, resulting in vast swathes of territory in Mali, Niger, Chad and Mauritania where central government presence is extremely weak. These areas have been colonised by smugglers, drugs traffickers and jihadists, who have been free to operate and create alternative economic systems and social arrangements. At the same time, the associated failure of Sahelian governments to provide economic opportunities and inclusive development to a population scraping an existence on the margins of the Sahara Desert has driven some into the arms of radical groups.

There was certainly significant local recruitment and cooperation with local elites during the Malian crisis, which allowed Islamist pseudo-governance to gain a toehold, but we have seen how the internal narratives of Malian Islam meant that reactions to the imposition of sharia law by AQIM, MUJAO and Ansar al-Din were extremely complex and varied. Rather than seeing a direct link between the failure of Sahelian governments to provide hope for their people and propelling people towards the adoption of Islamist ideologies, it may be more helpful to consider how a few very committed individuals – Mokhtar Belmokhtar and Iyad ag Ghali to name but a few – were able to use the chaotic circumstances in northern Mali to their advantage and impose their ideologies on populations, some of whom were receptive to their ideas.

In a further indictment of governance in the region, it is notable how little effort seems to have been made to challenge these radical ideas. While Mauritania has led some commendable efforts in its prisons to engage detained radical Islamists in theological debate, and even held a national social dialogue on the acceptability of violent actions in Islam, Mali's HIC has at times seemed more concerned with politics, and similar national dialogues are almost unheard of in Niger and Chad.[64] The Islamists have been dislodged but little has been done to dislodge their ideas. Recruitment continues as evidenced by several of the attackers involved in the assault on the Radisson Blu in Bamako being local Malians. As Andrew Lebovich argues: 'Despite the toll exacted on these groups by Operation Serval and Operation Barkhane ... their operations have not only increased in the last year in northern Mali but also spread increasingly to central and southern Mali.'[65]

It can be tempting to see the Sahel, and in particular Mali, as an accident waiting to happen. Years of neglect in the northern regions and, indeed, political failings in Bamako meant that a group of uniquely determined individuals – both Tuareg rebels and Islamist fighters – were able to take full advantage of the political stagnation and inability of government to control territory or provide basic services to many of its citizens. The potential for chaos in the region has long been acknowledged by regional leaders and the international community alike.

However, this analysis misses the significant impact of a series of extraordinary events. The collapse of Colonel Gaddafi's regime in Libya pushed a band of heavily armed and determined MNLA fighters back into Mali. This crisis could have been mitigated and turned into yet another brief skirmish with Tuareg rebels if the Malian army had been fit for purpose. Instead, Mali was hit by an unstoppable domino effect sparked by the 'accidental coup' of Amadou Sanogo on 22 March 2012.[66] The MNLA's weakness was easily exposed by the Islamists who defeated them and overran their territory in a matter of weeks. With President Touré gone, political paralysis set in and the army was unable to stop the Islamists claiming huge swathes of territory.

Thus, lack of governance did not so much create the ideologies themselves or even propel large numbers of people towards radical ideas. Rather, it created an environment in which a toxic mix of rebel groups, drugs smugglers, criminals and jihadists could thrive. Once the weak Malian state institutions were swept aside, the Islamist groups were able to claim territory, gain recruits and weapons, and carry out a social experiment in applying sharia law for nearly nine months. And while this experiment with controlling territory was quite easily uprooted by the vastly superior military capabilities of the French and Chadian armies, the Malian state has been unable to fully reassert itself since Operation Serval formally ended. Today, disillusionment with the government of Ibrahim Boubacar Keita (IBK), a prominent member of Mali's old Frenchleaning political class, is widespread. Anecdotal evidence from Bamako suggests that many people believe the status quo has returned.[67] In a recent survey of 5 000 Malians, poor governance and the failure of the state to deliver equitable development in the south and north, as well as urban and rural areas, was recently cited as one of the main obstacles to peace.[68]

Conclusion

In the aftermath of the attack on the Radisson Blu hotel in Bamako in November 2015 and the Splendid Hotel in Ouagadougou in early 2016, it was reported that Al-Mourabitoun had been reabsorbed into AQIM.[69] Andrew Lebovich argues that the reconciliation and merger of the two groups appears to have been the result of 'competition from a growing Islamic State presence in north Africa and the Sahara/Sahel region'.[70] The growing influence of ISIS in Africa, most markedly in the chaotic east of Libya, where there may be as many as 3 000 ISIS fighters, appears to have pushed AQIM and Al-Mourabitoun to put their differences aside and to attempt to reassert their pre-eminence in the Sahel region. AQIM has also recently been challenged for dominance in eastern Niger by the activities of Boko Haram, which also pledged allegiance to ISIS. The recent merger between Ansar al-Din, AQIM, Al-Mourabitoun and the Macina Liberation Front (FLM) should be seen as a way of maintaining supremacy in the region in the face of increased competition by the ISIS.

The focus for AQIM continues to be France and its activities in West Africa, and the scale and audacity of the Ouagadougou, Ivory Coast and Bamako attacks can only be seen as continuing proof of what the newly reunited group is capable of. In addition, militancy has spread to southern and central Mali in the aftermath of the French realignment under Operation Barkhane, with new groups emerging, such as the Macina Liberation Front led by radical preacher Amadou Kouffa, which claimed responsibility for several attacks across southern Mali during 2015.

Although some progress has been made to restore order in Mali, such as the largely peaceful 2013 elections which returned the former prime minister, Ibrahim Boubacar Keita, as president, there are still considerable obstacles in the way to the re-establishment of Mali's full territorial integrity and political systems. A locally unpopular UN peacekeeping mission, MINUSMA, continues to carry out much of the day-to-day patrols and security measures in the north, albeit under the constant threat of attack. In the first few months of 2016 alone, at least 15 UN soldiers were killed in ambushes on the UN camps in Kidal.[71] The status of Kidal, which has predominantly been under the control of a shifting alliance between Tuareg rebel groups, became a serious question mark. Efforts by the Malian government to reassert control were repeatedly rebuffed, including the humiliating visit of the former prime minister, Moussa Mara, to Kidal in May 2014, which sparked deadly clashes between the MNLA and government forces.[72] Although the Algiers Accord, a peace deal signed between the rebel CMA (Coordination of Movements of Azawad) and the Malian government in June 2015 was greeted with optimism by some in Bamako, when Algeria's foreign minister visited Bamako a year later it seemed that little concrete progress had been made.[73] This slow progress and lack of implementation is reminiscent of most of the peace accords signed with northern rebels over the last decade.

This pattern is repeated across the wider Sahel, where little progress has been seen in attempts to consolidate democracy and improve governance. Niger's elections in early 2016 took place in an environment of intense hostility between the government and opposition. Establishment figures have been largely discredited in the eyes of the opposition and ordinary citizens. In April 2016, the incumbent president, Idriss Déby Itno, successfully ran for a fifth term. Amid post-election recriminations, it was claimed by opposition figures that 60 military personnel disappeared without trace after failing to vote for Déby Itno. With a prolonged slump in the world oil price, Chad's public finances were severely impacted during 2015 and it was forced to seek a bail out from the IMF. In 2014, Burkina Faso's longstanding president, Blaise Compaore, was toppled in a coup, which was followed in 2015 by a violent botched counter coup by his supporters, who briefly arrested the country's transitional president and prime minister. It has been argued that this prolonged political crisis was a factor in Al-Mourabitoun's decision to attack Ouagadougou in early 2016. Perhaps of most concern is the ongoing crisis in Libya, where all attention is focused on the failing attempts to create a unity government in Tripoli. This has left the entire south of the country – the Sahelian hinterlands – as yet another enormous space where state institutions are weak and free for armed groups to exploit. Chad's President Déby Itno, in particular, has repeatedly warned about the dangers posed by this region.

Although there have been some attempts to create regional groupings to share intelligence and resources to combat terrorism and instability across the Sahel, such as the CEMOC (Algeria, Mali, Mauritania and Niger) and the Sahel G5 (Chad, Niger, Mauritania, Mali and Burkina Faso), in reality regional rivalries have tended to complicate these efforts. Chad and Niger have contributed troops to peacekeeping forces in Mali and in northeastern Nigeria against Boko Haram, but despite early gains in both conflicts, comprehensive peace solutions are lacking and resentment has built towards Nigeria's government for its own inability to deal with the crisis.

Looking at the region as a whole, it is clear that while the short-lived attempt of groups such as AQIM and Ansar al-Din to conquer and administer significant territory in northern Mali was easily defeated by the superior firepower of a Western army, tanks and guns have done little to change the fundamental political economy of all Sahelian states. France, with its 3 000-strong military presence in West Africa, is keen to push all those who remain obstacles to peace in northern Mali to accept the 2015 Algiers Accord, even if its provisions do not appear to represent a game-changing solution to the long-standing problems of the north. Islamist groups can and almost certainly will continue to move unhindered across huge swathes of desert, striking predominantly foreign targets at will.

If this continued instability is ever to be addressed, all the countries of the Sahel, and most importantly Mali and Niger, need to improve governance structures and offer their populations the realistic prospect of inclusive economic development. Particular attention needs to be paid to improving the region's security forces, including border patrols, intelligence and national armies, in order to help each country control the territory. At the same time, ordinary people in marginalised areas need to be given better access to schools, health care and employment opportunities. They need to feel that the state is 'investing' in them, as a way to counteract the narratives of rebellion and radicalism which have proved so popular. Failing to make these changes will undoubtedly see the region continue to suffer waves of instability and violence.

Endnotes

1 United Kingdom: Foreign and Commonwealth Office (2013) Traffickers and Terrorists: Drugs and violent jihad in Mali and the wider Sahel. Published 12 November 2013. Available at: http://www.refworld.org/docid/53f361204.html
2 Afsahi, K (2015) Are Moroccan cannabis growers able to adapt to recent European market trends? *Journal of Drug Policy*, **26** (3), pp. 327–329.
3 United Kingdom: Foreign and Commonwealth Office (2013).
4 De Waal, A (2004) Counter-insurgency on the cheap, *Review of African Political Economy*, **31** (102), pp. 716–725; Westenfelder, F (2011) *Soldiers of Misfortune: The history of mercenaries*. Norderstedt: Herstellung & Verlag.
5 DefenceWeb (2013) Niger Armed Forces. 13 September 2013. Available at: http://www.defenceweb.co.za/index.php?option=com_content&view=article&id=31880:niger-armed-forces&catid=119:african-militaries&Itemid=255
6 United Kingdom: Foreign and Commonwealth Office (2013).
7 Ibid.
8 Gberie, L (2016) *Crime, Violence, and Politics: Drug trafficking and counternarcotics policies in Mali and Guinea*. Foreign Policy at Brookings. Washington, DC: Brookings Institute. Available at: https://www.brookings.edu/wp-content/uploads/2016/07/Gberie-Mali-and-Guinea-final.pdf
9 *The Washington Post* (2014) Pentagon set to open second base in Niger as it expands operations in Africa. Published 31 July 2014. Available at: https://www.washingtonpost.com/world/national-security/pentagon-set-to-open-second-drone-base-in-niger-as-it-

expands-operations-in-africa/2014/08/31/365489c4-2eb8-11e4-994d-202962a9150c_story.html
10. Al Jazeera (2014) What do the Tuareg want? Published 13 September 2014. Available at: http://www.aljazeera.com/indepth/opinion/2014/01/what-do-tuareg-want-20141913923498438.html
11. International Crisis Group (2012) *Mali: Avoiding escalation*. Report No. 189, 18 July 2012. Available at: http://www.crisisgroup.org/~/media/Files/africa/west-africa/mali/189-mali-avoiding-escalation-english.pdf
12. Council on Foreign Relations (2015) Al-Qaeda in the Islamic Maghreb. Published 27 March 2015. Available at: http://www.cfr.org/terrorist-organizations-and-networks/al-qaeda-islamic-maghreb-aqim/p12717
13. Stanford University (2017) *Al-Qaeda in the Islamic Maghreb*. Stanford University's Mapping Militants Project. Published 6 June 2015. Available at: https://web.stanford.edu/group/mappingmilitants/cgi-bin/groups/view/65
14. *The Telegraph* (2016) 'France boosted al-Qaeda in Mali by paying £11m in ransoms', says US ambassador. Published 8 February 2013. Available at: http://www.telegraph.co.uk/news/worldnews/africaandindianocean/mali/9857723/France-boosted-al-Qaeda-in-Mali-by-paying-11m-in-ransoms-says-US-ambassador.html
15. Stratfor (2012) Mali besieged fighters fleeing Libya. Published 2 February 2012. Available at: https://www.stratfor.com/weekly/mali-besieged-fighters-fleeing-libya
16. Small Arms Survey (2015) *Small Arms Survey Yearbook*. Chapter 6: Expanding arsenals: Insurgent arms in northern Mali. Available at: http://www.smallarmssurvey.org/fileadmin/docs/A-Yearbook/2015/eng/Small-Arms-Survey-2015-Chapter-06-EN.pdf
17. Al Jazeera (2013) Investigating 'massacre' of soldiers in Mali. Published 25 April 2013. Available at: http://www.aljazeera.com/news/africa/2013/04/20134242218374249.html
18. *The Atlantic* (2012) How confused protesters seized an African country. Published 4 April 2012. Available at: http://www.theatlantic.com/international/archive/2012/04/the-accidental-coup-how-confused-protesters-seized-an-african-country/255442/
19. BBC (2017) Mali profile: Timeline. Last updated 28 June 2017. Available at: http://www.bbc.com/news/world-africa-13881978
20. Al Jazeera (2014) What do the Tuareg want? Published 13 September 2014. Available at: http://www.aljazeera.com/indepth/opinion/2014/01/what-do-tuareg-want-20141913923498438.html
21. Terrorism Research and Analysis Consortium (2017) *Movement for Unity and Jihad in West Africa*. Available at: http://www.trackingterrorism.org/group/movement-unity-and-jihad-west-africa-mujao
22. Ibid.
23. Al Jazeera (2012) Ansar Dine destroys more shrines in Mali. Published 10 July 2012. Available at: http://www.aljazeera.com/news/africa/2012/07/201271012301347496.html
24. BBC (2013) Mali Islamists 'enter' Konna after clashes with army. Published 10 January 2013. Available at: http://www.bbc.com/news/world-africa-20970604
25. Spet, S (2015) Operation Serval: Analysing the French strategy against jihadi in Mali, *Air and Space Power Journal – Africa and Francophonie*, **6** (3). Available at: http://www.au.af.mil/au/afri/aspj/apjinternational/aspj_f/digital/pdf/articles/2015_3/spet_e.pdf
26. United Nations (2017) Supporting political process and helping stabilize Mali. Available at: http://www.un.org/en/peacekeeping/missions/minusma/index.shtml
27. BBC (2013) Niamey Prison break: Niger confirms 22 escaped. Published 2 June 2013. Available at: http://www.bbc.com/news/world-africa-22749230
28. BBC (2013) Belmokhtar's militants 'merge' with Mali's Mujao. Published 22 August 2013.

Available at: http://www.bbc.co.uk/news/world-us-canada-23796920

29 Lebovich, A (2006) The hotel attacks and the militant realignment in the Sahara–Sahel Region, *CTC Sentinel*, **9** (1). New York: Counter Terrorism Centre at West Point. Available at: https://www.ctc.usma.edu/posts/the-hotel-attacks-and-militant-realignment-in-the-sahara-sahel-region

30 Ibid.

31 Interview with Zeini Moulaye, former minister and government adviser, Bamako, November 2015.

32 United Kingdom Parliament (2013) Address by Guy Lankester: Extremism and political instability in North and West Africa. Available at: http://www.publications.parliament.uk/pa/cm201314/cmselect/cmfaff/writev/extremism/m08.htm

33 *The Guardian* (2012) Mali: No rhythm or reason as militants declare war on music. Published 23 October 2012. Available at: http://www.theguardian.com/world/2012/oct/23/mali-militants-declare-war-music

34 *The Guardian* (2014) The book rustlers of Timbuktu: How Mali's ancient manuscripts were saved. Published 23 May 2014. Available at: https://www.theguardian.com/world/2014/may/23/book-rustlers-timbuktu-mali-ancient-manuscripts-saved

35 United Nations (2013) 'Arc of Instability' across Africa, if left unchecked, could turn continent into launch pad for larger-scale terrorist attacks, Security Council told. Published 13 May 2013. Available at: http://www.un.org/press/en/2013/sc11004.doc.htm

36 Brookings Institute (2016) Facing threats at home, France should still engage abroad. Published 25 July 2015. Available at: http://www.visionofhumanity.org/sites/default/files/English%20Media%20Release%20GTI%202015.pdf

37 *Daily Nation* (2012) Mali Islamists a threat to Europe: French minister. Published 12 November 2012. Available at: http://www.nation.co.ke/News/africa/Mali-Islamists-a-threat-to-Europe/-/1066/1617766/-/10pfpyu/-/index.html

38 BBC (2013) *Beyond the War: Faith and Culture in West Africa*. Video published 9 April 2013. Available at: http://www.bbc.co.uk/programmes/p016tmhv

39 Research on Islam and Muslims in Africa (RIMA) (2014) *Sufis vs Salafis: Winning Friends and Interdicting Enemies in Islamic Africa* by Dr T Furnish. Policy Paper Vol. 1, No. 1. Published April 2013. Available at: https://muslimsinafrica.wordpress.com/2013/04/11/sufis-v-salafis-winning-friends-and-interdicting-enemies-in-islamic-africa-dr-timothy-r-furnish/

40 BBC (2013) *Beyond the War*.

41 *Jeune Afrique* (2012) Mali: Mahmoud Dicko, imam médiateur. Published 12 April 2012. Available at: http://www.jeuneafrique.com/140316/politique/mali-mahmoud-dicko-imam-m-diateur/

42 Lebovich, A (2013) The local face of jihadism in northern Mali, *CTC Sentinel*, **6** (64). Available at: https://www.ctc.usma.edu/posts/the-local-face-of-jihadism-in-northern-mali

43 Lebovich (2006).

44 Lebovich (2013).

45 Interview with Habib Kane, Ministry of Religious Affairs, Bamako, November 2015.

46 Fund for Peace (2015) *Fragile States Index: 2015*. Available at: http://library.fundforpeace.org/library/fragilestatesindex-2015.pdf

47 From a series of interviews with ordinary Malians during research for my BBC *Heart and Soul* documentary, Bamako, February 2013.

48 International Crisis Group (2012) *Mali: Avoiding escalation*, Africa Report No. 189, 18 July 2012. Available at: http://www.crisisgroup.org/~/media/Files/africa/west-africa/mali/189-mali-avoiding-escalation-english.pdf

49 *The Washington Post* (2014) Pentagon set to open second drone base in Niger as it expands

50. BBC (2013) *Beyond the War*.
51. From my experience as a reporter for the BBC in Mali during 2007/08.
52. International Crisis Group (2012).
53. United Nations Development Programme (2015) *Mali 2015: Human Development Indicators*. Available at: http://hdr.undp.org/en/countries/profiles/MLI
54. International Crisis Group (2012).
55. Ibid.
56. African Arguments (2012). Malian crisis: Tuareg rebellion could spark regional violence in Mali, Niger and southern Algeria. Published 15 March 2012. Available at: http://africanarguments.org/2012/03/15/tuareg-rebellion-could-spark-regional-violence-in-mali-niger-and-southern-algeria-by-celeste-hicks/
57. Interview with Niger's Foreign Minister Bazoum Mohamed, Niamey, February 2013.
58. African Arguments (2016) Why Niger's elections may be less important than they seem. Published 19 February 2016. Available at: http://africanarguments.org/2016/02/19/why-nigers-elections-may-be-less-important-than-they-seem/
59. United Nations Development Programme (2015).
60. International Crisis Group (2015) *The Central Sahel: The perfect sandstorm*. Africa Report No. 227. Published 25 June 2016. Available at: http://www.crisisgroup.org/~/media/Files/africa/west-africa/227-the-central-sahel-a-perfect-sandstorm.pdf
61. Ibid.
62. Ibid.
63. Ibid.
64. Interview with Zeini Moulaye, former minister and government adviser, Bamako, November 2015.
65. Lebovich (2006).
66. *The Atlantic* (2012) How confused protesters seized an African country. Published 4 April 2012. Available at: http://www.theatlantic.com/international/archive/2012/04/the-accidental-coup-how-confused-protesters-seized-an-african-country/255442/
67. Informal interviews with people in Bamako, November 2015.
68. Institute Malien de Recherche Action pour la Paix (2015) *Autoportrait du Mali: Les obstacles à la paix*. Published March 2015. Available at: http://reliefweb.int/sites/reliefweb.int/files/resources/2015_03_02_Mali_Autoportrait_FR_0.pdf
69. Lebovich (2006).
70. Ibid.
71. BBC (2015) The world's most dangerous peacekeeping mission. Published 25 November 2015. Available at: http://www.bbc.com/news/world-africa-34812600
72. Interview with Zeini Moulaye, Bamako, November 2015.
73. *Africa News* (2016) Algerian foreign minister in Mali to assess reconciliation progress. Published 21 June 2016. Available at: http://www.africanews.com/2016/06/21/algerian-foreign-minister-in-mali-to-assess-reconciliation-progress/

References

African Arguments (2012) Malian crisis: Tuareg rebellion could spark regional violence in Mali, Niger and southern Algeria. Published 15 March 2012. Available at: http://africanarguments.org/2012/03/15/tuareg-rebellion-could-spark-regional-violence-in-mali-niger-and-southern-algeria-by-celeste-hicks/

African Arguments (2016) Why Niger's elections may be less important than they seem. Published 19 February 2016. Available at: http://africanarguments.org/2016/02/19/why-nigers-elections-may-be-less-important-than-they-seem/

Africa News (2016) Algerian foreign minister in Mali to assess reconciliation progress. Published 21 June 2016. Available at: http://www.africanews.com/2016/06/21/algerian-foreign-minister-in-mali-to-assess-reconciliation-progress/

Afsahi, K (2015) Are Moroccan cannabis growers able to adapt to recent European market trends? *Journal of Drug Policy*, **26** (3), pp. 327–329.

Al Jazeera (2012) Ansar Dine destroys more shrines in Mali. Published 10 July 2012. Available at: http://www.aljazeera.com/news/africa/2012/07/201271012301347496.html

Al Jazeera (2013) Investigating 'massacre' of soldiers in Mali. Published 25 April 2013. Available at: http://www.aljazeera.com/news/africa/2013/04/20134242218374249.html

Al Jazeera (2014). What do the Tuareg want? Published 13 September 2014. Available at: http://www.aljazeera.com/indepth/opinion/2014/01/what-do-tuareg-want-20141913923498438.html

BBC (2013) Belmokhtar's militants 'merge' with Mali's Mujao. Published 22 August 2013. Available at: http://www.bbc.co.uk/news/world-us-canada-23796920

BBC (2013) *Beyond the War: Faith and culture in West Africa*. Video published 9 April 2013. Available at: http://www.bbc.co.uk/programmes/p016tmhv

BBC (2013) Mali Islamists 'enter' Konna after clashes with army. Published 10 January 2013. Available at: http://www.bbc.com/news/world-africa-20970604

BBC (2013) Niamey Prison break: Niger confirms 22 escaped. Published 2 June 2013. Available at http://www.bbc.com/news/world-africa-22749230

BBC (2015) The world's most dangerous peacekeeping mission. Published 25 November 2015. Available at: http://www.bbc.com/news/world-africa-34812600

BBC (2017) Mali profile: Timeline. Last updated 28 June 2017. Available at: http://www.bbc.com/news/world-africa-13881978

Brookings Institute (2016) Facing threats at home, France should still engage abroad. Published 25 July 2015. Available at: http://www.visionofhumanity.org/sites/default/files/English per cent20Media per cent20Release per cent20GTI per cent202015.pdf

Council on Foreign Relations (2015) Al-Qaeda in the Islamic Maghreb. Published 27 March 2015. Available at: http://www.cfr.org/terrorist-organizations-and-networks/al-qaeda-islamic-maghreb-aqim/p12717

Daily Nation (2012) Mali Islamists a threat to Europe: French minister. Published 12 November 2012. Available at: http://www.nation.co.ke/News/africa/Mali-Islamists-a-threat-to-Europe/-/1066/1617766/-/10pfpyu/-/index.html

De Waal, A (2004) Counter-insurgency on the cheap, *Review of African Political Economy*, **31** (102), pp. 716–725.

DefenceWeb (2013) Niger Armed Forces. 13 September 2013. Available at: http://www.defenceweb.co.za/index.php?option=com_content&view=article&id=31880:niger-armed-forces&catid=119:african-militaries&Itemid=255

Fund for Peace (2015) *Fragile States Index, 2015*. Available at: http://library.fundforpeace.org/library/fragilestatesindex-2015.pdf

Gberie, L (2016) *Crime, Violence and Politics: Drug trafficking and counter-narcotics policies in Mali and Guinea*. Foreign Policy at Brookings. Washington, DC: Brookings Institute. Available at: https://www.brookings.edu/wp-content/uploads/2016/07/Gberie-Mali-and-Guinea-final.pdf

International Crisis Group (2012) Mali: Avoiding escalation, Africa Report No. 189, 18 July 2012. Available at: http://www.crisisgroup.org/~/media/Files/africa/west-africa/mali/189-mali-avoiding-escalation-english.pdf

International Crisis Group (2015) The Central Sahel: The perfect sandstorm, Africa Report No. 227. Published 25 June 2016. Available at: http://www.crisisgroup.org/~/media/Files/africa/west-africa/227-the-central-sahel-a-perfect-sandstorm.pdf

Institute Malien de Recherche Action pour la Paix (2015) *Autoportrait du Mali: Les obstacles à la paix*. Published March 2015. Available at: http://reliefweb.int/sites/reliefweb.int/files/resources/2015_03_02_Mali_Autoportrait_FR_0.pdf

Jeune Afrique (2012) Mali: Mahmoud Dicko, imam médiateur. Published 12 April 2012. Available at: http://www.jeuneafrique.com/140316/politique/mali-mahmoud-dicko-imam-m-diateur/

Lebovich, A (2006) The hotel attacks and the militant realignment in the Sahara–Sahel region, *CTC Sentinel*, **9** (1). Available at: https://www.ctc.usma.edu/posts/the-hotel-attacks-and-militant-realignment-in-the-sahara-sahel-region

Lebovich, A (2013) The local face of jihadism in northern Mali, *CTC Sentinel*, **6** (64). Available at: https://www.ctc.usma.edu/posts/the-local-face-of-jihadism-in-northern-mali

Research on Islam and Muslims in Africa (RIMA) (2014) *Sufis vs Salafis: Winning Friends and Interdicting Enemies in Islamic Africa* by Dr Timothy Furnish. Policy Paper Vol. 1, No. 1. Published April 2013. Available at: https://muslimsinafrica.wordpress.com/2013/04/11/sufis-v-salafis-winning-friends-and-interdicting-enemies-in-islamic-africa-dr-timothy-r-furnish/

Small Arms Survey (2015) *Small Arms Survey Yearbook*. Chapter 6: Expanding arsenals: Insurgent arms in northern Mali. Available at: http://www.smallarmssurvey.org/fileadmin/docs/A-Yearbook/2015/eng/Small-Arms-Survey-2015-Chapter-06-EN.pdf

Spet, S (2015) Operation Serval: Analysing the French strategy against jihadi in Mali, *Air and Space Power Journal: Africa and Francophonie*, **6** (3). Available at: http://www.au.af.mil/au/afri/aspj/apjinternational/aspj_f/digital/pdf/articles/2015_3/spet_e.pdf

Stanford University (2017) *Al-Qaeda in the Islamic Magrheb*. Stanford University's Mapping Militants Project. Published 6 June 2015. Available at: https://web.stanford.edu/group/mappingmilitants/cgi-bin/groups/view/65

Stratfor (2012) Mali besieged fighters fleeing Libya. Published 2 February 2012. Available at: https://www.stratfor.com/weekly/mali-besieged-fighters-fleeing-libya

Terrorism Research and Analysis Consortium (2017) *Movement for Unity and Jihad in West Africa*. Available at: http://www.trackingterrorism.org/group/movement-unity-and-jihad-west-africa-mujao

The Atlantic (2012) How confused protesters seized an African country. Published 4 April 2012. Available at: http://www.theatlantic.com/international/archive/2012/04/the-accidental-coup-how-confused-protesters-seized-an-african-country/255442/

The Guardian (2012) Mali: No rhythm or reason as militants declare war on music. Published 23 October 2012. Available at: http://www.theguardian.com/world/2012/oct/23/mali-militants-declare-war-music

The Guardian (2014) The book rustlers of Timbuktu: How Mali's ancient manuscripts were saved. Published 23 May 2014. Available at: https://www.theguardian.com/world/2014/may/23/book-rustlers-timbuktu-mali-ancient-manuscripts-saved

The Telegraph (2016) 'France boosted al-Qaeda in Mali by paying £11 m in ransoms,' says US ambassador. Published 8 February 2013. Available at: http://www.telegraph.co.uk/news/worldnews/africaandindianocean/mali/9857723/France-boosted-al-Qaeda-in-Mali-by-paying-11m-in-ransoms-says-US-ambassador.html

The Washington Post (2014) Pentagon set to open second base in Niger as it expands operations in Africa. Published 31 August 2014. Available at: https://www.washingtonpost.com/world/national-security/pentagon-set-to-open-second-drone-base-in-niger-as-it-expands-operations-in-africa/2014/08/31/365489c4-2eb8-11e4-994d-202962a9150c_story.html

United Kingdom Foreign and Commonwealth Office (2013) Traffickers and terrorists: Drugs and violent jihad in Mali and the wider Sahel. 12 November 2013. Available at: http://www.refworld.org/docid/53f361204.html

United Kingdom Parliament (2013) Extremism and political instability in North and West Africa. Address by Guy Lankester. Available at: http://www.publications.parliament.uk/pa/cm201314/cmselect/cmfaff/writev/extremism/m08.htm

United Nations (2013) 'Arc of Instability' across Africa, if left unchecked, could turn continent into launch pad for larger-scale terrorist attacks, Security Council told. Published 13 May 2013. Available at: http://www.un.org/press/en/2013/sc11004.doc.htm

United Nations (2017) Supporting political process and helping stabilize Mali. Available at: http://www.un.org/en/peacekeeping/missions/minusma/index.shtml

United Nations Development Programme (2015) *Mali 2015: Human Development Indicators*. Available at: http://hdr.undp.org/en/countries/profiles/MLI

Westenfelder, F (2011) *Soldiers of Misfortune: The history of mercenaries*. Norderstedt: Herstellung & Verlag.

Chapter 5
Why the Tuareg have been demonised

Jeremy Keenan

Fifteen years ago, a foreign tourist, or anyone else for that matter, could travel across the western Sahara–Sahel region of Africa, from the Atlantic shores of Mauritania, through Mali and Niger to the Lake Chad region in almost complete safety. The biggest danger might have been falling down a well, treading on a scorpion, too much sun, or not carrying enough water. Today, few places in the world are more dangerous.

Few parts of Africa have a more complex ethnographic make-up than the Sahel. If the traveller had passed through the northern parts of the Sahel – Timbuktu, Kidal, Ménaka, Tahoua and Agades – the majority of the people they would have met would have been Tuareg, whose lands traditionally extended over northern Mali and northern Niger, southern Algeria and south-west Libya, with small communities in most neighbouring states. The traveller would most likely have also made the acquaintance of some of the Arab tribes of the northern Sahel, such as the Kunta, Berabiche, Lamar and Tasara.

If the traveller's latitude had been a few degrees further south, passing through the southern Sahel, most of the peoples whom they would have met would have been members of the 'black African' Peul (Fulani), Bambara and the many other ethno-linguistic groups that inhabit the Sahel.

Today, such a journey would be extremely difficult. In recent years, the security situation in the region has deteriorated to the point where Western powers, notably France and the United States, aided by military contingents from Germany, Holland, Sweden, and soon possibly Canada, not to mention other European Union (EU) trainers and the United Nations (UN), are militarising the region in what their intelligence agencies are now referring to as the 'long war' against 'international jihadism'.

The region's first introduction to post-9/11 'terrorism' was in early 2003 when 32 European tourists were kidnapped in the Algerian Sahara and taken hostage to Mali.[1] At that time, local Tuareg tribesmen were quick to see the writing on the wall. They knew that the moment terrorism reared its head in the Sahara, Western tourism would collapse and with it the main cash base of their economy. For both ideological and economic reasons, Tuareg in Algeria,

Libya, Mali and Niger all sought to take up arms against the 'terrorists' and rid the region of this new enemy.

At the start of this saga in 2003, when the Global War on Terrorism (GWOT) was being introduced into the region, the Tuareg were still revered by most Westerners, or at least by those who knew much about them. Journalists and other writers invariably spoke of them in almost heroic terms as the true nomads and the fabled blue-veiled warriors of the Sahara. They had been immortalised, often romantically, in European colonial and post-colonial literature. There is no recent demographic survey of the Tuareg, but they are estimated to number around three million, with the biggest concentrations in Mali and Niger.[2] They had opposed French colonial forces in the 19th and 20th centuries, succumbed to the independence of their various countries in the 1960s, before standing opposed to Islamist extremism and terrorism during the first years of this century.

Today, their traditional reputation, albeit slightly exaggerated and romanticised, has virtually gone. Instead, Tuareg are now being demonised in much of the Western and regional media as terrorists and jihadists. One reason for this is because the leader of the most prominent jihadist groups in the Sahel is a Malian Tuareg – Iyad ag Ghali.

How is this possible? How can a whole people be rebranded, albeit largely in the popular media, so easily and in such a short space of time? More importantly, is the Tuaregs' current reputation – as terrorists and jihadists – true or merely propaganda or hyperbole, or based on the activities of only a few individuals? And, if it does bear any truth, how has it happened?

This chapter traces the situation of the Tuareg populations in Mali, Niger, Algeria and Libya since the start of this millennium, and explains how and why they have become demonised in much of the media, first as terrorists and more recently as jihadists, and whether such labels have any justification.

This chapter is divided into nine sections. Ideally, it should cover the entire pre-colonial, colonial and post-colonial histories of the Tuareg people – but that would entail several volumes. Instead, it starts at the turn of this millennium with one brief, crucial but little-known period of contemporary Tuareg history, which lasted barely four years.

The Tuaregs' Prague Spring

Czechoslovakia's Prague Spring was a period of political liberalisation during the Soviet Union's domination of the country. It began on 5 January 1968 when the reformist, Alexander Dubček, was elected First Secretary of the Communist Party of Czechoslovakia. Dubček introduced partial decentralisation of the economy, democratisation and freedoms that loosened restrictions on the media, speech and travel. It lasted seven and a half months, until 21 August, when the Soviet Union and other members of the Warsaw Pact invaded the country to halt the reforms.[3]

Although the Tuaregs' Prague Spring was felt in all Tuareg countries, it was most pronounced in Algeria, where it lasted about four years, from the election of Abdelaziz Bouteflika as president and the effective ending of the country's 'dirty war' in 1999, to the launch of the GWOT in Algeria in 2003.

For the prior seven to eight years, Ahaggar, the huge massif of southern Algeria (capital Tamanrasset), had been closed to the outside world. This was not simply because of Algeria's civil war (or 'dirty war' as it was commonly referred to), which prohibited foreign tourists from entering, but because the region was effectively cut off from access, at least to foreigners, on all other sides. Libya was closed to tourists because of the post-Lockerbie (1988) sanctions, while Tuareg rebellions in Niger, and especially Mali, during the 1990s effectively prohibited access through the Sahel.[4] The closure of the Algerian–Morocco border, along with the western Sahara dispute, cut off access from the west and northwest.

Ahaggar had been further isolated from the world by the antiquated nature of the Sahara's communications system. During the 1990s, there was no internet or satellite communications system in the region – only a dilapidated phone service, which, at best, might reach Algiers, and an equally decrepit postal service. The same was true for the Tuareg regions of Libya, Niger and Mali.

In the decade prior to 1992, the number of foreign tourists visiting Ahaggar and the Tassili n'Ajjer regions of southern Algeria, the Tuareg's traditional domain, reached about 10 000 a year. Aside from the Tuaregs' semi-nomadic husbandry, which had been reduced over the years to little more than subsistence level, tourism was their main source of income.

To a lesser extent, the same was true for Niger and Mali, at least prior to the Tuareg rebellions in these countries in the 1990s. Several Algerian Tuaregs became astute businessmen and registered themselves as tourist agencies. Several had European spouses or good contacts in Europe with whom they set up tourism partnerships.

The European business partner recruited tour groups, usually small in number and affluent, from within their local French, German, Swiss, British or other national markets, arranged their air travel, and sometimes even accompanied them to Algiers and then on to Tamanrasset.

The same had been true in Niger and Mali. Such Tuareg tourism agencies in Tamanrasset were invariably linked to Tuareg business partners in Niger and Mali, notably in Agades and Kidal respectively. They employed cameleers, guides, cooks, drivers and others, which saw a regular flow of cash into even the most distant nomadic camps. These Tuareg had usually built and staffed their own gîtes (lodges) and campsites in and around Tamanrasset and conducted tours – on foot, camel or four-wheel-drive vehicles – across the entire vast region. Similar operations, although on a smaller scale, were found in Agades and Kidal.

In 1992, Algeria's military regime, in an effective coup d'état, annulled the country's democratic elections that would have brought to power the world's first democratically elected Islamist government. The coup led to the start of Algeria's 'dirty war'. Almost overnight, the Algerian Tuareg's lucrative tourism industry came to a halt. The Tuareg were forced to rely once again on their own meagre resources and their wits. For the next seven or eight years, they were left to contemplate what might have been, and what they might do if Algeria's dirty war came to an end and foreigners once again dared venture into their land. In Niger and Mali, Tuareg rebellions against their governments in the 1990s had had a similar effect on the tourist industry.

For the Algerian Tuareg, these years of reflection led them to realise that the type of mass tourism that had developed in the 1980s was unsustainable. It was destructive of their fragile environment and cultural heritage, which were what had attracted tourists to the region in the first place. They, therefore, spent much of their seven years of global isolation planning and even registering local civil society organisations that would foster an eco-friendly, alternative tourism.[5] They reflected on and planned how the region in future could become a world centre for sustainable 'green' tourism. They had more than enough time to plan even the minutest details of what they foresaw as a new age, and spread the word around all the outlying villages and distant camps, as if they were spreading a new gospel. They also planned to open or reopen business links and partnerships with Tuareg agencies in Niger and Mali.

In Algeria especially, late 1999 was the beginning of a new dawn, a new venture and a new world that would be 'green', sustainable and democratic. This message was not limited to Ahaggar and the Tassili. Algeria's Tuareg had spread it to their Tuareg contacts and former tourism business associates in Niger, Mali and even Libya. The whole of the central Sahara stood on the brink of a planned transformation that was designed to transform the entire region into a global heritage site, based on sustainable, 'alternative tourism', as they called it, which would be managed democratically by and for the benefit and livelihoods of the predominantly Tuareg local communities.[6]

Central to this new world was the internet and the use of satellite phones, which arrived in Tamanrasset at around this time. They not only enabled the Tuareg to remain in immediate contact with their agents in Europe and their business partners in Libya, Niger and Mali, but also with one another when travelling in the desert. More importantly, it gave them control over their own communications and business arrangements, enabling them to jump over and bypass the repressive and grasping government of Algiers, as well as the not so pro-Tuareg governments in Niamey and Bamako.

Launching the Global War on Terror

The Tuaregs' Prague Spring lasted barely four years. It was cut short in February 2003 by the kidnapping of 32 European tourists in the Algerian Sahara by members of Algeria's Groupe Salafiste pour la Prédication et le Combat (GSPC or Salafist Group for Preaching and Combat) – which would in 2006 change its name to Al-Qaeda in the Islamic Maghreb (AQIM).[7]

Although this incident brought post-9/11 terrorism to the Sahara and, in part, helped to justify the Bush administration's launch of a second or Sahara–Sahelian front in the GWOT a few months later, Algeria itself was no stranger to terrorism. Indeed, the origins of the Sahara's post-9/11 terrorism were rooted firmly in the events of Algeria's 'black decade' (the 1990s), which effectively began when Algeria's military regime annulled democratic elections in 1992 and thus prohibited the Front Islamique du Salut (FIS) from winning an overwhelming victory.

The outcome was the bloody dirty war of the 1990s, ostensibly between Islamists and the army, which left some 200 000 dead and Algeria indelibly scarred. The essential strategy of the army and the Département du Renseignement et de la Sécurité (DRS), the Algerian state intelligence agency, had been to infiltrate the Armed Islamic Group (GIA). As a result, by the time the war began to wind down in 1999, it was difficult to know who was killing whom. Army units and the DRS, masquerading as Islamists, had committed many of the worst civilian massacres and other atrocities.[8]

The main agency in the emerging counterterrorism and black-ops that came to characterise the post-9/11 Bouteflika era, both in Algeria and most of the surrounding Maghreb and Sahel regions, was the DRS. The DRS became the real power in Algeria, a state-within-a-state, which, under its director, General Mohamed 'Toufik' Mediène, wielded this power through an elaborate patronage system, which co-opted the political and business elite, and provided them access to both political and business rents.[9]

The essence of the relationship between the DRS and Western intelligence agencies was the DRS's unique experience of both infiltrating and fighting Islamists, or terrorists as they became known in the post-9/11 era, and the DRS's ability to provide the West with experience, knowledge of and access to terrorist networks. In return, the West was able to provide the DRS and the Algerian army with the new, high-tech weapon systems that had been denied them during the 1990s because of sanctions against Algeria's military regime.[10]

In January 2004, the Pan-Sahel Initiative (PSI) was launched, which saw the deployment of some 1 000 US forces across the Sahelian states of Mauritania, Mali, Niger and Chad. According to the office of counterterrorism in the US state department, the PSI was a 'a state-led effort to assist Mali, Niger, Chad, and Mauritania in detecting and responding to suspicious movement of people and goods across and within their borders through training, equipment and co-operation. Its goals support two US national security interests in Africa: waging the war on terrorism and enhancing regional peace and security.'[11] Eighteen months later, in July 2005, the United States expanded the PSI into the Trans-Saharan Counterterrorism Initiative (TSCTI), involving an additional five countries: Algeria, Tunisia, Morocco, Senegal and Nigeria. Through the TSCTI, Washington succeeded in joining the two hydrocarbon-rich sides of the Sahara together in complex security arrangements, designed by America.[12] The problem for the Tuareg was that they found themselves virtually in the geographical centre of this US creation.

The decimation of Tuareg livelihoods

The region's residents did not welcome the PSI with open arms. While the US rhetoric at the time was that 'the Pan-Sahel Initiative [was] to enhance regional peace and security', many regional experts, as well as local people, notably the Tuareg, believed that the initiative would backfire by creating new problems and fuelling existing tensions in the region. That is precisely what has happened.[13][14]

As life in the desert became more difficult, especially in the wake of the Sahelian droughts in the 1970s and 1980s, followed by Tuareg rebellions in both Niger and Mali in the 1990s, the region's nomadic and semi-nomadic Tuareg pastoralists became increasingly dependent on tourism for their livelihood. However, it was tourism, more than any other component of their economy, that was decimated: first by the 2003 kidnapping of 32 European tourists by the GSPC and then by the US launch of its Sahara–Sahel front in its GWOT.

The decimation of tourism impoverished many households and forced many local people, especially the Tuareg (who thanks to their 'Prague Spring' had come to effectively control local tourism) to seek their livelihood through various activities such as smuggling enterprises.

In times of impoverishment, people resort to desperate means. As Amadou Bocoum, deputy chairman of Mali's government commission to combat the proliferation of small arms, told the UN's regional news network (IRIN) in 2004: 'cigarette, fuel and weapon smuggling is carried out by the population (especially the desert nomads) and it is difficult to consider them as bandits as it is their only source of income and allows them to survive'.[15]

Furthermore, the view of many senior people in the region was that the impact of the PSI was more likely to attract terrorists than dispel them. Hervé Ludovic de Lys, for instance, head of the UN's West African Office for the Coordination of Humanitarian Affairs (OCHA), expressed the fear that terrorists hiding in the desert could exploit local peoples' anger at the crackdown on their livelihoods, stating: '[Terrorist] groups taking refuge in barely controllable areas could easily take advantage of the frustration of the Tubus and Tuaregs.' Similar sentiments were expressed by Aboubacrim ag Hindi, professor of law at Bamako University. He told IRIN that, 'the biggest danger in this region is not Al-Qaeda. It is famine. If the development of these zones is not undertaken, we may see more rebellion.'[16] His fears, as we shall presently see, became horribly true.

Almost all residents in the Sahara–Sahel region seemed to recognise that poverty had increased to the extent that if groups associated with Al-Qaeda emerged, they would quite likely find some measure of local support if they were able to provide people with resources.

Local people's awareness of this possibility made them additionally resentful of the American 'invasion', which they saw as concentrating on little more than what was soon proven to be wholly ineffectual military counterterrorism training, rather than the actual development of the region.

It is particularly pertinent that the PSI coincided with the worst locust plagues to blight the Sahel for at least 15 years. With chronic food shortages imminent, West African leaders tried to impress on Washington that the locust invasion should be treated like a war, because its capacity to destroy human life, as one of them told IRIN, 'was far greater than that of the worst conflicts'. And, as another Sahelian resident remarked, voicing the views of many: 'If the US had spent the same [money] on locust control as on terrorist control, we would not have this imminent loss of life.'[17]

Governments' provocation of the Tuareg

Although US 'neo-con' think tanks frequently published strategic papers emphasising the international threat posed by Al-Qaeda-linked terrorism in the Sahara–Sahel, there were few further terrorist incidents in the region throughout much of this period. Following the 2003 kidnappings in Algeria, the two most frequently cited terrorist incidents in the region prior to late 2006 were the gun battle in Chad between GSPC fighters and troops from both Niger and Chad in which 43 GSPC fighters were killed, and the 2005 attack in Lemgheity, Mauritania, led by the GSPC, which left 15 Mauritanian soldiers dead.[18] [19]

Extracting terrorism rents: The Niger and Algerian examples

Most of the TSCTI countries were only too happy to go along with Washington's GWOT strategy, because it provided them with what can be described as 'terrorism rents' in the form of US military and financial largesse. In Mauritania, the autocratic Ould Taya took this to extremes and became an embarrassment to the Americans by labelling almost all his political opponents – who comprised much of the civil population – as terrorists.[20]

In Niger and Mali, however, where Islamism was marginal and where there was no terrorism in the conventional meaning of the term[21] prior to the GSPC's arrival in 2003, the governments were a little more ingenious in their attempts to extract terrorism rents.

Their ingenuity took the form of provoking opposition and minority elements of one sort or another into demonstrations of civil unrest or even taking up arms, enabling the region to be branded – in the language of the United States European Command (EUCOM) and Washington officials – as a potential haven for terrorists. Unsurprisingly, the victims of these exercises have been the already marginalised minority populations, notably the Tuareg.

The best examples of such Tuareg provocation at that time came from Algeria and Niger. With the launch of the PSI and TSCTI, all governments in the region became more repressive in the knowledge that they had the United States behind them.

In Algeria, for example, corruption, especially the embezzlement of local-authority funds, became more brazen. Repression became more widespread, especially crack-downs on elements of civil society that expressed concern for human rights and democratic organisation, as well as the harassment of individuals who could be seen as potential opposition spokesmen. The secret police became more pervasive, more visible and more openly confident in their abuse of power.[22]

Since 2003, almost every town in the Algerian Sahara has experienced outbreaks of civil unrest and rioting. The most serious incident, however, was the civil rioting that overwhelmed Tamanrasset in July 2005. One reason why the town did not erupt earlier was because the Tuareg, who had long suspected that government authorities were trying to provoke such a response from them, had been urging restraint.

On 10 July, a seemingly peaceful demonstration over high unemployment turned, within a matter of minutes, into a rampaging mob. The rioting, which continued for two days, was unparalleled by any other Saharan riots for its violence against state and public property. Numerous government offices and other symbols of the state, as well as some 40 properties in the commercial centre, including the main market, were attacked, with many looted and then set alight. The town literally went up in smoke.[23]

An estimated 150 youths, nearly all Tuareg, were immediately jailed. The townspeople, especially the Tuareg, were furious, demanding the youths be freed on the grounds that the police had provoked them into rioting. The court responded by sitting in closed session under heavy security. The surrounding streets were cleared and no one was allowed to attend the hearings at which 64 youths were given prison sentences, while the rest were given fines of around €60 each.

However, Tuareg elders claimed that *agents provocateurs* had incited the youths to riot and sought advice from lawyers based in Algiers. Evidence was eventually brought before the court proving that the riots, as the Tuareg had claimed, had indeed been whipped up and directed by police *agents provocateurs*. The court had no choice but to immediately free the 64 imprisoned youths.[24]

Tuareg provocation has been even more pronounced in Niger, one of the world's poorest countries and, therefore, especially appreciative of American largesse. By the end of 2007, Niger, the country in the region least able to excite the Americans with any significant Islamist activity, was engulfed in a Tuareg rebellion. However, long before then, the governments in the region had earmarked their marginalised Tuareg populations as the means to acquire terrorism rents.

Four weeks after the official launch of the PSI, the Nigerien government accused a prominent Tuareg, Rhissa ag Boula, of complicity in the killing of Adam Amangué, a young member of the ruling National Movement for the Development of Society – Nassara (MNSD-Nassara).[25]

During the 1990s Tuareg rebellion in Niger, Ag Boula took over the leadership of the Front de Libération de l'Aïr et de l'Azawak (FLAA) after the death of Mano Dayak in 1995. Ag Boula was, therefore, the FLAA's signatory to the 1995 peace accord, which formally marked the end of the Tuareg rebellion in Niger. As part of the post-rebellion reintegration process, Ag Boula was appointed minister of tourism and crafts.

Local people regarded Amangué's murder as most uncharacteristic, describing the three bullets in his head and two in his stomach as a 'mafia-style' killing. Ag Boula, who denied any involvement in the murder, was dismissed as minister on 12 February 2004. Three days later, he was arrested in a move many people believed was designed to provoke the Tuareg into taking up arms so that the government could secure more US military aid.

If that were so, Ag Boula's arrest and detention had the desired effect, increasing political tension among the Tuareg, especially in their traditional stronghold, the Aïr Massif. During the course of the summer, the region experienced an escalation in banditry, for which Ag Boula's brother, Mohamed ag Boula, reportedly claimed responsibility.

That was enough for the Nigerien government to send some 150 troops into the Aïr Massif in September, in a move that many thought would ignite a new Tuareg rebellion.[26] However, the troops, who were recently trained by the United States as part of its PSI, were ambushed by the Tuareg and at least one soldier was killed, four wounded and four taken hostage.

Radio France Internationale (RFI) subsequently carried an interview with Ag Boula's brother in which he said that he was leading a 200-strong group that was fighting to defend the rights of the Tuareg, Tubu and Semori nomadic populations of northern Niger, and that he was personally responsible for the ambush.[27]

Northern Aïr remained tense and effectively cordoned off from the outside world throughout the winter months of 2004 and into 2005. However, there were no further serious incidents, largely due to Tuareg restraint and the good offices of the Libyan leader, Muammar Gaddafi, who secured the Niger soldiers' release on 8 February.

On 4 March, Ag Boula was released after 13 months in prison without any charges being brought against him. In 2011, under the new presidency of Mahamadou Issoufou, Ag Boula was rehabilitated. In 2016, he was appointed as a minister and given charge of development programmes in the Agades region.

A new wave of Tuareg rebellions

A new Tuareg rebellion began in Niger in February 2007 and spread to Mali a few months later.[28] There were multiple possible causes of the Niger rebellion. In addition to a sense of political marginalisation, the Tuareg were aggrieved by the conditions and expansion of uranium mining in northern Niger. In particular, they were angered and concerned by the exploitative nature of these enterprises, the threat of an impending ecological disaster, and abuse of Tuareg indigenous rights by the government and foreign companies. Other grievances included the government's failure to adhere to the 1995 peace agreement, as well as the impact of the US's GWOT.

Although all of these grievances were legitimate and serious, none warranted a rebellion. Indeed, the circumstances that led to the first shots being fired in the village of Iferouane on 8 February, are still unexplained. Contemporaneous research in the region revealed that almost all Niger's Tuareg feared another rebellion and had no desire to take up arms again; government atrocities in the 1990s rebellion were still fresh in their minds.

The evidence from Niger and Mali suggests that both rebellions may well have been triggered by external parties. This was especially true of Niger, where there are allegations that President Mamadou Tandja and his interior minister,

Albadé Abouba, were determined to draw the Tuareg into a bloody conflict.

After a spate of atrocities committed by Niger's Armed Forces (FAN) during the spring and summer of 2007, in which they attacked villages and encampments, killing the disabled and old men, women and children, the Niger Tuareg – now organised in the Mouvement des Nigériens pour la Justice (MNJ) – feared a genocide.[29] Genocide fears were reinforced on 27 September, during Ramadan itself, when a FAN patrol stopped a small convoy of five vehicles in the extreme north of Aïr. The soldiers forced the passengers out of the vehicles, divided them into light-skinned and dark-skinned groups, and presuming them to be Tuareg, executed the 12 light-skinned ones in cold blood.

The following day, these troops came across a series of Tuareg encampments in the same region. The soldiers rampaged through the tents, killing 22 innocent men, women and children and slaughtering an unknown number of livestock.[30]

At the end of Ramadan, a government television station twice broadcast comments from a Nigerien civil society leader who said that ethnic Tuareg rebels could be exterminated in 48 hours.[31] Indeed, a report on the conflict in Niger, commissioned by the United Nations High Commissioner for Refugees (UNHCR) in August, had already warned that President Tandja was likely to unleash his armed forces on the Tuareg civilian population.[32] That is precisely what he did. In the week before Christmas 2007, the UK-based Amnesty International and the US-based Human Rights Watch, denounced Niger's armed forces for committing war crimes.[33]

Worse was to come, with the UN being notified in writing on 29 March 2008 that the policy and actions of President Tandja towards the Tuareg constituted genocide.[34] The letter, written on behalf of the Tuareg people of northern Niger, urged the UN 'to intervene as a matter of urgency and to protect them from such genocidal actions'.

In Mali, the rebellion was also triggered by government armed forces committing atrocities against Tuareg civilians, although of considerable less severity than in Niger.

In both countries, the governments refused to dignify the Tuareg by calling them rebels. Rather, they referred to them as insurgents, criminals and increasingly as terrorists, and tried to link them to AQIM and drug traffickers. Indeed, the Tuareg, except for Iyad ag Ghali and his small group of followers (who will be discussed shortly), were violently opposed to AQIM.

The number of people killed in the two rebellions has not been confirmed, but runs into the hundreds, not thousands. Nor did either rebellion come to an end in any sort of official peace and reconciliation process. Rather, they fizzled out in a state of exhaustion and bitterness.

In Niger, the key MNJ leader was deposed by his people and moved to Libya, while Tandja was overthrown in a coup d'état in 2010. While Issoufou's new government went to considerable ends to rehabilitate the Tuareg rebels, there were no such reconciliatory moves by Mali's government. This left the rebellion to flare up again on a much larger scale at the end of 2011.

The marginalisation and criminalisation of the Tuareg

With the rebellions petering out in a state of exhaustion, and with no peace agreements or attempts at reconciliation, the Tuareg populations in both countries found themselves even more marginalised and impoverished. The rebellions, along with the renewal of hostage taking in 2008, destroyed what was left of the tourism industry. Most international NGOs also left the region, taking with them the often lucrative cash flows attached to the international development sector.

As in the 1970s and 1980s, when drought devastated the Sahel, many Tuareg took the well-trodden path to Libya in search of employment: sometimes in the oil fields, but more often in Gaddafi's foreign legion and security forces. Others drifted into a life of banditry and lawlessness, with a growing number seeking money and excitement as guides, drivers and armed guards in the trans-Saharan cocaine-trafficking business. From around 2005/06 onwards, South American cocaine was, on an increasing scale, shipped or flown into West Africa and its Malian hub.[35]

Although mostly in the hands of the Berabiche, Lamhar and Tilemsi Arabs – and protected by the highest levels of the state and security services, especially in Mali, Mauritania and Algeria – most Tuareg tribes and rebel groups took protection money and 'rent' for safe passage through their territories. Drug trafficking increasingly became the financial mainstay of many Sahelian communities – Arab and Tuareg – and of the rebellions.[36]

In 2008, hostage taking resumed. The first Westerners taken hostage since 2003 were seized in Tunisia and taken to Mali.[37] By the end of 2011, some 70 Westerners, including the 32 in 2003, had been taken hostage in the Sahara–Sahel. Most kidnappings were attributed to AQIM and the Algerian outlaw Mokhtar Belmokhtar.[38] Nevertheless, as with drug trafficking, the Tuareg received much more than their fair share of blame.

In the same way that the highest levels of state were protecting drug trafficking, there are widespread allegations that the DRS was involved, to one degree or another, in all of these hostage-taking cases.[39]

However, one of the primary reasons why the Tuareg became branded as kidnappers was because of a small Tuareg group commanded by Iyad ag Ghali and his cousin, Hamada ag Hama (aliases Abdelkrim Taleb (preacher) and Abdelkrim al-Targui).[40] Both were closely associated with the DRS, along with Abdelkrim's nephews, Haïba ag Achérif and Mohamed Ali ag Wadoussène. The group was heavily involved in kidnapping Westerners; Taleb would do the kidnapping, while Ag Ghali negotiated the ransom and release.

With the Americans trying to link drug trafficking to Al-Qaeda and with Ag Ghali and Taleb so heavily involved in hostage taking, it is hardly surprising that the Tuareg as a whole were increasingly being branded as terrorists and linked to AQIM in the media and local governments.

The fall of Gaddafi brings crisis to the Sahel

The Libyan rebellion and the overthrow of Colonel Muammar Gaddafi in September 2011 had profound ramifications for the Tuareg and the Sahel. During the course of the rebellion, several hundred Tuareg had signed up as mercenaries to help Gaddafi. However, many of the thousands of Tuareg who migrated to Libya during the 1970s and 1980s, and who often lived as second-class citizens under his regime, were tarnished with the same brush as the mercenaries and forced to return to the Sahel.

The Niger government was aware of the potential problems posed by these returnees and went to considerable lengths to reincorporate them into civil society. The Mali government made no such effort. The result was that several hundred well-armed Tuareg fighters returning to Mali met up with Ibrahim ag Bahanga's remaining rebels in northeast Mali and formed the Mouvement National de Libération de L'Azawad (MNLA). This secessionist force was bent on creating the independent state of Azawad – the Tuareg name for northern Mali.

The MNLA posed a serious threat to Algeria as well, which realised that the well-armed secessionist force could easily defeat Mali's ill-led and ill-equipped armed forces and potentially ignite simmering Tuareg unrest in Algeria's south.

The first shots in the new rebellion were fired in January 2017, with the MNLA rebels and their Islamist allies quickly putting the Malian army to flight, which, in turn, triggered a coup d'état in Bamako and the collapse of the government.

On 6 April, the MNLA declared the independent state of Azawad. However, within days, the MNLA was effectively sidelined by the Islamists, led by Iyad ag Ghali, Abou Zaïd and the Mokhtar Belmokhtar. The Tuareg MNLA rebels were politically and militarily discredited and marginalised as the Islamists took control of northern Mali.

Western military intervention, and a fragile peace and divisions among the Tuareg

By January 2012, with the Islamists threatening to break out of Azawad and threaten the capital Bamako itself, the French intervened militarily. Within a week, France's Operation Serval had halted the Islamists' advance and began driving them back into the Tigharghar Mountains in the Adrar des Ifoghas. The number of Islamists killed has never been adequately accounted for but probably numbered at least 200, possibly more, with many escaping northwards into Algeria, Tunisia and Libya, while others melted back into civil society.[41]

The cities of Timbuktu and Gao were soon relieved from the ruthless, supposedly sharia rule that had been imposed on them through much of 2012, while Kidal remained in the hands of the MNLA.

Two and a half years later, in June 2015, an alliance of predominantly Tuareg rebels and the Malian government signed a peace agreement in Algiers. The French military intervention failed to oust the Islamists, now labelled jihadists, from Mali. Furthermore, the main jihadist threat in Mali, led primarily by Iyad ag Ghali, is once again expanding across the country and neighbouring states, notably Niger and Burkina Faso, and possibly threatening others, such as Mauritania, Senegal and Ivory Coast.

Moreover, the French military intervention has been expanded under Operation Barkhane, with some 4 000 to 5 000 French troops now deployed across Mali, Niger and Chad in an attempt to arrest the increasing jihadist threat. It is supported by some 13 000 UN peacekeepers in Mali, and an increasing number of other Western powers. The United States and Germany are building military bases in Niger, with smaller contingents from Holland and Sweden, and with Canada likely to join them.

The Malian Tuareg, like those in Niger, Algeria and Libya, have always been characterised by tribal and class divisions. Today, in addition to these traditional divisions, they are divided into at least six post-2012 political groupings, aligned across at least two broad and fast-changing alliances, which reflect the ethnic complexity of Azawad (northern Mali).

The two broad alliances are the Coordination des Mouvements de l'Azawad (CMA) and the Platform. The CMA consists of the core MNLA and the Haut Conseil pour l'Unité de l'Azawad (HCUA), which comprises mostly Tuareg of the 'noble' Ifoghas lineage and is suspected by many to have close links with Iyad ag Ghali's jihadist Ansar al-Din. It also consists of dissident Arabs who broke from the original Mouvement Arabe de l'Azawad (MAA); the Tuareg Coalition du Peuple pour l'Azawad (CPA), which split from the MNLA in 2014 but rejoined in late 2016; the Coordination des Mouvements et Forces Patriotiques de Résistance (CMFPR II), which split from CMFPR I and is comprised mostly of Peul (Fulani), Songhai and other militia, such as the Ganda Iso; and, since October 2016, the Congrès pour la Justice dans l'Azawad (CJA), comprising mostly Kel Intessar Tuareg.

The Platform consists of predominantly 'pro-government' groups, notably the Groupe Autodéfense Touareg Imghad et Alliés (GATIA), consisting of the Imghad (vassal) Tuareg and their allies, led by the former Tuareg Malian army colonel (now General) El Hadj ag Gamou; the original Mouvement Arabe de l'Azawad (MAA); the remains of CMFPR I; the Peul Mouvement pour la Défense de la Patrie (MDP), which switched from the CMA to the Platform in June 2016; and the Mouvement pour le Salut de l'Azawad (MSA), led by two Tuareg of the Chamanamas and Daoussak tribes, which split from the MNLA in September 2016.

The key parties in the CMA are the predominantly Tuareg MNLA and HCUA and the increasingly influential CMFPR II, led by Ibrahim Abba Kantao, a native of Gao (Cité des Askia) and also the leader of the Forces de Libération du Nord du Mali (FLN) and Ganda Iso. The key person in the Platform, although invariably operating more behind the scene, is El Hadj ag Gamou. In this complex and very dynamic post-2012 political landscape, the MNLA is now a relatively weaker entity than at the start of the 2012 rebellion, although it still effectively holds de facto power over Kidal.

Within this landscape, the major cleavages, at least potentially, are between the MNLA and GATIA, who spent much of 2015–2016 in a state of conflict, and between both the MNLA and GATIA and Iyad ag Ghali's Ansar al-Din, which is still outside both alliances (although with unofficial ties to the HCUA) and outlawed as a terrorist/jihadist organisation. The fight between GATIA and Ansar al-Din is based more on personal rivalries and ambitions than on ideology, with one bone of contention being that Iyad married Ag Gamou's first wife.

Since the start of the Tuareg rebellion and Islamist insurgency in January 2012, Mali's Tuareg have been subjected to demonisation in both the local and Bamako-based Western media. This is because these media platforms are reliant on information from Mali's south, the prejudices of the Bamako government against the Tuareg and Arabs of northern Mali, and a lack of understanding of northern Mali's fundamentals. There is also a complete lack of appreciation of the complex situations and tribulations most Tuareg groups have endured since the rebellions of the 1990s and the subsequent GWOT.

Indeed, the fact that it took two and half years to achieve a peace agreement, which has still not been implemented, is largely due to the Bamako government's ill will towards its northern populations, especially the Tuareg. As a result, the international and local media have been prone to follow Bamako authorities' example in demonising the Tuareg in general, not just as rebels, but also as terrorists and now even as jihadists.

The threat of Islamist extremism to Niger's Tuareg

Thanks to the more understanding and accommodating policies of the Issoufou government, Niger averted a Malian-type crisis. Brigi Rafini, a Tuareg from the Agades region, has been prime minister since 2011, while Rhissa ag Boula, a former Tuareg rebel, is now the minister responsible for developing the predominantly Tuareg Agades region.

Since the end of the 2007–2009 rebellion, the biggest difficulty faced by Niger's Tuareg has probably been Algeria's closure of its frontier with Niger in January 2013. Algeria's stated reason was to prevent terrorists, driven out of Mali by France's military intervention there, from entering Algeria. However, there are also allegations that the real reason was to control and divert much of Niger's food supply and other Algerian trade with Niger into the hands of local Algerian Arabs.[42]

After the rebellion, with the tourism industry decimated, increasing numbers of Tuareg sought alternative livelihoods as seasonal workers in Algeria's southern city of Tamanrasset and running illegal taxis between Agades and Tamanrasset. However, the closure of the Algerian frontier eliminated these opportunities. As a result, more young Tuareg drifted into the criminal margins of banditry and drug trafficking, while a growing number moved into the people-trafficking business, which, until 26 May 2015, was quite legal, and saw an estimated 100 000 or more trans-Saharan migrants passing through Agades annually.[43] However, under pressure from the EU, Niger voted for a new law, with immediate effect, that prohibited the transport of migrants. The EU's promise to pump huge funds into alternative sustainable projects has yet to come to fruition.

With people trafficking criminalised, and more and more people trying to seek their fortunes in a proliferation of gold-rush ventures in Djado, Tibarakaten and elsewhere, many Tuareg have established businesses transporting people and goods to the gold fields, or even searching for gold themselves, but with few, if any, reports of fortunes being made.

However, the most serious impact of the Algerian border closure on Niger's Tuareg is that it has led to a dangerous radicalisation of the youth, the one thing that all Sahelian countries are trying to counter.

Many of the seasonal workers who had previously sought work in Tamanrasset went to Libya instead. There, many of the younger men got indoctrinated by extremist Islamist movements and on their return to Niger began trying to impose extremist Islamist rules on their camps and villages. In several villages in Aïr, the Tuareg mountainous stronghold north of Agades, radicalised youths have stopped the people playing traditional 'tamtam' music, forced women to wear the hijab, and prohibited women from shaking hands with men. This is a particularly dangerous development in the Sahel, where jihadist groups are increasingly making their presence felt.

Conclusion

Life in the desert is always hard. For most Tuareg, it has become even harder during the 21st century, and not by their own making. Washington's launch of a Sahara–Sahel front in the GWOT was a catastrophe for the entire region, especially the Tuareg, as livelihoods were destroyed and both American and local governments tried to brand them as terrorists or, at best, putative terrorists.

The fall of the Gaddafi regime in 2011 compounded the economic problems that GWOT brought to the region and set in motion a further and more serious Tuareg rebellion in Mali, which was possibly undermined by Algerian DRS's promotion of an Islamist insurgency.

Algeria's support for terrorism, and its own policy of relocating jihadism further south into the Sahel, enabled DRS agents such as Iyad ag Ghali, Abou Zaïd and the Mokhtar Belmokhtar to effectively take control of much of this part of the Sahara–Sahel. A small number of Tuareg have joined them, more out of economic necessity and adventure than any ideological reasons.

However, it has been the spread of jihadism following the French military intervention, especially through Iyad ag Ghali, that has given the Tuareg a bad name and led to their further demonisation.

To refer to the Tuareg in general as terrorists or jihadists is absurd: they are the one people who have struggled more than any other to rid the region of terrorists, jihadists and their ideologies. And yet the leading jihadist in the region is a Tuareg – Iyad ag Ghali.

Iyad ag Ghali has his supporters among some of Mali's Tuareg and among other ethnic groups in Mali. However, since early March 2017, his jihadist star shines ever brighter and further afield.

On 2 March, he announced that he was in command of a new jihadist entity called Nusrat al-Islam Wal Muslimin, meaning The Support Group for Islam and Muslims, which, at this stage, comprises Ansar al-Din, AQIM in the Sahara, the Mokhtar Belmokhtar's Al-Mourabitoun (including MUJAO), Mali's Macina Liberation Front, and possibly a few other small jihadist groups in Mali and Burkina Faso.[44]

There are several people in Mali who believe that there will never be a proper peace until Iyad ag Ghali is brought into the negotiations. That may be his aim. But, he also has many enemies among the Tuareg population, as well as other ethnic and political groups.

Many believe that the only reason why he is still alive is because he is protected by the Algerians, and, according to many sources, also by the French, in addition to Malian government interests and connections in the gulf. He has been described as both a triple and a quadruple agent. However, the fact that he remains a war criminal (yet to be convicted), an internationally wanted terrorist, and the region's leading jihadist does not mean that all other Tuaregs should be tarred with the same brush.

If it is legitimate to talk of an ethnic group in such general terms, it is true to say that few, if any, other people have suffered more from the GWOT and its consequences than the Tuaregs – and for reasons that are still little known or understood, except by themselves.

Endnotes

1 BBC (2003) Missing Sahara tourists rescued. Published 14 May 2003. Available at: http://news.bbc.co.uk/2/hi/africa/3026181.stm
2 Imperato, PJ and Imperato GH (n.d.) *The Historical Dictionary of Mali,* 4th edn. Lanham, MD: The Scarecrow Press.
3 Williams, K (1997) *The Prague Spring and its Aftermath: Czechoslovak politics, 1968–1970.* Cambridge: Cambridge University Press.
4 Otman, W and Karlsberg, E (2007) *The Libyan Economy: Diversification and international repositioning.* Berlin: Springer Verlag.
5 The two most prominent were the Union Nationale des Associations des Agences de Tourisme Alternatif (UNATA) and the Association des Agences de Tourisme Wilaya de Tamanrasset (ATAWT).
6 Much of the Central Sahara is already protected by UNESCO as a designated World Heritage Site. World Heritage Sites in the Sahara include: the Tassili-n-Ajjer (Algeria), the Rock Art sites of Tadrart Acacus (Libya), Ghadames (Libya), Timbuktu (Mali), the Air and Ténéré Natural Reserves (Niger), the Historic Centre of Agades (Niger), the Ancient Ksours of Ouadane, Chinguetti, Tichitt and Oualata (Mauritania).
7 Cristiani, D (2011) *Al-Qaeda in the Islamic Maghreb (AQIM): Implications for Algeria's regional and international relations.* IAI Working Papers No. 1107. Rome: Istituto affari internazionali.
8 Keenan, J (2009) *The Dark Sahara: America's War on Terror in Africa.* Chapter 8, Algeria's 'black decade'. London: Pluto Press, pp. 132–141.
9 The DRS command began to be dismantled in September 2013, after the In Amenas 'terrorist' attack of that year. General Mediène was 'retired' in late 2015. See, Keenan, J (2016) *The In Amenas Report.* International State Crime Initiative (ISCI). Published November 2016. Available at: http://statecrime.org/data/2016/11/KEENAN-IN-AMENAS-REPORT-FINAL-November-2016.pdf
10 Schindler, JR (2012) The ugly truth about Algeria, *The National Interest.* Published 10 July 2007. Available at: http://nationalinterest.org/commentary/the-ugly-truth-about-algeria-7146
11 US Department of State, Office of Counterterrorism (2002) Pan Sahel Initiative. Published 7 November 2002. Available at: https://2001-2009.state.gov/s/ct/rls/other/14987.htm
12 See, Keenan, J (2013) *The Dying Sahara: US imperialism and terror in Africa*, Chapter 2. London: Pluto Press, pp. 1–13.
13 IRIN (2004) Famine not fanaticism poses greatest threat in Sahel. Published 14 October 2004. Available at: http://www.irinnews.org/feature/2004/10/14
14 A particularly good example of EUCOM's view of its role in the Sahara–Sahel can be gleaned from reading the evidence given to the US House of Representatives: Pope, WP (2005) Eliminating Terrorist Sanctuaries: The role of security assistance. Hearing before the

Subcommittee on International Terrorism and Non-proliferation of the Committee on International Relations, House of Representatives. One Hundred and Ninth Congress, First Session, 10 March 2005. Available at: https://2001-2009.state.gov/s/ct/rls/rm/43702.htm

15 IRIN (2004) Famine not fanaticism poses greatest threat in Sahel. Published 14 October 2004. Available at: http://www.irinnews.org/feature/2004/10/14
16 Ibid
17 Ibid.
18 Archer, T and Popovic, T (2007) *The Trans-Saharan Counter-Terrorism Initiative: The U.S. war on terrorism in North Africa*. The Finnish Institute for International Affairs, Report No. 16. Available at: https://www.files.ethz.ch/isn/32043/16_TransSaharanCounterTerrorism.pdf
19 Reuters (2013) U.S. transports suspected senior al-Qaeda members to Mauritania. Published 2 June 2013. Available at: http://www.reuters.com/article/us-mauritania-us-qaeda/u-s-transfers-suspected-senior-al-qaeda-member-to-mauritania-idUSBRE9500ER20130601
20 *The New York Times* (2005) Mauritania frees political prisoners jailed by ousted leader. Published 3 September 2005. Available at: http://query.nytimes.com/gst/fullpage.html?res=9802E7DC1431F930A3575AC0A9639C8B63
21 There are many definitions of terrorism. By 'conventional', I mean that terrorism is the threatened or employed use of violence against civilian targets for political objectives. 'Terrorism' does not include such fairly normal Saharan pursuits as smuggling, acts of political rebellion or the many forms of resistance of civil society to the corrupt and authoritarian regimes that hold sway over most of this part of Africa.
22 Amnesty International (2006) Algeria: Unrestrained powers: Torture by Algeria's military security. Published 10 July 2006. Available at: http://www.refworld.org/docid/44c614174.html
23 Keenan (2013) pp. 34–37.
24 For details of the riots, see Keenan (2013) pp. 34–37. Many of the imprisoned youths and their parents were interviewed by the author, as were the two lawyers who defended them and won their case. Algeria does not maintain accessible court records. However, the two lawyers were able to provide detailed accounts of what happened in the court.
25 *Jeune Afrique* (2014) Rhissa ag Boula: The end of a baroudeur? Published 1 March 2014. Available at: http://www.jeuneafrique.com/60077/archives-thematique/rhissa-ag-boula-la-fin-d-un-baroudeur/
26 Keenan, J (2010) Resisting imperialism: Tuareg Threaten US, Chinese and other foreign interests. In I Kohl and A Fischer (eds) *Tuareg Life Within a Globalized World: Saharan life in transition*. London: Tauris Academic Studies.
27 Keenan (2013).
28 See, Keenan (2013) pp. 74–91; 92–108.
29 Human Rights Watch (2007) Niger: Warring sides must end abuses of civilians. Published 19 December 2007. Available at: https://www.hrw.org/news/2007/12/19/niger-warring-sides-must-end-abuses-civilians
30 Eyewitness reports were collected and published less than two weeks later by the Society for Threatened Peoples. See: ReliefWeb (2007) Eye-witnesses report massacre of 32 Tuareg – independent investigation demanded. Published 9 October 2007. Available at: https://reliefweb.int/report/mali/eye-witnesses-report-massacre-32-tuareg-independent-investigation-demanded
31 Keenan (2010).
32 Keenan, J (2007) Niger: Tuareg unrest, its recent background and potential regional implications. A Writenet Report commissioned by the United Nations High Commissioner for Refugees, Emergency and Technical Support Service, August 2007.
33 Amnesty International (2007) Niger: Extrajudicial executions and population displacement

34 in the north of the country. Published 19 December 2007.
34 As defined in Resolution 260 (III) A of the United Nations General Assembly on 9 December 1948, namely the Convention on the Prevention and Punishment of the Crime of Genocide. Article 1 states that 'The Contracting Parties confirm that genocide, whether committed in time of peace or in time of war, is a crime under international law which they undertake to prevent and to punish.'
35 United Nations Office on Drugs and Crime (2011) *The Transatlantic Cocaine Market*. Published April 2011. Available at: http://www.refworld.org/pdfid/4e809c692.pdf
36 Ibid.
37 BBC (2008) Tricky dealings in hostage case. Published 28 March 2008. Available at: http://news.bbc.co.uk/2/hi/africa/7317495.stm
38 For details of all these kidnappings, see Keenan (2009). This number excludes 20 Italians taken hostage in Chad in 2006.
39 This was because Mokhtar Belmokhtar and AQIM leaders such as Abdelhamid Abou Zaïd were closely associated with Algeria's DRS. See: Archer and Popovic (2007) p. 11.
40 Wing, SD (2008) Mali: Politics of crisis, *African Affairs*, **112** (448), pp. 476–485. Available at: https://academic.oup.com/afraf/article-abstract/112/448/476/124663
41 Boeke, S and Schuurman, B (2015) 'Operation Serval': A strategic analysis of the French intervention in Mali, 2013–2014, *Journal of Strategic Studies*, **38** (6), pp. 801–825.
42 Keenan, J (2017) Algeria border closure has negative effects on Sahel, *New African*, No. 570. Published March 2017. Available at: http://newafricanmagazine.com/algeria-border-closure-negative-effects-sahel/
43 United Nations Office on Drugs and Crime (2011) The Role of Organized Crime in the Smuggling of Migrants from West Africa to the European Union. Publishing and Library Section, United Nations Office, Vienna. Available at: https://www.unodc.org/documents/human-trafficking/Migrant-Smuggling/Report_SOM_West_Africa_EU.pdf
44 *Newsweek* (2017) African jihadi groups unite and pledge allegiance to Al-Qaeda. Published 3 March 2017. Available at: http://www.newsweek.com/al-qaeda-groups-unite-sahel-563351

References

Amnesty International (2006) Algeria: Unrestrained powers: Torture by Algeria's military security. MDE 28/004/2006. Published 10 July 2006. Available at: http://www.refworld.org/docid/44c614174.html

Amnesty International (2007) Niger: Extrajudicial executions and population displacement in the north of the country. Published 19 December 2007.

Archer, T and Popovic, T (2007) *The Trans-Saharan Counter-Terrorism Initiative: The U.S. war on terrorism in North Africa*. The Finnish Institute for International Affairs, Report No. 16. Available at: https://www.files.ethz.ch/isn/32043/16_TransSaharanCounterTerrorism.pdf

BBC (2003) Missing Sahara tourists rescued. Published 14 May 2003. Available at: http://news.bbc.co.uk/2/hi/africa/3026181.stm

BBC (2008) Tricky dealings in hostage case. Published 28 March 2008. Available at: http://news.bbc.co.uk/2/hi/africa/7317495.stm

Boeke, S and Schuurman, B (2015) 'Operation Serval': A strategic analysis of the French intervention in Mali, 2013–2014, *Journal of Strategic Studies*, **38** (6), pp. 801–825.

Cristiani, D (2011) *Al-Qaeda in the Islamic Maghreb (AQIM): Implications for Algeria's regional and international relations*. IAI Working Papers No. 1107. Rome: Istituto Affari Internazionali.

Human Rights Watch (2007) Niger: Warring sides must end abuses of civilians. Published 19 December 2007. Available at: https://www.hrw.org/news/2007/12/19/niger-warring-sides-must-end-abuses-civilians

Imperato, PJ and Imperato, GH (n.d.) *The Historical Dictionary of Mali*, 4th edn. Lanham, MD: The Scarecrow Press.

IRIN (2004) Famine not fanaticism poses greatest threat in Sahel. Published 14 October 2004. Available at: http://www.irinnews.org/feature/2004/10/14

Jeune Afrique (2014) Rhissa Ag Boula: The end of a baroudeur? Published 1 March 2014. Available at: http://www.jeuneafrique.com/60077/archives-thematique/rhissa-ag-boula-la-fin-d-un-baroudeur/

Keenan, J (2007) Niger: Tuareg unrest, its recent background and potential regional implications. A Writenet Report commissioned by the United Nations High Commissioner for Refugees, Emergency and Technical Support Service, August 2007.

Keenan, J (2009) *The Dark Sahara: America's War on Terror in Africa*. Chapter 8: Algeria's 'black decade'. London: Pluto Press, pp. 132–141.

Keenan, J (2010) Resisting imperialism: Tuareg threaten US, Chinese and other foreign interests. In I Kohl and A Fischer (eds) *Tuareg Life within a Globalized World: Saharan life in transition*. London: Tauris Academic Studies.

Keenan, J (2013) *The Dying Sahara: US imperialism and terror in Africa*, Chapter 2. London: Pluto Press, pp. 1–13.

Keenan, J (2016) *The In Amenas Report*. International State Crime Initiative (ISCI). Published November 2016. Available at: http://statecrime.org/data/2016/11/KEENAN-IN-AMENAS-REPORT-FINAL-November-2016.pdf

Keenan, J (2017) Algeria border closure has negative effects on Sahel, *New African*, No. 570. Published March 2017. Available at: http://newafricanmagazine.com/algeria-border-closure-negative-effects-sahel/

Newsweek (2017) African jihadi groups unite and pledge allegiance to Al-Qaeda. Published 3 March 2017. Available at: http://www.newsweek.com/al-qaeda-groups-unite-sahel-563351

Otman, W and Karlsberg, E (2007) *The Libyan Economy: Diversification and international repositioning*. Berlin: Springer Verlag.

Pope, WP (2005) Eliminating Terrorist Sanctuaries: The role of security assistance. Hearing before the Subcommittee on International Terrorism and Non-proliferation of the Committee on International Relations, House of Representatives. One Hundred Ninth Congress, First Session, 10 March, 2005. Available at: https://2001-2009.state.gov/s/ct/rls/rm/43702.htm

ReliefWeb (2007) Eye-witnesses report massacre of 32 Tuareg: Independent investigation demanded. Published 9 October 2007. Available at: https://reliefweb.int/report/mali/eye-witnesses-report-massacre-32-tuareg-independent-investigation-demanded

Reuters (2013) U.S. transports suspected senior Al-Qaeda members to Mauritania. Published 2 June 2013. Available at: http://www.reuters.com/article/us-mauritania-us-qaeda/u-s-transfers-suspected-senior-al-qaeda-member-to-mauritania-idUSBRE9500ER20130601

Schindler, JR (2012) The ugly truth about Algeria, *The National Interest*. Published 10 July 2007. Available at: http://nationalinterest.org/commentary/the-ugly-truth-about-algeria-7146

The New York Times (2005) Mauritania frees political prisoners jailed by ousted leader. Published 3 September 2005. Available at: http://query.nytimes.com/gst/fullpage.html?res=9802E7DC1431F930A3575AC0A9639C8B63

United Nations Office on Drugs and Crime (2011) The Role of Organized Crime in the Smuggling of Migrants from West Africa to the European Union. Publishing and Library Section, United Nations Office at Vienna. Available at: https://www.unodc.org/documents/human-trafficking/Migrant-Smuggling/Report_SOM_West_Africa_EU.pdf

United Nations Office on Drugs and Crime (2011) *The Transatlantic Cocaine Market*. Published April 2011. Available at: http://www.refworld.org/pdfid/4e809c692.pdf

US Department of State, Office of Counterterrorism (2002) Pan Sahel Initiative. Published 7 November 2002. Available at: https://2001-2009.state.gov/s/ct/rls/other/14987.htm

Williams, K (1997) *The Prague Spring and its Aftermath: Czechoslovak politics, 1968–1970.* Cambridge: Cambridge University Press.

Wing, SD (2008) Mali: Politics of crisis, *African Affairs*, **112** (448), pp. 476–485. Available at: https://academic.oup.com/afraf/article-abstract/112/448/476/124663

Chapter 6

Visions of an alternative world: Understanding the background to Boko Haram

Graham Furniss

Introduction

Northeastern Nigeria is a land of savannah with rocky escarpment along the Cameroon border. A rich dark agricultural soil, *firki,* supports farming communities from Lake Chad to the regional capital Maiduguri. Borno, the name of the modern state whose capital is Maiduguri, was an important state in precolonial times with a long tradition of Islamic scholarship and trading relations across the Sahel and the Sahara. The majority of the population are Muslim Kanuri speakers, but speakers of many other languages live along the escarpment of the borderlands and in the south of the region. The primary northern Nigerian lingua franca, Hausa, is spoken widely as a second or third language. However, the larger towns, like much of Nigeria, have speakers of many languages living side by side. Rainy season agriculture is the mainstay of communities across the region, with intense manual labour in the fields between planting in May/June and harvest in September/October. Abundant rains are the salvation of these communities, providing sufficient millet, rice and vegetables to store and sustain a family through the dry season between November and April, as well as produce to sell, and seed to retain for the next sowing season. Late rains or extensive drought can limit a harvest and push families and communities to the limits of sustainability. This fragility is mitigated by dry season petty trading, moving the able-bodied to towns and cities in search of paid labour, thereby reducing the number of mouths to feed at home, and, if the system works, producing a cash income for the purchase of essential commodities. In a good year the cycle repeats as people return to their farms at the sign of rain in May and have the seed to plant, the land to till, and the labour to apply to the land. Across the tree-lined savannah and through patches of denser bush, the Fulani follow tracks, driving their cattle between grazing grounds and water. They move over farmland in the dry season and through the bush during the wet season, causing potential friction between farmers and herders if cattle damage crops. Maiduguri has for many years acted as a hub for cattle transported by road to the meat markets of the cities of the south. Some of these cattle are driven in from as far away as the other side of Lake Chad.

Economic decline

The mid to late 1970s was a period of economic boom in Nigeria. New oil revenues were accruing to the federal government, the reliance on agricultural produce, such as cotton and groundnuts for export, was disappearing, and government jobs, funded by oil revenues, were growing in reward and in number. The splitting of three regions into 12 states after the end of the civil war and then the creation of 21, then 30, and most recently, in 1996, 36 states multiplied bureaucracies and the number of government jobs. The boom years, until the crash came in the mid-1980s, created both a commercial and ruling elite in which some people rose fast and far. A burgeoning urban middle class was able to buy imported goods ranging from fridges to luxury cars, while the Naira traded at two to a British pound. When structural adjustments in the mid-1980s burst the economic bubble, the naira went to 200 to the pound, and spare parts for fridges or cars suddenly became hugely expensive, if not unobtainable, encouraging many Nigerians to become familiar with the 'make-do' culture of constant repairs. The aspiring middle class found their standard of living falling rapidly, while the mega rich seemed to be able to sustain their international lifestyles. Young people, who had aspired to join the older generation in promotion and reward, found that there was nowhere to go, no jobs that met their aspirations, or often no jobs at all. The industrial areas in places such as Bompai and Sharada in the great city of Kano, saw factory after factory close its doors, and school and university graduates had little or no prospects in government employment, while teaching salaries often went unpaid. A popular perception was that the rich had gained their wealth through corruption on a grand scale.

The early 1990s were years characterised by dislocation and disarray in many sectors. With the grim humour that typified many Nigerians' attitudes, the national electrical power authority, NEPA (Nigerian Electric Power Authority), became popularly known as Never Ever Power Anywhere. Ordinary Nigerians everywhere suffered from a lack of medicines in the clinics and hospitals, collapsing schools with no books or teachers, a corrupt and ineffective police and legal system, problems with water supply, transportation and safety on the roads, and few job opportunities. Stories of corruption abounded and people yearned for a way out of the apparent national chaos.

Islam in northern Nigeria

From before the 16th century in what is now northern Nigeria, walled towns and cities, such as Kano, Zaria, Rano, Daura and Katsina, were home to

Hausa aristocracies. There was a variety of craft and trade guilds supported by surplus production from agricultural communities, sometimes of slaves, in the surrounding farmlands. Islamic clerics were often resident in these towns and cities, providing religious and scribal services to the local ruler and to the urban community. Non-Islamic religious belief systems, particularly the *bori* spirit-possession cult, were practised in both rural and urban environments alongside Islam. In 1804, a jihad against un-Islamic practices in the Hausa city states led to the overthrow of the pre-existing Hausa rulers who were replaced by emirs of Fulani descent, led from a new capital at Sokoto and owing allegiance to the leader of the jihad, Shaikh Usman dan Fodio. The military overthrow was complemented by an ideological war to reform Islam as it was practised at the time, and to spread the Sunni Islamic faith through preaching and teaching throughout the land. The writings of the leaders of the jihad debated both the practice of the faith and the correct administration of the state, the practice of sharia law, and the promulgation of the branches of Islamic knowledge from theology and the traditions of the Prophet to Arabic grammar and the writing of religious verse. They translated and wrote in Arabic, Hausa and the language of the Fulani, Fulfulde. Among the issues they debated were the lawfulness of enslavement, the definition of a Muslim, and the prohibition against the enslavement of fellow Muslims.

Within the practice of Islam, there were a number of movements, including Sufi brotherhoods, which had their own ways of prayer, their own leaders, and their own forms of religious literature. The two major brotherhoods that spread and grew in adherents through the 19th and early 20th centuries were the Tijaniyya and the Qadiriyya. These were brotherhoods with members right across West Africa and beyond. Within the traditions of these movements, the importance of the founders, the role of saints revered by the membership, and a body of mystical knowledge were of central significance. By the 1960s and 1970s, with the rise of modern media and the introduction of printing presses, the Tijani or the Qadiri way of prayer was transformed from a set of beliefs and practices that were focused on the individual person and their own way of faith to a mass movement, where adherents would pray together in public, meet in brotherhood buildings, and distribute pamphlets and poetry as part of their proselytising. The Qadiriyya quickly matched this new style, led by the Tijaniyya in Kano, across the north generally. At the same time, there were many people who viewed themselves as pious Muslims but who did not belong to either brotherhood. With the greater public presence of the brotherhoods in the 1970s, there was a growth of anti-Sufi sentiment, arising from an abhorrence for the veneration of Sufi saints and mystical practices. A strong line of thought at the time of the jihad of 1804 (and ever since) has been the condemnation of introducing *bidi'a* (innovation) into the beliefs and practices of Islam. Adaptation, syncretism and addition have all been seen as movements away from the essential truths contained in the Qur'an and in the traditions of the Prophet. A return to the fundamentals is a rallying cry repeated often down the centuries. In the late 1970s, in northern Nigeria, an anti-Sufi movement called *izalat al-bidi'a* (removal of innovation), under the leadership of the cleric Abubakar Gumi, began to preach against adherence to the ways of the Sufi brotherhoods. The movement quickly spread, particularly among graduates, government employees and others outside the networks of the brotherhoods.

Traditions of rejection

The issue of what are the appropriate actions for a good Muslim faced with external or, indeed, internal threats has been the subject of debate over the years. A hundred years apart, around 1800 and 1900, there were discussions about options in the face of perceived threats. In 1800, the followers and extended family of Usman dan Fodio were faced with opposition from the rulers of a series of Hausa states, and their options were accommodation, fight or flight. In opting to fight, and declaring a jihad, the leaders of the jihad set out their justifications in terms of the maladministration and un-Islamic practices of previous regimes. A hundred years later, similar debates about options occurred when the descendants of the jihadists were faced with the arrival of the British in the first decade of the 20th century. The British defeated the military resistance they encountered, and the Sultan of Sokoto, Attahiru, a descendant of Usman dan Fodiyo, fled east and was killed at the battle of Burmi, while his followers dispersed. The options to fight, to flee, or to accommodate were illustrated in one of the first Hausa novels, *Gandoki*, published in 1934. The novel's eponymous warrior-hero, in the service of Sultan Attahiru, resists the British in battle. He escapes capture in defeat and flees eastward. His defeats in the real world are followed by a series of victories and conversions of infidels in a fantasy world, only for him to return to northern Nigeria at the end of the story and reach an accommodation with the presence of the British and their new technologies.

However, in the face of British colonisers there were other options. For example, rather than fight or flight, resistance could take the form of quietist non-engagement. Non-cooperation was typical of attitudes among many northerners to aspects of colonial government, on issues of taxation, for example, and the demand that northerners send their children to the new, Western-style schools that were being established in the north, schools which parents feared were synonymous with Christianisation.

Fight, flee, resist actively, resist passively, withdraw, engage – these were all options in dealing with what was seen as any illegitimate power, and by the middle of the 19th century, the geography of northern Nigeria allowed for a variety of such possibilities. Space and order were generally divided into three major categories. Cities and towns were the sites of aristocratic power, craft guilds, traders and markets, administration and sources of religious authority. The second, dependent category of space, was the agricultural hinterland to these towns and cities – hamlets, settled farms, slave settlements, paths, economic trees, land ownership and places to process produce. The third category was the unregulated bush – the domain of hunters, outlaws, dangerous animals and spirits – ventured into along dangerous paths only by outlaws, woodcutters and honey collectors. This land was beyond the control of authorities, but potentially available for clearing and occupation if someone was brave or foolhardy enough. Hausa stories and early novels trace characters into and between these spaces.

Two types of schooling

The north of Nigeria has long operated with two systems of schooling, with efforts at various times to combine the two. Islamic education starts from the age of five or six years with the learning of verses of the Qur'an and writing them in Arabic script. A child will go on to study a range of religious texts under the tutelage of a scholar (*malam*) into early adulthood. The child may leave home to live as part of the scholar's small community of religious students (*almajirai*) who, in addition to studying, may farm, pursue a craft and collect alms from neighbours for the *malam*'s community. This traditional model has been supplemented since the middle of the 20th century by more formalised schooling, where Islamic education has sat alongside history, geography, maths and other subjects in an integrated school curriculum in a formal school setting. Institutions of higher Islamic learning were established, such as the School for Arabic Studies, and the universities have had departments of Islamic Studies from which graduates have gone on to train at other institutions such as Al-Azhar University in Egypt and, in more recent years, the Islamic University of Medina.

Western secular education began in the north of Nigeria in the early colonial period with the establishment of a small number of primary schools and one secondary school, Katsina College, where teaching was in English and a range of subjects, including science, maths, English, history and geography, were taught. British colonial officials pressed the emirs to send their sons to school as a means of training a modernised ruling class. The early years of resistance in the lead up to independence began to crumble as the acknowledged political leader of the north, Ahmadu Bello, saw the need to train young northerners to compete with the larger number of southerners who had benefited from years of mission schooling and gained Western educational qualifications. The imbalance between the north and the south in terms of numbers and level of qualification in Western education was to remain a factor for many years after independence. A move to introduce universal primary education in 1976 and a further move to strengthen adult education produced a new generation of northerners who could read and write in English and in Roman script Hausa. However, the question became 'an education for what?' as the effects of the economic downturn hit from the mid-1980s onwards. In the boom years, some people went through primary, secondary and university education straight into positions of power and wealth, whether ill-gotten or not. When the crash came, it damaged the quality of all levels of education, and qualifications seemed to no longer lead anywhere. Modern state schooling was the key to advancement in the Nigerian state, yet the resistance of the colonial years was followed by a disillusionment that had started long before the economic collapse of the 1980s. A Hausa woman poet, Alhajiya 'Yar Shehu, wrote a poem called *Wakar Gargadi* (A Poem of Warning) in 1973, which illustrated the dilemma of the undereducated alienated from the lives of their parents. An extract is presented below:

> *Ka ce da ni an kai ka har ga uban gari,*
> *Wai ka ki ba da su Tanko har da Magajiya.*
> *Aka tilasa ka ka ba da su aka kai gari,*
> *Wai don sui yo ilmu ka huta dawainiya.*
> *Aikinka noma ka ga su ba su san shi ba,*
> *Su sai zama bisa kan kujera ka jiya.*
> *Ka kai su sun gama du Piramare sun fita,*
> *Kuma an hana su shiga Koleji gaba daya.*
> *Har ma da Certificate Piramare sun gama,*
> *Kuma an rubuta sun yi passing kun jiya.*
> *Sai anka ce musu wai akwai interview,*
> *Interview nan ne akai musu murdiya.*
> *Sai anka ja su aka hau su da tambaya,*
> *Ko sun ci ma ai dole ne sai an biya.*
> *To kun ga Kosau babu wanda ya san da shi,*
> *Kuma bai da kurdi wanda zai yai murdiya.*
> *Gona guda daya ga shi 'ya'ya sha biyar,*
> *Kuma ban da noman ba sana'a ko daya.*
> *To kun ga Tanko Magajiya duk sun rasa,*
> *Don babu wanda ya san ubansu a duniya.*

Daga nan su Mallam Tanko sai a shige gari,
An bar uwa da uba da bacin zuciya.
Daga nan a fada kantuna har campuna,
Har ofisoshi babu aiki ko daya.
Ilmin su Tanko bai wuce na Piramare,
Su 'yan Coleji suke bukata kun jiya.
To kun gan shi bai zauna gun babansa ba,
Kuma nan a birni babu aiki ko daya.
Irinsu ba su kidayuwa a Nijeriya,
Sun yiwo Piramare ba sana'a ko daya.
To kun ga guntun ilmi ba shi da fa'ida,
Kuma shi ya ke da yawa a nan Nijeriya.

You told me that you were taken before the authorities
For not handing over your children Tanko and Magajiya.
You were forced to give them up and they were taken to town
Seemingly so that they could be educated and you receive some relief.
Your work is farming but they now know nothing of it
They only know how to sit on chairs.
You sent them off and they graduated from primary
But they were prevented from going to College.
They even emerged with primary certificates
In which it indicates that they passed the exams.
They were told there would be an interview
And that was when they came under pressure to pay.
They were beset and beleaguered with questions
And even if they could answer them they were required to pay up.
Nobody has ever heard of Kosau
And he has no money with which to bribe.
He has just one farm and fifteen children
And apart from farming he has no other trade.
So you see Tanko and Magajiya lose out
Because no one knows their father in this big wide world.
And then those like Tanko make their way to town
Leaving mother and father desolate at home.
They go round to shops and companies
And offices where there is no work at all.
The education of the likes of Tanko goes no further than primary
But they need College graduates.
So neither does he stay with his father

Nor can he find work in the city.
There are innumerable people like him in Nigeria
Primary graduates with no trade.
So you see a little knowledge is not a good thing
And there is much little knowledge here in Nigeria.

Islamic schooling assisted with insertion into the economic activities of traders and merchants within, for example, the Sufi brotherhoods, but did little to provide direct access to employment within the Nigerian state or its agencies or, indeed, national commercial companies. However, the combination of early childhood Islamic education and universal primary education from 1976 onwards produced a new literate generation who were looking for a way forward for Nigeria in the years leading up to the return of civilian rule in 1999. Many looked at the mess they thought Nigeria was in and desperately wanted, with civilian rule, a dispensation that could bring some order, some discipline and some effectiveness to Nigerian economic and daily life.

Sharia as the way forward

For many northern Muslims faced with the conditions in Nigeria at the turn of the millennium, the extension of sharia beyond the field of civil law, where it had long since operated, into criminal law and the regulation of public life, was not only enjoined by their religion but constituted the only system that seemed to have the potential to restore order and discipline to society – a system that would apply to Muslims only, or to others by choice. My former neighbour in Gandun Albasa, a suburb of Kano, where I lived in the 1970s, told me in 2000 that an *alkali's* court operating under sharia would get you justice in one day for a theft, but nothing would come from a magistrate's court but delays, demands for bribes, extortionate legal fees and failure. So, when the governor of Zamfara State in 2000 declared that sharia law would be extended into many areas of public life, most people welcomed this as the only way to bring order and justice to the chaos of Nigeria. It would be as impossible for a northern public figure to publicly oppose the extension of sharia as it would be for a US politician to oppose motherhood and apple pie.

Central to the implementation of sharia is an agency, the *hisbah*, responsible for enforcing rules regarding public behaviour, particularly in relation to the mixing of the sexes in public places. Even more central to the implementation of sharia is the recognition of authority of those who pronounce on the interpretation of rules. In the years following the 2000 initiative in Zamfara State, other northern governors also set up *hisbah* organisations and recognised clerics' authority to speak on issues of rules and good practice. The authority of religious leadership has generally been based on scholarly reputation in the teaching of theological, legal and other texts – a reputation combining personal qualities of piety and wisdom with a charismatic ability to perform as a preacher and teacher. Such reputations are perceived as having nothing to do with what creates a position of power in the Nigerian state at large – money and influence. However, there were not only different religious leaders among the Tijaniyya and the Qadiriyya, there was also a leadership of anti-Sufi *izala*, which split into a variety of groups with a number of leadership contenders. For some years, there had also been a small but growing number of Nigerian Shia adherents under the leadership of Ibrahim Zakzaky in Zaria, who were opposed to all branches of Sunni Islam across Nigeria. Their numbers have grown in recent years and in 2015–2016 they clashed with the Nigerian military on a number of occasions.

For ordinary people, the post-2000 implementation of sharia law saw limited improvement in their daily lives, and among the proponents of sharia, more and more strident voices rejected the Nigerian state and all that it represented to them – theft, corruption, impoverishment and oppression. Disappointment with the implementation of sharia led to increasingly bitter denunciations by one scholar of another for endorsing backsliding and selling out to the authorities. Rejectionist positions not only opposed all agencies of the modern Nigerian state, they also fiercely criticised the factions from which they had split.

Twenty-five years earlier, in the early 1980s, another popular rejectionist movement, the Maitatsine rebellion, was put down by the army, air force and police in Kano and then in other cities. In this instance, a preacher called Muhammadu Marwa gathered followers from among the poor and the dispossessed and preached a wholesale rejection of all aspects of Nigerian modernity. Marwa and his followers went as far as to refuse to wear buttons and watches or ride bikes, and attacked those passersby who did. Marwa apparently claimed to be a prophet, denouncing majority views among Kano clerics, criticising the Qur'an and calling for the destruction of pagans. Marwa and many of his followers, known as *'Yan Tatsine* (those who curse) were killed by the police and army, while some fled to other northern cities where further outbreaks of violence were suppressed.

Schism and radicalism
A range of preachers took increasingly radical positions in reaction to what was seen by some as the failed implementation of sharia after 2000. Some had emerged within the *izala* movement and had broken away from the leadership of that movement. Others, who trained in Salafist thought at the

Islamic University of Medina in Saudi Arabia, learnt of new authorities and new sources of interpretation and began establishing their authority within mosques and educational institutions across the north. A return to a vision of a pre-modern society, justly governed in an egalitarian Islamic polity, was an attractive idea to the disenfranchised and the dispossessed, and this is what some preachers, most notably a man called Mohammed Yusuf, set out for their followers. A complex pattern of splitting and alliances between radical groups and preachers led to animosity and denunciation between groups, and in 2002–2003, a group of people moved away from the big cities and established themselves near the border with Niger in a place called Kanama, as far away from state control as they could get. Nevertheless, this retreat into supposed liminal areas, like the ungoverned bush of traditional stories, led to clashes with local people and subsequent attacks on nearby police and government offices. Police action defeated the group, who scattered and regrouped in Maiduguri under the leadership of Mohammed Yusuf. Local journalists started using the phrase Boko Haram (Western education is forbidden) for the movement led by Mohammed Yusuf at the time. In 2007, the BBC's Hausa Service conducted a radio interview with him following clashes between his followers and the police. In that interview, he called his group the *Jama'atu Ahlis-Sunnah Lidda'awati wal Jihad* (People who propagate the Prophet's teachings and the struggle). He went on to explain that conflict with the authorities began after a doctrinal rift in interpretation between himself and the imam of the mosque in Monguno. This led to the foundation of a separate mosque in Monguno and his followers were reported to the police and some of them unfairly arrested. Attempts were made to free those arrested from the police station, which quickly escalated into attack and counter-attack between his followers and Nigerian security forces. In the interview, he was asked whether he was opposed to education and he replied that he was fully in favour of education, but not an education that promoted falsehoods such as evolution and much of modern science. In his answers to questions he cited a range of authoritative religious texts, including the 14th-century Damascus scholar Ibn Taymiyyah. During the same year as Yusuf's BBC interview, an erstwhile teacher/colleague of his, Jaafar Adam, who had criticised him in a mosque in Kano, was assassinated in his own mosque, apparently by some of Yusuf's followers. Further clashes in towns near Maiduguri between 2007 and 2009 were followed by an event that proved to be the spark that ignited the flames between Boko Haram and the state.

June–July 2009

In June 2009, some of Yusuf's followers clashed with a police unit in an altercation about the wearing of motorbike helmets. The police opened fire, killing a number of people. Tensions quickly mounted and the next month the military put down a major Boko Haram uprising in which more than 800 people were killed and many arrested. Yusuf was captured, interrogated and summarily executed. Subsequent police action saw many people rounded up and jailed. Reports of mistreatment at the hands of the authorities began to emerge. A year later, a new leader, Abubakar Shekau, appeared on a videotape denouncing all those who opposed Boko Haram and threatening to destroy all those who supported the state. A campaign of assassination ensued, targeting Islamic clerics who criticised Boko Haram, village and district heads who cooperated with the security forces, and policemen and local representatives of state organisations. Churches, police stations, military outposts, customs offices, newspaper offices, bars, government buildings in Abuja, Kano, Bauchi, Potiskum, Gombe and Kaduna were the target of frequent bombings. Boko Haram began to arrive in armed columns in towns and villages, killing inhabitants, taking supplies, robbing banks and, in the case of police stations or army barracks, stripping them of their armaments, vehicles and munitions, to be used against security forces and civilians. A splinter group, called Ansaru, was implicated in the kidnapping and execution of foreigners. Complaints of reprisals against civilians by the Military Joint Task Force were reinforced by external reports of widespread human rights abuses by security forces and civilian militias. In April 2014, Boko Haram took more than 200 girls from their school in Chibok and Abubakar Shekau claimed he would marry them off to his fighters.

By the end of 2014

By the end of 2014, Shekau declared Gwoza to be the capital of his new caliphate in West Africa. A regional summit proposed military cooperation between Nigeria, Niger, Cameroon and Chad to tackle the now rampant threat of Boko Haram to the region. At this low point, Nigerian soldiers complained of being ill equipped and ill led, and soldiers mutinied against their superior officers. There started to be suicide bombs attached to children. However, by 2015, the army began to slowly take back towns that had been under the control of Boko Haram, including Gwoza in March of that year. Military collaboration with neighbouring states began to have an effect and Boko Haram largely withdrew into outlying areas such as the Sambisa Forest, south of Maiduguri. It appeared by mid-2016 that large-scale Boko Haram raids had become few and far between and, in most of the north, attacks by the group were primarily suicide bombings in crowded marketplaces using young children. However, by late 2016, the insurgency had led to the displacement of an estimated 2.5 million people in northeast Nigeria and the possibility of a major humanitarian crisis. While good rains came in May/June 2016, people's homes had been destroyed, their seed corn stolen, their livestock gone and their essential cycle of subsistence broken.

Some members of Boko Haram were, and are, committed to the cause, some were press-ganged into joining, and others or their families had suffered at the hands of the police and military. Others were paid mercenaries, or simply saw no alternative to achieving what was unavailable to them – a wife, wealth and power. Many will disperse and disappear into the urban populations of the north. Some may even manage to go home, if they still have one. Will that happen and will that be the end of it? It would appear that Boko Haram has split into at least two factions and armed groups still mount attacks in Cameroon, in Niger and on villages in the far northeast of Nigeria. While diminished, the insurgency is not yet over.

Solutions proposed

Commentators have commonly proposed a range of long-term solutions to the insurgency, including:

- Improve the economy of the north to provide jobs, prospects and reduce poverty;
- Strengthen moderate Islamic organisations and the propagation of moderate Islamic messages;
- Improve transparency and governance;
- Reduce levels of state corruption;
- Improve the quality and availability of Western education in northern Nigerian schools;
- Improve the quality of the state's intelligence services and counter-insurgency training of the military.

However, even if all these proposed measures were, indeed, put into effect, would that necessarily be the end of it?

Accommodating rejection – co-existence or violence

By the end of 2014, the idea of withdrawal of a community from a corrupt world into a separate society following its own true path was no longer viable, if it ever had been. For the leadership of Boko Haram, war was seen as the only way to establish an alternative world built on what they saw as Islamic principles. But the creation of a viable state, with a functioning local economy, was never achievable while at war with the Nigerian state.

As I write in early 2017, the insurgency is not over. The question remains as to whether a modern nation state can accommodate an ideology and a group of committed individuals who wish to have nothing to do with the daily manifestations of that state. Nigeria is a big country with over 400 languages, a federation of 36 states, and a multiplicity of lifestyles based on ethnicity and religion. Could it accommodate a group that wanted to live apart by its own rules and in its own way? To what extent does it already do so in accommodating local communities and a variety of religious and social practices? Is it the demand that others conform to self-created norms that inevitably leads to conflict and an escalation of violence? These questions come back to the limits of tolerance at all levels of the state. Is the idea of withdrawal into ungoverned space any longer possible in a world of modern communications and surveillance? A small peaceful group may be able to manage it, but Boko Haram's message was never a pacifist one – it was struggle (jihad) that would bring about the alternative vision. Boko Haram and the *'yan tatsine'* before them, were perceived as a threat when large numbers of people moved to join them. Is violent suppression the only solution for groups that reject the state, or is there a politics of accommodation that could come into play when, inevitably, the sentiments that drove the jihad of 1804, or the warped sentiments that inspired the Maitatsine uprising of 1980, or the radical sentiments of the Boko Haram movement, re-emerge in years to come?

Clearly, alternative visions constantly jostle for attention, and people *in extremis* will tend to resort to extreme visions and extreme measures. Casting around for possible points of comparison, the history of the United States offers the contrasting trajectories of groups who desired to follow their own path. There were clashes between Mormons and local communities before the followers of Brigham Young migrated to Utah in the middle of the 19th century. Violence was transformed into co-existence with and within the federal US state. The Amish of Pennsylvania live peaceably to this day in their separate communities. In a prosperous, well-educated, economically viable northern Nigeria, could the state accommodate an Amish-like group seeking to live a communal and religious life away from the trappings of modernity – not the conversion of the state, but accommodation within the state? Or, is it more likely that antagonism will lead to a crescendo of violence – not the peaceful life of the Amish, but the conflagration in Waco, Texas, where a religious group calling themselves the Branch Davidians fought a 10-day bloody battle with the US federal authorities.

Is that the way it will happen again? Simply transforming economic conditions may alleviate the material situation of people *in extremis*, but one lesson of Boko Haram is perhaps that a solution to the human condition requires an additional dimension in terms of parallel alternative visions.

Further reading

Comolli, V (2015) *Boko Haram: Nigeria's Islamist insurgency*. London: Hurst Publishers.

Last, M (1967) *The Sokoto Caliphate*. London: Longman.

Loimeier, R (1997) *Islamic Reform and Political Change in Northern Nigeria*. Evanston, IL: Northwestern University Press.

Mustapha, AR (ed) (2014) *Sects and Social Disorder: Muslim identities and conflict in northern Nigeria*. Martlesham, Suffolk: James Currey.

Perouse de Montclos, M-A (ed) (2014) *Boko Haram: Islamism, politics, security and the state in Nigeria*. Los Angeles, CA: African Academic Press.

Thurston, A (2016) *Salafism in Nigeria: Islam, preaching and politics*. London: Cambridge University Press for the International African Institute.

Walker, A (2016) *'Eat the Heart of the Infidel': The harrowing of Nigeria and the rise of Boko Haram*. London: Hurst Publishers.

Chapter 7

Boko Haram and counter-insurgency in Nigeria

Stephen Johnson

Introduction

Boko Haram emerged in the early 2000s as a small religious sect outside Maiduguri, the capital of Nigeria's Borno State, which borders Cameroon, Chad, and Niger in the northeast of the country. Led by the charismatic Mohammed Yusuf, a fiery Islamic cleric known for his notable oratory skills, few could have predicted that within a decade, the group would evolve from a few dozen to several thousand members, and lead an insurgency that would cause immense devastation and displace millions.

In 2014, at the height of the insurgency, the Global Terrorism Index ranked Boko Haram above the Islamic State of Iraq and Syria (ISIS) as the most violent terrorism organisation in the world.[1] The group had gained effective control of an area roughly 17 700 km^2 across Borno, Adamawa and Yobe states, and left thousands dead in its wake. In the following year, Muhammadu Buhari, a retired major general who ran on a platform that put defeating Boko Haram at centre stage, won the 2015 general election, defeating the incumbent, Goodluck Jonathan. Today, two years into President Buhari's term, significant military gains have been made against Boko Haram. The group holds little territory and the number of deaths per month have reduced drastically. However, they are far from 'defeated' and still pose a significant security threat in northern Nigeria and countries in the Lake Chad region. These provisional gains made against the group have taken the creation of a Multinational Joint Task Force (MNJTF), made up of troops from Benin, Cameroon, Chad, Niger and Nigeria – and the significant use of private military companies.

This chapter provides a history of Boko Haram and the context in which the group arose. An overview of the group's organisational structure and key objectives is sketched, as well as their funding and recruitment strategies. Finally, drawing on key literature from the field of counterterrorism and counter-insurgency, recommendations are made for how the Nigerian armed forces could improve operations and make changes that would help to ensure that short-term military gains translate into a sustainable and lasting peace in Nigeria.

The Nigerian context

Nigeria is Africa's largest country, both in terms of population and economy. With a population of 177 million in 2014, it accounts for 15.6 per cent of Africa's total population.[2] This population is very young, with 44.4 per cent being between the ages of 0 and 14 years in 2013. Nigeria's population growth rate was 2.2 per cent in 2013, which is below the African average of 2.6 per cent, but above the global rate of 1.2 per cent. The United Nations Department of Economic and Social Affairs (UN DESA) predicts that Nigeria's population is expected to grow from 122 million in 2000 to 913 million in 2100, or by a factor of 7.4.[3] Nigeria's Gross Domestic Product (GDP) was US$573.65 billion in 2014, making it US$223.57 billion larger than the next biggest economy, South Africa, and it accounted for 34.35 per cent of sub-Saharan Africa's total GDP.[4] Nigeria's economy has seen sustained growth over the past decade, with the average annual growth rate sitting at a healthy average of 7 per cent.[5] However, the country is still heavily reliant on oil exports, which accounted for 75 per cent of government revenue and 95 per cent of exports in 2013.[6]

Oil exports remain the mainstay of the Nigerian economy, despite the crash in oil prices that saw the price of crude go from around US$105 a barrel at the beginning of 2014 to US$38 in April 2016.[7][8] Currently, the sectors driving the highest growth are services, manufacturing, trade and agriculture. In 2014, the non-oil sector grew by 7 per cent, while oil sector growth fell by 1.2 per cent.[9] The growth in the non-oil sector is particularly important to Nigeria as most of the oil industry is based in the south of the country, while the north is more of an agrarian economy. Despite the advances of the non-oil sector, Nigerian society remains highly unequal, with a 2013 ranking of 152 out of 187 on the Human Development Index and a Gini coefficient score of 48.8 out of 100, where 0 indicates absolute equality.[10]

While Nigeria's growth is almost entirely based on the oil sector, this wealth is primarily concentrated in the south, with states such as Lagos having a GDP of US$33.6 billion in 2010 compared to Borno State's GDP of US$5.1billion for the same year. Even adjusted for population sizes, the GDP per capita for Lagos was US$3 469 in 2010 compared to Borno's US$1 214.[11] This north–south economic divide is even more starkly apparent when one considers the occurrence of poverty in Nigeria. According to the last comprehensive household survey in 2009/10, 46 per cent of Nigerians live in poverty, and 66 per cent of people living in poverty live in the north of the country. Poverty is also split along an urban–rural divide, with rural areas seeing more poverty.[12] Social and human development is also split in Nigeria, with development focused on urban areas where the net attendance rate for schools was 84.3 per cent, up from 62.2 per cent in 2014. There are further disparities when one takes into account that school attendance is lowest in the north, in rural areas and among the poorest demographic.[13]

Furthermore, social development is also skewed heavily along gender lines. In the eight northern states, 80 per cent of women cannot read compared to 54 per cent of men. In northeastern Nigeria, where Borno State sits, women own just 4 per cent of the land compared to the 10 per cent ownership in southeast and southsouth regions.[14] Women occupy 21 per cent of informal-sector positions regardless of education, fewer than 30 per cent in the public sector, and only 17 per cent at the most senior level. Less than a third of all loans are granted to women, and in certain cases women must receive their husbands' permission before getting a loan.[15] This gender-based discrimination is also apparent in the political sphere with only 9 per cent of candidates in the 2011 National Assembly elections being women. In 2012, out of the 360 members of the House of Representatives, only 25, or 6 per cent, were women.[16] Culturally, there is widespread indoctrinated gender discrimination that manifests itself in a myriad of ways, such as husbands being the head of families; strict gender roles mandated by fundamentalist religions, which subordinate women to men; a preference for male over female children; inheritance laws that favour men over women; a high prevalence of child marriages; and the persistence of female genital mutilation, with 30 per cent of women between the ages of 15 and 49 years being subjected to it in 2012 – even when 11 states prohibited the practice in 2008.[17]

In terms of health, Nigeria still performs poorly with 37 neonatal deaths per 1 000 live births, compared to the sub-Saharan average of 31 and the global average of 20 neonatal deaths per 1 000 live births in 2013. This trend is also reflected in deaths for children under 5 years, where Nigeria has an average of 117 deaths per 1 000 children, while the sub-Saharan average is 92 and the global average is 46 per 1 000.[18] The weaknesses of the Nigerian health system are also seen in its handling of the HIV/AIDS pandemic with 3.39 million people living with HIV in 2014 (1.97 per cent of the population), as well as 227 518 new infections in 2014, adding 17.7 per cent of new infections across Africa and 11.2 per cent to the global total of new infections. The number of people living with HIV who receive antiretroviral treatment stands at 22 per cent, showing that Nigeria still has a long way to go with containing its HIV/AIDS pandemic.[19]

As a result of all these factors, which are often concentrated in the north and rural areas of the country, providing a living, let alone improving one's position in society, has become largely unattainable for millions of Nigerians.

The legacy of colonialism

The modern Nigerian state is a construct built as a result of British conquest and colonial ambitions in the 19th and early 20th centuries. It wove a multiplicity of kingdoms, ethnicities, languages and cultures into a single area of governance. At the end of the imperial campaign, more than 200 groups had been amalgamated into a single national unit that gave little to no consideration to ethnic, linguistic or cultural boundaries.[20] The colonial administration then governed this area through what Nigerian academic Godwin Hembe describes as 'based on policies which tended to encourage ethnic consciousness and exclusiveness'.[21] According to Hembe, local administration and governance were based on indirect rule that relied on the use of precolonial institutions that were modified to suit the purposes of colonial rule.[22] This carried over into Nigeria's independence era and created a society in which Nigerians were divided along ethnic, regional, cultural and religious fault lines.[23] According to Robin Hallett: 'Before the 1890s there was no one term that could be used to embrace all the territories that today form part of the modern republic [Nigeria].'[24]

Under British rule, three distinct regions emerged in Nigeria: the Yoruba dominated the west, the Hausa-Fulani dominated the north and the Igbo the east. These formed the fault lines that have dominated the Nigerian political landscape ever since. This was demonstrated in Nigeria's first general elections in 1959, where the three major competitors were the Northern People's Congress (NPC), the Action Group (AG) representing the west, and the National Council for Nigeria and the Cameroons (NCNC) representing the east.[25] More than 50 years after independence, and 100 years after the creation of the modern Nigerian state, citizens still rely largely on cultural, religious, ethnic and linguistic identities to inform their political loyalties. These loyalties result in animosities that are not only self-reinforcing but also self-regenerating, leading to inter-regional enmity, suspicion and violent conflicts.[26]

In the post-independence era, local elites did not seek to cast off the colonial structures of governance but instead reinforced them as a means of maintaining control. Professor Kalu Kalu of Auburn University describes this pattern as such: 'What the colonial regime left, African leaders did not abandon, but instead, have perfected into the most predatory form of Machiavellian statecraft.'[27] Kalu further notes that 'as the state ceases to reflect society in general, and frustrated by the social and economic costs of rudderless governance, the average citizen withdraws and disengages himself from the sphere of public discourse'.[28] The consequence of such a non-representative state is that either its citizens do not get involved in politics due to a lack of space for participation, or they find alternative means to express political goals and desires.

Islam and identity in Nigeria

The spread of Islam in West Africa dates back to the 8th century AD when the religion was slowly introduced to what are now the states of Senegal, Gambia, Guinea, Burkina Faso, Niger, Mali and Nigeria.[29] Several reasons are given for the spread of Islam in this region, including economic motivations, spiritual messages, as well as the influence of Arabic literacy in facilitating state-building. While the motivations behind the early conversions remain unclear, it appears that the presence of Islam in West Africa developed from trade links between North and West Africa.[30] The history of Islam in West Africa can be explained in three stages: containment, mixing and reform. In the first stage, African kings contained Islam by segregating Muslim communities. In the second stage, African rulers blended Islam with local traditions as the population selectively appropriated Islamic traditions. And the final phase, in which African Muslims pressed for reform to remove mixed practices and work on the implementation of sharia law.[31]

The arrival of Islam in the region can be explained similarly in two phases. The first occurred when scholars and merchants arrived along the trade routes through the Sahara into what would become northern Nigeria. During the first phase of Islam's arrival, it was considered mainly the religion of the elite, with the Kanem Bornu Empire on the northeast of Lake Chad to be the first to become Islamised.[32] The second phase, and more relevant to our studies, is the arrival of Islam in Nigeria in the 19th century through the jihad of Usman dan Fodio. In 1804, Fodio began a campaign that within 50 years had swept all Hausa rulers off their thrones and established Fulani hegemony in most of northern Nigeria.[33] Within years, Islam had become dominant through trade, the social contract and war, spreading even to some southeastern Yoruba districts. The British recognised a number of administrative structures created during this period and integrated them into colonial rule.[34]

According to data from the Pew Forum on Religious and Public life, Nigeria's population in 2012 was 48.8 per cent Muslim and 49.3 per cent Christian. This means the country's total Muslim population is 82.3 million, making it the fifth largest Muslim country in the world.[35] Nigeria was also ranked the most religious country in the world in 2004, with 90 per cent of the population believing in God, praying regularly and affirming their willingness to die for their beliefs.[36] Geographically, the Fulani-Hausa north is largely Muslim, the Igbo southeast is largely Christian, and the Yoruba southwest is a mix of both Islam and Christianity.[37] Yet Nigerian Muslims cannot be seen as a homogenous group, as there are a range of different attitudes within Nigerian Islam. As Joseph Kenny noted: '[W]hile Northern Islam has been firmly reformist and separatist with regards to anything non-Islamic, Yoruba

Muslims have been accommodating. The Yoruba people are first of all Yoruba, secondly Muslims or Christians and lastly Nigerians, so that in one family you can find both Muslims and Christians and some involvement in the traditional religion.'[38]

These attitudinal differences can be traced to the northern jihads of the early 19th century, which saw a reform of Hausa-Fulani Islam and a closer adherence to sharia law, whereas the Yoruba southwest has been characterised by a more liberal version of Islam. In a deeply religious country such as Nigeria, the interplay between religion and identity is a real factor in political and social interactions. This creates a situation in which the dominant religious groups see God as the ultimate source and summit of power, and political power bases and leadership are accordingly formed along religious lines.[39] Often these contests for political power along ethno-religious lines can result in violence, as seen in the central Nigerian city of Jos, which saw 160 deaths due to the appointment of a Christian as the local council chairman in 2001.[40] While this is a small and somewhat isolated example, there have been much larger ones. The election of Goodluck Jonathan – a southern Christian – in 2011, resulted in clashes between Muslims and Christians, as well as bared the divides between the north and south. The potency of religion in Nigerian society as both a source of personal and political identity means that citizens often clash over religion, rather than directing their attention to how the country as a whole is being governed.[41] However, the importance and consequences of religion in Nigerian society is perhaps most strongly felt in the northern provinces.

Borno State

Borno State is a traditionally Muslim region in the northeast of Nigeria. It is where the Boko Haram insurgency originated – as will be discussed in more depth below – as well as being the organisation's natural stronghold. Borno State, with its capital in Maiduguri, is the largest of Nigeria's 36 states covering an area of 116 589 km^2 and has a population of 4.3 million, 80 per cent of whom are Muslim.[42] The state shares borders with Cameroon and Chad to the east and Niger to the north, with its major ethnic groups being Kanuri, Babur and Shuwa Arabs.[43] Infrastructure is severely underdeveloped, with 2 449 km of tarred all-season roads and 755 km of untarred seasonal roads. The city of Maiduguri is linked to the rest of Nigeria and the outside world by an international airport. While rail links do exist, they are yet to be upgraded as part of the rail modernisation project, so traffic on the lines is rare. Electricity supply is restricted to urban areas, particularly those where local government offices are situated; the State Rural Electrification Board is tasked with supplying electricity to rural regions but little progress has been made in doing so. Water shortages are common due to the climate of the region and there are 1 548 cemented wells throughout the state. State and local authorities have sunk 692 wells, but there is a culture of poor maintenance and less than half the boreholes sunk are operational.[44]

The origins and evolution of Boko Haram

Boko Haram emerged in the early 2000s as a small Sunni Islamic sect influenced by Wahhabist teachings, advocating a strict interpretation and implementation of Islamic law. Calling itself *Jama'a Ahl as-Sunna Li-da'wa wa-al Jihad* (roughly translated from Arabic as 'People Committed to the Propagation of the Prophet's Teachings and Jihad'), the group is more popularly known as Boko Haram (often translated as 'Western education is forbidden'), a nickname given by local Hausa-speaking communities to describe the group's view that Western education and culture have been corrupting influences, which is *haram* ('forbidden') under its conservative interpretation of Islam.[45] In Boko Haram's early days, there was no call for violence from its former leader, Muhammad Yusuf, but members were periodically involved in skirmishes with the police during the group's formation.[46]

The organisation seeks to establish an Islamic state in Nigeria. It is vehemently anti-Western and in a 2009 BBC interview, the former leader, Muhammad Yusuf, stated that the ideas of a spherical Earth, Darwinian evolution and democracy are incompatible with the teachings of Islam.[47] A major event in the development of Boko Haram was in 2009 when Nigerian security forces cracked down on the group. More than 700 people died in the crackdown, including the public execution of then leader, Muhammad Yusuf, at police headquarters in Maiduguri.[48] After Yusuf's death, Mallam Abubakar Shekau became the leader of the group. This was marked by a large increase in violence and attacks, starting with the Bauchi prison break on 7 September 2010 and a bomb attack outside a barracks in Abuja on 31 December 2010.[49] Since then, the number of attacks and fatalities attributed to the organisation has increased exponentially.

Between 2009 and 2013 Boko Haram was the third deadliest terrorist organisation in the world, behind the Taliban and Tehrik-i-Taliban Pakistan, with 801 attacks and 3 666 fatalities.[50] According to Africa Check, between 9 000 and 17 500 people have been killed by Boko Haram, with most sources agreeing that 13 000 have been killed. Another 1–2 million have been internally displaced by the insurgency.[51] Boko Haram has staged several high-profile attacks, such as the kidnapping of 276 girls from the Government Secondary School in Chibok between 14 and 15 April 2014.[52] This particular incident led to international efforts to rescue and return the girls, and the later deployment of 300 US special forces to Cameroon to fight Boko Haram.[53] Other high-profile attacks include Boko Haram's overrunning of security forces in the town of Baga, killing as many as 2 000 people and destroying 600 houses. The headquarters of the MNJTF, the military command in charge of fighting Boko Haram, also based in Baga, was overrun, with equipment and supplies falling into the group's hands.[54]

Organisation, strategy and objectives

Boko Haram, at least before 2009, had no clear organisational or political structure and, therefore, little was known of its command and control system. However, by 2011 and 2012, it became clear that members were organised into complex cell structures from which they operated locally and internationally. These cells, of which there are about 26, are headed by regional commanders who in turn take commands from Abubakar Shekau, the current leader. This diffuse structure makes it difficult for the Nigerian security forces to dismantle the group.

In August 2016 the movement split into two factions. Long-time leader Abubakar Shekau favoured a more indiscriminate attack profile, while the new ISIS-backed Abu Musab al-Barnawi faction preferred to engage security forces directly (such as in Bosso, Niger, in June). Despite these developments, the high rate of violence perpetrated by the group remains a consistent feature.[55] Al-Barnawi's Boko Haram faction appears to be gathering strength in the Lake Chad region and along the Komadugu River, which delineates the eastern Niger–Nigeria border, while Shekau's group is based further south in Nigeria's Sambisa Forest.[56]

The group also has a sophisticated leadership structure, comprising departments headed by highly trained personnel who are able to effectively execute designated assignments. Such departments include bomb manufacturing, suicide bombers, intelligence, research, welfare/health care and other logistics needed for proper execution of their goals. It has also been said that Boko Haram's highest decision-making body is run by a Shura Council.[57] Boko Haram's strategic and tactical goals seem to be aimed at destabilising the north of Nigeria. The group targets civilian, government and economic centres as a means to destabilise all civilian life by disrupting cultural, economic and government functions. High-profile attacks on Christian civilians and infrastructure have been particularly effective at destabilisation because they can result in reprisals on Muslim civilians, thus exacerbating ethno-religious tensions. These attacks are particularly effective at increasing tensions because they are routinely carried out during Sunday services.[58]

Boko Haram has also extensively targeted government installations, including police stations, military bases and government offices.[59] Although the targets they favour have changed since the 2010 attacks, it is possible to make some generalisations. During the first two years, the group focused its attacks on ideologically opposed targets. These included education and medical facilities, bars and gambling establishments, marketplaces where non-*halaal* meat was sold, and the targeted assassination of Muslims who opposed them.[60] During the second phase, 2011–2013, Boko Haram shifted its targets, while maintaining a high level of local terrorism. The group projected its power into two areas: the Fulani-Hausa heartland around Kano and Zaria (northwestern Nigeria) and the Middle Belt, especially the flashpoint city of Jos, where there are frequent clashes between Christians and Muslims. These attacks focused on symbolic centres such as churches, government buildings and army bases. To maximise casualties and the psychological effect of incidents, Christian locations were often attacked on key days.[61]

These types of attack have been effective at tactically limiting the government's ability to respond by destroying critical infrastructure and at undermining its legitimacy by reducing its ability to provide basic state functions such as security, education, health care and economic activity. The group uses a wide range of tactics in its operations that can be largely grouped into two methods. The first uses individuals or small groups, who will commit individualised terror such as assassinations, drive-by shootings, bombings, improvised explosive devices (IEDs) and suicide bombings. Since 2014, Boko Haram has also begun to use massed-attack tactics that rely on highly mobile units using motorcycles, pick-up trucks or technicals (pick-up trucks with larger weaponry mounted on them). These units choose vulnerable targets where they will have a large advantage in terms of firepower and numbers; an example is the attacks on Baga. After a successful mass attack, they will either imprison or execute whatever population remains behind.[62]

Boko Haram trains or arranges the training of its members in a wide variety of conventional and unconventional tactics. Both Al-Qaeda in the Islamic Maghreb (AQIM) and Al-Shabaab have been involved in the training of Boko Haram members, especially in the manufacturing and deployment of suicide bombers and IEDs, as can be seen by the sharp rise in the use of these tactics from 2013.[63]

Funding and recruitment
Funding for Boko Haram has expanded as the group has grown and has developed from its initial support base of wealthy members from Borno and Yobe states and its policy of charging members a daily amount of 100 NGN (US$0.62).[64] As the group expanded it became involved in more criminal activities such as

bank robberies, extortion and kidnapping. In more recent years, it has emerged that Al-Qaeda has been providing funding to the group, which correlates to the upswing in the scale of attacks since 2013.[65] There have also been worrying allegations that the governors of Kano and Bauchi have paid Boko Haram not to launch attacks in these states.[66]

While Boko Haram has neither the support nor the funding to threaten the existence of the Nigerian state, it has shown remarkable ability to use what resources it does have to cause havoc across the north of the country. The group has been able to create a humanitarian crisis for Nigeria not seen since the Biafran War. Along with the human impact, the political and social impact on the future stability of Nigeria cannot be underestimated as Boko Haram has shown that it is extremely accomplished at taking advantage of existing fault lines in the country, as well as creating new ones.

Boko Haram's recruitment typically targets men between the ages of 18 and 30 from Nigeria, Chad, Cameroon and Niger. The preferred recruits are those from impoverished backgrounds with little education or opportunity, who show enthusiasm or susceptibility to their radical interpretation of Islam. As the group grew, it also began to attract a more educated class of recruit, especially through its alleged funding links to Nigeria's upper classes, such as university-educated elites and men in uniform. Finally, Boko Haram also gained recruits by breaking prisoners out and integrating them into the group.[67]

Counter-insurgency and counterterrorism

To fully understand how to defeat Boko Haram it is necessary to look at the various counterterrorism and counter-insurgency options the Nigerian government has available. The US Department of Defense succinctly defines insurgency as 'an organised movement aimed at the overthrow of a constituted government through the use of subversion and armed conflict'. The issue with a definition like this is that it has remained unchanged for decades and 'fails to encompass the wider scope and context of insurgencies today, especially their protracted and transnational nature, as well as their political, economic and social dimensions.'[68] The other flaw with this definition is that it places emphasis on subversion and armed conflict, thereby framing insurgencies as purely military issues.[69]

Insurgencies seek radical change of the existing political and/or social order, and their primary means of achieving this is commonly through the use of sustained violence and political disruption. However, when considering insurgent groups such as Boko Haram, it is important to note that guerrilla warfare and terrorism form only one element of the greater insurgency and often more important aspects to consider – especially of successful insurgencies – are the political, social and economic ones. Insurgents do not seek to defeat conventional massed armies but rather chip away at the authority and legitimacy of the central state and those who represent it. Thus, disruption and subversion can be more effective than violence, regardless of how spectacular and horrifying that violence may be.[70] Therefore, the US Department of Defense's definition of an insurgency should be expanded to better fit the 21st century, by taking into account that military or violent aspects of insurgency are a means to disrupt social, political and economic activity and thus delegitimise the state.

Types and structures of insurgencies

One must also consider the differences between types of insurgencies when trying to develop effective counter-insurgency strategies. The US government has noted the following five typologies: (1) Revolutionary insurgencies, which seek to replace the existing political order with an entirely different system, often entailing transformation of the economic and social structures. (2) Reformist insurgencies, which do not aim to change the existing political order but, instead, seek to compel the government to alter its policies or undertake political, economic or social reforms. (3) Separatist insurgencies, which seek independence for a specific region. In some cases, the region in question spans existing national boundaries. (4) Resistance insurgencies, which seek to compel an occupying power to withdraw from a given territory. And lastly, (5) Commercialist insurgencies, which are motivated by the acquisition of wealth or material resources and where political power is simply a tool for seizing and controlling access to the wealth.[71]

In addition to the five typologies, there are four commonly used organisational structures for insurgencies. Firstly, politically organised insurgencies, which develop a complex political structure and try to consolidate control of territory through the use of shadow governments rather than through military power. They may also undertake military operations against the government but their military components are subordinate to their political structure. Secondly, militarily organised insurgencies, which emphasise military action against the government over political mobilisation of the population. The insurgents calculate that military success and the resulting weakening of the government will help to cause the population to rally to their cause. Militarily organised insurgencies begin with small, weak, ill-defined political structures, often dominated by military leaders. Thirdly, traditionally organised insurgencies draw on pre-existing tribal, clan, ethnic or religious affiliations. Established social hierarchies – a system of chiefs and sub-chiefs, for example – often substitute for political and military structures in traditionally organised insurgencies. And lastly, urban-cellular insurgencies, which develop and are centred in urban areas. These insurgencies lack hierarchical political and military leadership structures, instead organising around small, semi-autonomous cells.[72]

Of the above, Boko Haram can be seen as a revolutionary separatist movement because the organisation desires to overthrow the established government where it operates and replace it with its own form of government or a proposed caliphate. It can also be seen as organised along military and traditional lines because it focuses on militarily engaging the Nigerian government and not consolidating and setting up alternative forms of governance. It should also be seen as traditional due to its reliance on religion as a binding factor for its members.

What must always be considered when analysing insurgencies is that they are inherently political movements that seek to overturn real or perceived maladies endemic to a particular situation or set of conditions within their own environment.[73] This is important as it makes them fundamentally different from conventional armed conflicts that will see two military powers clash until one overcomes the other. The point of conventional warfare is not to annihilate one's opponent but rather to destroy their will to fight – two sides trying to push the other past its limit of endurance.[74] While this definition still rings partly true with Boko Haram and other insurgent and terrorist groups, the organisation's major goal is still to delegitimise the state through violence and terror. Boko Haram does not, and in all likelihood will never, have the capacity to militarily defeat the Nigerian state. Rather, it seeks to destroy the people's trust and faith in the state, thereby creating a power vacuum in which it can operate or create and attempt to set up its own system of governance and rule.

The actions, structures, and beliefs of insurgencies

Insurgencies reflect a complex interaction of actions, structures and beliefs. Actions consist of the events, behaviours and acts that characterise and shape conflicts. These actions are not limited to the insurgent or terrorist groups but rather all those involved: the military, local populace, local and national leaders, security forces and aid workers, among others. While these actions can be acts of terror and violence, they also encompass the security sector's response, how the local population reacts and how central government acts.[75] This was made especially clear when the Nigerian security service killed Muhammad Yusuf in July 2009 during a crackdown on Boko Haram. This was the watershed moment for a group that had evolved from an organisation that seemed more focused on an ideological rejection of Western and Christian values rather than on violent conflict with the Nigerian state.[76] Yusuf's extrajudicial killing in custody allowed his shadowy deputy, Abubakar Shekau, to take control of

Boko Haram and, on 24 December 2010, launch the group's first bombing campaign, using improvised explosive devices, killing 38 people in Jos and injuring another 74.[77] In this case, it is easy to make the link in which Yusuf's death at the hand of the Nigerian security services created a situation where Boko Haram was encouraged to increasingly turn to acts of violence.

The next thing to take into account when examining insurgencies and terrorist groups is the structure, or context, in which a group operates. These include the economic development and wealth of an area, the level of infrastructure, humanitarian aid, unemployment, security structures, poverty and urbanisation, among others.[78] These structures may have practical implications such as how a group operates and what tactics and strategies it uses. For example, Boko Haram's preferred tactic of using suicide bombers on market days in larger towns or using massed motorcycle and technical attacks on remote towns and bases to overrun them, illustrates how they have effectively adapted their tactics to suit their environment.[79] In the case of larger areas such as market towns, where there are more likely to be security forces, they will try to infiltrate with a suicide bomber. However, in areas where they have the advantage of mobility and numbers, such as in the remote areas of Borno State, they will risk a massed attack that puts more of their combatants at risk. These are a few examples of how the structure and environment affects strategy and tactics. However, implications of structure go further than merely the staging and tactics used during attacks. The economic development of an area will affect recruiting; the religious or ethnic make-up of an area will determine which groups are targeted; and the types and level of infrastructure will also help determine what the organisation targets and how it may plan its escape.

The final aspect to consider when discussing insurgencies is the belief system that animates the insurgent group. This may comprise the attitudes, perceptions, prejudices, worldviews, ideologies, culture and beliefs that fuel insurgencies and insurgents. Beliefs form the core of any insurgency or terrorist movement, as insurgents or terrorists are the ones perpetrating acts of violence in the name of a belief in how society should be or, at the very least, should not be. While some would associate the focus on the belief system of insurgents with the 'hearts and minds' approach to counter-insurgency, this is an over-simplification and inappropriate.[80] The term 'hearts and minds' was originally used by the British in their repression of the Malayan uprisings from 1948. However, it was popularised by the US military in the Vietnam and Afghanistan wars. The major criticism of this approach, which has been hugely popular among Western military and political elites when viewing the beliefs of insurgents as well as local populations, is that it does not portray the complexity of belief systems and sees them as something inanimate, controllable and constant. Beliefs rest not only with the individual, but also with the wider society and culture, and how they have been shaped over hundreds if not thousands of years.[81]

Insurgencies thus reflect an extremely complex interplay of actions, structures and beliefs. Every insurgency sees these factors play out differently and change over time, as none of them are static. To truly understand insurgencies, it is necessary to understand the interplay between these factors. While most insurgencies use some form of terrorism in their tactics, not all terrorist groups can be defined as insurgent, and with groups such as Boko Haram, which can be classified as both terrorist and insurgent in nature, it is necessary to examine both counter-insurgency and counterterrorism strategies.

Terrorism and counterterrorism

There is no universally applicable counterterrorism policy for democratic states as every conflict involving terrorism has its own unique characteristics and influences.[82] However, the *US Army/Marine Corps Counterinsurgency Field Manual* defines counterterrorism operations as 'operations that include the offensive measures taken to prevent, deter, pre-empt, and respond to terrorism'.[83] While this definition is fairly concrete, it has its own strengths and weaknesses. Its strength is that it recognises that counterterrorism operations are all-inclusive, including prevention, deterrence, pre-emption and responses which would require bringing to bear all aspects of a nation's power, not just its military and security forces.[84]

The challenge of such an all-encompassing approach of 'whatever we need, whenever we need it' is that it creates issues with developing effective counterterrorism strategies, allocating resources and determining accountability.[85] While a superpower such as the United States may have the resources and structures at its disposal to implement such a far-reaching strategy, which includes everything from a domestic transport security administration to sustained intelligence and offensive operations in multiple countries, developing countries such as Nigeria do not have the same capacity. Therefore, a different, more tailored and prudent approach in line with the resources at their disposal is required. This includes a plan that acknowledges the strategic and tactical aspects involved in militarily defeating terrorism and insurgencies, as well as acknowledging the root causes of these movements. Otherwise, any form of military or security success will always be temporary.

There has been much work done on the root causes of terrorism. However, it is difficult, if not impossible, to attribute terrorism to any one specific factor. For example, the links between poverty and terrorism, long thought to be the primary driver, have been researched in considerable depth. Even US President George W Bush said in 2002, at the beginning of the Global War on Terrorism, that, 'We fight against poverty because hope is an answer to terror.'[86] However, what academic studies, which have focused on the relationship between poverty and terrorism, have revealed is that it is too simplistic to say that poverty is the sole or largest cause of terrorism. If that were the case, we would see much more terrorism globally, as the World Bank estimated that in 2012 more than 1.2 billion people lived on less than US$3.10 a day, most concentrated in sub-Saharan Africa and South Asia.[87]

What is a more useful approach is to see poverty as just one of the many factors that foster the rise of terrorism. Tim Krieger of the University of Freiburg puts forward a more complete list of factors in his paper 'What causes terrorism'. He lists economic deprivation, modernisation strain, political and institutional order, political transformation and instability, identity and culture clash, the global economic and political order, and contagion.[88] Contagion is an especially interesting factor that is not featured in many analyses of the root causes of terrorism but it should not be discounted. Contagion could be explained as how terrorist activity in one environment may spur terrorist activity in another environment. These environments may be localised such as neighbourhoods, for instance, Hezbollah in southern Lebanon, or on a nation-state scale, such as ISIS in Syria and its spread to Iraq.[89]

Another, more classic, set of factors that can explain the rise of terrorism comes from Alex P Schmid's 2005 paper, 'Root causes of terrorism: Some conceptual notes, a set of indicators, and a model'. He states that if there is good governance, democracy, rule of law and social justice, terrorism is less likely. His argument is that when there is bad governance and corruption, resistance easily gains support and legitimacy. Democracy allows a voice for the people and a channel to remove unpopular rulers, thereby diminishing the impetus for oppositional voices to use violence. When rule of law becomes a tool for rulers, it loses legitimacy and thereby its ability to maintain public order. And finally, when long-standing social injustices are unresolved and there seems to be no possibility of resolving them through official channels, one should not be surprised when violence follows.[90]

The last important cause of terrorism to be highlighted is a concept raised in Akbar Ahmed's book, *The Thistle and the Drone: How America's War on Terror became a global war on tribal Islam*. The concept that Ahmed describes is one of a balancing act of give-and-take between the centralised state and its tribal periphery. More specifically, he speaks of how the modernisation of the centralised state and its attempts to modernise and exert its control over the tribal periphery have brought the two into conflict. Those living on the periphery are being forced to give up a way of life that has gone on for generations in favour of modernity, but are not necessarily reaping the rewards of a modernised society.[91] This theory may be of particular relevance to Boko Haram because a rejection of modernity is central to its ideology and beliefs.[92]

The three pillars of effective counter-insurgency

For counter-insurgency and counterterrorism to truly work it is necessary for the counter insurgents to employ proactive responses to insurgent or terrorist violence.[93] Dr David J Kilcullen, an Australian counter-insurgency and counterterrorism theorist, describes the three pillars of counter-insurgency in terms of security, political and economic factors. These three pillars sit on a base of information and support a 'roof' of control.[94] He goes on to comment on counter-insurgency as follows:

> You cannot command what you do not control. Therefore, 'unity of command' (between agencies or among government and non-government actors) means little in this environment. Instead, we need to create 'unity of effort' at best, and collaboration or deconfliction at least. This depends less on a shared command and control hierarchy, and more on a shared diagnosis of the problem, platforms for collaboration, information sharing and deconfliction. Each player must understand the others' strengths, weaknesses, capabilities and objectives, and inter-agency teams must be structured for versatility (the ability to perform a wide variety of tasks) and agility (the ability to transition rapidly and smoothly between tasks).[95]

The goal of the three pillars is to gain and maintain control of a space, but to do so each pillar needs to rest on a solid foundation of information. To break this framework down further, the security pillar is made up of the following organisations, factors and tasks: military, police, human security, public safety and population security. The second pillar is that of the political sphere: mobilisation, governance, institutional capacity and social reintegration. The final pillar is primarily economic and includes humanitarian assistance, development assistance, resource and infrastructure management, and growth capacity.

These pillars rest on a base of information made of two parts: military intelligence and social intelligence. Military intelligence consists of intelligence collection, information operations and media operations. Social intelligence is made up of counter-ideology, counter-sanctuary and counter-motivation.[96] Intelligence is the most important place to start when performing counterterrorism and counter-insurgency operations. If not, these operations will either fail or the current situation will get worse.

When considering the three pillars approach to counterterrorism it is necessary to examine the nature of each pillar. The security pillar includes military security (securing the population from attack or intimidation by guerrillas, bandits, terrorists or other armed groups) and police security (community policing, police intelligence or 'Special Branch' activities, and paramilitary police field forces). It also incorporates human security, building a framework of human rights, civil institutions and individual protections, public safety (fire, ambulance, sanitation and civil defence) and population security.[97] The security pillar mostly engages military commanders' attention but, of course, military means are applied across the model, not just in the security domain, while civilian activity is also critically important to the security pillar. However, security is not the basis for economic and political progress (as some commanders and political leaders argue). Nor does security depend on political and economic progress (as others assert). Rather, all three pillars must develop in parallel and stay in balance, while being firmly based on an effective information campaign.

The political pillar focuses on mobilising support. It comprises efforts to mobilise stakeholders in support of the government, marginalise insurgents and other groups, extend governance and further the rule of law.[98] Building institutional capacity in all agencies of government and non-government institutions is a key element, as well as social reintegration efforts such as the disarming, demobilisation and reintegration of combatants. Like the security pillar for military forces, the political pillar is the principal arena for diplomatic and civil governance assistance efforts – although, again, civil agencies also play a significant role in the security and economic pillars.[99]

The economic pillar includes a near-term component of immediate humanitarian relief, as well as longer-term programmes for development assistance across a range of agricultural, industrial and commercial activities. Assistance in effective resource and infrastructure management, including the construction of key infrastructure systems, is critically important. Tailoring efforts to the society's capacity to absorb spending, as well as efforts to increase absorptive capacity, underpin other development activities.[100]

All of these pillars work together to achieve the goal of control, not to defeat every insurgent or terrorist or to simply create stability. Creating stability is just a means to an end. In achieving control, the counter-insurgent force can manage the terrorist activity, the level of violence and the degree of stability in an environment. The end goal of counter-insurgency or counterterrorism should be to return 'normality' to an environment so that the control achieved can be transferred to permanent, effective and legitimate institutions.[101] In the light of this, the following section provides an overview of the Nigerian armed forces and outlines some of the key challenges and deficiencies they face, which impact on their ability to carry out effective and sustainable counterterrorism and counter-insurgency strategies as outlined earlier.

The Nigerian armed forces

The Nigerian armed forces had 162 000 personnel and a budget of US$2 billion in 2013, and spent more than US$700 million on arms imports between 2000 and 2014.[102] In terms of equipment, the Nigerian armed forces have 153 tanks, 699 reconnaissance vehicles, 527 armoured personnel carriers, 364 artillery pieces, 14 combat aircraft, 35 transport aircraft, 43 transport helicopters, 11 combat helicopters and nine unmanned aerial reconnaissance vehicles.[103] While impressive on paper, much of this equipment is old, poorly maintained and dates back to the days of Nigeria's military dictatorship.[104]

The Nigerian army, as a part of the larger Nigerian armed forces, is also particularly underfunded, receiving less than US$30 million in 2013 with which to equip itself. As Major General Abdullahi Muraina, the Nigerian army's chief of accounts and budget, stated when asked about this situation:

> For instance, the army budget for this year [2013/14] is just N4.8 billion. Now, to provide only one item for the troops engaged in the operation in the north-east will gulp most of the amount. Assuming we committed 20 000 troops, the jacket and the helmet is in the average of about US$1 000. This means US$20 million, about N3 billion. N3 billion as a percentage of N4.8 billion is more than 50 per cent and that is just one item; we are not talking about uniforms, or boots, or structure [sic] where they will stay; we are not talking about training, because training is key to enhancing the capability of the force.[105]

The Nigerian military also suffers from widespread corruption, which has seen security forces sent to counter Boko Haram often heading into combat underequipped, poorly trained, short of vital supplies and often unpaid for months at a time, leading to troops deserting or mutinying against their officers.[106] There is also an issue with understaffed units being sent to fight. This understaffing is caused by officers reporting that their units are at full strength, while pocketing the salaries of so-called 'ghost soldiers'. The most infamous case of this was when 54 soldiers of the 111th Special Forces Battalion were sentenced to death after they refused to join an operation against Boko Haram in August 2014 due to poor equipment and lack of soldiers. A month earlier, the unit had been ambushed by Boko Haram, leaving 26 soldiers dead and 83 injured. They went up against Boko Haram fighters armed with anti-aircraft guns and armoured personnel carriers, mostly looted from Nigerian army bases. The unit had approximately 174 soldiers in August, instead of the 750 that such battalions are expected to have.[107]

Another major issue blunting the Nigerian army's effectiveness is the large number of soldiers of all ranks who have been supplying weapons, supplies and intelligence to Boko Haram. In a high-profile case, 15 senior officers, including 10 generals, were court-martialled for supplying intelligence and troop movements to Boko Haram, allowing for a number of ambushes that caused the deaths of Nigerian soldiers.[108]

However, the most harmful aspect of the Nigerian army's performance in counterterrorism and counter-insurgency operations is its incredibly poor human rights record, allegations of crimes against humanity and extra-judicial killings. Amnesty International documented 27 incidents of extra-judicial killings committed by members of the military between 2013 and 2014, which saw at least 1 200 boys and men killed.[109] The precise number of extra-judicial killings is unknown due to a lack of records, official cover-ups and difficulty in locating witnesses in the areas where the crimes were committed. The highest-profile and horrific mass killing by the military happened on 14 March 2014 in Maiduguri, Borno State. In the aftermath of a Boko Haram attack on the military detention facility at Giwa barracks, during which the detainees were released, the military killed at least 640 men and boys, most of them recaptured detainees.[110] The military has also been accused of being responsible for many deaths in custody, with Amnesty International stating that more than 7 000 men and boys have died while in detention. Testimony from a 25-year-old carpenter from Maiduguri who was arrested in November 2012, paints a grim scene of conditions in Nigerian prisons:

> We have a sense that they just want us to die. Many people died in the cells. Any time we were denied water for two days, 300 people died [in those two days]. Sometimes we drink people's urine, but even the urine you at times could not get. Every day they died, and whenever someone died, we [the other detainees] were happy because of the extra space. And because we will be taken out, to take out the corpses, and the military will give us water to wash our hands and when washing our hands, we drink the water.[111]

Along with deaths in custody, the Nigerian security services have been accused of arbitrary arrests, unlawful detention, enforced disappearances and torture. According to Amnesty International, at least 20 000 people have been arbitrarily arrested. A few of those arrested were released shortly after, sometimes because their families had paid bribes. A small proportion have been prosecuted and tried, hundreds were executed and thousands died in detention. The rest are being held indefinitely in unauthorised and unacknowledged military detention, denied contact with lawyers or relatives, without formal charges and without ever appearing in court.[112]

Overall, the Nigerian military has proved woefully inadequate at best and criminally vicious at worst. The inability of the army to properly train, supply and equip its soldiers has resulted in a situation where, at its height, Boko Haram controlled more than 20 000 km² or about one-quarter of the total size of Borno State.[113]

Arguably, the Nigerian government's war against Boko Haram only turned around when it began to employ apartheid-era South African Defence Force (SADF) mercenaries to begin an assault on Boko Haram positions. In 2015, photos began to emerge of mercenaries, or contractors in more sanitised terms, operating in Borno State. Ostensibly in Nigeria to train the Nigerian army, it soon emerged, after Leon Lotz died in a friendly fire incident, that South African mercenaries were involved in frontline combat operations.[114] Led by Eeben Barlow, founder of the firm Executive Outcomes, which was hired by Sierra Leone to contain the Revolutionary United Front (RUF) in 1995,[115] they launched attacks on Boko Haram-held towns and regions, and with the support of armour and attack helicopters, managed to push Boko Haram back on all fronts.[116] Subsequently, by December 2015 President Buhari was able to claim a technical victory over the group.[117] Despite Buhari's claim in 2015, Boko Haram is far from 'defeated' and still poses a significant security threat in northern Nigeria and countries in the Lake Chad region. It is important, however, that recent short-term military gains are translated into a sustainable stability, which would allow the government to begin to rebuild its legitimacy in the region.

Conclusion

Based on the above, a number of policy recommendations can be made to improve both the efficacy of the Nigerian armed forces counter-insurgency and counterterrorism operations, and more successfully address some of the root causes of the Boko Haram insurgency. First and foremost, it is necessary to reform the Nigerian military, if not all of it at least the security forces responsible for maintaining peace and establishing government control in areas affected by Boko Haram. This will require training, equipping, paying, commanding and deploying soldiers who are combating Boko Haram in the most effective manner. To achieve this, the Nigerian government needs to stamp out officer-level corruption because soldiers who cannot trust their leaders will never make an effective fighting force.

Military approaches must focus not only on securing urban areas but also on securing rural areas to ensure displaced rural communities can return home. This will require training and equipping special force units more effectively to combat and disrupt Boko Haram operations, and continuously sweeping the areas targeted as strategic points of control by Boko Haram. These forces must be highly mobile and ready for deployment at a moment's notice. This will require equipping them with additional helicopters to alleviate reliance on poor roads, which slow down operations. It will also necessitate efficient command, control, communications, computers, intelligence, surveillance and reconnaissance (C4SIR) systems to ensure that these forces are proactive rather than reactive.

Second, regular troops must receive additional training, equipping and deployment to maintain control over areas that the special forces units have freed from Boko Haram control. These units will be the ones that interact with the local population and will, therefore, need to have sufficient training in this respect. As the face of the Nigerian government in rural areas, the relationship between these regular troops and the civilian population is key. They are there not only to stop Boko Haram attacks but also to rebuild the legitimacy of the state.

Third, human rights abuses by security forces must be dealt with harshly and publicly. There is little to no chance of the local population giving the Nigerian military the support, information and cooperation it needs while they are the victims of both Boko Haram and military abuses. Even if the Nigerian army does manage to suppress Boko Haram through sheer force of arms, it will be a temporary suppression if it does not involve and gain support among the local populace.

Fourth, those displaced by the insurgency need to be able to return to their homes, and to do so they are going to need significant humanitarian assistance. There is no point in securing a geographical space if the people will not or cannot return. This will take a concerted effort from the Nigerian Emergency Management Agency as well as other humanitarian organisations. Returning Nigerian citizens to their homes should be the ultimate goal of the counter-insurgency operations.

Fifth, the Nigerian government needs to rebuild the institutions destroyed by Boko Haram. This does not only mean the bureaucratic functions of state, but also the community institutions that manage daily life. This requires spaces for village and town councils to be rebuilt and operate safely. Local governance is key to returning power and agency to the people, and to ending the cycle of grievances that allow insurgencies to foment. Due to the importance of religion in the daily life of northern Nigeria, religious leaders who have been killed or driven away need to be replaced or returned to their communities. Rather than trying to manage the affected areas from Abuja, the government needs to encourage and train the local population to take control of local governance within the rule of law.

Sixth, the state needs to prioritise economic development. Economic development is an important factor in reducing the appeal of insurgency, as it gives people something to lose. Economic development must take place on a macro level, such as repairing and upgrading infrastructure, but also on a micro level, such as supplying farmers with the requisite tools they need to resume planting and harvesting. Furthermore, a concerted effort should be made to expand access to markets so that those who return can move beyond purely subsistence farming. A large investment is needed in education, but this should not focus only on basic literacy but also provide practical, skills-based curricula. The government should investigate the viability of options such as micro-finance, agricultural training and small-scale manufacturing throughout Borno State, as a means to develop both the region and the human capital within it.

Seventh, the state needs to embark on an extensive disarmament, demobilisation and reintegration programme, as well as a reconciliation process. People who fought for Boko Haram need to be returned to society. The reconciliation process needs to be started as soon as possible so that Boko Haram fighters are encouraged to defect without fear, while communities can begin to come to terms with the horror of what has been inflicted upon them. This reconciliation process should involve communities, local government, former combatants and members of the armed forces who have committed human-rights abuses. While the government continues to use harsh methods at all levels to combat Boko Haram, it is going to be difficult, if not impossible, to get the rank and file to desert them.

Finally, if the insurgence is to be truly defeated, governance must be addressed. Corruption must be stamped out, and those found guilty of it must not only be punished but also punished publicly. The Nigerian government must also acknowledge that its own poor governance was a contributing factor to the rise of Boko Haram. This will do more to secure the legitimacy of the state than any amount of deradicalisation education could hope to achieve. The government must be seen as responsive to the needs of the people, and communities must be offered legitimate avenues to air grievances and make recommendations, as they often understand local issues far better than a central bureaucracy based in a province's capital. If the Nigerian government seeks to turn recent, short-term military gains against Boko Haram into a sustainable and lasting peace, they need to govern proactively and provide citizens with a space in which to air their grievances, free from fear of retribution and in the knowledge that the government will listen and respond.

Endnotes

1. Institute for Economics and Peace (2016) *Global Terrorism Index 2015*. Available at: http://economicsandpeace.org/reports/
2. Good Governance Africa (2015) *Africa Survey 2015–2016*. Available at: http://www.gga.org/research-knowledge/knowledge-centre/africa-survey/
3. Ibid, pp. 6–10.
4. Ibid, p. 49.
5. African Economic Outlook (2015) *Nigeria 2015*, p. 3. Available at: http://www.africaneconomicoutlook.org/fileadmin/uploads/aeo/2015/CN_data/CN_Long_EN/Nigeria_GB_2015.pdf
6. Good Governance Africa (2015).
7. World Bank (2015) *Poverty Overview*, p. 1. Available at: http://www.worldbank.org/en/topic/poverty/overview
8. Oilprice.com (2016) *Commodity Prices Live*. Available at: http://oilprice.com/
9. African Economic Outlook (2015) p. 3.
10. United Nations Development Program (2013) *Human Development Index: Income Gini Coefficient, 2013*. Available at: http://hdr.undp.org/en/content/income-gini-coefficient
11. Organisation for Economic Co-operation and Development (2017) *Nigeria*. Available at: http://www.oecd.org/countries/nigeria/
12. African Economic Outlook (2015) p. 10.
13. Abara, CJ (2012) *Inequality and Discrimination in Nigeria: Tradition and religion as negative factors affecting gender*. Paper presented at the Federation of International Human Rights Museums, 8–10 October 2012.
14. Ibid, pp. 5–7.
15. Ibid, p. 7.
16. Ibid, p. 8.
17. Ibid, pp. 10–11.
18. Good Governance Africa (2015) p. 492.
19. Ibid, pp. 493–498.
20. Hembe, G (2000) The logic of more states and the nature of Nigerian Federalism, *African Journal of Economy and Society*, **2** (2), p. 3.
21. Cited in Vande, P (2012) Ethnicity and the politics of state creation in Nigeria, *European Scientific Journal*, **8** (16), p. 38.
22. Ibid, p. 4.
23. Ojochenemi, D, Asuelime, L and David, O (2015) *Boko Haram: The socio-economic drivers*. Gewerbestrasse: Springer International Publishing.
24. Cited in Ojochenemi et al (2015) p. 4.
25. Ibid, p. 3.
26. Ibid.
27. Kalu, K (2008) *State Power, Autarchy, and Political Conquest in Nigerian Federalism*. Plymouth: Lexington Books, p. 9.
28. Ibid.
29. SPICE (2009) *The Spread of Islam in West Africa: Containment, mixing, and reform from the eighth to the twentieth century*. Stanford Program on International and Cross-Cultural Education (SPICE), Spring 2009.
30. Ibid, p. 1.

31 Ibid.
32 Alao, A (2013) Islamic radicalisation and violence in Nigeria, *Security and Development*, **13** (2), pp. 127–147. Available at: http://www.securityanddevelopment.org/pdf/ESRC%20Nigeria%Overview.pdf
33 Ibid.
34 Ibid.
35 Good Governance Africa (2015) p. 33.
36 Agbiboa, D and Maiangwa, B (2013) *Boko Haram, Religious Violence and the Crisis of National Identity in Nigeria: Towards a non-killing approach*. London: Sage Publications, p. 381.
37 Alao (2013) pp. 127–147.
38 Alao (2013) p. 7.
39 Agbiboa and Maiangwa (2013) p. 383.
40 Ibid.
41 Ibid, p. 38.
42 Abu Bakar, A and Saleh, A (2011) A survey of information resources required by ulama to perform their work roles: A case study of Borno State, Nigeria, *Library Philosophy and Practice*, 2011, p. 2.
43 Borno State Ministry of Health (2010) *Strategic Health Development Plan 2010–2015*. Available at: http://www.mamaye.org/sites/default/files/evidence/Borno%20SSHDP%2006.01.11.pdf
44 Online Nigeria (n.d.) Borno State. Available at: http://links.onlinenigeria.com/bornoadv.asp?blurb=221
45 Blanchard, L (2014) Nigeria's Boko Haram: Frequently asked questions, *Current Politics and Economics of Africa*, **7** (2), pp. 153–172.
46 Ibid, p. 1.
47 Okemi, M (2013) A religious sect or a terrorist organization? *Global Journal of Politics and Law Research*, **1** (1), p. 3.
48 Anti-Defamation League (ADL) (2014) Boko Haram: The emerging jihadist threat in West Africa. Available at: http://www.adl.org/assets/pdf/combating-hate/boko-haram-jihadist-threat-west-africa-2013-1-11-v1.pdf
49 Connell, S (2012) To be or not to be: Is Boko Haram a foreign terrorist organization? *Global Security Studies*, **3** (3), p. 88.
50 Study of Terrorism and Response to Terrorism (2014) Boko Haram Recent Attacks: Background report, p. 9.
51 Ogunlesi, T (2014) Have over 13,000 people been killed in Nigeria's insurgency? The claim is broadly correct. Africa Check. Published 14 October 2014. Available at: https://africacheck.org/reports/have-13000-people-been-killed-in-nigerias-insurgency-the-claim-is-broadly-correct/
52 Blanchard (2014) p. 5.
53 Al Jazeera (2015) US troops deployed to Cameroon for Boko Haram fight. Published 7 October 2015. Available at: http://www.aljazeera.com/news/2015/10/usa-troops-deployed-cameroon-boko-haram-fight-151014212428195.html
54 United Nations Office for the Coordination of Humanitarian Affairs (2015) Nigeria: Northeast Crisis. Situation Report, 30 January 2015.
55 Mahmood, O (2017) *Boko Haram in 2016: A highly adaptable foe*. Pretoria: Institute of Security Studies.
56 Crisis Group (2017) *Watchmen of Lake Chad: Vigilante groups fighting Boko Haram*, Africa Report No. 244. Available at: https://d2071andvip0wj.cloudfront.net/244-watchmen-of-lake-chad-vigilante-groups-fighting-boko-haram.pdf
57 Liolio, SE (2013) Rethinking counterinsurgency: A case study of Boko Haram. Master's

thesis, European Peace University, Stadschlaining, Austria, pp. 55–56; Okeme (2013) p. 6.
58 Liolio (2013) p. 55.
59 Mantzikos, I (2013) *Boko Haram: The anatomy of a crisis*. Bristol: e-International Relations, p. 18.
60 Cook, D (2014) *Boko Haram: A new Islamic State in Nigeria*. Houston, TX: Rice University's Baker Institute for Public Policy, p. 9.
61 Ibid.
62 Ibid.
63 Connel (2012) p. 88.
64 Ibid.
65 Ibid.
66 Liolio (2013) p. 73.
67 Ibid, p. 74.
68 Moore, RS (2007) The basics of counterinsurgency, *Small Wars Journal*, **5** (5), p. 2.
69 Ibid, p. 2.
70 Ibid, p. 7.
71 Liolio (2013) p. 38.
72 Ibid.
73 Moore (2007) p. 3.
74 Brooks, M (2007) *World War Z*. New York: Crown Publishers, p. 187.
75 Moore (2007) p. 4.
76 Brigaglia, A (2012) Ja'far Mahmoud Adam, Mohammed Yusuf and Al-Muntada Islamic Trust: Reflections on the genesis of the Boko Haram phenomenon in Nigeria, *Annual Review of Islam in Africa*, **11**, p. 7.
77 START (2014) p. 8.
78 Moore (2007) p. 5.
79 Cook (2014) p. 9.
80 Valeyre, B (2011) *'Winning Hearts and Minds': Historical origins of the concept and its current implementation in Afghanistan*. Paris: Cahiers de la Recherche Doctrinale.
81 Moore (2007) p. 5.
82 Wilkinson, P (2006) *Terrorism Versus Democracy: The liberal state response*. New York: Routledge, p. 203.
83 United States, Department of Army (2006) *The US Army/Marine Corps Counterinsurgency Field Manual: US Army Field Manual No. 3–24*. Marine Corps Warfighting Publication No. 3-33.5. Available at: https://www.hsdl.org/?abstract&did=468442
84 Rineheart, J (2010) Counterterrorism and counterinsurgency, *Perspectives on Terrorism*, **4** (5).
85 Ibid.
86 United Nations (2002) United States of America, remarks by President George W Bush at the International Conference on Financing for Development. Monterrey, Mexico, 22 March 2002.
87 World Bank (2015) *Poverty Overview*. Available at: http://www.worldbank.org/en/topic/poverty/overview
88 Krieger and Meierrieks (2009) pp. 5–8.
89 Ibid, p. 8.
90 Schmid, AP (2005) Root causes of terrorism: Some conceptual notes, a set of indicators, and a model, *Democracy and Security*, **1** (2), p. 138.
91 Ahmed, A (2013) *The Thistle and the Drone: How America's War on Terror became a global war on tribal Islam*. Washington, DC: Brookings University Press.
92 Okemi (2013) p. 3.
93 Liolio (2013) p. 58.

94. Kilcullen, DJ (2006) Three Pillars of Counterinsurgency. Remarks at the US Government Counterinsurgency Conference, Washington, DC, 28 September 2006. Available at: www.au.af.mil/au/awc/awcgate/uscoin/3pillars_of_counterinsurgency.pdf
95. Ibid, p. 4.
96. Ibid.
97. Ibid, p. 6.
98. Ibid.
99. Ibid.
100. Ibid.
101. Ibid.
102. Good Governance Africa (2015) pp. 694–714.
103. DefenceWeb (2016) *Nigerian Armed Forces*. Available at: http://www.defenceweb.co.za/index.php?option=com_content&view=article&id=32118:nigerian-armed-forces&catid=119:african-militaries
104. Okemi (2013) p. 3.
105. Ibid, p. 4.
106. *Bloomberg* (2017) Nigeria sets up special court to battle graft. Published 28 September 2017. Available at: https://www.bloomberg.com/news/articles/2017-09-28/nigeria-setting-up-special-courts-for-graft-cases-minister-says
107. *The Washington Post* (2015) The Nigerian military is so broken, its soldiers are refusing to fight. Published 10 May 2015. Available at: https://www.washingtonpost.com/world/africa/the-nigerian-military-is-so-broken-its-soldiers-are-refusing-to-fight/2015/05/06/d56fabac-dcae-11e4-b6d7-b9bc8acf16f7_story.html?utm_term=.ddcb97018600
108. *The Atlantic* (2014) Nigerian military officers court-martialed for giving Boko Haram weapons. Published 3 June 2014. Available at: https://www.theatlantic.com/international/archive/2014/06/nigerian-generals-arrested-for-giving-boko-haram-weapons/372052/
109. Amnesty International (2015) *Stars on Their Shoulders, Blood on their Hands: War crimes committed by the Nigerian military*, p. 3. Available at: https://www.amnesty.org/en/documents/afr44/1657/2015/en/
110. Ibid, p. 5.
111. Ibid.
112. Ibid.
113. *The Atlantic* (2014).
114. Smith D (2015) South Africa's ageing white mercenaries who helped turn tide on Boko Haram, *The Guardian*. Published 14 April 2015.
115. Cilliers, J and Mason, P (1999) *Peace, Profit or Plunder? The privatisation of security in war-torn African societies*. Pretoria: Institute for Security Studies, p. 85.
116. Freeman, C (2015) South African mercenaries' secret war on Boko Haram, *The Telegraph*. Published 10 May 2015.
117. Bhutia, J (2015) Buhari claims 'technical' victory over Boko Haram, *IB Times*. Published 24 December 2015.

References

Abara, CJ (2012) *Inequality and Discrimination in Nigeria: Tradition and religion as negative factors affecting gender*, Federation of International Human Rights Museums, 8–10 October 2012.

Abdul'Aziz, I and Mbachu, D (2014) Nigerian troops say corruption saps will to fight Islamists. *Bloomberg*. Published 16 July 2014.

Abu Bakar, A and Saleh, A (2011) A survey of information resources required by ulama to perform their work roles: A case study of Borno State, Nigeria, *Library Philosophy and Practice*, **2011**, p. 2.

African Economic Outlook (2015) *Nigeria 2015*. Available at: http://www.africaneconomicoutlook.org/fileadmin/uploads/aeo/2015/CN_data/CN_Long_EN/Nigeria_GB_2015.pdf

Agbiboa, D and Maiangwa, B (2013) *Boko Haram, Religious Violence and the Crisis of National Identity in Nigeria: Towards a non-killing approach*. London: Sage Publications.

Ahmed, A (2013) *The Thistle and the Drone: How America's War on Terror became a global war on tribal Islam*. Washington, DC: Brookings University Press.

Al Jazeera (2015) US troops deployed to Cameroon for Boko Haram fight. Published 7 October 2015. Available at: http://www.aljazeera.com/news/2015/10/usa-troops-deployed-cameroon-boko-haram-fight-151014212428195.html

Alao, A (2013) Islamic radicalisation and violence in Nigeria, *Security and Development*, **13** (2), pp. 127–147. Available at: http://www.securityanddevelopment.org/pdf/ESRC%20Nigeria%Overview.pdf

Amnesty International (2015) *Stars on Their Shoulders, Blood on their Hands: War crimes committed by the Nigerian military*. Available at: https://www.amnesty.org/en/documents/afr44/1657/2015/en/

Anti-Defamation League (ADL) (2014) Boko Haram: The emerging jihadist threat in West Africa. Available at: http://www.adl.org/assets/pdf/combating-hate/boko-haram-jihadist-threat-west-africa-2013-1-11-v1.pdf

Bhutia, J (2015) Buhari claims 'technical' victory over Boko Haram, *IB Times*, 24 December.

Blanchard, L (2014) Nigeria's Boko Haram: Frequently asked questions, *Current Politics and Economics of Africa*, **7** (2), pp. 153–172.

Bloomberg (2017) Nigeria sets up special court to battle graft. Published 28 September 2017. Available at: https://www.bloomberg.com/news/articles/2017-09-28/nigeria-setting-up-special-courts-for-graft-cases-minister-says

Borno State Ministry of Health (2010) *Nigeria: National Strategic Health Development Plan 2010–2015*. Available at: http://www.mamaye.org/sites/default/files/evidence/Borno%20SSHDP%2006.01.11.pdf

Brigaglia, A (2012) Ja'far Mahmoud Adam, Mohammed Yusuf and Al-Muntada Islamic Trust: Reflections on the genesis of the Boko Haram phenomenon in Nigeria, *Annual Review of Islam in Africa*, **11**, pp. 35–45.

Brooks, M (2007) *World War Z*. New York: Crown Publishers.

Cilliers, J and Mason, P (1999) *Peace, Profit or Plunder? The privatisation of security in war-torn African societies*. Pretoria: Institute for Security Studies.

Connell, S (2012) To be or not to be: Is Boko Haram a foreign terrorist organization? *Global Security Studies*, **3** (3), p. 88.

Cook, D (2014) *Boko Haram: A new Islamic State in Nigeria*. Houston, TX: Rice University's Baker Institute for Public Policy.

Crisis Group (2017) *Watchmen of Lake Chad: Vigilante groups fighting Boko Haram*, Africa Report No. 244. Available at: https://d2071andvip0wj.cloudfront.net/244-watchmen-of-lake-chad-vigilante-groups-fighting-boko-haram.pdf

DefenceWeb (2016) *Nigerian Armed Forces*. Available at: http://www.defenceweb.co.za/index.php?option=com_content&view=article&id=32118:nigerian-armed-forces&catid=119:african-militaries

Ehiabhi, V (2015) Army court-martials 10 generals, 5 others for helping Boko Haram, Naij.com.

Ejiofor, C (2015) Boko Haram control over 20 000 km^2 of Nigeria, Naij.com.

Freeman, C (2015) South African mercenaries' secret war on Boko Haram, *The Telegraph*. Published 10 May 2015.

Good Governance Africa (2015) *Africa Survey 2015–2016*. Available at: http://www.gga.org/research-knowledge/knowledge-centre/africa-survey/

Hembe, G (2000) The logic of more states and the nature of Nigerian federalism, *African Journal of Economy and Society*, **2** (2), p. 3.

International Monetary Fund, *Nigeria Country Profile 2014*. Available at: http://www.imf.org/external/pubs/ft/scr/2014/cr14103.pdf

Institute for Economics and Peace (2016) *Global Terrorism Index 2015*. Available at: http://economicsandpeace.org/reports/

Kalu, K (2008) *State Power, Autarchy, and Political Conquest in Nigerian Federalism*. Plymouth: Lexington Books.

Kilcullen, DJ (2006) Three Pillars of Counterinsurgency. Remarks at the US Government Counterinsurgency Conference, Washington, DC, 28 September 2006. Available at: www.au.af.mil/au/awc/awcgate/uscoin/3pillars_of_counterinsurgency.pdf

Krieger, T and Meierrieks, D (2009) What causes terrorism? University of Freiburg, Department of Economics.

Liolio, SE (2013) Rethinking counterinsurgency: A case study of Boko Haram. Master's thesis, European Peace University, Stadschlaining, Austria.

Mahmood, O (2017) *Boko Haram in 2016: A highly adaptable foe*. Pretoria: Institute of Security Studies.

Mantzikos, I (2013) Boko Haram: The anatomy of a crisis. Bristol: e-International Relations.

Moore, RS (2007) The basics of counterinsurgency, *Small Wars Journal*, **5** (5), p. 2.

Ogunlesi, T (2014) Have over 13,000 people been killed in Nigeria's insurgency? The claim is broadly correct. Africa Check. Published 14 October 2014. Available at: https://africacheck.org/reports/have-13000-people-been-killed-in-nigerias-insurgency-the-claim-is-broadly-correct/

Oilprice.com (2016) *Commodity Prices Live*. Available at: http://oilprice.com/

Ojochenemi, D, Asuelime, L and David, O (2015) *Boko Haram: The socio-economic drivers*. Gewerbestrasse: Springer International Publishing.

Okemi, M (2013) A religious sect or a terrorist organisation? *Global Journal of Politics and Law Research*, **1** (1), p. 3.

Omeni, AE (2015) Insurgency COIN in Nigeria. Presentation to Defence Studies Department, Kings College.

OnlineNigeria (n.d.) Borno State. Available at: http://links.onlinenigeria.com/bornoadv.asp?blurb=221

Organisation for Economic Co-operation and Development (2017) *Nigeria*. Available at: http://www.oecd.org/countries/nigeria/

Rineheart, J (2010) Counterterrorism and counterinsurgency, *Perspectives on Terrorism*, **4** (5).

Schmid, AP (2005) Root causes of terrorism: Some conceptual notes, a set of indicators and a model, *Democracy and Security*, **1** (2).

Sieff, K (2015) The Nigerian military is so broken, its soldiers are refusing to fight, *Washington Post*, 10 May 2015.

Smith D (2015) South Africa's ageing white mercenaries who helped turn tide on Boko Haram, *The Guardian*, Published 14 April 2015.

SPICE (2009) *The Spread of Islam in West Africa: Containment, mixing, and reform from the eighth to the twentieth century*. Stanford Program on International and Cross-Cultural Education (SPICE), Spring 2009.

START (Study of Terrorism and Response to Terrorism) (2014) Boko Haram Recent Attacks: Background report 2014. Available at: https://www.start.umd.edu/pubs/STARTBackgroundReport_BokoHaramRecentAttacks_May2014_0.pdf

The Atlantic (2014) Nigerian military officers court-martialled for giving Boko Haram weapons. Published 3 June 2014. Available at: https://www.theatlantic.com/international/archive/2014/06/nigerian-generals-arrested-for-giving-boko-haram-weapons/372052/

United Nations, United States of America, remarks by President George W Bush at the International Conference on Financing for Development. Monterrey, Mexico, 22 March 2002.

United Nations Development Program (2013) *Human Development Index: Income Gini Coefficient, 2013*. Available at: http://hdr.undp.org/en/content/income-gini-coefficient

United Nations Office for the Coordination of Humanitarian Affairs (2015), North East Nigeria Crisis: Humanitarian Snapshot (as of 30 January 2015). Available at: https://reliefweb.int/report/nigeria/north-east-nigeria-crisis-humanitarian-snapshot-30-january-2015

United States, Department of Army (2006) *The US Army/Marine Corps Counterinsurgency Field Manual: US Army Field Manual No. 3–24*. Marine Corps Warfighting Publication No. 3-33.5. Available at: https://www.hsdl.org/?abstract&did=468442

Valeyre, B (2011) *'Winning Hearts and Minds': Historical origins of the concept and its current implementation in Afghanistan*. Paris: Cahiers de la Recherche Doctrinale.

Vande, PT (2012) Ethnicity and the politics of state creation in Nigeria, *European Scientific Journal*, **8** (16), p. 38.

Washington Post (2015). The Nigerian military is so broken, its soldiers are refusing to fight. Published 10 May 2015. Available at: https://www.washingtonpost.com/world/africa/the-nigerian-military-is-so-broken-its-soldiers-are-refusing-to-fight/2015/05/06/d56fabac-dcae-11e4-b6d7-b9bc8acf16f7_story.html?utm_term=.ddcb97018600

Wilkinson, P (2006) *Terrorism Versus Democracy: The liberal state response*. New York: Routledge, p. 203.

World Bank (2015) *Poverty Overview*. Available at: http://www.worldbank.org/en/topic/poverty/overview

Chapter 8

The rise of ISIS and its implications for East Africa

Stephen Buchanan-Clarke

Introduction

The emergence and spread of militant Islamist groups in East Africa has had profound consequences for the region, which transcend national security. The ongoing Al-Shabaab conflict in Somalia, for example, has generated massive refugee flows in the region, putting pressure on the often already strained economic systems in neighbouring states. In several cases, this has provoked an increase in xenophobic and anti-immigrant violence, provoked ethnic and religious tensions, and led to governments passing new security measures, which both threaten the core values of open societies and impede democratic consolidation among states in the region.

The ability of violent extremist organisations to spread and recruit members is contingent on a number of environmental factors, such as porous borders, weak governance, high youth unemployment, corruption and ethnic divisions, to name a few. However, Al-Shabaab's spread out of Somalia has in part been enabled by the presence of local violent Islamist organisations in neighbouring states who show support and then pledge allegiance to the group – as has been the case in both Kenya and Tanzania.[1] Their progression from a local insurgency to a transnational actor should, therefore, be understood not simply as a product of the group's military success but also partly as the result of the rise and evolution of various brands of Islamist ideology in East Africa.

In 2012, after the gradual realignment of their ideology, Al-Shabaab pledged allegiance to Al-Qaeda and began to espouse Al-Qaeda's brand of global Salafi jihadism more actively. This translated to stark changes in the organisation's ideology, battlefield tactics, targets and ultimate goals. By elevating their *raison d'être* from a local insurgent group to a member of the 'global jihad', Al-Shabaab was able to attract both foreign fighters and revenue streams. Furthermore, their union with Al-Qaeda had significant implications for both the United States' Global War on Terrorism (GWOT) and the mandate of the African Union Mission in Somalia (AMISOM).

Over the past two years, the Islamic State of Iraq and Syria (ISIS) has made increasing inroads in Africa and begun to compete with Al-Qaeda for the allegiance of local violent Islamist groups, including Al-Shabaab.² In 2015, East Africa saw both an increase in the number of citizens attempting to travel abroad to fight for ISIS and several local Islamist organisations declaring their loyalty to the group – including a faction of Al-Shabaab in Puntland. In 2016, with the support of local actors, ISIS was able to carry out attacks in both Somalia and Kenya.³

While often viewed by the casual observer as one and the same, Al-Qaeda and ISIS differ in a variety of ways, including their core ideologies, how they recruit, battlefield tactics, who they target and their ability to encourage acts of 'lone wolf' terrorism. The growing influence of ISIS in the region will likely define the nature of terrorism in East Africa for years to come. As such, this chapter will provide a historical overview of violent Islamist movements in East Africa, including Al-Shabaab, and examine the impact their alignment to the broader Al-Qaeda network has had on the organisation. The extent to which ISIS has been successful in gaining local support will be discussed, in addition to the effects this may have on local violent Islamist organisations and state and human security in the region.

The evolution of Islamist movements in East Africa

Over the past decade, East Africa has seen an exponential growth in terrorist attacks perpetrated by militant Islamist groups seeking to further their political goals in the region.⁴ Islamist movements are not new to East Africa and emerged largely as a post-independence phenomenon in the 1960s and 1970s, predominantly inspired by Egypt's Muslim Brotherhood. As Boukhars (2006) writes, Islamism in East Africa can be divided into three distinct types of activism: political, missionary and jihadi.⁵ While Islamism is often perceived as a pejorative term, Fuller (2003) argues, that 'Islamism/Islamist' should be neutral in character as Islamist movements run the gamut from 'radical to moderate, violent to peaceful, democratic to authoritarian, and traditional to modernist'.⁶ However, throughout the latter half of the 20th century, successive waves of socially conservative Islamist movements, particularly Salafism and Wahhabism, emanating from the Middle East, have found a home in both political parties and non-political social movements in East and North Africa with varying levels of success.⁷

It can be difficult to make clear distinctions between some of the terms commonly used to denote ideological trends within Islam, such as Islamism, Salafism, neo-Salafism, Salafi-Takfirism and Wahhabism. Islamic scholars themselves offer varying and opposing definitions. However, it is generally agreed that Salafism is an ultra-conservative movement within Sunni Islam that developed during the 18th century. Its followers seek to return to the traditions of the *Salaf*, the first three generations of Muslims. Salafism does not inherently condone violence and terrorism. Some Salafis, for example, abstain from the political process, preach non-violence and seek to simply focus on *Da'wa* (the preaching of Islam). However, Wahhabism, which can be understood as a subset of Salafism, seeks to introduce an ultra-conservative religious way of life *and* generally legitimises the use of violence to achieve this goal.[8] Further still, some Wahhabis follow the *takfiri* school of thought, which either condones or actively promotes violence against both non-believers (*kafir*) and other Muslims they deem to be 'impure', such as Shi'a and Alawites.[9]

It is important here to emphasise the difference between violent Salafism and Wahhabism and other forms of Islam so as not to risk scapegoating an entire religion. Furthermore, it is important to also recognise that recruitment into organisations such as Al-Shabaab and Al-Hijra is driven by a range of factors, of which religious ideology is but one. However, as will be shown later, the founders and leaders of these movements almost exclusively follow the Salafi/Wahhabi school of thought within Islam.

Islam has been in East Africa for centuries and has helped contribute to the region's rich cultural heritage and diversity. Trade and cultural exchanges are thought to have begun in the 11th century, predating European colonisation and Christian missionaries by several centuries. Today, most Muslims in East Africa are Sunni, although there are also Shi'a and Sufi communities, in addition to members of the Ahmadiyya sect. Historically, religion has not been a significant social fault line in the region, with members of the various Islamic schools of thought and Christians living together in tolerance. Abisaid Ali (2016) argues that this has changed in recent decades, primarily as a result of the growing influence of Salafi ideology.[10] As Ali (2016) notes: 'A small but growing number of Muslims have adopted more exclusivist interpretations of their religion, thereby changing their relationship with other Muslims, with other faiths, and with the state. The radical view of a global struggle for Islam is by no means pervasive but it is very much present in a way it was not before.'[11] While, as mentioned earlier, not all those who subscribe to Salafism endorse violence (non-violent Salafis are a key community to engage with in the fight against violent extremism), it is a highly puritanical and exclusionary belief system.[12] As Abdi (2015) writes:

> The attraction of Salafism lies in the simplicity and accessibility of its theology; its absolute certitude; its disdain for hierarchy and intermediaries; and its emphasis on active faith. The true believer is not simply preoccupied with individual salvation; he or she is also an active agent for social change and for creating Dar ul Islam – a polity

governed by sharia. It is these latter qualities that have allowed Salafism to tap youthful idealism effectively and attract idealists impatience for social reform and revolution. Salafi dominance in political, social and economic spheres is in no small part a function of this activist view of faith.[13]

The genesis for the rise of Salafism in the region is largely due to external factors. The global oil boom in the 1970s, 1980s and 1990s afforded the Gulf states the ability to spread Salafism through the funding of mosques, madrassas and Muslim youth centres throughout the region. In the absence of formal education systems, many communities have come to rely heavily on these madrassas.[14] Furthermore, scholarship opportunities in the Gulf states have also increased over the past two decades, exposing scholars to fundamentalist forms of Islam, which they have brought back with them to the region. The presence of well-funded foreign Islamist groups who sponsor religious, educational, humanitarian and social programmes has also helped spread Salafism by integrating proselytisation into all their activities.[15]

For example, in Kenya, the Saudi government has for decades provided financial support and scholarships to the Kisauni College of Islamic Studies in Mombasa, where radical preacher Aboud Rogo Mohammed studied. There are 'likely dozens, if not hundreds, of Islamic schools and centres similarly underwritten by the Saudi government in the country'.[16] Rogo was well known for denigrating non-Muslims, declaring other schools of Islamic thought as *haram*, publicly supporting Al-Shabaab and Al-Qaeda, and instructing his followers to forsake inter-religious dialogue, abstain from politics and boycott all elections.[17] In his speeches, Rogo claimed that 'most Muslims in East Africa do not understand Islam. They only know the pillars of Islam but not the substance'.[18] He also consistently claimed it was the duty of all Muslims to wage war against infidels and 'fake religions' and that Muslims lived in poverty and ghettoes as divine retribution for abandoning the 'authentic teachings' of Islam.[19] He openly supported violent *jihad* by claiming that 'every Muslim should do everything to lose their lives, wealth and whatever they can for the sake of Allah'.[20] He also argued against the idea propagated by other Muslim scholars that Islam is a religion of peace stating that 'Islam is not supposed to be weak and be patronised [because] without the sword, Islam will not stand'.[21]

In Tanzania, Sheikh Ponda Issa Ponda, who is often considered the public face of radicalism in the country, was convicted of inciting religious hatred in 2013. Like Rogo, Ponda has become well known for his fiery speeches. His network includes hundreds of mosques and madrassas across the country, largely funded by Saudi Arabia. As Gilsaa (2015) notes: 'All major cities in Tanzania host at least one organisation that is run with the specific aim of propagating basic Salafi thought and purifying local Islamic practices from "un-Islamic innovations."[22] It is estimated that Saudi Arabia spends roughly US$1 million a year on building mosques, madrassas and Islamic centres in Tanzania alone.[23]

In Somalia, the Revival of Islamic Heritage Society, a Kuwaiti non-governmental organisation, was found to have provided financial and material support to Al-Itihaad al-Islamiya (AIAI), whose leaders would later help to establish Al-Shabaab. Furthermore, practically all of AIAI's leadership was educated in the Middle East, and predominantly in Saudi Arabia. As Ali (2016) notes:

> Whether universities or bare-bones madrassas, educational institutions have obvious strategic value in shaping the beliefs of youth. Some of these schools do provide valuable instruction in math, sciences, and more. However, they also inculcate a rigid interpretation of Islam that is exclusionary and emphasises *da'wa*, or the further proselytisation of this brand of Islam … Over time, students absorb very definitive ideas of what is and what is not Islamic and who is and who is not a Muslim – and are encouraged to actively advance these same views. This is a recipe for confrontation, even if the programmes that initially promoted such views did not advocate violence.[24]

The growing influence of Salafism and Wahhabism in East Africa has led to an increasing number of groups in the region adopting progressively more aggressive and confrontational positions against both the state and other Muslim and Christian communities. Where governments have handled the situation with excessive force, such as the alleged extra-judicial killing of Rogo in Kenya, and the alleged attempted killing of Ponda in Tanzania by security forces, radical preachers become martyrs and gain further sympathy for their cause. The growth of these networks across East Africa has created enormous pools of potential recruits, who may be easily drawn into violent jihad, and laid the ground for the local collaboration required for Al-Shabaab to carry out attacks in Kenya, Tanzania and Uganda.[25]

The birth of Al-Shabaab

In Somalia, initial inroads made by Egyptian Islamist groups in the 1960s and 1970s were superseded by the influence of Saudi charities, which brought significant resources in humanitarian aid, along with a puritanical Salafi brand of Islamism.[26] As mentioned, one such group who was the recipient of this charity was Al-Itihaad al-Islamiya (AIAI), which emerged as Somalia's leading

Islamist social movement in the early 1990s. The group's leadership, while Somali, comprised mostly of graduates from Islamic universities in Pakistan, Kuwait and Saudi Arabia – several of whom had gained military experience fighting in Afghanistan against the Soviet Union.[27] By the early 2000s, Somalia had been without a functioning central government for over a decade. The collapse of the Siad Barre regime in 1991 represented the failure of prior efforts by nationalist and socialist governments to improve the lives of Somali citizens and overcome divisive clan politics. As Hansen (2013) writes: 'The various ideologies that had influenced Somali history, nationalism, fascism, Marxism and clanism, were all discredited. By the late 2000s, Islam was the only belief system in Somalia that had not been discredited, and the citizens went to religious leaders with their needs for protection.'[28] The Islamic Courts Union (ICU) emerged in this period as an indigenous method of conflict resolution and governance. While the ICU was effective in stabilising Mogadishu, both Ethiopia and the US government feared the organisation's fiery rhetoric, claims to the Ogaden region of Ethiopia, and the possibility that the state would come to harbour Al-Qaeda operatives. In 2007, Ethiopia, backed by the United States, invaded Somalia and overthrew the ICU. The more radical elements within AIAI, who sought to transform the movement from *da'wa* (proselytising or preaching of Islam) to militant jihad merged with elements of the now defunct ICU to form Al-Shabaab.[29]

Today, a decade since its formation, Al-Shabaab is the predominant militant Islamist organisation in East Africa. The group's territorial control within Somalia has vacillated. At its strongest, it controlled much of the country's capital, Mogadishu; the main port city of Kismayo; and territory in the south and centre of the country equal to the size of Denmark, with an estimated troop strength of between 10 000 and 15 000.[30] The African Union's Mission in Somalia (AMISOM), a regional peacekeeping force tasked with supporting the government and reducing the threat posed by Al-Shabaab and other armed groups, has been able to recapture most of this territory. However, Al-Shabaab still poses an asymmetrical threat to the state, and routinely carries out attacks against government, AMISOM forces and civilians.

Since the group's emergence in 2007, it has evolved from a national insurgency against the Transitional Federal Government (TFG) of Somalia to a transnational actor with ties to global jihadist networks. They have been active to varying degrees throughout the Horn of Africa, including in Djibouti, Ethiopia, Kenya, Tanzania and Uganda. Their first attack outside of Somalia occurred on 11 July 2010. Twin suicide bombings were carried out against crowds gathered to watch the FIFA World Cup final at two locations in Kampala, Uganda. The attacks left 74 dead and another 70 injured.[31] On 25 May 2014, two Al-Shabaab suicide bombers blew themselves up in a popular restaurant in Djibouti City, Djibouti. The attack killed a Turkish national and wounded several others.[32] In July 2014, the group claimed responsibility for attacking and killing a number of moderate Muslim clerics in Tanzania. In 2015, their operational footprint in Tanzania increased with multiple attacks on police stations and checkpoints, resulting in the death of several officers and civilians.[33] To date, Ethiopia has uncovered several local Al-Shabaab terrorist plots but has largely managed to escape any large scale attacks on its soil.[34] Outside of Somalia, Kenya has borne the brunt of Al-Shabaab's attacks, of which there have been an estimated 272 in the country between 2011 and 2015.[35]

Al-Shabaab joins the Al-Qaeda network

Al-Shabaab is usually perceived as a unified entity, which can be misleading. Rather, Al-Shabaab is the amalgamation of several Islamist groups which often differ considerably in both ideology and objectives. Perhaps unsurprisingly, there have been episodes of disagreement among the group's leading *shura* council, which have at times turned violent. Most notably, in 2013, Ahmed Godane was able to purge Al-Shabaab's *shura* council of his critics thereby solidifying himself as leader and giving him the ability to fulfil his vision of allying Al-Shabaab with Al-Qaeda.[36] The implications for Al-Shabaab and the region as a whole were profound. As Bryden (2014) writes: 'Al-Shabaab's leadership was once relatively heterogeneous, including nationalists and politically pragmatic figures … internal debates raged over the value of a relationship with Al-Qaeda, the wisdom of attacks on civilians, and the role of foreign fighters within the organisation.'[37] The ascent of Godane signified Al-Shabaab's evolution into a chapter in Al-Qaeda's franchise, a recommitment to international jihad, and the triumph of the leadership's most radical fringe who adhere to a *takfiri* ethos, which legitimises the killing of civilians, both Muslim or otherwise.[38] The ideological alignment of Al-Shabaab had critical implications in the organisation's modus operandi, its ability to attract foreign fighters, and for the security of the region as a whole. A study by Taarnby and Hallundbaek (2010) sought to evaluate the implications of Al-Shabaab's alignment with Al-Qaeda, both at an ideological and operational level. Their study, along with others of a similar nature, found stark changes in how this ideological realignment translates to a change in operational behaviour.[39] First, Taarnby and Hallundbaek (2012) found Al-Shabaab's increasing alignment to Al-Qaeda and its Salafi jihadist ideology translated to a hardening of the group's religious and political vision:

[A]l-Shabaab became much more vocal in outlining an international agenda and called for a regional offensive against imperialist and Christian forces threatening Somalia. The arch enemy, Ethiopia, was blamed for all sorts of evils. This perception also included the USA, which was seen as controlling Ethiopia. Threats were issued against Ethiopia, Kenya, Uganda, and Burundi for their meddling in Somali affairs, but also Denmark attracted attention. On several occasions the infamous cartoons were mentioned and used explicitly as a reverence for future retaliation for insulting the Prophet.[40]

Among a range of Islamist groups in the country, Al-Shabaab increasingly began to self-identify as the only true bearers of Islam in Somalia, regardless even of the government's efforts to institutionalise sharia law. Secondly, the authors noted a change in how Al-Shabaab governed areas under its control. This included the application of social control mechanisms based on strict interpretations of sharia law, as used by the Taliban in Afghanistan. Al-Shabaab began to desecrate Sufi shrines, impose a mandatory dress code for both men and women, ban cultural practices such as music and dancing, and impose a strict interpretation of sharia law. Third, their study noted Al-Shabaab's ideological shift translated into specific perspectives on both the use of violence and operational tactics. Suicide bombings and other forms of martyrdom increased, civilians were targeted directly, and highly ritualistic and symbolic acts of violence were perpetrated more frequently.[41]

ISIS in East Africa, and Al-Shabaab's crisis of allegiance

ISIS has actively been seeking to establish itself in East Africa since at least 2014, releasing a series of propaganda videos and circulating memos calling for Islamist organisations in the region to pledge allegiance to its leader, Abu Bakr al-Baghdadi, and support the establishment of a *wilayat* (province) of the Islamic State in the Horn of Africa. Their efforts appear to be paying dividends as several Islamist groups from Kenya, Uganda and Tanzania have pledged allegiance to the group.[42]

In October 2015, Abdiqadir Mumin, leader of Al-Shabaab's Puntland faction, publically declared allegiance to ISIS, thereby establishing the first confirmed ISIS franchise in East Africa. This came after a year of reports indicating increasing disagreement within Al-Shabaab's leadership over whether allegiance should be transferred from Al-Qaeda to the quickly expanding ISIS. In a video released on social media, in the company of approximately 70 fighters, Mumin pledged *bayah* (an oath of allegiance) to ISIS leader Abu Bakr al-Baghdadi and recognised him as the rightful *Khalifa* – leader of all Muslims.[43]

In April 2016, another violent Islamist group calling itself Jhaba East Africa emerged, releasing a video publically declaring allegiance to ISIS leader Abu Bakr al-Bhagdadi. The organisation is made up of militants fighting in Somalia, including Kenyans, Tanzanians and Ugandans. The group released a public statement via social media stating that:

> We in Jahba East Africa are advising all East Africans to leave Al-Shabaab and their sponsor groups, like Al-Muhajiroun, Al-Hijra and Ansar Islam … Like Al-Shabaab, the sponsor groups have not understood the binding obligation of the Khalifah (caliphate). We are telling the mujahideen in East Africa that Al-Shabaab has now become a psychological and physical prison. To pledge *bayah* to Caliph Abu Bakr al-Baghdadi is freedom for the mujahideen in East Africa and opportunity to wage jihad according to the Sunnah against the enemies of Allah.[44]

A month later, in May 2016, Ahl al-Kahf (people of the cave), a radical Salafi sect in Tanzania, similarly released a video via social media, publically threatening to carry out attacks in the country in support of ISIS.[45]

ISIS has also had some initial successes in boosting its profile in the region through low-impact attacks orchestrated by ideological converts. In April 2016, the first attack in East Africa for which ISIS publically claimed responsibility occurred in Mogadishu, with several more occurring in Somalia since then. In September 2016, ISIS claimed responsibility through their media wing for an attack on a Mombasa police station in Kenya, where three women walked into a police station, stabbed and shot three police officers, before setting fire to the building.[46] In October, a self-proclaimed follower of ISIS was responsible for an attack on a Kenyan police officer outside the US embassy in Nairobi.[47] Furthermore, while precise figures differ, Kenyan authorities estimate at least 100 Kenyans have left to fight for ISIS in Libya and the Middle East.[48]

ISIS has already established itself across North Africa, with organisations from Algeria, Egypt, Libya, Niger and Tunisia declaring allegiance to the group. As analysts have noted, as ISIS continue to lose territory in both Iraq and Syria, both North and sub-Saharan Africa are increasingly gaining importance as an area of expansion for the group. This has been confirmed by ISIS itself through its online magazine, *Dabiq*, where the consolidation and expansion of the group into Africa is identified as a leading strategic goal.[49]

Increasing power struggles and turf wars between Al-Qaeda and ISIS for allegiance of East Africa's local violent Islamist movements pose a new threat to the region's security. The emergence of ISIS in East Africa will change the nature of violent jihad in the region. As seen in other contexts, ISIS promotes a different approach to jihad than its predecessor, Al-Qaeda. This translates into different battlefield tactics and goal structures. Furthermore, the organisation has proven adept at motivating sympathisers to take up arms in their countries of residence, thereby spreading the threat of terrorism to states which, to date, have been relatively insulated.

Al-Qaeda and ISIS: Origins and divergence

Al-Qaeda and ISIS are often understood by the casual observer to be one and the same. In fact, what is today called ISIS, was just a few years ago an affiliate of Al-Qaeda and went by the name Al-Qaeda in Iraq (AQI). Ideologically, both groups adhere to Salafi jihadism, which can be characterised by two criteria: 'First, the group emphasises the importance of returning to a "pure" Islam, that of the *Salaf*, the pious ancestors. Second, the group believes that violent jihad is *fard 'ayn* (or a personal religious duty)'.[50] However, there are a number of important differences between the organisations, which determines the type and nature of the threat each poses to society and the state.

Al-Qaeda emerged in 1988 out of the anti-Soviet jihad in Afghanistan. Throughout the 1980s, a growing number of Arabs joined the fight against the Afghan Marxist regime and their Soviet Union backers. These individuals were largely funded by the Saudi government and a number of global Muslim organisations.[51] One of these was Maktab al-Khidamat (MAK), funded by wealthy Saudi businessmen, of which Osama bin Laden was the most prominent. In 1984, MAK established a 'service office' in Peshawar, Pakistan, which was run by Bin Laden and Abdullah Yusuf Azzam, a Palestinian Islamic scholar and member of the Muslim Brotherhood. MAK served to construct paramilitary training camps for foreign recruits for the Afghan war front. Bin Laden became a major financier of the Afghan mujahideen, using his own money and influence among Saudi royalty and Gulf petro-billionaires to influence public opinion and raise awareness among Muslims about the jihad against the 'atheist' Marxist forces.[52] In 1988, the soviet military withdrew from Afghanistan, which was perceived as a major victory for the mujahideen. Bin Laden saw this victory as a road map from which to expand their operations to other parts of the world, such as Palestine and Kashmir. As Byman (2015) writes:

> Osama bin Laden and a few of his close associates – high on their perceived victory over the mighty Soviet Union – decided to capitalise on the network they had built to take jihad global. Bin Laden's vision was to create a vanguard of elite fighters that could lead the global jihad project in a clear, strategic direction. His goal was to bring together

under a single umbrella the hundreds of small jihadist groups struggling, often feebly, against their own regimes. By the mid-1990s, he wanted to re-orient the movement as a whole, focusing it on what he saw as the bigger enemy underwriting all these corrupt local regimes – the United States.[53]

Al-Qaeda saw itself as the backer of jihadist groups around the globe. Its goal was to provide local violent Islamist organisations with the technical skills and financial support to attack US targets everywhere. Unlike ISIS, Al-Qaeda's priority has always been to undertake operations against the 'far enemy' (Western nations). Bin Laden believed this would lead the United States to invade the Middle East, and thus draw the country into a long-term conflict where, like the Soviet Union, they would be slowly defeated in an asymmetrical guerrilla-style war.[54] While Bin Laden and the Al-Qaeda leadership would often publically ridicule Middle Eastern governments for being 'puppet governments' of the West, he was careful not to directly target these governments in attacks, as he feared losing Muslim public support for Al-Qaeda's cause.[55] Al-Qaeda's 1998 attacks on US embassies in Kenya and Tanzania are indicative of their early modus operandi. In both cases, the capacity of local violent Islamist groups was developed through support by Al-Qaeda to carry out complex and well-planned attacks on US targets. Al-Qaeda has, over the years, structured itself into a network of affiliate groups, who are coordinated under Al-Qaeda Central based in the Pakistani tribal areas. There are estimated to be roughly 21 direct affiliates or Al-Qaeda 'chapters', including Al-Qaeda in the Islamic Maghreb, Al-Qaeda in Yemen, Al-Qaeda in Somalia (Al-Shabaab) and Al-Qaeda in the Arabian Peninsula, among others.

What today is called alternatively the Islamic State of Iraq and Syria (ISIS), the Islamic State in Syria and the Levant (ISIL), the Islamic State (IS) or Daesh evolved from one such Al-Qaeda chapter: Al-Qaeda in Iraq (AQI), led by Abu Musab al-Zarqawi, who earned the nickname 'the Butcher of Baghdad' for his extreme use of violence.[56] Whereas Bin Laden was the son of a well-respected billionaire construction magnate and studied economics at King Abdulaziz University, Al-Zarqawi was an orphan and school dropout, with a long prison record. As Weaver (2006) writes: 'Al-Zarqawi had been a bully and a thug, a bootlegger and a heavy drinker, and even, allegedly, a pimp in Zarqa's underworld.'[57] The points of contention, which led to the split between Al-Qaeda and Al-Qaeda in Iraq, were primarily related to Al-Zarqawi's alacrity when it came to targeting Muslim civilians whom he personally deemed as *takfir* and, therefore, apostates who should be killed.[58] Al-Zarqawi's punishment for those he deemed as *takfir* often included public beheadings, which were filmed and posted online: now a trademark of ISIS propaganda. Furthermore, unlike Bin Laden, Al-Zarqawi was focused on defeating the 'near enemy' – any government that did not institute the strictest form of puritanical Salafi-Wahhabism.[59] All Shi'a Muslims, for example, were proclaimed by him to be apostates and beheaded whenever captured. Whereas Bin Laden was reticent to attack local governments or Shi'a Muslims for fear of creating unnecessary infighting among Muslims, Al-Zarqawi specifically targeted Shi'a Muslims as a means of instigating a sectarian war in Iraq. In communications intercepted following a notorious wave of hostage beheadings and truck bombings of Shi'a shrines and mosques in Iraq, Al-Zarqawi wrote: 'If we succeed in dragging [the Shi'a] into a sectarian war, this will awaken the sleepy Sunnis who are fearful of destruction and death at the hands of the Shia'.[60] Bin Laden believed these actions would have a negative effect on Muslim opinion of Al-Qaeda as a franchise, and lose them global support. By 2006, Al-Qaeda in Iraq and Al-Qaeda Central no longer communicated, and after Al-Zarqawi was killed by the US bombing campaign, Abu Bakr al-Baghdadi took over the leadership of AQI's remaining elements to form ISIS.

A new face of Islamist extremism in East Africa?

The above serves to illustrate some of the theological and operational differences between Al-Qaeda and ISIS, which directly translates to the type of threat they pose in East Africa. In January 2017, the director of the African Centre for the Study and Research on Terrorism (ACSRT) warned of an estimated influx of 2 500 ISIS fighters into North and East Africa should the organisation's strategic stronghold in Mosul fall.[61] The nature of this evolving threat should determine how counterterrorism operations, and broader efforts to address extremism, are conceptualised and implemented.

First, the increasing influence of ISIS in East Africa may result in an increase in the proportion of attacks directed against local governments. Abu Muhammad al-Adnan, a senior leader and spokesperson for ISIS, has on multiple occasions made calls for ISIS followers the world over to take up arms against their governments wherever they live.[62] Whereas Al-Qaeda's operational focus has been to prioritise the 'far enemy' (Western nations), ISIS has proven to be more focused on state-building and governance by immediately seizing land from the 'near enemy' to create a caliphate.[63] Therefore, ISIS may pose more of a threat to governments in the region than they do to Western embassies and interests – which have long been the primary focus of Al-Qaeda (as witnessed in the 1998 US embassy bombings in Tanzania and Kenya).

Al-Qaeda has effectively used women in their operations since their inception in the late 1980s. However, women within Al-Qaeda have largely taken up roles relating to communications and material support.[64] Bin Laden and Al-Zawahiri have been critical of women being used as suicide bombers or frontline fighters. ISIS, however, has no such qualms, and routinely uses women to carry out bombing operations, as they see them as less likely to be stopped at checkpoints and border crossings.[65] Their recruiting videos and magazines often appeal directly to women and spell out the roles they can play within the movement. In September 2016, three women who had publically declared allegiance to ISIS walked into a police station in Mombasa, Kenya, stabbed one officer and set fire to the building with a petrol bomb.[66] While Al-Shabaab have used women as both recruiting agents and to courier weapons, they have generally not served in frontline positions. The rise of ISIS in East Africa may thus result in more women being recruited and used to carry out suicide bombings, as has been seen in Iraq and Syria.

Both Shi'a and Sunni Muslims, who do not follow the hard-line Salafi-Wahhabism of ISIS, have always been a primary target of the organisation. Where Al-Qaeda is generally reluctant to direct violence against fellow Muslims, ISIS actively attempts to foment sectarian violence by engaging in attacks against both Sunni and Shi'a Muslims. In East Africa, while the majority of the Muslim population is Sunni, there are small populations of Sufis and Shi'as. ISIS may seek to direct operations against them, including their cultural and historical sites of importance, as a way of further polarising the Muslim community and galvanising local support.

In Kenya and elsewhere in East Africa there has been an increase in ISIS recruitment in recent years. Moreover, whereas in the past Al-Qaeda had sought to gain the allegiance of prominent sheiks and religious scholars, a major strength of ISIS has been its ability to appeal to the youth. Al-Qaeda's propaganda largely comprises poor quality videos of grey-bearded clerics giving long sermons denouncing the West. In comparison, ISIS's communication techniques are far more sophisticated. Young fighters are encouraged to capture their own exploits in high-quality videos, which are then well edited with soundtracks and subtitles added. The clerics and religious leaders who do give sermons for ISIS are young and engaging. Abu Bakr al-Baghdadi, the current leader of ISIS, is about 30 years younger than Ayman al-Zawahiri, today's leader of Al-Qaeda. ISIS has also been adept at exploiting social media in a way that the older leadership of Al-Qaeda never could. In particular, their use of Twitter bots has been extremely effective in amplifying their message and making it difficult for authorities to identify from which accounts they originate. Internet connectivity within East Africa is growing exponentially year by year. Today, Kenya currently leads in African connectivity with the highest bandwidth per person on the continent, the fastest speeds, and some of the lowest internet costs.[67]

Of course, acts of terrorism are also designed as a form of communication, often to generate fear or to broadcast a message to both an organisation's enemies and allies. Whereas Al-Qaeda was often reluctant to widely publish beheadings and other acts of violence, extreme brutality has become a defining aspect of ISIS. Indeed, the recording and publishing of execution videos by Al-Qaeda in Iraq was one of the disagreements that eventually led to the two groups splitting and the formation of ISIS.[68] On 8 January 2017, Al-Shabaab militants in Kenya beheaded nine civilians in an attack on the village of Jima in southeast Kenya. As a change from their primary tactic of IEDs and mass assaults, this may indicate that Al-Shabaab is learning from the notoriety gained by ISIS and adapting accordingly. The way in which Al-Shabaab has adapted its social media engagement and communications strategy in recent years, such as increasing the amount of high-quality video content they produce, using Twitter bots and sending mass texts, already shows signs that ISIS has had a considerable effect on how violent Islamist movements can market themselves to potential recruits.[69] As exposure to digital propaganda grows in the region, ISIS will likely gain a greater foothold among vulnerable youth, while Al-Qaeda continues to lose relevance.

An increase in influence of ISIS in East Africa may also precipitate an increase in 'lone wolf' terrorist incidents – something that was rarely seen among Al-Qaeda recruits and supporters. The term 'lone wolf' gives the impression that individuals who carry out acts of terrorism act alone and without contact to a broader network of terrorist actors. However, in reality, usually individuals who commit 'lone wolf' acts of terrorism are actively encouraged and supported (sometimes financially and materially), either online or through person-to-person interactions by the greater ISIS network. As Worth (2016) writes:

> The phenomenon of lone wolf attacks by radical jihadis can be traced to the late 1990s when Al-Qaeda-affiliated writer and strategist Abu Musab al-Suri began advocating within the organisation for the decentralisation. In late 2004, Al-Suri's 1 600-page manifesto, *The Global Islamic Resistance Call*, laid out his vision: 'A leaderless jihad, with individuals or small cells around the world acting independently, united only by a common ideology.'[70]

However, despite Al-Suri's strategy, the Al-Qaeda leadership, reticent to relinquish control and influence of their movement, never truly embraced it. By contrast, ISIS was quick to see the usefulness of the strategy and strongly advocated it. The organisation also established protocols for claiming credit for acts of violence it had no direct hand in orchestrating, thereby creating the illusion of a sophisticated and extensive reach. For example, ISIS has claimed responsibility for both the San Bernardino and Orlando shootings, where there is no evidence of direct support for the individuals responsible. The organisation's official online magazine, *Dabiq*, routinely encourages supporters to carry out any form of attack in any location they are able. In June 2016, a spokesperson for ISIS encouraged potential lone wolf supporters by saying: 'The smallest action you do in the heart of their land is dearer to us than the largest action by us and more effective and more damaging to them'.[71] Hence, it is likely that East Africa will see an uptick in lone wolf terrorist attacks directed at 'soft-targets' such as places where civilians congregate.

Conclusion

Since 2000, there has been close to a tenfold increase in the number of deaths from terrorism, rising from an estimated 3 361 in 2000 to 29 376 in 2015.[72] Furthermore, the rapid expansion of activities by some of the world's deadliest violent extremist organisations to countries considered insulated from this threat was largely unforeseen by terrorism analysts. For example, between 2015 and 2016, ISIS and its affiliates became active in 15 new countries, many African, raising the total number of countries in which the group now operates to 28.[73] It is clear that governments and policy-makers have been unable to effectively address transnational violent extremism as an evolving security threat.

In recent years, there has at least been a growing convergence among government and policy-makers around appropriate responses to violent extremism. This includes a recognition that purely militaristic and kinetic responses to organisations that use terrorism have proven ineffective in solving the phenomenon in the medium to long term, and the need to take a more comprehensive approach which addresses the underlying drivers of violent extremism. This is reflected in the United Nations Secretary-General's Plan of Action on Preventing Violent Extremism, which emphasises the need for a whole-of-society approach, and the growing number of regional and national P/CVE frameworks in East Africa, including in Kenya, Somalia and Tanzania.[74] However, as highlighted in this chapter, the threat posed by violent Islamist organisations in East Africa is complex and rapidly changing. It is often easy to group the multitude of Islamist organisations operating in the region (Al-Qaeda, Al-Shabaab and ISIS in particular) as one and the same, or at the very least, sharing an equivalent objective. However, a more nuanced evaluation illustrates the stark differences they have in ideology, goals and modi operandi. In the coming years, it is likely that ISIS will gain further traction in East Africa, and be able to encourage lone-wolf attacks in countries previously considered insulated against the threat of terrorism, and reshape the marketplace of violent extremism. While ISIS may find resilience among some local Islamist organisations, their notoriety and power may entice others to realign themselves in support. This will likely occur on a case-by-case basis and be contingent on the specific power dynamics in the region. Both security-led and developmental frameworks to prevent and counter violent extremism in East Africa are bound to fail if they do not differentiate between violent Islamist organisations and craft nuanced policy that speaks to the characteristics of each organisation.

Endnotes

1. Al-Hijra, for example, is a local Kenyan group, which pledged allegiance to Al-Shabaab in 2013. They are thought to be responsible for helping plan the 2013 attack on the Westgate Mall. See https://www.trackingterrorism.org/group/muslim-youth-center-al-hijra-kenya
2. Reuters (2015) Shabaab and East African Front compete for notoriety. Published 12 April 2015. Available https://www.nytimes.com/2016/04/13/world/africa/militant-groups-compete-for-notoriety-in-east-africa.html
3. Centre for Security Policy (2015) Jahba East Africa Jihadists Encroaching Upon al-Shabaab. Published 2 April 2015. Available at: http://www.centerforsecuritypolicy.org/2016/04/12/jahba-east-africa-jihadists-encroaching-upon-al-shabaab/ p. 1.
4. Institute for Economics & Peace (2016) *Global Terrorism Index 2015*. Available at: http://economicsandpeace.org/reports/
5. Boukhars, A (2006) Understanding Somali Islamism, *Terrorism Monitor*, 4 (10). Published 18 May 2006. Available at: https://jamestown.org/program/understanding-somali-islamism/
6. Fuller, GE (2003) *The Future of Political Islam*. New York: Palgrave Macmillan, p. 12.
7. Most notably, in the 1991 Algerian local government elections, the Islamic Salvation Front (ISF) was the first Islamist party to win a majority vote in a democratic election. However, as it became increasingly clear the party would win the national elections, the Algerian army seized power, sparking a bloody decade-long civil war. In Sudan, the National Islamic Front (NIS) became one of only two Islamic revivalist movements to gain political power in the 20th century (the other being the followers of Ayatollah Ruhollah Khomeini in the Islamic Republic of Iran). See: Esposito, JL & Piscatori, JP (1991) Democratization and Islam, *Middle East Journal*, 45 (4). Available at: http://www.jstor.org/stable/4328314?seq=1#page_scan_tab_contents
8. Moussalli, A (2009) *Wahhabism, Salafism and Islamism: Who is the enemy?* A Conflicts Forum Monograph. Beirut, London, Washington: Conflicts Forum. Published 30 January 2009. Available at: http://conflictsforum.org/briefings/Wahhabism-Salafism-and-Islamism.pdf p. 3.
9. Ibid, p. 3.
10. Ali, AM (2016) *Islamist Extremism in East Africa*. Africa Centre for Strategic Studies, Africa Security Brief No. 32. Available at: http://africacenter.org/publication/islamist-extremism-east-africa/#fn8
11. Ibid, p. 3.
12. The word 'jihad' is often understood by the general public to mean 'holy war'. However, in a purely linguistic sense, the Arabic word translates to 'struggle' or 'effort'. The term is interpreted by religious scholars in a variety of ways, and there are 164 mentions of it in the Qur'an. While it can be understood as a believer's 'struggle' or 'effort' to live out the Muslim faith as well as possible, it is usually interpreted by violent Islamist movements as a 'struggle' or 'holy war' to defend Islam, and the duty of all Muslims Therefore, this

chapter makes sure to use the term 'violent jihad' to distinguish it from other non-violent definitions of the term. See: Delong-Bas, N (2004) *Wahhabi Islam: From revival and reform to global jihad*. New York: Oxford University Press.

13 Abdi, R (2015) East Africa's s Sufi path to Countering Violent Extremism must not shun Salafists if it is to succeed. *Mail & Guardian*. Published 15 September 2015. Available at: http://mgafrica.com/article/2015-09-15-east-africas-sufi-path-to-countering-violent-extremism-must-not-exclude-salafists-if-it-is-to-succeed

14 Haynes, J (2007) Islam and democracy in East Africa. In F Volpi and F Cavatorta (eds) *Democratization in the Muslim World: Changing patterns of power and authority*. New York: Routledge. p. 491.

15 Ali (2016) p. 3.

16 Ibid, p. 3.

17 Ibid, p. 3.

18 Ochami, D (2012) How fiery cleric Rogo developed, propagated extremism, *The Standard*. Published 2 September 2012. Available at: http://www.standardmedia.co.ke/article/2000065268/how-fiery-cleric-rogo-developed-propagated-extremism

19 Ali (2016) p. 4.

20 Ochami (2012).

21 Ibid.

22 Gilsaa, S (2015) Salafism(s) in Tanzania: Theological roots and political subtext of the Ansar Sunna, *Islamic Africa*, **6**, pp. 30–59. Available at: https://www.deepdyve.com/lp/brill/salafism-s-in-tanzania-theological-roots-and-political-subtext-of-the-dQH4XNv0cH

23 Haynes (2007).

24 Ali (2016), p. 5.

25 Ibid, p. 5.

26 Menkhaus, K (2004) *Somalia: State collapse and the threat of terrorism*. Adelphi Paper 364. London and New York: Routledge, p. 65.

27 Tadesse, M (2002) *Al-Ittihad: Political Islam and the Black Economy in Somalia: Religion, money, clan, and the struggle for supremacy over Somalia*. Addis Ababa: Maeg Press.

28 Hansen, SJ (2013) *The History and Ideology of a Militant Islamist Group*. Oxford: Oxford University Press p. 23.

29 Samatar, I (2007) Ethiopian invasion of Somalia, US warlordism and AU shame, *Review of African Political Economy*, **34** (111), pp. 155–165. Available at: http://www.jstor.org/stable/20406369?seq=1#page_scan_tab_contents, p. 156.

30 Hansen (2013) p. 72.

31 *The Guardian* (2010) Uganda bomb blast kills at least 74. Published 12 July 2010. Available at: http://www.theguardian.com/world/2010/jul/12/uganda-kampala-bombs-explosions-attacks

32 Reuters (2014) Al-Shabaab claims responsibility for Djibouti suicide attack. Published 27 May 2014. Available at: http://www.reuters.com/article/uk-djibouti-attacks-idUSKBN0E72AA20140527

33 LeSage, A (2014) The Rising Threat in Tanzania: Domestic Islamist Militancy and Regional Threats. Institute for National Strategic Studies No. 288. Available at: http://ndupress.ndu.edu/portals/68/documents/stratforum/sf-288.pdf

34 Al Jazeera (2013) Is Ethiopia on Al Shabaab's hit list? Published 21 October 2013. Available at: https://www.aljazeera.com/indepth/features/2013/10/ethiopia-al-shabab-hit-list-201310211211366477.html

35 National Consortium for the Study of Terrorism and Responses to Terrorism (2016) *Global Terrorism Database*. Available at: http://www.start.umd.edu/gtd

36 Anzalone, C (2014) The life and death of Al-Shabab Leader Ahmed Godane, *CTC Sentinel*,

7 (9), pp. 19–23. Available at: https://www.ctc.usma.edu/posts/the-life-and-death-of-al-shabab-leader-ahmed-godane
37 Bryden, M (2014) *The Reinvention of Al-Shabaab: A strategy of choice or necessity?* A report of the CSIS Africa Program. Washington, DC: Center for Strategic & International Studies. Available at: https://csis-prod.s3.amazonaws.com/s3fs-, p. 1.
38 Ibid, p. 1.
39 See: Enders, W and Sandler, T (2000) Is transnational terrorism becoming more threatening? *Journal of Conflict Resolution*, **44**, pp. 307–332. University of Alabama. Available at: http://jcr.sagepub.com/content/44/3/307.full.pdf+html; Hoffman, B (2010) Al-Qaeda, trends in terrorism, and future potentialities: An assessment, *Studies in Conflict and Terrorism*, **26** (6). Available at: http://www.tandfonline.com/doi/abs/10.1080/10576100390248275
40 Taarnby, M and Hallundbaek, L (2010) Al-Shabaab: The internationalization of militant Islamism in Somalia and the implications for radicalization processes in Europe. Justice Ministry of Denmark. Available at: http://justitsministeriet.dk/sites/default/files/media/Arbejdsomraader/Forskning/Forskningspuljen/2011/2010/alshabaab.pdf, p. 13.
41 Ibid, p. 40.
42 Centre for Security Policy (2015) p. 1.
43 Reuters (2015) Small group of Somali al Shabaab swear allegiance to Islamic State. Published 23 October 2015. Available at: https://www.reuters.com/article/us-mideast-crisis-somalia/small-group-of-somali-al-shabaab-swear-allegiance-to-islamic-state-idUSKCN0SH1BF20151023
44 Dearden, L (2016) Isis: New terrorist group Jahba East Africa pledges allegiance to 'Islamic State' in Somalia, *The Independent*. Published 12 April 2016. Available at: http://www.independent.co.uk/news/world/africa/isis-new-terrorist-group-jahba-east-africa-pledges-allegiance-to-islamic-state-in-somalia-a6974476.html
45 *Daily Maverick* (2016) Militants rising: Islamic State's East Africa ambitions. Published 10 January 2017. Available at: https://www.dailymaverick.co.za/article/2017-01-10-militants-rising-islamic-states-east-african-ambitions/#.Wt8X5tNubVo
46 *Newsweek* (2016) Kenya: ISIS claims responsibility for police station attack, its first in country. Published 14 September 2016. Available at: http://europe.newsweek.com/isis-kenya-police-station-mombasa-498226?rm=eu
47 Reuters (2016) Islamic State claims responsibility for attack outside PS embassy in Nairobi. Published 29 October 2016. Available at: http://www.reuters.com/article/us-kenya-usa-islamicstate-idUSKCN12T0QS?il=0
48 Bryson, R (2016) Where does ISIS stand in Somalia? Tony Blair Institute for Global Change. Published 8 July 2016. Available at: http://tonyblairfaithfoundation.org/religion-geopolitics/commentaries/backgrounder/where-does-isis-stand-somalia
49 Ibid.
50 Jones, S (2014) A Persistent Threat: The evolution of al Qa'ida and other Salafi jihadist. RAND Corporation, p. 6.
51 Wright, L (2006) *The Looming Tower: Al Qaeda and the road to 9/11*. Random House: New York, p. 56.
52 Ibid. p. 57.
53 Byman, D (2015) *Comparing Al-Qaeda and ISIS: Different goals, different targets*. Washington, DC: Brookings Institute. Published 29 April 2016. Available at: https://www.brookings.edu/testimonies/comparing-al-qaeda-and-isis-different-goals-different-targets/
54 Stern, J and Berger, JM (2016) *ISIS: State of terror*. HarperCollins: New York, p. 38.
55 Ibid, p. 14.
56 Ibid, p. 15.
57 Weaver, MA (2006) The short, violent life of Abu Musab al-Zarqawi, *The Atlantic*. Published

July/August 2006. Available at: https://www.theatlantic.com/magazine/archive/2006/07/the-short-violent-life-of-abu-musab-al-zarqawi/304983/
58   Ibid.
59   Stern and Berger (2016) p. 38.
60   Weaver (2006).
61   ACSRT (African Centre for the Study and Research on Terrorism) (2017) ACSRT and ACSS hold seminar on analyzing the membership on African terrorist movements. Available at: http://caert.org.dz/?p=2183
62   *The Guardian* (2014) Isis instructs followers to kill Australians and other 'disbelievers'. Published 23 September 2014. Available at: https://www.theguardian.com/world/2014/sep/23/islamic-state-followers-urged-to-launch-attacks-against-australians
63   Byman, D and Williams, J (2015) ISIS vs Al-Qaeda: Jihadism's global civil war, *The National Interest*. Published 24 February 2014. Available at: http://nationalinterest.org/feature/isis-vs-al-qaeda-jihadism%E2%80%99s-global-civil-war-12304?page=show
64   Wright (2006).
65   Byman and Williams (2015).
66   Al Jazeera (2016) Kenya: Three female attackers killed in police station. Published 11 September 2016. Available at: http://www.aljazeera.com/news/2016/09/kenya-female-attackers-killed-police-station-160911151409114.html
67   IT News Africa (2015) East Africa tops Africa for internet access. Published 10 September 2014. Available at: http://www.itnewsafrica.com/2014/09/east-africa-tops-africa-for-internet-access-connectivity/
68   Stern and Burger (2016) p. 40.
69   Farwell, JP (2014) The media strategy of ISIS, *Global Politics and Strategy*, **6** (6). Available at: http://www.tandfonline.com/doi/abs/10.1080/00396338.2014.985436
70   Worth, K (2016) Lone wolf attacks are becoming more common – and more deadly, *PBS: Frontline*. Published 14 July 2016. Available at: http://www.pbs.org/wgbh/frontline/article/lone-wolf-attacks-are-becoming-more-common-and-more-deadly/
71   Ibid.
72   Institute for Economics and Peace (2016).
73   Ibid.
74   UN General Assembly, Plan of Action to Prevent Violent Extremism: Report of the Secretary-General, A/70/674, 24 December 2015, pp. 16–19.

References

Abdi, R (2015) East Africa's s Sufi path to Countering Violent Extremism must not shun Salafists if it is to succeed. Mail & Guardian. Published 15 September 2015. Available at: http://mgafrica.com/article/2015-09-15-east-africas-sufi-path-to-countering-violent-extremism-must-not-exclude-salafists-if-it-is-to-succeed

ACSRT (African Centre for the Study and Research on Terrorism) (2017) ACSRT and ACSS hold seminar on analyzing the membership on African terrorist movements. Available at: http://caert.org.dz/?p=2183

Al Jazeera (2013) Is Ethiopia on Al Shabaab's hit list? Published 21 October 2013. Available at: https://www.aljazeera.com/indepth/features/2013/10/ethiopia-al-shabab-hit-list-201310211211366477.html

Al Jazeera (2016) Kenya: Three female attackers killed in police station. Published 11 September 2016. Available at: http://www.aljazeera.com/news/2016/09/kenya-female-attackers-killed-police-station-160911151409114.html

Ali, AM (2016) *Islamist Extremism in East Africa*. Africa Centre for Strategic Studies, Africa Security Brief No. 32. Available at: http://africacenter.org/publication/islamist-extremism-east-africa/#fn8

Allison, S (2014) The Islamic State: Why Africa should be worried. Pretoria: The Institute for Security Studies. Published 12 September 2014. Available at: https://www.issafrica.org/research/policy-brief/the-islamic-state-why-africa-should-be-worried

Anzalone, C (2014) The life and death of Al-Shabab leader Ahmed Godane, *CTC Sentinel*, **7** (9), pp. 19–23. Available at: https://www.ctc.usma.edu/posts/the-life-and-death-of-al-shabab-leader-ahmed-godane

Boukhars, A (2006) Understanding Somali Islamism, *Terrorism Monitor*, **4** (10). Published 18 May 2006. Available at: https://jamestown.org/program/understanding-somali-islamism/

Bryden, M (2014) *The Reinvention of Al-Shabaab: A strategy of choice or necessity?* A report of the CSIS Africa Program. Washington, DC: Center for Strategic & International Studies. Available at: https://csis-prod.s3.amazonaws.com/s3fs-public/legacy_files/files/publication/140221_Bryden_ReinventionOfAlShabaab_Web.pdf

Bryson, R (2016) Where does ISIS stand in Somalia? Tony Blair Institute for Global Change. Published 8 July 2016. Available at: http://tonyblairfaithfoundation.org/religion-geopolitics/commentaries/backgrounder/where-does-isis-stand-somalia

Byman, D (2015) *Comparing Al-Qaeda and ISIS: Different goals, different targets*. Washington, DC: Brookings Institute. Published 29 April 2016. Available at: https://www.brookings.edu/testimonies/comparing-al-qaeda-and-isis-different-goals-different-targets/

Byman, D and Williams, J (2015) ISIS vs Al-Qaeda: Jihadism's global civil war, *The National Interest*. Published 24 February 2014. Available at: http://nationalinterest.org/feature/isis-vs-al-qaeda-jihadism%E2%80%99s-global-civil-war-12304?page=show

Centre for Security Policy (2015) *Jahba East Africa Jihadists Encroaching Upon al-Shabaab*. Published 2 April 2015. Available at: http://www.centerforsecuritypolicy.org/2016/04/12/jahba-east-africa-jihadists-encroaching-upon-al-shabaab/

Daily Maverick (2016) Militants rising: Islamic State's East Africa ambitions. Published 10 January 2017. Available at: https://www.dailymaverick.co.za/article/2017-01-10-militants-rising-islamic-states-east-african-ambitions/#.Wt8X5tNubVo

Dearden, L (2016) Isis: New terrorist group Jahba East Africa pledges allegiance to 'Islamic State' in Somalia, *The Independent*. Published 12 April 2016. Available at: http://www.independent.co.uk/news/world/africa/isis-new-terrorist-group-jahba-east-africa-pledges-allegiance-to-islamic-state-in-somalia-a6974476.html

Delong-Bas, N (2004) *Wahhabi Islam: From revival and reform to global jihad*. New York: Oxford University Press.

Enders, W and Sandler, T (2000) Is transnational terrorism becoming more threatening? *Journal of Conflict Resolution*, **44**, pp. 307–332. University of Alabama. Available at: http://jcr.sagepub.com/content/44/3/307.full.pdf+html

Esposito, JL and Piscatori, JP (1991) Democratization and Islam, *Middle East Journal*, **45** (4). Available at: http://www.jstor.org/stable/4328314?seq=1#page_scan_tab_contents

Farwell, JP (2014) The media strategy of ISIS, *Global Politics and Strategy*, **6** (6). Available at: http://www.tandfonline.com/doi/abs/10.1080/00396338.2014.985436

Fuller, GE (2003) *The Future of Political Islam*. New York: Palgrave Macmillan.

Gilsaa, S (2015) Salafism(s) in Tanzania: Theological roots and political subtext of the Ansar Sunna, *Islamic Africa*, **6**. Available at: https://www.deepdyve.com/lp/brill/salafism-s-in-tanzania-theological-roots-and-political-subtext-of-the-dQH4XNv0cH

Hansen, SJ (2013) *The History and Ideology of a Militant Islamist Group*. Oxford: Oxford University Press.

Haynes, J (2007) Islam and democracy in East Africa. In F Volpi and F Cavatorta (eds) *Democratization in the Muslim World: Changing patterns of power and authority*. New York: Routledge.

Hoffman, B (2010) Al-Qaeda, trends in terrorism, and future potentialities: An assessment, *Studies in Conflict and Terrorism*, **26** (6). Available at: http://www.tandfonline.com/doi/abs/10.1080/10576100390248275

Institute for Economics and Peace (2016) *Global Terrorism Index* 2015. Available at: http://economicsandpeace.org/reports/

IT News Africa (2015) East Africa tops Africa for internet access. Published 10 September 2014. Available at: http://www.itnewsafrica.com/2014/09/east-africa-tops-africa-for-internet-access-connectivity/

Jones, S (2014) A Persistent Threat: The evolution of al Qa'ida and other Salafi Jihadist. RAND Corporation.

LeSage, A (2014) The Rising Threat in Tanzania: Domestic Islamist militancy and regional threats. Institute for National Strategic Studies No. 288. Available at: http://ndupress.ndu.edu/portals/68/documents/stratforum/sf-288.pdf

Menkhaus, K (2004) *Somalia: State collapse and the threat of terrorism*. Adelphi Paper 364. London and New York: Routledge.

Moussalli, A (2009) *Wahhabism, Salafism and Islamism: Who is the enemy?* A Conflicts Forum Monograph. Beirut, London, Washington: Conflicts Forum. Published 30 January 2009. Available at: http://conflictsforum.org/briefings/Wahhabism-Salafism-and-Islamism.pdf

National Consortium for the Study of Terrorism and Responses to Terrorism (2016) *Global Terrorism Database*. Available at: http://www.start.umd.edu/gtd

Newsweek (2016) Kenya: ISIS claims responsibility for police station attack, its first in country. Published 14 September 2016. Available at: http://europe.newsweek.com/isis-kenya-police-station-mombasa-498226?rm=eu

Ochami, D (2012) How fiery cleric Rogo developed, propagated extremism, *The Standard*. Published 2 September 2012. Available at: http://www.standardmedia.co.ke/article/2000065268/how-fiery-cleric-rogo-developed-propagated-extremism

Reuters (2014) Al-Shabaab claims responsibility for Djibouti suicide attack. Published 27 May 2014. Available at: http://www.reuters.com/article/uk-djibouti-attacks-idUSKBN0E72AA20140527

Reuters (2015) Shabaab and East African Front Compete for Notoriety. Published 12 April 2015. Available at: https://www.nytimes.com/2016/04/13/world/africa/militant-groups-compete-for-notoriety-in-east-africa.html

Reuters (2015) Small group of Somali al Shabaab swear allegiance to Islamic State. Published 23 October 2015. Available at: https://www.reuters.com/article/us-mideast-crisis-somalia/small-group-of-somali-al-shabaab-swear-allegiance-to-islamic-state-idUSKCN0SH1BF20151023

Reuters (2016) Islamic State claims responsibility for attack outside PS embassy in Nairobi. Published 29 October 2016. Available at: http://www.reuters.com/article/us-kenya-usa-islamicstate-idUSKCN12T0QS?il=0

Samatar, I (2007) Ethiopian invasion of Somalia, US warlordism and AU shame, *Review of African Political Economy*, **34** (111), pp. 155–165. Available at: http://www.jstor.org/stable/20406369?seq=1#page_scan_tab_contents

Stern, J and Berger, JM (2016) *ISIS: State of terror*. HarperCollins: New York.

Taarnby, M and Hallundbaek, L (2010) Al-Shabaab: The internationalization of militant Islamism in Somalia and the implications for radicalization processes in Europe. Justice Ministry of Denmark. Available at: http://justitsministeriet.dk/sites/default/files/media/Arbejdsomraader/Forskning/Forskningspuljen/2011/2010/alshabaab.pdf

Tadesse, M (2002) *Al-Ittihad: Political Islam and the black economy in Somalia: Religion, money, clan, and the struggle for supremacy over Somalia*. Addis Ababa: Maeg Press.

Terrorism Research and Analysis Consortium (2016) Muslim Youth Center/Al-Hijra. Available at: https://www.trackingterrorism.org/group/muslim-youth-center-al-hijra-kenya

The Guardian (2010) Uganda bomb blast kills at least 74. Published 12 July 2010. Available at: http://www.theguardian.com/world/2010/jul/12/uganda-kampala-bombs-explosions-attacks

The Guardian (2014) Isis instructs followers to kill Australians and other 'disbelievers'. Published 23 September 2014. Available at: https://www.theguardian.com/world/2014/sep/23/islamic-state-followers-urged-to-launch-attacks-against-australians

The Guardian (2017) Nine Kenyans beheaded by Somali al-Shabaab terrorists. Published 8 July 2017. Available at: https://www.theguardian.com/world/2017/jul/08/nine-kenyans-beheaded-by-somali-al-shabaab-terrorists

UN General Assembly (2015) Plan of Action to Prevent Violent Extremism: Report of the Secretary-General, A/70/674. Published 24 December 2015, pp. 16–19.

Weaver, MA (2006) The short, violent life of Abu Musab al-Zarqawi, *The Atlantic*. Published July/August 2006. Available at: https://www.theatlantic.com/magazine/archive/2006/07/the-short-violent-life-of-abu-musab-al-zarqawi/304983/

Williams, JR (2015) ISIS vs Al-Qaeda: Jihadism's global civil war, *The National Interest*. Published February/March 2015. Available at: https://www.brookings.edu/articles/isis-vs-al-qaeda-jihadisms-global-civil-war/

Worth, K (2016) Lone wolf attacks are becoming more common – and more deadly, *PBS: Frontline*. Published 14 July 2016. Available at: http://www.pbs.org/wgbh/frontline/article/lone-wolf-attacks-are-becoming-more-common-and-more-deadly/

Wright, L (2006) *The Looming Tower: Al Qaeda and the road to 9/11*. Random House: New York.

Chapter 9

The evolving threat of violent extremism and terrorism in the SADC region

Richard Chelin and Stephen Buchanan-Clarke

Introduction

Over the past decade, Africa has seen a rapid increase and spread of transnational terrorist organisations operating within regional 'hot spots' on the continent. Al-Shabaab, which emerged as a local insurgency against the Somali state in 2005, now maintains an active presence in neighbouring Kenya, and has attempted or successfully carried out attacks in several other East African states, including Djibouti, Uganda and Ethiopia.[1] Boko Haram, which also emerged as a local insurgency against the Nigerian state in 2009, has spread into the Lake Chad region, and is now a major security threat in Chad, Cameroon and Niger.[2] North African states lying along the Sahel have also been particularly affected, as groups like Al-Qaeda in the Islamic Maghreb (AQIM) and the Islamic State of Iraq and Syria (ISIS) exploit the region's porous borders and low levels of governance to their advantage.[3] While the Southern African Development Community (SADC) countries have not experienced the same levels of terrorism as other regions on the continent, in recent years, several member states have seen rising levels of extremism and an increase in activity by local actors connected with transnational terrorist networks.

In response to the changing nature of conflict and rise of transnational terrorist organisations over the past two decades, governments, intergovernmental organisations and civil society have looked to develop a range of policy options to address the challenge. In 2005, the European Union (EU) adopted a counterterrorism strategy focused on four pillars: prevent, protect, pursue and respond.[4] In 2006, the United Nations (UN) adopted a global counterterrorism strategy, also comprising four pillars, which are designed for: (1) 'Addressing the conditions conducive to the spread of terrorism'; (2) 'Preventing and combating terrorism'; (3) 'Building states' capacity and strengthening the role of the United Nations'; and (4) 'Ensuring human rights and the rule of law'.[5] In 2014, the African Union (AU) adopted the 2004 Protocol of the Algiers Convention, which recognised the 'linkages between terrorism and mercenarism, weapons of mass destruction, drug trafficking, corruption, transnational organised crimes, money laundering, and the illicit proliferation of small arms' as increasingly prevalent risks associated with terrorism.[6] The protocol mandated the AU's Peace and Security Council to monitor and facilitate implementation of counterterrorism policies and to encourage Regional Economic Communities (RECs) to play a more active role. Consequently, the SADC's regional counterterrorism strategy was adopted at the SADC Heads of State Summit on 18 August 2015. However, to date, both the SADC and member states lack the capacity and coordinating mechanisms to effectively implement these policies. Furthermore, as will be seen later, the threat and nature of terrorism across SADC states differ vastly. Thus, these frameworks often lack the nuance and detail to deal with the root causes and local drivers of violent extremism.

An exhaustive evaluation of the threat of terrorism in each of the 16 SADC member states is beyond the scope of this chapter. Therefore, to illustrate the different ways in which states experience violent extremism and terrorism in the region, Tanzania and South Africa will serve as case studies: the former, due to its increasing religious polarisation and the emergence of local violent extremist organisations, and the latter, due to the role it plays as a logistical hub for transnational terrorist networks. Finally, an overview of the SADC's response to this emerging security threat will be provided, along with an evaluation of some of its strengths and weaknesses.

Violent extremism and terrorism in the SADC region

The SADC was established on 17 August 1992 in Windhoek, Namibia, where the SADC Treaty was adopted, redefining the basis of cooperation among member states of the Southern African Development Coordinating Conference (SADCC) – a forerunner to the SADC signed in Lusaka, Zambia in 1980. Today, the SADC is headquartered in Gaborone, Botswana, with its primary goal to further socio-economic cooperation and integration as well as political and security cooperation among its 16 member states. These 16 member states include Angola, Botswana, Comoros, Democratic Republic of Congo (DRC), Lesotho, Madagascar, Malawi, Mauritius, Mozambique, Namibia, Seychelles, South Africa, Swaziland, Tanzania, Zambia and Zimbabwe.[7]

The United Nations Development Programme (UNDP), as part of a recently launched long-term engagement to prevent the spread of violent extremism in Africa, splits countries into three categories. These include 'epicentre countries' such as Mali, Nigeria and Somalia; 'spill-over countries' such as Cameroon, Chad, Kenya and Mauritania; and 'at risk' countries such as the Central African Republic (CAR), Sudan, Tanzania and Uganda.[8] Countries within the SADC would largely fall under the 'at risk' category, as to date there have been no large-scale insurgencies by a transnational violent extremist organisation in the region.

However, this is not to say that transnational terrorist groups have not been active in the region, or are not trying to actively establish a presence. For example, in 2015, in the DRC, reports indicated the Alliance of Democratic Forces – National Army for the Liberation of Uganda (ADF-NALU) had made early connections with Al-Shabaab.[9] In Mauritius, while authorities claim that ISIS has no presence in the country, in May 2016 gunshots were fired at the French embassy and a hotel in the capital, Port Louis. Graffiti with the words, 'you will no longer live here in peace' and the ISIS symbol were found on the wall of the embassy.[10] Furthermore, in 2015, ISIS released a propaganda video featuring a young Mauritian, speaking Creole and exhorting Muslims to come and join the promised land and to 'free Mauritius'.[11] Alleged ISIS supporters have also been arrested in Madagascar, while the country's close proximity to piracy off the Somali coast, political instability and lax visa restrictions have been identified as preconditions for the spread of regional and international militant Islamist organisations in the country.[12] In recent years, there have been several reports from Mozambique and Malawi, alleging the existence of Al-Shabaab training camps.[13] While the validity of these claims has not been proven, it is likely that the organisation, given the geography of the region, at the very least profits from the ivory trade and refugee flows along the coastlines of both countries.

Several SADC member states have witnessed various forms of civil conflict since independence from colonial rule. However, to date, few have experienced significant levels of transnational terrorism perpetrated by organisations such as Al-Qaeda and ISIS. Tanzania and South Africa, however, present two interesting case studies, which illustrate the role different countries can play in providing a space for the emergence and spread of transnational terrorism.

The case of Tanzania

Over the past decade, a growing number of terrorist attacks in Tanzania have targeted local Christian leaders, tourists and 'soft' targets such as bars and restaurants. This has raised the question of whether the country is becoming a target and a recruitment ground for regional terrorist networks, such as Al-Shabaab, Al-Qaeda and ISIS. Scholars emphasise that while relations between Christian and Muslim groups are increasingly tense, evidence suggests that Tanzania is not 'a battleground for conflicting civilisations'.[14] Heilman and Kaiser (2002), for example, argue that while various political, religious and ethnic identity groups have served as the basis for political organisation and conflict at one point or another, no particular identity has crystallised as a major dividing line. Furthermore, rather than religious identity, the authors argue that class division and political-party affiliation are more likely sources of conflict.[15]

However, in recent years, there is increasing evidence that Islamist mobilisation has grown in strength to challenge more moderate and state-run Islamic associations. For example, analysts have highlighted evidence showing the links between Tanzanian individuals and associations and regional terrorist groups.[16] This has included the discovery of training camps and indoctrination centres; the arrest of Somali nationals suspected of Al-Shabaab affiliation; and discovery of communication between Islamist leaders in Tanzania and Al-Shabaab in Somalia and Al-Hijra in Kenya.[17]

According to LeSage (2014), Tanzania has a population of approximately 48 million people, divided into three main religious traditions: Christian (35 per cent), Islamic (45 per cent) and traditional animists (20 per cent), with Jews, Buddhists and Hindus forming a small minority. Muslims and Christians co-exist in all major Tanzanian cities with the exception of Zanzibar. There, 95 per cent of the population of 750 000 is Muslim, as well as the mainland Tanzanian coastline, where the population is also mostly Muslim. More than 80 per cent of Tanzanian Muslims are Sunni, while other Islamic groups include Shi'a (both Ithna Asheris and Ismailis), Ibadites and Ahmadiyya.[18]

Vittori et al (2009) traces the Islamic history of eastern Africa along three separate chronological phases. The first epoch was the early settlement of Muslims along the coastal regions of East Africa, where they were eventually incorporated under Bantu ethnic leadership. The second, called Shirazi (or Shirazian) involved the configuration of a number of small community dynasties alongside the eastern coast of the continent and on the Comoros Islands, which reached its climax between the 13th and 15th centuries. The third phase was distinguished by the growth of the island of Zanzibar in modern-day Tanzania and brought about the influence of Hadrami Shafi'i Islam.[19] With regards to Tanzania, Islam arrived from Arabia in the 11th century, and by the 13th century, several dynastic settlements had been established along the coast, which then spread inland along precolonial trade routes. European colonisation – the British in Zanzibar and the Germans on the mainland – did little to disrupt the spread of Islam. Rather, the establishment of railroads, where the Germans often employed Muslims as officials, police and soldiers, served to spread the religion further into the continent.[20]

The first Christian missionaries, who arrived in Tanzania from the mid-19th century, strongly impacted on the country's social structures by establishing Christian schools with modern education. Education in these schools was more suited for the modern nation state and its bureaucratic structures in the late 19th and early 20th century. This created a reversal of power relations between Christians and Muslims, as Christians began to replace Muslims in positions within the state bureaucracy.[21] This led to a gradual decline in the socio-economic status of Muslims and, as Mesaki (2011) writes, 'By mid-1950s a more significant distinction in access to education in the territory had emerged between Christians and Muslims.'[22] This inequitable access to educational opportunities resulted not only in social and class differentiation, but also created a schism between Christians and Muslims, the effects of which are still felt today and are clearly seen in the rise of Islamism.[23] For example, according to Heilman and Kaiser (2002), Islamic revival in Tanzania in recent decades has been based primarily on 'an Islamic-centric interpretation of history that maintains Muslims have been discriminated against by a Christian-dominated state since the colonial period'.[24]

In addition to tensions between Christians and Muslims, it is important to note that there are also internal divisions among Muslim groups. In Tanzania, the majority of the Muslim population is Sufi, which is one of the most tolerant orders of Islam. Sufism has been able to adapt to fit local traditions and incorporate traditional animist practices.[25] However, in recent decades, Sunni Islamists in the region have increasingly targeted Sufism, which they perceive as a 'primitive' and 'degraded' form of Islam that needs to be 'purified'.[26]

From a study conducted in the southern Tanzanian town of Rwangwa, Becker (2006) highlights the ability of Islamists to combine an 'unchanging and consciously universalist message' with very specific local concerns.[27] This connects two previously distinct agendas: a religious reformist agenda and a potentially violent political one.[28] Despite the fact that Islamists failed to take over local politics in 2006, they managed to establish a claim to primacy regarding religious scholarship, thus weakening claims to religious legitimacy by Sufi elders. As Becker (2006) notes, Islamist groups in Tanzania have challenged the notion that the state is the main purveyor of modernity.[29] In a context where young people are increasingly disenchanted with the political and economic liberalisation that is a hallmark of modernity, the Islamist agenda is growing in resonance.

Indeed, Haynes (2005) argues that 'there appear to be signs of a gradual hardening of indigenous Muslim identity in Tanzania, a development with political connotations'.[30] This has been especially present in Zanzibar, where a study by Glickman (2011) found a rapid rise in recent years of revivalist groups closely linked to conservative religious movements originating in the Arabian Peninsula, such as Wahhabism and Salafism.[31]

The rise of Islamism in Tanzania: The case of Zanzibar

Zanzibar's local communities have long felt excluded from representation in the national politics of Tanzania. This discontent has its genesis in the union of Zanzibar with Tanganyika, which was unfavourably looked upon by much of Zanzibar's population.[32] Tanganyika secured independence from the British in 1961, while Zanzibar was granted formal independence two years later, which established a constitutional monarchy for the archipelago ruled by Sultan Jamshid bin Abdullah and an Arab government. However, Abdullah's reign was short-lived. The majority African population, who had become increasingly resentful of the political and economic dominance of the minority Arab communities, rose up to topple the regime in a violent revolution just two years later. The Zanzibar Revolutionary Council was established, which was composed of members of the Afro-Shirazi Party (ASP), and signed an act of union with Julius Nyerere in 1964 to create modern Tanzania.[33] Despite the union, tensions between Arab islanders, who resent their loss of power and the perceived forced union, and Africans from the mainland, who still feel economically marginalised, continue today. In 1993, for example, the Tanzanian government forced Zanzibar to withdraw its application to the Organisation of Islamic States (OIC).[34]

The political discontent between mainland Tanzania and Zanzibar continues to alienate many Zanzibaris. The result is the growth of violent Islamist organisations – which has at times turned militant, as seen in attacks on Christian Tanzanians and Western tourists. Currently, Zanzibar is the home to several violent Islamist movements, including *Imam Majlis* (Imam Society) and *Da'awa Islamiya* (Islamic Call). These movements capitalise on Zanzibar's historical background and political grievances against the state to mobilise youth on the islands.[35]

One group in particular, *Jumikior Jumuiya ya Uamsho na mihadhara ya kiislam* (The Association for Islamic Mobilisation and Propagation or UAMSHO) has been at the forefront of calling for separation from the mainland. Led by Sheikh Farid Hadi, UAMSHO has consistently called for Zanzibar to secede from Tanzania and implement sharia law.[36] The group, which began as an Islamic NGO in 2001, has also allegedly been involved in multiple violent protests since 2012. However, the chairman of UAMSHO's trustees, Abdulrahim Salim, insists the group is peacefully pursuing independence for Zanzibar and has dismissed claims that it is looking to impose sharia law.[37]

Glickman (2011) argues that UAMSHO has been particularly effective because it employs the language of human rights and good governance in its critique of the government, while blaming the state for the moral decline of the country. Although the group has been classified as a fundamentalist group by the Tanzanian government, the British, US and Danish embassies all considered the group 'non-violent' following an official inquiry.[38]

UAMSHO has been involved in multiple protests since 2012, several of which ended in violence and virtually shut down Zanzibar City. One such protest in 2012 led to the arrest of the group's leader; a day after his arrest, Muslim rioters set two churches ablaze.[39] It is important to note that following its inception in 2001, UAMSHO was not publically active for a number of years. It was only after the formation of a government of national unity prior to elections in 2010 that UAMSHO's demands for Zanzibar to secede began receiving strong support from the Muslim population.[40] The first violent clashes between UAMSHO's supporters and police in 2012 set a precedent for more violence in the ensuing years.[41]

In addition to protests and riots, UAMSHO is believed to have been responsible for a series of unsophisticated attacks, using crude homemade explosives, handguns and acid, against Christians, moderate Muslims and tourists in Zanzibar.[42] Three Catholic priests were attacked in separate incidents in 2012 and 2013. In 2013, two British tourists were attacked with acid. In January 2014, a bomb was thrown from a car at followers as they left a mosque where a moderate Muslim cleric had just finished giving a sermon on peace in the face of violent jihad. In February 2015, three separate attacks on churches in Zanzibar took place. According to the Jane's *Intelligence Review* (cited in Burchard, 2015):'The nature of Islamist militancy in Tanzania is likely to change drastically over the next few years ... Although the capacity of Zanzibar-based militant groups is still rudimentary, their skill-set is fast improving and their target set is expanding.'[43]

While attacks have taken place largely in Zanzibar, there have been reports of activity on the mainland in cities such as Arusha and Dar es Salaam, and in rural areas surrounding Tanga and Mtwara. However, as Burchard (2015) notes, the government and media are relatively quiet when it comes to reporting on UAMSHO's activities due to media restrictions on reporting terrorism.[44] Since 2013, there has also been an increase in groups other than UAMSHO that have capitalised on the rise of violent Islamist ideologies in Tanzania.

In July 2015, an Al-Shabaab attack on the Stakishari police station near the Dar es Salaam airport killed seven people. Press reports indicated that four police officers, two civilians and one of the attackers were killed.[45] In the first four months of 2015, Al-Shabaab militants were directly involved in five battles with Tanzanian security forces in which eight policemen and soldiers died. Al-Shabaab's increased presence in early 2015 was in stark contrast to the previous year, when no such incidents were recorded – although the July 2014 attacks on moderate Muslim clerics and foreign tourists in Arusha were thought to be in retaliation for alleged Al-Shabaab arrests in the country.[46]

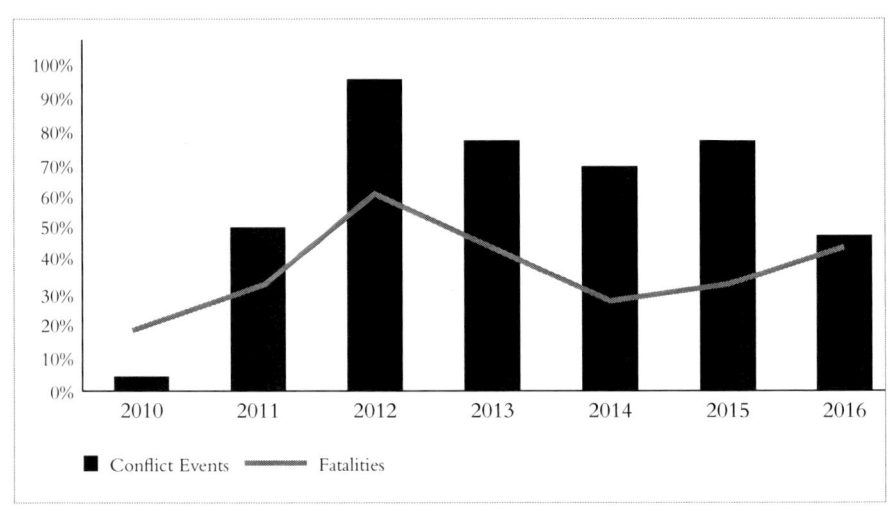

Figure 9.1: Conflict events and fatalities, Tanzania, 2010–2016
Source: ACLED[47]

Al-Shabaab-related attacks in 2015 concentrated on the eastern regions of Morogoro, Pwani and Tanga. For example, an Al-Shabaab group led by Abu Qays bin Abdullah claimed responsibility for two attacks on 15 January 2015 – one on a police station in Kilombero in Morogoro and the other on Ushirombo police post in the northern Shinyanga Region. On 21 January 2015, Al-Shabaab killed two police officers in Ikwiriri in Pwani Region, west of Dar es Salaam. These attacks contributed to January 2015 having the highest number of conflict events (17) and the highest number of fatalities (eight) in the country over the prior 12 months. Although just six conflict events occurred in February, eight fatalities were recorded, including a soldier killed in an exchange of fire with suspected Al-Shabaab militants.[48]

In February 2015, local police attempted to arrest individuals who were thought to be bandits hiding deep in the Amboni Caves near the city of Tanga in northern Tanzania. Following an intense 20-minute gunfight, the local police were forced to call for military backup from the Tanzanian defence force. During the initial exchange of gunfire, a police officer was killed and five others were wounded.[49] The militants eventually escaped by using a complex system of ladders and ropes. Shortly after the event, Al-Shabaab posted a video online claiming responsibility for the incident.

Table 9.1: List of terror-related attacks in Tanzania and Zanzibar

November 2011	Tanzanian government issues a warning of potential Al-Shabaab attacks after 10 Tanzanian nationals were arrested on the Kenya–Somalia border attempting to join Al-Shabaab.
June 2012	Arrest of Emrah Erdogan, a German national who had joined Al-Shabaab, at Dar es Salaam airport.
October 2012	A Tanzanian policeman is hacked to death with machetes in Zanzibar.
November 2012	Acid attack on moderate, anti-UAMSHO Muslim imam in Zanzibar.
December 2012	Shooting of a Catholic priest in Zanzibar.
February 2013	Interfaith rioting in Mwanza area, related to Muslim protests against Christian butchery practices, leads to beheading of a local priest.
February 2013	Murder of a Catholic priest and the torching of a church in Zanzibar.
March 2013	Rioting by Sheikh Ponda Issa Ponda supporters in Dar es Salaam.
May 2013	Hand-grenade attack at St Joseph's church in Arusha, killing three and wounding 63, during a celebration by the Vatican nuncio.
May 2013	Burning of a Christian church in Tanga Region.
May 2013	Arrest in Dar es Salaam of five men in possession of explosives and improvised explosive-device-related materials.
July 2013	The arrest of British terrorism suspect, Hassan Ali Iqbal in Kyele, in Mbeya Region, as he tried to cross into Malawi.
August 2013	Acid attack on two young British women in Zanzibar's Stone Town.
August 2013	Homemade petrol-bomb attack on a Christian church in Dar es Salaam.
September 2013	Acid attack on a Catholic priest in Zanzibar's Stone Town.
September 2013	Attempted hand-grenade attack at shopping area in Zanzibar's Stone Town.
September 2013	Killing of an elderly priest in Zanzibar's Stone Town.
October 2013	Arrest of 13 suspected Al-Shabaab-linked militants at a military-style training camp at Makolionga Mountain in Mtwara Region.
October 2013	Arrest by Kenyan military forces of three Tanzanians travelling to Somalia to join Al-Shabaab.
October 2013	Arrest of Tanzanian businessman Juma Abdallah Kheri for financing terrorism in Kenya and Tanzania.
November 2013	Arrest of 69 people running an 'Al-Shabaab child indoctrination camp' in Tanga for more than 50 4- to 13-year-olds.
January 2014	Explosives attack at New Year's Eve celebration at Christian church in Arusha.
February 2014	Three IED attacks in Zanzibar, targeting two Christian churches and a restaurant popular with tourists.

February 2014	Acid attack on moderate Muslim preacher and his son in Arusha.
April 2014	Bombing of a crowded bar popular with tourists in Arusha, injuring 15 people.
June 2014	Explosives attack on a mosque in Zanzibar's Stone Town, killing one person and wounding four others.
July 2014	Explosives attack on a private house in Arusha where moderate clerics were gathered.
July 2014	Explosives attack on an Indian restaurant popular with tourists and local residents in Arusha.
January 2015	Attacks on a police station in Kilombero in Morogoro and on Ushirombo police post in the northern Shinyanga Region.
January 2015	Al-Shabaab kill two police officers in Ikwiriri in Pwani Region.
February 2015	Al-Shabaab militants kill soldier in the Amboni Caves.
April 2015	10 suspected members of Al-Shabaab arrested in a mosque in Dar es Salaam.
July 2015	Seven people killed in an Al-Shabaab attack on the Stakishari police station near Dar es Salaam airport.
May 2016	Three people killed in a mosque in Mwanza.

Sources: *Independent Newspapers, BBC, Al Jazeera*

Government responses to terrorism

According to the US Department of State (2016), in 2015, Tanzania's security services investigated and were involved in active operations against several alleged violent extremists who had conducted numerous attacks on police and police installations. Security services made multiple arrests, and officials prosecuted these cases at the end of 2015. Tanzania's National Counterterrorism Centre (NCTC) also reported concerns over escalating radicalism and inadequate border security.[50]

However, Tanzanian security forces – including the Tanzanian police force, defence force and intelligence and security service – are considered generally too weak, under-resourced and poorly coordinated to ensure the security of the country's borders.[51] The Jamestown Foundation (2005) argued that the situation was further complicated by the fact that the region has 'highly porous land and sea borders, it is also beset by largely dysfunctional structures of law and enforcement, endemic organised criminal activity (involving everything from drugs and people smuggling to weapons trafficking) and relative proximity to known Islamist logistical hubs such as Yemen and the United Arab Emirates'.[52]

Today, the mobilisation and radicalisation of aggrieved Muslim youth by both UAMSHO in Zanzibar and other militant Islamist movements based in Dar es Salaam pose a significant security threat. While terrorist attacks have been relatively unsophisticated and loosely coordinated, the gradual encroachment and influence of more experienced militant organisations in the region, such as Al-Shabaab and Al-Hijra, may see the operational capabilities of local organisations improve and their reach expand. As these local organisations evolve into transitional terrorist organisations, as has been the case with Al-Shabaab, ISIS and others, improved regional security measures and coordination is required by bodies such as the AU and SADC. To operate effectively, transnational terrorist organisations often need to find logistical hubs from where they can source and channel funding and garner other material and operational support. As will be seen later in this chapter, evidence suggests that South Africa, to a degree, serves as an example of one such logistical hub for transnational terrorist organisations operating in Africa.

The case of South Africa

In 1999, Khalfan Khamis Mohamed, 'a Tanzanian trained by Al-Qaeda, was arrested in Cape Town, South Africa, for his role in the 1998 US embassy bombings', where nearly simultaneous truck-bomb explosions at the US embassies in Dar es Salaam, Tanzania, and Nairobi, Kenya, killed more than 200 people.[53] While the 9/11 attacks are commonly identified as a defining moment in the modern history of terrorism, the US embassy bombings in Kenya and Tanzania were an early demonstration of Al-Qaeda's ability to garner local support and draw on cross-continental networks to successfully execute complex terrorist attacks.[54] It was a wake-up call for South Africa and other African governments, who had likely never given considerable attention or thought to dealing with the newly emerging threat of transnational terrorist networks. Just two years later, after the 9/11 attacks gained worldwide attention and the subsequent US Global War on Terrorism began to gain momentum, governments across the world were forced to engage with the issue.

The threat of violent extremism and terrorism has only grown since 2001, and evidence suggests that South Africa, while not experiencing anywhere near the same level of terrorism by violent extremist organisations as other countries on the continent, does play a role as a logistical hub for transnational terrorist networks.

South Africa has a long and complicated history with terrorism. The apartheid government used the term 'terrorist' as a way of delegitimising the African National Congress and other anti-apartheid resistance movements. In 1967, the National Party introduced the Terrorism Act, which defined the term as 'any activity that may endanger the maintenance of law and order'.[55] As Dugard (1978) writes, 'The Terrorism Act was the most comprehensive, all-encompassing and police-empowering piece of apartheid legislation.'[56] Under this law, 'terrorism suspects' could be detained for 60 days without trial on the authority of a senior police officer, while there was no requirement to release information as to who was being held, or where.

However, after 1994, the newly elected democratic government undertook a complete review of security legislation. This included the promulgation of a comprehensive new counterterrorism law that would conform to the tenets of the country's new democratic dispensation.[57]

Unlike Tanzania, South Africa has not experienced any significant terrorist incidents in recent years. Moreover, the county does not suffer the same inter- and intra-religious divides, which are so often exploited by violent extremist organisations. Under apartheid rule, South Africa was clearly segregated by race through a number of legislative measures, such as the Bantu Education Act (1953), the Population Registration Act (1950), the Group Areas Act (1950) and the Prohibition of Mixed Marriages Act (1949). However, there was no legislation that specifically called for the division of people by religion. Despite being a secular state, South Africa is deeply religious. A recent survey by Statistics South Africa revealed that more than 90 per cent of citizens associate themselves with a religion, while 36.6 per cent of Hindus, 52.5 per cent of Christians and 75.6 per cent of Muslims attend religious ceremonies at least once a week.[58] After apartheid, under South Africa's new Constitution, a commitment was made to overcome social divisions by fostering a society that tolerated diversity and did not position one religion above another.[59] In fact, as Amien (2012) writes, 'Unlike Europe and North America, the discussions in South Africa relating to religious freedom do not centre on the extent to which religion can be excluded from the public domain but rather the extent to which it can be accommodated.'[60] This has undoubtedly served to develop relatively harmonious relations between religious communities in South Africa. However, this is not to say the country has been free from incidents of terrorism since 1994.

Between 1994 and 2001, People Against Gangsterism and Drugs (PAGAD) committed several acts of terrorism. Initially, the group used explosives in the context of internecine gang warfare and vigilante action against suspected drug dealers in the Western Cape. However, as Boshoff et al (2001) posit, as hard-line Islamist elements within PAGAD began to gain influence within the leadership structure, so the modus operandi of the group began to change. Bombing campaigns shifted from the Cape Flats to central Cape Town, and began to include popular tourist spots.[61] Over the course of two years, PAGAD is alleged to have been responsible for more than 20 bombings. While elements within the organisation increasingly adopted more fundamentalist rhetoric, Hough

(2007) writes that it is 'unclear to what extent the incidents were criminally or politically motivated, or whether a combination of motives was present'.[62]

In addition to acts of terrorism perpetrated by PAGAD, South Africa has also seen a number of attacks by violent far-right extremist groups seeking to establish an independent Afrikaner nation state, most notably, the *Afrikaner Weerstandsbeweging* (AWB) and the Boeremag. In 1996, members of the *Boere Aanvalstroepe*, an offshoot of the AWB, detonated two bombs, killing a woman and three children, while injuring another 67 people.[63] In 2012, members of the *Boeremag* detonated eight bombs in Soweto, seven of which destroyed railway lines, and the eighth damaged a mosque.

While transnational terrorist organisations such as Al-Qaeda, Al-Shabaab and ISIS have not staged attacks on South African targets, there is evidence to suggest that the country serves as a financial and logistical hub for these networks. There are a number of facilitating factors which make this possible, including:

- South Africa's role as a transport, business and communications hub on the continent;
- The ease of travelling on a South African passport relative to other African passports;
- High levels of corruption;
- High levels of internet connectivity and a well-established telecommunications sector;
- South Africa's proximity to illicit and unregulated trade networks in southern Africa;
- Limited investigative intelligence capabilities; and
- Low levels of corporate awareness of terrorism-funding mechanisms.[64]

Indeed, as Cummings (2016) suggests, the fact that South Africa has not experienced a terrorist attack by a transitional terrorist organisation may be due to these organisations' unwillingness to compromise networks that help to fund and facilitate terrorism across the continent. Furthermore, he states that South Africa's relatively neutral foreign policy, secular government, 'discernible lack of Salafi ideologues radicalising its thriving Muslim community, is also incongruent with the development of homegrown terrorism as witnessed in other African countries.'[65]

In instances where terrorist networks have been exposed in South Africa, the government and the State Security Agency in particular have chosen to remain largely silent. At a press conference in July 2016, following the arrest of four people suspected of planning attacks on US- and Jewish-owned targets, Minister of Home Affairs Malusi Gigaba stated that 'the South African government is aware that there are people who are using South Africa as a logistic hub, as a hideout, and there are sleeper cells'. When asked what actions the South African government was taking, Gigaba stated that 'we don't talk about those things. Our security forces are acting on those issues in a manner which we think is best for us … we don't want to be mobilised into other people's fights.'[66]

While specific illicit financial streams, such as the ivory and drug trades, are often rumoured to be used to fund regional and international terrorist organisations, in reality, transnational terrorist organisations will use any illicit or poorly regulated financial flow to fund operations.[67] These methods also change and evolve over time, depending on the security landscape. However, there have been several cases which the government has been unable to keep concealed, which help shed light on the issue. On such example is that of Khalfan Khamis Mohamed, who, as mentioned earlier, was arrested in Cape Town in 1999 for his role in the 1998 US embassy bombings. As Schoeman notes, 'He escaped detection by South African law enforcement for over a year before his arrest and handover to the US Federal Bureau of Investigation (FBI) in a covert rendition in 2001.'[68] Hussein Solomon documents several cases in which South African nationals, suspected of engaging in terrorist activities, have been picked up by police and security agencies abroad. For example, in 2004, South African citizens Dr Feroze Abubaker Ganchi and Zubair Ismail were arrested in Pakistan, along with a senior Al-Qaeda operative, Ahmed Khalfan Ghailan.[69] Ghailan was on the FBI's most-wanted terrorist list for the instrumental role he played in the 1998 US embassy bombings. It later emerged that Ganchi and Ismail had received training in Afghanistan and had entered Pakistan with fake passports.[70]

Indeed, high levels of corruption within the Department of Home Affairs have seen South African passports being used extensively by terrorist operatives on the African continent and abroad.[71] For example, Ibrahim Tantouche, a Libyan national with ties to Al-Qaeda in the Islamic Maghreb (AQIM), who set up two Al-Qaeda financing fronts in South Africa – the Afghan Support Committee and the Revival of Islamic Society – both of which fronted as charities, was captured in Libya travelling on a fake South African passport in 2012.[72]

In 2009, the US embassy in Pretoria was compelled to temporarily close following reports of a terrorist plot targeting American interests in South Africa. This was seen as a response by Al-Shabaab to the assassination by US forces of a senior Al-Qaeda operative, Saleh Ali Saleh, in Somalia. The plot was uncovered through a number of intercepted mobile phone communications, which were allegedly traced back to a Somali group in Khayelitsha, Cape Town.[73]

In 2014, following the Al-Shabaab attack on Westgate Shopping Mall in

Nairobi, Kenya, it was discovered that Samantha Lewthwaite, a British national who had acquired a fake South African passport and who was instrumental in the planning of the attack, had lived in South Africa since at least 2008. Lewthwaite had fled the United Kingdom for South Africa after her husband, Germaine Lindsay, an Al-Qaeda operative, died in the London 7/7 bombings a year earlier.

In 2008, Lewthwaite was introduced to her future second husband in Durban, South Africa, by Abdullah al-Faisal, a Jamaican-born radical Islamist preacher who had been jailed for four years on terrorism charges in the United Kingdom (2003–2007), before being deported to Jamaica and making his way to South Africa. Indeed, a Kenyan Intelligence Agency (KIA) report, made public by Al Jazeera, indicates that KIA operatives have uncovered several Al-Shabaab plots that involved South African-based operatives and financiers.[74]

ISIS in South Africa

The emergence of the ISIS from Al-Qaeda in Iraq in 2006, has fundamentally changed the global militant jihadist landscape.[75] By 2013, ISIS leader Abu Bakr al-Baghdadi had declared a caliphate in Iraq and the Levant, and began to attract vast numbers of foreign nationals to his cause.[76] While the two groups espouse similar ideologies, they differ substantially in structure, strategies, tactics and targets. Through a slick propaganda campaign, ISIS has been adept at attracting foreign nationals to its cause at a far higher rate than Al-Qaeda. Furthermore, in line with the group's shifting modi operandi, Al-Baghdadi has been successful in encouraging adherents to rise up and carry out attacks in their home countries.[77]

The risk ISIS poses to South Africa is twofold. First, there is concern that an estimated 60–100 South African nationals, who have joined ISIS and gone to fight for them in Iraq and Syria, will return to radicalise others or carry out domestic attacks.[78] The second is that ISIS will encourage supporters already in South Africa to carry out attacks on government or 'Western targets'. In June 2016, the US government received information that ISIS was planning attacks at popular tourist destinations in South Africa and publically released a warning to US citizens. The United Kingdom and Australia quickly followed suit. The US diplomatic mission to South Africa, through their website, stated that:

> US government has received information that terrorist groups are planning to carry out near-term attacks against places where US citizens congregate in South Africa, such as upscale shopping areas and malls in Johannesburg and Cape Town. This information comes against the

backdrop of the Islamic State of Iraq and the Levant's public call for its adherents to carry out terrorist attacks globally during the upcoming month of Ramadan.[79]

The South African government and a number of media outlets were quick to refute these claims, arguing that the warning was a ploy by the United States to meddle in SA's domestic politics and was not substantiated by sufficient evidence. However, as Opperman (2017) writes,

> Official responses missed the point, focusing on reasons why South Africa is not vulnerable to attack. These included South Africa's democratic foundations, the country's neutral foreign policy which provides little motivation for an attack, the risk of exposure for supporters already in South Africa, and the (incorrect) assumption that support for terrorist groups on South African soil is the result of self-radicalisation only, and not part of a broader strategy on the part of the terrorist groups in question.[80]

A month later, in July 2016, two brothers, with alleged ties to ISIS, were arrested in South Africa for plotting to blow up the US embassy and Jewish facilities in Cape Town. Their trial is ongoing. However, as per the government's discreet approach in dealing with terrorism cases, information surrounding the case has been restricted.[81] In January 2017, a top ISIS bomb maker named Abu Osama was arrested at a Turkish airport while boarding a plane to Johannesburg. The Iraqi Ambassador to South Africa, Saad Kindeel, told *The Sunday Times* that intelligence officials believed Osama was not coming to South Africa to recruit but to identify specific targets that would later be attacked.[82]

While South Africa has not experienced the levels of domestic terrorism that has marked many African countries over the past decade, it is clear that within the SADC, the country has at times functioned as a logistical and financial hub for transnational terrorism organisations, both on the continent and internationally. Evaluating the extent and nature of the threat is difficult, given the government's approach of keeping any indication of terrorist activity in the country to a minimum. As has been seen in countries across Europe, attacks carried out by 'lone wolves' inspired by ISIS are extremely challenging to predict or prevent. South Africa already suffers from sporadic bouts of xenophobic violence. In the event of a terrorist attack on South African soil by a violent Islamist organisation, it is easy to foresee xenophobic, racial and anti-immigrant sentiments rapidly spreading and leading to increased violence and instability.

The SADC's response to the threat of violent extremism and terrorism

Despite the changing nature of global conflict and significant threat posed by transnational terrorist organisations within member states, addressing violent extremism and terrorism has received relatively little attention from the SADC. The SADC was founded in August 1992 to succeed the SADCC, which grew out of cooperation between the frontline states during the liberation struggle in southern Africa. According to Cawthra (1997), the transition from apartheid in South Africa has had profound effects on southern Africa's strategic environment.[83] The formation of the SADC came at a time of change in African politics, precipitated largely by the end of the Cold War. The SADC Treaty emphasises human and state security, committing member states to uphold human rights, democracy and the rule of the law, as well as setting objectives, which include economic integration and the promotion of peace and security.[84]

In June 1996, at the SADC summit, heads of state endorsed and established the SADC Organ on Politics, Security and Defence (OPSD), which incorporates the Inter-State Defence and Security Committee (ISDSC). The creation of such a security-focused mechanism within the SADC was essential since the SADC is, as implied in its name, focused on economic development for which security is paramount. The region faces a number of broad challenges, which impact on the defence sector, namely the transnational nature of crime, terrorism, HIV/AIDS, limited resources, protection of maritime resources and food security. Among these challenges, international terrorism has received little attention. It is in many ways a far less pressing threat than issues such as violent crime, poverty, public health and corruption. However, because of its relative prosperity, coupled with relatively weak institutions and other vulnerabilities, the sub-region is a potentially attractive operating environment and target for transnational terrorist groups.[85]

Prior to devising a sub-regional response mechanism to address terrorism, the SADC adopted a number of protocols related to security that, although not explicitly couched in the language of counterterrorism, nevertheless addressed related issues, such as small arms and drug trafficking. Most of these activities, however, were carried out by individual SADC members, not by or through the organisation itself.[86] The SADC secretariat did not have the staff or resources devoted to counterterrorism during this period, although its legal unit did try to provide guidance on the implementation of the international conventions and protocols related to terrorism and the relevant UN Security Council resolutions.[87]

As the threat of transnational terrorist organisations continued to grow over the next decade, SADC heads of state eventually drafted a sub-regional response to terrorism known as the SADC Regional Counterterrorism Strategy and Action Plan,[88] which was adopted at the SADC Heads of State Summit on 18 August 2015. The strategy was developed in response to requests for assistance from the SADC secretariat and the African Union's African Centre for the Study & Research on Terrorism (ACSRT) and focused on the prevention of terrorist activities that threatened to spill over from other regions. It is modelled on the UN counterterrorism strategy and the Bogota Guiding Principles for Counterterrorism Strategies. The regional counterterrorism strategy emerged out of various workshops organised by the United Nations Counterterrorism Centre (UNCCT). These included:

- Southern African Development Community (SADC) regional counterterrorism strategy drafting workshop on measures to prevent and combat terrorism. Held in Harare, Zimbabwe, on 5–7 November 2014.
- Integrated counterterrorism and non-proliferation of arms strategy for Central Africa drafting workshop on conditions conducive to the growth of terrorism and human rights and the rule of law. Held in Luanda, Angola, on 24–26 February 2015.
- SADC regional counterterrorism strategy drafting workshop on addressing the conditions conducive to the spread of terrorism and upholding the rule of law. Held in Livingstone, Zambia, on 24–26 March 2015.
- Integrated counterterrorism and non-proliferation of arms strategy for Central Africa drafting workshop on terrorist financing and money laundering. Held in Libreville, Gabon, on 19–21 May 2015.
- SADC regional counterterrorism strategy drafting workshop on counterterrorism capacity-building needs in the southern Africa region. Held in Gaborone, Botswana, on 10–11 June 2015. This workshop also reviewed the draft strategy and associated plan of action that had been prepared by the SADC secretariat, with extensive input from UNCCT, ACSRT and the SADC troika.[89]

Another crucial issue facing the SADC is that of organised crime, which is a major impediment to good governance and the economy in the region.[90] It is also a potential source of funding for terrorist organisations. In 2012, the United Nations Office on Drugs and Crime (UNODC) and the SADC jointly developed a regional programme for 2013–2016 entitled 'Making the Southern African Development Community (SADC) Region Safer from Crime and Drugs', which aimed to: 'Support the member states in responding to these and other challenges related to organised crime, security, effectiveness and integrity of criminal justice systems, as well as drug abuse and HIV/AIDS through strengthening capacities at the national level and promoting regional cooperation, in line with the priorities and needs of the countries concerned.'[91]

The regional programme focuses on three interdependent substantive pillars: (1) Countering illicit trafficking and organised crime; (2) Criminal justice and integrity; and (3) Improving drug abuse prevention, treatment and care, and HIV prevention, treatment and care. The remainder of this section will focus on the first of these as it is the most relevant to the discourse of this chapter.

This pillar aimed to strengthen the capabilities of SADC member states to effectively address organised crime and illicit trafficking through promoting regional cooperation and coordination, which is supported through corresponding capacity-building at the national level. In particular, attention is given to regional border control and management; counter-narcotics efforts, with special regard to precursor chemicals; the regional response to urban and emerging crimes; anti money-laundering (AML); and improving the forensic capacity of member states. According to the programme, a central element of the pillar was to support the creation of transnational organised crime units (TOCUs) to undertake investigations, and to promote and facilitate regional cooperation among them.

Another aim of the regional programme is to promote a regionally coherent border control management response by SADC countries, with respect to trafficking flows to, from and within the region. SADC countries will be given support to assist victims and combat human trafficking and migrant smuggling. This will be achieved 'through targeted training, development of a cooperation manual and contact list of focal points, and the establishment of a regional forum for specialised investigators and prosecutors'.[92] With regard to border-control management, the programme promises to facilitate increased coordination in counter-narcotics efforts by the countries in the region, especially with regard to precursor control. Through the regional programme, UNODC will support SADC countries to develop and, where possible, implement a regionally consolidated strategy to address emerging crimes and urban crime.

Moreover, the UNODC has assured SADC member states of its support in combating money laundering. This will be achieved by creating or strengthening financial intelligence units (FIUs), delivering training courses, as well as mentorship and placement programmes for prosecutors and investigators, based on the UNODC's own experiences. It will also aim to promote an integrated approach to the investigation of financial crimes, which will contribute to the adoption of effective multi-agency approaches. On 23 November 2015, a regional programme steering committee meeting was held to review the implementation of the SADC–UNODC joint regional programme.[93] However, the results of the meeting are yet to be published.

Building policy frameworks is, however, only the first and perhaps easiest step to effectively address the issues of violent extremism and terrorism. As has been seen in the case of the AU, the ratification and implementation of these frameworks can be a major challenge. For example, in July 1999 in Algiers, the OAU Convention on the Prevention and Combating of Terrorism, or the 'Algiers Convention' was adopted by the 35th ordinary session of the OAU heads of state, but it only came into effect three years later, in December 2002, after 30 states ratified it. In addition to providing a definition of terrorism, the Algiers Convention set out the importance of promoting areas of cooperation among member states, the institution of state jurisdiction over acts of terror, as well as initiating a system for extradition, inter-state investigation and mutual legal assistance. The Algiers Convention also required that member states adhere to a fourfold commitment to countering terrorism.[94]

In July 2002, after the amalgamation of the OAU and the African Economic Community (AEC), the newly formed African Union (AU) set out to align itself with the global fight against terror. The Algiers Convention, coupled with the reality of international terrorism in the wake of the 9/11 attacks, led counterterrorism to become a major element of the AU's peace and security framework. In September 2002, as part of its efforts to firm up the commitments and strategies in the Algiers Convention, the AU adopted its plan of action to prevent and combat terrorism.

In addition to calling on all member states to ratify and implement the Algiers Convention, this plan sought to adopt practical counterterrorism measures, including police and border controls, legislative and judicial measures, policies to stop illicit financing of terrorism, and methods to improve the exchange of information. To this end, the plan of action initiated the creation of the AU's Peace and Security Council (PSC) with the objective to 'harmonise and coordinate continental efforts in the prevention and combating of terrorism' and the creation of the African Centre for the Study & Research on Terrorism (ACSRT or CAERT in French) within the PSC.[95] The objectives of this centre include researching all aspects of terrorism, developing counterterrorism capacity-building programmes and providing advice to member states based on recommendations on a needs basis.

In July 2004, the AU adopted the 2004 Protocol of the Algiers Convention, which recognised the 'linkages between terrorism and mercenarism, weapons of mass destruction, drug trafficking, corruption, transnational organised crimes, money laundering, and the illicit proliferation of small arms' as increasingly prevalent risks associated with terrorism.[96] The purpose of this protocol was to rectify a significant weakness of the OAU convention, which did not have sufficient implementation mechanisms. To this end, the protocol mandated the AU PSC to monitor and facilitate implementation and to encourage Regional Economic Communities (RECs) to play a more active role.

Although the protocol was adopted in 2004, it only came into force on 26 February 2014. The reason behind the delay was that the AU required 16 countries to ratify the protocol before it could be put into effect; a number achieved this only a decade later. Thus far, states at the forefront of the fight against transitional terrorist organisations such as Kenya, Nigeria, Somalia, Mauritania and Chad have still not ratified the protocol. To date, after much urging and continuous pleading by the AU, only 41 member states have ratified the convention.[97] In addition, it took just over a decade for the 2004 protocol to come into effect and thus far there have only been 17 ratifications.[98]

In an effort to continue implementing counterterrorism measures in Africa in accordance with the relevant regional and international mechanisms, the AU has developed the African Model Anti-Terrorism Law that would serve as a comprehensive legal instrument member states could adopt to 'strengthen their criminal justice system and effectively prevent and combat terrorism'.[99] However, only three member states (Ghana, Mauritius and Burkina Faso) have approached the AU for assistance in implementing the new model into their national legislation.

In addition to the challenges faced in implementing conventions and counterterrorism mechanisms, efforts by the AU to address terrorism are often eclipsed by the actions of the United States, Britain, France and the UN. Moreover, the AU has received little support from Western powers in implementing anti-terrorism instruments on the African continent. Instead of collaborating with the AU, these Western powers prefer working directly with member states, as exemplified in the US establishment of the Pan-Sahel Initiative (PSI) in 2002 to assist Mali, Mauritania, Niger and Chad in their fight against terrorism.

Additionally, the AU lacks a system for monitoring implementation of measures in states that do ratify. A lack of funds, resources and technical knowledge remain the greatest challenges contributing to the AU's failure to fully implement its counterterrorism strategies. This, in turn, leaves the AU reliant on the UN and Western states for help, all of which prefer to function or implement their strategies independently.

Conclusion

Over the coming decades, the threat of terrorism and violent extremism is likely to grow in the SADC region. While there are considerable differences in the socio-economic profiles and level of development across the 15 SADC member states, a youth bulge, high levels of unemployment, poor governance, rapid urbanisation and a range of other potential drivers of violent extremism are present in many of the countries that make up the region.[100] Furthermore, the changing religious landscape in countries such as Tanzania, and the arrival of new religious ideologies that are averse to cultural and religious pluralism, threaten to polarise religious communities and create an opportunity for violent extremist organisations to establish themselves and gain local support.

To date, the responsibility of meeting the challenges posed by the emergence and spread of local violent extremist organisations has largely fallen on individual states. However, as migration flows grow and access to the internet and the international financial system increases, allowing these local organisations to merge and evolve into transnational threats, regional cooperation and coordination become paramount. The SADC has taken important steps in developing a regional counterterrorism strategy. However, this strategy remains largely on paper and has not been effectively implemented by member states. As illustrated by the difficulties the AU has faced, the real challenge is building capacity, developing coordinating mechanisms and implementing counterterrorism policies at state level. Furthermore, while regional counterterrorism frameworks are important for coordination and cooperation, the drivers of violent extremism can be highly localised and, thus, require localised solutions. There is a paucity of research on violent extremism and terrorism within the SADC region, and so the potential threat posed by transnational terrorist organisations across member states is difficult to evaluate. More research is needed within SADC member states to identify local push and pull factors, which enable violent extremism, before any meaningful measures to address these issues can be taken.

Endnotes

1. Brandon, J (2016) Al-Shabaab attack keeps pressure on Kenyan military and government. *Briefs. The Jamestown Foundation Terrorism Monitor*, **14** (2). Available at: http://www.jamestown.org/single/?tx_ttnews%5Btt_news%5D=45008andtx_ttnews%5BbackPid%5D=228andcHash=c4321643a91f6367fccc4b6580b8b2a8#.V0w9FJN97Vo
2. Council on Foreign Relations (2017) *Nigeria Security Tracker*. Available at: http://www.cfr. org/nigeria/nigeria-security-tracker/p29483
3. Cilliers, J (2015) *Violent Islamist Extremism and Terror in Africa*. Institute for Security Studies Paper No. 286. Available at: https://www.issafrica.org/uploads/ Paper%20286%20_v3.pdf.
4. European Union (2014) *Revised EU Strategy for Combating Radicalisation and Recruitment to Terrorism*. Published 19 May 2014. Available at: http://data.consilium.europa.eu/doc/document/ST-9956-2014-INIT/en/pdf
5. United Nations (2006) *Global Counter-Terrorism Strategy*. Available at: https://www.un.org/counterterrorism/ctitf/en/un-global-counter-terrorism-strategy
6. African Union (2004) *Protocol To The OAU Convention On The Prevention And Combating Of Terrorism*. Available at: http://www.peaceau.org/uploads/protocol-oau-convention-on-the-prevention-combating-terrorism-en.pdf
7. SADC (1992) *Treaty of the Southern African Development Community*. Available at: http://www.sadc.int/files/9113/5292/9434/SADC_Treaty.pdf
8. United Nations Development Programme (2015) *Preventing and Responding to Violent*

Extremism in Africa: A development approach. *Available at: https://www.google.co.za/ search?q=Preventing+and+Responding+to+Violent+Extremism+in+Africa%3A+A+ Development+Approachandq=Preventing+and+Responding+to+Violent+ Extremism+in+Africa%3A+A+Development+Approachandqs=chrome..69i57. 284j0j4andsourceid=chromeandie=UTF-8*

9. West, S (2015) The rise of ADF-NALU in Central Africa and its connections with Al-Shabaab, *Terrorism Monitor,* **13** (1). The Jamestown Foundation. Available at: https://jamestown.org/program/the-rise-of-adf-nalu-in-central-africa-and-its-connections-with-al-shabaab/

10. Reuters (2016) Mauritius ramps up security after gunshots fired on French embassy. Published 30 May 2016. Available at: http://uk.reuters.com/article/uk-mauritius-security-idUKKCN0YL1AY

11. Reuters (2015) Mauritius investigates ISIS video. Published 12 November 2015. Available at: http://www.newsweek.com/mauritius-investigates-islamic-state-video-404352

12. Rakawski, S (2015) Madagascar wakes up to ISIS, *The National Interest*. Published 24 December 2015. Available at: http://nationalinterest.org/feature/madagascar-wakes-isis-14721

13. Benjamin, C (2015) SA an attractive destination for terrorism funding networks, *Mail & Guardian*. Published 4 February 2015. Available at: https://mg.co.za/article/2015-02-04-sa-an-attractive-destination-for-terrorism-funding-networks

14. Heilman, BE and Kaiser, PJ (2002) Religion, identity and politics in Tanzania, *Third World Quarterly,* **23** (4), pp. 691–709.

15. Ibid, p. 494.

16. See, Glickman, H (2011) The threat of Islamism in sub-Saharan Africa: The case of Tanzania. Available at: http://www.fpri.org/docs/media/201104.glickman.islamismsubsaharanafrica. pdf; LeSage, A (2014) *The Rising Terrorist Threat in Tanzania: Domestic Islamist militancy and regional threats*, Strategic Forum No. 288. Washington, DC: National Defense University. Available at: http://ndupress.ndu.edu/Portals/68/Documents/stratforum/SF-288.pdf

17. LeSage, A (2014).

18. Ibid, p. 3.

19. Vittori, J, Bremer, K and Vittori, P (2009) Islam in Tanzania and Kenya: Ally or threat in the war on terror? *Studies in Conflict and Terrorism*, **32** (12), pp. 1075–1099.

20. Ibid, p. 1076.

21. Vittori et al (2009) p. 1078.

22. Mesaki, S (2011). Religion and the state in Tanzania, *Cross-Cultural Communication*, **7** (2), pp. 249–259.

23. Bondakero, DM (2004) The 'Fruit of Enlightenment': Education, politics and Muslim–Christian relations in contemporary Tanzania, *Islam and Christian-Muslim Relations*, **15** (4), pp. 443–468.

24. Heilman and Kaiser (2002) p. 702.

25. Ibid, p. 692.

26. Haynes, J (2005) Islamic militancy in East Africa, *Third World Quarterly*, **26** (8), p. 1333.

27. Becker, F (2006) Rural Islamism during the 'War on Terror': A Tanzanian case study, *African Affairs*, **105** (421) p. 583.

28. Ibid, p. 584.

29. Ibid, p. 602.

30. Haynes (2005) p. 1333.

31. Glickman (2011).

32. Brent, G and Mshigeni, DS (2004) Terrorism in Context: Race, Religion, Party, and Violent Conflict in Zanzibar, *The American Sociologist*, **35** (2), pp. 60–74. Available at: https://faculty.

unlv.edu/brents/research/terrorZanzibar.pdf
33 Lopez LE (2015) *Islamist Radicalisation and Terrorism in Tanzania*. GSDRC Helpdesk Research Report No. 1223. Birmingham: GSDRC, University of Birmingham.
34 Mesaki, S (2011) Religion and the state in Tanzania, *Cross-Cultural Communication*, **7** (2), pp. 249–259.
35 Brent and Mshigeni (2004) p. 64.
36 Howden, D (2012) Trouble in paradise as radical Islam grows in Zanzibar, *The Independent* (UK). Published 30 October 2012. Available at: http://www.independent.co.uk/news/world/africa/trouble-in-paradise-as-radical-islam-grows-in-zanzibar-8231626.html
37 IRIN (2012) Protests on both Zanzibar and mainland threaten stability. Published 25 October 2012. Available at: https://www.irinnews.org/fr/node/252711
38 Glickman (2011).
39 United Nations Integrated Regional Information Networks (2012) Tanzania: Islamist riots threaten Zanzibar's stability. Published 24 October 2012.
40 Becker, F (2006) p. 583.
41 Gatsiounis, I (2013) After Al-Shabaab, *Current Trends in Islamist Ideology*, **14**, p. 79.
42 LeSage (2014) p. 26.
43 Burchard, S (2015) *Violent Extremist Organizations and the Electoral Cycle in Africa: A framework for analyzing the 2015 Tanzanian elections*. Alexandria, VA: Institute For Defense Analyses, p. 20.
44 Ibid. p. 14.
45 Reuters (2015) Gunmen kill seven in attack on Tanzanian police station. Published 13 July 2015. Available at: http://af.reuters.com/article/africaTech/idAFKCN0PN1Q520150713
46 LeSage (2014) p. 6.
47 Armed Conflict Location and Event Database (ACLED) (2016) *Al-Shabaab in Tanzania: Current status and potential future patterns*. Available at: http://www.crisis.acleddata.com/al-shabaab-in-tanzania-current-status-and-potential-future-patterns/
48 Ibid.
49 World Bulletin (2015) Fear in Tanzania town after alleged Al-Shabaab attack. Published 16 February 2015. Available at: http://www.worldbulletin.net/news/155095/fear-in-tanzania-town-after-alleged-al-shabaab-attack.
50 Unites States Department of State (2016) *Country Reports on Terrorism 2015 Africa Overview: Tanzania*. Available at: https://www.state.gov/j/ct/rls/crt/2015/257514.htm
51 LeSage (2014) p. 5.
52 Jamestown Foundation (2005) Tanzania: Al-Qaeda's East African beachhead? *Terrorism Monitor*, **1** (5), p. 5.
53 Institute for Security Studies (2016) South Africa and Terrorism. The links are real, by A Schoeman. Published 9 August 2016. Available at: https://issafrica.org/iss-today/southafrica-and-terrorism-the-links-are-real
54 Steinburg, G and Weber, A (2015) Jiihadism in Africa: An introduction. In G Steinburg and A Weber (eds) *Jihadism in Africa: Local causes, regional expansion, international alliances*. Berlin: German Institute for International and Security Affairs.
55 South African History Archive (2017) Terrorism Act, Act No. 83 of 1967. Available at: http://www.saha.org.za/nonracialism/terrorism_act_act_no_83_of_1967.htm
56 Dugard, J (1978) *Human Rights and the South African Legal Order*. Princeton, NJ: Princeton University Press.
57 In 2004, the Protection of Constitutional Democracy against Terrorist and Related Activities Act (Act No. 33 of 2004) was adopted by Parliament. In the aftermath of 9/11, President Thabo Mbeki also reiterated the South African government's commitment to combating terrorism, and ensured that the country actively participated in a number of

international initiatives designed to address terrorism, including initiatives led by the Non-Aligned Movement, the Organisation of African Unity (OAU) and the United Nations. See, South African Police Services (2014) Protection of Constitutional Democracy Against Terrorism and Related Activities Act 33 of 2004. Available at: https://www.saps.gov.za/resource_centre/acts/downloads/juta/terrorism_act.pdf

58 Statistics South Africa (2015) *General Household Survey*. Statistical Release P0318. Available at: http://www.statssa.gov.za/publications/P0318/P03182015.pdf

59 This is evident in sections 15 and 31 of the 1996 Constitution: s 15(1) protects every individual's right to freedom of religion; s 15(2) allows religious observances to be conducted at state or state-aided institutions; s 31(1) protects the collective right of religious communities to practise their religion and to establish and maintain religious associations; s 15(3)(a) permits the enactment of legislation to recognise religious marriages or religious personal or family law systems. In fact, s 15(2)–(3) enables the establishment of a semi-secular, legally pluralistic society that involves an intersection between religion and the state where government is encouraged to support religion.

60 Amien, W (2012) Politics of religious freedom in South Africa, *The Immanent Frame*. Published 24 July 2012. Available at: https://tif.ssrc.org/2012/07/24/politics-of-religious-freedom-in-south-africa/

61 Boshoff, H, Botha, A and Schonteich, M (2001) *Fear in the City: Urban terrorism in South Africa*. Institute for Security Studies, Monograph No. 63. Pretoria: Institute for Security Studies. Available at: https://oldsite.issafrica.org/publications/monographs/monograph-63-fear-in-the-city-urban-terrorism-in-south-africa-henri-boshoff-anneli-botha-and-martin-schonteich

62 Hough, J (2007) Urban terror in South Africa: A new wave? *Terrorism and Political Violence*, **12** (2). Available at: http://www.tandfonline.com/doi/abs/10.1080/09546550008427561

63 Ibid.

64 Cummings, R (2016) Terrorism in South Africa: What is the risk? Tony Blair Institute for Global Change. Published 23 December 2016. Available at: http://www.religion-andgeopolitics.org/sub-saharan-africa/terrorism-south-africa-what-risk

65 Ibid.

66 Reuters (2016) Militant cells lying low in South Africa, minister says. Published 11 November 2016. Available at: http://www.reuters.com/article/us-safrica-security-idUSKBN13614C

67 Benjamin, C (2015) SA an attractive destination for terrorism funding networks, *Mail & Guardian*. Published 4 February 2015. Available at: https://mg.co.za/article/2015-02-04-sa-an-attractive-destination-for-terrorism-funding-networks

68 Institute for Security Studies (2016) 'South Africa and terrorism: The links are real, by A Schoeman. Published 9 August 2016. Available at: https://issafrica.org/iss-today/south-africa-and-terrorism-the-links-are-real

69 Solomon, H (2013) Researching terrorism in South Africa, *Scientia Militaria*, **40** (2), pp. 142–165. Available at: http://www.ajol.info/index.php/smsajms

70 Ibid, p. 146.

71 Al Jazeera (2013) South Africa bears down on al-Shabaab. Published 6 October 2013. Available at: http://www.aljazeera.com/indepth/features/2013/09/south-africa-bears-down-al-shabab-2013930112321530266.html

72 Solomon (2013), p. 144.

73 Ibid.

74 Cummings, R (2016).

75 ISIS evolved from Al-Qaeda in Iraq (AQI) around 2006 after a series of disputes between Al-Qaeda Central and Al-Qaeda in Iraq led the former to publically cut ties with the latter.

76 Byman, DL (2015) *Comparing Al-Qaeda and ISIS: Different goals, different targets*. Washington, DC: Brookings Institute. Published 29 April 2015. Available at: https://www.brookings.edu/testimonies/comparing-al-qaeda-and-isis-different-goals-different-targets/
77 Ibid.
78 Cachalia, RC and Schoeman, A (2017) *Violent Extremism in South Africa: Assessing the current threat*. Institute for Security Studies, Policy Brief. Published May 2017. Pretoria ISS: 155. Available at: https://issafrica.org/research/southern-africa-report/violent-extremism-in-south-africa-assessing-the-current-threat; *Daily Maverick* (2017) ISS today: Are Islamic State returnees a risk for South Africa? Published 22 May 2017. Available at: https://www.dailymaverick.co.za/article/2017-05-22-iss-today-are-islamic-state-returnees-a-risk-for-south-africa/#.WcvNN9MjHVo
79 United States Embassy (2017) Threats to shopping areas and malls. Published 4 June 2017. Available at: usembassy.gov/Threats to Shopping Areas and Malls/04 June 2017
80 Opperman, J (2017) Is an ISIS attack likely in South Africa? *Daily Maverick*. Published 16 January 2017. Available at: https://www.dailymaverick.co.za/article/2017-01-16-2017-is-isis-attack-likely-in-south-africa/#.WPdkqFOGPVo
81 Njanji, S (2016) South African brothers charged with terrorism, accused of planning attacks against US embassy and Jewish institutions, *Mail & Guardian*. Published 12 July 2016. Available at: https://mg.co.za/article/2016-07-12-sa-in-islamic-state-first-as-twins-accused-over-us-embassy-plot
82 Wa Afrika, M and Hofstatter, S (2017) Top terror bomber bust on his way to SA, *Sunday Times*. Published 15 January 2017. Available at: http://www.timeslive.co.za/sundaytimes/stnews/2017/01/15/Top-terror-bomber-bust-on-his-way-to-SA
83 Cawthra, G (1997) *Securing South Africa's Democracy: Defence, development and security in transition*. London: Palgrave Macmillan.
84 SADC (1992) *Treaty of the Southern African Development Community*. Available at: http://www.sadc.int/files/9113/5292/9434/SADC_Treaty.pdf
85 Rosand, E and Ipe, J (2008) Enhancing counterterrorism cooperation in southern Africa, *African Security Review*, **17** (2). Available at: https://issafrica.s3.amazonaws.com/site/uploads/17NO2ROSAND.PDF
86 McCoubrey, H and Morris, J, (2000) *Regional Peacekeeping in the Post-Cold War Era*. The Hague: Kluwer Law International.
87 Nyang'oro, J (2007) Terrorism threats and responses in the Southern African Development Community region. In A LeSage (ed) *African Counterterrorism Cooperation: Assessing regional and sub-regional initiatives*. Washington, DC: National Defense University Press and Potomac Books, p. 106.
88 SADC (2015b) SADC Experts meet to draft a Regional Counter-Terrorism Strategy. Available at: https://www.sadc.int/news-events/news/sadc-experts-meet-draft-regional-counter-terrorism-strategy/
89 UNCCT (2017) *Facilitating The Development Of Regional Counter-Terrorism Strategies*. Available at: https://www.un.org/counterterrorism/ctitf/en/uncct/facilitating-development-regional-counter-terrorism-strategies
90 Tshwete, S (2011) Legislative responses to organised crime in the SADC region. In C Goredema (ed) *Organised Crime in Southern Africa: Assessing legislation*. Pretoria: Institute for Security Studies.
91 UNODC (2012) *Making the Southern African Development Community (SADC) Region Safer from Crime and Drugs: Regional Programme: 2013 – 2016*. Pretoria: UNODC Regional Office for Southern Africa, p. 5.
92 Ibid.
93 SADC (2015b).

94 Firstly, as Article 2*(c)* of the convention noted: states must 'implement the actions, including enactment of legislation and the establishment as criminal offences of certain acts as required in terms of the international instruments' (African Union, 1999). As such, these states should ratify these international instruments and apply them within their domestic statutes. An example of such an international instrument is the International Convention against the Taking of Hostages of 1979. The second commitment emphasises the importance of establishing and supporting inter-agency cooperation at a national level prior to an inter-state level (Article 5). The third commitment follows from the second, requiring that states improve cross-border policing and surveillance so as to 'develop and strengthen methods of controlling and monitoring land, sea and air borders and customs and immigration check points' (Article 4 (2)*(c)*). The final commitment pertains to states not providing any type of support to terrorist groups such as 'providing safe sanctuaries both directly or indirectly, financing groups, committing or inciting to commit terrorist acts through provisions of weapons or issuing of travel documents and visas' (Article 4(1)). Although the Algiers Convention predated the establishment of the African Union, it remained the foundation for subsequent counterterrorism frameworks. See, African Union (1999) *OAU Convention on the Prevention and Combating of Terrorism, 1999*. Available at: https://treaties.un.org/doc/db/Terrorism/OAU-english.pdf

95 African Union (1999) *OAU Convention on the Prevention and Combating of Terrorism, 1999*. Available at: https://treaties.un.org/doc/db/Terrorism/OAU-english.pdf

96 African Union (2004) *Protocol to The OAU Convention on the Prevention and Combating of Terrorism*. Available at: http://www.peaceau.org/uploads/protocol-oau-convention-on-the-prevention-combating-terrorism-en.pdf

97 African Union (2016a) *List of Countries Which Have Signed, Ratified/Acceded to The OAU Convention On the Prevention and Combating of Terrorism*. Available at: https://www.au.int/web/sites/default/files/treaties/7779-sl-protocol_to_the_oau_convention_on_the_prevention_and_combating_of_terrorism_14.pdf

98 African Union (2016b) *List of Countries which have Signed, Ratified/Acceded to The Protocol to The OAU Convention On the Prevention and Combating of Terrorism*. Available at: https://www.au.int/web/sites/default/files/treaties/7787-sl-protocol_on_terrorism.pdf

99 African Union (2012) *Report of The Chairperson of the Commission on Terrorism and Violent Extremism in Africa*. Available at: http://caert.org.dz/Reports/Report-terrorism-13-11-2012.pdf

100 SADC (2015c) *SADC Statistical Yearbook 2015*. Published 10 June 2015. Available at: https://reliefweb.int/report/world/sadc-statistical-yearbook-2015

References

African Union (1992) *Resolution on The Strengthening of Cooperation and Coordination among African States*, AHG/Res. 213. Available at: http://caert.org.dz/AU-Res-Dec-Decl/AHG-Res-213-Dakar.pdf

African Union (1992) *Declarations and Resolutions Adopted by the Thirtieth Ordinary Session of The Assembly of Heads of State and Government*. Available at: https://issafrica.org/ctafrica/uploads/OAU%20Declaration%20on%20the%20Code%20of%20Conduct%20for%20Inter-African%20Relations.PDF

African Union (1999) *OAU Convention on the Prevention and Combating of Terrorism, 1999*. Available at: https://treaties.un.org/doc/db/Terrorism/OAU-english.pdf

African Union (2004) *Protocol to the OAU Convention on the Prevention and Combating of Terrorism*. Available at: http://www.peaceau.org/uploads/protocol-oau-convention-on-the-prevention-combating-terrorism-en.pdf

African Union (2012) *Report of the Chairperson of the Commission on Terrorism and Violent Extremism in Africa*. Available at: http://caert.org.dz/Reports/Report-terrorism-13-11-2012.pdf

African Union (2016a) *List of Countries Which Have Signed, Ratified/Acceded to the OAU Convention on the Prevention and Combating of Terrorism*. Available at: https://www.au.int/web/sites/default/files/treaties/7779-sl-protocol_to_the_oau_convention_on_the_prevention_and_combating_of_terrorism_14.pdf

African Union (2016b) *List of Countries which have Signed, Ratified/Acceded to The Protocol to The OAU Convention On the Prevention and Combating of Terrorism*. Available at: https://www.au.int/web/sites/default/files/treaties/7787-sl-protocol_on_terrorism.pdf

Al Jazeera (2013) South Africa bears down on al-Shabaab. Published 6 October 2013. Available at: http://www.aljazeera.com/indepth/features/2013/09/south-africa-bears-down-al-shabab-2013930112321530266.html

Amien, W (2012) Politics of religious freedom in South Africa, *The Immanent Frame*. Published 24 July 2012. Available at: https://tif.ssrc.org/2012/07/24/politics-of-religious-freedom-in-south-africa/

Armed Conflict Location and Event Database (ACLED) (2016) *Al-Shabaab in Tanzania: Current status and potential future patterns*. Available at: http://www.crisis.acleddata.com/al-shabaab-in-tanzania-current-status-and-potential-future-patterns/

Bakari, MA (2012) Religion, secularism, and political discourse in Tanzania: Competing perspectives by religious organisations, *Interdisciplinary Journal of Research on Religion*, **8** (1), pp. 1–34.

Becker, F (2006) Rural Islamism during the 'War on Terror': A Tanzanian case study, *African Affairs*, **105** (421), pp. 583–603.

Benjamin, C (2015) SA an attractive destination for terrorism funding networks, *Mail & Guardian*. Published 4 February 2015. Available at: https://mg.co.za/article/2015-02-04-sa-an-attractive-destination-for-terrorism-funding-networks

Bondakero, DM (2004) The 'Fruit of Enlightenment': Education, politics and Muslim–Christian relations in contemporary Tanzania, *Islam and Christian-Muslim Relations*, **15** (4), pp. 443–468.

Boshoff, H, Botha, A and Schonteich, M (2001) *Fear in the City: Urban terrorism in South Africa*. Institute for Security Studies, Monograph No. 63. Pretoria: Institute for Security Studies. Available at: https://oldsite.issafrica.org/publications/monographs/monograph-63-fear-in-the-city-urban-terrorism-in-south-africa-henri-boshoff-anneli-botha-and-martin-schonteich

Brandon, J (2016) Al-Shabaab attack keeps pressure on Kenyan military and government. *Briefs. The Jamestown Foundation Terrorism Monitor*, **14** (2). Available at: http://www.jamestown.org/single/?tx_ttnews%5Btt_news%5D=45008andtx_ttnews%5BbackPid%5D=228andcHash=c4321643a91f6367fccc4b6580b8b2a8#.V0w9FJN97Vo

Brent, G and Mshigeni, DS (2004) Terrorism in Context: Race, religion, party, and violent conflict in Zanzibar, *The American Sociologist*, **35** (2), pp. 60–74. Available at: https://faculty.unlv.edu/brents/research/terrorZanzibar.pdf

Burchard, S (2015) *Violent Extremist Organizations and the Electoral Cycle in Africa: A framework for analyzing the 2015 Tanzanian elections*. Alexandria, VA: Institute For Defense Analyses, p. 20.

Byman, DL (2015) *Comparing Al-Qaeda and ISIS: Different goals, different targets*. Washington, DC: Brookings Institute. Published 29 April 2015. Available at: https://www.brookings.edu/testimonies/comparing-al-qaeda-and-isis-different-goals-different-targets/

Cachalia, RC and Schoeman, A (2017) *Violent Extremism in South Africa: Assessing the current threat*. Institute for Security Studies, Policy Brief. Published May 2017. Pretoria: ISS. Available at: https://issafrica.org/research/southern-africa-report/violent-extremism-in-south-africa-assessing-the-current-threat

Cawthra, G (1997) *Securing South Africa's Democracy: Defence, development and security in transition.* London: Palgrave Macmillan.

Cilliers, J (2015) *Violent Islamist Extremism and Terror in Africa.* Institute for Security Studies Paper No. 286. Pretoria: Institute for Security Studies. Available at: https://www.issafrica.org/uploads/ Paper%20286%20_v3.pdf

Council on Foreign Relations (2017) *Nigeria Security Tracker.* Available at: http://www.cfr.org/nigeria/nigeria-security-tracker/p29483

Cummings, R (2016) Terrorism in South Africa: What is the risk? Tony Blair Institute for Global Change. Published 23 December 2016. Available at: http://www.religionandgeopolitics.org/sub-saharan-africa/terrorism-south-africa-what-risk

Daily Maverick (2017) ISS today: Are Islamic State returnees a risk for South Africa? Published 22 May 2017. Available at: https://www.dailymaverick.co.za/article/2017-05-22-iss-today-are-islamic-state-returnees-a-risk-for-south-africa/#.WcvNN9MjHVo

Dugard, J (1978) *Human Rights and the South African Legal Order.* Princeton, NJ: Princeton University Press.

European Union (2014) *Revised EU Strategy for Combating Radicalisation and Recruitment to Terrorism.* Published on 19 May 2014. Available at: http://data.consilium.europa.eu/doc/document/ST-9956-2014–INIT/en/pdf.

Gatsiounis, I (2013) After Al-Shabaab, *Current Trends in Islamist Ideology*, **14**, pp. 74–89.

Glickman, H (2011) The threat of Islamism in sub-Saharan Africa: The case of Tanzania. Available at: http://www.fpri.org/docs/media/201104.glickman.islamismsubsaharanafrica.pdf

Haynes, J (2005) Islamic militancy in East Africa, *Third World Quarterly*, **26** (8), pp. 1321–1339. Available at: http://dx.doi.org/10.1080/01436590500336807

Haynes, J (2006). Islam and democracy in East Africa, *Democratization*, **13** (3), pp. 490–507.

Heilman, BE and Kaiser, PJ (2002). Religion, identity and politics in Tanzania, *Third World Quarterly*, **23** (4), pp. 691–709.

Hough, J (2007) Urban terror in South Africa: A new wave? *Terrorism and Political Violence*, **12** (2). Available at: http://www.tandfonline.com/doi/abs/10.1080/09546550008427561

Howden, D (2012) Trouble in paradise as radical Islam grows in Zanzibar, *The Independent* (UK). Published 30 October 2012. Available at: http://www.independent.co.uk/news/world/africa/trouble-in-paradise-as-radical-islam-grows-in-zanzibar-8231626.html

IRIN (2012) Protests on both Zanzibar and mainland threaten stability. Published 25 October 2012. Available at: https://www.irinnews.org/fr/node/252711

Institute for Economics and Peace (2016) *Global Terrorism Index 2015.* Available at: http://economicsandpeace.org/reports/

Institute for Security Studies (2016) South Africa and terrorism: The links are real, by A Schoeman. Published 9 August 2016. Available at: https://issafrica.org/iss-today/south-africa-and-terrorism-the-links-are-real

Jamestown Foundation (2005) Tanzania: Al-Qaeda's East African beachhead? *Terrorism Monitor*, **1** (5), pp. 1–6.

LeSage, A (ed) (2007) *African Counterterrorism Cooperation: Assessing regional and sub-regional initiatives.* Washington, DC: National Defense University Press and Potomac Books, p. 106.

LeSage, A (2014) *The Rising Terrorist Threat in Tanzania: Domestic Islamist militancy and regional threats*, Strategic Forum No. 288. Washington, DC: National Defense University. Available at: http://ndupress.ndu.edu/Portals/68/Documents/stratforum/SF-288.pdf

Lopez LE (2015) *Islamist Radicalisation and Terrorism in Tanzania.* GSDRC Helpdesk Research Report No. 1223. Birmingham: GSDRC, University of Birmingham.

McCoubrey H and Morris, J (2000*) Regional Peacekeeping in the Post-Cold War Era.* The Hague: Kluwer Law International.

Mesaki, S (2011) Religion and the state in Tanzania, *Cross-Cultural Communication*, **7** (2), pp. 249–259.

Njanji, S (2016) South African brothers charged with terrorism, accused of planning attacks against US embassy and Jewish institutions, *Mail & Guardian*. Published 12 July 2016. Available at: https://mg.co.za/article/2016-07-12-sa-in-islamic-state-first-as-twins-accused-over-us-embassy-plot

Nyang'oro, J (2007) Terrorism threats and responses in the Southern African Development Community region. In A LeSage (ed) *African Counterterrorism Cooperation: Assessing regional and sub-regional initiatives*. Washington, DC: National Defense University Press and Potomac Books, p. 106.

Opperman, J (2017) 2017: Is an ISIS attack likely in South Africa? *Daily Maverick*. Published 16 January 2017. Available at: https://www.dailymaverick.co.za/article/2017-01-16-2017-is-isis-attack-likely-in-south-africa/#.WPdkqFOGPVo

Potgieter, DW (2012) Meet the youngest Worcester Bomber – now a poster boy for reconciliation, *The Daily Maverick*. Published 12 December 2012. Available at: https://www.dailymaverick.co.za/article/2012-12-20-meet-the-youngest-worcester-bomber-now-a-poster-boy-for-reconciliation/#.WVDJ2xOGPVo

Rakawski, S (2015) Madagascar wakes up to ISIS, *The National Interest*. Published 24 December 2015. Available at: http://nationalinterest.org/feature/madagascar-wakes-isis-14721

Reuters (2015) Gunmen kill seven in attack on Tanzanian police station. Published 13 July 2015. Available at: http://af.reuters.com/article/africaTech/idAFKCN0PN1Q520150713

Reuters (2015) Mauritius investigates ISIS video. Published 12 November 2015. Available at: http://www.newsweek.com/mauritius-investigates-islamic-state-video-404352

Reuters (2016) Militant cells lying low in South Africa, minister says. Published 11 November 2016. Available at: http://www.reuters.com/article/us-safrica-security-idUSKBN13614C

Reuters (2016) Mauritius ramps up security after gunshots fired on French embassy. Published 30 May 2016. Available at: http://uk.reuters.com/article/uk-mauritius-security-idUKKCN0YL1AY

Rosand, E and Ipe, J (2008) Enhancing counterterrorism cooperation in southern Africa, *African Security Review*, **17** (2). Available at: https://issafrica.s3.amazonaws.com/site/uploads/17NO2ROSAND.PDF

SADC (1992) *Treaty of the Southern African Development Community*. Available at: http://www.sadc.int/files/9113/5292/9434/SADC_Treaty.pdf

SADC (2015a) *35th SADC Summit Brochure*. Gaberone: SADC Secretariat.

SADC (2015b) SADC experts meet to draft a Regional Counter-Terrorism Strategy. Available at: https://www.sadc.int/news-events/news/sadc-experts-meet-draft-regional-counter-terrorism-strategy/

SADC (2015c) *SADC Statistical Yearbook 2015*. Published 10 June 2015. Available at: https://reliefweb.int/report/world/sadc-statistical-yearbook-2015

Solomon, H (2013) Researching terrorism in South Africa, *Scientia Militaria*, **40** (2), pp. 142–165. Available at: http://www.ajol.info/index.php/smsajms

South African History Archive (2017) Terrorism Act, Act No. 83 of 1967. Available at: http://www.saha.org.za/nonracialism/terrorism_act_act_no_83_of_1967.htm

South African Police Services (2014) Protection of Constitutional Democracy Against Terrorism and Related Activities Act 33 of 2004. Available at: https://www.saps.gov.za/resource_centre/acts/downloads/juta/terrorism_act.pdf

Statistics South Africa (2015) *General Household Survey*. Statistical Release P0318. Available at: http://www.statssa.gov.za/publications/P0318/P03182015.pdf

Steinburg, G and Weber, A (2015) Jiihadism in Africa: An introduction. In G Steinburg and A Weber (eds) *Jihadism in Africa: Local causes, regional expansion, international alliances*. Berlin: German Institute for International and Security Affairs.

Tshwete, S (2011) Legislative responses to organised crime in the SADC region. In C Goredema (ed) *Organised Crime in Southern Africa: Assessing legislation*. Pretoria: Institute for Security Studies.

UNCCT (2017) *Facilitating the Development of Regional Counter-Terrorism Strategies.* Available at: https://www.un.org/counterterrorism/ctitf/en/uncct/facilitating-development-regional-counter-terrorism-strategies

United Nations Development Programme (2015) *Preventing and Responding to Violent Extremism in Africa: A development approach.* Available at: https://www.google.co.za/search?q=Preventing+and+Responding+to+Violent+Extremism+in+Africa%3A+A+Development+Approachandoq=Preventing+and+Responding+to+Violent+Extremism+in+Africa%3A+A+Development+Approachandaqs=chrome..69i57.284j0j4andsourceid=chromeandie=UTF-8

United Nations (2006) *Global Counter-Terrorism Strategy.* Available at: https://www.un.org/counterterrorism/ctitf/en/un-global-counter-terrorism-strategy

United Nations Integrated Regional Information Networks (2012) Tanzania: Islamist riots threaten Zanzibar's stability. Published 24 October 2012.

UNODC (United Nations Office on Drugs and Crime) (2012) *Making the Southern African Development Community (SADC) Region Safer from Crime and Drugs: Regional Programme: 2013 – 2016.* Pretoria: UNODC Regional Office for Southern Africa.

United States Department of State (2016) *Country Reports on Terrorism 2015. Africa Overview: Tanzania.* Available at: https://www.state.gov/j/ct/rls/crt/2015/257514.htm

United States Embassy (2017) Threats to shopping areas and malls. Published 4 June 2017. Available at: usembassy.gov/Threats to Shopping Areas and Malls/04 June 2017

Vittori, J, Bremer, K and Vittori, P (2009) Islam in Tanzania and Kenya: Ally or threat in the war on terror? *Studies in Conflict and Terrorism*, **32** (12), pp. 1075–1099.

Wa Afrika, M and Hofstatter, S (2017) Top terror bomber bust on his way to SA, *Sunday Times*. Published 15 January 2017. Available at: http://www.timeslive.co.za/sundaytimes/stnews/2017/01/15/Top-terror-bomber-bust-on-his-way-to-SA

West, S (2015) The rise of ADF-NALU in Central Africa and its connections with al-Shabaab, *Terrorism Monitor*, **13** (1). The Jamestown Foundation. Available at: https://jamestown.org/program/the-rise-of-adf-nalu-in-central-africa-and-its-connections-with-al-shabaab/

World Bulletin (2015) Fear in Tanzania town after alleged Al-Shabaab attack. Published 16 February 2015. Available at: http://www.worldbulletin.net/news/155095/fear-in-tanzania-town-after-alleged-al-shabaab-attack

Chapter 10

Identity politics and the re-emergence of South Africa's far-right

Stephen Buchanan-Clarke

Introduction

In recent decades, the threat posed by violent extremist organisations has gained prominence in states across the world. Al-Qaeda, ISIS and Boko Haram, among others, have gathered considerable media attention and are responsible for the overwhelming majority of terrorist violence on the continent today. Few countries have remained entirely shielded from the threat of violent Islamist extremism, and its emergence and spread has had profound effects on both domestic and international politics. However, while receiving comparatively less media attention, the membership of 'right-wing movements', including 'alt-right', 'white nationalist' and 'neo-Nazi' political parties and organisations, has also steadily risen, especially in Europe and the United States. The ideologies that animate these organisations, while often perceived as homogenous, differ in significant ways, and shift and realign in response to political events.

While not posing the same level of threat to state security as violent Islamist organisations, far-right extremist movements have undoubtedly had a significant impact on the political landscape in countries across Europe and in the United States, and pose a direct threat to the advancement of democratic and pluralist societies. In the digital age, the spread of ideas occurs rapidly and is unpredictable. Both individuals and organisations of the far-right, which in the past would have existed in relative isolation, are today easily able to connect through a variety of online forums, identify similitude in each other, and form strategic alliances to further their respective political agendas. This has led some to ask whether recent developments abroad, such as the electoral successes of nationalist parties across Europe and the rise of the alt-right in the United States, has or will serve to animate and motivate far-right movements in South Africa.[1]

This chapter provides a brief taxonomy of some of the key themes common to far-right movements, before going on to examine recent trends in far-right extremism in the United States and Europe. Ehud Sprinza's iceberg model of political extremism and Thomas Blume's social cognition theory are drawn on in an attempt to explain the concurrent decline in the number of far-right acts of terrorism and the rising number of hate crimes and other forms of political violence in these regions. Finally, this chapter provides a brief history of far-right organisations in South Africa and discusses recent social and political developments that are shaping the country's political spectrum. While it is difficult to make direct comparisons between the far-right in the United States, Europe and South Africa due to the vastly different histories and societies across these regions, these case studies will be drawn on to discuss possible scenarios for the South African context and the threat the far-right currently poses to the country.

Defining the 'far-right'
A central challenge that makes the study of far-right extremism difficult is a lack of definitional consensus around terms. As Mudde (1996) writes:

> Even though the term right-wing extremism is accepted by a large number of scholars, there is no consensus on the extract definition of the term. Authors have defined it in a variety of ways. This has been partly caused by the fact that the term is not only used for scientific purposes but also for political purposes … Notwithstanding this, there is a broad consensus in the field that the term right-wing extremism describes primarily an ideology in one form or another.[2]

Since the 1980s, as the ability of right-wing parties to obtain or hold their positions in various European party systems has increased, so too has the amount of academic literature around the topic. Two opposing schools of thought have emerged in relation to the rise of right-wing political parties in Europe since the 1980s. Von Beyme (1988), for example, argues that right-wing extremist parties come and go in waves across Europe; while others, such as Buijs and Van Donselaar (1994), argue that what seems to be a European development may be the temporary and accidental coming together of national developments in countries across the region.[3] However, comparative studies, which may help to solve this disagreement, are hindered by the lack of definitional consensus described above.

Most authors tend to define the term as a political ideology that constitutes several features. However, the selection and weighting of these features differ considerably across definitions. Macridis (1989:101), for example, forwards a relatively short definition of right-wing extremism: 'ideology that revolves around the same old staples: racism, xenophobia, and nationalism'. Other authors, such as Falter and Schumann (1989:231), pose definitions containing a far more exhaustive list of features, including: 'extreme nationalism, ethnocentrism, anti-communism, anti-parliamentarianism, anti-pluralism, militarism, law-and-order thinking, a demand for a strong political leader and/or executive, anti-Americanism and cultural pessimism'.[4] In a literature review on right-wing extremism in Europe, Mudde (1996) identified 26 different definitions of the term, in which no less than 58 different features were mentioned at least once.[5] However, five were mentioned by just over half the authors. These included nationalism, racism, xenophobia, anti-democracy and the strong state.

However, this lack of definitional consensus, while making cross-national comparative analyses between right-wing parties difficult, should not, as Mudde (1996) argues, 'be seen as a reason to ignore our collective hunch that there is something common about these parties ... instead of putting so much effort into defining the object of study *a priori* on the basis of some (vague) notion of historical continuity, it would be more useful to study the object itself first and to try and define it later.'[6]

Terrorism versus hate crime

Not only is there a lack of definitional consensus around the terms 'far-right' and 'right-wing' extremism, but also around the forms of political violence such groups periodically employ. Many incidents of far-right terrorism have been analysed under the concept of 'hate crime' as both forms of political violence share similar characteristics. For example, Blazak (2011) has defined a 'hate crime' as 'a criminal act that is motivated by a bias toward the victim or victims' real or perceived identity group and which may be intended to terrorise a broader group'.[7] This definition shares similarities with common definitions of terrorism, such as that laid out in the United Nations Security Resolution 1566 (2004), which defines terrorism as 'criminal acts, including against civilians, committed with the intent to cause death or serious bodily injury, or taking of hostages, with the purpose to provoke a state of terror in the general public or in a group of persons or particular persons, intimidate a population or compel a government or an international organization to do or to abstain from doing any act.'[8]

Both terrorism and hate crimes may include ideology as a motivating factor and seek to intimidate a wider population group. However, for the purposes of this chapter, emphasis is given to the scale and level of planning involved in the act. Typically, acts of terrorism involve a considerably higher level of planning, and targets are chosen to make a symbolic statement. Furthermore, as Koehler (2016) argues, 'It is reasonable to assume that the step from committing hate crimes to committing terrorism is much smaller and easier to take than that from "ordinary crime" (or no criminal activity) to terrorism. Hate crimes seem to provide a bridge and an ideological testing phase for catalysing potential motivations for violent action (for example, hate, fear, aggression, power) with the ideological call to act.'[9]

The American far-right

The United States has a long history of far-right extremism. Many far-right organisations operating today can trace their roots back to the first years of the nation's history. The Ku Klux Klan (KKK), for example, perhaps the most well-known white supremacist group, has been in existence since 1866. Over the years, it has fluctuated significantly in strength and numbers. In the organisation's heyday in the 1920s, the KKK boasted chapters across every southern state in the United States. After a period of decline, the organisation was revived in response to the civil rights movement by white Protestant nativists. During this era, the group bombed a number of black schools and churches and committed various acts of violence against black and white activists in the South. Today, there are still an estimated 5 000 to 8 000 active clan members.[10] However, the far-right landscape in America is populated not only by avowed white supremacist groups such as the KKK, but also by movements that espouse anti-federalist and Christian fundamentalism ideologies. Perliger (2012) identifies three major ideological movements within the American violent far right: racist/white supremacy movements, anti-federalist movements and Christian fundamentalist movements.[11]

Racist/white supremacist movements are made up of groups such as the KKK and neo-Nazi and skinhead groups like the National Alliances and Aryan Brotherhood. The core ideological motivator of these groups is to preserve or restore what they perceive as an appropriate and natural racial and cultural hierarchy by enforcing political and social control over non-whites ('non-Aryans'), such as African Americans, Jews and various immigrant communities.[12] Members of the KKK and other neo-Nazi groups are more associated with acts of vandalism and violent individual assaults than large-scale terrorist attacks. It is often difficult to untangle the different factions and figures that animate white supremacist factions. This results in terms such as 'white nationalist' and 'white supremacists' being used interchangeably. However, there are ideological differences between the two. White supremacists believe that people of European descent are biologically and culturally superior to people of non-European descent. In a multiracial society, such as the United States, this leads them to espouse a racial hierarchy in which white people enjoy a privileged status. White nationalists, on the other hand, oppose multicultural societies and espouse the creation of a white ethno-state.[13]

The anti-federalist movement rationale is multifaceted. It espouses the strong conviction that the federal government is corrupt, tyrannical and determined to encroach on individual and civil liberties. This is often mixed with a conspiracy theory that the American political system has been hijacked by external 'Jewish forces interested in promoting a new world order'. Anti-federalist extremists have been responsible for some of the deadliest terrorist attacks in US history, such as the 1995 Oklahoma City bombing, which killed 168 and injured more than 600. More recently, in January 2016, members of the Sovereign Citizen Movement (SCM) seized and occupied the headquarters of a national wildlife park in Oregon.[14] The SCM is an anti-federalist group, which believes that the US government is illegitimate and whose members answer only to their particular interpretation of the common law. As such, most of their violence is directed against the federal government and its proxies in law enforcement. Lastly, Perliger (2012) identifies a Christian fundamentalist stream, including movements such as the Aryan Nations, who fuse elements of white supremacy with biblical scripture. Their promotion of nativism and racial superiority is derived from their unique interpretation of biblical scripture that it is not the people of Israel, but Anglo-Saxons who are the 'chosen people'. This fusing of religious scripture with political grievance against minorities tends to elevate conflict to a zero-sum game and thus Christian fundamentalists have a higher tendency to engage in mass-casualty terrorist attacks, hoping to incite a biblically prescribed 'holy war'.[15]

The recent emergence of the 'alt-right'

In recent years, the United States has seen the rise of what is often referred to as the alt-right, short for 'alternative right'. Rather than a highly structured organisation, such as the KKK or Aryan Brotherhood, the alt-right is better understood as a loose organisation of far-right movements, which emphasises internet activism and is hostile to both multicultural liberalism and mainstream conservatism.[16] The alt-right gained prominence through their support for Donald Trump, which elevated the movement into the national debate. It brings together different ideological components of far-right movements mentioned earlier, including elements of pseudoscientific racism, but also encompasses ideologies that do not centre on race. For example, the alt-right generally opposes feminism and any other form of progressive politics. Richard Spencer introduced the term 'alternative right' in 2008 on AlternativeRight.com, an online magazine, which he founded and edited from 2010 to 2012, and helped to set the parameters of the movement.[17] Spencer's magazine served as a forum for a range of dissident and rightist' views, including scientific racism, libertarianism, male tribalism, anarchism, white nationalism, and other rightists at odds with the conservative establishment. In 2010, influential alt-right columnist Richard Hoste published an article on the website titled 'Why the

Alternative Right is necessary'. The following excerpt from the article provides insight into the various ideological components of the movement:

> One would think that the odds of a major terrorist attack happening would depend on how many Muslims are allowed to live in the United States. Reducing Islamic immigration in the name of fighting terror would receive widespread public support, be completely practical in a way installing a puppet regime in Afghanistan wouldn't, and not lead us to kill or torture anybody. Yet the 'Conservative of the Year' whose entire *raison d'être* has been 'keeping us safe' acts as if such a thing isn't even possible. The idea that nothing must be done to stop the March Of Diversity is so entrenched in the minds of those considered of the Right that they will defend America policing the entire planet, torture, indefinite detentions, and a nation on permanent war footing but won't mention immigration restriction or racial profiling.
>
> It's because of so-called 'conservatives' like Cheney that an Alternative Right is necessary.
>
> Besides our disagreements with mainstream conservatives on the issue of foreign policy and the relative importance of fighting terrorism, there is the topic of race and, more broadly, IQ and heredity. We've known for a while through neuroscience and cross-adoption studies – if common sense wasn't enough – that individuals differ in their inherent capabilities. The races do, too, with whites and Asians on the top and blacks at the bottom. The Alternative Right takes it for granted that equality of opportunity means inequality of results for various classes, races, and the two sexes. Without ignoring the importance of culture, we see Western civilization as a unique product of the European gene pool.[18]

The above excerpt contains a number of the views commonly expressed by members of the alt-right movement. There are arguments for isolationism, xenophobia, sexism and elitism grounded in a pseudoscience that people (mostly males) of European descent are culturally and biologically superior to those of non-European descent.

As several authors have argued, the ascendancy of Donald Trump to the presidency has not only served to electrify the far-right, but his campaign messaging itself played an important role in his ultimate victory by appealing either implicitly or explicitly to far-right ideologues.[19] For example, Trump vilified Mexican immigrants in one of his campaign's opening speeches, stating that, 'When Mexico sends its people, they are not sending the best ... they

263

are sending people who have lots of problems, and they're bringing those problems to us, they're bringing drugs, they're bringing crime, they're rapists, and some, I assume, are good people.'[20] He retweeted fake crime statistics, claiming that, in 2015, African Americans were responsible for 81 per cent of murders where the victim was white, a statistic that is wildly inaccurate and originally published by a white supremacist Twitter account.[21] He also went on the Alex Jones show, a well-known conspiracy theorist with a considerable online following.[22] His victory was met with applause from several prominent members of the far right. Andrew Anglin, who runs the neo-Nazi Stormer website wrote: 'Make no mistake about it: we did this. If it were not for us, it wouldn't have been possible.' Richard Spencer, the self-declared leader of the alt-right wrote: 'Trump's victory was, at its root, a victory of identity politics.'[23] Trump sought the chairman of Breitbart Media, Steve Bannon, to lead his presidential election campaign, and upon victory, installed Bannon as chief strategist in his administration. Bannon has candidly spoken of his support for the alt-right movement and called Breitbart News, under his editorship, the 'platform for the alt-right'.[24] In Steve Bannon, the alt-right, once a loose assembly of libertarians, white supremacists and anti-immigrationists, has been elevated into the mainstream political culture in the United States.

Competing frameworks

The elevation of far-right ideology into mainstream political culture in the United States has led to many analysts of terrorism and political violence to ask whether this has corresponded with an increased number of terrorist attacks and other acts of politically or ideologically motivated violence.[25] The relationship between acts of terrorism and political violence and perceived changes in the socio-political structure is contested in the literature, with two schools of thought predominating. Israeli political scientist Ehud Sprinzak developed the iceberg model of political extremism. Originally a theoretical framework to explain the *Gush Emunim* – an Israeli orthodox messianic, right-wing settler movement active during the 1970s and 1980s in Palestine and Israel – Sprinzak's theory has been influential in explaining the link between a changing socio-political culture and the prevalence and frequency of acts of political extremism.[26]

Sprinzak posits that the tip of the theoretical iceberg is the extremist movement, which is most likely to engage in acts of terrorism and political violence in support of its political and ideological objectives. The base (which, like that part of the iceberg, is submerged) is a complete social and cultural system. The extremist group is not detached from its base but makes use of all of its resources. It receives tacit and explicit ideological and material support, and provides a pool of potential recruits. When there is an enabling socio-political climate (warm weather) the base of the iceberg melts somewhat and the tip (the extremist group) loses much of its acuity. When there is a constraining political environment (cold weather), the iceberg freezes again and the tip of the iceberg regains its acuity. Sprinzak argued that the *Gush Emunim*, from the beginning of the Likud government in Israel up until the Camp David Accords two years later, lost its acuity as an extremist group and carried out less acts of political violence because the base of the iceberg (the social and cultural system, which either implicitly or explicitly supported or at least sympathised with the *Gush Emunim*) gained considerable political power, creating an enabling socio-political climate for the organisation. In a similar vein, the 'pressure cooker theory', developed by Ruud Koopmans, argues that when radical-right parties obtain substantial electoral support, followed by political influence, this may function as a 'safety valve', releasing pressure from dissatisfied activists who may otherwise have engaged in political violence.[27] Both Sprinzak's and Koopmans's models would suggest that the rise of far-right figures, such as Steve Bannon, to the White House, and the mainstreaming of far right-causes, such as the attempted ban on immigration from several Muslim majority countries, would create an enabling socio-political climate for their base and thus far-right extremist groups would engage in fewer acts of political violence.

However, there are others that may disagree with Sprinzak's model. Social cognitive theorists such as Thomas Blume, for example, emphasise the role that social perspectives have on generating violence, and identify factors within certain social situations that explain why violence is not universal but varies in frequency and intensity.[28] Blume argues that an individual's experiences become social as they are shared, either through person-to-person communication or via other means of communication such as social-media platforms. It is the combined experiences of many individuals shared in these ways that make up a culture, a society or a family. Blume (1996) states:

> The social construction of reality occurs naturally at an informal level … An older person is jostled by a group of young people, returns to his or her peers, and talks about how and where it occurred, about who was present and how the bystanders responded, and about the characteristics of the assailants, etc. As such accounts are shared, a social group builds a model of common experience in which the personal experience becomes universal and members of the group see each other and their social world in similar ways.[29]

Blume (1996) and other social cognitive theorists would argue that an enabling social environment, in which the political system is seen as increasingly open to far-right ideas, such as the cultural and biological superiority of people of European descent or the obligation to defend one's homeland from 'invasive' foreign cultures, would, indeed, encourage acts of political violence. However, it is important here to differentiate between acts of terrorism and hate crimes. Where Sprinzak and Koopmans's models speak to the likeliness of terrorist violence, Blume's theory emphasises the relation between social perspectives and a rise in hate crimes.

Political violence in America by the numbers
In a report prepared by the United States Governmental Accountability Office (GOA) and delivered before Congress in April 2017, all recorded far-right violent extremist attacks perpetrated by individuals or organisations since 2001 were collated.[30] The information on each attack, including the motivation of the attackers was taken from the US Extremist Crime Database (ECDB), maintained by the world's leading database on acts of terrorism: the National Consortium for the Study of Terrorism and Responses to Terrorism (START) at the University of Maryland.[31] 'Far-right' violent extremist attackers are characterised by the ECDB as holding some or all of a number of different beliefs. Some of these include 'anti-global' and 'fiercely nationalistic' (as opposed to universal and international in orientation) beliefs; the belief that one's personal and/or national 'way of life' is under attack and is either already lost or that the threat is imminent'; and a belief 'in conspiracy theories that involve a grave threat to national sovereignty and/or personal liberty'. The ECDB also notes in its definition that the majority of far-right attackers express support for some version of white supremacy, the Ku Klux Klan and neo-Nazism.

Between 12 September 2011 and 31 December 2016, in 62 separate incidents, 106 people were killed by far-right extremists. During the same time, 119 people were killed by Islamist extremists in 23 separate incidents. The two deadliest attacks during this period occurred during 2015. The first was the killing of nine African Americans in a shooting at a church in Charleston, South Carolina, by avowed white supremacist Dylann Roof on 17 June 2015. Prior to the attack, in a 2 000-word text published on The Last Rhodesian, his personal website, Roof explained his motivation, writing:

> I am not in the position to, alone, go into the ghetto and fight. I chose Charleston because it is the most historic city in my state, and at one time had the highest ratio of blacks to Whites in the country. We have no skinheads, no real KKK, no one doing anything but talking on the

internet. Well someone has to have the bravery to take it to the real world, and I guess that has to be me.[32]

On 10 October 2015, Christopher Harper-Mercer shot and killed nine people at a community college in Oregon. During the police investigation, Harper-Mercer was described as having both anti-religious and white-supremacist leanings, and to have been especially vocally opposed to the Black Lives Matter movement.[33] The data of deadly attacks by far-right extremist individuals and organisations are not strong enough to make a causal inference with reasonable confidence, especially with regard to the recent rise of alt-right and far-right political views in mainstream American political culture. However, 2015 was the deadliest year for attacks by far-right extremists during the past 15 years, with 23 civilian deaths – three times the yearly average.[34]

While deadly attacks by violent extremists resulting in mass casualties are rare, these numbers tell only a small part of the story. Hate crimes, intimidation and other incidents motivated by racism and xenophobia may also help to shed light on a country's current socio-political culture, and be used to gauge the presence and extent of far-right ideology within a society. The Southern Poverty Law Centre (SPLC) has sought to collect reports of bias-related harassment and intimidation around the United States to determine whether a surge in right-wing populism correlates with an increase in such incidents. The SPLC's methodology is based largely on anecdotal self-reporting on such incidents.[35] This may well result in false incidents being captured in the data. Nonetheless, the SPLC recorded a surge in such incidents in the month after Donald Trump was elected president: 1 094 reported incidents were captured between 9 November and 12 December 2016. Overall, anti-immigrant incidents (315) were the most reported, followed by anti-black (221), anti-Muslim (112), and anti-LGBT (109). The SPLC maintains that this surge in incidents is a direct result of Trump's ascendance to the presidency due to the fact that 'around 37% of all incidents directly referenced either President-elect Donald Trump, his campaign slogans, or his infamous remarks about sexual assault'.[36] In addition, the SPLC has recorded a dramatic increase in the number of hate groups in America since 2000, with a rise from 892 to 917 organisations last year alone. The SPLC writes that

> ... there has been an explosive rise in the number of hate groups since the turn of the century, driven in part by anger over Latino immigration and demographic projections showing that whites will no longer hold majority status in the country by around 2040. The rise accelerated in 2009, the year President Obama took office, but declined after that, in

part because large numbers of extremists were moving to the web and away from on-the-ground activities. In the last two years, in part due to a presidential campaign that flirted heavily with extremist ideas, the hate group count has risen again.[37]

The SPLC's methodology in defining a 'hate group' is largely predicated on their reading of a group's published literature and public speeches made by individual members of the group. This undoubtedly will result in some groups being defined as 'hate groups' when, in fact, they are simply a conservative group who may have members that hold and express far-right extremist views. However, the SPLC's published list of hate groups includes a large and growing number of organisations whose far-right ideology is made abundantly clear in their name, such as the Knights of the White Disciples, American Nazi Party and Aryan Renaissance Society, to name a few.

Europe and the rise of the far-right

As several authors have argued, the global migrant crisis, sluggish economic growth, growing disillusionment with the European Union (EU), and violent Islamist terrorist attacks, have meant that far-right parties, both new and old, have achieved unprecedented electoral success in several European nations.[38] Currently, 39 European countries have nationalist and extreme right-wing parties represented in their parliaments (excluding Turkey and Russia). In Germany, the Alternative for Germany Party was established in 2014 as a protest movement against the Eurozone, and by March 2016 was able to win 25 per cent of the votes in the German state elections. The Party's platform is vehemently anti-Muslim, and calls for the immediate halt on immigration and banning of the construction of mosques. Following the Party's success in the state elections, Sylke Tempel of the German Council on Foreign Relations wrote that the new party won 'not just because of the vacuum on the right, but because they attracted voters who were anti-establishment, anti-liberalization, anti-European, anti-everything that has come to be regarded as the norm'.[39] In France, the National Front was able to use similar populist rhetoric to promote its anti-immigration and anti-European positions to propel party leader Marine Le Pen to win a plurality of votes in the first round of voting in the regional elections. In the Netherlands, the Party for Freedom, which promotes a platform calling for an exit from the EU, a ban on immigration, the closure of Islamic schools, and even a record of the ethnicity of all Dutch citizens, was a leading frontrunner in the 2017 parliamentary elections. Other far-right parties that have been remarkably successful across several other countries in Europe, including the Golden Dawn party in Greece, the Jobbik party in Hungary, the Sweden Democrats party in Sweden, the Freedom Party of Austria, and the People's Party-Our Slovakia in Slovakia, to name a few.[40] While these parties generally run on anti-immigrant, anti-globalist, and anti-EU platforms, many of their leaders have made speeches which either implicitly or explicitly emphasise policies that favour nativism, ethno-solidarity or white supremacy. Furthermore, as is the case with the Sweden Democrats, the National Front, the People's Party-Our Slovakia, and the Freedom Party of Austria, many of their founding members have direct relations with neo-Nazi or white-supremacist organisations.[41]

Terrorist incidents perpetrated by individuals or organisations associated with far-right ideologies have declined in Europe over the past two decades, despite the recent successes of far-right political parties in the region. While there are several datasets that track incidents of 'right-wing' terrorism in states across Europe, these are of limited value and ultimately uncomparable when trying to identify regional trends. This is due in part to European countries using differing definitions of 'terrorism', 'extremism', 'hate crime' and other relevant terms. There are also different registration methods and inclusion criteria for each database. Furthermore, owing to changes in discourse around terrorism, countries tend to change their criteria from time to time, making timeseries analysis difficult. However, Jacob Ravndal developed a Right-Wing Terrorism and Violence (RTV) dataset, which has done well to overcome these challenges by using a limited criteria of inclusion to create a small dataset with extensive information on each incident. Due to the strict criteria for selection, the number of incidents (578) recorded in the dataset between 1990 and 2015 may well be lower than the number of incidents that actually occurred during this period. However, it provides a strong enough sample size to extrapolate on whether there has been a general increase or decrease in far-right terrorist incidents over time in Europe. According to Ravndal (2016), there has been a steady decline in the number of far-right terrorist attacks since 2000, which he states 'may come as a surprise at a moment in time when experts are warning about rising levels of right-wing militancy and violence across Europe'.[42] Ravndal (2016) puts forward a number of hypotheses to explain this declining trend in significant far-right terrorist incidents, including a less politically active youth, more internet activism, and better law enforcement.

However, as with the United States, far-right terrorist attacks, which produce mass casualties, are only a small part of the story. While terrorist operations carried out by these organisations have declined over the past decade, in recent years, the region has seen a spike in hate crimes. The European Union Agency for Fundamental Rights (EUAFR) defines hate crimes as 'violence and offences motivated by racism, xenophobia, religious intolerance, or bias against a person's disability, sexual orientation or gender identity'.[43] It is difficult to quantify the extent to which levels of hate crime have risen in Europe, as EU member states differ markedly in the data they record and publish on motivations behind incidents of political violence. For example, only eight EU member states record crime motivated by the victim's sexual orientation. However, if one takes Britain, Germany and France as case studies, it is clear that hate crimes have risen exponentially in recent years, and seemingly in response to specific political developments. In Britain, in a report compiled by the Home Office, incidents of racist or religious abuse recorded by police in England and Wales increased sharply in the months during and following the EU referendum. In July 2015, 3 886 such crimes were logged, compared with over 5 000 crimes logged in June 2016. Of these, 79 per cent were motivated by race hate, 12 per cent by sexual orientation, 7 per cent by religion, 6 per cent by disability and 1 per cent were transgender hate crimes.[44] The UN Committee on Eliminating Racial Discrimination (CERD) cites 'divisive, anti-immigrant and xenophobic rhetoric' as a major influence on the spike in hate crimes surrounding the Brexit referendum.[45] Similarly, Germany reported a 77 per cent increase in hate crimes between 2014 and 2015: data collected by the interior ministry show that attacks on asylum shelters surged to 1 031 in 2015, up from 199 the previous year and 69 in 2013.[46] Attacks on asylum shelters were especially common during anti-immigrant protests. In France, the National Human Rights Commission (CNCDH) reported 429 anti-Muslim threats and attacks in 2015 – a striking 223 per cent increase from the previous year, and 808 anti-Semitic threats and attacks in 2015 – a 5 per cent decrease from the previous year.[47]

A decline in strategic and planned terrorist operations perpetrated by far-right organisations, with the simultaneous rise in the number of hate crimes, and other forms of racially, religiously or ethnically motivated violence, is somewhat counter-intuitive. However, understood using Sprinzak's iceberg model of political extremism, the success of far-right and nationalist political parties at the parliamentary level across Europe may be helping to appease dissatisfied far-right ideologues who may otherwise have turned to planning acts of terrorism. At the same time, the political mainstreaming of xenophobic and anti-immigrant sentiments professed by far-right political parties may be serving to normalise discrimination and drive up incidents of everyday hate crimes. However, a more thorough analysis drawing on more substantial datasets is needed to confirm these trends.

South Africa's far-right
In the age of social media, the spread of ideas is both global and unpredictable. The recent emergence of the alt-right in the United States and the rise and

success of the far-right in Europe has led some in South Africa to question whether these developments will serve to animate far-right elements locally. The re-emergence of the far-right in South Africa poses concerns at two levels. First, there is the possibility that militant far-right organisations are able to gain more adherents and carry out terrorist attacks that may lead to the loss of life and plunge the country into instability. Second, a proliferation of narratives common to far-right movements, such as white supremacy, white victimhood, and isolationism, among others, could translate into an increase in hate speech and racially or religiously motivated hate crimes, adversely effecting race relations in South Africa.

South Africa has an extensive and complex history with far-right extremism. The National Party (NP) and the apartheid system it established were based on ideologies shared by many far-right movements today. At the core of apartheid ideology was the idea that black South Africans were biologically and culturally inferior to white South Africans. This can be seen in legislation such as the 1953 Bantu Education Act, which established an inferior education system for Africans based on a curriculum intended to produce manual labourers and obedient subjects. In addition to ideas of white supremacy, apartheid was built on other ideological components that are common to the far-right. The apartheid government discouraged multiculturalism through legislation such as the Population Registration Act (1950), the Group Areas Act (1950) and the Prohibition of Mixed Marriages Act (1949). They stood firmly against communism, passing legislation such as the Suppression of Communism Act (1950), and had prominent members who routinely espoused anti-Semitic ideologies. During the 1960s, for example, Oswald Mosley, founder of the British Union of Fascists, was a frequent visitor to South Africa, where the prime minister and other members of the cabinet received him. On Hendrik Verwoerd's assassination in 1966, the NP elected BJ Vorster to replace him. 'Vorster had been a supporter of Hitler during the Second World War, and his policy towards Jews in his own country can best be described as ambivalent.'[48] The National Party was also suspicious of globalism and routinely encouraged a return to 'traditional values'. However, while the NP may have held far-right ideologies, a feature, which set the party apart from other far-right organisations such as the *Afrikaner Weerstandsbeweging* (AWB), was the party's willingness to engage in a political process that would create a democratic and multicultural South Africa.

As Cachalia and Schoeman (2017) write: 'Far-right extremist groups in the country have traditionally been based on Afrikaner nationalism, with many aimed at establishing an independent Afrikaner nation state, built on the notion of a shared language and religion, and a common Afrikaner history.'[49] The AWB and the *Boeremag* are two of the more prominent examples of Afrikaner nationalist organisations that committed acts of terrorism in pursuit of their desire to secede from South Africa and create an independent Boer republic. The largest attack committed after 1994 by a far-right organisation was the 'Worcester bombing' in 1996, in which members of the *Boere Aanvalstroepe*, an offshoot of the AWB, detonated two bombs, killing a women and three children, while injuring another 67 people.[50] In 2002, members of the *Boeremag* detonated eight bombs in Soweto, seven of which destroyed railway lines, and the eighth damaged a mosque. Twenty-three suspects were charged with treason and acts of terrorism, sabotage and the possession of explosives and firearms, while 3 000 kg of explosives were seized during the arrests. It was revealed, during the 10-year-long trial, that members of the organisation were plotting to assassinate Nelson Mandela with the hopes of creating a 'race war', during which the *Boeremag* would seize power in a military coup.[51] However, as Cachalia and Schoeman's (2017) assessment of the threat of violent extremism in South Africa reveals, since the death of AWB leader Eugène Terre'blanche and the dismantling of the *Boeremag* after the 2002 Soweto bombings, Afrikaner nationalists have seemed to be in disarray and lacking the coherent leadership structure that would allow them to execute complex terrorist plots.[52] However, despite the failure of Afrikaner nationalist movements to achieve their political goals over the past two decades, there are still individuals and small cells, which actively seek a secessionist agenda or look to reinstate 'white rule'. The *Kommandokorps* is perhaps the most subscribed militant Afrikaner nationalist organisation operating today. Led by a former South African Defence Force (SADF) colonel, Franz Jooste, the group organises paramilitary training camps for youths between the ages of 13 and 19 years. The 1 500 youth the organisation claims to have trained since 2000 are taught self-defence and how to combat a perceived 'black enemy'.[53] Central to the propaganda of the *Kommandokorps* is that white Afrikaners are being systematically targeted by black South Africans in the new South Africa and that Afrikaners will eventually have to band together and take up arms to defend themselves. This separatist, ethno-nationalist narrative is infused with pseudoscientific neo-Darwinism that is common in white supremacist ideology. Jooste teaches that black people have smaller cerebral cortexes than white people, and are thus unable to effectively govern.[54] While the *Kommandokorps* and other Afrikaner nationalist movements may play on fears and prejudices held by wider segments of the white South African population, Professor Hermann Giliomee argues that: 'There are a few right-wing splinter groups, though I think they have no more than a thousand active members.'[55] The most recent attempted act of terrorism by individuals associated with the far-right occurred in 2012, when a group of four men planned an attack on the African National Congress (ANC) national conference in Mangaung with the goal of killing President Jacob Zuma. The plan was thwarted when the group's leader, Johan Prinsloo, trying to buy mortars for the operation, approached an undercover police officer.[56]

A re-emergence of the far-right?

An analysis of articles and posts published on the website Stormfront helps to provide insight into some of the key themes that animate the far-right in South Africa today. Stormfront.org began as an online bulletin board system in the early 1990s, before former Ku Klux Klan leader Don Black launched it as a website in 1995. Stormfront has been the subject of controversy; it was removed from French, German and Italian Google indexes due to violations of hate speech laws. The website describes itself as a 'community of racial realists and idealists', stating that: 'We are white nationalists who support *true* diversity and homeland for *all* peoples.'[57] However, the website is well known for being the world's largest white supremacist and neo-Nazi website. By its 20th anniversary in 2015, it had nearly 300 000 members and, globally, averages 734 972 unique page views per month. The site has country specific message boards for 15 countries, including Australia, France, Russia, Serbia, Ireland and South Africa, among others. A two-year study by the SPLC shows that registered Stormfront users have been disproportionately responsible for some of the most lethal hate crimes and mass killings since the site was launched in 1995. In the past five years alone, Stormfront members have murdered close to 100 people in the United States.[58] Beirich (2016) argues that these individuals follow a predictable trajectory towards violence:

> From right-wing anti-government websites and conspiracy hatcheries, he migrates to militant hate sites that blame society's ills on ethnicity and shifting demographics. He soon learns his race is endangered – a target of 'white genocide'. After reading and lurking for a while, he needs to talk to someone about it, signing up as a registered user on a racist forum where he commiserates in an echo chamber of angry fellow failures where Jews, gays, minorities and multiculturalism are blamed for everything.[59]

To determine the most prominent discussion points on Stormfront's South African board, 32 forum threads from 2017 that received a minimum of one reply were analysed. Collectively, these 32 threads were viewed 137 670 times. However, without an extensive analysis of IP addresses and where each originated, there is no way of knowing what percentage of these views were by South Africans living in the country. From a textual analysis of these 32 threads, several themes consistently arise. The notion of 'white victimhood' is prominent throughout the majority of posts. This notion centres on the idea that the wider 'black' population is systematically targeting white South Africans, and especially farmers. The term 'white genocide' is used regularly as a label to describe violent crime in which white South Africans are the victims. Zimbabwe is commonly used as an example of a 'white genocide' and land expropriation features highly. There are several threads that discuss immigration to Europe and the United States, and the possibility of gaining refugee status as a persecuted minority group. Some threads discuss the possibility of building white-only communities and prepping for a future 'race war'. The cultural and biological differences between 'blacks' and 'whites' are also discussed at length, with people of European descent generally being characterised as culturally and biologically superior. Moreover, there are a number of threads that argue against the pitfalls of multiculturalism, with South Africa's Democratic Alliance often being cited as traitors to the wider white South African population.

While South African Stormfront members perhaps represent the very fringe of far-right extremism in the country, there are other developments within mainstream society that may indicate these ideologies are growing more popular. South African singer Steve Hofmeyr regularly shows his support on social media for right-wing causes, including retweeting the campaign messaging of prominent European far-right parties, such as UKIP, the National Front and the Alternative for Germany party. After Trump was elected, a farmers' rights activist, Henk van de Graaf, started a crowdfunding campaign through his Facebook group called *Kommando Sorg* (commando support). The campaign sought to send Hofmeyr to meet Trump in an effort to 'grant the white people of South Africa their independence'. Other links also exist between the Trump administration and the South African far-right. The alt-right news website Breitbart, of which Steve Bannon was a founding member before becoming the White House chief strategist in August 2017, has a South African-born editor-at-large, Joel Pollak. He was a speechwriter for Tony Leon when he was leader of the DA, and the Trump administration is currently touting Pollak as the next US ambassador to South Africa.[60] In 2015, a petition, appealing to the EU Council to allow white South Africans the right to 'return' to the continent, was started. The petition was endorsed by the Nationale Front (NF) and gained 62 568 supporters. After Trump's election, the petition was updated to appeal to the United States to accept white South Africans as refugees or as legal immigrants. The petitioner states on Change.org:

> The USA has a new President, one who was largely elected by a predominantly pro-western electorate who see America as undergoing

an existential threat in the form of massive illegal immigration from Mexico. The election showed the divided opinions of Americans down not only party lines, but also cultural and racial lines. It showed a resurgent white America no longer willing to back down and surrender its identity to the false siren song of globalism. What this means is that we have a renewed opportunity to push the plight of the White South Africans. We have a new administration that could lend a sympathetic ear. We have an administration largely elected by white Americans who want the USA to continue to be a western nation and a majority white nation.

Other political parties and civil society organisations have launched similar initiatives. In 2015, the Freedom Front Plus (FF+) approached the United Nations Human Rights Commission (UNHRC) in a bid to force the ANC to deal with farm murders. Following the move, the Party stated that 'compared to international norms, farm murders in South Africa can justifiably be viewed as genocide ... this latest actions of the FF+ follow on the visit of its leader, Dr Pieter Mulder, to the UN in Geneva at the end of 2014, where the international community had been informed about farm murders, Afrikaans, affirmative action and other abuses against minorities'.[61]

Black-on-white crime features prominently among far-right rhetoric in South Africa. It serves as a rallying call, and is used as a powerful political tool to garner support. However, often implicit in the idea that a peaceful white minority is being targeted by a violent black majority is the racist belief that black South Africans are either biologically or culturally more violent than white South Africans. Not only is this historically inaccurate, given the country's history of colonialism and apartheid, but it is easily debunked by the data. Africa Check, a non-profit organisation set up in 2012 to promote accuracy in public debate and in the media in Africa, has undertaken a considerable amount of research and analysis on the topic. Drawing on data from 1 378 murder dockets conducted by police in 2009, Africa Check found that whites, while making up 8.85 per cent of the population, accounted for only 1.8 per cent of the cases.[62] Further studies, drawing on data from the South African Police Service (SAPS) annual report, a 2012 Victims of Crime Survey and the United Nations Office of Drugs and Crime (UNODC) Global Report on Crime and Justice, result in similar findings. As Brodie (2013) writes: 'The fact is that whites are *less likely* to be murdered than any other race in South Africa. The current murder rate of white South Africans is also *equivalent to, or lower than,* murder rates for whites recorded between 1979 and 1991.'[63] In 2013, Ernst Roets, a prominent member of AfriForum, a non-governmental organisation that aims to protect the rights of Afrikaners, told the

BBC that 400 000 white South Africans lived in squatter camps. Research by Africa Check has similarly disproved these figures, with the number of white South Africans living in informal housing closer to 30 000.[64] However, regardless of the facts, the perception that white South Africans, especially Afrikaners, are becoming a persecuted minority is still strong enough to drive racial polarisation. The growth of organisations like AfriForum may be indicative of South Africa's increasingly troubled identity politics. The institution was established in 2006, but has seen an exponential growth in supporters, and today has the backing of around 200 000 members. In her 2016 analysis of AfriForum, Fairbanks (2017) argues:

> Nelson Mandela's African National Congress (ANC) – the liberation movement that helped free the country from white minority rule, but also championed forgiveness and racial reconciliation – is suffering a decline in influence. Today, a new, more radical generation of young black people is finding its voice, arguing that whites still maintain far too much power in institutions like the country's universities and banks.[65]

Between 2015 and 2016, membership of AfriForum's Pretoria branch increased from 300 to 1 200, with the average member being just 27 years old. AfriForum attribute this dramatic rise in membership to increasingly polarised racial politics, especially on college campuses.[66] Due to a lack of data, it is difficult to determine whether hate crimes based on racial identity have increased. It is fair to assume, however, that increased racial polarisation and a perception of white victimhood could lead to an increased frequency of such incidents. However, further research is needed to confirm this.

Conclusion

South Africa has not seen a terrorist incident perpetrated by far-right individuals or organisations since 2012. While there is evidence of some attempts at training and organising, current far-right support of militant organisations seems minimal and diffuse among a number of small groups with no central coordination. The ideologies that animate far-right militant groups such as *Kommandokorps*, and the vitriol espoused by far-right extremists on websites such as Stormfront are strongly fuelled by racism and are antithetical to transformation and co-existence. However, by playing on more legitimate concerns held by many South Africans, such as the weakening of democratic institutions and perceptions of white victimhood held by more mainstream institutions such as AfriForum, the far-right may be able to gain a growing number of members in years to come. The success of nationalist parties in Europe and the rise of the alt-right in the United States may also help to further motivate the far-right in South Africa.

However, it seems unlikely at this stage that a growth of the far-right would translate into an increase in terrorist attacks in the absence of other forms of civil conflict. White nationalist organisations are often motivated to commit acts of terrorism as a means of polarising societies into competing racial or cultural factions when they feel they already have the upper hand. However, unlike in the United States and many European societies, white South Africans are a minority group. Therefore, the high cost of seeking to create a hypothetical 'race war', to use the words of white supremacist Dylann Roof, would likely produce little or no tangible rewards. This may be one of the reasons why the rise of the alt-right in America and nationalist populist parties in Europe has led South African far-right extremists to discuss the possibility of immigration, rather than militancy, on platforms such as Stormfront.

While the political landscape in South Africa may be becoming increasingly fractious and contested, it is still an open political system, which allows for the voicing of political grievances and political opportunities to promote one's agenda. There is a robust media and civil society, increasingly strong political opposition, and relatively low barriers to entry for new political parties. This may serve to alleviate some of the tensions, which produce acts of political violence and terrorism in closed political systems. As per Sprinzak's iceberg model of political extremism, while political and economic conditions are favourable for a given sociopolitical structure, the chance of political extremism by a far-right minority within the group is reduced. While Black Economic Empowerment (BEE) and other economic transformation initiatives have attempted to reduce economic inequality by race, ANC economic policies have had relatively minor financial effects on white South Africans. However, this is not to say that the chance of future far-right acts of terrorism will remain as they are today. A decline in race relations, increasing authoritarianism or radical economic transformation initiatives, which result in certain populations seeing no legitimate future for themselves, may serve to increase the likelihood of political violence.

Endnotes

1. See, Van Gelder, E (2015) How a right-wing South African group incites a new wave of white fear, *Time Magazine*. Published 26 June 2015. Available at: http://time.com/3931773/how-a-right-wing-southafrican-group-incites-a-new-wave-of-white-fear/; Davis, R (2017) President Trump, SA's white right's white knight? *The Daily Maverick*. Published 17 January 2017. Available at: https://www.dailymaverick.co.za/article/2017-01-17-president-trump-sas-white-rights-white-knight/#.WVDX3BN97Vo
2. Mudde, C (1996) The war of words defining the extreme right party family, *West European Politics*, **19** (2), p. 228. Available at: https://www.tcd.ie/Political_Science/undergraduate/module-outlines/ss/political-parties/PolP/MuddeWEP96.pdf

3   Buijs, FJ and Van Donselaar, V (1994) Extreem rechts: Aanhang, geweld en onderzoek (The extreme right: Adherents, violence and research). Leiden: LISWO, pp. 55–64; Von Beyme, K (1988) Right-wing extremism in post-war Europe, *West European Politics*, **11** (2).
4   Macridis, RC (1989) *Contemporary Political Ideologies: Movements and regimes*. Glenview, IL: Scott, Foresman and Co, p. 101; Falter, JW and Schumann, S (1989) Affinity towards right-wing extremism in Europe, *West European Politics*, **11** (2), p. 231.
5   Mudde (1996), p. 229.
6   Ibid, p. 226.
7   Blazak, R (2011) Isn't every crime a hate crime? The case for hate crime laws, *Sociology Compass*, **5** (4) p. 245.
8   United Nations (2004) Security Council Resolution 1566 (2004) on Threats to International Peace and Security caused by Terrorist Acts. Available at: https://www.un.org/ruleoflaw/blog/document/security-council-resolution-1566-2004-on-threats-to-international-peace-and-security-caused-by-terrorist-acts/
9   Koehler, D (2016) Right-wing extremism and terrorism in Europe: Current developments and issues for the future, *PRISM*, 6 (2). Available at: http://cco.ndu.edu/Publications/PRISM/PRISM-Volume-6-no-2/Article/839011/right-wing-extremism-and-terrorism-in-europe-current-developments-and-issues-fo/
10 Southern Poverty Law Centre (2016) *Ku Klux Klan*. Available: https://www.splcenter.org/fighting-hate/extremist-files/ideology/ku-klux-klan
11 Perliger, A (2012) *Challenges from the Sidelines: Understanding America's violent far-right*. New York: Combating Terrorism Center, US Military Academy at West Point. Available at: https://info.publicintelligence.net/CTC-ViolentFarRight.pdf
12 Ibid, p. 32.
13 Ibid.
14 *The Guardian* (2016) Bundy brothers found not guilty of conspiracy in Oregon militia standoff. Published 28 October 2016. Available https://www.theguardian.com/us-news/2016/oct/27/oregon-militia-standoff-bundy-brothers-not-guilty-trial
15 Perliger (2012) p. 34.
16 Lyons, MN (2017) Ctrl-Alt-Delete: The origins and ideology of the alternative right. Political Research Associates, January 2017. Available at: http://www.politicalresearch.org/2017/01/20/ctrl-alt-delete-report-on-the-alternative-right/#sthash.dbd3RszV.jxN91wyS.dpbs
17 Ibid.
18 Full article available at: http://www.toqonline.com/blog/why-an-alternative-right-is-necessary/
19 Southern Poverty Law Centre (SPLC) (2016). Update: 1 094 bias-related incidents in the month following the election. *SPLC Hatewatch*. Available at: https://www.splcenter.org/hatewatch/2016/12/16/update-1094-bias-related-incidents-month-following-election
20 BBC (2016) 'Drug dealers, criminals, rapists': What Trump thinks of Mexicans. Published 31 August 2016. Available at: http://www.bbc.com/news/av/world-us-canada-37230916/drug-dealers-criminals-rapists-what-trump-thinks-of-mexicans
21 Ibid.
22 SPLC (2016).
23 Ibid.
24 Ibid.
25 See: Van Gelder (2015); Davis (2017).
26 Sprinzak, E (1985) *The Impact of Gush Emunim: Politics and settlement in the West Bank*. London: Croom Helm Publishers.
27 Koopmans, R (1996) Explaining the rise of racist and extreme right violence in Western

Europe, *European Journal of Political Research,* **30** (2).

28 Blume, TW (1996) Social perspectives on violence, *Michigan Family Review,* **2** (1). Available at: https://quod.lib.umich.edu/m/mfr/4919087.0002.102/--social-perspectives-on-violence?rgn=main;view=fulltext

29 Ibid, p. 28.

30 United States Government Accountability Office (2017) Report to Congressional Requesters. Countering Violent Extremism: Actions Needed to Define Strategy and Assess Progress of Federal Reports. Published April 2017. Available at: http://www.gao.gov/assets/690/683984.pdf

31 'Far-right' violent extremist attackers are characterised by the ECDB as having beliefs that include some of or all of the following: Fiercely nationalistic (as opposed to universal and international in orientation); Anti-global; Suspicious of centralized federal authority; Reverent of individual liberty (especially right to own guns; be free of taxes); Belief in conspiracy theories that involve a grave threat to national sovereignty and/or personal liberty; Belief that one's personal and/or national 'way of life' is under attack and is either already lost or that the threat is imminent. In addition, ECDB rates the confidence in this assessment of ideological motivations using standard definitions of the factors that lead a confidence level on a scale from 0 to 4, where 0 is the lowest level of confidence and 4 is the highest level of confidence.

32 Mejia, P (2015) Apparent Dylann Roof racist manifesto unearthed online, *Newsweek*. Published 20 June 2015. Available at: http://www.newsweek.com/apparent-dylann-roof-racist-manifesto-unearthed-online-345325

33 Healy, J and Lovett, I (2015) Oregon killer described as man of few words, except on topic of guns, *New York Times*. Published 2 October 2015. Available at: https://www.nytimes.com/2015/10/03/us/chris-harper-mercer-umpqua-community-college-shooting.html

34 United States Government Accountability Office (2017).

35 The SPLC collected reports from news articles, social media, and direct submissions via their #ReportHate intake page. The SPLC states that they 'made every effort to verify each report, but many included in the count remain anecdotal'.

36 Southern Poverty Law Centre (2016). Update: 1,094 bias-related incidents in the month following the election. Available at: https://www.splcenter.org/hatewatch/2016/12/16/update-1094-bias-related-incidents-month-following-election

37 Southern Poverty Law Centre (2016). Active hate groups 2016. Available at: https://www.splcenter.org/fighting-hate/intelligence-report/2017/active-hate-groups-2016

38 See, Chakelein, A (2017) Rise of the nationalists: A guide to Europe's far-right parties, *The New Statesman*. Published 8 March 2017. Available at: http://www.newstatesman.com/world/europe/2017/03/rise-nationalists-guide-europe-s-far-right-parties; Werts, H, Scheepers, P and Lubbers, M (2012) Euro-scepticism and radical right-wing voting in Europe, 2002–2008: Social cleavages, socio-political attitudes and contextual characteristics determining voting for the radical right, *European Union Politics*, **14** (2). Available at: http://journals.sagepub.com/doi/abs/10.1177/1465116512469287

39 Smale, A (2016) German state elections point to vulnerability for Angela Merkel, *New York Times*. Published 14 March 2016. Available at: https://www.nytimes.com/2016/03/15/world/europe/german-state-elections-point-to-vulnerability-for-angela-merkel.html

40 Chakelein (2017).

41 Ibid.

42 Ravndal, JA (2016) Right-wing terrorism and violence in Western Europe: Introducing the RTV dataset, *Perspectives on Terrorism*, **10** (3).

43 European Union Agency for Fundamental Human Rights (2017) Hate Crimes. Available at: http://fra.europa.eu/en/theme/hate-crime

44 Corcoran, H and Smith, K (2016) Hate Crime, England and Wales 2015/16. *Home Office*. Available at: https://www.gov.uk/government/uploads/system/uploads/attachment_data/file/559319/hate-crime-1516-hosb1116.pdf
45 BBC (2016) Race and religious hate crimes rose 41% after EU vote. Published 13 October 2016. Available at: http://www.bbc.com/news/uk-politics-37640982
46 Human Rights Watch (2016) Take on hate crime. Published 29 November 2016. Available at: https://www.hrw.org/news/2016/11/29/take-hate-crime
47 L'Antisemitisme et La Xenophobie. Available at: http://www.cncdh.fr/sites/default/files/les_essentiels_-_rapport_racisme_2015_page_a_page.pdf
48 Louw, P (2015) History of anti-free market policies in South Africa. In: A Hayek. *A Collaborative Biography*. E Leeson (ed). London: Palgrave Macmillan.
49 Cachalia, RC and Schoeman, A (2017) *Violent Extremism in South Africa: Assessing the current threat*. Pretoria: Institute for Security Studies p. 3. Published May 2017. Available at: https://issafrica.org/research/southern-africa-report/violent-extremism-in-south-africa-assessing-the-current-threat
50 Potgieter, D (2012) Meet the youngest Worcester Bomber – now a poster boy for reconciliation, *The Daily Maverick*. Published 12 December 2012. Available at: https://www.dailymaverick.co.za/article/2012-12-20-meet-the-youngest-worcester-bomber-now-a-poster-boy-for-reconciliation/#.WVDJ2xOGPVo
51 Cachalia and Schoeman (2017) p. 3.
52 Ibid, p. 8.
53 Ibid.
54 Van Gelder, E (2015).
55 Ibid.
56 *Times* (2012) Blueprints for 'death plot.' Published 19 December 2012. Available at: https://www.timeslive.co.za/news/south-africa/2012-12-19blueprints-for-death-plot/
57 Stormfront.org. Accessed 12 July 2017.
58 Southern Poverty Law Centre (2016). Active hate groups 2016. Available at: https://www.splcenter.org/fighting-hate/intelligence-report/2017/active-hate-groups-2016
59 Beirich, H (2016) *White Homicide Worldwide*. Southern Poverty Law Centre. Available at: https://www.splcenter.org/sites/default/files/d6_legacy_files/downloads/publication/white-homicide-worldwide.pdf
60 Davis, R (2017) In Trump he trusts: Meet the man who could be the next US ambassador to South Africa, *The Daily Maverick*. Published 6 February 2017. Available at: https://www.dailymaverick.co.za/article/2017-02-06-in-trump-he-trusts-meet-the-man-who-could-be-the-next-us-ambassador-to-south-africa/#.WVD_HRN97Vp
61 Chernick, I (2015) FF+ to approach UN over farm murders, *The Star Early Edition*. Published 3 July 2015. Available at: http://www.pressreader.com/south-africa/the-star-early-edition/20150703/281573764355495
62 Brodie, N (2013) Are SA whites really being killed 'like flies'? Why Steve Hofmeyr is wrong, *Africa Check*. Published 24 June 2013. Available at: https://africacheck.org/reports/are-white-afrikaners-really-being-killed-like-flies/
63 Brodie (2013).
64 Rademeyer, J (2013) Do 400 000 whites live in squatter camps in South Africa? No. Africa Check. Published 22 May 2013. Available at: https://africacheck.org/reports/do-400-000-whites-live-in-squatter-camps-in-south-africa-the-answer-is-no/
65 Fairbanks, E (2017) The last white Africans, *Foreign Policy*. Published 16 January 2017. Available at: http://foreignpolicy.com/2017/01/16/the-last-white-africans/
66 Fairbanks (2017).

References

Bandura, A (2001) Social Cognitive Theory: An Agentic Perspective, *Annual Review of Psychology*, **52**, pp. 1–26. Available at: https://www.uky.edu/~eushe2/Bandura/Bandura2001ARPr.pdf

BBC (2016) 'Drug dealers, criminals, rapists': What Trump thinks of Mexicans. Published 31 August 2016. Available at: http://www.bbc.com/news/av/world-us-canada-37230916/drug-dealers-criminals-rapists-what-trump-thinks-of-mexicans

BBC (2016) Race and religious hate crimes rose 41% after EU vote. Published 13 October 2016. Available at: http://www.bbc.com/news/uk-politics-37640982

Beirich, H (2016) *White Homicide Worldwide*. Southern Poverty Law Centre. Available at: https://www.splcenter.org/sites/default/files/d6_legacy_files/downloads/publication/white-homicide-worldwide.pdf

Blazak, R (2011) Isn't every crime a hate crime? The case for hate crime laws, *Sociology Compass*, **5** (4).

Blume, TW (1996) Social perspectives on violence, *Michigan Family Review*, **2** (1). Available at: https://quod.lib.umich.edu/m/mfr/4919087.0002.102/--social-perspectives-on-violence?rgn=main;view=fulltext

Brodie, N (2013) Are SA whites really being killed 'like flies'? Why Steve Hofmeyr is wrong, Africa Check. Published 24 June 2013. Available at: https://africacheck.org/reports/are-white-afrikaners-really-being-killed-like-flies/

Buijs, FJ and Van Donselaar, V (1994) *Extreem rechts: Aanhang, geweld en onderzoek* (The extreme right: Adherents, violence and research). Leiden: LISWO, pp. 55–64.

Healy, J and Lovett, I (2015) Oregon killer described as man of few words, except on topic of guns, *The New York Times*. Published 2 October 2015. Available at: https://www.nytimes.com/2015/10/03/us/chris-harper-mercer-umpqua-community-college-shooting.html

Cachalia, RC and Schoeman, A (2017) *Violent Extremism in South Africa: Assessing the current threat*. Pretoria: Institute for Security Studies. Published May 2017. Available at: https://issafrica.org/research/southern-africa-report/violent-extremism-in-south-africa-assessing-the-current-threat

Chakelein, A (2017) Rise of the nationalists: A guide to Europe's far-right parties, *The New Statesman*. Published 8 March 2017. Available at: http://www.newstatesman.com/world/europe/2017/03/rise-nationalists-guide-europe-s-far-right-parties

Change.org (2017) Allow all white South Africans the right to return to Europe. Petition. Available at: https://www.change.org/p/european-commission-allow-all-white-south-africans-the-right-to-return-to-europe

Change.org (2017) Donald Trump: A new hope for White South Africans? Petition Update. Available at: https://www.change.org/p/european-commission-allow-all-white-south-africans-the-right-to-return-to-europe/u/18505106

Chernick, I (2015) FF+ to approach UN over farm murders, *The Star Early Edition*. Published 3 July 2015. Available at: http://www.pressreader.com/south-africa/the-star-early-edition/20150703/281573764355495

Commission Nationale Consultative Des Droits De L'Homme (2015) Rapport sur La Lutte Contre Le Racisme L'Antisemitisme et La Xenophobie. Available at: http://www.cncdh.fr/sites/default/files/les_essentiels_-_rapport_racisme_2015_page_a_page.pdf

Corcoran, H and Smith, K (2016) Hate Crime, England and Wales 2015/16. *Home Office*. Available at: https://www.gov.uk/government/uploads/system/uploads/attachment_data/file/559319/hate-crime-1516-hosb1116.pdf

Davis, R (2017) In Trump he trusts: Meet the man who could be the next US ambassador to South Africa, *Daily Maverick*. Published 6 February 2017. Available at: https://www.dailymaverick.co.za/article/2017-02-06-in-trump-he-trusts-meet-the-man-who-could-

be-the-next-us-ambassador-to-south-africa/#.WVD_HRN97Vp
Davis, R (2017) President Trump, SA's white right's white knight? *The Daily Maverick*. Published 17 January 2017. Available at: https://www.dailymaverick.co.za/article/2017-01-17-president-trump-sas-white-rights-white-knight/#.WVDX3BN97Vo
Ebrahims, S (2017) Trump's alt-right coming to SA, *IOL*. Available at: http://www.iol.co.za/news/opinion/trumps-alt-right-coming-to-sa-7803189
ENCA (2013) Red October: The plight of whites in the new South Africa. Published 10 October 2013. Available at: http://www.enca.com/south-africa/red-october-plight-whites-new-south-africa
European Union Agency for Fundamental Human Rights (2017) Hate Crimes. Available at: http://fra.europa.eu/en/theme/hate-crime
Fairbanks, E (2017) The last white Africans, *Foreign Policy*. Published 16 January 2017. Available at: http://foreignpolicy.com/2017/01/16/the-last-white-africans/
Falter, JW and Schumann, S (1989) Affinity towards right-wing extremism in Europe, *West European Politics*, **11** (2).
Global Terrorism Database (2017), The National Consortium for the Study of Terrorism and Responses to Terrorism (START), University of Maryland.
Grobler, A (2014) Mangaung plot accused sought mortars, *IOL*. Available at: http://www.iol.co.za/news/crime-courts/mangaung-plot-accused-sought-mortars-1687089
Healy, J and Lovett, I (2015) Oregon killer described as man of few words, except on topic of guns, *New York Times*. Published 2 October 2015. Available at: https://www.nytimes.com/2015/10/03/us/chris-harper-mercer-umpqua-community-college-shooting.html
Hoste, R (2010) Why the alternative right is necessary, *Radix Journal*. Published 24 February 2010. Available at: http://www.radixjournal.com/altright-archive/altright-archive/main/the-magazine/why-an-alternative-right-is-necessary
Human Rights Watch (2016) Take on hate crime. Published 29 November 2016. Available at: https://www.hrw.org/news/2016/11/29/take-hate-crime
Koehler, D (2016) Right-wing extremism and terrorism in Europe: Current developments and issues for the future, *PRISM*, **6** (2). Available at: http://cco.ndu.edu/Publications/PRISM/PRISM-Volume-6-no-2/Article/839011/right-wing-extremism-and-terrorism-in-europe-current-developments-and-issues-fo/
Koopmans, R (1996) Explaining the rise of racist and extreme right violence in Western Europe, *European Journal of Political Research*, **30** (2).
Louw, P (2015) History of anti-free market policies in South Africa. In: A Hayek. *A Collaborative Biography*. E Leeson (ed). London: Palgrave Macmillan.
Lyons, MN (2017) Ctrl-Alt-Delete: The origins and ideology of the alternative right. Political Research Associates, January 2017. Available at: http://www.politicalresearch.org/2017/01/20/ctrl-alt-delete-report-on-the-alternative-right/#sthash.dbd3RszV.jxN91wyS.dpbs
Macridis, RC (1989) *Contemporary Political Ideologies: Movements and regimes*. Glenview, IL: Scott, Foresman and Co.
Mejia, P (2015) Apparent Dylann Roof racist manifesto unearthed online, *Newsweek*. Published 20 June 2015. Available at: http://www.newsweek.com/apparent-dylann-roof-racist-manifesto-unearthed-online-345325
Mudde, C (1996) The war of words defining the extreme right party family, *West European Politics*. **19** (2). Available at: https://www.tcd.ie/Political_Science/undergraduate/module-outlines/ss/political-parties/PolP/MuddeWEP96.pdf
Mudde, C (2011) Radical right parties in Europe: What, who, why? *Participation*, **35** (1), Available http://works.bepress.com/cas_mudde/46/
Perliger, A (2012) *Challenges from the Sidelines: Understanding America's violent far-right*. New York:

Combating Terrorism Center, U.S. Military Academy at West Point. Available at: https://info.publicintelligence.net/CTC-ViolentFarRight.pdf

Potgieter, D (2012) Meet the youngest Worcester Bomber – now a poster boy for reconciliation. *The Daily Maverick*. Published 12 December 2012. Available at: https://www.dailymaverick.co.za/article/2012-12-20-meet-the-youngest-worcester-bomber-now-a-poster-boy-for-reconciliation/#.WVDJ2xOGPVo

Rademeyer, J (2013) Do 400 000 whites live in squatter camps in South Africa? No. Africa Check. Published 22 May 2013. Available at: https://africacheck.org/reports/do-400-000-whites-live-in-squatter-camps-in-south-africa-the-answer-is-no/

Ravndal, JA (2016) Right-wing terrorism and violence in Western Europe: Introducing the RTV dataset, *Perspectives on Terrorism*, **10** (3).

Sanchez, R and Payne, E (2016) Charelston Church shooting: Who is Dylann Roof? CNN Online. Published 12 December 2016. Available at: http://edition.cnn.com/2015/06/19/us/charleston-church-shooting-suspect/index.html

Smale, A (2016) German state elections point to vulnerability for Angela Merkel, *New York Times*. Published 14 March 2016. Available at: https://www.nytimes.com/2016/03/15/world/europe/german-state-elections-point-to-vulnerability-for-angela-merkel.html

Southern Poverty Law Centre (2016) A year in hate and extremism, *Intelligence Report*, Spring. Available at: https://www.splcenter.org/fighting-hate/intelligence-report/2017/year-hate-and-extremism

Southern Poverty Law Centre (2016) Active hate groups 2016, *Intelligence Report*, Spring. Available at: https://www.splcenter.org/fighting-hate/intelligence-report/2017/active-hate-groups-2016

Southern Poverty Law Centre (2016) *Ku Klux Klan*. Available at: https://www.splcenter.org/fighting-hate/extremist-files/ideology/ku-klux-klan

Southern Poverty Law Centre (2016). Update: 1 094 bias-related incidents in the month following the election, *SPLC Hatewatch*. Available at: https://www.splcenter.org/hatewatch/2016/12/16/update-1094-bias-related-incidents-month-following-election

Sprinzak, E (1985) *The Impact of Gush Emunim: Politics and settlement in the West Bank*. London: Croom Helm Publishers.

The Guardian (2016) Bundy brothers found not guilty of conspiracy in Oregon militia standoff. Published 28 October 2016. Available at: https://www.theguardian.com/us-news/2016/oct/27/oregon-militia-standoff-bundy-brothers-not-guilty-trial

United States Government Accountability Office (2017) Report to Congressional Requesters. Countering Violent Extremism: Actions Needed to Define Strategy and Assess Progress of Federal Reports. Published April 2017. Available at: http://www.gao.gov/assets/690/683984.pdf

Van Gelder, E (2015) How a right-wing South African group incites a new wave of white fear, *Time Magazine*. Published 26 June 2015. Available at: http://time.com/3931773/how-a-right-wing-southafrican-group-incites-a-new-wave-of-white-fear/

Villet, C (2017) Donald Trump, white victimhood and the South African far-right, *The Conversation*. Published 23 February 2017. Available at: http://theconversation.com/donald-trump-white-victimhood-and-the-south-african-far-right-73400

Von Beyme, K (1988) Right-wing extremism in post-war Europe, *West European Politics*, **11** (2).

Werts, H, Scheepers, P and Lubbers, M (2012) Euro-scepticism and radical right-wing voting in Europe, 2002–2008: Social cleavages, socio-political attitudes and contextual characteristics determining voting for the radical right, *European Union Politics*. **14** (2). Available at: http://journals.sagepub.com/doi/abs/10.1177/1465116512469287

Chapter 11

The rehabilitation and reintegration of children associated with armed groups in Borno State, Nigeria

Emmanuel Bosah & Mustapha al-Hassan

'It is easier to build strong children than to repair broken men'
Frederick Douglass
(African–American social reformer, abolitionist, orator, writer and statesman)

Introduction

The threat of violent extremism and terrorism continues to pose a serious global challenge both to the physical and mental well-being of societies. Hostilities and uprisings involving armed groups in recent times have become increasingly protracted and brutal, especially towards civilian populations and mostly affecting women and children. Worldwide, an estimated 300 000 children under the age of 18 years are involved with military forces and/or armed rebel groups, with many coerced, abducted or drugged into participating in violence and conflict.[1] The recruitment and use of children by armed forces and groups has been a focus of international attention and widely condemned. Yet children continue to be involved in adult wars. Many of these children, on their release and return to civilian life, have returned home on their own, often to face an uncertain future and a fight for acceptance from their families and communities.[2]

Nigeria, which continues to fight against the violent insurgent group, Boko Haram, has experience of children in armed conflict: armed groups involved in the insurgency in the northeast of the country have recruited and used children. However, this phenomenon is not unique to Nigeria. Uganda, Sudan and Rwanda have all experienced conflicts during which significant numbers of child soldiers were used. Much like the Lord's Resistance Army (LRA) in Uganda, which is estimated to have abducted 10 000 children over the past 15 years, Boko Haram has recruited children, primarily through force.[3] While the number of children Boko Haram has used in the insurgency is difficult to ascertain, the extremist group's sustained campaign of violence has had, and will continue to have, enormous ramifications for children across the region.

The tragic incident that took place in Chibok in April 2014, in which 276 schoolgirls were abducted from a secondary school, is merely one example of the horrific violence the group has committed against children.[4]

Boko Haram's capabilities have been significantly degraded by military gains over recent years, beginning the process of returning stability to Borno State. But the group's activities have severely and adversely affected the socio-economic, physical and emotional well-being of the northeast of Nigeria and the country as a whole. Children have been among those most seriously affected in Boko Haram's violent quest for power, with reports indicating that hundreds of children have been directly involved in hostilities and used in a variety of roles.[5]

Thousands of these children have had their childhood truncated by their exposure to unspeakable levels of violence, loss and instability, and have suffered severe disruption to family life and development. The insurgency has had a hugely negative impact on education in Borno State – the region worst affected most by the insurgency – with 524 out of 1 716 schools destroyed, affecting more than 400 000 children.[6] Furthermore, the sheer scale of insecurity in the region has led to the fairly widespread involvement of children in armed groups. Both Boko Haram and vigilante groups that sprung up to protect communities as a result of the insurgency, such as the Civilian Joint Task Force (CJTF), have used children in a variety of roles, including, but not limited to, full combat roles, intelligence gathering, cooking, cleaning and performing sexual roles. This chapter outlines some of the causes and effects of children associated with armed forces and armed groups (CAAFAG) in the northeast Nigerian context, and provides an overview of the Neem Foundation's recently established community-based, socio-economic rehabilitation and reintegration programme developed to support these children.

Children and armed groups in the era of Boko Haram

The chaos and trauma created by the Boko Haram insurgency has seen an increase in inter- and intra-communal violence and suspicion, and a general breakdown in social cohesion. Children associated with Boko Haram and community vigilante groups, such as CJTF, as well as other armed groups, have been exposed to extreme levels of violence, sexual and drug abuse, and in many cases have missed out on valuable and formative years of their life and education. As a result, psychological trauma has become a pervasive problem – as identified in a recent research study carried out by the Neem Foundation.[7] According to the research findings, a number of Boko Haram and CJTF group members stated that they have at some point experienced symptoms of psychological trauma. Moreover, interactions with local community actors in Borno State revealed that not every child that was associated with Boko Haram was abducted. Some children joined the group as a result of coercion in the form of peer pressure and familial ties. A key informant who participated in the study asserted that there were instances in which parents gave their children to Boko Haram. The Neem Foundation research also revealed that Boko Haram made calculated attempts to attract and recruit children in its early days through, for instance, *mallams* (religious teachers and scholars) who operated in schools on behalf of the group's founder, Mohammed Yusuf. These schools targeted secondary school dropouts and, until about 2014, were major platforms for indoctrination and recruitment. Children from these schools went on to become Yusuf's ideological mouthpiece, challenging their parents on aspects of belief and spreading radical views.

Irrespective of how they were recruited, children were routinely drugged during the indoctrination process and before they were sent to commit attacks or on suicide missions. In other research conducted by the Neem Foundation, joining the CJTF was seen as a way to defend communities vulnerable to Boko Haram attacks; many children joined voluntarily to support their families and their communities. The research indicated that children were used mainly for intelligence gathering and to staff guard posts, even though some may have participated in combat during the initial emergence of the CJTF.

Arguably, the situation of children associated with the CJTF could be said to be markedly better than that of their Boko Haram counterparts, although there are several reasons for concern. Children in the CJTF are also exposed to extreme levels of violence, with some taking part in killings, body mutilation and even parading with body parts. Drug abuse is also common among the CJTF, which presents a danger to children within their ranks and to wider society. CJTF members have acknowledged the use of drugs 'but only after the children were asleep'. Psychological trauma also represents a significant problem for the CJTF, with 84 per cent of survey participants stating that they experienced symptoms of trauma and psychological distress.[8]

Military successes have improved the general state of security in many parts of Nigeria's northeast and changed the dynamics of the conflict. However, many of the root causes of the conflict remain and, in some cases, may have been complicated and compounded by the ongoing humanitarian crisis in the region. Boko Haram's 'technical defeat', as it has lost control of territory, has enabled the Nigerian government, supported by national and international humanitarian actors, to launch interventions focused on providing humanitarian relief. This includes the reconstruction of some affected infrastructure such as schools, local government buildings and homes for victims. In part, these efforts have contributed to restoring stability and helping some displaced populations back to their homes. However, the realities of the post-conflict environment in the region has shown that part of any comprehensive response must include rehabilitation and reintegration, which targets not only victims of the insurgency but also others such as the perpetrators, and especially children.

Rehabilitation, peace-building and reintegration

According to the United Nations Children's Fund (UNICEF), approximately 8 000 children and young people were associated with various armed groups during the insurgency, with a proportion of these children used in direct combat roles.[9] Therefore, these children, who in many cases have been neglected and ostracised by their families and communities, pose a serious threat not only to the well-being and long-term peace of their own communities but also to society as a whole. This is of particular concern when considering Boko Haram's recent apparent regrouping, which may inspire these disenfranchised children and youths to return to their ranks where they are provided for.

Having had key years of their development substituted by indoctrination and violence, these children may be liable to turn to violence and crime in the future. There are already concerns that the neglect of children associated with armed groups could lead to a similar sense of marginalisation and disaffection that fuelled the rise of Boko Haram. These children could potentially morph into the state's next violent movement, posing a significant long-term threat to Nigerian society. As Nigeria seemingly moves closer towards a post-conflict denouement, the scope of the problem will only grow. To be fully reintegrated back into society, these children require varying degrees of psychosocial support, re-socialisation, drug rehabilitation, remedial education, skills acquisition and economic empowerment. However, despite this dire need, little is being done to help them do this in a holistic, sustainable and contextually appropriate way. Their rehabilitation and reintegration must be a policy and investment priority for both the state and non-government organisations to ensure long-term peace and stability in insurgency-affected areas.

In response to this need, the Neem Foundation, a non-profit, non-governmental organisation founded as a direct response to the problem of insecurity in Nigeria, has recently established a community-based, socio-economic rehabilitation and reintegration programme aimed at children associated with armed forces and groups (CAAFAG).[10] This pioneer programme uses individual and community-wide trauma counselling and psychological support, creative education initiatives, religious engagement, sports and mentoring, as well as economic empowerment to rehabilitate and support the reintegration of these children in a way that is context-specific, culturally appropriate and sustainable. This is achieved using credible community leadership structures to promote and support the rehabilitation, acceptance and peaceful reintegration of these children back into their communities, and in giving developing community leaders the capacity to provide ongoing support, long after the programme ends.

The components of this community-based model are designed to:

- Comprehensively address widespread psychological distress by providing psychosocial support services and counselling.
- Use creative education and play therapy to improve vulnerable children's social and emotional learning and create opportunities to heal, undergo value-based learning and psychosocial development, as well as build resilience to radicalisation.
- Counter and discuss themes and narratives on extremism and religious ideology, using credible religious leaders to preach religious tolerance, peace and reconciliation; and provide a safe space for beneficiaries to receive counselling and discuss ideas around the role of religion in a contemporary and pluralistic society.
- Build tolerance, peace, trust and unity through sports and mentoring within communities and between children of different faiths and ethnic backgrounds.
- Work with and develop the capacity of community leadership structures, including local government authorities, to promote and directly support acceptance, tolerance, unity and peace-building among communities.
- Create opportunities for beneficiaries to engage in skills development, or economic empowerment so that they are able to engage in activities that are viable within the context of their local economies.
- Strengthen collaboration between state and non-state actors (more specifically, small community-based organisations) to scale up and share capacity/resources to meet the needs of communities in the short term, and build the capacity of communities to continue to support their beneficiaries in the long term when the programme ends.

When discussing the key components of the community-based, socio-economic rehabilitation and reintegration approach, it is important to examine the experiences and outcomes for CAAFAG in northeast Nigeria, and the challenges associated with supporting these children. The objective is to set out an implementable model, which can be adopted and adapted in other conflict contexts to rehabilitate and reintegrate children who have participated in violent conflicts.

Trauma counselling and psychosocial support
There is no single systematised, context-specific approach that holistically

addresses the psychological state of victims associated with or affected by conflict or violent extremism. Western conceptions of childhood tend to regard children as vulnerable and passive victims and not as active members of a community. Nevertheless, though many young people suffer from the consequences of conflict, it has been shown that children and youths in conflict-affected regions tend to demonstrate extraordinary levels of resilience, thereby calling into question the wide applicability of the concept of the passive victim.[11]

These victims, as experienced by many individuals that have associated with violent extremist groups, are often ostracised by the wider community and receive little to no support. Their exposure to violence and radical ideology means that psychosocial rehabilitation is key, both to the issue of deradicalisation and to addressing their psychological trauma. Unless more is done to address these needs, communities risk not only allowing such individuals to spread their radical ideology, but also the problem of continued violence in all its forms. In Borno State, for example, disorders triggered by trauma are often misunderstood and communities often treat these disorders using many traditional and religious methods. However, the healing process will be incomplete without an evidence-based and systematic process of understanding and dealing with mental health challenges.[12]

Therefore, it is important to consider the provision of psychosocial support and trauma counselling as part of any rehabilitation and reintegration strategy. The purpose of psychosocial support and counselling is to provide individuals with a platform to come together, with the support of counsellors and psychologists, to work through their challenges, discuss their experiences, and develop the key skills required to cope with their trauma and build resilience. A key outcome of this intervention is that it creates a positive sense of belonging within the community, which ultimately supports their reintegration.

Services take the form of group counselling sessions, which provides beneficiaries with the opportunity to share experiences and collectively support one another's recovery. This is important for the sustainability of such an intervention because it helps to prevent isolation and stigma. For victims with higher level needs, one-on-one counselling is provided to support their rehabilitation. Where necessary, individuals requiring specialised support are identified and referred through existing mental health structures or social services so that they can receive long-term support to aid their recovery.

Building resilience and religious counselling
Violent extremist groups such as Boko Haram use religion to justify their campaigns of violence and destruction. Ideology and religion are often not

the direct cause of violent extremism and conflict, but there is little doubt that they can be contributing factors. Equally, religion can also play a crucial role in the de-escalation of violence, peace-building and reconciliation, especially in a region such as Nigeria's northeast where religion and religious leaders are highly respected and influential. Therefore, it is important that, as part of any rehabilitation and reintegration model adopted, religious leaders are included as key stakeholders in promoting religious tolerance and understanding, and they support rehabilitation, community healing and reintegration efforts.

As credible and prominent voices across Nigeria, religious leaders in almost every community across the northeast enjoy the implicit trust of victims and survivors, which gives them an opportunity to provide religious guidance and counselling that speaks to the relevant challenges faced by populations affected by the insurgency. Religious leaders are also essential in transforming the mindsets and narrative(s) within communities as they relate to peaceful co-existence, community cohesion and healing. They are also essential in encouraging communities to support the reintegration of displaced populations (especially in communities that have to receive these returnees), including certain categories of perpetrators, such as children. Religion can be an invaluable tool in instilling positive coping mechanisms, psychological well-being and resilience. Religious leaders are undoubtedly best placed to provide this aspect of support.

Moreover, as the Nigerian government works towards returning displaced populations to their communities, the role of religious leaders as part of a community leadership structure is fundamental to achieving sustainable community reintegration. To achieve this, religious leaders must evolve their approach to religious counselling, understand how to provide psychosocial support, raise awareness about the need for rehabilitation and, most importantly, facilitate community healing and peace-building. Religious leaders must be empowered to disseminate and amplify messages focused on the need for forgiveness, reconciliation and reintegration. By leveraging religion as a force for positive change, religious leaders can promote and ensure community buy-in and begin to address the distrust and anger that still exists across Borno State and the wider northeast region.

As part of the Neem Foundation's Yellow Ribbon Initiative, the principal role of religious leaders is not only to provide religious instruction and disseminate the 'right' religious understanding of Islam to confront extremist propaganda and narratives, they also serve as moral guides and authority figures who actively preach and promote the importance of tolerance, acceptance, peace and reconciliation. They provide a safe space for children to discuss ideas around the role of religion in a contemporary and pluralistic society, and counter misconceptions about Islam and other faiths. Through counselling, they also support families dealing with difficult issues, such as rape of and pregnancy in young girls who may have been rejected and ostracised by their families or communities. Religious leaders also have a role to play in supporting advocacy campaigns targeted at peace-building and conflict prevention at the community level.

Creative education and play therapy

There is little doubt that poor levels of education across the northeast region contributed to the recruitment of children during the Boko Haram insurgency. According to the Millennium Development Goals Performance Tracking Survey 2015, net primary school attendance in the northeast stood at 42.5 per cent, with literacy rates among young women as low as 33 per cent and primary school completion at 49.5 per cent.[13] In all three metrics, the northeast recorded the worst figures in the country.

In addition, an assessment carried out by the State Universal Basic Education Board (SUBEB) in the aftermath of the violent insurgency found that 524 schools were destroyed during the insurgency, with approximately 943 schools closed across Borno State, affecting over 400 000 children of school age. Not only has the insurgency stalled the educational development of thousands of children, it has also created a vicious cycle that makes the region more vulnerable to radicalisation and instability.

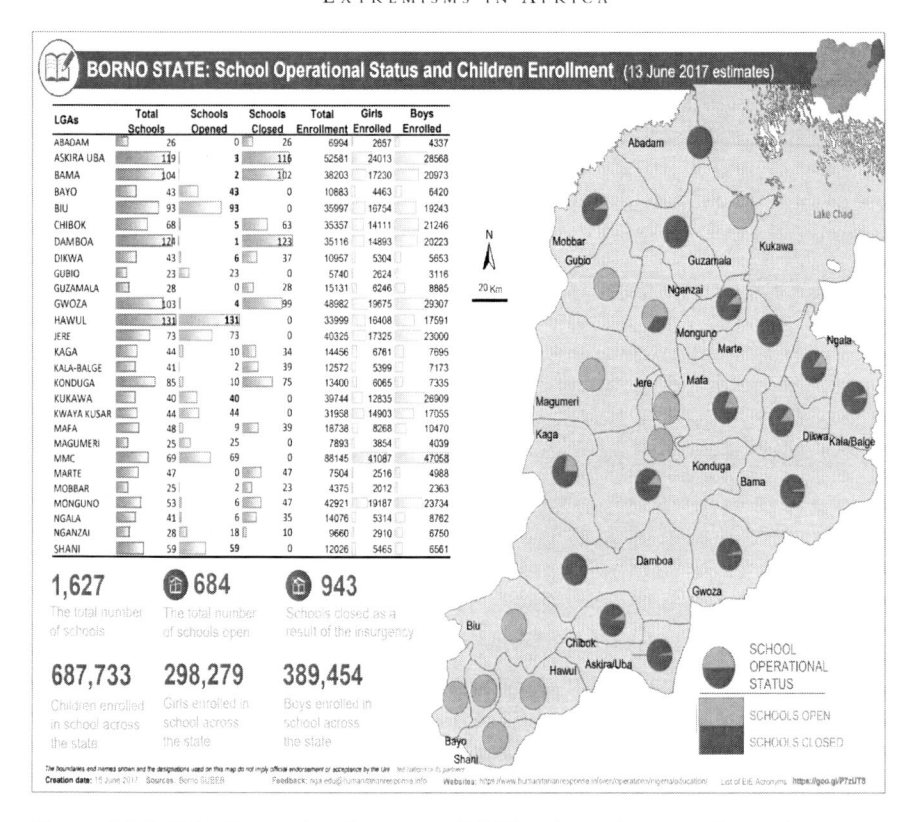

Figure 11.1: School operational status and children's enrolment in Borno State
Source: Humanitarian Response[14]

Communities devastated by conflict often find it difficult to provide conventional education because learning facilities have been destroyed, or are inaccessible or non-existent. Such conflict-affected communities lack teachers with the requisite training and skills, and, in most cases, spending on education is often insufficient to meet the demand for access to education. For the most part, current interventions in the education sector in the northeast, and Borno State in particular, have focused on infrastructure. As necessary as these efforts are, there is a need for a greater focus on the content and quality of the education provided. To effect significant and sustainable change, infrastructural development must be coupled with enhancements to teaching methodology and lesson content. Education plays a crucial role in national development because it inculcates in children the knowledge and skills required to build a more open, tolerant and resilient society.

In the wake of the insurgency, the desired conventional form of education is difficult to achieve in the short term. However, learning cannot wait, as education is critical for the successful rehabilitation and reintegration of children. It is vital to develop an approach that will enable refugees from violence and the struggles of daily life to play, express themselves creatively and develop new skills, especially in conflict-ridden communities.

As part of the comprehensive approach to rehabilitation and reintegration, creative arts and activities such as music, dance, crafts, painting, reading and drama are used to support the therapeutic interventions planned for CAAFAG. Not only do such activities directly address the psychological needs of CAAFAG, and build their resilience to radicalisation and violence, but they also challenge Boko Haram's radical ideology and narratives, and promote a greater sense of community and national identity.

By embedding concepts such as creativity, critical thinking, tolerance, character-building, acceptance, etiquette and hygiene in children, the Neem Foundation's creative education initiative supports CAAFAG to develop life skills, improve the quality of their learning experiences, and prevent radicalisation by raising the overall standard of education. The aim is to give children the capacity to envision bright futures for themselves, building their resilience to extremism. Most importantly, the Neem Foundation's creative education initiative is designed to give beneficiaries the necessary tools to ensure they succeed at both school and in life.

Alongside conventional education, unstructured play and, in more serious cases, trauma-informed integrated play, is incorporated into the psychosocial rehabilitation of CAAFAG (especially for younger children below the age of 16 years). Play has long been recognised as a natural form of communication for children and play therapy can have a lasting positive effect, allowing children to resolve emotional difficulties, overcome inner conflict and return to their pre-crisis state of being. It is important, therefore, to include the construction of playgrounds and child centres to encourage children to express themselves freely and engage in their psychological healing and social integration.

Community structures, stakeholders and partnerships

A peculiar challenge, often compounded by complex community structures, especially in parts of the northeast where the insurgency occurred, is the nature and role of key stakeholders who are best placed to support and champion the importance of rehabilitation and reintegration of populations affected by the conflict. According to available research,[15] the persistence of conflicts in many places where peace-building has been tried, illustrates the significant difficulties in establishing conditions for sustainable peace and reintegration. In the context of Borno State and the northeast, key stakeholders, especially those within communities, are an important constituent in defining and supporting conditions for sustainable peace and reintegration.

The Boko Haram insurgency has fractured community relationships across the region. Community acceptance of the reintegration of child victims that were kidnapped, held and used by Boko Haram, remains largely unresolved and there is still stigmatisation. The question then is, how does one implement an effective rehabilitation and reintegration programme? Community engagement and trust-building, using credible community stakeholders, represents one part of the solution and is crucial to the success of any intervention. Through engagement, the Neem Foundation has brought communities together to talk openly and honestly about issues around rehabilitation and reintegration. Thus, understanding community structures aids in the development of any programmatic approach and decision-making relating to rehabilitation and reintegration. Alongside this, developing such relationships is essential to ensure that existing fault lines are not exacerbated.

Anchored by credible community voices such as traditional leaders, district heads and local government leadership structures, the Neem Foundation understands that in an environment such as Borno State, it is important to create a platform for community stakeholders, concerned groups and individuals to directly address past and present issues. This is essential to ensuring community buy-in and a sense of communal ownership of the process of defining community priorities, conditions for peace and transitional justice, and ultimately healing and reintegration. In addition, this approach helps develop concrete, action-oriented solutions to identified challenges in combating factors that either hamper rehabilitation or reintegration, or the factors that led to the violence.

By sensitising stakeholders to the importance of leading the rehabilitation and reintegration process, communities are able to move forward with difficult issues that may be holding them back from rebuilding their lives and livelihoods. By listening to multiple perspectives and finding a common ground between opposing views and diverse populations, communities have a better understanding of the relevant challenges and are able to begin the process of building trust, commitment and participation, and take responsibility for solving critical issues such as stigmatisation.

As part of this response, the Neem Foundation has developed the capacity of community stakeholder groups and leadership structures to understand, promote and support the holistic socio-economic rehabilitation and reintegration of their communities. It is essential to empower stakeholders such as the police, traditional and religious leaders, local government leaders, teachers, parents, community-based organisations and other significant community actors and local community members to establish response mechanisms and internal structures to address issues locally in a manner that takes cultural sensitivities into account.

Specifically, the capacity-building workshops were designed to cover key areas such as preventing violence and de-escalating tension within communities. For example, building the capacity of teachers helps to create an inclusive atmosphere for children, which is conducive to respectful dialogue, understanding, openness and critical thinking. It also empowers teachers to incorporate value-based and citizenship-centred teaching methods for vulnerable children at risk of radicalisation. Meanwhile, community-based organisations have been designed to encourage youth-focused activities, foster community dialogue, and promote measures that prevent violent conflict by, for example, empowering young people to stay away from vices that may be detrimental to the community. Moreover, training targeted at parents and guardians reflects how to strengthen family-based social networks, particularly parental influence, to build resilience to violence.

Promoting tolerance and unity through sports
Sports are widely recognised as one of the most unifying instruments of peace and development. It is a key social activity that transcends ethnicity, age, gender, creed, religion, economic status or political affiliation, and has the capacity to bring people together in great numbers. In Nigeria, as in many countries, football has a huge following. The game is enjoyed by most Nigerians, irrespective of ethnicity, tribe or religion, and is a great source of national pride and identity. The fundamental elements of football make it a viable and practical tool for supporting the rehabilitation and reintegration of children affected by and used during the insurgency. Football can be used to support the holistic development of children, including their physical and emotional health, soft skills and sense of community, as well as social connections and healthy relationships. It offers opportunities for play and self-expression, and the game represents a healthy alternative to harmful activities such as drug use and crime. This is especially so for children with few other options for engaging in meaningful activities.

Football is a powerful tool for addressing mutual suspicion and mistrust, and supporting peace-building and conflict prevention. If implemented effectively, football programmes can promote social integration and tolerance, helping to reduce tensions and generate dialogue. According to the United Nations Inter-Agency Task Force on Sport for Development and Peace, 'well-designed, sport-based initiatives are practical and cost-effective tools for achieving development and peace'.[16]

The Neem Foundation understands that as part of the comprehensive response to rehabilitation and reintegration, football can serve as a platform for engaging children, strengthening community cohesion and building resilience to conflict, radicalisation and violent extremism. Football provides a fun entry point into the Neem Foundation's integrated model and helps to promote personal development and growth, encourage pro-social thinking and behaviour, and provides opportunities for peace-building.

The football and peace mentorship programme educates children on non-violent strategies for responding to conflict among peers, which also serves to support the prevention of violence and conflict at community level. Perhaps most importantly, the objective of this programme is to bring together marginalised children who have encountered violence with the broader community. By doing so, the Neem Foundation's Football Peace Programme directly addresses the disaffection and ostracisation faced by these children and acts as a vital first step to community acceptance and, ultimately, reintegration.

Establishing partnerships

To ensure a coordinated and sustainable approach, and expand the resource base and capacity, it is vital to synergise, strengthen and establish a close working relationship with state and non-state actors. Collaboration and regular stakeholder engagement allows government agencies, non-government organisations and international development partners working in the area of rehabilitation and reintegration to share experiences and best practices. For example, by establishing a strong partnership with the Borno State's departments of education, and women's affairs and social development, the process of enrolling as many vulnerable children as possible in school becomes achievable. Furthermore, by working with state agencies in charge of social and economic protection, such as the ministries of justice, poverty and youth empowerment, to identify existing initiatives that could support beneficiaries, it becomes easier to support and strengthen the operation of an efficient referral system, which allows all partners to share resources, experiences and expertise in meeting the needs of vulnerable children across affected communities.

Economic opportunities and engagement

For interventions to be successful and sustainable, the rehabilitation and reintegration of CAAFAG must take place within an economic context that supports their livelihoods, enables them to recover from the upheaval they have been through, and ensures that they do not have to engage in a life of crime to survive. This is especially important because poverty and economic exclusion were key reasons why children were easily recruited during the insurgency. Moreover, post-conflict economies typically face reduced productive capacities and livelihoods, destroyed infrastructure, collapsed markets, raging inflation, and widespread underemployment and unemployment.

Such situations inadvertently create unregulated black markets, which further affect the local economies of conflict-affected areas and push affected populations further into poverty and deprivation. Economic revitalisation is, therefore, an important aspect of post-conflict reconstruction of communities. This means that there must be economic support and opportunities for CAAFAG and their families as part of any comprehensive response to the issue of rehabilitation and reintegration. Skills development and direct economic support represent vital ways through which these and other vulnerable children can be supported under any socio-economic reintegration programme.

Owing to this vital consideration, the Neem Foundation provides training to aid them in developing relevant technical skills and qualities such as teamwork, dispute resolution, punctuality, respect for authority and problem-solving, among others. Specific skills-development training is provided after the children have completed an economic and opportunities mapping exercise, designed to determine viable economic activities in the geographical area in which they live.

Reintegration efforts must be appropriate for children and, therefore, strike a balance between their need for skills and genuine concerns for their welfare. Having missed out on the formative years of their lives and development, vocational training is an especially important path in successfully reintegrating CAAFAG back into society. Providing children with economic opportunities and the skills required will help, over time, to have them accepted back into the community – as their contribution to the economic redevelopment of their communities is perceived as a form of restitution.

The International Labour Organization (ILO) convention stipulates that 'the minimum age for work should not be below the age for finishing compulsory schooling'.[17] Therefore, to operate within the confines of the law, the Neem Foundation ensures that only children who are the right age are accepted into the economic reintegration programme. For children under the age of 16 years, it is their families who need the economic support necessary for the rehabilitation and reintegration of a child. Once they have successfully completed the skills-development programme, the beneficiaries are provided with economic support in the form of equipment, livestock and raw materials to build small-scale enterprises, under a cooperative or self-employment model, or they engage in some form of economic activity relevant to the skills they have acquired. In addition, economic support training is designed to provide children with the necessary information to choose skills or training relevant to their capacity to learn, abilities, interests and available economic opportunities in the chosen sector. Having done that, training takes the form of technical skills development, basic education and life skills, and entrepreneurial skills development. Keeping in mind that economically productive lives bring the greatest satisfaction to CAAFAG and their communities, the education provided cannot be purely theoretical, but must be linked to apprenticeships and internship-type work. By offering opportunities to gain work experience to selected CAAFAG, it helps them develop a life that is productive, industrious, profitable and rewarding. This helps to sustain reintegration efforts and restoration to normalcy in affected communities.

Conclusion: Heal, restore, renew

The recruitment and use of children in armed forces and groups is very clearly a war crime.[18] Existing national, regional and international legal instruments protect children under the age of 18 years from recruitment and use by armed forces/groups, especially during armed conflicts.[19] Nevertheless, girls and boys under the age of 18 years represent up to 50 per cent of armed groups in all the major conflicts in the world today.[20] As seen in the case of Nigeria, the reasons and ways in which children are recruited into armed groups vary. Poverty, poor education, the breakdown of family and community structures, coercion and the need to satisfy immediate needs all play a role.

Irrespective of the method of recruitment or rationale, participation in armed conflict is extremely damaging to a child's development and harmful to their future well-being. It also makes these children vulnerable to future radicalisation and violent extremism, as well as other forms of antisocial behaviour. Participation in warfare is synonymous with separation from parents, school and community support structures; the activities of groups like Boko Haram and CAAFAG have proven extremely damaging to these support structures in northeast Nigeria.

The comprehensive socio-economic rehabilitation and reintegration model outlined earlier is an attempt to create a truly holistic approach to addressing this problem, by improving the capacity available to respond to the needs of CAAFAG, from policy to funding for special interventions.

Moreover, it makes room for a robust, consistent and sustained advocacy, targeted at state and non-state actors to support and promote the immediate reintegration of CAAFAG. This model also sensitises community stakeholders, government institutions, representatives from various sectors, non-governmental organisations (international and national) and civil society groups to help in the prevention and recruitment of children, while providing communities with platforms to monitor and support the rehabilitation and reintegration of CAAFAG.

Moreover, this model seeks to improve the quality of care services for CAAFAG and move from the provision of general psychosocial support to the provision of specialised, child-centred and culturally appropriate psychosocial support services. By engaging communities and seeking their buy in, it improves these children's chances of being accepted by their communities, and it places children in need at the centre of programming for the transition to peace, while taking cognisance of their own capacities and potential contributions.

The conventional structures to achieve normality in Nigeria's northeast have been largely destroyed. In most affected communities, the root causes that led to the Boko Haram insurgency are still present, and the same environmental factors that led to children being recruited and used by armed groups remain. Failing to address these issues will likely lead to a recurrence of these events in the future.

Therefore, it is of the utmost importance that initiatives like the one outlined here are implemented to support the development of children by providing them with the necessary tools to ensure that they succeed in life, even in the absence of conventional support structures. In adopting this unconventional approach, the Neem Foundation is restoring hope and renewing the capacity of affected communities to build their resilience in a fragile environment in which state structures are weak. Ensuring this model is community based helps to ensure that it is locally owned and sustainable. The practical implementation of the initiative can inform policy and set out a globally acceptable model to ensure that communities and children devastated by conflict are helped to heal and return to their normal lives.

Endnotes

1. Youth Advocate Programme International (2017) Children Affected by Armed Conflict/Child Soldiers. Available at: http://yapi.org/youth-wellbeing/children-affected-by-armed-conflict-child-soldiers/ (accessed September 25, 2017)
2. United Nations Children's Fund (UNICEF) (2016) *Missing Childhoods: The impact of armed conflict in children in Nigeria and beyond*. Available at: https://www.unicef.org/media/files/Child_Alert_MISSING_CHILDHOODS_Embargo_00_01_GMT_13_April.pdf
3. SOS Children's Villages (2016) Children in Conflict: Child soldiers. Available at: http://www.child-soldier.org/
4. *The Guardian* (2017) Boko Haram releases dozens of Chibok schoolgirls, say Nigerian officials. Published 6 May 2017. Available at: https://www.theguardian.com/world/2017/may/06/boko-haram-releases-dozens-of-kidnapped-chibok-schoolgirls
5. BBC (2017) Nigeria's Boko Haram conflict: Huge rise in child 'human bombs'. Published 22 August 2017. Available at: http://www.bbc.com/news/world-africa-41010993
6. Assessment carried out by Borno State Universal Basic Education Board (SUBEB), 2015; Human Rights Watch (2016) *Nigeria: Northeast children robbed of education*. Published 11 April 2016. Available at: https://www.hrw.org/news/2016/04/11/nigeria-northeast-children-robbed-education
7. Neem Foundation (2017) Research and Messaging. Available at: http://www.

neemfoundation.org.ng/what-we-do/research-and-messaging
8   Ibid.
9   United Nations News Centre (2016) 'If you want to protect your image, protect children,' Ban tells debate on war-affected children. Published 2 August 2016. Available at: http://www.un.org/apps/news/story.asp?NewsID=54610#.WfGbNBOCzVo
10 Neem Foundation (2017) About Us. Available at: http://www.neemfoundation.org.ng/what-we-do/research-and-messaging
11 GTZ (2007) Psychosocial Support for Children and Youth: Approaches of international cooperation in post-conflict countries. Available at: https://www.giz.de/fachexpertise/downloads/gtz2007-en-psychosocial-support-children.pdf
12 Burina, DA and Burina, EA (2016) Mental health and psychosocial support in areas affected by conflict: Review of programs in the Chechen Republic, *Archives of Psychiatry and Psychotherapy*, **18**, pp. 40–47.
13 United Nations (2015) *The Millennium Development Goals Report 2015*. Available at: http://www.un.org/millenniumgoals/2015_MDG_Report/pdf/MDG%202015%20rev%20%28July%201%29.pdf
14 Humanitarian Response (2017) Borno State School Status and Children Enrolment by Local Government Authority. Available at: https://www.humanitarianresponse.info/system/files/documents/files/borno_state_school_status_and_children_enrollment_by_local_government_authority_as_of_june_2017-tbl.pdf
15 Knight, A (2008) Disarmament, demobilization and reintegration, and peacebuilding in Africa: An overview, *African Security*, **1** (1). Available at: http://www.tandfonline.com/doi/full/10.1080/19362200802285757
16 United Nations Inter-Agency Task Force on Sport for Development and Peace (2005) Sport as a Tool for Development and Peace: Towards Achieving the United Nation's Millennium Development Goals. Available at: https://www.un.org/sport2005/resources/task_force.pdf
17 International Labour Organization (ILO) (1998) *ILO Declaration on Fundamental Principles and Rights at Work*. Available at: http://www.refworld.org/docid/425bbdf72.html
18 See the definition of 'war crime' under the Rome Statute of the International Criminal Court: UN General Assembly, *Rome Statute of the International Criminal Court:* Article 8, paragraph 2*(b)* (xxvi) *(last amended 2010)*, 17 July 1998. Available at: http://www.refworld.org/docid/3ae6b3a84.html; See also, United Nations (2006) *Integrated Disarmament, Demobilization and Reintegration Standards*: Section 1, Introduction. Available at: http://www.iddrtg.org/wp-content/uploads/2013/05/IDDRS-5.30-Children-and-DDR1.pdf
19 United Nations Human Rights Office of the High Commission (2017) *Optional Protocol to the Convention on the Rights of the Child on the Involvement of Children in Armed Conflict*. Available at: http://www.ohchr.org/EN/ProfessionalInterest/Pages/OPACCRC.aspx
20 United Nations (2006) *Integrated Disarmament, Demobilization and Reintegration Standards:* Section 1, Introduction. Available at: http://www.iddrtg.org/wp-content/uploads/2013/05/IDDRS-5.30-Children-and-DDR1.pdf

References

BBC (2017) Nigeria's Boko Haram conflict: Huge rise in child 'human bombs'. Published 22 August 2017. Available at: http://www.bbc.com/news/world-africa-41010993

Burina, DA and Burina, EA (2016) Mental health and psychosocial support in areas affected by conflict: Review of programs in the Chechen Republic, *Archives of Psychiatry and Psychotherapy*, **18**, pp. 40–47.

GTZ (2007) Psychosocial Support for Children and Youth: Approaches of international cooperation in post-conflict countries. Available at: https://www.giz.de/fachexpertise/

downloads/gtz2007-en-psychosocial-support-children.pdf

Human Rights Watch (2016) Nigeria: Northeast Children Robbed of Education. Published 11 April 2016. Available at: https://www.hrw.org/news/2016/04/11/nigeria-northeast-children-robbed-education

Humanitarian Response (2017) Borno State School Status and Children Enrolment by Local Government Authority. Available at: https://www.humanitarianresponse.info/system/files/documents/files/borno_state_school_status_and_children_enrollment_by_local_government_authority_as_of_june_2017-tbl.pdf

International Labour Organization (ILO) (1988) *ILO Declaration on Fundamental Principles and Rights at Work*. Available at: http://www.refworld.org/docid/425bbdf72.html

Knight, A (2008) Disarmament, demobilization and reintegration, and peacebuilding in Africa: An overview, *African Security*, **1** (1). Available at: http://www.tandfonline.com/doi/full/10.1080/19362200802285757

Neem Foundation (2017) About Us. Available at: http://www.neemfoundation.org.ng/what-we-do/research-and-messaging

Neem Foundation (2017) Research and Messaging. Available at: http://www.neemfoundation.org.ng/what-we-do/research-and-messaging

SOS Children's Villages (2016) Children in Conflict: Child soldiers. Available at: http://www.child-soldier.org/

The Guardian (2017) Boko Haram releases dozens of Chibok schoolgirls, say Nigerian officials. Published 6 May 2017. Available at: https://www.theguardian.com/world/2017/may/06/boko-haram-releases-dozens-of-kidnapped-chibok-schoolgirls

United Nations (2006) *Integrated Disarmament, Demobilization and Reintegration Standards:* Section 1, Introduction. Available at: http://www.iddrtg.org/wp-content/uploads/2013/05/IDDRS-5.30-Children-and-DDR1.pdf

United Nations (2015) *The Millennium Development Goals Report 2015*. Available at: http://www.un.org/millenniumgoals/2015_MDG_Report/pdf/MDG%202015%20rev%20%28July%201%29.pdf

United Nations Children's Fund (UNICEF) (2016) *Missing Childhoods: The impact of armed conflict in children in Nigeria and beyond*. Available at: https://www.unicef.org/media/files/Child_Alert_MISSING_CHILDHOODS_Embargo_00_01_GMT_13_April.pdf

United Nations General Assembly. *Rome Statute of the International Criminal Court (last amended 2010)*, 17 July 1998. Available at: http://www.refworld.org/docid/3ae6b3a84.html

United Nations Human Rights Office of the High Commission (2017) *Optional Protocol to the Convention on the Rights of the Child on the Involvement of Children in Armed Conflict*. Available at: http://www.ohchr.org/EN/ProfessionalInterest/Pages/OPACCRC.aspx

United Nations Inter-Agency Task Force on Sport for Development and Peace (2005) Sport as a Tool for Development and Peace: Towards achieving the United Nation's Millennium Development Goals. Available at: https://www.un.org/sport2005/resources/task_force.pdf

United Nations News Centre (2016) 'If you want to protect your image, protect children', Ban tells debate on war-affected children. Published 2 August 2016. Available at: http://www.un.org/apps/news/story.asp?NewsID=54610#.WfGbNBOCzVo

Youth Advocate Programme International (2017) Children Affected by Armed Conflict/Child Soldiers. Available at: http://yapi.org/youth-wellbeing/children-affected-by-armed-conflict-child-soldiers/

Chapter 12

Accounting for the rise and trajectory of Islamist extremism in Africa

Hussein Solomon

Introduction

The facts are indisputable. Terrorism is on the rise in Africa. Terrorists have killed more than 20 000 people over the past five years.[1] Tens of thousands more have been maimed. According to the Mo Ibrahim Foundation, there has been more than a 1 000 per cent increase in terrorism since 2006.[2] More than the sheer number of terror attacks is the fact that the lethality of individual attacks has increased. On Saturday 14 October 2017, Al-Shabaab Islamist militants targeted the Somali capital, Mogadishu. A deadly truck bombing killed more than 300 people, while hundreds more were injured.[3] These developments raise the question of how Africa's Muslims – the overwhelming majority of whom are peaceful – allow foreign jihadi ideologies to make inroads into their communities?

Those who have researched and travelled to Africa are struck by the distinctive, moderate and tolerant Islam practised on the continent. Indeed, Eva Rosander (1997) has referred to this phenomenon as 'African Islam'.[4] By this she meant an Islam which takes into consideration local context and is accommodating and flexible – not one that is dogmatically rigid. This African Islam is intimately tied to the mystical and spiritual aspects of Islam known as Sufism, or in Arabic *tasawwuf*.[5] Unlike the formal, ritualistic aspects of those subscribing to a more scriptural Islam, which stresses the chasm between man and God,[6] Sufi brotherhoods or paths (*tariqa* in Arabic) stress the need to bridge that gap through love and knowledge of the true inner self. Many African Muslims are Sufi in orientation. This form of the Islamic faith was more personal and more emotional, stressing the love of God as opposed to the fear of God. Moreover, Sufi Islam co-existed[7] with the richness of pre-Islamic folk customs.[8] The accommodating and tolerant aspects of Sufi Islam are seen in its dominant traits being '… ecstatic dancing *(hadra),* spirit possession and expulsion and visits to 'saints' and tombs'.[9] These traits, in turn, are in keeping with many African traditional religious practices and this accounts for Sufi Islam's popularity across the length and breadth of Africa and Sufi Islam continues to attract the largest number of adherents to Islam in Africa.[10] In recent years, this Sufi Islam has come under increasing threat from Islamism. But what is Islamism and how is it that it has increasingly displaced traditional Sufi practices across the length and breadth of Africa?

Understanding Islamist ideology

Islamism – whether the Iranian Shi'a version or the radical Sunni[11] version popularised by the likes of the Islamic State – is a 20th-century totalitarian ideology that seeks to mould Islamic religious tradition to serve narrow political ends of domination.[12] Indeed, Islamism is sometimes interchangeably used with political Islam. According to Zeynep Kuru and Ahmet Kuru (2008), 'Political Islamism aims to create an "Islamic state" ruled according to the Sharia.'[13] Although political Islamist movements can be characterised as part of the Islamic religious resurgence, these movements are primarily political. Political Islamists regard the foundation of the Islamic state as the *sine qua non* for the attainment of a complete Muslim life. The key ideological components of the political Islamists' programme are taking the Qur'an as the source of political, legal and social systems and claiming to return to the example of the Prophet Muhammad. Unlike Sufi Islam, which is more inward looking, attempting to purify the soul of the individual believer, Islamists seek to capture political power to dogmatically enforce the central tenets of their faith on those living under their rule. Whether Al-Shabaab in Somalia, Ansar al-Din in Mali, Al-Qaeda in the Islamic Maghreb, Boko Haram in Nigeria or the various Islamic State franchises in Egypt and Libya – they all subscribe to these fundamentals of Islamism.

Khaled Abou El Fadl (2005) also refers to this as a 'puritanical' tradition within Islam noted for its 'fanatical reductionism and narrow-minded literalism'.[14] Although moulded and brought together as a somewhat coherent ideology in the 20th century, its ideological roots go all the way back to the 13th century to the time of the Iraqi, Ahmad ibn Taymiyya (CE 1263–1328), and the Arabian,[15] Muhammad ibn Abd al-Wahhab (CE 1703–1792). As with other totalitarian ideologies, Islamists do not tolerate difference or accept the proverbial 'other'. Al-Wahhab infamously declared that all those who did not conform to his purist vision of Islam were apostates and worthy of death.[16] Indeed, violence is part of its creed. Maulana Abul Ala-Maududi (CE 1903–1979), the founder of the Pakistani Jamaat-e-Islami argued that 'force may be used, in fact should be used to prevent people from doing wrong. Non-Muslim countries and cultures cannot be allowed to practise immoral deeds'.[17] We saw this dogmatic intolerance in Nigeria when the Islamist Abubaker Gumbi (d. 1992) attacked Sufism, arguing that there were no Sufi orders during the time of the Prophet and that it was, thus, a recent innovation and, therefore, unacceptable. Given the austere nature of Wahhabism, Gumbi also attacked the employment of Sufi amulets to ward off evil spirits and the use of drums in mosques.[18] It should come as no surprise, therefore, that radical Islamist groupings in Africa, such as Al-Shabaab in Somalia, Ansar al-Din in Mali and Boko Haram in Nigeria, targeted Sufi shrines and practices. The desecration of Sufi places of worship in historical Timbuktu during the Islamist takeover of northern Mali in 2012 was no less than a cultural genocide.[19]

Another Islamist ideologue, the Egyptian Hassan al-Banna (1906–1949), founder and Supreme Guide of the Muslim Brotherhood remarked that, 'It is the nature of Islam to dominate and not to be dominated, to impose its laws on all nations and to extend its power to the entire planet'.[20] Violence and intimidation, then, are tools of the propagation of their creed. Neither is this confined to Sunni Islam; Shi'a Islam has its own violent ideologues of the Islamist creed, despite their theological differences. Iran's Ayatollah Khomeini proclaimed, 'Whatever good there is exists thanks to the sword and in the shadow of the sword! People cannot be made obedient except with the sword! The sword is the key to paradise, which can only be opened for holy warriors'.[21] Islamists aim to create an ideal society, drawing inspiration from 7th-century Arabia during the time of the Prophet Muhammad and the first four caliphs to succeed him. Following from this is their aversion to any form of secularism – the separation between faith and state. According to Westerlund (1997), 'The Islamist goal is to establish Islamic law, sharia, as the basis of Muslim societies and Islamic states. Since God is the legislator and ruler on earth as in heaven, human beings are not supposed to legislate. The secular idea of human legislation is regarded as *shirk* (polytheism), putting humans on a par with God, which is seen as the most serious sin.'[22] In Shi'a Iran, while this Sunni argument of God's sovereignty is accepted, it is also proposed that God can have an agent on Earth acting for Him ('Her' in Islamist thought is inconceivable!). Ayatollah Khomeini developed the concept of *velayat-e-faqhi* – the rule of the supreme jurisprudent.[23] Flowing from this, according to Articles 56 and 57 of the Iranian Constitution, the guardian or supreme religious leader holds God's absolute sovereignty over the world and man. In the process, elections, and the democratic will of the people these represent, become passé.

Indeed, the Islamists' ideal state strongly resembles Stalin's gulag. Here it is important to understand what Ala-Maududi's government of God consists of. According to Ala-Maududi:

> In our domain we will neither allow any Muslim to change his religion nor allow any other religion to propagate its faith. Whenever the death penalty for apostasy is enforced in a new Islamic state, then Muslims are

kept within Islam's fold. But there is a danger that a large number of hypocrites will live alongside them. They will pose a danger of treason. My solution to the problem is this. That whenever an Islamic revolution takes place, non-practising Muslims should, within one year, declare their turning away from Islam and get out of Muslim society. After one year, all born Muslims will be considered Muslim. All Islamic law should be enforced upon them. They will be forced to practise all the tenets of their religion and, if anyone wishes to leave Islam, he will be executed.[24]

It is no wonder then that Ala-Maududi's beliefs spawned the Taliban in Afghanistan and Pakistan. When Boko Haram first emerged in Maiduguri, northern Nigeria, they were calling themselves the Nigerian Taliban.

With the growing strength of Islamism on the continent, it should come as no surprise that Africa has witnessed an intensification of inter-religious strife. Islamists declare Sufi practices as pagan[25] and have attacked Sufi shrines in Somalia as well as in northern Mali. At the same time, Coptic Christian monasteries in Egypt have been set alight, while Christian churches have been attacked in northern Nigeria. This, in turn, raises an intriguing question. Why is it that Islamism is on the rise on the African continent? After all, at face value why would people move from tolerant, accommodating Sufi Islam to the nihilistic creed, which is Islamism? Two sources – one external, the other internal – account for the rise of Islamism in Africa. External factors include the enduring legacy of Arabism and Islamism, and the issue of Islamist charities operating on the continent.

The enduring legacy of Arabism and Islamisation
When referring to the Arabisation and Islamisation of sub-Saharan Africa, Arab scholars generally adopt a romantic and positive tone. Helmy Sharawi (2004) strongly argues that the Arabic language, together with Islamic teachers and Islamic sciences, played a major role in the development of the African continent.[26] In a similar vein, Yusuf Fadl Hasan (1985) argues, 'The process of conversion was both slow and generally peaceful and in time Islam became an important agent of social cohesion, which brought together Sudanese peoples of different racial, cultural and linguistic origins.'[27]

The historical record, however, points to a far more nuanced picture. While Swahili, Tanzania's national language, has certainly borrowed much from the Arabic language,[28] in other cases the local languages of the Borgo, Berti and Maal of Sudan were transplanted by Arabic and the sense of identity of these local communities was forever lost.[29] Indeed, Kokole (1984) convincingly argues that the twin forces of Arabism and Islamism worked to disintegrate other social and tribal groups operating in the same space.[30] Tamura (2008) is more blunt in his assessment: 'The contacts between Arabs and Black Africans have been largely asymmetrical, in which Arabs have penetrated Africa, enslaved Africans and imposed their religion (Islam) and language (Arabic). They have viewed themselves as superior, as the conveyors of a higher civilisation and tended to be patronising towards those considered as inferior.'[31] The issue of Arabisation cannot be separated from Islamism. Wahhabi Islamists in Saudi Arabia, for instance, view their version of Islam as the only correct one and that African Islam is un-Islamic. Similarly, they argue that since the Qur'an was revealed in Arabic, this language is superior to all other languages. In the process, Arabic language and culture forms part and parcel of Islamist ideological hegemony. In multi-ethnic, multilinguistic, multicultural African polities, this culturally chauvinistic attitude is bound to increase conflict dynamics.

The issue of Arabisation is not merely a cultural issue, but one intimately connected to issues of power. The use of Arabisation as an element of Arab power projection was clearly understood by the Arab League. In its September 1978 report, it noted with satisfaction the Arabisation activities taking place in Djibouti, Kenya and Mali and urged that budgets be increased for further Arabisation activities on the continent.[32] Arabisation was also about access to power in countries like Sudan where the country's political mandarins all claimed Arabic descent.[33] Lusk (2008) points out that Sudan is run by a clique of 'Arab' people from the Ja'alin, Shaigiya and Danagla tribes, to the exclusion of the majority 'black'[34] Sudanese.[35] Indeed, this was one of the drivers behind the conflict in Darfur. Small wonder then that issues of Arabisation reinforce the fault lines between the political elite and those who feel disempowered in countries like Sudan, Mauritania and Algeria. Small wonder, too, that when the new government of South Sudan came into being (following their secession from Sudan), they introduced English into the school curriculum and have generally adopted processes of de-Arabisation as they seek to assert their independence.

In a similar fashion, the historical record also demonstrates that the spread of Islam may not be as peaceful as Sharawi and Hasan would indicate. While there have certainly been cases of the peaceful conversion to Islam as a result of Muslim merchants and the *ulema* (clerics), there have also been conversions as a result of intimidation and outright violence.[36] Under the influence of purist Wahhabist interpretations of the Qur'an taking place on the Arabian Peninsula, similar movements emerged in West Africa and vast swathes of territory were conquered in the name of Islam during the 18th and early 19th centuries. These include Ibrahim Mousa who led militant Islam in Vota Kalon, the westernmost tip of Africa, Suleiman Bal who carried the Islamic flag into battle in Senegal, and perhaps the most famous of them all, Sheikh Othman Dan Foudy,[37] who greatly expanded the realm of the Sokoto caliphate throughout much of northern Nigeria, beginning in 1804.[38] Modern-day Islamists like Boko Haram draw inspiration from Dan Fody's jihad and consciously attempt to emulate his example, especially in their rhetoric. The problem with many counterterrorism measures is that they are based on historical amnesia. History matters. Not recognising this truism results in superficial responses to extremism that merely exacerbate, as opposed to ameliorate, the problem. Religious terrorism on the African continent, in other words, has a long pedigree.

Therefore the spread of Islam on the continent was not only violent but it also was increasingly of a kind that was intolerant of other faiths. One example of this occurred on 17 May 1985, when Libyan leader Colonel Muammar Gaddafi gave a speech at the opening of a Muslim centre in Kigali, Rwanda:

> First, you must stick to your Islamic religion and insist that your children are taught the Islamic religion, and you teach the Arabic language because without the Arabic language we could not understand Islam. Furthermore, you must encourage the children of Christians to embrace Islam and the doors of the Islamic centre, the Islamic school and hospital should be opened to the children of Christians. You must teach the children of Christians that Christianity is not the religion of Africans, that is the religion of colonialism, that Islam is the religion of God. Christianity is the religion of the French, Belgians, Germans and American enemies. It is also a religion of Jews … Muslims must become a force to defend their religion. You must raise your head high in Rwanda, Burundi, Uganda and Zaire. You must raise your voice higher and declare that Allah is great because Africa must be Muslim. Africa is not Christian. Christians are intruders in Africa. Christians in Africa are agents of colonialism. We must wage a holy war so that Islam may spread in Africa …[39]

Given the necessary financial incentives, various African dictators – including Uganda's Idi Amin[40] and Central African Republic's (CAR's) Emperor Bokassa I – were quite willing to play to Gaddafi's agenda and to turn Muslims against Christians.[41] Given Africa's ethnic and religious diversity, this was a sure way to promote further conflict. Given the inherent fragility of African polities, insecurity only increased across the length and breadth of the continent. Indeed, tensions between Muslims and Christians surfaced not only in Sudan but also in Ethiopia and Eritrea.[42] The attacks by Boko Haram in northern Nigeria against Christians and more moderate Muslims is a continuation of these historical trajectories, as is the sectarian strife between Muslims and Christians in the CAR.

There is, however, another dimension to this religious conflict and this relates to the thousands of students who have left Africa to further their Islamic studies at Islamic institutions of higher learning such as Al-Azhar in Egypt, Al-Uzai in Lebanon, the University of Damascus in Syria and scores of other institutions in Saudi Arabia. It has been noted that most of these students, upon their return to their respective countries, are more radical than those who remained behind.[43] Indeed, according to John Yoh (2001):

> Most of the students from Africa who studied in the Middle East are accused of being behind the religious conflicts that have been going on in Nigeria, Ghana, Kenya and Tanzania. In fact, some reports in most West and East African media suggest that those students who studied in the Middle East are often recruited before their departure to their various countries into some radical religious group operating in guise, a humanitarian agency, causing inter-religious conflicts in Africa. It is this group of students that are considered to be the source of the so-called Islamic radicalism in Africa. Some of these groups are said to be connected with Islamic organisations operating in Africa under the guise of religious agencies, some of which were accused a couple years ago to be behind domestic conflicts and public insecurities in Zanzibar, Tanzania; Kampala, Uganda; Cape Town, South Africa; and Addis Ababa, Ethiopia.[44]

These students then become the conduits of Islamism in sub-Saharan Africa. Students, however, are not the only conduit for radical thought entering Africa. The annual pilgrimage, which sees tens of thousands of Africans going to Mecca, serves as another conduit for the spread of radical Islam. In West Africa, the introduction of Wahhabi classics such as Muhammad ibn Abd al-Wahhab's *Kitab al Tawhid* (The Book about the Oneness of God) had such a profound impact on Islamists in Mali that they took inspiration from the title of this book to name themselves Movement for Unity and Jihad in West Africa (MUJAO).[45] Radical ideologies are also spread online. Indeed, there are over 6 000 websites around the world spreading extremism.[46] With the spread of these technologies in Africa, Islamism, too, has spread. In a recent study of Saudi clerics' online activities (including Twitter, Facebook and YouTube), Jonathan Schanzer and Steven Miller[47] found that up to 75 per cent of over 40 000 entries collected and coded were hostile to the West, non-Muslim and secular cultures, as well as openly hostile to non-Wahhabi Muslims. In addition, the Saudi-funded

Channel Islam International, which is beamed into 60 African and Middle Eastern countries, also serves to propagate the Wahhabi ideology.[48] Under the circumstances, should we be surprised by the likes of Boko Haram ranting against secular states, or the Islamists of Ansar al-Din and Al-Shabaab violently tearing down Sufi shrines in Mali and Somalia respectively?

One manifestation of resurgent Islamism is the phenomenal growth of huge mosques with Gulf funding across Africa.[49] Examples of Saudi-funded West African mosques alone include the King Faisal Mosque and Centre in Guinea (US$21.3 million), the King Faisal Mosque in Chad (US$16 million), Bamako Mosque in Mali (US$6.7 million) and the Yaoundé Mosque in Cameroon (US$5.1 million).[50] The magnificent opulence of these mosques can be particularly alluring to Muslims who view it from the perspective of the rudimentary housing in which they often have to live on account of the years of neglect they have suffered as a result of an uncaring state. More important than the establishment of the physical structures, the funding of these mosques is, as David McCormack (2005) has argued, often contingent on the appointment of a Saudi-approved imam, which means, de facto, the propagation of Wahabbi Islamism.[51]

These mosques, however, serve as more than places of prayer. Rather, they often offer educational facilities and even basic health-care facilities. More importantly, perhaps, the mosque offers a social space for discussions within the community – especially those of a political nature. In situations in which authoritarian states have either restricted or shut down entirely the political space, the mosque provides an avenue for alternative political expression.[52] Under the circumstances, political opposition to the state often has an Islamist flavour.

The capture by radical Islamists of an African state, with the help of Gulf charities, does not only have negative repercussions for the local citizens; these are also felt much further afield.[53] A case in point is Sudan following the 1989 coup, which brought Omar al-Bashir and the National Islamic Front (renamed the National Congress Party after 1999) to power. Peter Kagwanja (2006) notes that Sudan quickly became the epicentre of the militant Islamist world,

> providing shelter to Islamist fighters, including Abu Nidal, the Egyptian Islamic Jihad; Gama' al Islamiyya; Hamas; Hezbollah; and the Palestinian Islamic Jihad. In 1991–1996, Osama bin Laden used his base in Sudan to consolidate his networks and to support terrorist groups in Algeria, Tunisia, Egypt and other sub-Saharan countries. Khartoum not only provided aid and shelter to extremist groups such as the Islamic Front for the Liberation of Oromia in Ethiopia, the Eritrean Islamic Jihad, and

the Ugandan Lord's Resistance Army (LRA), but also covertly aided Gama' al-Islamiyya's abortive attempt on President Hosni Mubarak's life in Addis Ababa in July 1995.[54]

Moreover, Islamist Sudan's chief ideologue, Hassan al-Turabi, became an inspiration to many Islamist movements across the region, including Mali, Nigeria and Somalia. In the 1980s in Mogadishu, for instance, small Islamic study groups were established, hoping to apply the principles of the Sudanese Islamist revolution to Somalia.[55]

Charities, terrorist funding and indoctrination

Closely connected to the issue of radical Islamism, and its attendant terrorism, is the issue of funding. It is incumbent on every Muslim to give a portion of their earnings for some charitable purpose (*zakat*). It is also a religious duty to support charitable works through voluntary deeds or contributions (*sadaqah*). Whilst *zakat* is collected by the government, local mosques and religious centres in the Middle East, *sadaqah* is paid directly to the Islamic charity.[56] This is, however, where the problem begins. According to Robert Looney (2006) because *zakat* and *sadaqah* are viewed as religious duties, there has been little oversight of these activities.[57] Moreover, the fact that donations have been made anonymously, coupled with the opaque financial and operating structures of Islamic charities, has created a perfect environment which terrorists can exploit. One indication of this comes from Somalia where one survey points out that 70 per cent of Arab donors allowed the recipient complete autonomy to manage and disperse funds with little or no accountability.[58]

Recently leaked US State Department cables to the whistle-blowing website Wikileaks illustrate American diplomats' frustrations with getting Arab countries to monitor these charitable donations. Indeed, Saudi Prince Mohammed bin Nayef, who leads his kingdom's anti-terrorism activities, was quoted as saying that 'if the money wants to go to terrorist causes, it will go'.[59] A similarly fatalistic attitude was adopted by the Qatari and Kuwaiti leadership. This compelled US officials to bemoan Islamic militants' 'ability to generate money almost at will from wealthy individuals and sympathetic groups throughout the Middle East while often staying ahead of counterterrorism officials'.[60]

The size of these charitable donations has been immense. Josh Martin (2005) estimates that since the early 1970s, Middle East charities distributed US$110 billion, of which US$40 billion found its way to sub-Saharan Africa, making Arab states the largest donor bloc to this region.[61] There is, however, a strong belief that this figure of US$110 billion is too conservative. After all, the

Saudi-based and funded Muslim World League alone disbursed US$75 billion between 1962, when it was founded, and 2002.[62] Jonathan Manthorpe (2013), meanwhile, believes that between 1983 and 2013, the Saudi kingdom spent US$100 billion to promote their violent, intolerant and puritanical Islamist creed around the world.[63] To put matters into perspective, the Soviet Union's communist party and its Communist International spent a measly US$7 billion propagating its ideology around the world between 1921 and 1991.[64] Under the circumstances, it is understandable why former US Under Secretary of the Treasury for Terrorism and Financial Intelligence, Stuart Levey, told ABC News in September 2007, 'If I could somehow snap my fingers and cut off the funding from one country, it would be Saudi Arabia'.[65]

More important than the amounts disbursed, however, are the actual activities of these charities. While many of these charities are involved in useful social-welfare activities, providing schools and clinics to the poor, they can also contribute to political tensions by proselytising a radical Islamism that can undermine security in a given African state by exacerbating tensions between Muslims, Christians and Animists, and between Wahhabi and Sufi-inclined Muslims. Salih, for instance, powerfully argues that 'some Muslim NGOs have been used as a vehicle for spreading political Islam at an accelerated rate, combining faith and material rewards among the disenfranchised Muslim poor ... becoming cronies to militant Muslim groups, including an emergent tide of indigenous African Islamic fundamentalist movements'.[66]

In Somalia, for instance, the Saudi-funded Al-Islah organisation supports and runs numerous schools, health facilities and community centres. While the organisation is not violent itself, its long-term political goal is to establish a theocratic Islamic state, not only within Somalia's borders but also in Somali-inhabited regions of neighbouring countries.[67] At an ideological level, such a position hardly differs from the Al-Qaeda-linked Al-Shabaab terrorist grouping in Somalia today. Indeed, many Al-Islah members went on to become active members of the Islamic Courts Union and then went on to join Al-Shabaab. It should be noted that the diverse Sufi orders did resist Al-Islah and its radical ideology, 'viewing it as a form of religious and cultural imperialism'.[68] However, these Sufi orders lacked access to the external funds of Al-Islah, which allowed it to propagate its Wahhabist creed and win over converts. Al-Islah received its funding from two Saudi entities – the Muslim World League and Al-Haramain. The latter was subsequently designated by the United States as a terrorist entity on account of its financial ties to Al-Qaeda.[69]

Approximately 20 per cent of the world's Muslims reside in sub-Saharan Africa, and Gulf countries have targeted these for proselytisation of the Islamist variety.[70] Flush with petro dollars, Saudi Arabia has played a key role in propagating its version of Islam onto the African continent. The Saudi Muslim World League (MWL) has 16 of its foreign offices in sub-Saharan Africa (comprising nearly half of its foreign operations) as well as 36 offices of its International Islamic Relief Organization and several offices of the World Assembly of Muslim Youth (WAMY) on the continent – the latter two are subsidiary organisations of the League. WAMY played a key role in war-torn Somalia where it targeted the youth for the propagation of Wahhabi Islam.[71]

More than just providing such organisations with money, Saudi and Kuwaiti backers also allegedly provide them with protection through corruption. Peter Kagwanja (2006) asserts that funds from the Africa Muslim Agency (a Kuwaiti charity), the CIFA Development Group (a joint Tanzanian–Saudi investment venture) and the Saudi-based petroleum company Oilcom were used to bribe corrupt members of Tanzania's ruling Chama Cha Mapinduzi party to turn a blind eye to the spread of Wahhabist Islam.[72] Indeed, throughout East Africa, security officials have witnessed the close relationships between some Gulf-funded Muslim charities and local extremist groupings, which have been undermining the respective countries' security. Following the August 1998 Nairobi bombing, the Kenyan government banned five Islamic NGOs on account of their alleged terrorist sympathies and funding of local Islamic fundamentalists. Those banned included Mercy Relief International, the Al-Haramain Islamic Foundation, Help African People, the International Islamic Relief Organization (IIRO), and the Ibrahim Bin Abdul Aziz Al Ibrahim Foundation.[73] In similar vein, the European Intelligence Agency contends that Uganda's Islamist extremists are receiving support from the IIRO, the Islamic African Relief Agency, the World Islamic Call Society, the International Islamic Charitable Foundation, the African Charitable Society for Mother and Child Care and the Sudanese National Islamic Front.[74]

Despite the progressive tone of Qatar's state-owned propaganda arm, Al Jazeera, this Gulf state has been involved in arming, funding and even providing direct military support for Islamists[75] in northern Mali.[76] Indeed, the tiny (and super-rich) Gulf emirate had established networks of madrassas, schools and charities pushing the Islamist message in northern Mali.[77] Moreover, Islamist extremists like Ansar al-Din and MUJAO have both received funds from Doha.[78] Saudi Arabia, meanwhile, has laid special emphasis on Africa's largest economy – Nigeria – for proselytisation, given the country's growing influence, oil resources, and the fact that it is the most populous African country, of which half are Muslim.[79] Indeed, Nigeria is the world's sixth-largest oil producer and can play a crucial role as a swing producer in the event of oil shortages. This is especially important in a world that consumes one-billion barrels of oil every 12 days and where demand is growing rapidly.[80] Saudi

Arabia's support for Islamists in northern Nigeria began in the 1960s with support to Ahmadu Bello and then Alhaji Abubakar Gumi.[81] In 1978, Gumi went on to establish the Saudi-funded Jamaat Izalat al-Bida wa Iqamat al-Sunna (commonly referred to as the Yan Izala) or the Society for the Eradication of Evil Innovation and the Establishment of the Sunnah).[82] In many ways, Yan Izala was the ideological progenitor of today's Boko Haram. It should come as no surprise then that Boko Haram, too, receives financial support from Saudi Arabia.[83] The underlying point being made is that without Arab radical Islamist indoctrination and financial support emanating from the Arab states, Islamic militancy in sub-Saharan African would not have been as severe a problem, both in scale and magnitude, as it is currently.

Internal factors contributing to the rise of Islamism
Here a caveat is urgently needed. Even though this Islamist ideology in Africa is being propagated by various Persian Gulf entities, this does not necessarily mean that a society would be prone to Islamist violence. Reflecting on this, Eva Rosander (1997) poses an intriguing question: why is it that Senegal, whose population is 90 per cent Muslim, has experienced little religious conflict, while Nigeria, whose population is only 50 per cent Muslim, has seen internal strife among Muslims, as well as violence between Muslims and Christians?[84] The answer to the question lies in the fact that the external variables are mediated by domestic conditions: economic crises, the democratic deficit and the crisis of the African State since independence.

In recent years, far from being viewed as the 'hopeless continent', Africa is being characterised as 'hopeful' by publications such as *The Economist* (2011). There seems to be some empirical evidence to support such an optimistic view. After all, half a dozen African economies have been growing at more than 6 per cent per year for the past six years, and two out of every three African countries hold elections.[85] However, such optimism is seriously misplaced. While economic growth is taking place, such growth is occurring from a low base – reflected in the fact that Africa accounts for a dismal 2.5 per cent of world output at purchasing power-parity, despite accounting for a sixth of the world's population.[86] This growth was also heavily dependent upon the export of primary products, and the rapid decline of commodity prices has led to growth being slashed by more than half. In 2016, growth was a mere 3.3 per cent (Solomon, 2017:63). Living standards have consequently rapidly deteriorated across the continent. Consider here the following statistics from the African Development Bank (2013):
- 60 per cent of Africans are engaged in low-paid, unpredictable and informal jobs;

- Half of Africa's population of one billion subsists on less than US$1.25 a day – the international poverty threshold;
- Only half of Africa's youth is economically active.[87]

Here, an important caveat is needed: not all people within states are similarly affected by the distressing economic conditions. In Mali, for instance, the average poverty rate is 64 per cent. In the Tuareg-dominated and Muslim north, the corresponding figures were much higher. In Timbuktu, the poverty rate was 77 per cent, for Gao it was 78.7 per cent and for Kidal it was a staggering 92 per cent.[88] Should we then be surprised that Tuaregs responded to the call of the Islamists of Ansar al-Din (Defenders of the Faith) in 2012 to declare jihad from Bamako? A similar dynamic is also at play in Nigeria. While 27 per cent of the population in the largely Christian south lives in poverty, the figure for the overwhelming Muslim north is an astounding 72 per cent.[89] Should we then be surprised when thousands of young men flocked to Boko Haram when it began its insurrections against an uncaring state in Abuja?

On the political front, while more elections have been taking place on the continent, these have not necessarily led to liberal democracy. This is reflected in the fact that only 11 African countries have been classified as 'Free' by Freedom House (2013), while 23 have been classified as 'Partly Free' and 22 as 'Not Free'.[90] In its 2015 survey, Freedom House found that only 12 per cent of sub-Saharan Africa could be defined as free.[91] In attempting to explain the discrepancy between holding elections while perpetuating authoritarian rule, Fareed Zakaria coined the phrase 'illiberal democracy'. He defined this as 'the troubling phenomenon of elected governments systematically abusing individual rights and depriving people of liberty'.[92] However, not all people within a polity are equally politically marginalised. Consider the case of Somalia, which is a state organised along clan lines. Not all clans are equal, however. The Darod, Dir, Hawiye and Isaq are nomadic pastoralists and are, therefore, regarded as *bilis* (noble) while the Rahanweyn, who are mostly cultivators, hold a subordinate position in society. This subordinate position has led to the Rahanweyn being marginalised in political and economic terms by successive regimes in Mogadishu. At the same time, the Rahanweyn are historically a weapons-carrying clan and have established the largest and most powerful of the clan militia forces in the country. Is it any wonder then that 70 per cent of Al-Shabaab fighters emanate from the Rahanweyn?[93] This volatile mix of economic disparities and the democratic deficit has provided the ideal recipe for sustained conflict within African polities, laying the seeds of state failure or state collapse. While state contraction/failure has not affected all African states to the same extent, and while the form it takes is context dependent, it is also true that the dubious honour of occupying the top six positions in the

2015 Fragile State Index all belong to African states – South Sudan, Somalia, the Central African Republic, Sudan, the Democratic Republic of Congo (DRC) and Chad. To compound matters still further, regional powerhouses such as Nigeria, Ethiopia and Kenya also find themselves at the top end of the index, occupying the 14th, 20th and 21st positions, respectively.[94] Indeed, the African State has lurched from crisis to crisis since achieving independence. Post-colonial Africa has experienced 85 coups d'état, and this figure passes 100 if one takes into consideration the various bloody failed attempts at regime change by the men in the military.[95] Since 1945 there have been 95 conflicts on the continent, with over 45 of these being civil wars. To compound matters further, Africa has hosted some of the longest-running conflicts in recent times. Consider here the fratricidal conflicts in Chad and Sudan lasting four decades and more, or the almost three-decade-long civil war in Angola. Of course, certain regions seem to be more conflict-prone than others. The 16 West African states, for instance, have experienced 82 forms of political conflict, including 44 military coups.[96] In the process, the African State enjoys scant legitimacy in the eyes of long-suffering citizens. Under these conditions, the 2015 Global Peace Index lists several African countries at the bottom, including the DRC (number 155 out of 162 countries surveyed), Sudan (157), the CAR (158) and Somalia (159). What is particularly worrisome is that regional powerhouses like Nigeria (151), Kenya (135) and South Africa (136) all feature at the lower end of the Peace Index.[97] The existence of these conflicts entails a ready supply of weapons for jihadists. Following the capture and killing of Libyan strongman Colonel Muammar Gaddafi on 20 October 2011, Libyan armouries were plundered and weapons from these soon found their way into northern Mali, helping to fuel the Islamist takeover in 2012.[98]

Islamists have often exploited the deteriorating economic and political conditions in African countries to expand their reach among the disaffected.[99] Because of their superior organisation (relative to the ineptitude and corruption of government bureaucracies), their use of volunteers and (of course) their access to funds from the Gulf, Islamists have been able to step in and assist desperate communities across Africa. In Mali, for instance, Islamists and their grassroots economic development have been able to establish mosques, modern schools, clinics, pharmacies and cultural centres since the 1980s.[100] Similarly, Islamists in the 1990s established a small Islamist community in Luuq in southern Somalia, where they engaged in innovative cultivation techniques and fed villagers. In the process, the loyalty of citizens in these areas transferred to these Islamist groupings.

A similar dynamic where local economic conditions are exploited is clearly evident in the manner in which the Lebanese terrorist movement and the

Iranian-funded Hezbollah (Party of God) emerged on the African continent. As Major James Love notes, Hezbollah's tried and tested modus operandi is also used on the African continent to great effect. Fledgling Hezbollah cells use subtle infiltration techniques to gain access to an area without drawing attention. They gain the trust of the local populace by conducting charity fund-raising activities and other social-welfare programmes. This resonates very well among Africa's poor, whose own politicians seem unresponsive to the needs of their citizens, while they themselves accumulate wealth. Once it has gained the trust of the locals, the Hezbollah cell begins to recruit from the local population, allowing the cell to begin operations. Cells would be unable to operate without building a popular support base.[101]

Having created a popular support base through the exploitation of economic conditions and government neglect of its own citizens, Hezbollah began supporting local organisations, for example, the radical Shi'a cleric Sheikh Ibrahim Zakzaky's Islamic Movement of Nigeria (IMN), which also serve to destabilise existing regimes. This was graphically illustrated when IMN members audaciously attacked the motorcade of the Emir of Zazzau, Alhaji Shehu Idris, who was on his way to a security meeting in Kaduna where the IMN was under discussion. It subsequently emerged that IMN members were instructed on religious and military matters in Iran.

The problem with counterterrorism policies

Islamist terrorism on the African continent is also on the rise because existing counterterrorism policies have exacerbated the problem and seem to be ignorant of the reasons why citizens are likely to be recruited by terrorist groups. Instead, the focus seems to be on militarily defeating these groups. A recent study by the UNDP illustrates the need for a more holistic approach to extremism on the African continent. The UNDP engaged in an exhaustive survey of militants across the length and fbreadth of the continent. The salient findings were the following:

- Those more prone to join militant movements had little exposure to people of other religions and ethnicities.
- Individuals whose overall levels of literacy and education are low, are more likely to join extremist groupings.
- If an individual was either studying or working, such a person was less likely to join a jihadist group. Indeed, employment, the UNDP study stressed, was the single most frequently cited 'immediate need' faced at the time of joining.
- Those who joined militant groups also had low levels of trust (78 per cent) in politicians and the security services, believing them to be corrupt.

Perhaps more poignantly, for the majority of respondents, the catalyst for them joining an extremist organisation was 'government action'. Indeed, 71 per cent pointed to the killing or arrest of a family member or a friend by security forces, which prompted them to join extremist organisations to avenge their loved ones.[102] This latter point has been emphasised time and time again, as under-resourced and poorly trained military and police officials attempt to stem the tide of extremism in Africa. In the process, these have often turned to brutal means of suppression, making little distinction between innocent civilians and guilty jihadis. The Joint Military Task Force (JTF) in Borno State in Nigeria, for instance, has resorted to unlawful killings, dragnet arrests, and extortion and intimidation of the hapless residents of Borno. Far from intelligence-driven operations, the JTF simply cordoned off areas and carried out house-to-house searches, at times shooting young men in these homes. Similar tactics were pursued by the JTF at homes searched in the Kaleri Ngomari Custain area on 9 July 2011. Twenty-five people were shot dead by security services, women and children were beaten, homes were burnt, and many boys and men were reported missing. Such excesses on the part of the security services can only further alienate citizens from the state and its security forces – something that Abuja can ill afford. This situation is compounded by the fact that the Nigerian soldiers and police patrolling against Boko Haram in northern states are national, not local, and therefore unlikely to share either ethnic or cultural backgrounds with the local population, who view themselves as being under siege in an occupation by 'foreign forces'.[103] Under the circumstances, the author endorses the position of the United Nations Secretary General, António Guterres, when he asserted, 'I am convinced that the creation of open, equitable, inclusive and pluralist societies, based on the full respect of human rights and with economic opportunities for all, represents the most tangible and meaningful alternative to violent extremism'.[104] In practice, this means that the international community must use the aid they disburse to African governments as leverage to get them to open up democratic spaces and open up economic opportunities for their citizens, while also engaging in responsive and accountable governance. It also means more resources need to be directed towards governance and development initiatives in the fight against extremism rather than military means. Currently, government budgets are skewed towards the men in uniform. Commenting on US expenditure in the fight against extremism globally, Daniel Aldrich reminds us that only 5 per cent of funds between 2001 and 2012 have gone towards public diplomacy and development programmes.[105] The lion's share went to the military.

The limitations of a military-centred paradigm have already been explored but to emphasise the point being made, allow me to quote the former US

Joint Chiefs of Staff chairman, Admiral Mike Mullen. Explaining the fact that the military is a particularly blunt instrument when fighting terrorist ideologies, Admiral Mullen opined that the United States cannot 'kill our way to victory'.[106] In similar fashion, Colonel Thomas Dempsey of the US Army War College argues that the use of direct military action against terrorists is counter-productive since it increases their status and confers on them greater legitimacy within marginalised communities in these states (Solomon, 2015b: 124). While military means are not to be excluded, these cannot be the primary means by which one fights a malevolent ideology. Moreover, when military measures are used, they should be applied to ensure only the minimum loss of life of innocent civilians. Part of the problem here is that African militaries use conventional warfare methods to engage with the guerrilla tactics of terrorist insurgents. What is needed is for the international community to assist African armies with their asymmetrical warfare capabilities. A good beginning here is for African armies to develop highly mobile 600-troop battalions as opposed to bigger and more rigid brigades of 3 000 troops or a corps of 10 000 troops.[107]

In recent years, it has become increasingly recognised that in an ideological struggle one should stress other Islamic ideas, emphasising tolerance, pluralism, diversity and respect for the proverbial 'other'. For instance, in December 2017, Moroccan King Mohammad VI gathered 300 Islamic clerics from across the continent in Fez in an effort to promote Sufi values of moderation.[108] Laudable as this initiative was, one of the major problems undermining Sufi Islam is its proximity to the incumbent government. Sufi brotherhoods grew exponentially during the colonial period, partly as a result of their cooperation with the colonial powers. Donal Cruise O'Brien[109] concludes that 'most Sufi orders came to collaborate willingly, even enthusiastically, with European rulers'. The British, for instance, incorporated the Qadiriyya Sufi brotherhoods as part of the colonial administration in northern Nigeria. In Senegal, meanwhile, the Mouridiyya Sufi brotherhoods worked with the French colonial authority to introduce commercial agricultural production.[110]

In the post-colonial period, this cooperation between Sufi orders and the respective authorities continued, with many Sufi leaders receiving financial benefits from government.[111] The proximity of Sufi leaders to corrupt and authoritarian government caused them to lose credibility and popularity in the eyes of ordinary citizens and formed the basis of vehement Islamist attacks on them. Consequently, moderate Sufi Islam could not serve as a bulwark to radical Islamism since the Sufi leadership was perceived to be an extension of a corrupt state.

In similar fashion, other Muslim organisations aiming to foster peace and tolerance between faiths were tarnished on account of their proximity to an often predatory and authoritarian state. In Nigeria in the 1980s, an Advisory Committee on Religious Affairs, representing both Muslims and Christians, was established and aimed to mitigate religious tensions. Similar structures came into being across the continent: the Supreme Council of Muslims in Tanzania, the Supreme Council of Kenya Muslims, the Uganda Muslim Supreme Council, the Association des Musulmans au Rwanda and the Muslim Association of Malawi.[112] Few of these have been able to mitigate sectarian strife. Because of their perceived proximity to regimes which are viewed as illegitimate, Muslims who participated in these structures were viewed as co-opted. The fact that these Muslims often defended the incumbent governments merely served to reinforce this perception.[113] With moderate Muslims discredited, it left the door open for Islamists to spread their message of hate. What is needed is a Sufi Islam that articulates the concerns of ordinary Muslims, even when those concerns mean criticism of incumbent governments. A co-opted Islam, which is uncritical of the West and whose members serve as praise singers to rapacious political elites, will only serve to delegitimise moderate Muslims, while giving further ammunition to militants. These Sufi Muslims, however, must be given space to articulate their criticism in public platforms without sanction. The opening up of the democratic space is essential if moderate Islam is to turn the tide against Islamist extremism.

A concomitant of this is the opening up of economic opportunities. Abundant research has indicated that the bulwark of liberal democratic values, such as pluralism, tolerance and secularism, is a vibrant middle class. Where such a middle class does not exist, extremism will take root in whatever form – be it religious fundamentalism or vile ethnocentric nationalism.[114] Finally, the international community needs to pressure Gulf countries, charities and organisations to stop exporting their radical extremist ideologies to the African continent.

Endnotes

1   Solomon, S (2017a) Terrorism in Africa falling after reaching highs, *Voice of America*. Published 9 July 2017. Available at: https://www.voanews.com/a/africa-terrorism-deaths-falling
2   Cochi, M (2017) Terrorism Africa, *Sub-Saharan Monitor*. Published 19 May 2017. Available at: eastwest.eu/en/opinion/sub-saharan-monitor/terrorism-since-2006-attacks-in-africa-increased-by-1000
3   Burke, J (2017) Mogadishu truck bomb: 500 casualties in Somalia's worst terrorist attack. *The Guardian*. 16 October 2017. Available at: https://www.theguardian.com/world/2017/oct15/truck-bomb-mogadishu-kills-people-somalia
4   Rosander, EE (1997) Introduction: The Islamization of 'Tradition' and 'Modernity'. In *African Islam and Islam in Africa: Encounters Between Sufis and Islamists*, edited by D Westerlund and EE Rosander. London: Hurst and Co, 1–27. p. 1.

5   Ibid, p. 3.
6   Ibid, p. 3.
7   McCormack, D (2005) *An African Vortex: Islamism in Sub-Saharan Africa*. Occasional Paper Series No. 4. Washington, DC: The Centre for Security Policy. p. 1.
8   Viorst, M (1995) Sudan's Islamic experiment, *Foreign Affairs*, **74** (3), p. 48.
9   Ibid, p. 48.
10 Westerlund, D (1997) Reaction and action: Accounting for the rise of Islamism. In D Westerlund and E Evers Rosander (eds) *African Islam and Islam in Africa: Encounters Between Sufis and Islamists*. London: Hurst and Co, p. 330.
11 Shi'a and Sunni Islam refers to the two main divisions of Islam which have their origins at the time of the death of the Prophet Muhammad in 632 CE when the thorny question of succession emerged. The Shi'a or Partisans of Ali believed that succession should stay in the House of the Prophet, while the Sunnis believed that Abu Bakr, a close companion of the Prophet should succeed him. Since this time each have developed their own respective theology with sharp differences (Rogerson, 2006).
12 Solomon, H (2013) *Jihad: A South African perspective*. Bloemfontein: SUN Press. p. 14.
13 Kuru, Z and Kuru, A (2008) A political interpretation of Islam: Said Nursi's faith-based activism in comparison with political Islamism and Sufism, *Islam and Christian-Muslim Relations*, **19** (1), p. 100.
14 El Fadl, KA (2005) *The Great Theft: Wrestling Islam from the extremists*. New York: Harper Collins.
15 At the time there was no Saudi Arabia, just the Arabian Peninsula, so it is fitting to refer to Al-Wahhab as Arabian.
16 Armstrong, K (2000) *Islam: A Short history*. New York: The Modern Library. p. 135.
17 Ahmad, MT (1989) *Murder in the Name of Allah*. Cambridge: Lutterworth Press. p. 21.
18 Westerlund (1997) p. 309.
19 Solomon, H (2015b) *Terrorism and Counter-terrorism in Africa: Fighting insurgency from Al Shabaab, Ansar Dine and Boko Haram*. London: Palgrave Macmillan. p. 75.
20 Post, JM (2007) *The Mind of the Terrorist: The psychology of terrorism from the IRA to Al-Qaeda*. New York: Palgrave Macmillan. p. 175.
21 Quoted in: Wright, L (2007) *The Looming Tower: Al-Qaeda's Road to 9/11*. London: Penguin Press. p. 47.
22 Westerlund (1997), p. 309.
23 Armstrong (2000), p. 122.
24 Ahmad, MT (1989) *Murder in the Name of Allah*. Cambridge: Lutterworth Press. p. 55.
25 Rosander (1997), p. 4.
26 Sharawi, Helmy (2004) Arab-African Relations: From Liberation to Globalisation. *African Renaissance* **1** (1), p. 4.
27 Hasan, YF (1985) The historical roots of Afro-Arab Relations. In Khair El-Din Haseeb (ed) *The Arabs and Africa*. London: Croom Helm and Centre for Arab Unity Studies, p. 35.
28 Ibid, p. 32.
29 Bankie, FB (2004) Arab slavery of African in the Afro–Arab borderlands, *African Renaissance* **1** (1), p. 80.
30 Kokole, OH (1984) The Islamic factor in African–Arab Relations, *Third World Quaterly*, **6** (3), p. 690.
31 Tamura, S (2008) Rethinking Pan-Africanism under African Union-led continental integration: Revival of Afro-Arab solidarity or clash of civilizations? *Journal of Global Change and Governance* **1** (4), p. 7.
32 Yoh, JGN (2001) Reflections on Afro-Arab relations: An African perspective. A Paper Presented to the Arab Thought Forum, Amman, Jordan. Available at: http://johngaiyoh.

com/pdf/Reflections%20%20Afro-Arab%20Relations.pdf, p. 16.
33 Al Medani, KA (2010) From assimilation to confrontation: Macro-micro-level processes of acculturation and cultural pluralism in the Blue Nile Region, the Sudan, *International Journal of African Renaissance Studies*, **5** (1), p. 111.
34 'Arab' and 'black' are placed in inverted commas on account of the fact that there was a tremendous amount of intermarriage between Arabs and indigenous peoples over the years and that these categories in Sudan are cultural in orientation rather than ethnic.
35 Lusk, G (2008) False premise and false response to the Darfur crisis, *Peace Review*, April–June, **20** (2), p. 168.
36 Al Medani (2010) p. 115.
37 Kokole (1894), p. 689.
38 Hasan (1985), pp. 39–40.
39 Yoh (2001), pp. 20–21.
40 Huliaris, A (2001) Qadhafi's comeback: Libya and sub-Saharan Africa in the 1990s, *African Affairs* 100 (398), p. 6.
41 Tamura (2008), p. 8.
42 Ibid, p. 8.
43 Yoh (2001), p. 14.
44 Ibid, pp.14–15.
45 Westerlund (1997) p. 311.
46 Schanzer, J and Miller, S (2012) *Facebook Fatwa: Saudi Clerics, Wahhabi Islam and Social Media*. Washington, DC: FDD Press. p. 57.
47 Ibid, p. v & p. 61.
48 McCormack, D (2005) *An African Vortex: Islamism in Sub-Saharan Africa*. Occasional Paper Series No. 4. Washington, DC: The Centre for Security Policy. p. 7.
49 Westerlund (1997), p. 313.
50 Ibid, p. 7.
51 Ibid, p. 7.
52 Westerlund (1997), p. 314.
53 Schanzer & Miller (2012), p. 11.
54 Kagwanja, P (2006) Counter-terrorism in the Horn of Africa: New security frontiers, old strategies, *African Security Review*, **15** (3), p. 75.
55 Menkhaus, K (2002) Political Islam in Somalia, *Middle East Policy*, **9** (1), p. 111.
56 Looney, R (2006) The mirage of terrorist financing: The case of Islam charities, *Strategic Insights*, **5** (3), p. 1.
57 Ibid, p. 1.
58 Arab Donor Policies and Practices in Education in Somalia/Somaliland (2004) Available at: http://www.soma-li-civilsociety.org/downloads/NOVIB-WAMY-FINAL.pdf
59 Lichtblau, E and Schmitt, E (2010) Cash flow to terrorists evades US efforts, *The New York Times*. Published 5 December 2010. Available at: www.Nytimes.com/2010/12/06/world/middleeast/06wikileaks-financing.html
60 Ibid.
61 Martin, J (2005) Arab countries eye new giving guidelines: Arab and Islamic charities, which suffered in the wake of 9/11 revelations of links to extremists, have been working hard to clean up their image. But are they doing and giving enough? *The Middle East*. Published July 2005. p. 1.
62 Looney (2006), p. 3.
63 Manthorpe, J (2013) Saudi Arabia funding fuels jihadist terror, *Vancouver Sun*. Published 28 May 2013. Available at: www.vancouversun.com/Jonthan+Manthorpe+Saudi+Arabia+fudning+fuels+jihadist+terror/8445917/story/html#

1xzz33Ypjup5

64 Winsor, C (2007) *Saudi Arabia, Wahhabism and the Spread of Theo-Fascism*. Available at: www.globalpolitician.com/print/asp?id=3661

65 Ehrenfeld, R (2011) Their oil is thicker than our blood, *Terror Finance.org*. Available at: www.terrorfinance.org/the-terror-finance-blog/2011/12/their-oil-is-thicker-than-our-blood.html

66 Quoted in: Haynes, J (2005) Islamic militancy in East Africa. *Third World Quarterly* **26** (8), p. 322.

67 International Crisis Group (2002) *Somalia: Countering terrorism in a failed state*, ICG Africa Report No. 45. Nairobi/Brussels: International Crisis Group. p. 13.

68 Ibid, p. 13.

69 Ibid, p. 13.

70 McCormack (2005), p. 1.

71 Ibid, p. 6.

72 Kagwanja, P (2006) Counter-terrorism in the Horn of Africa: New security frontiers, old strategies, *African Security Review*, **15** (3), p. 77.

73 Hayns (2005), p. 1324.

74 Ibid, p. 1525.

75 See: Makhmudov, M and Walker, LJ (2012) Islamists in Mali: Funding and ideological ratlines linking Saudi Arabia and Qatar, *Global Security News*. Published 3 July 2012. Available at: http://global-security-news.com/2012/07/03/islamists-in-mali--funding-and-ideological-ratlines-linking-saudi-arabia-and-qatar; Barillas, M (2013) Qatar extends influence to Africa with support to rebels in Mali, *Cutting Edge News*. Published 22 January. Available at: www.thecuttingedgenews.com/index.php?article=78562

76 Cartalucci, T (2013). Destroying a nation-state: US-Saudi funded terrorists sowing chaos in Pakistan, *Global Reach*, February. Available at: www.globalreach.ca/destroying-a-nation--state-us-saudi-funded-terrorists-sowing-chaos-in-pakistan/5323295

77 Allemandou, S (2013) Is Qatar fuelling the crisis in north Mali? *France 24*. Published 23 January. Available at: www.france24.com/en/20130121-qatar-mali-france-ansar-dine-mnla-al-qaeda-sunni-islam-doha

78 Ibid.

79 Mandaville, P (2007) *Global Political Islam*. London: Routledge. p. 5.

80 Ghorbani, A, Assoulin, Y and Al Zahrani, S (2014) *The Syrian War, Saudi Arabia's Struggle for Global Influence, and Control in Africa*. Available at: www.elombah.com/index.php/special-reports/21954-the-sytian-war-saudi-arabia-s-struggle-for-global-influence-and-control-of-Africa

81 McCormack, D (2005) p. 9.

82 Ibid, p. 10.

83 Ghorbani et al (2014).

84 Rosander (1997), p. 5.

85 *The Economist* (2011) Africa's Hopeful Economies, *The Economist*. Published 3 December 2011. Available at: www.economist.com/node/21541008

86 Ibid.

87 African Development Bank (2013) *African Statistical Yearbook*. Tunis: African Development Bank. pp. 30-36.

88 Solomon, H (2015a) Critical terrorism studies and its implications for Africa, *Politikon: South African Journal of Political Studies*, **42** (2), p. 230.

89 Ibid, p. 228.

90 Freedom House (2013) *Freedom in the World 2013: Democratic breakthroughs in the balance*. Available at: www.freedomhouse.org/report/freedomworld/freedom-world-2013

91 Solomon, H (2017) Beyond the state: Reconceptualizing African security in the 21st century, *African Security Review*, **26** (1), p. 63.
92 Zakariya, F (2013) After the coup: Egypt must reach out to the Islamists it is now jailing, *Time*. Published 22 July. p. 23.
93 Solomon, H (2015b) *Terrorism and Counter-terrorism in Africa: Fighting insurgency from Al Shabaab, Ansar Dine and Boko Haram*. London: Palgrave Macmillan, pp. 41, 45.
94 Solomon (2017b), p. 63.
95 Araoye, A (2012) Hegemonic agendas, intermesticity and conflicts in the post-colonial state, *African Journal of Conflict Resolution*, **12** (1), p. 10.
96 Ibid, p. 10.
97 Solomon (2017b) p. 63.
98 Solomon, H (2016) *Islamic State and the Coming Global Confrontation*. London: Palgrave Pivot. p. 29.
99 McCormack (2005) p. 1.
100 Westerlund (1997) p. 321.
101 Love, J (2010) *Hezbollah: Social services as a source of power*, JSOU Report No. 10–5. Hurlburt Field, FL: Joint Special Operations University. Available at: www.globalsecurity.org/military/library/report/2010/1006-jsou-report-10-5.pdf
102 United Nations Development Programme (2017) *Journey to Extremism in Africa: Drivers, incentives and tipping point for recruitment*. New York: United Nations. pp. 4, 5.
103 Solomon (2015b) p. 91–92.
104 UNDP (2017) p. iii.
105 Aldrich, D (2012) *First Steps towards Hearts and Minds? USAID's Countering Violent Extremism Policies in Africa*. Available at: http://ssrn.com/abstract=2156060, p. 2.
106 Quoted in Aldrich (2012) p. 2.
107 Solomon (2015b) p. 134.
108 Moroccan World News (2017) 300 African Ulema gather in Fez to promote values of moderate Islam. *Moroccan World News*, 7 December. Available at: https://www.moroccoworldnews.com/201712/235742/african-ulemas-fez-moderate-islam
109 Quoted in Westerlund (1997) p. 310.
110 Ibid, pp. 310–311.
111 Ibid, p. 311.
112 Ibid, p. 318.
113 Ibid, p. 319.
114 Solomon, H and Liebenberg I (2000) *Consolidation of Democracy in Africa: A view from the South*. London. Ashgate Publishing.

References

African Development Bank (2013) *African Statistical Yearbook*. Tunis: African Development Bank.

Ahmad, MT (1989) *Murder in the Name of Allah*. Cambridge: Lutterworth Press.

Al Medani, KA (2010) From assimilation to confrontation: Macro–micro-level processes of acculturation and cultural pluralism in the Blue Nile Region, the Sudan, *International Journal of African Renaissance Studies*, **5** (1), pp. 111–122.

Aldrich, D (2012) *First Steps towards Hearts and Minds? USAID's Countering Violent Extremism Policies in Africa*. Available at: http://ssrn.com/abstract=2156060

Allemandou, S (2013) Is Qatar fuelling the crisis in north Mali? *France 24*. Published 23 January. Available at: www.france24.com/en/20130121-qatar-mali-france-ansar-dine-mnla-al-qaeda-sunni-islam-doha

Arab Donor Policies and Practices in Education in Somalia/Somaliland (2004) Available at: http://www.soma-li-civilsociety.org/downloads/NOVIB-WAMY-FINAL.pdf

Araoye, A (2012) Hegemonic agendas, intermesticity and conflicts in the post-colonial state, *African Journal of Conflict Resolution*, **12** (1), pp. 9–32.

Armstrong, K (2000) *Islam: A Short History*. New York: The Modern Library.

Bankie, FB (2004) Arab slavery of African in the Afro–Arab borderlands, *African Renaissance* **1** (1), pp. 78–81.

Barillas, M (2013) Qatar extends influence to Africa with support to rebels in Mali, *Cutting Edge News*. Published 22 January. Available at: www.thecuttingedgenews.com/index.php?article=78562

Burke, J (2017) Mogadishu truck bomb: 500 casualties in Somalia's worst terrorist attack. *The Guardian*. Published 16 October 2017. Available at: https://www.theguardian.com/world/2017/oct15/truck-bomb-mogadishu-kills-people-somalia

Cartalucci, T (2013). Destroying a nation-state: US-Saudi funded terrorists sowing chaos in Pakistan, *Global Reach*, Published February 2013. Available at: www.globalreach.ca/destroying-a-nation--state-us-saudi-funded-terrorists-sowing-chaos-in-pakistan/5323295

Cochi, M (2017) Terrorism Africa, *Sub-Saharan Monitor*. Published 19 May 2017. Available at: eastwest.eu/en/opinion/sub-saharan-monitor/terrorism-since-2006-attacks-in-africa-increased-by-1000

Ehrenfeld, R (2011) Their oil is thicker than our blood, *Terror Finance.org*. Available at: www.terrorfinance.org/the-terror-finance-blog/2011/12/their-oil-is-thicker-than-our-blood.html

El Fadl, KA (2005) *The Great Theft: Wrestling Islam from the extremists*. New York: Harper Collins.

Freedom House (2013) *Freedom in the World 2013: Democratic breakthroughs in the balance*. Available at: www.freedomhouse.org/report/freedomworld/freedom-world-2013

Fund for Peace (2013) *2013 Failed States Index*. Available at: http://ffp.statesindex.org

Ghorbani, A, Assoulin, Y and Al Zahrani, S (2014) *The Syrian War, Saudi Arabia's Struggle for Global Influence, and Control in Africa*. Available at: www.elombah.com/index.php/special-reports/21954-the-sytian-war-saudi-arabia-s-struggle-for-global-influence-and-control-of-Africa

Hasan, YF (1985) The Historical Roots of Afro-Arab Relations. In Khair El-Din Haseeb (ed.) *The Arabs and Africa*. London: Croom Helm and Centre for Arab Unity Studies, pp. 27–57.

Haynes, J (2005) Islamic militancy in East Africa. *Third World Quarterly* **26** (8), pp. 1321–1339.

Hoensball, M (2010) Obama's 'Intelligence Czar' plugs a new counter-terrorism catchphrase. *Newsweek*. Published 6 April. Available at: www.newsweek.com/blogs/declassified/2010/04/06/obama-s-intelligence-czar-plugs-a-new-terrorist-catchphrase.html

Huliaris, A (2001) Qadhafi's comeback: Libya and sub-Saharan Africa in the 1990s, *African Affairs* 100 (398), pp. 5–25.

International Crisis Group (2002) Somalia: Countering terrorism in a failed state. ICG Africa Report No. 45. Nairobi/Brussels: International Crisis Group.

Kagwanja, P (2006) Counter-terrorism in the Horn of Africa: New security frontiers, old strategies, *African Security Review*, **15** (3), pp. 72–86.

Kokole, OH (1984) The Islamic factor in African–Arab Relations, *Third World Quaterly*, **6** (3), pp. 687–702.

Kuru, Z and Kuru, A (2008) A political interpretation of Islam: Said Nursi's faith-based activism in comparison with political Islamism and Sufism, *Islam and Christian-Muslim Relations*, **19** (1), pp. 99–111.

Lichtblau, E and Schmitt, E (2010) Cash flow to terrorists evades US efforts, *The New York Times*. Published 5 December 2010. Available at: www. Nytimes.com/2010/12/06/world/middleeast/06wikileaks-financing.html

Looney, R (2006) The mirage of terrorist financing: The case of Islam charities, *Strategic Insights*,

5 (3), pp. 1–13.

Love, J (2010) *Hezbollah: Social services as a source of power*, JSOU Report No. 10–5. Hurlbert Field, FL: Joint Special Operations University. Available at: www.globalsecurity.org/military/library/report/2010/1006-jsou-report-10-5.pdf

Lusk, G (2008) False premise and false response to the Darfur crisis, *Peace Review*, April–June, **20** (2), pp. 166–174.

Lynch, G (2013) The politics of ethnicity. In N Cheeseman, DM Anderson and A Scheiber (eds) *Routledge Handbook of African Politics*. London: Routledge.

Makhmudov, M and Walker, LJ (2012) Islamists in Mali: Funding and ideological ratlines linking Saudi Arabia and Qatar, *Global Security News*. Published 3 July 2012. Available at: http://global-security-news.com/2012/07/03/islamists-in-mali--funding-and-ideological-ratlines-linking-saudi-arabia-and-qatar

Mandaville, P (2007) *Global Political Islam*. London: Routledge.

Manthorpe, J (2013) Saudi Arabia funding fuels jihadist terror, *Vancouver Sun*. Published 28 May 2013. Available at: www.vancouversun.com/Jonthan+Manthorpe+Saudi+Arabia+fudning+fuels+jihadist+terror/8445917/story/html#1xzz33Ypjup5

Martin, J (2005) Arab countries eye new giving guidelines: Arab and Islamic charities, which suffered in the wake of 9/11 revelations of links to extremists, have been working hard to clean up their image. But are they doing and giving enough? *The Middle East*. Published July 2005.

McCormack, D (2005) *An African Vortex: Islamism in Sub-Saharan Africa*. Occasional Paper Series No. 4. Washington, DC: The Centre for Security Policy.

Menkhaus, K (2002) Political Islam in Somalia, *Middle East Policy*, **9** (1), pp. 109–123.

Moroccan World News (2017) 300 African Ulema gather in Fez to promote values of moderate Islam. *Moroccan World News*. Published 7 December. Available at: https://www.moroccoworldnews.com/201712/235742/african-ulemas-fez-moderate-islam

Post, JM (2007) *The Mind of the Terrorist: The Psychology of Terrorism from the IRA to Al-Qaeda*. New York: Palgrave Macmillan.

Rogerson, B (2006) *The Heirs of the Prophet Muhammad and the Roots of the Sunni-Shia Schism*. London: Abacus.

Rosander, EE (1997) Introduction: The Islamization of 'Tradition' and 'Modernity'. In *African Islam and Islam in Africa: Encounters Between Sufis and Islamists*, edited by D Westerlund and EE Rosander. London: Hurst and Co, pp. 1–27.

Schanzer, J and Miller, S (2012) *Facebook Fatwa: Saudi Clerics, Wahhabi Islam and Social Media*. Washington, DC: FDD Press.

Sharawi, H (2004) Arab-African Relations: From Liberation to Globalisation. *African Renaissance* **1** (1), pp. 43–54.

Solomon, H (2012) The challenges confronting political science in the twenty-first century: A South African perspective, *Politeia: South African Journal for Political Science and Public Administration*, **31** (3).

Solomon, H (2013) *Jihad: A South African Perspective*. Bloemfontein: SUN Press.

Solomon, H (2015a) Critical terrorism studies and its implications for Africa, *Politikon: South African Journal of Political Studies*, **42** (2), pp. 219–234.

Solomon, H (2015b) *Terrorism and Counter terrorism in Africa: Fighting insurgency from Al Shabaab, Ansar Dine and Boko Haram*. London: Palgrave Macmillan.

Solomon, H (2016) *Islamic State and the Coming Global Confrontation*. London: Palgrave Pivot.

Solomon, S (2017a) Terrorism in Africa falling after reaching highs, *Voice of America*. Published 9 July 2017. Available at: https://www.voanews.com/a/africa-terrorism-deaths-falling

Solomon, H (2017b) Beyond the state: Reconceptualizing African security in the 21st century,

African Security Review, **26** (1), pp. 62–76.
Solomon, H and Liebenberg I (2000) *Consolidation of Democracy in Africa: A view from the South*. London. Ashgate Publishing.
Tamura, S (2008) Rethinking Pan-Africanism under African Union-led continental integration: Revival of Afro-Arab solidarity or clash of civilizations? *Journal of Global Change and Governance* **1** (4), pp. 1–21.
The Economist (2011) Africa's hopeful economies, *The Economist*. Published 3 December 2011. Available at: www.economist.com/node/21541008
United Nations Development Programme (2017) *Journey to Extremism in Africa: Drivers, incentives and tipping point for recruitment*. New York: United Nations.
Viorst, M (1995) Sudan's Islamic experiment, *Foreign Affairs*, **74** (3), pp. 45–58.
Westerlund, D (1997) Reaction and action: Accounting for the rise of Islamism. In D Westerlund and E Evers Rosander (eds) *African Islam and Islam in Africa: Encounters between Sufis and Islamists*. London: Hurst and Co, 308–334.
Winsor, C (2007) *Saudi Arabia, Wahhabism and the Spread of Theo-Fascism*. Available at: www.globalpolitician.com/print/asp?id=3661
Wright, L (2007) *The Looming Tower: Al-Qaeda's Road to 9/11*. London: Penguin Press.
Yoh, JGN (2001) Reflections on Afro-Arab Relations: An African perspective. A Paper Presented to the Monthly Seminar Arab Thought Forum, Amman, Jordan. Available at: http://johngaiyoh.com/pdf/Reflections%20%20Afro-Arab%20Relations.pdf
Zakariya, F (2013) After the coup: Egypt must reach out to the Islamists it is now jailing, *Time*. Published 22 July 2013.

Chapter 13

Transnational evangelical Christianity and political culture in sub-Saharan Africa

Robert A. Dowd

Evangelical Christianity, especially its more Pentecostal expressions, has been one of the more popular exports from the United States to sub-Saharan Africa. While not all evangelical churches in sub-Saharan Africa trace their roots to 'America', and even many that do are now thoroughly 'indigenised' and 'independent', there remain significant connections between several American and African evangelical communities. In fact, during the past few decades, with easier travel and communication, there is evidence that the connections have grown stronger.[1] Further, this 'American export' has done so well in Africa that Africans themselves have started to export their own versions of evangelical Christianity to various parts of the world, including the United States.[2]

We cannot help but wonder what effects, if any, sub-Saharan Africa's evangelical churches, particularly those with connections to evangelical churches and faith-based organisations (FBOs) in the United States, are having on political culture, particularly support for democratic institutions and respect for civil liberties. While there is plenty of evidence to suggest that Africa's evangelical communities, including Pentecostal churches, have become increasingly active in politics,[3] the effects of this political activity are not always and everywhere clear. Is evangelical Christianity undermining or promoting support for political rights and respect for civil liberties? Is it encouraging or discouraging national unity? Does it exacerbate or alleviate the inter-ethnic and interreligious divides that threaten peace and security within and across some of the region's countries?

In this chapter, I point to evidence from three countries – Nigeria, Uganda and Zambia – to suggest that the political activities of evangelical churches, including those connected with evangelical organisations in the United States, have encouraged support for political rights but discouraged support for some basic civil liberties. While recognising that evangelicals do not always apply their Christian faith to politics in the same way, there is evidence to suggest they have supported democracy to the extent that they have encouraged participation in democratic institutions. They have, however, undermined civil liberties to the extent that they have supported government leaders who have violated freedom of speech and association. There is also evidence to suggest that evangelicals have jeopardised fragile political stability, national integrity and regional security by engaging in activities to spread their faith that have increased tensions between Christians and Muslims. In this sense, there is evidence that evangelicals have encouraged a type of illiberal democracy, a regime characterised by a high degree of political participation and activism but a low degree of ideological and social tolerance.

In this chapter I first briefly define what I mean by evangelical Christianity, note its dramatic growth in and beyond Africa, and describe the nature of the connections between evangelical communities in the United States and sub-Saharan African countries. I go on to discuss the evangelical political agenda in sub-Saharan Africa and whether, and the extent to which, American evangelical ministers, churches and FBOs shape or influence that agenda. After exploring how that agenda is being carried out in three countries in which the evangelical presence is significant, namely Nigeria, Uganda and Zambia, I discuss possible implications for political culture and the directions that future research might take.

Evangelical Christianity and its growth in sub-Saharan Africa

While evangelical Christianity is a religious movement that cuts across various Christian churches, this chapter focuses on Protestant evangelical churches rather than evangelical, Pentecostal, or charismatic renewal movements within mainline Protestant and Roman Catholic churches. Although there are many different kinds of evangelical Christian communities, I define evangelical churches here as those with certain characteristics in common. Drawing on the insightful work of Paul Freston (2001), these characteristics include: conversionism (emphasis on a need for a change in one's own life), activism (an emphasis on efforts to convert others), biblicism (a special emphasis placed on the Bible as a guide for living and a reading of the Bible that tends to accept Biblical passages as being literally true), and crucicentrism (an emphasis on the sacrifice of Jesus on the cross).[4]

Pentecostalism is an expression of evangelical Christianity that has become increasingly popular in sub-Saharan Africa. Pentecostals generally place a special emphasis on being 'born again' and the gifts of the Holy Spirit of Christ that manifest themselves through speaking in tongues, deliverance from demons, and healing miracles.[5] Pentecostals typically forbid drinking alcohol, and many churches have started to place emphasis on material blessings, in the form of health and wealth, that accrue to those who are faithful to God and tithe or give generously to the church. The Pew Research Center (2006) estimates that the percentage of Christians who are Pentecostal in sub-Saharan Africa grew by 20 per cent between 1980 and 2009.[6] This growth has typically occurred at the expense of the mainline churches, such as the Anglican, Lutheran, Presbyterian and Roman Catholic churches.[7] Some Pentecostals are known for their poor opinion of the mainline Christian churches, which they believe have wandered from the Bible, tolerate too much sinful behaviour, and are not open to the healing power of the Holy Spirit of Christ.[8]

While many of Africa's evangelical churches, especially those more Pentecostal in orientation, have been founded by or inspired by American missionaries and preachers, it is important to note that most of these churches have become thoroughly indigenised. What are often called African-initiated churches (AICs) have sprung up throughout the region.[9] Many such churches are either loosely associated with founding churches or completely independent of them. Most 'rank-and-file' African evangelicals, particularly members of the AICs, have little direct contact with American evangelicals and it would be completely inaccurate to consider many of Africa's evangelical churches to be subsidiaries of 'mother churches' in the United States.

Nonetheless, there are a significant and growing number of transnational evangelical and Pentecostal networks that connect ministers and their churches in the United States with those in sub-Saharan Africa. In fact, thanks to greater ease of travel and advances in media and electronic communication, there is some evidence that the connections have been strengthened in recent decades. Many American evangelical churches sponsor 'mission trips' to various African countries, which provide church members with opportunities to interact with one another and build networks for sharing ideas and financial resources. A considerable number of African evangelical ministers and pastors have spent considerable time in the United States studying, attending conferences and fundraising. American-based evangelical organisations, such as the Institute on Religion and Democracy (IRD), the Association for Church Renewal (ACR), and Samaritan's Purse, have been actively internationalising their efforts, particularly in sub-Saharan Africa.[10] Further, evangelical Christian media in the United States has grown dramatically in its international reach. For example, the Christian Broadcasting Network (CBN) and the Trinity Broadcasting Network (TBN) are beamed into an increasing number of African households. Of course, television is becoming old fashioned and more recently social media platforms have become the communication tools of choice as evangelical organisations, such as the IRD, the ACR, and others seek to build transnational alliances and networks of evangelical and Pentecostal churches.

While there are studies that show that evangelical Christianity, particularly Pentecostalism, has discouraged participation in public life,[11] there is a great deal of evidence to suggest that evangelicals, including Pentecostals, have become much more politically active in various parts of the world.[12] In their book, *Global Pentecostalism: The new face of Christian social engagement* (2007), Miller and Yamamori describe how Pentecostal religious involvement has actually encouraged civic engagement in many parts of the world, including sub-Saharan Africa. Marshall (2009) and others have noted that many of Nigeria's Pentecostals have become thoroughly immersed in and engaged with local, state and federal politics.[13]

The growth of evangelical Christianity, the increase in transnational connections, and the rise in evangelical political activism, raises important questions: (1) What are the objectives of this evangelical political activism in sub-Saharan Africa, and to what extent are these objectives influenced by evangelicals in the United States? (2) What are the effects of this political activism on support for democracy, respect for civil liberties, and the prospects for inter-ethnic and interreligious harmony in the region?

American evangelicals and the evangelical political agenda in sub-Saharan Africa

While it is important to recognise that not all evangelicals apply their religious faith to politics in the same way and that there is no single evangelical political agenda, there is evidence to suggest that there has been an attempt to build an evangelical political agenda in sub-Saharan Africa.[14] While it would be inaccurate to suggest that American evangelicals have created a political agenda that they have imposed on African evangelicals, there is evidence to suggest evangelical ministers, churches and FBOs in the United States have helped shape and have bolstered a political agenda in significant ways. That agenda has focused largely on promoting greater respect for religious freedom and a particular version of evangelical Christian morality in political culture and law. This raises important questions: what do evangelical Christians mean by 'religious freedom' and what are the threats to religious freedom that must be confronted? Further, what does a political culture shaped by evangelical Christianity look like to these evangelicals and to what extent is it conducive to liberal democracy, good interreligious relations, peace and security?

It is important to note that evangelicals are not the only Christians concerned about the state of religious freedom in the world. Many Christians, including Roman Catholics and mainline Protestants, have become understandably concerned about the persecution of Christians.[15] Many agree that the two major threats to religious freedom in the early decades of the 21st century are (1) violent Islamic extremism and (2) 'Western liberal-secular ideology' that seeks to marginalise religion and prevent people from allowing the faith to influence public life.[16] Nonetheless, Christians do not all agree on how best to address these perceived threats. Most Roman Catholic and mainline Protestant leaders, and many evangelical leaders, have stressed the importance of good interreligious relations and dialogue as the best way to check politically aggressive Islam and promote religious freedom in the long run.[17] Some evangelical leaders, however, take a different approach and have called on their followers to counter politically aggressive Islam and Western secular ideology by promoting politically aggressive Christianity and seeking to get government leaders to proclaim their countries to be 'Christian nations'.[18] American evangelicals are especially concerned that Christianity and Christian values are under attack worldwide. Some have encouraged and supported those evangelicals who call for a more politically assertive Christianity. In the view of some observers, they have taken the American 'culture wars', focused as they have been on issues like abortion and gay rights, to other parts of the world.[19] In Africa, these evangelicals claim not only to be promoting Christian values but also African values. They argue that they are seeking to defend African traditional values, conducive as they are with Christian values, from secular-liberal ideology that Western governments, intergovernmental organisations (especially the United Nations and the European Union), and non-governmental organisations seek to impose.[20] These transnational evangelical efforts to promote a certain version of Christian values have appeared to gain considerable traction in Africa, where the evangelical Christian population is significant and many political leaders are only too happy to embrace critiques of Western institutions, since such critiques promise to bolster their efforts to curtail civil liberties and concentrate their power.

In African countries with large evangelical populations, such as Nigeria, Uganda and Zambia, evangelical Christians have become increasingly active in politics. They have also become increasingly influential and have shaped political discourse in many ways. In all three countries, American evangelical ministers, churches and FBOs have been connected with local evangelical communities. American evangelical media outlets have been very popular. While it is difficult to establish whether, and the extent to which, American evangelicals have helped shape and support the political agenda of local evangelicals in these three countries, there is good reason to think their efforts have not been without consequence.

Nigeria

Perhaps nowhere in sub-Saharan Africa have evangelical Christians been more concerned about the threat of politically aggressive Islam than in Nigeria, a country with a population of more than 170 million people, which is roughly

50 per cent Christian and 50 per cent Muslim.[21] This concern is understandable. In 1986, the federal government decided to leave it up to the states as to whether Sharia, Islamic religious law, should be constitutionally enshrined.[22] By the end of the 1990s, Sharia had been enshrined in 12 predominantly Muslim northern states. In 1986, the Nigerian government revealed that it had joined the Organization of the Islamic Conference [OIC].[23] Although most observers of Nigerian society and politics have noted that ethnic differences were more disruptive than religious differences during the decade or two after independence,[24] many suggest that religious differences, which often overlap with ethnic differences, have become more politically significant and destabilising since the early 1980s.[25] Nigeria is widely known as a place where Christianity and Islam have met and clashed. Usman (1987) notes that Nigerian politicians have increasingly attempted to manipulate religious differences to their advantage.[26] Falola (1998) suggests that religious dominance has become the major issue in Nigeria's politics, with proponents of Christianity and Islam seeking to impose their own values and to control the state.[27] Christian versus Muslim violence of the 1980s and 1990s claimed thousands of lives.[28] Inter-communal violence along religious lines has been sporadic since then. Between the years 2000 and 2010, Boko Haram (translated as 'Western education is a sin') emerged and became a threat to Christians and a menace to most Muslims. The Islamist group rejected Western influence and promoted the integration of Islamic religious authority and the state. Boko Haram is thought to be responsible for as many as 13 000 deaths since the insurgency began in Borno State in northeastern Nigeria, with more than 6 000 of these deaths occurring in 2014 alone, which is more than the deaths attributed to Islamic State of Iraq and Syria (ISIS) in the same year.[29] The Christian community in Nigeria is diverse and the country's Christians have not always agreed on how best to respond to the threat they all seem to recognise in politically aggressive Islam. While many of Nigeria's Christian leaders have indicated that any effective response to politically aggressive Islam must include interreligious mediation and cooperation to promote mutual respect at the grassroots, others have seemed less than enthusiastic about reaching out to Muslims. While the differences do not break down perfectly along denominational lines, most of the sceptics of interreligious dialogue tend to be evangelical Christians.[30] The differences in opinion are not just about what would be most effective in ending the violence and persecution perpetrated by groups like Boko Haram; they also seem to be about how Christians called to evangelise should relate to Muslims and people of different religions. In other words, they seem to concern different theologies of evangelisation, some of which leave little room to respect religious differences. Whereas most mainline Christian churches

in Nigeria respect the religious identity of Muslims and have not mounted efforts to convert them,[31] some evangelical Christian leaders have ascribed to a theology of evangelisation that calls for the conversion of all, including Muslims, to Christianity.[32] This has made cooperation with Muslim leaders very difficult, if not totally impossible, for many evangelical leaders.

The Christian Association of Nigeria (CAN) is a multi-denominational organisation formed by Christian churches in 1976 to develop greater Christian unity and promote the influence of Christianity in the public realm. Founded by mainline Protestant and Catholic churches, CAN has become much more diverse in make-up and evangelical churches, particularly those with a Pentecostal orientation, have become increasingly powerful members of the organisation.[33] Once a bastion of inter-denominational cooperation and a vehicle for Christian unity in the face of common concerns, CAN has become divided over how best to respond to the challenge of politically aggressive Islam. Increasingly powerful evangelical and Pentecostal leaders have disagreed with mainline Christian leaders, especially Roman Catholic leaders, as to how best to address the challenge. For example, one of the complaints lodged by some of CAN's evangelical members against Cardinal John Onaiyekan, the Catholic Archbishop of Abuja and President of CAN from 2007 to 2010, was that he was soft on Islam. With the help of evangelical members of the association, Pentecostal pastor Ayo Oritsejafor garnered more votes than Archbishop Onaiyekan to win the CAN presidency in 2010. As leader of the Word of Life Bible Church and President of the Pentecostal Fellowship of Nigeria [PFN], with his own television programme (Hour of Deliverance), Pastor Oritsejafor has a huge following across Nigeria. According to many observers, Oritsejafor took control of CAN by appealing to the large numbers of evangelicals, particularly Pentecostals, who thought Onaiyekan was overly compromising in his approach to Muslims and not dedicated enough to making Nigeria a Christian country.[34] Some American evangelicals and FBOs have encouraged and supported the more aggressive approach to the threat posed by political Islam that some of Nigeria's evangelical leaders have adopted.[35] They have joined Nigerian evangelicals in implying that Nigeria's mainline Christian leaders are naïve appeasers or enablers of politically aggressive Islam.[36] In this sense, they have fuelled the divisions that have emerged within CAN. Through television broadcasts, social-media campaigns and preaching at religious revivals, the message that many American evangelicals have sent is that Islam, the religion itself, is the problem that Christians in Nigeria must confront. They have implied, or openly stated, that Islam as a religion is by nature aggressive and violent.[37] Therefore, the only way for Nigeria to be at peace is to check the growth of Islam by more actively and unapologetically promoting the spread of Christianity, even among Muslims, and to elect Christian leaders to public office.[38] The approach to halting the spread of politically aggressive Islam that Nigerian evangelicals have taken is a totalitarian one; one that seeks control over political institutions. Marshall (2009) quotes one Pentecostal pastor as saying, 'If we don't take active part by helping them choose the right person [to be governor or president] you will see that it is the enemy coming to rule us again.'[39] And another, 'If we do what God wants us to do, if we can get at least 80 per cent of the people of Nigeria born again [ie, evangelical Christian], you can be sure a Christian will be president'.[40]

When it comes to countering the perceived threat posed by Western secular-liberal values, many of Nigeria's evangelicals focus on different issues or take a different approach than many of Nigeria's mainline Christian leaders. While many of Nigeria's Roman Catholic and mainline Protestant leaders are as concerned as evangelical leaders about the prospects of homosexuality becoming more socially acceptable and abortion legally acceptable, the Roman Catholic and mainline churches have tended to also focus on other challenges they see as related to the spread of Western secular-liberal values, such as materialism and individualism.[41] A significant segment of Nigeria's evangelical leaders have focused their efforts on promoting the passage of legislation that has reinforced the criminalisation of homosexuality and increased the severity of punishment for homosexual acts.[42]

Some American evangelicals and FBOs have implicitly or explicitly encouraged and supported efforts to resist 'Western secular-liberal' values and make Nigeria a 'Christian nation', as they have in Zambia and other countries of the region.[43] There are American evangelical ministers, churches and FBOs that have played an especially important role in promoting support for legislation for harsher penalties for those caught in homosexual activities.[44] Pat Robertson is an example of one such American evangelical preacher who focused on the challenge homosexuality posed to traditional Christian marriage. Using CBN, which was reportedly watched by over 74 million people in Nigeria,[45] Robertson explicitly used television broadcasts to support the passage of the 'anti-gay Bill' which President Goodluck Jonathan, himself an evangelical Christian, signed into law in 2014.[46] The Same Sex Marriage Prohibition Act criminalised homosexuality and '*homosexual* clubs', associations and organisations, with penalties of up to 14 years in jail.[47] While there is good reason to expect that such a Bill would have passed even without support from American evangelicals, many have argued that such legislation would never have been introduced in the first place, in Nigeria and elsewhere in Africa, without their encouragement.[48] Whereas homosexuality has generally not been socially acceptable in Nigeria, as well as in many other African societies, observers claim that it was never, even before colonial times, considered an issue worthy of public debate or one that would require legislation to ensure its criminalisation.[49] In sum, there is reason for concern as to how some expressions of evangelical Christianity may be affecting political culture in Nigeria, and the role that some American evangelical ministers, churches and organisations have played in stoking fears and exacerbating societal divisions in the country. Some of Nigeria's evangelical Christians have refused to temper their zeal to convert others, including Muslims, to their version of Christianity. Many have also refused to countenance interreligious dialogue as a way to greater peace and security, and have publicly stated that they intend to make Nigeria (or at least part of Nigeria) a 'Christian nation', where Christian values are enshrined not only in the hearts of Christians, but also in the law.[50] It is clear that these stances, in a religiously plural country like Nigeria, which has as many (if not more) Muslims as Christians, is problematic to say the least. They diminish the prospects for good interreligious relations and respect for civil liberties. While it is difficult to know what effect American evangelicals have had on these efforts, there is reason to think it has been significant. Directly and indirectly, some American evangelicals have, at the very least, encouraged and supported efforts to politically mobilise Nigerian evangelicals to fight a culture war in ways that may make predictions of such a war a self-fulfilling prophecy – feeding directly into a narrative promoted by the country's Islamist movements. Such a culture war would be severely destabilising both in and beyond Nigeria.

Uganda

In predominantly Christian Uganda, where, unlike in Nigeria, the Muslim population is relatively small, evangelicals have been less focused on the threat presented by politically aggressive Islam than on the perceived threat posed by Western secular-liberal values.[51] As Uganda's mainline Christian leaders have distanced themselves from the increasingly authoritarian tendencies of President Yoweri Museveni, many of the country's evangelical leaders have remained openly supportive of the president. As in Nigeria, Uganda's evangelical Christian groups have been at the forefront of efforts to reinforce laws that criminalise homosexuality and Bills that introduce more stringent penalties, including the death sentence, for those caught in homosexual activities. In Uganda, as in Nigeria, there is evidence to suggest that American evangelicals, with significant influence over members of Uganda's Parliament who are evangelicals, have initiated the movement to focus attention on the threat posed by Western liberal-secular values, as epitomised by greater acceptance of homosexuality. It is also thought that many prominent American evangelicals have implicitly encouraged support for President Museveni's stay in office, despite his authoritarian tendencies. This is largely because he appears open to promoting much of their evangelical political agenda.

Christians make up at least 80 per cent of Uganda's population of 37 million. Although Muslims represent a sizeable minority in Uganda, and were estimated to make up 12 per cent of the population in 2000, Islamic movements are thought to have played a negligible role in the country's politics since the fall of Idi Amin in 1979.[52] Although two Christian churches, the Roman Catholic and the Church of Uganda (part of the Anglican communion), have dominated the religious landscape, Uganda has grown in intra-Christian diversity since 1986, when President Museveni opened the country to other Christian groups. In 2000, about 41 per cent of Uganda's population was Roman Catholic and 39 per cent belonged to the Church of Uganda.[53] The religious demographics have almost certainly changed since 2000 and there is good reason to think that evangelical churches, especially Pentecostal or born-again churches, have grown largely at the expense of the Roman Catholic Church and the Church of Uganda. Exact figures are hard to come by, and often Pentecostals are lumped together with members of charismatic movements that exist within the Catholic and mainline Protestant churches. According to the World Christian Database (2002), as of 2000, 20 per cent of Ugandans were either Pentecostal or charismatic.

While religion has not always been a stabilising or liberalising force in Uganda, in recent decades the country's major Christian churches are thought to have contributed mostly positively to efforts to promote a political culture conducive to liberal democracy. However, the growth of assertive Pentecostal Christianity, which seeks to convert Muslims, threatens to weaken already weak Christian–Muslim relations in Uganda. While not nearly as contentious or violence-prone as in Nigeria, Christian–Muslim relations in Uganda can be described as painfully polite.

While initially supportive of President Museveni, who came to power in 1985, Uganda's major Christian churches have become more openly critical of him and more outspoken about their concern that he intends to remain in power indefinitely. Mainline Christian leaders have spoken out through organisations such as the Uganda Joint Christian Council (UJCC), which includes representatives from the Church of Uganda, the Roman Catholic Church and the much smaller Orthodox Church. They have also spoken out through the Inter-Religious Council of Uganda (IRCU), which includes Christian and Muslim religious leaders. The Roman Catholic Church, the Church of Uganda, the Seventh Day Adventist Church, the Orthodox Church and the Uganda Muslim Supreme Council are members of the IRCU. It is important to note that some evangelical churches are also part of the IRCU.

Through the UJCC and the IRCU, and as individuals, leaders of both the Catholic Church and the Church of Uganda called for an end to the 'no-party' or 'movement system' and the return to multiparty politics. In 2007, Museveni did act to reinstate political parties. However, that same year he also managed to convince Uganda's Parliament to amend the Constitution to remove presidential-term limits. Protestant and Catholic religious leaders came out strongly against this amendment to Uganda's Constitution. Emmanuel Cardinal Wamala, then Catholic Archbishop of Kampala, openly criticised this move by Museveni and Parliament.[54] Since then, Archbishop Luke Orombi of the Church of Uganda and the Catholic Archbishop Cyprian Lwanga have called for the reintroduction of presidential-term limits.[55] These religious leaders have also accused Museveni of violating freedom of speech when he closed down radio stations and newspapers for publishing stories critical of his rule.[56]

Even as mainline Christian leaders have grown critical of Museveni, many Ugandan evangelical Christian leaders have jumped to his defence as someone whose leadership is necessary to maintain stability and security and as someone willing to protect religious freedom and promote their version of Christian values in public life.[57] It would seem that many of Uganda's evangelical leaders have sensed an opportunity to strengthen the political influence they and their churches enjoy by stepping into the vacuum of support left by mainline Christian churches.[58] Museveni stands to benefit from their endorsement because Uganda's evangelical leaders have grown increasingly influential in their own right due to the dramatic growth in their membership, largely at the expense of the mainline churches.

Evangelicals have been at the forefront of efforts to defend 'Christian' and 'African' family values and promote the so-called 'anti-gay' legislation, first introduced in the Ugandan Parliament in 2009.[59] Ugandan evangelical pastor Steve Langa has conducted anti-gay workshops and has claimed that the international gay movement aimed to recruit children.[60] Pastor Martin Ssempa, in a letter to Human Rights Watch, indicated that its agenda to protect the rights of homosexuals conflicted with Uganda's strong family values.[61]

Many observers have noted that prominent American evangelicals were extremely supportive of MP David Bahati's efforts in 2009 to promote the draft and the passage of legislation that would increase the severity of penalties for homosexual acts.[62] There is evidence that a broad network of evangelical organisations called the Fellowship, largely made up of American evangelicals, have been active in efforts to encourage support for this Bill in Uganda. Pastors like Ssempa have close ties with American Pastor Rick Warren.[63] American evangelicals have also influenced Steve Langa's anti-gay workshops, which featured their writings.[64] They have also spoken at church rallies, where they have promoted the idea that because homosexuality is a choice that goes against God and nature, it is not a human-rights issue. While it is difficult to establish a causal relationship, this rhetoric certainly did little to decrease the likelihood of violence. In the Kampala area there was a significant spike in violence against gay and lesbian people, and those thought to be gay and lesbian. A prominent Ugandan gay activist, David Kato, was killed in 2011.[65]

There is evidence to suggest that some American evangelicals consider Museveni to be an important ally in their transnational efforts to promote their version of Christian values.[66] Recently they have seemed to turn a blind eye to the president's violation of free speech by closing down radio stations and newspapers for publishing stories critical of his rule. There is reason to think that Museveni has established these close relationships with fast-growing Pentecostal churches, in the hope that they might check the influence of mainline, particularly Anglican and Catholic, churches, which have grown more critical of his rule.

To conclude, the growth of Uganda's evangelical and Pentecostal population has been followed by an increase in the political clout of evangelical leaders, many of whom have strong connections to American evangelical ministers, churches and FBOs. This political influence has been used to encourage Uganda's evangelical religious and governmental leaders to defend Uganda against the perceived threat of Western secular-liberal values. Those in power, particularly but not only Museveni, are only too willing to cooperate since this plays into their efforts to dismiss calls for a greater respect for civil liberties – including freedom of speech and association – as an attempt to impose Western secular-liberal values on Uganda. To the extent that this is the case, some of these evangelical and Pentecostal churches, with the support of American evangelicals and Pentecostals, are impeding more transparent, open and accountable government in Uganda. By condoning the ways in which Museveni has curtailed basic freedoms and refused to build more democratic institutions, they may also be increasing the likelihood that Museveni's rule will end with a power vacuum and Uganda's next political transition will be a destabilising one.

Zambia

Of the three countries examined in this chapter, Zambia is the one in which evangelical Christianity has arguably had the most discernable impact on politics and political discourse. In the predominantly Christian country of 16 million people, where it is estimated that almost half the population is evangelical Christian,[67] evangelical Christianity has featured prominently in political discourse since the reintroduction of multiparty democracy in 1991.[68] Frederick Chiluba, Zambia's first president of the new multiparty era, openly campaigned for president as a born-again Christian. On his election in 1991, Chiluba declared Zambia a 'Christian nation'.[69] Since then, there has been a raging debate about the place of Christian values in public life, with considerable implications for the deepening of democratic institutions and a greater respect for political rights and civil liberties. While this debate has been dominated by Zambian Christians of various denominations, some American evangelicals have also sought to influence it. They have implicitly or explicitly endorsed politicians who support laws that reflect their version of 'Christian values'. As in Uganda, political leaders in Zambia have been happy to embrace critiques of Western institutions, as offered by evangelical Christians, since these promise to bolster their efforts to curtail civil liberties and concentrate their power.[70] It is estimated that Christians make up at least 85 per cent of Zambia's population. Most of the non-Christian population follows traditional religions, with Muslims making up about 2 per cent of the population.[71] As in Nigeria and Uganda, the Christian population is diverse, but the proportion of evangelicals is significantly higher in Zambia than in the other two countries, making the Christian community in Zambia extremely diverse. Evangelical Christians belong to a variety of churches and a large number of Pentecostal churches compete with one another for adherents and for influence.[72]

Despite the diversity and the competition within Christianity, Zambia's Christians have been more highly organised than those in Nigeria and Uganda. Christian organisations have at times worked together across denominations to exert considerable political influence. The most influential of these has been the Evangelical Fellowship of Zambia (EFZ). Its counterparts include the Christian Council of Zambia (CCZ), made up of mainline Protestant churches such as the Anglican Church and the United Church of Zambia, and the Zambian Episcopal Conference (ZEC) comprising the country's Catholic bishops.

By most accounts, the three major Christian organisations, the EFZ, the CCZ and the ZEC, worked together effectively to promote greater respect for political rights and civil liberties in the late 1980s and early 1990s. They implicitly or explicitly endorsed the Movement for Multiparty Democracy (MMD) and its candidate, Frederick Chiluba, who won the presidency in 1991.[73] Chiluba, a trade-union leader and self-described born-again Christian, openly spoke of his intention to renew the country's political, social and economic institutions through Christian values.[74]

Ironically, Christian unity on political matters weakened after Chiluba publicly declared Zambia to be a 'Christian nation' in 1991. Some evangelical

Christian leaders, particularly more Pentecostal-oriented ones, were more supportive of such a declaration than mainstream Christian leaders.[75] Leaders of the Roman Catholic and Anglican churches expressed concern about this declaration and its implications for interreligious and interdenominational relations.[76] There is good reason to think that leaders of mainline churches opposed this declaration because they perceived it to imply that evangelical Christianity would have a privileged place in Chiluba's government and that he would seek to use the state to spread this version of Christianity.[77] The rift between Chiluba and some evangelical/Pentecostal churches, on the one side, and the mainline churches, on the other, widened even further as Chiluba successfully enshrined the 'Christian nation' declaration in Zambia's Constitution in 1996.[78]

Although not all agree, evangelicals, especially Pentecostals, have been among the most openly supportive of the Christian-nation declaration. Pastor Nevers Mumba, president of Victory Ministries International, enjoyed nationwide prominence through televised church services and rallies, which he used to support Chiluba and promote the special status of Christianity in the Constitution.[79] As Gifford (1998) and Phiri (2008) have noted, many other Zambian Pentecostal leaders followed suit.

In an apparent effort to bolster his waning political support in the midst of a declining economy and growing opposition from Zambian Christian leaders across the denominational divide, Chiluba invited American evangelical preachers to Zambia who, in the course of their rallies, explicitly or implicitly endorsed him.[80] Ernest Angely, Benny Hinn and Richard Roberts of Oral Roberts Ministries were among these invited American evangelicals who endorsed him or gave him a speaking platform.[81] At the same time, many Zambian Christian leaders turned against Chiluba because of his efforts to concentrate his hold on power, curtail freedom of speech and association, and amend the Constitution to allow for a third term in office.[82]

Despite his endorsement by some evangelical Christian leaders within and beyond Zambia's borders, his efforts to amend the Constitution to allow for a third term in office were thwarted. There is reason to think that the Christian organisations, which had been instrumental in Chiluba's election to the presidency, namely the EFZ, CCZ and the ZEC, were now instrumental in efforts to prevent him from continuing in the presidency.[83] Mumba, a popular Pentecostal media personality, who had been one of Chiluba's greatest supporters, voiced his opposition to Chiluba on the grounds that he had tarnished the idea of the 'Christian nation' by not living up to its ideals.

Because the idea of Zambia as a Christian nation is ill-defined, it has engendered much debate among Christians, which continues to this day.

What does it mean that Christianity has been declared the official religion of Zambia? Does it mean that all laws are to be based on Christian morality? Is this appropriate in a country that aspires to respect equality before the law of all Zambians, regardless of religious affiliation? There has been considerable disagreement between and within Christian denominations, with some evangelical and Pentecostal Christians taking relatively extreme positions.

For some Christian leaders, Zambia can be a Christian nation only if it promotes Christian morality in culture and law. As in Nigeria and Uganda, some Christian leaders, particularly evangelicals and Pentecostals, emphasise the importance of promoting and enforcing laws that punish what they consider to be deviant behaviour, especially homosexuality.[84] Other Christian leaders, particularly those represented by the CCZ, ZEC and the EFZ, emphasise the importance of promoting a culture and laws conducive to social justice.[85] Nonetheless, it is important to note that the CCZ and the EFZ have both issued statements opposing calls to liberalise Zambia's laws on homosexuality and have encouraged Zambia's government to resist Western pressure to recognise gay rights.[86]

While it is important to recognise that, as in the case of Nigeria and Uganda, it is difficult to know how much influence American evangelical ministers, churches and FBOs have had on efforts to define what it means for Zambia to be a Christian nation, some have weighed in on the matter. American evangelicals like Scott Lively and organisations such as the Association for Church Renewal and the Institute on Religion and Democracy have joined Zambian evangelicals in their battle to defend Zambia against efforts to promote gay rights.[87] In so doing, they have argued that they are not only defending Christian values, but also traditional African values, against the godless agenda of Western liberal institutions such as the UN, EU and the World Bank.[88]

Besides the chilling effects these efforts may have on the well-being of individuals and their basic human rights, they play into the hands of politicians who wish to concentrate their power by labelling all efforts to promote greater respect for civil liberties as foreign meddling by a godless West. Just as Chiluba sought to appeal to his evangelical base to concentrate his power, subsequent Zambian political leaders have sought to gain, maintain or concentrate their power by endorsing the more extreme positions taken by some Zambian churches.[89] President Ruphia Banda noted that Zambians should blame the Western donor community for homosexuality. 'Some sections of the donor community had embarked on a campaign aimed at making Zambians believe that homosexuality was a human-rights issue,' Banda said.[90] In early 2011, some politicians challenged the late leader of the Patriotic Front, Michael Sata, as being pro-gay and, therefore, unfit to govern a Christian nation.[91] While such efforts were ultimately unsuccessful and Sata won the presidency, the question remains, will they be successful in the long run in altering Zambia's political discourse? How will their efforts affect political culture and the prospects for greater respect for political rights and civil liberties in Zambia? Future research is necessary to address these questions.

Discussion

What does a comparison of the three countries reveal about an evangelical political agenda, the extent to which it is shaped and supported by American Evangelicals, and the effects of this political agenda on political culture? First of all, it is important to note that evangelical Christianity is diverse and there is no single evangelical political agenda.[92] Nonetheless, there is plenty of evidence that some American evangelicals have been using their transnational networks to promote and support a political agenda in various parts of Africa. In Nigeria, that agenda has largely focused on promoting religious freedom through countering politically aggressive Islam with politically aggressive Christianity. In Zambia and Uganda, that agenda has focused largely on countering the threat posed by Western secular-liberal ideology through promoting tough new laws that keep homosexual acts illegal and harsher penalties for violation of such laws.

While we do not have direct evidence of the impact of the efforts of some evangelical Christians to affect the political actions and attitudes in these three countries, there is reason to expect that such efforts have been consequential. There is reason to think that they have strengthened democratic institutions, particularly electoral institutions, by encouraging participation in them. However, there is evidence to suggest that they have undermined respect for civil liberties by promoting support for draconian laws regarding homosexuality and endorsing governmental leaders because of their support for such legislation, despite the fact that these leaders have violated freedom of speech and association.

In a sense, it seems as if some evangelical Christians across all three countries featured in this chapter, supported by some American evangelicals, are encouraging a type of illiberal democracy.[93] By this, I mean a regime that is characterised by a high degree of political participation and activism but a low degree of ideological and social tolerance. In an illiberal democracy, the rights of minorities are called into question and often violated by the will of the majority. Minorities of various kinds become scapegoats for governments interested in deflecting criticism for persisting or worsening economic or social problems. In illiberal democracies, governments may allow, condone or encourage violence against minorities and those who do not conform to the cultural expectations of the majority. In a sense, it is reasonable to expect illiberal democracy and nationalism to go together.[94] There is a long history of association between religious institutions and nationalism, particularly in Europe, but also in south Asia (India, Pakistan and Bangladesh). In India, the Bharatiya Janata Party (BJP), formerly a fringe party, gained electoral traction by equating Hindu and Indian identity and stoking fears among the Hindu majority about the growth of non-Hindu minorities.[95] In some countries, including those featured in this chapter, there is reason to be concerned that some evangelical Christians are attempting to construct an exclusive form of cultural nationalism that may lead to violence against cultural or religious minorities and anyone who speaks out to criticise governments that privilege their religious institutions and beliefs.

Nonetheless, there is variation to explain. First of all, evangelicals are not always promoting the illiberal agenda I describe in this chapter. Thus, research is needed to understand where and why we find evangelicals seeking to further the illiberal political agenda and stoking the kind of cultural nationalism I describe here. In this regard, there is variation across countries and within countries that begs explanation. Secondly, it appears that the evangelical political agenda I describe is not gaining popular traction everywhere, even where evangelicals are seeking to promote it. Grossman (2015) points to evidence from across Africa to suggest that the salience or the attractiveness of the evangelical agenda described here depends in large part on the proportion of the population that is evangelical/Pentecostal, the degree of popular legitimacy of those in public office and the level of political competition in the country. Grossman finds that the illiberal evangelical political agenda is more salient in countries with a high percentage of evangelicals, where governments have a low or decreasing degree of popular legitimacy and there is a high level of political competition. This is supported by the examination of the three countries featured in this chapter, where governmental leaders seem to have sought to boost their legitimacy by claiming to be champions of the evangelical cause.

Because there is a great deal of variation within and between countries, further study might fruitfully focus on discerning any relationship between social conditions, such as changes in religious demography, and the political content of evangelical preaching. While there have been some studies on the content of preaching, they have often been limited to one country or one religious tradition and have not attempted to systematically relate the changes in local environment to differences in preaching content.[96] Although some studies have looked at the impact of preaching with political content, few have attempted to explain the variation in the content in the first place. Those that have done so have focused on differences between denominations rather than differences in the environment. In other words, there has been little focus on the variation we find among evangelicals and Pentecostals themselves, which may be explained by studying differences in social, economic, political and religious conditions across settings, or changes in these conditions across time in the same setting.

Conclusion

In this chapter, I have pointed to evidence from three countries to suggest that, while there is no single evangelical political agenda in Africa, there is a transnational network of evangelicals that are seeking to further a political agenda. There is reason to believe that this agenda, in some ways, is having a chilling effect on interreligious relations, basic human rights and respect for civil liberties. Nonetheless, Christians, including evangelicals, may apply religious ideas to politics in various ways with varying degrees of effectiveness. We have more work to do before we can say that we understand and can explain this variation. Assuming that religion, including evangelical Christianity, will continue to be an immensely powerful social force in Africa and many other parts of the world, we would do well to redouble our efforts to identify and foster social conditions that increase the likelihood of it being applied in ways that encourage the social tolerance necessary for peace and human flourishing.

Endnotes

1 See: Haynes, J (2012) *Religious Transnational Actors and Soft Power*. Aldershot: Ashgate Publishing; Oliver, M (2013) Transnational sex politics, conservative Christianity, and political activism in Uganda, *Studies in Social Justice*, **7** (1), pp. 83–105; Banchoff, T (2007) *Democracy and the New Religious Pluralism*. New York: Oxford University Press.
2 Micklethwait, J and Wooldridge, A (2010) *God is Back: How the global revival of faith is changing the world*. New York: Penguin Books.
3 Marshall, R (2009) *Political Spiritualities: The Pentecostal revolution in Nigeria*. Chicago, IL: University of Chicago Press.
4 Freston, P (2001) *Evangelicals and Politics in Asia, Africa and Latin America*. Cambridge: Cambridge University Press.
5 Pew Research Center (2006) *Spirit and Power: A 10-country study of Pentecostals*. Washington, DC: Pew Forum on Religion and Public Life.
6 Ibid. See also: Yong, A (2010) *In the Days of Caesar: Pentecostalism and political theology*. Grand Rapids, MI: WB Eerdmans Publishing Company.
7 Ibid.
8 In the book *To the Ends of the Earth: Pentecostalism and the transformation of world Christianity* (Oxford University Press, 2013), Allan Heaton Anderson does an excellent job of synthesising the most plausible explanations for the growth in Pentecostal Christianity in the world since the early 20th century.
9 Haynes (2012).
10 Hayes (2009); Kaoma, KJ (2012) *Colonizing African Values: How the US Christian right is transforming sexual politics in Africa*. Somerville, MA: Political Research Associates.
11 Steigenga, T (2001) *Politics of the Spirit: The political implications of Pentecostalized religion in*

Costa Rica and Guatemala. New York: Lexington Books; Marshall (2009).

12 Some theorists have argued that Pentecostalism, in particular, encourages people to spiritualise social and political problems and to blame them on personal sin rather than on political institutions or bad governance. Corruption may be seen as a problem but, according to some Pentecostals, it is not a problem that can be tackled by political activism. Pentecostals are thought to believe that society's problems are due to personal immorality and evil that can only be addressed spiritually. Energy focused on politics is misplaced. Born-again Christians, as Pentecostals often call themselves, simply focus on living out their Christian lives according to Biblical directives until Christ comes again and brings an end to the evil in the world as only He can do. See: Yong (2010).

13 Falola, T (1998) *Violence in Nigeria: The crisis of religious politics and secular ideologies*. Rochester, NY: University of Rochester Press.

14 Kaoma (2012); Haynes (2012); Oliver (2013).

15 Philpott, D and Shah T (eds) (2018) *Under Caesar's Sword: How Christians respond to persecution*. New York: Cambridge University Press.

16 Buss, D and Herman D (2003) *Globalizing Family Values: The Christian right in international politics*. Minneapolis, MN: University of Minnesota Press.

17 Dowd, RA (2017) Understanding how Christians respond to religious persecution: Evidence from Kenya and Nigeria, *The Review of Faith and International Affairs*, **15** (1), pp. 31–42.

18 Gifford, P (1998) *African Christianity: Its public role*. Bloomington, IN: Indiana University Press.

19 Koama (2012); Hayes (2012); Ranger, TO (2008) Introduction: Evangelical Christianity and democracy in Africa. In TO Ranger (ed) *Evangelical Christianity and Democracy in Africa*. New York: Oxford University Press.

20 Koama (2012); Van Klinken, AS (2014) Homosexuality, politics and Pentecostal nationalism in Zambia, *Studies in World Christianity*, **20** (3), pp. 259–281.

21 Although we lack official census figures on the percentages of Muslims and Christians that make up Nigeria's population, since questions on religion have not appeared on Nigeria's census since the 1980s (Paden, 2005), it is clear that Nigeria is a country that is roughly half Christian and half Muslim. As of the mid-1990s, Barrett (2001) estimate that approximately 45 per cent of Nigeria's population professed Christianity and 43 per cent professed Islam. Other estimates put the percentage of Muslims closer to 50 per cent and of Christians closer to 40 per cent.

22 Ahanotu, AM (1992) *Religion, State and Society in Contemporary Africa: Nigeria, Sudan, South Africa and Zaire*. Berkeley and Palo Alto, CA: Joint Center for African Studies pp 24–25.

23 Kukah, M (1995) Christians and Nigeria's aborted transition. In P Gifford (ed) *Christian Churches and the Democratization of Africa*. Leiden, Netherlands: EJ Brill, p. 227.

24 Mention here might be made of the Biafran War (1967–1970), in which southeastern provinces attempted to secede from Nigeria.

25 See: Paden, JN (2005) *Muslim Civic Cultures and Conflict Resolution: The challenge of democratic federalism in Nigeria*. Washington, DC: Brookings Institution Press; Falola, T (1998) *Violence in Nigeria: The crisis of religious politics and secular ideologies*. Rochester, NY: University of Rochester Press; Quinn, C and Quinn, F (2003) *Pride, Faith and Fear: Islam in sub-Saharan Africa*. Chicago, IL: University of Chicago Press; Usman, YB (1987) *The Manipulation of Religion in Nigeria 1977–1987*. Kaduna, Nigeria: Vanguard Printers and Publishers; Falola (1998).

26 Usman (1987), p. 31.

27 Falola (1998), p. 2.

28 Quinn & Quinn (2003); Paden (2005).

29 Institute for Economics and Peace (2016) *Global Terrorism Index, 2016*. Available at: http://economicsandpeace.org/reports/
30 Dowd (2017).
31 Kukah, M and Falola, T (1996) *Religious Militancy and Self-Assertion*. Aldershot: Ashgate Publishing.
32 Falola (1998); Marshal (2009).
33 Kukah (1995); Dowd (2017).
34 Dowd, RA (2015) *Christianity, Islam, and Liberal Democracy: Lessons from sub-Saharan Africa*. New York: Oxford University Press.
35 Campbell, J (2013) *Nigeria: Dancing on the brink*, 2nd edn. Lanham, MD: Rowman and Littlefield; Haynes (2012).
36 Cimino, R (2005) 'No God in Common' American Evangelical Discourse on Islam after 9/11. *Review of Religuos Research*. Vol 47, No 2, pp. 162–174. Available at: http://www.jstor.org/stable/3512048?seq=1#page_scan_tab_contents; Marshall (2009).
37 Campbell (2013).
38 Marshall (2009).
39 Marshal (2009), p. 217.
40 Ibid, p. 201.
41 See, Nigerian Catholic Bishops: Good families make good nations, Vatican Radio, 26 February 2015. Available at: http://en.radiovaticana.va/news/2015/02/26/nigerian_catholic_bishops_good_families_make_good_nations/1125751
42 Kaoma (2012).
43 Gifford (1998).
44 Kaoma (2012).
45 Ibid.
46 Baptiste, N (2014) It's not just Uganda: The Christian right's onslaught on Africa, *The Nation*. Published 4 April 2014. Available at: https://www.thenation.com/article/its-not-just-uganda-behind-christian-rights-onslaught-africa/
47 *The Telegraph* (2014) Nigeria passes law banning homosexuality Published 14 January 2014. Available at: http://www.telegraph.co.uk/news/worldnews/africaandindianocean/nigeria/10570304/Nigeria-passes-law-banning-homosexuality.html
48 Oliver (2013).
49 Kaoma (2012).
50 Marshall (2009).
51 It is important to note that the threat posed by the Somali-based Islamist group Al-Shabaab, which has claimed responsibility for deadly attacks in Uganda, has been a concern. See: *The Atlantic* (201) Why Al-Shabaab would attack Uganda. Published 12 July 2010. Available at: https://www.theatlantic.com/international/archive/2010/07/why-al-shabaab-would-attack-in-uganda/59551/
52 This figure is the percentage reported by the Uganda Population and Housing Census (UPHC) of 2002.
53 Barret, D (ed) (2001) *World Christian Encyclopedia*, 2nd edn. Oxford: Oxford University Press.
54 *Daily Monitor* (2007) Cardinal meets politicians over life presidency. Published 9 August 2007.
55 *Daily Monitor* (2012) Archbishop rallies for smooth power transfer. Published 28 March 2012.
56 *Daily Monitor* (2010) 'Respect press freedom,' says Church. Published 28 April 2010.
57 Oliver (2013).
58 Anderson, J (2003) *Religious Liberty in Transitional Societies: The politics of religion*. Cambridge:

Cambridge University Press.
59 It is important to note that Uganda's mainline Christian leaders have, in their own way, also expressed concern over the spread of Western secular-liberal values and either did not distance themselves from or openly supported legislation to stiffen criminal penalties for homosexual behaviour. For example, in 2011 and 2012, the UJCC expressed its support for a very controversial 'anti-gay law' that called for long prison sentences and even punishment by death for those known to engage in homosexual behaviour. See: *Daily Monitor* (2012) Bishops want shelved anti-gay bill dusted. Published 12 June 2012.
60 Oliver (2013).
61 Ibid.
62 Kaoma (2012); Anderson, J (2011) Conservative Christianity, the Global South and the battle over sexual orientation, *Third World Quarterly*, **32** (9), pp. 1589–1605; Oliver (2013).
63 Oliver (2013).
64 Langa, S (2009) Follow up meeting on the homosexuals' agenda, Kampala. Available at: http://www.boxturtlebulletin.com/2009/03/28/10171
65 BBC (2011) Uganda gay rights activist killed. Publised 27 January 2011. Available at: http://www.bbc.com/news/world-africa-12295718
66 Gifford (1998).
67 Phiri, I (2008) President Frederick Chiluba and Zambia: Evangelicals in a Christian nation. In TO Ranger (ed) *Evangelical Christianity and Democracy in Africa*. New York: Oxford University Press, pp. 95–121.
68 Gifford (1998).
69 Phiri (2008).
70 Phiri (2008); Van Klinken, AS (2014) Homosexuality, politics and Pentecostal nationalism in Zambia, *Studies in World Christianity*, **20** (3), pp. 259–28; Grossman, G (2015) Renewalist Christianity and the political saliency of LGBTs: Theory and evidence from Sub-Saharan Africa, *The Journal of Politics*, **77** (2), pp. 337–351.
71 Central Statistical Office Zambia (2018) 2010 Census of Population and Housing (PDF). Accessed 10 February 2018.
72 Gifford (1998); Phiri (2008).
73 Ibid; Ibid.
74 Gifford (1995); Freston, P (2001) *Evangelicals and Politics in Asia, Africa and Latin America*. Cambridge: Cambridge University Press.
75 Phiri (2008).
76 Gifford (1998).
77 Ibid.
78 Freston (2001).
79 Burgess, RH (2015) Pentecostals and development in Nigeria and Zambia: Community organizing as a response to poverty and violence. *Pentacostal Studies*. Vol 14, Issue 2. Available at: https://www.researchgate.net/publication/282475552_Pentecostals_and_Development_in_Nigeria_and_Zambia_Community_Organizing_as_a_Response_to_Poverty_and_Violence
80 Gifford (1998); Phiri (2008); Van Klinken (2014).
81 Freston (2001).
82 Ibid.
83 Freston (2001); Phiri (2008).
84 Kaoma (2012).
85 Phiri (2008).
86 Phiri, I (1999) Why African churches preach politics: The case of Zambia, *Journal of Church and State*, **41** (2), pp. 232–347.

87 Kaoma (2012); Oliver (2013).
88 Kaoma (2012); Van Klinken (2014).
89 Van Klinken (2014); Grossman (2015).
90 *Lusaka Times* (2011) Gay and lesbianism illegal – Kunda. Published 18 March 2011. Available at: http://www.lusakatimes.com
91 Veep challenges Sata, HH over gays, *Lusaka Times*. Published 1 January 2011. Available at: http://www.lusakatimes.com/2011/01/01/veep-challenges-sata-hh-gays/. Originally published in *Zambia Daily Mail*.
92 Miller, D and Yamamori, T (2007) *Global Pentecostalism: The new face of Christian engagement*. Berkeley, CA: University of California Press.
93 Zakaria, F (2003) *The Future of Freedom: Illiberal democracy at home and abroad*. New York: WW Norton.
94 Ibid.
95 Varshney, A (2002) *Ethnic Conflict and Civic Life: Hindus and Muslims in India*. New Haven, CT: Yale University Press; Chandra, K (2004) *Why Ethnic Parties Succeed: Patronage and ethnic headcounts in India*. New York: Cambridge University Press.
96 Reeber, M (1993) Islamic preaching in France: Admonitory addresses or political platform? *Islam and Christian-Muslim Relations*, **4** (2), pp. 210–222.

References

Ahanotu, AM (1992) *Religion, State and Society in Contemporary Africa: Nigeria, Sudan, South Africa and Zaire*. Berkeley and Palo Alto, CA: Joint Center for African Studies.

Aminzade, R and Perry E (2001) The sacred, religious, and secular in contentious politics: Blurring the boundaries. In R Aminzade, JA Goldstone, D McAdam, EJ Perry, WH Sewell Jr, S Tarrow and C Tilley (eds) *Silence and Voice in the Study of Contentious Politics*. Cambridge: Cambridge University Press.

Anderson, AH (2013) *To the Ends of the Earth: Pentecostalism and the transformation of world Christianity*. New York: Oxford University Press.

Anderson, J (2003) *Religious Liberty in Transitional Societies: The politics of religion*. Cambridge: Cambridge University Press.

Anderson, J (2011) Conservative Christianity, the Global South and the battle over sexual orientation, *Third World Quarterly*, **32** (9), pp. 1589–1605.

Baptiste, N (2014) It's not just Uganda: The Christian right's onslaught on Africa, *The Nation*. Published 4 April 2014. Available at: https://www.thenation.com/article/its-not-just-uganda-behind-christian-rights-onslaught-africa/

Banchoff, T (2007) *Democracy and the New Religious Pluralism*. New York: Oxford University Press.

Barret, D (ed) (2001) *World Christian Encyclopedia*, 2nd edn. Oxford: Oxford University Press.

BBC (2011) Uganda gay rights activist killed. Publised 27 January 2011. Available at: http://www.bbc.com/news/world-africa-12295718

Burgess, RH (2015) Pentecostals and development in Nigeria and Zambia: Community organizing as a response to poverty and violence. *Pentecostal Studies*. Vol 14, Issue 2.

Buss, D and Herman D (2003) *Globalizing Family Values: The Christian right in international politics*. Minneapolis, MN: University of Minnesota Press.

Campbell, J (2013) *Nigeria: Dancing on the brink*, 2nd edn. Lanham, MD: Rowman and Littlefield.

Central Statistical Office Zambia (2018) 2010 Census of Population and Housing (PDF). Accessed 10 February 2018.

Chandra, K (2004) *Why Ethnic Parties Succeed: Patronage and ethnic headcounts in India*. New York: Cambridge University Press.

Cimino, R (2005) 'No God in Common' American Evangelical Discourse on Islam after 9/11.

Review of Religous Research. Vol 47, No 2, pp. 162–174 Available http://www.jstor.org/stable/3512048?seq=1#page_scan_tab_contents

Daily Monitor (2007) Cardinal meets politicians over life presidency. Published 9 August 2007.

Daily Monitor (2010) 'Respect press freedom,' says Church. Published 28 April 2010.

Daily Monitor (2012) Archbishop rallies for smooth power transfer. Published 28 March 2012.

Daily Monitor (2012) Bishops want shelved anti-gay bill dusted. Published 12 June 2012.

Dowd, RA (2015) *Christianity, Islam, and Liberal Democracy: Lessons from sub-Saharan Africa.* New York: Oxford University Press.

Dowd, RA (2017) Understanding how Christians respond to religious persecution: Evidence from Kenya and Nigeria, *The Review of Faith and International Affairs*, **15** (1), pp. 31–42.

Ellis, S and Ter Haar, G (2004) *Worlds of Power: Religious thought and political practice in Africa.* Oxford: Oxford University Press.

Falola, T (1998) *Violence in Nigeria: The crisis of religious politics and secular ideologies.* Rochester, NY: University of Rochester Press.

Freston, P (2001) *Evangelicals and Politics in Asia, Africa and Latin America.* Cambridge: Cambridge University Press.

Gifford, P (ed) (1995) *Christian Churches and the Democratization of Africa.* Leiden, Netherlands: EJ Brill, pp. 225–238.

Gifford, P (1998) *African Christianity: Its public role.* Bloomington, IN: Indiana University Press.

Grossman, G (2015) Renewalist Christianity and the political saliency of LGBTs: Theory and evidence from Sub-Saharan Africa, *The Journal of Politics*, **77** (2), pp. 337–351.

Haynes, J (2012) *Religious Transnational Actors and Soft Power.* Aldershot: Ashgate Publishing.

Institute for Economics and Peace (2016) *Global Terrorism Index, 2016.* Available at: http://economicsandpeace.org/reports/

Kaoma, KJ (2012) *Colonizing African Values: How the US Christian right is transforming sexual politics in Africa.* Somerville, MA: Political Research Associates.

Kukah, M (1995) Christians and Nigeria's aborted transition. In P Gifford (ed) *Christian Churches and the Democratization of Africa.* Leiden, Netherlands: EJ Brill, pp. 225–238.

Kukah, M and Falola, T (1996) *Religious Militancy and Self-Assertion.* Aldershot: Ashgate Publishing.

Langa, S (2009) Follow up meeting on the homosexuals' agenda, Kampala. Available at: http://www.boxturtlebulletin.com/2009/03/28/10171

Lusaka Times (2011) Gay and lesbianism illegal – Kunda. Published 18 March 2011. Available at: http://www.lusakatimes.com

Marshall, R (2009) *Political Spiritualities: The Pentecostal revolution in Nigeria.* Chicago, IL: University of Chicago Press.

Micklethwait, J and Wooldridge, A (2010) *God is Back: How the global revival of faith is changing the world.* New York: Penguin Books.

Miller, D and Yamamori, T (2007) *Global Pentecostalism: The new face of Christian engagement.* Berkeley, CA: University of California Press.

Nigerian Catholic Bishops: Good families make good nations, Vatican Radio, 26 February 2015. Available at: http://en.radiovaticana.va/news/2015/02/26/nigerian_catholic_bishops_good_families_make_good_nations/1125751

Ohadike, D (1992) Muslim-Christian conflict and political instability in Nigeria. In J Hunwick (ed) *Religion and National Integration in Nigeria: Islam, Christianity and politics in the Sudan and Nigeria.* Evanston, IL: Northwestern University Press.

Oliver, M (2013) Transnational sex politics, conservative Christianity, and political activism in Uganda, *Studies in Social Justice*, **7** (1), pp. 83–105.

Paden, JN (2005) *Muslim Civic Cultures and Conflict Resolution: The challenge of democratic federalism in Nigeria.* Washington, DC: Brookings Institution Press.

Pew Research Center (2006) *Spirit and Power: A 10-country study of Pentecostals.* Washington, DC: Pew Forum on Religion and Public Life.

Philpott, D and Shah T (eds) (2018) *Under Caesar's Sword: How Christians respond to persecution.* New York: Cambridge University Press.

Phiri, I (1999) Why African churches preach politics: The case of Zambia, *Journal of Church and State*, **41** (2), pp. 232–347.

Phiri, I (2003) President Frederick JT Chiluba of Zambia: The Christian nation and democracy, *Journal of Religion in Africa*, **33** (4), pp. 401–428.

Phiri, I (2008) President Frederick Chiluba and Zambia: Evangelicals in a Christian nation. In TO Ranger (ed) *Evangelical Christianity and Democracy in Africa.* New York: Oxford University Press, pp. 95–121.

Quinn, C and Quinn, F (2003) *Pride, Faith and Fear: Islam in sub-Saharan Africa.* Chicago, IL: University of Chicago Press.

Ranger, TO (2008) Introduction: Evangelical Christianity and democracy in Africa. In TO Ranger (ed) *Evangelical Christianity and Democracy in Africa.* New York: Oxford University Press.

Reeber, M (1993) Islamic preaching in France: Admonitory addresses or political platform? *Islam and Christian-Muslim Relations*, **4** (2), pp. 210–222.

Rudolph, S (1997) Introduction: Religion, states and transitional civil society. In S Hoeber Rudolph and J Piscatori (eds) *Transitional Religion and Fading States.* Boulder, CO: Westview Press.

Smith, C (ed) (1996) *Disruptive Religion: The force of faith in social movement activism.* New York: Routledge.

Steigenga, T (2001) *Politics of the Spirit: The political implications of Pentecostalized religion in Costa Rica and Guatemala.* New York: Lexington Books.

The Atlantic (2010) Why Al-Shabaab would attack Uganda. Published 12 July 2010. Available at: https://www.theatlantic.com/international/archive/2010/07/why-al-shabaab-would-attack-in-uganda/59551/

The Telegraph (2014) Nigeria passes law banning homosexuality Published 14 January 2014. Available at: http://www.telegraph.co.uk/news/worldnews/africaandindianocean/nigeria/10570304/Nigeria-passes-law-banning-homosexuality.html

Usman, YB (1987) *The Manipulation of Religion in Nigeria 1977–1987.* Kaduna, Nigeria: Vanguard Printers and Publishers.

Van Klinken, AS (2014) Homosexuality, politics and Pentecostal nationalism in Zambia, *Studies in World Christianity*, **20** (3), pp. 259–281.

Varshney, A (2002) *Ethnic Conflict and Civic Life: Hindus and Muslims in India.* New Haven, CT: Yale University Press.

Yong, A (2010) *In the Days of Caesar: Pentecostalism and political theology.* Grand Rapids, MI: WB Eerdmans Publishing Company.

Zakaria, F (2003) *The Future of Freedom: Illiberal democracy at home and abroad.* New York: WW Norton.

Chapter 14

The United States' approach to countering terrorism and violent extremism

Lindsay Cohn

The chapters in this book have demonstrated that despite the great diversity of contexts and actors, poor governance plays a significant role in the emergence and spread of violent extremism on the African continent. Every chapter has argued, in one way or another, that poor governance allows for violent extremist and criminal groups to gain a foothold in territory, creates pools of potential recruits and impedes conflict resolution. This, of course, is not surprising to anyone who pays attention to terrorism, insurgency, transnational criminality or violent extremism. However, it bears expanding on, as it holds considerable significance for how the international community – both at regional and global levels – can better address these important issues.

This chapter reviews the various explanations commonly given for the emergence and spread of violent extremism in Africa and the responses to this issue that appear to have had success. It draws on the European Union and the United Nation's countering violent extremism (CVE) frameworks and provides a summary of some of the global responses to violent extremism and terrorism and contrasts these against the United States' current approach to counterterrorism (CT) and CVE. An overview of the structural factors within US political culture illustrates why militarised approaches to CVE and CT usually get precedence over 'softer' developmental responses. Finally, this chapter provides insights into how, under the new administration, US approaches to CVE and CT are likely to look in the near future.

What causes the problem?
Explanations for the emergence of political violence in Africa tend to fall into three key categories. First, it is often argued that both former colonial and current post-colonial governments on the continent tend to hold little legitimacy among their citizenry, govern poorly and have generally failed to develop sustainable economic systems. Second, the prevalence of local 'big man' cultures has created environments in which corruption is endemic, inhibiting the development of 'modern' state structures. Finally, the prevalence of neo-

patrimonialism in African states, where rational-legal bureaucracies mix with client-patronage systems, has created environments of uncertainty, where the population is unsure about which system will determine decision-making at any given moment. As Clapham (1985) writes, 'Officials hold positions in bureaucratic organisations with powers which are formally defined, but exercise those powers ... as a form ... of private property.'[1] This inherently creates factionalism between the haves and have-nots (or can-gets and cannot-gets), which often falls along ethnic or religious lines.

These three categories of explanations relate closely and often overlap with drivers highlighted in the larger scholarly literature on violent extremism and terrorism. These drivers include the concepts of relative deprivation,[2] weak governance,[3] and a feeling among the population that they do not have effective non-violent means to agitate for change.[4] Assuming these explanations all have some merit, the obvious conclusion is that the main goal must be to improve the legitimacy and effectiveness of governance in weaker African states and to support government and civil society in the stronger states.

How is the world responding?

Strengthening governance is easier said than done and, of course, telling a weak state that it needs to be stronger is no solution at all. It is very difficult to assess the effectiveness of efforts to strengthen governance or specifically to counter violent extremism. As with all such efforts, it is nearly impossible to know what did *not* happen, thanks to those efforts, and whether things would have been worse, better or the same without them. That being said, programmes that have been put in place in Europe (since the early 2000s), by the United Nations (since 2006) and in the United States (since 2011) give us some idea of what practitioners think works well.

The European response

In 2005, the European Union (EU) created a counterterrorism strategy based on four pillars: prevent, protect, pursue and respond. This strategy emphasises that addressing terrorism in Europe involves 'tackling the ... root causes which can lead to radicalisation and recruitment, in Europe and internationally', as well as improving defences, strengthening law-enforcement's ability to discover, apprehend and prosecute those engaged in violence, and improving states' ability to manage the human and infrastructural aftermath of violent attacks.[5] The EU strategy specifies the need to 'limit the activities of those playing a role in radicalisation; prevent access to terrorist training; establish a strong legal framework to prevent incitement and recruitment; and examine ways to impede terrorist recruitment through the internet'.[6]

This strategy explicitly recognises that some of the conditions contributing to radicalisation are: 'poor or autocratic governance ... lack of political or economic prospects and of educational opportunities' and that these factors may be experienced differently among distinct populations within a society.[7] The strategy states that 'to counter this, outside the Union we must promote even more vigorously good governance, human rights, democracy as well as education and economic prosperity, and engage in conflict resolution'.[8]

For weak states, especially those with dense urban populations, scattered rural populations, or a combination of both, the EU counterterrorism strategy's 'protect' pillar will inevitably be difficult, if not impossible, to implement fully. Part of the reason why weak states experience political violence is simply because it is fairly easy to engage in political violence (although the risk is high for those who are caught). Therefore, this is probably not the best place to focus CVE efforts in weaker states, as hardening some targets will simply channel violence towards a plethora of other, softer targets. However, one area in which interventions under the 'protect' pillar may make a significant impact in addressing violent extremism is border security. This would require significant cross-border cooperation from those African states where violent extremism and transnational criminal organisations are active. In weak states, the EU counterterrorism strategy's 'pursue' pillar will require significant international assistance. This is recognised in the EU strategy's call for improved efforts to build partner capacity in 'priority third countries'.[9] This will include improving information sharing; cooperation on tracking and freezing terrorist/insurgent financing; cooperation on fighting trafficking; and cooperation on capture, prosecution and incarceration (or rehabilitation, depending on the situation).

However, despite growing levels of violent extremism in Africa, the EU counterterrorism strategy is seemingly more focused on addressing violent extremism in states such as Iraq and Syria, which are more likely to produce foreign fighters who may launch attacks in Europe. In 2016, the European Peacebuilding Liaison Office (EPLO) released a briefing paper indicating the importance of assisting weaker states with security sector reform, the prevention of radicalisation and the protection of soft targets such as tourism sites.[10] The paper also notes the need for socio-economic development, the empowerment of women, and other developmental issues that may contribute to the emergence and spread of violent extremism. However, it specifies that the EU's efforts in the Middle East and North Africa (MENA) region would focus primarily on Jordan, Lebanon and Tunisia.[11]

The United Nations' response

The United Nations (UN) also has a global counterterrorism strategy, similarly built around four pillars, including: (1) addressing the conditions conducive to the spread of terrorism; (2) preventing and combating terrorism; (3) building states' capacity; and (4) ensuring human rights and the rule of law.[12] In 2015, the UN Secretary General released a Plan of Action on Preventing Violent Extremism, which identifies several conditions the UN believes are conducive to the emergence of violent extremism. These included a lack of socio-economic opportunity, marginalisation/discrimination against certain populations, poor governance/human-rights violations/a lack of rule of law, the presence of prolonged unresolved conflicts, and a climate in which radicalisation in prisons can occur.[13]

The UN's action plan primarily calls for member states to develop their own plans to prevent and counter violent extremism, and offers guidelines on how to do so. It offers seven categories of recommended action, including: dialogue and conflict prevention; strengthening good governance; human rights and the rule of law; engaging communities; empowering youth; gender equality and empowering women; education, skills development and employment facilitation; and strategic communications.[14]

The UN does undertake some direct capacity-building work, for example, through its Integrated Assistance on Countering Terrorism (I-ACT), which now has programmes in Nigeria and Burkina Faso. Similarly, there is the United Nations Counterterrorism Centre (UNCCT), which, to date, has 'initiated more than 30 non-military counterterrorism projects around the world'.[15] These have primarily consisted of programmes designed to train border security guards and youth engagement/education programmes. However, the majority of the UNCCT's work is focused on the coordination and production of guidelines, best practices and information, rather than direct P/CVE activities.

Both the EU and UN strategies recognise that there are certain particularly vulnerable populations, including those in prison, in marginal communities or unemployed. Both these strategies place an emphasis on the need to develop and disseminate a narrative to counter violent extremism. While the UN works mainly to coordinate and facilitate global CVE activities, the EU primarily focuses on countries that send migrant flows to Europe.

What has been the United States' response to violent extremism in Africa?

While the specific approach has changed slightly from one US administration to the next, the general tenor of US policy towards terrorism and violent extremism has stayed the same since the end of the Cold War. That general tenor has been to provide some focus on infrastructure building and economic aid, some training for justice and law enforcement, and a heavy emphasis on military training, equipment and exercises.

Approximately US$12 to US$14 billion foreign aid money is spent in Africa each year.[16] Close to US$9 billion of that is long-term development aid, focused primarily on health initiatives such as the President's Emergency Plan for AIDS Relief (PEPFAR). Approximately US$5 billion is spent on various economic and development assistance initiatives, while about US$57 million (excluding about US$1.3 billion to Egypt) is spent on security assistance.[17]

At first glance this seems like a fairly good balance of economic/development aid and security assistance. It is important to recognise, however, that most of the assistance goes towards population policies/reproductive health, basic health, emergency response and food aid/agriculture development, most of which focuses on providing humanitarian assistance and not on building government/national capability. Thus, it can be linked only loosely – if at all – to countering violent extremism, and is sometimes criticised as 'propping up' corrupt and illegitimate governments.[18] In sub-Saharan Africa, only about US$375 million goes to programmes categorised as 'government and civil society', whereas about US$556 million goes to programmes categorised as 'conflict, peace and security'.[19]

The US State Department's Bureau of African Affairs (which focuses on sub-Saharan Africa, while North Africa is handled by the department's Bureau of Near-Eastern Affairs) lists the pillars of US policy towards Africa as: (1) strengthening democratic institutions; (2) supporting African economic growth and development; (3) advancing peace and security; and (4) promoting opportunity and development.

The bureau's website touts its recent contributions to the first pillar as including: helping democratic transitions to occur in Côte d'Ivoire, Guinea and Niger; supporting democratic elections in Nigeria and supporting the peace agreement and independence referendum that led to an independent South Sudan.[20] The US State Department also points to its efforts in fighting trafficking, hunger, violence against women and children, infant/maternal mortality, the adverse effects of climate change and infectious diseases. In these efforts, the State Department often partners with the defence department, the US Center for Disease Control, USAID and various UN agencies.

The Department of Defense focuses its efforts almost entirely on counterterrorism (with some counter-narcotics and counter-trafficking), primarily through military-to-military contacts involving training, equipment, advice/assistance and multinational exercises. The US government lacks a consensus definition of 'countering violent extremism', but most of the agencies couple it with or discuss it in terms of counterterrorism. This means that most of the non-security assistance discussed above is not integrated into an overall

CVE strategy, but more into a standard neo-liberal economic development strategy. Most of the US government's thinking about CVE falls under its thinking about CT, and its CT strategy is primarily a military one. Furthermore, given indications in the current US administration, the budgets of USAID and the State Department will be cut significantly, and the Department of Defense's attention to Africa will likely become more militarised.

The US State Department defines CVE as 'domestic and international efforts to prevent violent extremists and their supporters from radicalising, recruiting or inspiring individuals or groups in the United States and abroad to commit acts of violence'.[21] Tellingly, however, even the State Department's own page for the Bureau of Counterterrorism and Countering Violent Extremism describes its mission purely in terms of counterterrorism: 'to promote US national security by taking a leading role in developing coordinated strategies and approaches to defeat terrorism abroad and securing the counterterrorism cooperation of international partners'.[22] This is the office that lists groups considered to be terrorist organisations, puts out country reports on terrorism, participates in the Global Counterterrorism Forum and runs a number of programmes aimed at countering terrorism and violent extremism around the world. The CVE part of its title appears to have been tacked on recently. The US Department of Defense did not host a global forum on CVE strategy until 2016, but produced no clear statement of what the CVE strategy was or what actions and initiatives it involved.[23]

When discussing CVE, the United States tends to focus purely on terrorism rather than other potential sources of political violence, and thus may miss out on larger patterns – especially those involving insurgency or criminal activity, all of which may be related to the same causes.[24]

Why is it that, when we know that military training, funding and equipment will do very little in the absence of a functioning government with tax revenue and professional civil servants, the US approach continues to have a primarily military focus? Mainly, this comes down to domestic politics, including the increased size, role and resources of the Department of Defense since 1947; the way in which incentives for members of Congress all point to Department of Defense rather than Department of State solutions; and the general scepticism that many Americans have towards state-directed systems of health, education and other social infrastructure.

How the Department of Defense became leviathan

Before the Second World War, the United States pursued a consistent pattern of maintaining a large navy but a small army, which focused on irregular operations (mostly against native Americans). These forces would be augmented in times of need by volunteer call ups, state militias and, occasionally, national conscripts. After conflict, the vast majority of troops would be demobilised. The Department of the Navy was fairly powerful, but focused on its own specific issues. The Department of War held little power and only really played a significant role in policy in times of conflict. The implications of this were that the departments of War and that of the Navy had very little influence on the conduct or aims of US foreign policy; the State Department reigned supreme over all things foreign until and unless there was large-scale fighting involved.

In the aftermath of the Second World War, all of this changed. In 1947 and 1949, Congress passed and then amended the National Security Act, which, among other things, combined the departments of War and the Navy into the National Military Establishment (and then the Department of Defense). This created an environment where the army and navy were far less in competition with each other but increasingly came together in competition with the State Department.

In 1948/49, the Soviets blockaded Berlin and the United States decided that full demobilisation of the armed forces would be unwise. In 1940, the US armed forces had less than 500 000 active members.[25] Manpower peaked in May 1945 at 12.124 million members, dropped down to 1.4 million in March 1948 and then went back up to over 3 million for the Korean War, before slowly dropping back down (with only a slight uptick during the Vietnam War). By 1975/76 it was down to just over 2 million and stayed that way through the 1980s until it dipped below 2 million in 1991. Since then, it has continued to slowly drop in number and has been hovering around 1.15–1.3 million for the past several years.[26]

Maintaining these troop numbers costs a considerable amount of money and resources, much more than is allocated to the State Department. Moreover, during the Cold War the Department of Defense increasingly came to play a more important role in making, communicating and executing US foreign policy, and challenged the idea that the State Department should monopolise foreign policy decision-making. By creating the Joint Chiefs of Staff and the Chairman position, the 1947/49 Acts had effectively placed a larger number of military/defence people in the room, versus only one chief diplomat. In short, the Department of Defense gained a significant voice and leverage in the world of foreign policy, and instead of thinking primarily in terms of 'foreign affairs' the United States began to think primarily in terms of 'national security'.

This brings us to the second point: constituency and congressional incentives. The Department of Defense has more than 3 million employees. In recent years, much has been made of how military bases and personnel are concentrated in certain parts of the country, but where they are, they are large, visible, unmistakable parts of the landscape. They provide the economic basis for whole towns; they employ contractors and other civilian workers; they buy large, expensive items or smaller items in bulk. In short, they are important constituents. And instead of being a weakness, this concentration is a strength when one is talking about getting the attention of Congress; being concentrated in one district gets one a lot more attention than being dispersed over many districts.

Many members of Congress have a direct interest in getting resources for the Department of Defense. They want to be able to go before their constituents and advertise how they were able to procure funding for a new ship or the refurbishment of base facilities, which will benefit the local economy. Even more members of Congress want to be able to go back to their constituents and announce how they were able to support the American troops, whether this be in the form of a pay rise or training and equipment that will ensure their safety while on mission.

There is no comparable constituency for foreign-service officers or the foreign-policy world in general. In human terms, it is a tiny group, and in geographic terms, they are either outside the United States or concentrated in and around Washington DC (which has no representative in Congress). No member of Congress reaps electoral benefit from getting resources for the State Department. The State Department buys no submarines, supports no places like Jacksonville or Fayetteville, and puts in no orders for several hundred thousand new uniforms.

Furthermore, no member of Congress looks forward to a photo opportunity with diplomats in suits in the same way as they look forward to a photo op with a starched and gleaming flag officer. No member of Congress expects rousing cheers at rallies when they discuss how they have got support for the on-going public diplomacy efforts in Djibouti. However, they can expect those cheers when announcing their success procuring better boots for US troops in Afghanistan. Much of this has to do with the general popular appeal of the military in American society, which has been reinforced in popular culture and captured in countless films which emphasise the action, personal sacrifice and tragedy experienced by American troops. Even those Americans who know very little about the military, or the conflicts in which they are engaged, have seen countless films in which they are prominently featured. How many Americans, however, know anything about the daily work of a foreign-affairs diplomat?

Secondly, in the realm of congressional attention, the Constitution itself produced unintended consequences, which favour the Department of Defense over the State Department. The framers, feeling that it was important to protect the new country against the frightening consequences of a standing, powerful military, made sure to include a provision in the Constitution that said that Congress 'shall have power to … raise and support armies, but no appropriation of money to that use shall be for a longer term than two years' (Article 1, Section 8). As a result, Congress has had to think explicitly about the authorisation and appropriation for defence every year. The National Defense Authorization Act is, next to the budget, the most predictable Bill of every legislative cycle. This means that the committees schedule time for it, every member is aware of it, and everyone has to spend at least a few minutes thinking about whether they agree with it or not. No such provision was made for the money allocated to the Department of State and there is, therefore, no urgency associated with thinking hard about the funding and authorisations for the State Department. Thus, instead of there being a push mechanism associated with the State Department's needs, the only way for it to get on Congress's docket is to reach out and convince someone in Congress to take on a specific issue.

Finally, US political culture is simply sceptical of state-driven solutions to problems like health, agriculture, education, job training and other developmental-related initiatives often included in CVE programming. It is far easier to get the average US citizen to support a military approach to a problem because military (defence/security) activity is seen as the most legitimate realm of government activity. Most other activities, in the standard American narrative, ought to be left to the private sector and market forces. Americans cannot even agree on whether to provide education and health care to all citizens. Therefore, it is very difficult to convince American citizens that their tax dollars ought to be spent on similar efforts abroad.

All of these factors combine to give the Department of Defense a great deal of weight in US foreign policy, both in terms of influence and resources. As a result, no inter-agency consensus exists on the precise meaning of CVE. Rather, the agency with the most weight, which is usually the Department of Defense, is likely to drive interpretation and policy.

Conclusion: What will US policy towards Africa look like in the near future?

The structural factors in US politics that tend to militarise foreign policy remain unchanged. Therefore, the current US approach to violent extremism in general is unlikely to change any time soon – regardless of the administration. The Trump administration has already indicated its intention to cut State Department and USAID budgets, and is likely to curtail many of the Bush and Obama initiatives regarding health and education. The core of US policy towards violent extremism in African countries is likely to remain focused on 'the terrorist problem' and on security assistance and cooperation.

Furthermore, as we saw in October 2017 in General Joseph Dunford's explanation of the US/Nigerien mission which resulted in the deaths of four US and five Nigerien personnel, it appears that the US military/defence community expects the focus of counterterrorism to shift from the Middle East to the northern half of the African continent in the near future.

The Department of Defense is limited in how much help it can offer to governments struggling to end corruption or professionalise their civil service. It does not focus on these tasks, and is often prevented by statute or by turf battles with other agencies from spending money on such initiatives.

The bottom line is that the structure and culture of US politics makes it likely that American activity on the continent will remain weighted strongly towards military and security assistance and counterterrorism operations, rather than governance and support to civil society. It is not that no one in the US foreign policy establishment recognises the value of such programmes, it is that the incentives for Congress to support such programmes are limited.

Endnotes

1 Clapham, C (1985) *Third World Politics: An introduction*. Abingdon: Routledge.
2 Gurr, TD (1970) *Why Men Rebel*. Princeton, NJ: Princeton University Press.
3 See Crenshaw, M (1990) The causes of terrorism. In CW Kegley Jr (ed) *International Terrorism: Characteristics, causes, controls*. New York: St Martin's Press, pp. 113–126; Koopmans, R (1996) Explaining the rise of racist and extreme right violence in western Europe, *European Journal of Political Research*, **30** (2), pp. 185–216; Ellingsen, T and Gleditsch, NP (1997) Democracy and conflict in the Third World. In K Volden and D Smith (eds) *Causes of Conflict in the Third World Countries*. Oslo: PRIO & North/South Coalition, pp. 69–81.
4 See Eckstein, H and Gurr, TD (1975) *Patterns of Authority: A structural basis for political inquiry*. New York: Wiley; Rummel, RJ (1995) Democracy, power, genocide, and mass murder, *Journal of Conflict Resolution*, **39** (1), pp. 3–26; Gissinger, R and Gleditsch, NP (1999) Globalization and conflict: Welfare, distribution, and political unrest, *Journal of World-Systems Research*, **5** (2), pp. 274–300.
5 European Union (EU) (2005) *European Union Counterterrorism Strategy*, p. 8. Available at: http://data.consilium.europa.eu/doc/document/ST-14469-2005-REV-3/en/pdf
6 Ibid, p. 8.
7 Ibid.
8 Ibid, p. 9.
9 Ibid, p. 15.
10 European Peacebuilding Liaison Office (EPLO) (2016) *Overview of the EU's Policy and Programming on Preventing/Countering Violent Extremism (PVE/CVE)*. Briefing Paper 1/2016. Available at: http://eplo.org/wp-content/uploads/2015/10/EPLO-Briefing-Paper-on-CVE-Sept-16.pdf
11 Ibid, p. 3.
12 See United Nations General Assembly (UNGA) (2015) UNGA Res A/70/674.

Available at: http://www.un.org/en/ga/search/view_doc.asp?symbol=A/70/674; United Nations (2015) Global Counter-Terrorism Strategy. Available at: https://www.un.org/counterterrorism/ctitf/sites/www.un.org.counterterrorism.ctitf/files/plan_action.pdf_

13   Ibid, pp. 7–8.
14   Ibid, pp. 9–10.
15   United Nations (2017) United Nations Counter-Terrorism Centre. Available at: https://www.un.org/counterterrorism/ctitf/en/uncct/main-projects_
16   This does not include the approximately US$1.3–1.5 billion in military aid to Egypt per year. All dollar figures are rough estimates due to the difficulty of getting exact numbers. This aid is administered by multiple US agencies through multiple authorities and is very hard to track. See McBride, J (2017) How does the US spend its foreign aid? *Council on Foreign Relations Backgrounder*. Available at: https://www.cfr.org/backgrounder/how-does-us-spend-its-foreign-aid
17   Bearak, M and Gamio, L (2016) The US foreign aid budget, visualized, *The Washington Post*. Available at: https://www.washingtonpost.com/graphics/world/which-countries-get-the-most-foreign-aid/
18   Swanson, A (2015) Does Foreign Aid Always Help the Poor? World Economic Forum. Available at: https://www.weforum.org/agenda/2015/10/does-foreign-aid-always-help-the-poor
19   USAID (2017) Data Dashboard. Available at: https://explorer.usaid.gov/aid-dashboard.html
20   United States Department of State (2017) Bureau of African Affairs: Our mission. Available at: https://www.state.gov/p/af/188266.htm
21   United States Department of State (2017) Countering violent extremism. Available at: https://www.state.gov/j/cve/
22   United States Department of State (2017) Bureau of Counterterrorism and Countering Violent Extremism. Available at: https://www.state.gov/j/ct/index.htm
23   Garamone, J (2016b) Dunford hosts Chiefs of Defense to discuss counter-extremism strategy, US DOD News. Available at: https://www.defense.gov/News/Article/Article/975734/dunford-hosts-chiefs-of-defense-to-discuss-counter-extremism-strategy/
24   McCants, W and Watts, C (2012) *US Strategy for Countering Extremism: An assessment*. Foreign Policy Research Institute. Available at: https://www.fpri.org/docs/media/McCants_Watts_-_Countering_Violent_Extremism.pdf
25   Defense Manpower Data Center (2017) Available at: https://www.dmdc.osd.mil/appj/dwp/stats_reports.jsp
26   Ibid.

References

Adams, G and Murray, S (2014) *Mission Creep: The militarization of U.S. foreign policy?* Washington, DC: Georgetown University Press.

Bearak, M and Gamio, L (2016) The U.S. foreign aid budget, visualized, *The Washington Post*. Available at: https://www.washingtonpost.com/graphics/world/which-countries-get-the-most-foreign-aid/

Clapham, C (1985) *Third World Politics: An introduction*. Abingdon: Routledge.

Crenshaw, M (1990) The causes of terrorism. In CW Kegley Jr (ed) *International Terrorism: Characteristics, causes, controls*. New York: St Martin's Press, pp. 113–126.

Crenshaw, M (1995) Thoughts on relating terrorism to historical contexts. In M Crenshaw (ed.) *Terrorism in Context*. University Park, PA: Pennsylvania State University Press, pp. 3–24.

Defense Manpower Data Center (2017) Available at: https://www.dmdc.osd.mil/appj/dwp/stats_reports.jsp

Eckstein, H and Gurr, TD (1975) *Patterns of Authority: A structural basis for political inquiry*. New York: Wiley

Ellingsen, T and Gleditsch, NP (1997) Democracy and conflict in the Third World. In K Volden and D Smith (eds) *Causes of Conflict in the Third World Countries*. Oslo: PRIO & North/South Coalition, pp. 69–81.

European Peacebuilding Liaison Office (EPLO) (2016) *Overview of the EU's Policy and Programming on Preventing/Countering Violent Extremism (PVE/CVE)*. Briefing Paper 1/2016. Available at: http://eplo.org/wp-content/uploads/2015/10/EPLO-Briefing-Paper-on-CVE-Sept-16.pdf

European Union (EU) (2005) *European Union Counterterrorism Strategy*, p. 8. Available at: http://data.consilium.europa.eu/doc/document/ST-14469-2005-REV-3/en/pdf

Garamone, J (2016a) Dunford explores ways to better-integrate counter-extremism efforts, *US Department of Defense News*. Available at: https://www.defense.gov/News/Article/Article/743160/dunford-explores-ways-to-better-integrate-counter-extremism-efforts/

Garamone, J (2016b) Dunford hosts Chiefs of Defense to discuss counter-extremism strategy, *US DOD News*. Available at: https://www.defense.gov/News/Article/Article/975734/dunford-hosts-chiefs-of-defense-to-discuss-counter-extremism-strategy/

Gissinger, R and Gleditsch, NP (1999) Globalization and conflict: Welfare, distribution, and political unrest, *Journal of World-Systems Research*, **5** (2), pp. 274–300.

Gurr, TD (1970) *Why Men Rebel*. Princeton, NJ: Princeton University Press.

Koopmans, R (1996) Explaining the rise of racist and extreme right violence in western Europe, *European Journal of Political Research*, **30** (2), pp. 185–216.

McBride, J (2017) How does the US spend its foreign aid? *Council on Foreign Relations Backgrounder*. Available at: https://www.cfr.org/backgrounder/how-does-us-spend-its-foreign-aid

McCants, W and Watts, C (2012) *US Strategy for Countering Extremism: An assessment*. Foreign Policy Research Institute. Available at: https://www.fpri.org/docs/media/McCants_Watts_-_Countering_Violent_Extremism.pdf

Rummel, RJ (1995) Democracy, power, genocide, and mass murder, *Journal of Conflict Resolution*, **39** (1), pp. 3–26.

Swanson, A (2015) Does Foreign Aid Always Help the Poor? World Economic Forum. Available at: https://www.weforum.org/agenda/2015/10/does-foreign-aid-always-help-the-poor

United Nations (2015) Global Counter-Terrorism Strategy. Available at: https://www.un.org/counterterrorism/ctitf/sites/www.un.org.counterterrorism.ctitf/files/plan_action.pdf

United Nations (2017) United Nations Counter-Terrorism Centre. Available at: https://www.un.org/counterterrorism/ctitf/en/uncct/main-projects_

United Nations General Assembly (UNGA) (2015) UNGA Res A/70/674. Available at: http://www.un.org/en/ga/search/view_doc.asp?symbol=A/70/674. See also https://www.un.org/counterterrorism/ctitf/sites/www.un.org.counterterrorism.ctitf/files/plan_action.pdf

United States Department of State (2017) Bureau of African Affairs: Our mission. Available at: https://www.state.gov/p/af/188266.htm

United States Department of State (2017) Bureau of Counterterrorism and Countering Violent Extremism. Available at: https://www.state.gov/j/ct/index.htm

United States Department of State (2017) Countering violent extremism. Available at: https://www.state.gov/j/cve

USAID (2017) Data Dashboard. Available at: https://explorer.usaid.gov/aid-dashboard.html

Index

Page numbers in *italics* indicate figures and tables. Arabic names are filed under the first element of the name, for example Al-Qaeda is filed under 'A'.

A

Abdi, R 207–208
abductions *see* kidnappings
Abouba, Albadé 150
Adam, Jaafar 171
Afghanistan
    and Al-Qaeda 10, 214
    becomes pariah state 12–13
    Soviet occupation 10
    US cruise missiles against 9, 16
    US-led invasion 10, 14, 17
Africa
    Fragile State Index 122, 314–315
    Global Peace Index 315
    'hopeless' vs 'hopeful' continent 313–314
    see also sub-Saharan Africa (SSA)
Africa Check 182, 275, 276
Africa Muslim Agency 312
African Centre for the Study & Research on Terrorism 216, 244, 246
African Model Anti-Terrorism Law 247
African Union (AU)
    Algiers Convention 246, 253n94
    Protocol of the Algiers Convention 227–228, 246–247
African Union Mission in Somalia (AMISOM)
    and Al-Shabaab 205, 210
    participation of Kenyan forces 23, 48, 51, 52, *52*, 53, *53*
AFRICOM (United States Africa Command) 110
AfriForum 275–276
Afrikaner nationalist movements 239, 271–273, 275–276

Afrobarometer 36
    see also security-related surveys
Ag Achérif, Haïba 152
Ag Alambo, Aghlay 125, 126
Ag Bahanga, Ibrahim 111, 114, 124, 125, 152
Ag Boula, Mohamed 148–149
Ag Boula, Rhissa 126, 148, 149, 155
Ag Gamou, El Hadj 154
Ag Ghali, Iyad
    cooperation of local populations 121
    creation of Ansar al-Din 115
    and demonisation of Tuareg 141, 151–152, 156–157
    exploits poor governance in Mali 129
    leader of Group for the Support of Islam and Muslims 90–91
    leader of main jihadist threat in Mali 153
    sidelining of MNLA 152
    see also Tuareg people
Ag Hama, Hamada 151–152
Ag Hindi, Aboubacrim 146
Ag Najem, Mohamed 114
Ag Wadoussène, Mohamed Ali 152
age, as survey demographic
    security concerns (Kenya) *49*, 50, 52, *53*
    security concerns (Mali) 55, *55*
    security concerns (Nigeria) *60*, 61
    security concerns (North African countries) *72*
Ahaggar (Algeria) 142
Ahl al-Kahf (people of the cave) 213
Ahmed, Akbar 190
airstrikes 96, 97
AIS (Islamic Salvation Army) 87
Al-Adnan, Abu Muhammad 216
Al-Afghani, Jamal al-Din 85
Al-Awlaki, Anwar 17
Al-Baghdadi, Abu Bakr
    leader of ISIS 11–12, 92, 216, 217
    pledges of allegiance to 94, 212, 213
    refusal to operate under Al-Qaeda's

umbrella 93
support of foreign nationals 241
Al-Banna, Hassan 304
Al-Barnawi, Abu Musab 183
Al-Bashir, Omar 309
Al-Faisal, Abdullah 241
Al-Haramain 311
Al-Hijra 48, 207, 213, 220n1, 230, 237
Al-Islah 311
Al-Itihaad al-Islamiya 209, 209–210
Al Jazeera 89, 241, 312
Al-Libi, Abu Irhayyim 96
Al-Masri, Abu Bakr 118
Al-Mourabitoun
    activities aided by poor governance 122
    formation of 110, 118
    mergers with other organisations 90, 107, 131
    part of Support Group for Islam and Muslims 156
    terrorist attacks 54, 90, 91, 107, 132
Al-Mua'qi'oon Biddam (Signed in Blood Battalion) 110, 118, 122
Al-Qaeda
    background/overview 10–11, 214–215
    adherence to Salafi jihadism 214
    alliance with GSPC 113
    attacks (9/11) 9, 10, 13, 25
    attacks (embassy bombings) 9, 12, 16, 48, 215, 237, 312
    attacks (Tunisia) 84
    competition with ISIS 205–206, 213
    decentralised units/chapters 10–11, 215
    disrupted by targeted killings 97
    expulsion of ISIS 92, 93
    focus on 'far enemy' 215, 216
    funding for Boko Haram 185
    links with Taliban 10, 12, 13
    merger with GSCP 89
    propaganda/communication techniques 217
    severs ties with GIA 88
    strategy of lone wolf attacks 218
    as transnational terrorist organisation 229, 237
    use of women in operations 216–217
    see also Bin Laden, Osama
Al-Qaeda Central 11, 118, 215, 216, 251n75
Al-Qaeda in Iraq (AQI) 11, 20, 89, 214, 215, 216, 218, 251n75
Al-Qaeda in the Arabian Peninsula (AQAP) 11, 215
Al-Qaeda in the Islamic Maghreb (AQIM)
    ability to adapt to military pressure 100
    ideological motivations questioned 118
    ideology/historical origins 84–86
    kidnappings/hostage-taking 113–114
    mergers with other organisations 90–91, 131
    networks of local relationships 81, 121
    part of Support Group for Islam and Muslims 156
    public opinion survey 45
    rebranding of GSPC as AQIM 113
    terrorist attacks 54, 89–90, 91, 107, 128
    training of Boko Haram 184
    as transnational terrorist organisation 227
Al-Shabaab
    background/overview 209–210
    alliance with Al-Qaeda 205, 211–212
    beheadings of civilians 218
    as regional security threat 227
    terrorist attacks 48, 53, 210–211, 227, 233–236, 240–241, 302
    training of Boko Haram 184
    as transnational terrorist organisation 210, 227, 229, 241
    use of women in operations 217
Al-Suri, Abu Musab 218
Al-Tilemsi, Ahmed 116, 118
Al-Turabi, Hassan 310
Al-Wahhab, Muhammad ibn Abd 85, 303, 308
Al-Zarqawi, Abu Musab
    accord between GSPC and AQI 89
    death of 216
    extreme use of violence 11, 215–216
    original leader of ISIS 92
    targeting of Shi'a Muslims 20, 216
Al-Zawahiri, Ayman 10, 11, 85, 89, 91, 118, 217
Ala-Maududi, Maulana Abul 85, 303, 304–305
Algeria
    activities of the DRS 144, 151, 152, 156
    founding member of GCTF 31n70
    part of TSCTI 145
    political overview 86–89, 143, 144
    survey, impact of Arab Spring 42

INDEX

survey, security vs human rights 46, *46*
surveys, security-related 44, *45*, *66*, *68*, *70*, *72–73*
terrorist attacks in *72*, 88, 89–90, 113, 118
threat posed by MNLA 152
Tuareg people, provocation of 147–148
Tuareg's Prague Spring 142–143
see also Al-Qaeda in the Islamic Maghreb (AQIM); North Africa (Maghreb)
Algiers Accords 112, 132, 133
Algiers Convention 246, 253n94
see also Protocol of the Algiers Convention
Ali, AM 207, 209
Alliance of Democratic Forces – National Army for the Liberation of Uganda 229
Alliance Tuareg du Nord-Mali pour le Changement 111
alt-right movements 262–264
see also far-right movements
Alternative for Germany Party 268, 274
Amadou, Hama 127
Amangué, Adam 148
American Nazi Party 268
Amien, W 238
AMISOM *see* African Union Mission in Somalia (AMISOM)
Amnesty International 16, 150, 194
Anacko, Mohamed 126
Anglican churches 329, 336, 338, 339, 340
Anglin, Andrew 264
Angola 228, 315
Ansar al-Din (Defenders of the Faith)
attacks on cultural/religious sites 116, 119, 304, 309
formed by Ag Ghali 115
funding from Qatar 312
mergers with other organisations 90, 107, 131
support of local Malians 121
terrorist attacks 54
Traoré calls on France for help 116
Ansar al-Din (Haidara's movement) 121
Ansar al-Sharia 91, 94, 95
anti-federalist movement 261–262
see also far-right movements
anti-immigrant incidents 267
apartheid ideology 237–238, 271
AQAP (Al-Qaeda in the Arabian Peninsula) 11, 215

AQI (Al-Qaeda in Iraq) 11, 20, 89, 214, 215, 216, 218, 251n75
Arab Spring protests 11, 41–43, 114
Areva (nuclear firm) 113, 118, 125, 127
armed forces *see* armies; police; security forces
Armed Islamic Group (GIA) 81, 87–88, 89, 113, 144
Armed Islamic Movement/Movement Islamique du Azawad (MIA) 87, 117
armies
attacks on soldiers 114, 118, 125, 131, 146, 149
mutinies by soldiers 115, 123, 172, 193–194
in need of international assistance 318
Nigerian armed forces 193–195, 195–196
small armies in Niger/Mali 109
survey (36 countries) *38*
survey (Kenya) 40, *41*, 51–53
survey (Mali) 40, *41*
survey (North African countries) 43, *44*
surveys (Nigeria) 40, *41*, 64, *64*
in United States 357
see also police; security forces
arms trafficking 95
Aryan Brotherhood 261, 262
Aryan Nations 262
Aryan Renaissance Society 268
assassinations 97, 98
Association des Musulmans au Rwanda 319
Association for Church Renewal 329, 341
Association for Islamic Mobilisation and Propagation (UAMSHO) 232–233, 236
Azoulay, R 95
Azzam, Abdullah Yusuf 214

B

Bakr, Abu 320n11
Bal, Suleiman 306
Banda, Ruphia 341
Bannon, Steve 264, 265, 274
Barlow, Eeben 195
Becker, F 231
beheadings 53, 94, 215–216, 218, *235*
Beirich, H 273
Bello, Ahmadu 166, 313
Belmokhtar, Mokhtar
ability to operate in the desert 117–118
exploits poor governance in Mali 129

kidnappings in Sahara–Sahel 151
leader of Al-Mourabitoun 90, 91, 110
loyalty to Al-Qaeda Central 118
marriage into local tribe 121
power struggle with Droukdel 113
sidelining of MNLA 152
see also Al-Mourabitoun
Benin 67, *68*, *70*, 83, 84, 176
Berber populations 82, 108, 111
Bin Abdullah, Abu Qays 234
Bin Abdullah, Sultan Jamshid 232
Bin Laden, Osama
  activities in Sudan 10, 309
  allegiance pledged to 89
  close ties with Taliban 11, 12, 13
  critical of using women as fighters 217
  death of 10, 11, 26
  fear of creating infighting among Muslims 216
  formation of Al-Qaeda 10
  funding for Afghan mujahideen 214
  troubled by Al-Zarqawi's brutality 11
  US embassy bombings 9
  vision of global jihad 214–215
  writings on jihad 85
  see also Al-Qaeda
Bin Nayef, Mohammed 310
Black, Don 273
Blazak, R 260
Blume, Thomas 265–266
Bocoum, Amadou 145
Boere Aanvalstroepe 239, 272
Boeremag 239, 271, 272
Bokassa, Emperor I 307
Boko Haram
  background/overview 59, 171–173, 176, 182–183
  allegiance to ISIS 131
  children, use of 285–286
  co-existence or violence 173–174
  funding 184–185, 313
  government attempts at negotiation 19
  government use of SADF 195
  kidnappings 19, 59, 172, 182, 185, 285
  proposed long-term solutions 173
  ranking in terms of violence 176, 182
  recruitment 184–185
  response of Christian community 332
  as revolutionary separatist movement 187
  strategy/objectives 183–184, 187

'technical defeat' of 286
terrorist and insurgent in nature 189
terrorist attacks 59, 128, 172–173, 182–183, 183–184, 188, 193–194, *194*
ties to jihadist networks 61
training from AQIM/Al-Shabaab 184
as transnational terrorist organisation 227
bombings
  Algeria 88, 89–90, 113
  Britain 241
  Djibouti 211
  Ethiopia 212
  France 88
  Iraq 216
  Kenya 9, 53, 217
  Mali 91, 117
  Niger 118, 128
  Nigeria 172, 182, 184, 188
  Somalia 302
  South Africa 238–239, 272
  Tanzania/Zanzibar 233, *235*, *236*
  Tunisia 43
  Uganda 210
  United Kingdom 241
  United States 10, 261, 262
  US embassies (Kenya/Tanzania) 9, 12, 16, 48, 215, 237, 312
  see also terror attacks/bombings
Borno State (Nigeria)
  overview 177, 178, 181–182
  attacks by Boko Haram 188
  children in armed conflict 286, 289
  education/schooling 285, 291–292, 296
  military atrocities 194
  see also Boko Haram; Nigeria
Boukhars, A 206
Bouteflika, Abdelaziz 142
Breitbart News 264, 274
bribery 39, 195, 312
Britain
  colonisation of Nigeria 165–166, 179, 318
  colonisation of Tanzania/Zanzibar 230, 232
  founding member of GCTF 31n70
  hate crimes 270
  terrorist attacks 241
Bryden, M 211
Buhari, Muhammadu 59, 65, 176, 195
Buijs, FJ 259
Bures, Oldrich 15

366

Index

Burkina Faso
   African Model Anti-Terrorism Law 247
   dictatorships/coups d'état 84, 132
   French military presence 110, 117
   jihadist threat from Ag Ghali 153
   joint counterterrorism force 58–59
   security-related surveys 67, 68, 70
   target of AQIM's expansion 99
   terrorist attacks in 91, 107
   UN capacity-building work 354
Bush, President GW 9, 17, 144, 189–190, 359
Byman, D 214–215

C

Cachalia, RC 271, 272
Cameroon
   classified as 'spill-over country' 228
   growing threat from extremist activity 37
   part of MNJTF 176
   security-related surveys 40, 67, 68, 70
   under threat from Boko Haram 173, 227
capacity building 244, 245, 246, 295, 354
Central African Republic
   classified as 'at-risk country' 228
   dictatorships/coups d'état 84
   Fragile State Index ranking 315
   Global Peace Index ranking 315
   Libyan troops sent to 114
   P/CVE policy approaches 27
   tensions between Christians and Muslims 307
Chad
   classified as 'spill-over country' 228
   failure to ratify Algiers Convention 247
   Fragile State Index ranking 122, 315
   French military presence in 110, 117
   gun battles with GSPC 146
   joint counterterrorism force 58–59
   Libyan troops sent to 114
   loans from IMF 132
   and Operation Serval 116–117
   Pan-Sahel Initiative 144–145, 247
   part of MNJTF 176
   under threat from Boko Haram 227
Chafer, T 83
charities, Muslim 310–313
children in armed conflict
   in Boko Haram 285–286
   in the CJTF 286
   in Lord's Resistance Army 284
   psychological trauma 285
   rehabilitation/reintegration measures 287–299
Chiluba, Frederick 339, 339–340, 341
Christian Association of Nigeria 333
Christian Broadcasting Network 329
Christian Council of Zambia 339
Christianity
   Christian fundamentalists 262
   in Tanzania 230–231
   tensions between Christians and Muslims 181, 184, 230–231, 307–308, 313, 318–319, 328, 332
   see also evangelical Christianity; United States evangelicals
churches, attacks on 129, 172, 183, 184, 233, 235, 261, 305
CIFA Development Group 312
Civilian Joint Task Force (Nigeria) 285, 286
Clapham, C 352
CMFPR (Coordination des Mouvements et Forces Patriotiques de Résistance) 153, 154
Coalition du Peuple pour l'Azawad (CPA) 153
Colombia 18, 31n70
colonisation
   of Nigeria 165–166, 179, 318
   of Tanzania/Zanzibar 230, 232
community structures/stakeholders 293–295
Compaore, Blaise 132
Congrès pour la Justice dans l'Azawad 153
Constitution (South Africa) 238, 251n59
Convention on the Prevention and Combating of Terrorism (OAU) 246
Coordination des Mouvements de l'Azawad 153
Coordination des Mouvements et Forces Patriotiques de Résistance (CMFPR) 153, 154
corruption
   Algeria 86, 147
   links with terrorism 190, 205, 227, 246, 351
   Mali 123
   Nigeria 163, 170, 173, 193, 195–196, 197
   Pentecostal views on 345n12
   South Africa 239, 240
   survey on police 70–71
   Tanzania 312

Côte d'Ivoire *see* Ivory Coast (Côte d'Ivoire)
counter-insurgency 185–186, 188, 191–193
  see also insurgencies
counterterrorism
  definition of 189
  African Union measures 227–228, 246–247
  based on historical amnesia 307
  categories of policy intervention 15–22
  countering ISIS in Libya 96–99
  EU strategies 14–15, 18, 227, 352–353
  military responses not enough 100, 219, 316, 317–318
  Pan-Sahel Initiative 110, 144–145, 146, 147, 247
  role of economic development 21, 63, *64*, 197, 319
  SADC strategies 228, 243–247
  standard measures of 97
  strategic policy choices 22–25
  survey (Mali) 55–56, *55, 56*
  surveys (Kenya) 49–53
  surveys (Nigeria) *60–61*, 63–65
  three pillars of 191–193
  training in Sahel 110
  UN strategies 12–13, 14, 15, 227, 353–354
  US strategies 354–356, 359–360
  see also preventing/countering violent extremism (P/CVE)
CPA (Coalition du Peuple pour l'Azawad) 153
crime
  black-on-white (SA) 275
  citizens' concerns about 37–38, 43, *44*, 68–69
  organised crime 90, 227, 236, 244, 245, 246
culture, political 24–25
Cummings, R 239
Czechoslovakia 141–142

D

Da'awa Islamiya (Islamic Call) 232
Dabiq (ISIS magazine) 213, 219
Dan Fodio, Usman 120, 164, 165, 180, 307
De Lys, Hervé Ludovic 146
Déby Itno, Idriss 123, 132
'decapitation' 97
Defenders of the Faith *see* Ansar al-Din (Defenders of the Faith)
democracy
  illiberal democracy 314, 328, 342–343
  lessens possibility of terrorism 190
  not just about elections 124, 314
  promotion of 21–22
  and role of Christians/evangelicals 327–328, 336
  see also governance
Democratic Republic of the Congo (DRC) 114, 229, 315
Dempsey, Colonel Thomas 318
denial strategy 17–18
Department of Defense (USA) 185, 355–359, 360
deradicalisation programmes 20, 21, 26, 27
Derna (Libya) 93, 94
development aid 191, 317, 355
dialogue, promotion of 19–20
Dicko, Imam Mahmoud 120, 121
Djibouti 210, 211, 227, 306
donations *see* charities, Muslim
Douglass, Frederick 284
DRC (Democratic Republic of the Congo) 114, 229, 315
drone flights 110–111, 123
drone strikes 17, 96, 97, 98
Droukdal, Abdelmalek 84, 89, 113
drug smuggling/trafficking 90, 95, 108–109, 110, 151
Dugard, J 237–238

E

East Africa
  links between Muslim charities/extremist groups 312
  rise of militant Islamic groups 205, 206–209
  use of P/CVE strategies 219
  see also Al-Shabaab; Islamic State of Iraq and Syria (ISIS)
economic development
  as counterterrorism strategy 21, 63, *64*, 197, 319
  and operations of terrorist groups 188
  and rehabilitation of CAAFAG 296–298
  see also poverty
education
  Islamic schools/centres 208, 209, 308
  schooling in Nigeria 165, 166–167, 285,

368

286, 291–293, 296
    schooling in Tanzania 230–231
    vocational/skills training 297–298
education, as survey demographic
    motivations for extremist behaviour *45*, 46, 62, *62*
    security concerns (Kenya) *49*, 52, *53*
    security concerns (Mali) *55*, 56
    security concerns (Nigeria) 60, *60*
Egypt
    founding member of GCTF 31n70
    negotiations with jihadist groups 19
    ranking of extremist activity 43
    survey, confidence in security forces 40, *70*
    survey, impact of Arab Spring *42*
    survey, security indicators *67*
    survey, security vs human rights 46, *46*, *48*
    surveys, security-related 43, 44, *44*, *45*, 65, *68*, *70*, *72*
    terrorist attacks in *72*
    US development aid 355
    see also North Africa (Maghreb)
Ehrlich, Paul 14
embassy bombings 9, 12, 16, 48, 215, 237, 312
employment *see* unemployment
Erdogan, Emrah *235*
Eritrea 307
Ethiopia
    Al-Shabaab's arch enemy 212
    Fragile State Index ranking 315
    invasion of Somalia 210
    tensions between Christians and Muslims 307
    terrorist attacks in 211, 227
European far-right movements 268–270
European Union
    alternatives to GWOT strategy 26
    counterterrorism strategies 14–15, 18, 227, 352–353
    founding member of GCTF 31n70
    and migrant smuggling in Niger 155
evangelical Christianity
    definition/overview 328–330
    illiberal political agenda 342–343
    Nigeria 330, 331–335
    Uganda 335–338, 347n59
    Zambia 334, 338–342

    see also Christianity; United States' evangelicals
executions
    by AQI 218
    by GIA 88
    by GSPC 89
    by ISIS 94
    by MNLA 114
    by Nigerian security forces 182
Executive Order 13129 12
Executive Outcomes 195

F
Faggaga, Hassan 111
Fairbanks, E 276
Falter, JW 259–260
FAMA (Forces Armées et de Sécurité du Mali) 54, 56, 59
far-right movements
    definition/overview 258–261
    competing frameworks 264–266
    Europe 268–270
    South Africa 239, 270–277
    United States 261–264, 266–268, 273
FARC (Revolutionary Armed Forces of Colombia) 18
Feltou, Rhissa 126
Financial Action Task Force (FATF) 23
financing of organisations
    AQIM 90
    Boko Haram 184–185
    EU counterterrorism measures 18
    FATF objectives 23
    ISIS 94–95, *95*
    via Muslim charities/donations 310–313
    via organised crime 244
FIS (Front Islamique du Salut) 86–87, 113, 144, 220n7
FLAA (Front de Libération de l'Aïr et de l'Azawak) 148
FLN (Forces de Libération du Nord du Mali) 154
FLN (National Liberation Front) 86–87
food crises 54, 124, 128, 146
football 295–296
Forces Armées et de Sécurité du Mali (FAMA) 54, 56, 59
Forces de Libération du Nord du Mali (FLN) 154
Fragile State Index 122, 314–315

France
- armed forces in Mali 56, *56*, 58, 59
- criticised for paying ransoms 113–114
- export of jihadi terrorism to 88
- founding member of GCTF 31n70
- hate crimes 270
- intelligence-gathering operations 123
- Le Drian's warnings on Islamism 119
- military presence in Sahel 110–111
- National Front 268, 269, 274
- Operation Barkhane 59, 117, 130, 131, 153
- Operation Serval 59, 116–117, 130, 153
- push for 2105 Algiers Accord 133
- relationship with North/West Africa 58, 82, 83–84, 110–111, 133, 318
- targeted by AQIM 131
- terrorist attacks in 88, 129

Freedom Front Plus (FF+) 275
Freedom Party of Austria 268–269, *269*
Front de Libération de l'Aïr et de l'Azawak (FLAA) 148
Front Islamique du Salut (FIS) 86–87, 113, 144, 220n7
Fuller, GE 206
funding *see* financing of organisations

G

Gaddafi, Muammar
- encouragement of 'holy war' 307
- interventions in Niger 126, 149
- overthrow of 41, 54, 81, 114, 130, 152, 156, 315
- vision of a United Africa 109, 114

Ganchi, Feroze Abubaker 240
Ganda Iso 116, 153, 154
gas facilities, attacks on 5, 90, 118
GATIA (Groupe Autodéfense Touareg Imghad et Alliés) 154
GCTF (Global Counterterrorism Forum) 26, 31n70
gender, as survey demographic
- security concerns (Kenya) 49, 52, *53*
- security concerns (Mali) 55, *55*
- security concerns (Nigeria) 60, 61, 64–65
- security concerns (North African countries) *72*
- *see also* women

gender discrimination 178
Germany
- colonisation of Tanzania 230
- far-right movements 268, 274
- founding member of GCTF 31n70
- hate crimes 270
- military bases in Niger 153

Ghailan, Ahmed Khalfan 240
Ghana 67, *68*, *70*, 247
GIA (Groupe Islamique Armee) 81, 87–88, 113, 144
Gigaba, Malusi 239–240
Giliomee, H 272
Gilsaa, S 208–209
Global Counterterrorism Forum (GCTF) 26, 31n70
Global Peace Index 315
Global Terrorism Database 36, 42
Global Terrorism Index *66–68*, 71, *71*, *72*, 176
Global War on Terrorism (GWOT)
- militarised focus of 1, 16
- as response to 9/11 attacks 9, 13
- Sahara–Sahelian front 142, 144, 145, 147, 149, 156
- US/EU alternatives to 26
- use of 'axis of evil' term 17

Godane, Ahmed 211
governance
- based on Allah/sharia law 85
- ISIS's structures/methods 92, 94
- more resources needed 317
- in Sahelian countries 54, 84, 107–108, 110, 122–131, 133
- and spread of violent extremism 107–108, 129–130, 190, 197–198, 247, 351, 352, 353
- US aid for 355, 360
- and US anti-federalist movement 261–262

government, surveys on
- Kenya 49, 50
- Mali 55–56, *55*
- Nigeria *60–61*, 61, *62*, *63*, *64*, 75
- North African countries *44*
- survey of 36 countries *68–69*
- UNDP survey 317

Gregoire, E 83
Group for the Support of Islam and Muslims 90, 156
Groupe Autodéfense Touareg Imghad et Alliés (GATIA) 154

370

GSCP (Salafist Group for Preaching and Combat) 88–89, 113, 144, 145, 146
Guinea 67, 68, 70, 180, 309, 312, 355
Gulf states 208, 309, 311
Gumbi, Abubaker 303–304
Gumi, Abubakar 165, 313
Gush Emunim 264–265
Guterres, António 317
GWOT *see* Global War on Terrorism (GWOT)

H
Haidara, Sheikh Cherif Ousmane 121
Hallett, Robin 179
Hallundbaek, L 211–212
Hama, Cheibane Ould 118
Hansen, SJ 210
Harmon, S 89
Harper-Mercer, Christopher 267
Hasan, Yusuf Fadl 305
Hashim, A 96
hate crimes 260–261, 267, 269–270, 273
hate groups 267–268
Hattab, Hassan 88, 89, 113
Haut Conseil pour l'Unité de l'Azawad (HCUA) 153, 154
Haynes, J 231
'hearts and minds' approach 188
Hegemann, H 15
Heilman, BE 229–230, 231
Hembe, G 179
Hezbollah 190, 309, 316
HIV/Aids 178, 244, 245, 355
Hofmeyr, Steve 274
homosexuality 334, 334–335, 335, 337–338, 341, 347n59
Horn of Africa 210, 212
hostage-taking *see* kidnappings
Hoste, Richard 262–263
hotels, attacks on 43, 54, 90, 107, 229
Hough, J 238–239
human development indicators 109, 124, 127, 177
human rights
 atrocities committed by security forces 150, 194–195, 196, 317
 security-related surveys 46–48
human trafficking 95, 99, 109, 245
humanitarian aid
 as counterterrorism strategy 191, 192, 196

by ISIS 92
from Islamist charities/groups 208, 209, 308
in Nigeria 286–287
and operations of terrorist groups 188
from USA 355

I
Ibrahim Index of African Governance 37, 66–68
ideology
 AQIM's motivations questioned 118
 promotion of other Islamic ideas 318
 role in driving extremists 98–99, 188–189, 289–290
 see also Islamist ideology
Idris, Alhaji Shehu 316
Imam Majlis (Imam Society) 232
India 31n70, 343
Institute for Justice and Reconciliation 27
Institute on Religion and Democracy 329, 341
insurgencies 185–189
 see also counter-insurgency; terrorism
intelligence-gathering operations 110–111, 123, 132, 144–145, 191, 286
Inter-Religious Council of Uganda 336–337
International Islamic Relief Organization (IIRO) 312
International Security Assistance Force (ISAF) 10, 13
internet connectivity 142, 143, 217, 239, 248, 352
Iqbal, Hassan Ali 235
Iran 17, 18, 304, 316
Iraq
 'axis of evil' state 17
 background to rise of ISIS 21
 EU's counterterrorism strategy 353
 recruitment in detention facilities 11–12
 terrorist attacks in 216
 US-led invasion of 16, 89
 see also Islamic State of Iraq and Syria (ISIS)
ISAF (International Security Assistance Force) 10, 13
ISIS *see* Islamic State of Iraq and Syria (ISIS)
Islam
 concept of 'African Islam' 302, 306
 in East Africa 206–209, 230

evangelicals' response to 333–334
five pillars of 85
Islamic schools/centres 208, 209, 308
   in Mali 119–122
   need to stress other Islamic ideas 318
   in northern Nigeria 163–165
   tensions between Christians and Muslims 181, 184, 230–231, 307–308, 313, 318–319, 328, 332
   writings of Al-Afghani 85
   see also religious beliefs; Salafism; Sufism; Wahhabism
Islamic Army for Iraq 11
Islamic Call (*Da'awa Islamiya*) 232
Islamic Courts Union 210, 311
Islamic Movement of Nigeria 316
Islamic Movement of Uzbekistan 11
Islamic Salvation Army (AIS) 87
Islamic Salvation Front (FIS) 86–87, 113, 144, 220n7
Islamic State of Iraq and Syria (ISIS)
   overview 91–93, 251n75
   and Al-Qaeda 92, 93, 205–206, 214–216
   communication/recruitment 100, 217, 229, 241
   counterterrorism measures against 96–99
   disowned by Al-Zawahiri 11
   in East Africa 206, 212–214, 217
   end of caliphate project 12
   growing influence in Africa 131, 219
   in Iraq 11–12, 21
   in Libya 81, 93–96, 131
   lone wolf attacks 218–219
   public opinion survey 45, *45*
   rapid expansion of activities 219
   risks to South Africa 241–242
   targeting of non-Salafi Muslims 93, 217
   terrorist attacks 12, 206, 213, 216, 217, 229
   as transnational terrorist organisation 227, 229
   use of extreme brutality 11, 218
   use of women in operations 213, 217
Islamic Youth Shura Council 94
Islamist ideology 303–305, 306, 308–310, 313–316, 318–319, 333–334
   see also ideology; Salafism; Wahhabism
Ismail, Zubair 240
Israel 18–19, 264, 265
Issoufou, Mahamadou 123, 126, 127, 128, 149, 151, 155
Ivory Coast (Côte d'Ivoire)
   security-related surveys 67, *68*, 70
   target of AQIM's expansion 99
   terrorist attacks in 90, 91, 107
   US assistance to 355

J

Jama'at Nusrat al-Islam wal-Muslimin 90, 156
Jemaah Islamiyah 11
Jhaba East Africa 213
jihad 85, 86, 174, 208, 214–215, 220n12
Joint Military Task Force (Nigeria) 317
Jonathan, Goodluck 59, 176, 181, 334
Jooste, Franz 272
Jordan 31n70, 353
Joustra, Tjibbe 26

K

Kadi, Yassin Abdullah 13
Kagwanja, P 309, 312
Kaiser, PJ 229–230, 231
Kalu, K 179
Kantao, Ibrahim Abba 154
Kato, David 338
Keita, Ibrahim Boubacar 130–131, 131
Kenny, J 180–181
Kenya
   banning of Islamic NGOs 312
   beheadings by Al-Shabaab 218
   classified as 'spill-over country' 228
   failure to ratify Algiers Convention 247
   Fragile State Index ranking 315
   Global Peace Index ranking 315
   increase in ISIS recruitment 217
   leader in internet connectivity 217
   new Constitution in 2013 21
   Operation Usalama Watch 16–17
   P/CVE policy approaches 27
   provision of forces to AMISOM 23
   religious tensions 319
   Saudi support for Islamic studies 208
   support for ISIS 213
   survey, direction of country *73*
   survey, fear of violence *73*–74
   survey, public opinion indicators *68*
   survey, security indicators *67*
   surveys, confidence in security forces 40, 41, *41*, 70, 71–72

surveys, security-related 39, *40*, 48–53, 65
terrorist attacks in 48, 53, *71*, 211, 213, 217, 240–241
US embassy bombings 9, 12, 16, 48, 215, 237, 312
Kenya Defence Forces 51–53
Khomeini, Ayatollah 304
kidnappings
    by AQIM 90, 113, 151
    by Boko Haram 19, 59, 172, 182, 185, 285
    by GIA 88
    by GSPC 89, 140, 144, 145
    by ISIS 95
    by MUJAO 115–116, 122
    in Sahara–Sahel 151
    by Tuareg 151–152
Kilcullen, DJ 191
Knights of the White Disciples 268
Koehler, D 260
Kommando Sorg 274
Kommandokorps 272, 276
Konaré, Alpha Oumar 123
Koopmans, Ruud 265, 266
Kouffa, Amadou 131
Krieger, Tim 190
Ku Klux Klan (KKK) 261, 266, 273
Kurdistan Workers' Party (PKK) 18
Kuwait 26, 209, 210, 310, 312

L
Langa, Steve 337, 338
Layada, Abdelhak 87, 113
Lazarevic, Serge 90
Le Drian, Jean Yves 119
Lebanon 308, 353
Lebovich, Andrew 121, 130, 131
LeSage, A 230
Lewthwaite, Samantha 241
Libya
    activities of ISIS 81, 93–96, 131
    counterterrorism against ISIS 96–99
    indoctrination of Tuareg 155
    ongoing political crisis 132
    ranking of extremist activity 43
    as 'sponsor of terrorism' 17
    terrorist attacks in *72*
    see also Gaddafi, Muammar; North Africa (Maghreb)
Lindsay, Germaine 241
Lively, Scott 341

Lord's Resistance Army (LRA) 284, 310
Lotz, Leon 195
Lum, C 22
Lwanga, Archbishop Cyprian 337

M
Macina Liberation Front 90, 131, 156
Macridis, RC 259
Madagascar *67*, *69*, *70*, 229
Maghreb *see* North Africa (Maghreb)
Maktab al-Khidamat 214
Malawi *67*, *69*, *70*, 229, 319
Mali
    activities of AQIM 81, 119
    average poverty rate 314
    broad political alliances 153–154
    classified as 'epicentre country' 228
    coup d'état in 2017 152
    donations from Arab countries 312
    Fragile State Index ranking 122
    French military presence in 110, 117
    human development indicators 124
    insurgency in northern Mali 54, 91, 111–112
    joint counterterrorism force 58–59
    lack of border controls 109
    Operation Serval 116–117
    overthrow of Touré 114–115, 123
    Pan-Sahel Initiative 144–145, 247
    poor governance 54, 84, 123, 123–125, 130–131
    relationship with Islam 119–122
    self-defence groups 56, *56*, 77n39, 124
    small national army 109
    support from Islamist groups 315
    survey, direction of country *73*
    survey, public opinion indicators *69*
    survey, security indicators *67*
    surveys, confidence in security forces 40, *40*, 41, *41*, 70, *71*–*72*
    surveys, security-related 53–59, 66, *73*–*74*
    terrorist attacks in *71*, 90, 91, 107, 117, 131
    see also Tuareg people: Mali Tuareg
Marwa, Muhammadu 170
Material Support Act (USA) 19
Mauritania
    attacks by GSPC 146
    classified as 'spill-over country' 228
    engagement with extremists 129–130

failure to ratify Algiers Convention 247
joint counterterrorism force 58–59
kidnappings 90
labelling of political opponents as terrorists 147
MUJAO's early focus on 116
Operation Barkhane 117
Pan-Sahel Initiative 144–145, 247
terrorist attacks 146
Mauritius 67, 69, 70, 229, 247
Mbeki, Thabo 250n57
McKenna, A 82
Mecca, pilgrimages to 308
Mediène, Mohamed 'Toufik' 144
MENA *see* Middle East and North Africa (MENA)
mercenaries 152, 173, 195, 227
Mesaki, S 231
metro stations, attacks on 88
MIA (Armed Islamic Movement/Mouvement Islamique du Azawad) 87, 117
Middle East and North Africa (MENA)
 Arab Spring period 11
 EU's counterterrorism strategy 353
 focus of extremist activity 41
Middle East charities 310–313
migrant smuggling
 by ISIS 95
 SADC response to 245
 Sahel region 109, 155
military *see* armies
military bases, attacks on 91, 172, 184, 194
mines, attacks on 113, 118, 125
MINUSMA (UN Multidisciplinary Integrated Stabilization Mission in Mali) 54, 56, *56*, 58, 59, 117, 131
missionaries 207, 230, 329
MNJ (Nigerien Movement for Justice) 125, 126, 150, 151
MNJTF (Multinational Joint Task Force) 176, 183
MNLA *see* National Movement for the Liberation of Azawad (MNLA)
Mohamed, Khalfan Khamis 237, 240
Mohammad VI, King 318
monasteries, attacks on 88, 305
money laundering 18, 23, 245, 246
Morocco
 founding member of GCTF 31n70
 part of TSCTI 145

survey, impact of Arab Spring *42*
survey, public opinion indicators *69*
survey, security indicators *67*
survey, security vs human rights 46, *46*
surveys, security-related *44*, *45*, *70*, *72*
terrorist attacks in *72*
see also North Africa (Maghreb)
Morsi, Mohamed 19
Mosley, Oswald 271
mosques
 attacks on 116, 216, 233, *236*, 239, 272
 growth across Africa 120, 309
 and spread of Salafism 208, 208–209
Mousa, Ibrahim 306
Moussa, Mansa 119–120
Mouvement des Nigériens pour la Justice (MNJ) 125, 126, 150, 151
Mouvement pour le Salut de l'Azawad (MSA) 154
Movement for Unity and Jihad in West Africa (MUJAO) 110, 115–116, 118, 121, 122, 308, 312
Movement Islamique du Azawad/Armed Islamic Movement (MIA) 87, 117
Mozambique 5, *67*, *69*, *70*, 229
Mudde, C 259, 260
Muhammad (prophet) 12, 85, 212, 303, 304, 320n11
Mullen, Admiral Mike 318
Multinational Joint Task Force (MNJTF) 176, 183
Mumba, Pastor Nevers 340
Mumin, Abdiqadir 212
Muraina, Abdullahi 193
museums, attacks on 43
Museveni, Yoweri 335, 336, 337, 338
Muslim Association of Malawi 319
Muslim World League 311, 312

N

National Coordinator for Counterterrorism in The Hague 26
National Front (France) 268, 269, 274
National Islamic Front (NIS) 220n7, 309, 312
National Liberation Front (FLN) 86–87
National Movement for the Liberation of Azawad (MNLA)
 advance on/retreat from northern Mali 114–115, 116, 123, 125

association with MNJ 126
conflict with GATIA 154
defeated by Islamists 130, 152
formation of 114, 152
part of CMA alliance 153, 154
rejection of PSPSDN 125
renewed rebellion in 2011 112
see also Tuareg people
National Party (SA) 237, 271
national security *see* security-related concerns
NATO (North Atlantic Treaty Organization) 13
navy, USA 356–357
Neem Foundation 285–286, 287, 290, 296, 297
negotiations, as counterterrorism strategy 18–19
neo-Nazism 261, 264, 266, 268, 269, 273
see also far-right movements
Netherlands 31n70, 268
Niger
  Boko Haram as security threat 227
  deaths of US/Nigerien personnel 360
  Fragile State Index ranking 122
  French military presence in 110, 117
  human development indicators 109, 127
  jihadist threat from Ag Ghali 153
  joint counterterrorism force 58–59
  kidnappings in 90
  Niger's Armed Forces (FAN) 150
  Pan-Sahel Initiative 144–145, 247
  part of MNJTF 176
  poor governance 123, 125–129
  public opinion surveys 40, 67, 69, 70
  small national army 109
  terrorist attacks in 91, 118, 125, 128, 129
  US assistance to 355
  see also Tuareg people: Niger Tuareg
Nigeria
  background/overview 162–163, 177–178, 181–182, 312
  armed forces 193–196, 317
  British colonial period 165–166, 179, 318
  Civilian Joint Task Force 285, 286
  classified as 'epicentre country' 228
  and corruption 163, 170, 173, 193, 195–196, 197
  counter-insurgency policy recommendations 195–198

education/schooling 165, 166–167, 285, 286, 291–293, 296
evangelical Christianity 330, 331–335
failure to ratify Algiers Convention 247
founding member of GCTF 31n70
Fragile State Index ranking 315
Global Peace Index ranking 315
Islamic practices 163–165, 169–170, 180–181, 331–332
P/CVE policy approaches 27
part of MNJTF 176
part of TSCTI 145
poverty rates 177–178, 314
support from Saudi Arabia 312–313
survey, confidence in security forces 40, 41, *41*, 70, 71–72
survey, direction of country 73
survey, fear of violence 73–74
survey, public opinion indicators 69
survey, security indicators 67
surveys, security-related 39, *40*, 59–65, 65–66, 75
tensions between Christians and Muslims 313, 319, 332
terrorist attacks in 59, *71*, 172–173, 182–183, 183–184, 188, 193–194, *194*
UN capacity-building work 354
US assistance to 355
see also Boko Haram
Nigerien Movement for Justice (MNJ) 125, 126, 150, 151
NIS (National Islamic Front) 220n7, 309, 312
North Africa (Maghreb)
  background/overview 82
  Al-Qaeda attacks in 84
  allegiance to ISIS 213
  focus of extremist activity 41–42, 81, 227
  see also Algeria; Egypt; Libya; Morocco; Sudan; Tunisia
North Atlantic Treaty Organization (NATO) 13
Northern Ireland 18, 19
Nusrat al-Islam Wal Muslimin 90, 156

O

Oklahoma City bombing 262
Omar, Mullah Mohammed 10
Onaiyekan, Cardinal John 333
Operation Barkhane 59, 117, 130, 131, 153

Operation Epervier 110–111, 116
Operation Flintlock 110, 123
Operation Infinite Reach 16
Operation Linda Nchi 48, 50
Operation Serval 59, 116–117, 130, 153
Operation Usalama Watch 16–17
Opperman, J 242
Orehek, E 24
Organisation of African Unity (OAU) 246
organised crime 90, 227, 236, 244, 245, 246
Organization of the Islamic Conference 332
Oritsejafor, Pastor Ayo 333
Orombi, Archbishop Luke 337
Osama, Abu 242
Oumarou, Seyni 127

P

P/CVE *see* preventing/countering violent extremism (P/CVE)
PAGAD (People Against Gangsterism and Drugs) 238–239
Pakistan
    and Al-Qaeda 10, 11, 97, 215
    establishment of MAK office 214
    formation of Taliban 29n24
    founding member of GCTF 31n70
    Tehrik-i-Taliban Pakistan 182
    use of retaliatory strikes 16
Pakistani Jamaat-e-Islami 303
Palestinian Liberation Organization (PLO) 19
Pan-Sahel Initiative 110, 144–145, 146, 147, 247
Panait, A 19
Party for Freedom (Netherlands) 268
Pate, Amy 15–16
Pentecostal churches
    overview 328–329, 345n12
    active in politics 327, 329–330, 338
    in SSA 333, 334, 336, 338, 339, 340
People Against Gangsterism and Drugs (PAGAD) 238–239
People of the Cave (Ahl al-Kahf) 213
People's Party-Our Slovakia 269
personal security *see* security-related concerns
Plan of Action on Preventing Violent Extremism (UN) 98, 219, 354
police
    attacks on 213, 217, 233, 234, *235*, *236*

provocation of Tuareg 147, 148
public confidence in *38*, 39, 40, *41*, *70–71*
see also armies; security forces
police stations, attacks on
    Algeria 88, 89
    Kenya 213, 217
    Nigeria 172, 184
    Tanzania/Zanzibar 211, 233, 234, *236*
political culture 24–25
political Islam *see* Islamist ideology
political parties, far-right 268–269, 271, 275
political violence 266–268
    see also terror attacks/bombings; terrorism
Pollak, Joel 274
Ponda, Sheikh Ponda Issa 208, 209, *235*
poverty
    ADB statistics 313–314
    among Tuareg people 145–146
    human development indicators 109, 124, 127, 177
    Lived Poverty Index 76n19
    as motivation for extremist behaviour 45, *45*, 46, *62*, 189–190
    in Nigeria 177
    rates in Africa 314
    and security concerns (Kenya) *49*, 50, 52, 53
    and security concerns (Mali) 55–56, *55*
    and security concerns (Nigeria) *61*, 62, *62*
Prague Spring (Czechoslovakia) 141–142
preventing/countering violent extremism (P/CVE)
    background/overview 25–27
    countering ISIS in Libya 98–99
    emphasis on local communities 39
    use in East Africa 219
    see also counter-insurgency; counterterrorism
Prinsloo, Johan 273
Protestant churches 330–331, 334
Protocol of the Algiers Convention 227–228, 246–247
PSI (Pan-Sahel Initiative) 110, 144–145, 146, 147, 247
PSPSDN (Special Programme for Peace, Security and Development in Northern Mali) 125
psychological trauma 285, 286
psychosocial support 287, 288–289, 290, 293, 299

Q
Qadiriyya 164, 170, 318
Qatar 31n70, 310, 312
Qsiyer, K 93–94
Qutb, Sayyid 85

R
racist attacks 266–267, 270
  see also far-right movements
radicalisation 20, 26, 352–353
Radicalisation Awareness Network 26
Rafini, Brigi 126, 155
Rapoport, David 9
Ravndal, Jacob 269
recruitment
  Boko Haram 184–185
  of children in armed conflict 286
  driven by a range of factors 207
  ISIS 217
  linked to poverty 46
rehabilitation/reintegration programmes 287–299
religious beliefs
  as motivation for extremism 45, *45*, 62, *62*, 229–230, 289–290
  and sense of identity 82, 181
  tensions between Christians and Muslims 181, 184, 230–231, 307–308, 313, 318–319, 328, 332
  see also Christianity; evangelical Christianity; Islam; United States' evangelicals
religious leaders
  attacks on 88, 229, 233, *235*
  recruitment for Boko Haram 286
  in rehabilitation/reintegration measures 290–291
religious sites, attacks on
  churches 129, 172, 183, 184, 233, *235*, 261, 305
  destruction of Buddhas of Bamiyan 119
  monasteries 88, 305
  mosques 116, 216, 233, *236*, 239, 272
  shrines 116, 119, 212, 216, 304, 305
  synagogues 84
resilience of children 289, 289–290
restaurants, attacks on 90, 211, 229, *235*, *236*
retaliation, as counterterrorism strategy 16–17
Revival of Islamic Heritage Society 209, 240
Revolutionary Armed Forces of Colombia (FARC) 18
right-wing organisations *see* far-right movements
Robertson, Pat 334
Roets, Erst 275–276
Rogo, Aboud Mohammed 208, 209
Roman Catholicism 330–331, 333, 334, 336, 337
Roof, Dylann 266–267, 277
Rosander, Eva 302, 313
Rudolph, RM 87
rural *see* urban–rural, as survey demographic
Rwanda 284, 307, 319

S
SADC *see* Southern African Development Community (SADC)
Sahara Desert
  kidnappings in 89, 140, 144
  trade routes 108, 180
Sahel region
  background/overview 82–83, 108–111
  complex ethnographic make-up 140
  focus of extremist activity 53–54
  joint counterterrorism force 58–59
  links between governance and extremism 122–131, 133
  regional rivalries 132
  see also Burkina Faso; Chad; Mali; Niger
Sahraoui, Nabil 89, 113
Salafism
  overview 85, 86, 206–208
  Ahl al-Kahf (people of the cave) 213
  Al-Qaeda's adherence to 214
  Al-Shabaab's adherence to 205, 211–212
  criteria of Salafi jihadism 214
  in East Africa 207–208, 209
  influence on Mali 120
  ISIS's adherence to 93, 214
  see also Islamist ideology, Wahhabism
Salafist Group for Preaching and Combat (GSPC) 88–89, 113, 144, 145, 146
Saleh, Saleh Ali 240
Salim, Abdulrahim 232
Samaritan's Purse 329
sanctions, as counterterrorism strategy 12–14, 18, 97
Sanogo, Amadou 115, 130
Sata, Michael 341–342

Saudi Arabia
  Arabisation of Africa 306
  deradicalisation programmes 20
  founding member of GCTF 31n70
  funding for Islamism in Africa 311, 311–312, 312–313
  funding for mosques/madrassas 208, 209
  social media/TV stations 308–309
Schmid, AP 190
Schoeman, A 240, 271, 272
schools *see* education
Schumann, S 259–260
security forces
  atrocities committed by 150, 194–195, 196, 317
  crackdown on Boko Haram in Nigeria 182, 187–188
  surveys (Kenya) *49*, 50, *71–72*
  surveys (Mali) *55*, *56*, 58, *71–72*
  surveys (Nigeria) *60–61*, 61, 63–64, 64, *71–72*, 75
  in Tanzania 236
  see also armies; police
security-related concerns
  vs human rights (surveys) 46–48
  survey, public opinion indicators *68–69*
  surveys (Kenya) 48–53, *67*, *68*, *70*, *71–72*, *73–74*
  surveys (Mali) 53–59, *67*, *69*, *70*, *71–72*, *73–74*
  surveys (Nigeria) 59–65, *69*, *70*, *71–72*, *73–74*, 75
  surveys (North African countries) 41–48, *72–73*
  surveys, security indicators 38–39, *66–67*
  vary across African countries 37
self-defence groups 56, *56*, 77n39, 124
Senegal *67*, *69*, *70*, 120, 145, 313, 318
sharia law
  as goal of Islamists 303, 304
  Mali 116, 119, 120–121
  Niger 155–156
  Nigeria 169–170, 332
  Somalia 212
Shekau, Abubakar 172, 182, 183, 187–188
Shi'a Islam 304, 320n11
Shi'a Muslims
  targeted by Al-Qaeda 20
  targeted by Al-Zarqawi 216
  targeted by ISIS 93, 217

ships, attacks on 10
shopping malls, attacks on 48, *235*, 240–241
shrines, attacks on 116, 119, 212, 216, 304, 305
Sierra Leone 37, *67*, *69*, *70*, 195
Signed in Blood Battalion 110, 118, 122
skills training 297–298
skinhead groups 261
  see also far-right movements
smuggling
  cigarettes/fuel/weapons 145
  drugs 90, 95, 108–109, 110, 151
  migrants 95, 109, 155, 245
social media
  evangelical organisations 329, 333
  extremist organisations 99, 212, 213, 217, 218, 274
  Saudi clerics' online activities 308
Somalia
  Al-Itihaad al-Islamiya 209, 209–210
  classified as 'epicentre country' 228
  donations from Arab countries 310, 311
  economic/democratic deficits 314
  failure to ratify Algiers Convention 247
  Fragile State Index ranking 315
  Global Peace Index ranking 315
  invaded by Ethiopia 210
  role of WAMY 312
  support from Islamists 315
  terrorist attacks in 10, 206, 210, 212, 213, 302
  see also African Union Mission in Somalia (AMISOM); Al-Shabaab
South Africa
  apartheid era 237–238, 271
  bombings 238–239, 272
  'commitment to combating terrorism' 250n57
  Constitution 238, 251n59
  far-right movements 239, 270–277
  founding member of GCTF 31n70
  Global Peace Index ranking 315
  hub for transnational terrorist organisations 237, 239–241, 242
  SADF mercenaries 195
  surveys, security-related *67*, *69*, *70*
  threat from ISIS 241–242
South Sudan 306, 315, 355
Southern African Development Community (SADC)

Index

overview 228
presence of transnational terrorist groups 229
regional counterterrorism strategies 228, 243–247
see also under names of member countries
Southern Poverty Law Centre 267, 268
Sovereign Citizen Movement 262
Soviet Union 10, 141–142, 311, 357
Special Programme for Peace, Security and Development in Northern Mali (PSPSDN) 125
Spencer, Richard 262, 264
sports 295–296
Sprinzak, Ehud 264–265, 266, 277
Ssempa, Pastor Martin 337
Stone, General Douglas 11
stonings 119
Stormfront.org 273–274, 276, 277
strikes, drone 17, 96, 97, 98
strikes, retaliatory 16
sub-Saharan Africa (SSA)
  Arabisation/Islamisation of 305–310
  area of expansion for ISIS 213
  classification as 'free' 314
  and evangelical Christianity 327, 328–331
  Middle East donations 310, 311–312
  US development aid to 355
  see also under names of countries
Sudan
  base for Bin Laden 10, 309
  child soldiers 284
  classified as 'at-risk country' 228
  epicentre of militant Islamist world 309–310
  Fragile State Index ranking 315
  Global Peace Index ranking 315
  National Islamic Front (NIS) 220n7, 309, 312
  'run by a clique of Arabs' 306
  survey, impact of Arab Spring *42*
  survey, security vs human rights *46*, 46
  surveys, security-related *44*, *67*, *69*, *70*, *72–73*
  tensions between Christians and Muslims 307
  terrorist attacks in *72*, 210
  US cruise missiles against 9
  see also North Africa (Maghreb)
Sufi shrines, attacks on 116, 119, 212, 304, 305
Sufism
  anti-Sufi sentiment 164–165
  cooperation with colonial powers 318–319
  mystical/inward-looking 120, 303
  in Tanzania 231
  under threat from Islamism 231, 302–303, 303–304
suicide bombings
  Al-Mourabitoun 91
  Al-Shabaab 210–211, 212
  AQIM 89–90, 128
  Boko Haram 172, 184, 188
  GIA 88
  GSPC 113
  by Islamists in Mali 117
  Signed in Blood Battalion 118
  women as suicide bombers 217
  see also bombings
Sunni Islam 164, 304, 320n11
  see also Salafism; Wahhabism
Sunni Muslims
  in East Africa 207, 230, 231
  ISIS as legitimate ruler of 92, 93
  in Libya 96
  and rise of ISIS 21
  targeted by ISIS 217
Support Group for Islam and Muslims 90, 156
Supreme Council of Kenya Muslims 319
Supreme Council of Muslims (Tanzania) 319
Sweden Democrats 268, 269
synagogues, attacks on 84
Syria
  EU's counterterrorism strategy 353
  as 'sponsor of terrorism' 17
  see also Islamic State of Iraq and Syria (ISIS)

T

Taarnby, M 211–212
takfirism
  and Al-Shabaab 211
  Al-Zarqawi's use of 11, 215–216
  and AQIM 86, 90
  and GIA 87
  and ISIS 21, 93
  and Wahhabism 86, 207
Taliban

379

background 29n24
based on Ala-Maududi's beliefs 305
destruction of Buddhas of Bamiyan 119
links with Al-Qaeda 10, 12, 13
ongoing talks with US 18
US sanctions against 12
world's deadliest organisation 182
Tandja, Mamadou 126, 149–150, 150, 151
Tantouche, Ibrahim 240
Tanzania
    background/overview 229–231
    Ahl al-Kahf (people of the cave) 213
    classified as 'at-risk country' 228
    religious tensions 208, 319
    spread of Wahhabist Islam 312
    surveys, security-related 68, 69, 70
    terrorist attacks in 211, 229, 233–236, 237
    US embassy bombings 9, 12, 16, 48, 215, 237, 312
    Zanzibar 230, 231–236
targeted killings 97, 98
Taya, Ould 147
Tehrik-i-Taliban Pakistan 182
Tempel, Sylke 268
terror attacks/bombings
    Algeria 72, 88, 89–90, 113, 118
    Britain 241
    Burkina Faso 91, 107
    Djibouti 211, 227
    Egypt 72
    Ethiopia 211, 227
    France 88, 129
    Iraq 216
    Ivory Coast (Côte d'Ivoire) 90, 91, 107
    Kenya 48, 53, 71, 211, 213, 217, 240–241
    Libya 72
    Mali 71, 90, 91, 107, 117, 131
    Mauritania 146
    Morocco 72
    Mozambique 5
    Niger 91, 118, 125, 128, 129
    Nigeria 59, 71, 172–173, 182–183, 183–184, 188, 193–194, 194
    Somalia 10, 206, 210, 212, 213, 302
    South Africa 238–239, 272
    Sudan 72, 210
    Tanzania/Zanzibar 211, 229, 233–236, 237
    Tunisia 43, 72, 84

Uganda 209, 210, 227
US embassies (Kenya/Tanzania) 9, 12, 16, 48, 215, 237, 312
World Trade Centre 9, 10, 13, 25, 237
terrorism
    definitions of 14, 158n21, 237, 246, 260, 269
    causes/motivations of 14, 25–26, 189–191, 317, 351–352
    competing frameworks 264–266
    concentrated in sparsely populated areas 66
    critical need for research 37
    evolution/operations of transnational organisations 227, 237, 240
    extraction of terrorism rents 147–148
    global number of incidents 12
    vs hate crimes 260–261
    increase in deaths since 2000 219
    lone wolf attacks 218, 219, 242
    NATO charter 13
    OAU Convention on the Prevention and Combating of Terrorism 246
    public opinion surveys 45–46, 45, 61–62
    on the rise in Africa 302
    United States' approach to 354–356, 359–360
    see also counter-insurgency; counterterrorism; far-right movements; insurgencies; Islamist ideology
Terrorism Act (SA) 237–238
The Platform (Mali) 153–154
Tijaniyya 164, 170
Timbuktu (Mali) 108, 116, 119, 120, 153, 304, 314
Touré, Amadou Toumani
    introduction of Family Code 120
    overthrow of 115, 123
    poor governance of 112, 123, 124
tourism
    impact of extremism in Kenya 48
    Tuareg tourism ventures 142–144
tourists, attacks on/kidnappings
    France 88
    Ivory Coast (Côte d'Ivoire) 90
    Sahara–Sahel region 89, 140, 144, 145
    Tanzania/Zanzibar 229, 232, 233, 235, 236
    Tunisia 90
Trans-Saharan Counterterrorism Initiative

110, 145, 147
Trans-Saharan Counterterrorism Partnership 110, 123
Traoré, Dioncounda 115, 116
Traoré, Moussa 123
trauma counselling 287–288, 288–289
trauma, psychological 285, 286
Trinity Broadcasting Network 329
Trump, Donald 262, 263–264, 267, 274, 359
Tuareg people
    decimation of livelihoods 145–146
    first prime minister elected 112
    loyalty to Gaddafi 114
    main inhabitants of the Sahel 83
    Mali Tuareg 54, 109, 111–112, 124, 142–143, 149–151, 152, 153–154
    Niger Tuareg 109, 125–126, 142–143, 149–151, 152, 155–156
    opposition to Islamist extremism 140–141, 150
    poverty rates 314
    provocation/marginalisation of 146–149
    tourism opportunities 142–144
    see also Ag Ghali, Iyad; National Movement for the Liberation of Azawad (MNLA)
Tunisia
    EU's counterterrorism strategy 353
    kidnappings 90
    part of TSCTI 145
    ranking of extremist activity 43
    survey, impact of Arab Spring 42, *42*
    survey, public opinion indicators *69*
    survey, security indicators *68*
    survey, security vs human rights 47, *47*, 48
    surveys, security-related 44, *44*, 45, 70, 72–73
    terrorist attacks in 43, 72, 84
    see also North Africa (Maghreb)
Turkey 18, 31n70, 84
Twitter 217, 218, 264, 308

U

UAMSHO (Association for Islamic Mobilisation and Propagation) 232–233, 236
Uganda
    ADF-NALU connections with Al-Shabaab 229
    Christianity/evangelicals 335–338, 347n59
    classified as 'at-risk country' 228
    donations from Arab countries 312
    Lord's Resistance Army (LRA) 284, 310
    religious tensions 307, 319
    support for ISIS 212, 213
    surveys, security-related *68*, *69*, *71*
    terrorist attacks in 209, 210, 227
UN Counterterrorism Centre 244, 354
UN counterterrorism strategy 14, 15, 227, 353–354
UN Development Programme (UNDP) 27, 109, 228, 316
UN Multidisciplinary Integrated Stabilization Mission in Mali (MINUSMA) 54, 56, *56*, 58, 59, 117, 131
UN Office on Drugs and Crime 108, 244, 245, 275
UN Secretary-General
    call for open societies 317
    Plan of Action on Preventing Violent Extremism 98, 219, 354
UN Security Council
    sanctions measures 12–13
    various resolutions 10, 12, 13, 117
unemployment
    as motivation for extremist behaviour 45, *45*, 62, *62*, 316
    a primary concern for Africans 37
United Arab Emirates 31n70, 236
United Kingdom *see* Britain
United States
    alternatives to GWOT strategy 26
    attack on *USS Cole* 10
    closure of embassy in SA 240
    cruise missiles strikes 9, 16
    Department of Defense 185, 355–359, 360
    downing of US helicopters 10
    embassy bombings 9, 12, 16, 48, 215, 237, 312
    far-right/alt-right movements 261–264, 266–268, 273
    founding member of GCTF 31n70
    global expenditure against extremism 317
    initiatives in Sahel region 110, 144–145, 146, 147
    intelligence-gathering operations 111, 123

invasion of Afghanistan 10, 14, 17
Material Support Act 19
policy towards Africa 354–356, 359–360
sanctions against Taliban 12
targeted by Bin Laden/Al-Qaeda 215
World Trade Centre attacks 9, 10, 13, 25, 237
see also Global War on Terrorism (GWOT)
United States Africa Command (AFRICOM) 110
United States evangelicals
 'American export' to SSA 327
 founders of African churches 329
 influence in Nigeria 331, 333, 334, 335
 influence in Uganda 335–336, 337–338, 338
 influence in Zambia 339, 340, 341
 organisations/media outlets 329, 331
 and political agendas in SSA 330, 331, 342
urban–rural, as survey demographic
 security concerns (Kenya) *49*, 50, *53*
 security concerns (Mali) 55, *55*
 security concerns (Nigeria) 60, *60*, 61
 security concerns (North African countries) 45, *72*
US Extremist Crime Database 266, 279n31

V
Van de Graaf, Henk 274
Van der Laan, Lousewies 25, 26
Van Donselaar, V 259
vocational training 297–298

W
Wahhabism
 growing influence in Africa 120, 209, 231, 308, 309, 312
 influence on AQIM 85, 86
 influence on Boko Haram 182
 ISIS's adherence to 216, 217
 puritanical form of Islam 85–86, 207, 303, 306
 see also Islamist ideology; Salafism
Wakar Gargadi (A Poem of Warning) 167–169
WAMY (World Assembly of Muslim Youth) 312

Warren, Pastor Rick 337
websites, extremist 262–263, 264, 273–274, 308
West Africa
 French military presence in 58–59, 110–111, 133, 318
 French presence in 58, 83, 133
 spread of Islam to 83, 119–120, 180, 306–307, 308, 309
 widespread political conflict 315
 see also Sahel region
white supremacy 261, 262, 266, 269, 271, 273
 see also far-right movements
women
 in extremist organisations 213, 216–217
 gender-based discrimination 178
 imposition of Islamic codes 94, 119, 155–156, 212
 as target of extremist violence 150, 284, 317
 see also gender, as survey demographic
World Assembly of Muslim Youth (WAMY) 312
World Trade Centre attacks 9, 10, 13, 25, 237
Worth, K 218

X
xenophobia 242, 259, 260, 263, 267, 269, 270

Y
Yan Izala 129, 313
'Yar Shehu, Alhajiya 167
Yemen 10, 13, 16, 215, 236
Yoh, JGN 308
Yusuf, Mohammed 171–172, 176, 182, 187–188, 286

Z
Zaïd, Abou 152, 156
Zakaria, F 314
Zakzaky, Ibrahim 170, 316
Zambia
 Christianity/evangelicals 334, 338–342
 surveys, security-related *68*, *69*, *71*
Zanzibar 230, 231–236
Zartman, W 82